THE
SPARTAN
WAY

Now, as every passerby knows,
there is an age-old legend that goes
laconic Leonidas held the Hot Gates
with just three-hundred Spartiates.
Each one was a father chosen by lot,
yet most passers by have since forgot,
the seven-hundred Thespians who volunteered to stand
together with the crimson professionals from Pelops' land.

And so, the sun scorched stones
were sown with Thespian bones
and watered too, with their gore.
Upon that sulphurous threshing floor,
smashed under the myriad Median flail,
comrades who had fought tooth and nail.
Unyielding Thespians, free husbandmen of a lesser town,
but no less deserving of Memory's immortal renown.

THE
SPARTAN
WAY

by

Nic Fields

Pen & Sword
MILITARY

First published in Great Britain in 2013 by
PEN & SWORD MILITARY
An imprint of
Pen & Sword Books Ltd
47 Church Street
Barnsley
South Yorkshire
S70 2AS

Copyright © Nic Fields 2013

ISBN 978-1-84884-899-3

Typeset in Ehrhardt by
Concept, Huddersfield, West Yorkshire.

Printed and bound in England by
CPI Group (UK) Ltd, Croydon, CR0 4YY.

Pen & Sword Books Ltd incorporates the Imprints of Pen & Sword Aviation, Pen &
Sword Family History, Pen & Sword Maritime, Pen & Sword Military, Pen & Sword
Discovery, Wharncliffe Local History, Wharncliffe True Crime, Wharncliffe Transport,
Pen & Sword Select, Pen & Sword Military Classics, Leo Cooper, The Praetorian
Press, Remember When, Seaforth Publishing and Frontline Publishing.

For a complete list of Pen & Sword titles please contact
PEN & SWORD BOOKS LIMITED
47 Church Street, Barnsley, South Yorkshire, S70 2AS, England
E-mail: enquiries@pen-and-sword.co.uk
Website: www.pen-and-sword.co.uk

Contents

Maps and Plans

The following maps are diagrammatic rather than geographical, and their purpose is only to give a rough indication of the manner in which Spartan battle tactics and manoeuvres panned out. These maps were composed mainly from notes and sketches made in the course of personally observing the battle sites in question.

There are still those who are not interested in physically studying the topography of ancient warfare, and so tranquilly ignore what they consider a frightful chore. Suffice to say, the study of ancient warfare is replete with topographical problems. But this, after all, is mere A-B-C. Yet still there have been plenty of attempts of late years to prove this and that and the other happened at this and that and the other battle, commonly by those who have never set foot upon the battleground in question. Many go to pieces at the first contact with the facts. So be it. I could go into quite an extended rant about how awful this is and what a disservice it does to the study of ancient warfare, but that might be poor taste, so I will leave the matter with my simple slogan: better boots, not books.

Map 1a: Pylos, summer 425 BC

Demosthenes

     5 triremes (later reduced to three), a thirty-oared Messenian privateer and a
          Messenian pinnace (Thucydides 4.9.1)
   60 Athenian hoplite marines (ibid. 4.9.2)
   40 Messenian hoplites (ibid. 4.9.1)
   20 Athenian archers ('a few', ibid. 4.9.2)
c. 980 armed sailors (later reduced to *c.* 640)

Thrasymelidas

  c. 60 Peloponnesian triremes (ibid. 4.16.3), of which 43 are used in the
          amphibious assault on Demosthenes' position (ibid. 4.10.2)
12,000 total available manpower (Diodoros 12.61.2)

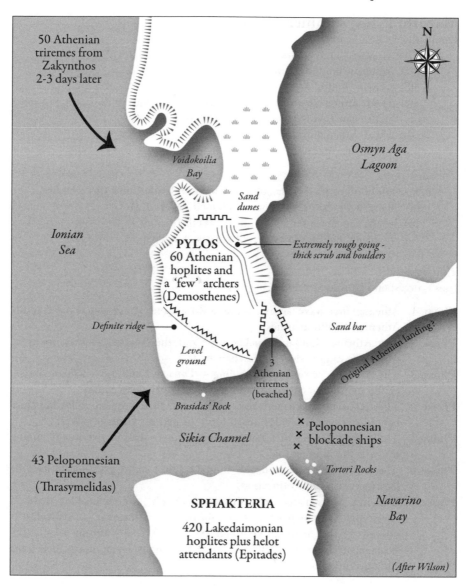

50 Athenian triremes from Zakynthos 2-3 days later

N

Voidokoilia Bay

Osmyn Aga Lagoon

Sand dunes

Ionian Sea

PYLOS
60 Athenian hoplites and a 'few' archers (Demosthenes)

Extremely rough going - thick scrub and boulders

Definite ridge

Level ground

Sand bar

Original Athenian landing?

3 Athenian triremes (beached)

Brasidas' Rock

43 Peloponnesian triremes (Thrasymelidas)

Sikia Channel

× Peloponnesian
× blockade ships
×

Tortori Rocks

SPHAKTERIA

420 Lakedaimonian hoplites plus helot attendants (Epitades)

Navarino Bay

(After Wilson)

Map 1b: Pylos, summer 425 BC

Demosthenes & Kleon
      70 triremes (Thucydides 4.32.2)
    800 Athenian hoplite marines (ibid. 4.30.4)
    800 archers (ibid. 4.32.2)
    800 lightly armed troops (loc. cit.), *peltastai* from Ainos in the main, but some
          psiloi from Lemnos and Imbros too (ibid. 4.28.4)
c. 8,000 armed Athenian sailors (ibid. 4.32.2)
     ? Messenians under Komon (loc. cit., Pausanias 4.26.2)

Epitades
   420 Spartan hoplites (and their attendant helots) divided into three bodies:
     (a) 30-strong picket force, south (Thucydides 4.31.2)
     (b) 360-strong main force, 'Grundy's Well' (loc. cit.)
     (c) 30-strong holding force, Profitis Elias (loc. cit.)

Phases
(nos. correspond to those on Pylos map 2)

Phase 1. Athenian first-wave landing – 'Santa Rosa Landing' –which consists of the Athenian hoplite marines.

Phase 2. The Athenian hoplites quickly wipe out the Spartan pickets, many of whom are caught sleeping in their beds.

Phase 3. The Athenian second-wave landing – 'Panagia Landing' – which consists of the lightly armed troops and the armed Athenian sailors.

Phase 4. The Athenian skirmishers and sailors, with their hoplites following close behind, torment Epitades' main force posted at 'Grundy's Well'.

Phase 5. The main force falls back northward in some confusion, eventually joining up with the holding force.

Phase 6. The remaining Spartans decide to make a 'last stand' at Profitis Elias, the location of an old fortification.

Phase 7. Komon's Messenians scale 'Pritchett's *Skala*', which enables them to attack the Spartan position from above and in the rear. A cease-fire is offered by the Athenian commanders, which finally results in the 292 Spartan survivors (inc. 120 Spartiates) agreeing to laying down their arms and surrendering.

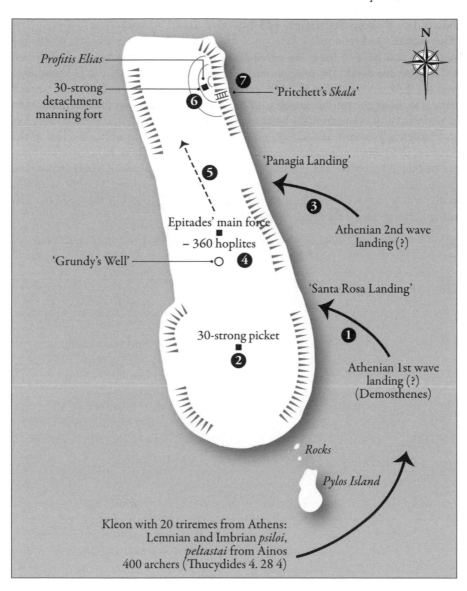

N

Profitis Elias

30-strong detachment manning fort

⑦

⑥ 'Pritchett's *Skala*'

'Panagia Landing'

③

Athenian 2nd wave landing (?)

⑤

Epitades' main force – 360 hoplites

'Grundy's Well' ○ ④

'Santa Rosa Landing'

①

Athenian 1st wave landing (?) (Demosthenes)

30-strong picket

②

Rocks

Pylos Island

Kleon with 20 triremes from Athens: Lemnian and Imbrian *psiloi*, *peltastai* from Ainos 400 archers (Thucydides 4. 28 4)

Map 1c: Pylos, Summer 425 BC, the final stand

The eastern flank of Profitis Elias in a forbidding cliff facing the sea, while the northern and western flanks are precipitous, the best (and most obvious) approach being from the south, the route in all likelihood taken by Kleon and Demosthenes and the bulk of their command. We are assuming that Komon and his men worked their way along the eastern shoreline of the island (unobserved, of course), and then scaled what is now known in the business as 'Pritchett's *Skala*' (the Greek *skala* refers to a 'stairway') to reach the unguarded high ground just above and to the rear of the Spartan defensive position. As regards to the latter, the rocks here, as elsewhere, are of folded limestone, the poriferous cavities of which support a profusion of ilex, gorse, sage, cistus, brooms and other thorny evergreen shrubs. Vestige of rubble walls, which may well have once served as part of the defences of the Spartans' last refuge, can be seen below spot height 168 metres.

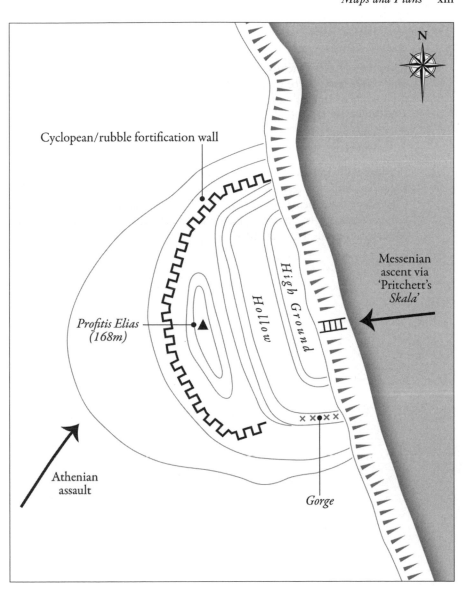

N

Cyclopean/rubble fortification wall

High Ground

Hollow

Messenian
ascent via
'Pritchett's
Skala'

*Profitis Elias
(168m)*

Athenian
assault

Gorge

Map 2: Amphipolis, 422 BC

Key to map

Kl = Kleon with 1,200 Athenian hoplites and 300 horsemen (Thucydides 5.2.1), plus 'a still larger force from the allies' (loc. cit.), which includes *psiloi* from the islands of Imbros and Lemnos (ibid. 5.8.2)

    1. = Athenian 'left wing'

    2. = Athenian 'centre'

    3. = Athenian 'right wing'

B = Brasidas with 150 picked hoplites (ibid. 5.6.4)

K = Klearidas with 'the rest' (loc. cit.), viz. some 2,000 hoplites (loc. cit.), 300 Chalcidian horsemen (ibid. 5.6.4, 10.9), 1,000 Chalcidian and Myrkinian *peltastai* (ibid. 5.6.4), ? Amphipolians (ibid. 5.6.4, 9.7), plus (?) 1,500 Thracian mercenaries (ibid. 5.6.4, cf. 10.9)

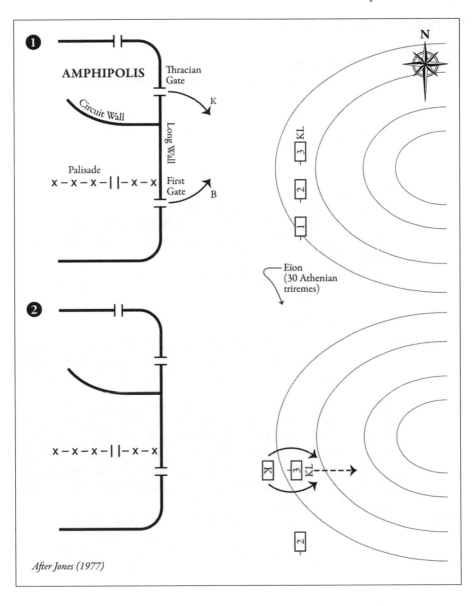

After Jones (1977)

Map 3: Mantineia, summer 418 BC

Key to map

M   = *c.* 3,000 Mantineians (Diodoros 12.78.4, Lysias 34.7)
A^1 = ? 1,000 Arcadian allies of Mantineia (Thucydides 5.67.2)
1,000 = thousand picked Argives (loc. cit.)
A^3 = ? 5,000 Argives including Kleonaians and Ornaians (loc. cit.)
A^2 = 1,000 Athenian hoplites and 300 horsemen under Laches and Nikostratos
          (ibid. 5.61.1)
S   = six *morai* of Spartiates minus 'the oldest and youngest men' (ibid. 5.64.3)
Sk   = 600 *skiritai* (ibid. 5.68.3)
Br   = 512 *brasideioi* plus other *neodamôdeis*
H   = 300 *hippeis* around King Agis (ibid. 5.72.4)
T   = ? Tegeans and other Arcadian allies, including Heraians and Mainalians
          (ibid. 5.67.1, cf. Diodoros 12.18.4, who gives 3,000 as the figure for the
          Spartan allies)
L   = 'a few' Lakedaimonians (Thucydides 5.67.1)

Phases
(nos. correspond to those on map)

Phase 1. As they advance to contact the two armies inch to the right as each man
seeks the protection of the *aspis* of the man to his right, and the man on the
extreme right tries to avoid exposing his unshielded side to the enemy.
The Mantineians therefore start to overlap the Spartan left.

Phase 2. Concerned about this development, King Agis orders the *skiritai* and
brasideioi to shift to their left until they can cover the Mantineians. But
when the 'two *lochoi*' (in Thucydides' words) of Hipponoïdas and Aristokles
from the right wing, ordered to plug the resulting gap, refuse to do so,
the confederate right rushes into the gap and routs the Spartan left.
Meanwhile, the confederate left wing takes to its heels before it even comes
to grips with the Spartan right.

Phase 3. The Spartan centre and right allow the confederates opposite them to
make good their escape, screened as they are by the stout-hearted Athenian
cavalry, and, by wheeling to their left, hit the victorious confederate right
wing on its unshielded flank as it streams back across the field.

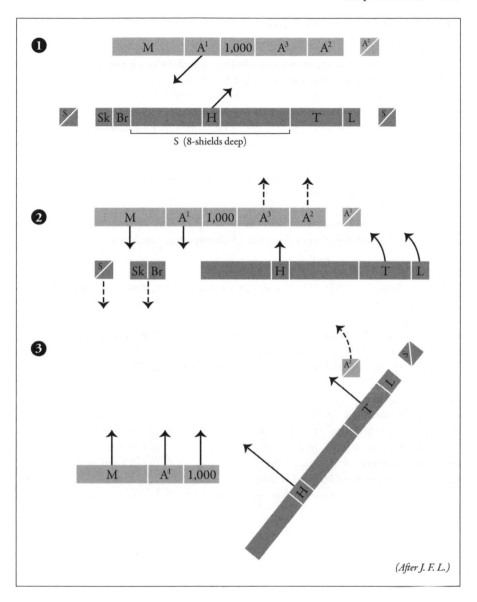

(After J. F. L.)

Map 4: the Nemea, summer 394 BC

Key to map

L	= 6,000 Lakedaimonians, including *perioikoi* (Xenophon *Hellenika* 4.2.16)
T	= ? Tegeans (cf. ibid. 4.2.13, 19, 22)
Ep	= 3,000 Epidaurians and others from Argolid *poleis* (ibid. 4.2.16)
M	= ? 2,000 Mantineians and other Arcadians (cf. ibid. 4.2.13)
E	= 3,000 Eleians, Triphylians, Akrorians and Lasioninas (ibid. 4.2.16)
Si & Ak	= ? 1,500 Sikyonians and other Achaians such as the men of Pellene (cf. ibid. 4.2.14, 20)
A	= 6,000 Athenians in ten tribal units (Xenophon *Hellenika* 4.2.17)
Eu	= 3,000 Euboians (loc. cit.)
Ar	= 7,000 Argives (loc. cit.)
C	= 3,000 Corinthians (loc. cit.)
B	= 5,000 Boiotians minus the Orchomenians (loc. cit.)

Frontages
(following Lazenby 1985: 138–9, and assuming one metre frontage per hoplite)

Spartan army
(a) option one: 13,500 hoplites @ 8-shields deep   = 1,688 metres
(b) option two: 13,500 hoplites @ 10-shields deep   = 1,350 metres
(c) option three: 13,500 hoplites @ 12-shields deep = 1,125 metres

Confederate army

(a) 5,000 Boiotians @ 25-shields deep	= 200 metres
(b) 3,000 Corinthians @ 16-shields deep	= 187/8 metres
(c) 7,000 Argives @ 16-shields deep	= 438 metres
(d) 3,000 Euboians @ 16-shields deep	= 187/8 metres
(e) 6,000 Athenians @ 16-shields deep	= 375 metres
Total frontage	= 1,388 metres

❶

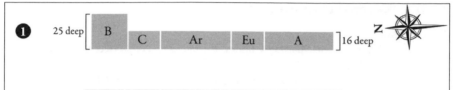

25 deep

B C Ar Eu A] 16 deep

Si & Ak E M Ep T L] 8-12 deep

❷ The opposing armies march to the right in column until they partially overlap the enemy left, then wheel left into line-of-battle.

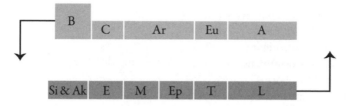

B C Ar Eu A

Si & Ak E M Ep T L

❸ Most of Sparta's allies flee on contact, as do six tribes of the Athenians, which are facing the Spartans.

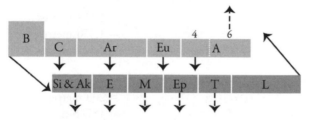

B C Ar Eu 4 6 A

Si & Ak E M Ep T L

❹ The Spartans wheel left and smash into the shieldless side of the enemy right as it attempts to withdraw across the battlefield, thereby rolling it up.

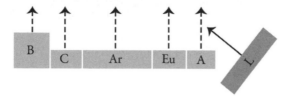

B C Ar Eu A L

(After J. F. L. (1985))

Map 5: Koroneia, summer 394 BC

Key to map

S   = 1½ *morai* of Spartiates under *polemarchos* Gylis (Xenophon *Hellenika* 4.3.15, 21)

N   = < 2,000 *neodamôdeis* from Asian campaign (ibid. 4.3.15, cf. 3.4.2)

10,000 = *c.* 5,000 Cyreans (inc. Xenophon) under the Spartiate Herippidas (ibid. 4.3.15, cf. 4.2.5, *Agesilaos* 2.11, *Anabasis* 5.3.6, Plutarch *Agesilaos* 18.1)

EG   = East Greeks, including Ionians, Hellespontines and Aeolians from Asian campaign (Xenophon *Hellenika* 4.3.15)

P   = Phokians (loc. cit.)

O   = *c.* 1,000 Orchomenians (loc. cit., cf. 4.2.17)

Ar   = ? 3,000 Argives

A   = ? 6,000 Athenians

C   = ? 3,000 Corinthians

Eu   = ? 3,000 Euboians

Lo   = Opountian and Ozolian Lokrians

B   = ? 6,000 Boiotians minus the Orchomenians

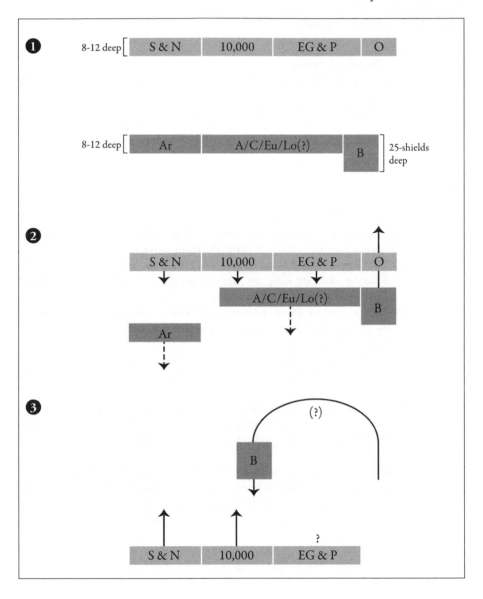

Map 6: Leuktra, summer 371 BC

Key to map
1   = 300 Boiotian horsemen
2   = 400 Theban horsemen (cf. Frontinus *Strategemata* 4.2.6, Polybios 2.3.8, 12)
M   = *mora* (x4) each under a *polemarchos* (Xenophon *Hellenika* 6.4.17)
H   = 300 strong *hippeis* around King Kleombrotos (ibid. 6.4.14)
3 & 4 = 1,000 horsemen from Lakedaimon, Phleious and Herakleia (ibid. 6.4.9,
       10, Plutarch *Pelopidas* 20.1)
5   = King Kleombrotos and his 'tent companions'

Phases
(nos. correspond to those on map)

Phase 1. The Theban horsemen screening the Theban phalanx advance against the
        Lakedaimonian horsemen. A brisk skirmish ensues.

Phase 2. (a) The Boiotians right and centre hold fast, i.e. refuse to offer battle,
        while on the left wing the heavily weighted Theban phalanx under
        Epameinondas advances to contact.

        (b) As he moves to attack, Kleombrotos attempts to increase the depth of
        his phalanx (viz. from twelve- to sixteen-shields deep) and shift to his
        right *at the same time.*

        (c) The Lakedaimonian horsemen, having been sorely compromised, burst
        through the Spartan battleline with the Theban horsemen in hot
        pursuit.

Phase 3. (a) The unusually deep Theban phalanx, spearheaded by the élite Sacred
        Band under Pelopidas, ploughs through the disorganized Spartan
        battleline and annihilate the *hippeis* and those Spartans to either side of
        them.

        (b) Witnessing the demise of the Spartan phalanx, the Lakedaimonians,
        mercenaries, etc. on the centre and left wilt and vanish from the field.
        The Thebans have carried the day and are now in possession of the
        battlefield and the tokens of victory – the bodies of the dead.

Frontages
(following Lazenby 1985: 155–6, and assuming one metre frontage per hoplite)

Spartan army
(a) × 4 *morai*, viz. 4,480 hoplites, + 300 *hippeis* @ 12-shields deep   = 400 metres
(b) Lakedaimonians, mercenaries, etc., viz. 5,000 hoplites @ 10-shields deep = 500 metres
                                                    Total frontage = 900 metres

Boiotian army
(a) 4,000 Thebans + 300 Sacred Band (front four ranks) @ 50-shields deep = 80 metres
(b) 3,000 other Boiotian hoplites @ 10-shields deep   = 300 metres
                                                    Total frontage = 380 metres

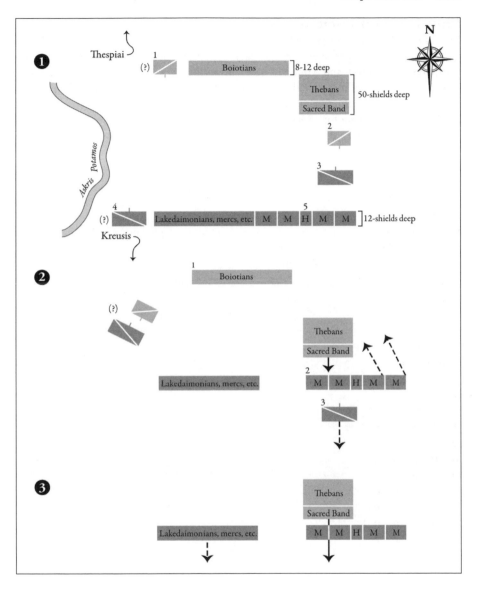

Plan 1: organisation of a Spartan *enômotia*

Spartan hoplites were organised into tactical subunits called *enômotiai*. Each had a paper strength of forty men, but usually contained thirty to thirty-five men on campaign, the oldest and youngest age classes being left to defend Sparta. The number and depth of files varied according to the number of shields deep the phalanx was deployed, viz. eight, twelve or even sixteen. For sake of argument, here we depict a full strength *enômotia* for a phalanx eight shields deep. In battle, hoplites formed up shoulder to shoulder, shields touching or even overlapping (top), but for some manoeuvres, such as the countermarch, a more open order would have been used (bottom).

Key to Plan

e = *enômotarchos*
f = file leader
r = rear marker

```
f f f f e
o o o o o
o o o o o
o o o o o
o o o o o
o o o o o
o o o o o
r r r r r


f   f   f   f   e
o   o   o   o   o
o   o   o   o   o
o   o   o   o   o
o   o   o   o   o
o   o   o   o   o
o   o   o   o   o
r   r   r   r   r
```

Plan 2: organisation of a Spartan *mora*

If we follow the controversial Lazenby, then four *enômotiai* made up a *pentekostys*, four *pentekostyes* made a *lochos* and two *lochoi* formed a *mora*.[1]

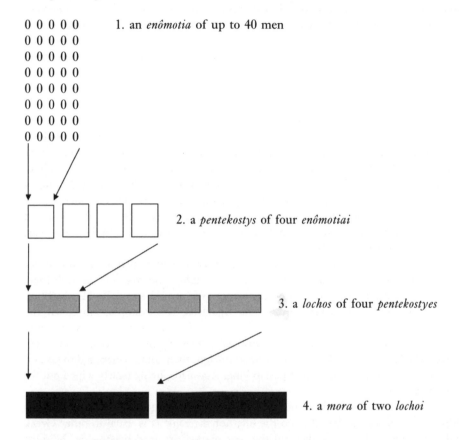

0 0 0 0 0
0 0 0 0 0
0 0 0 0 0
0 0 0 0 0
0 0 0 0 0
0 0 0 0 0
0 0 0 0 0
0 0 0 0 0   1. an *enômotia* of up to 40 men

2. a *pentekostys* of four *enômotiai*

3. a *lochos* of four *pentekostyes*

4. a *mora* of two *lochoi*

Whoever you follow, there is little doubt that the articulation into small units enabled the Spartans to perform manoeuvres such as the countermarch and the *anastrophê*.

Plan 3: Lakonian countermarch

'Meanwhile the Greeks saw the King advancing again, as it seemed, from their rear, and they accordingly countermarched and made ready to meet his attack in case he should advance in that direction.'[2] So wrote Xenophon, veteran of Cunaxa. The verb he uses, *pareskeuázonto* literally means 'to extend the front from the rear', viz. to countermarch.[3] The Ten Thousand had pursued straight forward from their position on the right wing of Cyrus' army and the enemy king, Artaxerxes, had wheeled round from his centre; hence the two had passed by one another at a considerable distance. With the king and his forces now to their rear, the Greeks decided to countermarch and thus face this new threat.

Now, there were two forms of countermarching, the Lakonian countermarch, and the Cretan or Macedonian countermarch. The first, as described by Xenophon, involves each man in the file performing an about turn, the original rear marker (now in front) standing fast, while the original file leader (now at the rear) leads his file to take up their original places again in front of the rear marker, thus giving the enemy the impression of advancing on an enemy appearing in the rear.[4] This manoeuvre was used to reverse the phalanx if the enemy appeared in the rear. Since officers would normally be in the front rank, a simple about turn would have left them in the rear, unable to control their units.

The Spartans were always anxious to keep men in order, that is the file leader always at the front, the rear marker to the rear, right-hand man on the right, etc. Moreover, the Spartans, when using this manoeuvre, would appear to be advancing towards the enemy by seven ranks. The Spartans, for example, employed the Lakonian countermarch at Koroneia (394 BC), the Spartan right smashing through the Boiotian left while the Theban contingent, forming the Boiotian right wing, enjoyed similar success. The victorious Spartan right then countermarched to take on the retiring Theban phalanx, the Spartan king, Agesilaos, being nearly wiped out for his efforts.[5]

The *enômotia* is the basis of manoeuvre. The secret is that all drill movements within the *enômotia* are based upon the file, not the rank as is usual in other Greek phalanxes. Thus, the file leader and the rear marker are in consequence the most experienced. All drill movements are initiated by these two, and the remaining members of the *enômotia* merely have to follow the man in front. As Xenophon writes:

> The formation is so easy to understand that anyone who can recognise another man cannot go wrong, for some are designated to lead, others to follow. Deployments are ordered by the *enômotarchoi* orally, acting as heralds, and the depth of the line of battle is established as they deploy. There is nothing remotely difficult to learn in this.[6]

In this way, what is difficult to perform for other Greeks, is easy for the Spartans.

Key to Plan
f = file leader
r = rear marker
2, 3, 4, 5, 6, 7 = other ranks
▲ = direction of facing

Stages 1	Stage 2	Stage 3	Stage 4
▲			
f	f		
2	2		
3	3		
4	4		
5	5		
6	6	6	
7	7	7 5	
r	r	r 4	r
	▼	3	7
		2	6
		f	5
		▼	4
			3
			2
			f
			▼

To reverse the phalanx: the phalanx adopts open order (Stage 1); each man about faces (Stage 2); the rear marker stands fast, while the file leader leads the rest of his file down the phalanx (Stage 3); the file is now facing the other way with the file leader again in the front rank and the rear marker in the rear rank (Stage 4).

Plan 4: Cretan or Macedonian countermarch

The second type of countermarch involves the file leader turning about to face his men and standing fast (Stages 1 and 2); his file then march around to his left, peeling off one by one and turning to line up behind him (Stage 3) until the file is restored but now all facing the opposite direction (Stage 4).

Key to Plan

f = file leader
r = rear marker
2, 3, 4, 5, 6, 7 = other ranks
▲ = direction of facing

Stage	Stage 2	Stage 3	Stage 4
			r
			7
			6
			5
			4
		3 ▲	3
▲		2 4	2
f	**f** ▼	**f** 5	**f**
2	2 ▲	▼ 6	▼
3	3	7	
4	4	**r**	
5	5		
6	6		
7	7		
r	**r**		

Note that, unlike the Lakonian countermarch, the formation will appear to give ground to an enemy appearing in its rear.

Plan 5: Lakonian *anastrophê*

> When they were over against the left wing of the Greeks, the latter conceived
> the fear that they might advance against that wing and, by outflanking them on
> both sides, cut them to pieces; they thought it best, therefore, to draw the wing
> back and get the river in their rear.[7]

Again, we have here the eyewitness testimony of Xenophon at Cunaxa. The verb
anastréssein literally means 'to fold back', viz. to deepen the phalanx by means of a
march from front to rear[8], or 'to open out the wing', viz. to extend the line of the
phalanx by means of a march from rear to front.[9] The Greek line was now, as in the
beginning, at right angles to the Euphrates. The manoeuvre described here would,
once executed, have made it parallel to the river, the latter thereby serving as a
defence to the rear of the Ten Thousand.

Key to Plan

□ = *enômotia* (at rest)
■ = *enômotia* (in motion)
▲ = direction formation (in this case a *lochos*) is facing
→ = direction of movement

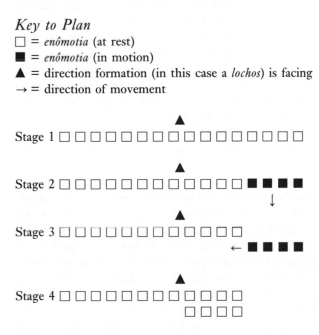

This was, therefore, the manoeuvre used by the Spartans to double all or part of the
depth of their phalanx (the above illustrates the doubling of the right wing of a
phalanx). A number of files (in this example those that make up four *enômotiai*) about
turn (Stage 1), march to the rear (Stage 2), and wheel right (Stage 3) to come up
behind the files in front (Stage 4). This was rather dangerous if the enemy attacked
during the manoeuvre, as may have happened at Leuktra (371 BC).

Prologue:
Holocaust at the Hot Gates

Conquest is an addictive habit. It is possible to argue that Xerxes invaded Greece, interests and revenge aside, simply because he thought it would be an easy fix. But after the affair at Thermopylai, that first flush of royal arrogance sat less and less comfortably about the shoulders of the Great King of Persia. Thermopylai was a small affair, in itself, but there is a thick layer of popular legend woven about the battle, and it seems to have been acquired unusually early. Its importance is less what it was, than what people think it was, a battle to which a slender, not to say suicidally small, Spartan force was despatched with orders to stand and die. Making one of those glorious but bad idea last stands at Thermopylai certainly casts a better, more heroic light on the Spartans than they generally deserved; it shows them at their audacious best. Rather than yield an inch at Thermopylai, Leonidas had sacrificed his men's lives and his own. He was a great and generous man, a man grown grey in the service of Sparta, and his death was a warrior's death and a king's death. Posterity was to remember him, and to this day he remains in the stream of popular history.

Tyrtaios (*fl. c.* 650 BC), favourite resident poet in Sparta, summed up the laconic ethos of the Spartans in his ode to the so-called noble death in battle: 'So let each stand his ground firmly with his feet well set apart and bite his lip'.[1] Sparta was essentially a military state, and elsewhere the poet, who may have been a general too, calls on the Spartans to fight aggressively and to plunge shoulder to shoulder into the thick of the fray, 'regarding life as their enemy and black death as dear as the rays of the sun'.[2] Yet the self-chosen and, in truth, avoidable death of Leonidas marked the end not the beginning of the battle. Indeed, the Spartan king had chosen his terrain wisely and his tactics logically. He reasoned that in the defile of Thermopylai a small number of resolute men could hold off the Persian juggernaut. There is no reason to believe that Leonidas and his men thought that they were doomed to swift extinction, except perhaps on the morning of the final day. A contemporary of Tyrtaios, Archilochos of Paros, offers us a much better, and far less treacly, analogy in his anti-heroic preference for the here-and-now, down-to-earth general 'set firmly on his feet and is full of guts'.[3] No reminders here of the glory to be won on the battlefield. But it was, after all, his heroic death at the head of his battling men at Thermopylai that has ensured Leonidas' name in legend.

It is a question of point of view, usually highly coloured by sentiment and spiced with short, pithy sayings. 'Yet being dead they have not died,' wrote Simonides of Leonidas and his fellow Spartans. 'Since from on high their excellence raises them gloriously out of the house of Hades.'[4] No doubt Leonidas had a difficult task, but when he stood at Thermopylai there was only a narrow passage between the mountains on his left and the sea to his right (since 480 BC the sea has retreated considerably). These mountains, the Kallidromos range, stretch in an east-west direction hugging the coast of the Malian Gulf, and at three points they came very close to the sea. Two of these points were even narrower, one to the east (East Gate) and one to the west (West Gate), than his chosen position (Middle Gate), which itself was barely fifteen metres wide. Yet Leonidas eliminated them from his plan because in both of them the landward slopes, though steep, were far from sheer. He opted, therefore, for a slightly wider front, but one where his vulnerable left flank was protected by a sheer wall of rock towering nearly a thousand metres over the Middle Gate. It would be here that he would attempt to compress the Persian host within natural features. There was another advantage to be gained from the site he chose. At the Middle Gate the Phokians had thrown up a defensive wall designed to protect them from their archenemies to the north, the horse-taming Thessalians. That was when Thermopylai was just a geographic reference point, long before the pass had taken on the proportions of a heroic struggle and lodged itself as an obsession in the collective psyche of the Spartans, long before a single Persian had stepped foot there and contested its ownership, long before it became an impromptu position held to the last man and then overrun.

The days before the battle

The old Phokian wall was in a ruinous condition, so the Greeks immediately set about repairing it. But the strength of the Thermopylai position was lessened by the existence of a number of flanking routes either southwards or eastwards round the gates. At the most dangerous of these, the Anopaia path, Leonidas stationed a thousand Phokian hoplites, local men, who might be supposed to be the best watch-and-ward force in a situation where local knowledge would be at a premium. They also had immediately the most to lose. Herodotos specifically says that the Greeks knew nothing of this mountain track until they learned of it from the people of Trachis on the spot,[5] a salutary reminder to us that we are not dealing with people equipped with trained staffs and good maps, but with people who had never faced a war on this scale before or fought at such distances from their homes.

After the Persian host had arrived at Thermopylai, there was a delay of four days before the actual assault began. In that well-known story of Herodotos the Spartans, calmly awaiting the Persian onslaught, pass their time in taking exercise and combing their hair in front of the Phokian wall, biceps, triceps and ringlets all out for breakfast.[6] Questioned about this, so Herodotos' tale continues, the former Eurypontidai king of Sparta, Demaratos, is said to have told Xerxes that combing their hair was a sign that the Spartans were preparing for battle.[7] Herodotos may have been a most entertaining gossip and snapper up of detail (and we should bless him for that),[8] but surely the point of his story here is that the Spartans, at some point in their history, adopted the idea of wearing the hair long as a symbolic reminder of belligerent arrogance, almost inverted snobbery. Hair cutting, after all, was a universal Greek token of mourning. This is certainly the view promoted by Xenophon, a man who certainly knew Sparta much better than Herodotos did, when he explains how men who had just entered manhood were not only permitted to don the highly prized crimson military cloak, but also to wear their hair long in the belief that it made them look taller, more dignified and more terrifying.[9] It is not surprising, therefore, to find young Spartan men entering battle with their hair immaculately groomed and oiled, 'looking cheerful and impressive'.[10]

Whether or not Herodotos' story is apocryphal, it does illustrate the awe in which the Spartans were held, not by the Persians, who had yet to view their adversaries as they snarled at them over the business ends of Dorian spears, but by their fellow Greeks. At Thermopylai there suddenly appeared from ages past what seemed a warrior band of fighting men trained from childhood, led by a tribal chief, the greatest warrior among them. In his version of events Diodoros says that Xerxes sent envoys to order the Greeks to surrender their arms and depart to their own territories, promising to grant them more and better lands if they did so.[11] This is not too improbable, since diplomacy was part-and-parcel of the Persian art of war, sparing the sword and sending in the purse instead, but in Diodoros' account Xerxes' demand elicits a most un-laconic reply from Leonidas. Far better is the answer of the king as Plutarch conjured it, doubtless delivered in a hard Lakonian dialect: '*molôn labê*' – 'Come and take them'.[12] Without flurry or rhetoric, this was a truly laconic quip emblematizing the quality of the Spartan way and, it will be agreed, deserved its ranking as a *mot historique*. The Great King must have thought the Spartan king was as defiant as he was simple and stupid. He did not know his man. Leonidas had stepped upon his stage at last, and was ready to begin.

First day

When the Persian assault was at last launched, it was the first day of what was celebrated as an epic three-day encounter. Herodotos' explanation for the prior four-day lull is that Xerxes was waiting 'in constant expectation that the Greeks would make good their escape'.[13] And if Xerxes could wait, the Greek temperament might prevail and their coalition crumple into an untidy mass of men, wasting their substance in quarrels among themselves. Besides, what was a diminutive stone wall to a monarch who had marched his vast army across the straits of the Hellespont (the crossing took a biblical seven days and seven nights)[14] and sailed his magnificent navy through the land behind the promontory of Mount Athos? A mere show of force and the opposition will prove but a morning mist that shall soon vanish. If not, then a quick scuffle in the hot dust of Thermopylai should see Leonidas and his ragtag band off and the pass safely in Xerxes' hands. So early in the morning of his fifth day before Thermopylai, Xerxes gave the order for a frontal assault on the paltry army of Greeks obstinately lodged in the pass, hardly a mouthful for his Olympian host. Like all great lords, if they are wise, Xerxes used others as his weapons, ruling from the rear, high and puissant and protected by the gold-pommelled spears of his élite royal guard, driving his slaves in submissive madness on before. The Median and Kissian contingents, in other words Xerxes' best type of infantrymen, marched forward to carry out their master's wish, which, after all, was to them a royal command. Battle then commenced.

Herodotos is somewhat vague about the epic fight that ensured, but he does make the obvious point that the Persians could not make full use of their numerical superiority because of the confined terrain; only the outer ranks of the mass of infantry crowded together could get at the enemy to fight. We can well imagine that the Persians suffered fearful casualties, ill-protected as they were and, Herodotos tells us, 'using shorter spears than the Greeks'.[15] The redoubtable defenders of the pass were indeed extremely competent in the use of such a weapon as many an unwary assailant realized to his chagrin. The unarmoured Persians, who were all principally armed with bows and preferred to settle matters from a distance, clearly committed themselves to an engagement that could only suit the enemy. It seems Xerxes' satisfaction had been premature.

Quickly bundling the Greeks out of the pass was the plan. But as any commander worth his salt knows it is the nature of a battle that such plans never unfold as they should. Xerxes was not going to enjoy the military walkover he had expected. Surprise is a weapon. Often underestimated, it is one of the most effective and cheapest of all force multipliers as well as one of the most versatile. It is possible to surprise your foe not only in time or place of battle but in the manner of fighting. The use of *ruse de guerre* is a constant theme in Xenophon's writings. He urged unequivocally that every commander should 'himself devise a ruse for every occasion, since in war nothing is more profitable than deceit ... Think about successes in war, and you will find that most of the greatest have been achieved by means of deceit'.[16] Among the qualities he admired in his role model, the Spartan king Agesilaos, was superior skill at deception 'once war had been declared and in consequence deceit had become legitimate and right'.[17] Indeed, according to Xenophon, Spartan boys were expected to supplement their inadequate diet by stealing food, and accordingly learnt the techniques of ambush and deception from an early age.[18]

The Spartans, representing the only force in Greece approaching what we moderns would call a professional army, brought the tactical development of the hoplite phalanx to its highest degree. And so it was that at Thermopylai they used the classic stratagem of turning and pretending to retreat in what seemed a disorderly fashion and then, once they had deceived the Persians into pursuing them, changing direction in an instantaneous turnabout and, in the words of Herodotos, 'inflict in the new struggle innumerable casualties'.[19] The full advantage of such a formidable hedgehog-like formation, such as the phalanx, was its ability to switch from a defensive to an attacking role, but to do this, its hoplites' standard of drill had to be high and the ground relatively smooth. Clearly such belligerent tactics, which denied the Persians a static target for their customary, deadly hail of arrows, had the effect of bringing about a series of hand-to-hand encounters in which the Spartans had the upper hand.

The essential Persian weapon was the composite bow.[20] The Persians habitually relied on arrow-fire to shred the opposition, and so with their massed deployment and rapid rate of fire – having their quivers hanging at their side at waist level afforded them a higher rate of fire – would blanket the opposition, dealing death at a distance.[21] It is the Spartan Dienekes' bravura remark days before the battle, as recorded by Herodotos, which probably gives us our best impression of Persian archery. One of the Trachinians, presumably unfriendly to the Spartans for choosing his country to fight in, told him:

'Such was the number of the barbarians, that when they shot forth their arrows the sun would be darkened by their multitude'. Dienekes, not at all frightened at these words, but making light of the Median numbers, answered, 'Our Trachinian friend brings us excellent tidings. If the Medes darken the sun, we shall have our fight in the shade.'[22]

This description of blotting out the sun suggests that the Persians launched their arrows skywards in a long-ranging, arcing trajectory to beat upon the target by the weight of their own fall. To the target the arrows must have seemed everywhere at once, and yet nowhere specially. As for Dienekes' wit, well it belongs to that peculiar rough soldiers' humour, universal and timeless, which springs from the experience of shared pain and misery. It often translates poorly for those not on the spot and enduring the same hardships. Sometimes in reading military history it would appear as though for success the first requisite must be a lack of humour, and inability to look upon what one is attempting except with absolute seriousness. But I digress.

It was growing late in the afternoon, probably about the same time that the Greek fleet was achieving its tactical if limited success against the Persians out at Artemision, when Xerxes decided to clear the pass ahead before sundown. The crack troops of the empire, the very ones that gave it its military sheen, the Immortals of Persian legend themselves, were ordered up and 'advanced to the attack in full confidence of bringing the business to a quick and easy end'.[23] In this they failed. Vainly the Immortals tried to break the hedgerow of Greek spears but were no more successful than the Medes and Kissians had been before them. When the sun cast its last red spangles over the piles of dead, the situation was stalemate. With ecstatic bravery, unnecessary and provocative, the Persians had hammered away but the Greeks had stood without buckling. But of course, it could not last.

Second day

Xerxes' battle plan was hardly complicated, a full frontal assault on the Greek force occupying the pass. If unimaginative, the plan demonstrated supreme confidence in his crushing superiority. His basic error was overconfidence. Little wonder, therefore, the second day's fighting was much like the first, with no better success for the Persians despite the Greeks being so few in number. Herodotos does add, however, the interesting detail that the latter fought in relays, each contingent, apart from the Phokians, of course, taking 'its turn in the line'.[24] Thus those not engaged had the opportunity to lick their wounds and catch their breath. At the end of the day, albeit a few Greeks had been killed, Xerxes was no nearer to his objective, and we can well imagine his increasing frustration and irritation at the turn of events. Yet to Xerxes the only immediate route lay through the pass ahead. At Thermopylai an irresistible force had met an immovable object. The irresistible force was the Great King and his myriads. The immovable object was the Greek band in the pass. Twice confounded, Xerxes needed a miracle.

What the Persian high command lacked, although they had well-informed Greek advisors in tow, was that salient thing, local knowledge. Since there were no maps and military intelligence depended chiefly on word-of-mouth reports delivered directly by messenger, local knowledge was of prime consequence in ancient warfare: something that meant that the invader of a foreign land was always at a grave disadvantage. Still, traitors and deserters are the common currency of war, and so it was for the

Persians when a local man from Trachis, Ephialtes son of Eurydemos, came forward in the hope of receiving a worthwhile reward from Xerxes. Apparently the gods made no rock so steep that men could not climb it, particularly driven by gold. Ephialtes offered to show the Persians the hard-to-follow mountain track and guide them along it and back down to the East Gate to take the Greek position in the rear.

Starting at the West Gate, this route follows the valley of the Asopos, which passes through a precipitous gorge. The route climbs up the hillside about a kilometre east of the gorge, the easiest and shortest ascent up the mountainside, and then runs over the hills above the gorge and stretches along the spine of the Kallidromos range, and ends at Alpênoi, the first settlement of Opountia Lokris. Leonidas was of course aware of this route and had stationed the local Phokian contingent, a thousand-strong, to guard it. Herodotos clearly implies that all the Immortals, that is, 10,000 men, accompanied Ephialtes, and there is no real reason to dispute him here, as the route he guided them along was comparatively easy.[25]

Third day

Kallidromos ('beautiful running track'), the name is used by Strabo and not Herodotos,[26] is in fact, as the name suggests, not a spiny ridge of limestone. Along its crest there are two parallel ridges, between which lies a narrow but fertile upland plain that was at that time fringed by dense oak-woods. 'This, then,' says Herodotos, 'was the mountain track, which the Persians took, after crossing the Asopos'.[27] Of course, the beauty of this wild place would not have appealed to the Persians. For them, the approach route to the Kallidromos had simply meant hard physical work, hauling themselves and their equipment up rocks and around sudden twists and turns, concentrating only on keeping their footing, and in the dark too. Still, by exploiting night's orphan light, starlight and moonshine, their nocturnal hike was swift and silent and marked by only one brush: just as dawn was breaking, Hydarnes, the commander of the Immortals under Xerxes, and his command reached the Phokian position. Both sides were surprised, but the Immortals rapidly drew their bows and opened fire on the Phokians. After a lofted volley or two, the citizen militia, naturally believing themselves the primary target, retired to a high position and prepared to sell their lives as dearly as they could. The disciplined professionals of Persia paid no heed to them, however, but hurried on their way to take the main Greek force in the rear. And so on this occasion too, the truth of that dictum of Napoléon, 'The battlefield is a scene of constant chaos', was entirely borne out.

The first warning to the Greeks of 'the death that was coming with the dawn' came from the *mantis* Megistias of Akarnania, and we would call this gentleman a seer, when he examined the first sacrificial victims of the day.[28] Leonidas then received the news that the Persians were crossing the mountains first from deserters, who came in during the night, and then from lookouts posted on the heights who ran down to inform him just after dawn. So began the famous fateful final day at Thermopylai.

Upon receipt of the news that his position was about to be turned, Leonidas held a council of war, which revealed a split in the allies' opinions between retreat and resistance. It is worth knowing that a combination of Greek states would only act in concert if all the commanders agreed. Indeed, nothing was stranger to Greek eyes than a Persian council of war presided over by the Great King, where each commander not only spoke in strict rotation, but kept silence while others were doing so. Anyhow, in his lively council of war Leonidas ended up ordering the allies to retreat, with the exception of the Spartans, Thespians and Thebans, 1,400 men, less the casualties from previous days fighting. This was done, in Herodotos' own opinion, because the Spartan king perceived there was a lack of will to fight in his battered little army, and did not want such a potentially damaging and divisive split to be made public. His decision to stay with his Spartans, Herodotos continues, was motivated by a Delphic oracle, which prophesied that either Sparta 'must be laid waste by the foreigner or a Spartan king be killed'.[29]

Herodotos is close to the epic poets and the early tragedians, believing that the rule of events was down to fate, and thus man's lot was already preordained; his uncle, Panyassis of Halikarnassos, had been a reader of signs. Yet to Herodotos fate is not a blind force. On the contrary, it is determined by heaven. Such a belief has little to do with the traditional Greek anthropomorphic religion. It is for this reason that Herodotos attacks Homer and Hesiod for giving the gods their 'appropriate titles, offices, and powers'.[30] In this context, he can be compared with an Ionian contemporary of his uncle, Xenophanes of Kolophon (*fl.* 520 BC), who was utterly disgusted at man's attempt to represent the gods in his own image. For Herodotos there exists a single and eternal being (whether it is *ó theós* or the more general *tò theîon*) who takes an interest in human affairs, provides a function that is moral,[31] and maintains a strict balance between man and nature.[32] We are all familiar with this school of thought: when mighty men fall they are paying the price for upsetting this balance. The Spartan king was doomed because the oracle had decreed that it was so. And so it came to be.

Even if one has little faith in prophesies and omens, such a tale is of interest as indicating Leonidas' high reputation. His ultimate failure and death have to be explained in ways that will not undermine his heroic stature. Once he had come to Thermopylai, his failure was inevitable, for he was fighting against fate, which no man can overcome. The ancient world, we have to appreciate, was a world peopled so sparsely that nature was not yet overshadowed by man, and nature must have hit people in the eye so plainly and grabbed them so fiercely and so tangibly by the scruff of the neck that perhaps it really was still full of gods. It was these gods, spiteful when mishandled, which marked out a destiny for each man, and he must walk down that path, without turning back. However true this may be, and the oracle is a little too neat and thus could be a *post eventum* attempt to boost morale after the death of the Spartan king, there was a much more prosaic reason for Leonidas staying and engaging the Persians on the third day: the need to buy time for the other Greeks to escape. If the whole Greek force had retreated, the Persians, with their strength in cavalry and lightly armed troops, would have rolled clear through the pass and soon overtaken them and destroyed them. Hence a fighting rearguard would be necessary. It was a gutsy and ingenious plan.

The inclusion of Leonidas and his Spartans, presumably with their attendant helots, was inevitable, since he could hardly hope to be obeyed if he ordered others to stay put, while he and the Spartans departed. He may have called for volunteers. So, as Herodotos says, all the allies went off in obedience to Leonidas' orders, except the Thespians and Thebans, the latter under compulsion because Leonidas wanted to keep them as hostages, the former simply because they 'refused to desert Leonidas and his men'.[33] As for the Thebans, as was pointed out long ago by an indignant Plutarch, a priest at Delphi, humane and likable, if Leonidas had really wanted to keep them hostage, he would have sent them off under guard with the rest of the Greeks.[34] Our likeable Boiotian has a point. Retaining people of doubtful loyalty in such a situation would have surely weakened Leonidas' position.

And why should we not believe that the Thespians, and for that matter the Thebans too, volunteered to stay with Leonidas? Perhaps a guess is permissible. Some indication that men were willing to volunteer is shown by the case of Megistias. When Leonidas tried to dismiss the seer, a man not expected to stand in the front line and fight, he refused to go, sending his only son instead, who was serving with the army as a hoplite. Simonides, in an epitaph he personally put up for friendship's sake, said of Megistias that 'he scorned to save himself, but shared the Spartans' grave'.[35]

On the morning of what would be his last day, Leonidas, in the words of Plutarch, 'passed the word to his soldiers to eat breakfast in the expectation that they would be having dinner in Hades'.[36] Laconic gallows humour, maybe so, but this was an oblique reference to the fact that living Spartans when in Sparta took just one compulsory meal a day, the communal evening mess meal – to the abstemious Spartans the rest in the Greek world thought only to stuff their bellies and slake their throats. Anyway, with the amount of energy used in hand–to–hand fighting it seemed an eminently sensible suggestion. As the first streaks of dirty grey stained the eastern sky, the Spartans at Thermopylai, no doubt, also found time to comb their hair and prepare fresh garlands. Lying behind the Phokian wall, the other Greeks knew themselves to be desperately placed and in all likelihood marked for early death.

The Great King celebrated the rising of the sun by pouring libations, and then waited until 'about the time that the marketplace is full' before giving the order for his army to move forward.[37] This evocative Herodotean phrase places the time of day somewhere between the ninth and the tenth hour, before all sensible Mediterranean people retire into the shade like lizards to escape the 'teeth of the sun'. Herodotos adds that Xerxes had been asked to do so by Ephialtes, presumably so that Xerxes' attack on the Middle Gate was intended to coincide with Hydarnes' blocking of the East Gate. In the event it appears that Hydarnes was late, but this is understandable in view of the difficulty of synchronizing a military operation of this nature. When we reconstruct a battle, we have a tendency to present it as a matter of carefully drawn up forces, well–thought out plans and logical decisions made by rational men in command of events. In truth, if we want to be more convincing, we should talk of haste, muddle, confusion and improvisation. We should, at all cost, resist the temptation to turn our reconstruction into what ought to have happened rather than what the sources say happened.

However, to return to Herodotos. The Persians were met by the Greeks, who on the two previous days had occupied the narrowest part of the pass by the Phokian wall, and relieved the frontline hoplites in relays. But today Leonidas changed his tactics and led them into the wider part of the pass so that all were to be committed at once. Whether this was wise or not is impossible to say, though some would argue that he had committed his command to a situation permitting no escape, the tiny Greek phalanx *ipso facto* being given a last chance to score heavily prior to liquidation.

At first sight, to advance from a good defensive position against a vastly superior enemy seems folly, but Leonidas knew his men (or at least his fellow Spartans among them). The fighting they knew best and excelled in, was the measured advance to contact followed by personal close quarter combat with the enemy in the open. A noteworthy feature of a Spartan battleline, and on this particular occasion we should also include those gallant Thespians and Thebans, was that it advanced in an organized and measured way to the wailing music of the *aulos*, flute. The Spartans had enough confidence and skill to do without the initial advantage, which most Greek armies sought from the impact of as quick a charge as a hoplite could possibly achieve with the burden of his arms and armour under a Mediterranean sun.

Meanwhile, the Persians were beginning to flex their bows and eye the unbroken shield wall of slow-moving hoplites, ready to empty death into their ranks. Arrows thick as hail came whistling over, and fell clinking and glancing on the Greeks. Some found a mark. The final battle had begun. It was at this point that the Greeks made their customary blood sacrifice and continued the advance. Then, as the enemy's missiles began to fly again, Leonidas probably broke with Spartan custom and ordered his men to sprint towards the Persians, whereupon a furious engagement commenced. The king, leading from the front of the mêlée and as he had no mechanical means of communicating, his primary function that desperate morning was to maintain the morale of his minuscule command at the highest possible pitch by personal example. He could not have done otherwise and held the loyalty of the Greek volunteers. They were expecting of him what he was demanding of them that day: commitment to something else than personal safety. And then there were his compatriots. To the members of a warrior society, as the Spartans surely were, the individual skills and exploits of a king who takes his place with spear and shield amid the manslaughter conferred greater renown than the skills of a king whose will and pleasure was to direct battles from a safe distance, atop a hill, perched upon a golden throne, rather than fight in them.

Herodotos claims the losses among the Persians were even heavier than those sustained on the previous two days, many of the enemy being forced into the sea or trampled underfoot by their comrades 'as their commanders plied their whips indiscriminately'.[38] Even allowing for a degree of exaggeration, he may well be right. After all, where there's a whip there's a will. Once again the Greeks were denying the Persian archers a static target at which to shoot, by advancing (or running) at a vengeful pace into contact, and if they were deployed on a broader front the losses they would have inflicted would have been all the greater.

Here they fought with reckless abandon. But then events overtook them when Leonidas himself fell under the crush of the enemy, and not only would this have left the Greeks momentarily leaderless, but the Spartans, being such proud, fierce men, who never shirked a fight, would never have been prepared to leave the king's body where it lay, in the dust and debris of battle. Thus, far from the Greeks retreating, an even more furious hand-to-hand struggle developed over the king's dead body. In a scene that might have come straight out of the *Iliad*, Herodotos describes how there was 'much shoving',[39] and, after flinging the enemy back four times, the Greeks dragged it back within their battle-worn ranks. But for the Greeks losing Leonidas was like the Trojans losing their greatest warrior, Hector. He gave some amount of reason to fight.

At last, the remaining Greeks learned of the approaching Immortals and fell rearward from the open killing ground to the narrow part of the pass crossing the Phokian wall and taking up a position on the hillock, where Herodotos says 'the stone lion in memory of Leonidas stands today'.[40] Here the survivors took their stand and braced for the inevitable, except for the Thebans, who broke away from the rest and ran towards the enemy, throwing aside what weapons they had and holding out their hands in a token of surrender. Some of them were inevitably killed by men who were still hot for blood, but the majority of those who gave themselves up were taken prisoners. They were branded with the Great King's mark. The Thebans were lucky.

The final act in the drama was soon over. The other Greeks, the Spartans and Thespians, knew they were doomed, and if anything, it probably relaxed them. They went on to cover themselves with glory, killing as many Persians before they were wiped out. Herodotos tells of the last stand that none of the defenders had spears left, and were fighting 'with their swords, if they had them, and, if not, with their hands and teeth'.[41] In the warlike words of an ancient adage: there isn't any point in dying without a struggle, like sheep.

But the attackers pushed down the Phokian wall and poured through the breach, and Hydarnes and his men arrived at last to take them in the rear. It could only have one end: the throat-parched survivors were caught between the hammer and the anvil, and all died on the fetid, fluid-soaked hillock. Significantly, Herodotos says that the Persians 'finally overwhelmed them with missile weapons',[42] so even at the finish the Persian weapon of choice was the arrow, safely released at a distance, rather than swarm up the hillock and sweep away the defenders. Still, even with the switch from hand-to-hand fighting to the long-range missile, the butchery became a massacre. The sun was high now, and the day was hot. The hillock soon stank of death. A butcher-shop rather than a battleground. Great King Xerxes had won a victory.

Introduction:
The Setting and the People

The Spartans reportedly sent an embassy to the new rising star in the east, Cyrus of Persia,[1] telling the Achaemenid king rather grandly to keep his hands off their fellow Greeks in Asia.[2] Cyrus replied with a chilling putdown, 'who are these Spartans?'[3] As we have just discussed, within two generations his successor Xerxes would have good cause to know who they were at firsthand. By whatever means people become acquainted with ancient Sparta – the present book will hardly be the last written about it – they naturally want to come to their own assessment of the Spartans. With people who flourished some twenty-five centuries ago they can hardly do without some understanding of their society and a glimpse of the primary colours, at least, which helped to make up that vivid and intricate tapestry that was Sparta. A discerning traveller coming to Sparta usually prepares him or herself by reading about the town's ancient past. But on arriving in the modern town, he or she may reflect on how antiquity was transformed into the Sparta of today.[4] What happened to the Spartans in all those centuries from the time of the so-called Dorian invasion up to today?

Inquiring into a standard guidebook is usually of little use. The history of the Spartans is often summed up in a vague paragraph, and mostly deals with the more sensational side of things. But Sparta was far more than a self-invented tribal reserve offering, amongst other exotic fare, stolen cheeses and whipped boys. Why did they expose their young and liberate their women? Why were they so feared by the other Greeks? What is the Lykourgan constitution that they preserved? The *agôgê*, the Lakonian countermarch, ephors and kings, Brasidas and Agesilaos? All these names pop up occasionally in our general readings only to sink back as vague and amorphous as if in a mist. There is one exception, of course. While the outside world might have difficulty with Spartan names, one is known all over the world or ought to be known – Leonidas, with his Three Hundred, who died fighting the Persian host at the pass of Thermopylai. The glory that they reaped in the heat and the dust there was their own to keep in perpetuity.

How to fit the old cloth into the new garment? This present book is designed to introduce the interested reader to ancient Sparta and its extraordinary people. Yet this is not just the history of a military state, however. It is the history of an idea, the idea of a military utopia that has attracted so many other peoples over the centuries. We are used to thinking in terms of ancient Greece as democratic Athens alone – in truth, a democracy adrift in a sea of oligarchies and monarchies. Sparta, which considered democracy as little more than civil disorder and mob rule, has its own history, mostly revolving around the fortunes of its warriors and women rather than politicians and philosophers. This book is about heroes and villains. It is also about deeds, glory, honour, lands, empires, might, dominion, greed, and naked power. But above all, it is about war, blood and gore. About the whole of authentic history of Sparta is comprised in one large episode: the rise and fall of the military power.

Sparta was virtually a society of tribal warriors, for whom warfare was necessary to prove their manhood and bind them tightly together in the elation of aggression, the pride of success, the determination of defeat. Indeed, for Sparta warfare was the highest art form, and periodic violence was an essential and honourable part of Spartan life. It was Spartan society and its traditions, real or imagined, that provided that essential motivation that made the Spartan war machine what it was. Thus, Spartans, from the age of seven years, when they entered military training, to sixty, when they retired from military service, lived to fulfil the demands of the state. Individual freedom – whatever that is – responsibility and initiative were suppressed, and the state took care of everything. Sparta was a model of the same sort of social experiment that in recent times was to shred the Soviet paper tiger. The state's sole purpose was the conduct of war, nothing else. Every Spartan was trained to be fearless, hardy, and to follow orders – not to reason why. This is what made them such fearsome foes on the battlefield. Many scholars (both ancient and modern) have written about the reasons underlying Sparta's autocratic rules. One of the most insightful was perhaps a visitor to Sparta who wrote that it finally dawned on him why Spartans were willing to die – after he tasted Spartan cuisine, but such tales do not come into this story.

I feel a word of caution is in order. By the time of Leonidas, the Spartans are said to have displayed all those features that were to make them, according to the observation point selected by an observer, either the object of undiluted admiration or the object of total disdain. Between these two extremes approaches to a historical evaluation of their role – one of which saw them as brute instruments of state power, while the other praised them as the embodiment of all those virtues a man could ever hope to attain – it has been left for unbiased observers to view the Spartans as the sadly uncomfortable example of that rigid conditioning to which historical circumstances can subject man if and when he slides into an unreserved commitment to any dogma or creed. Militarism and militaristic feeling, so integral a part of ancient Spartan society, is not something that can be catalogued and itemized in a neat academic manner to serve as a record for historians, sociologists, or even psychologists, for that matter. True, we live in a world where apparently irrational or non-empirical experience has been marginalized, and is often ridiculed. But looking at Spartan life from such a cold and objective perspective completely ignores the human capacity to rise above the limitations of the rational. Such a methodology, in other words, can have no real object of study and is (even in scientific terms) unsatisfactory. I have not chosen to follow it here.

And there is another point to be made. However much we look at the growth of a tree in spring we see it as motionless. And such also is the immobility to our eyes of the eternally growing, ceaselessly changing life of society, of history moving as invisibility in its incessant transformations as a tree in only a few days in springtime. If we truly reflect upon the course of history, we should deny that history was set in motion by Caesar or Napoléon or any other 'great man'. History is not made by fanatical men of action who are narrow-minded to the point of genius. They cannot make history, neither can they see the march of history, any more than you and I can watch the grass growing in our gardens. Wars and revolutions, kings and Lenins, are in truth no more than history's organic agents, its yeast. It is said that revolutions cannot be achieved without leaders. Wrong, the people make revolutions, make history indeed, but 'the people' is an epithet that customarily carries contempt with it.

There is a modern fashion of coddling a man who moves in a loftier sphere, exalting him above the rest of the people and worshipping him. Sociology built on this false premise and served up as politics should really strike us as pathetically homemade and amateurish. It is a strange attitude, for at the bottom we know that the great man is supported by that vast underlying force called the people, and when that support is removed nothing in this world can save him. The people will rise when they are discontented, having lost faith because the great man they have supported turns out to be an autocrat who claims absolute power for himself in their name and gives them not benefits but burdens. As the great man does not hold the destiny of the people in his hands, since destiny deals with him as it does with everyone else, the invidious cult of personality should be rejected out of hand; it is a conjuring trick. The real life of peoples and cultures is usually cacophonous, occasionally choral, but seldom solo.

Even in our globally interconnected world, there is much to learn both about and from ancient Sparta. But most of all, I feel that us moderns, who have a propensity to measure our place in history in split-second images rather than centuries or epochs, can benefit from the study of a world radically different from our own, questioning our ever-so-sure view of society, progress and historical development. After all, is it not said that the pursuit of knowledge was the greatest adventure ever discovered by humanity, though I would hesitate to go as far as Plato and suggest its pursuit makes one the best possible human being, a kind of spiritual rebirth of the soul from darkness to light. So it is the author's fond hope that this book may prove as stimulating to the reader as its production was to him, especially when they surveyed the multiform landscape of an ancient culture and often tragic but brave attempts of its citizens to cope, in their own singular way, with the demands of a harsh reality. Now that our cycles of tit-for-tat violence have broken out of their tribal enclaves and become global, with no immediate prospect of resolution, the story of Sparta tells us that the humiliation and attempted annihilation of the enemy will never bring peace. The rulers of our world could not, had they internalized the fate of triumphant Sparta, be pursuing their calamitous strategies of winner-takes-all.

Confronted as we are today with social and political turbulence, with a world that keeps devising new methods of destruction, even though these soon become obsolete, which, in turn, necessitates the development of even more destructive devices, *ad infinitum*, all studies of humanity's experience in the art of violent confrontation have acquired particular relevancy. Almost everyone seems to agree that we must attempt to determine whether humanity will be forever trapped by its apparently constitutional inclination to employ any method, however lethal, to ensure its dominance over its fellow kind, or whether it may – in time – be capable of ritualizing and then, ultimately, transforming that pattern. In this endeavour, thoughtful studies of humanity's past, with all its pitfalls and bloody errors, may prove to be necessary and valuable in the final equation. After all, history should be the subservient handmaiden of posterity not its imperious mistress, and a historian its chronicler not its maker.

Saga, it is said, presupposes strife. According to the Athenian historian Thucydides, the Trojan War, thought by far the most celebrated feat of Greek arms, was followed by a long period of political strife in the Greek chiefdoms. The glory days of late Bronze Age Mycenaean Greece had ended in tears, with widespread destruction of citadels and wide dispersal of communities. The most portentous event recorded by Thucydides is the occupation of the Peloponnese by the warlike Dorian Greeks from the north, together with the sons of Herakles, 'in the eightieth year after the war'.[5] This folk movement is recounted by several other Greek writers as well, often with great accumulation of detail. It has become known in modern times simply as the 'Dorian invasion', although the Greeks themselves spoke of the 'return of the Herakleidai', the sons of Herakles who led the reconquest of the Peloponnese. According to one tradition, the sons of Herakles were expelled from the Peloponnese by Eurystheus, the tyrannical ruler of Argos, before they could reach manhood and depose him. After an unsuccessful attempt to come back, they settled in central Greece, until the Delphic oracle informed them that 'the due time' had come for their return, whereupon they divided into three groups, fell upon the Peloponnese, and conquered most parts of it. Another version has them, after long wandering and many hardships, reaching Doris, a small kingdom in central Greece, where they settled on land given by the king of those parts. With that friendly gesture is established a friendship with the Dorian people, who would later help the Herakleidai reconquer the whole Peloponnese in the fourth generation. None of these writers, however, ever suggest that the Dorian migration was a destructive affair and, like them, we should not allow it to play a role in the historical explanation that it does not really warrant.

There is a possibility that the 'Dorian invasion' was actually an infiltration of peoples into a half empty land rather than a military invasion. This infiltration, if indeed there was such, is intimately bound up with the history of the Peloponnese in the early Iron Age, and above all with that of Sparta, for in historical times it regarded itself, and was regarded by the other Greeks, as the Dorian state *par excellence*. The Spartan kings, for instance, traced their descent in a direct line from Herakles. Leonidas, for instance, is provided by Herodotos with a pedigree reaching back through seven centuries to Hyllos the son of Herakles.[6] Genealogies of this calibre were reserved for men of heroic distinction, in the Homeric tradition.[7]

Herakles (now better known in the Latin form, Hercules) was really a panhellenic champion (all-Greek and only Greek), the bastard son of Zeus who in his adventuresome lifetime rescued cities from pests and oppressors and who, after his death, was deified. During his lifetime Herakles was for a long time enslaved to Eurystheus, in whose service he performed his seemingly impossible labours. But the Dorians revered him as their particular ancestor, since his sons regained the Peloponnese after they had been wrongfully expelled from it. In one legend it is Peloponnesian Tiryns, and not Boiotian Thebes, that is recorded as the birthplace of the footloose Herakles, later serving as the base for his labours.[8] As a minor point of interest, a generation before the 'bronze armoured' Achaians sailed against Troy under the leadership of

Agamemnon of Mycenae,[9] Herakles, leading the crews of six vessels, stormed Troy (then ruled by Priam's father, Laomedon) and 'widowed all her streets'.[10] Other versions say that Herakles came with eighteen shiploads of men,[11] but all agree that he brought only a small force to destroy Troy. Laomedon's only surviving son, Priam, was placed on the throne of Troy, which flourished under his long reign. Sadly Priam, when a very old man, also had to witness the final fall of Troy.

The dominators

The Spartans, the Dorian conquerors of the south-eastern quarter of the Peloponnese, were strange in two ways: they kept themselves totally separate from the people they had subdued or enslaved, and they made soldiering their sole occupation. Not that the Spartan style of fighting was anything special: they used armoured spearmen, hoplites, drawn up in a close-packed formation, the phalanx, in the same way as other Greeks. But they trained hard and did it better than the rest. Possessing a distinctive political and cultural tradition of its own, Sparta was a totally militarized society, the one *polis* in which the army could truly be said to be equivalent to the citizen body. The transformation began before puberty, when the young boys were taken from their mothers and immersed in a disciplined environment in which only the warrior ethic was allowed to penetrate. They were taught to be austere, daring and brave, and not to be reckless, for bravery and recklessness was justifiably considered a dangerous combination. The end product was a citizen who was tough, courageous, disciplined, and highly motivated. No other Greek *polis* appears to have put its young through such a rigorous régime as the Spartan *agôgê*, and by and large, there was a prejudice, born from the militia ethos of the citizen farmer, against any training in war.

It was common currency in the rest of the Greek world that when the Spartan men went to war, the Spartan mother had only one injunction for her son: 'Come back with your shield, or on it',[12] that is to say, either alive and victorious carrying the warlike shield, or lying dead upon it after a fight to the finish. Spartan mothers were made of stern stuff. Take the cast-iron demeanour of this mother in mourning:

> Argileonis, mother of Brasidas, when her son had died, and some of the citizens of Amphipolis came to Sparta to visit her, asked them whether her son had died nobly and as befitted a Spartan. When they praised him to skies and told that he was the best of all the Spartans in such deeds of valour, she replied: 'Strangers, my son was indeed noble and brave, but Sparta has many better men than he'.[13]

For us there could not be anything worse for a mother if she had a son and he grew up to fight and die in a war. For the Spartan son, however, most of his life would be spent in wars or near them, and if he fell he was commemorated as a hero not mourned as a victim. Such was the Spartan way.

With its peculiar practices, the *agôgê* being one of many, it is easy to over simplify the social divisions within Spartan society – full Spartan citizens and their families, the Spartiates, often referred to as *homoioi* ('similars'), *perioikoi* ('those who live around', i.e. the inhabitants of the largely autonomous communities dotted around the area of the fertile valley of the Eurotas river since Homer's day), and *heilôtai*, helots ('captives in war'). In truth, however, there were many subordinate groups, such as the *neodamôdeis* ('new citizens'), helots emancipated for services rendered as hoplites in the Spartan army,[14] and the *hupomeiones* ('inferiors'), either Spartans whom through misfortune or poverty had lost their status as full citizens, or those of mixed-birth or whose ancestry was suspect, who, together with the *homoioi*, made up the chosen group known as the *Spartiãtai*, Spartiates.[15] Here we should also include those unfortunates who could not brave out the *agôgê*,[16] or those who played the coward in battle, *oi trésantes*, 'the tremblers'.[17] The latter condition, which also applied to those who survived a defeat, was worse than death, for no one wanted eat or wrestle or play ball games, let alone form marriage ties, with a convicted 'trembler'. He had to give way in the street and surrender his seat to a full citizen. In a theatrical gesture, a 'trembler' was also forbidden personal grooming, a serious social stigma in a warrior community where carefully dressed long hair, in particular, was a status symbol of the highest degree, and were humiliatingly forced to shave off half their beards so as to advertise their status as half men.[18]

So it was the *Spartiãtai* who were the much feared warriors of Sparta. At the age of twenty years, having successfully survived the *agôgê*, the new warrior was now eligible for election into to one of the communal messes at which all Spartans had to eat and sleep until he was thirty.[19] According to Plutarch the existing members had a right of veto on the candidate to their communal mess and, it seems, he had only one chance. At that age he was admitted to the full rights of a citizen as one of the *homoioi* and officially allowed to inherit an estate, or an allotment, *klãros*, on which his household would be supported by the labours of helots, and from which he had to provide the stipulated contribution to maintain the communal mess, to pay tribute to the state, and to provide his own weapons and equipment as a hoplite. Indeed, a Spartiate's citizenship depended on his ability to do all this. He was also granted leave to marry if he so wished, though not allowed to lead an 'ordinary' home life. Indeed, he was not allowed to set up home with his wife until the age of thirty, that is after ten years of fully effective military life, though it was still expected of him to dine with his comrades in the communal mess. Even the kings could be penalized for failing to do so.[20] It seems kings took first place only in times of danger and hardship.

Other free men outside the charmed circle of *homoioi* were the *mothakes*. Lysandros, a larger-than-life figure we shall be meeting in due course, was a *mothax*,[21] that is to say, he was said to have been a Spartan citizen by adoption, brought up in the household of a Spartan other than his father and put through the full rigours of the *agôgê* with the son or sons of that other Spartan, after which he would have been elected to a *sussition*.[22] If this story is correct, Lysandros could have had a mother who could have been a helot woman belonging to his father's household rather than being the son of his father's Spartan wife, or his father could have been too poor to raise and provide for him, though he was legitimately born – Lysandros himself claimed to be a descendant of the Herakleidai, the sons of Herakles.[23]

Another notable *mothax* was a contemporary of Lysandros, Gylippos. As a product of Sparta, not Syracuse, Gylippos was the closest to what we would consider a professional soldier, and would turn what seemed like an inevitable Syracusan defeat into a resounding victory. Gylippos, whose birth date is not recorded, was brought up in penury. He was the son of the Kleandridas whom in 446 BC was the adviser to King Pleistoanax, on the occasion of his sudden unexplained withdrawal from

Attica.[24] Accused of having taken bribes from the agents of Perikles, Kleandridas fled to Thourioi (Sibari), a panhellenic colony then being founded in the instep of Italy with Athenian help and participation. What is more Gylippos' mother, it was said, was a helot, which meant he was a man of inferior status, in other words a *mothax*. Despite his mean birth, however, he was sponsored and enrolled in the *agôgê*. From an early childhood, therefore, Gylippos was trained for war as any other blood issue of a citizen and on reaching maturity had been elected to a *sussition*, his dues contributed by a wealthier Spartiate patron. For an individual of marginal origins, plucked as he was from dire straits and elevated to this station, war was an opportunity to gain honour and eminence, which would probably have been denied him in more peaceful times.

It is significant that Gylippos became famous as a result of being sent to Sicily, where he never commanded full Spartan citizens, Spartiates. He was possibly chosen as an *ad hoc* generalissimo because of his family connections with Thourioi. Condemned to death in his absence, Kleandridas nevertheless survived to help the men of Thourioi in a war against the Tarentines. Curiously, however, after his outstanding performance at Syracuse Gylippos hardly features again in our historical record. That said, it was alleged that he stole money from Lysandros, who had instructed him to convey a large amount of money home to Sparta. He could not resist the temptation to dip into the bags of cash, but he failed either to take note of the receipt tallies, or to alter them. A search of Gylippos' house revealed the stolen funds stashed beneath his roof beams. Like father like son, it seems, 'for Gylippos himself, after his brilliant exploits, was also convicted of taking bribes and banished from Sparta in disgrace'.[25] An alternative version of the story has Gylippos starving himself to death 'after he had been found guilty by the ephors of filching from the money of Lysandros'.[26] Impoverished exile or slow starvation, either way it was a sad demise for the audacious Gylippos, the Spartan who had saved Syracuse. Yet the case raised public interest and precipitated discussion of the impropriety of employing coined money, Sparta of course having no usable currency of its own.

That individuals of inferior origins, men such as Lysandros and Gylippos, could rise to high military commands during war, thereby attaining honour and eminence, meant that others could aspire to do the same, if only they could acquire a wealthy *homoios* patron. Here we are reminded of that old axiom, 'good iron is not used for nails', and in Sparta, with its singular warrior code, membership of a communal mess was the basic criterion of full citizenship and formed the basis of all military training and organization, from the *agôgê* onwards. The *homoioi* were held to be equal, subject only to distinctions of age and honour due to achievement. However, it is clear that an aristocracy of some form continued to exist in Spartan society. This is seen most clearly in the record of a significant number of Spartans who were victors in the chariot races at Olympia,[27] horseracing having been always an expensive hobby. Moreover, as alluded to above, failure to provide the annual contribution of rations to their mess would result in the loss of full citizenship.[28] In such a system of competition as at Sparta there must have been losers as well as winners, men who were not fish or fowl or good red herring, mongrels at best. Despite Spartans living highly public lives, competing to be seen as the best in obeying their iron laws, we certainly cannot believe that all of them reacted in the way Plutarch describes: 'When

Paidaretos was not selected as one of the *hippeis* [viz. Royal Guard], he withdrew looking very cheerful, thus expressing his happiness that the *polis* possessed three hundred men better than he was'.[29]

The dominated

Though the Greeks often referred to the two together as Lakedaimonians, there was a considerable difference between the Spartiates in Sparta and those who lived around Sparta, the *perioikoi*. Strabo says there were around one hundred perioikic settlements, each of them dignified with the label of *polis*,[30] but we know the names of eighty and they were more likely villages in fact, many far removed from Sparta. There were those that guarded important frontier routes into Lakedaimon, Pellana and Belmina, for instance, which sat astride the north-eastern routes from Tegea and Argos and feature in Epameinondas' invasion of 370/69 BC.[31] Others were dotted along the eastern seaboard of Lakedaimon, such as Prasiae, burnt to the ground by the Athenians in 430 BC and visited by them again in 414 BC,[32] while during the Arcadian troubles after Leuktra it witnessed the landing of Corinthian troops,[33] or Zarax nestled on a promontory and with its 'good harbour'.[34]

Personally free but subject to Sparta, the *perioikoi* can be seen as internally largely autonomous communities with no political rights under Spartan law but providing valuable hoplite manpower for the army. For example, Herodotos says 5,000 *perioikoi* stood alongside an equal number of Spartiates at Plataia (479 BC),[35] an army on foot that would have gratified the dead Leonidas. Likewise, Xenophon specifically mentions on a number of occasions perioikic contingents on campaign without and within the Peloponnese.[36] Even though they were expected to fight in the Spartan army, the *perioikoi* lacked citizen rights – apart from whatever rights their own communities might accord them – and their main tasks within the Spartan system were that of trading and manufacturing. Their settlement of Gytheion was Sparta's main port and naval dockyard, while the stone quarries at Krokeai supplied *lapis lakedaimonius*.[37] Xenophon says that many of these perioikic communities surrendered up to the kings of Sparta part of their land, which apparently symbolized the subjugation of these people to the Spartan state.[38] Nevertheless, unlike the conquered peoples of the Spartan state, the helots, the *perioikoi* occupied a privileged position, being protected by the Spartans and their military system and yet not subjected to its full rigours. This made them totally loyal to the Spartan state, a classic case of 'divide and rule', and the politically unambitious *perioikos* could be a happy, if dull man.

It is less easy to picture a happy helot, with his 'cruel and bitter lot'.[39] Even way back then the status of helots was obscure since they were not differentiated from the conquered Messenians. Thucydides, for instance, pointed out that 'the majority of the helots were descended from the Messenians who were enslaved of old. Hence all were called Messenians'.[40] The first reference to helots is to be found in two fragments of Tyrtaios' poetry. In the first of these fragments the poet sketches the position of the Messenians, 'like asses worn down by great burdens,/bringing to their masters out of grievous necessity/the half of all the crop tilled land bears'. In the second we hear that the helots 'wailing for their masters, the wives and the men alike,//whenever the destruction doom of death comes upon any'.[41] On the other hand, Plutarch suggests that it was a fixed quota, *apophora*, which was handed over to the master.[42] This difference is best explained by assuming that Tyrtaios is painting a picture that is atypical, belonging to a period of crisis, while Plutarch could be representing the requirement after this period of crisis. Either way, the main responsibility of the helots was to provide their individual Spartan masters with a fixed quota of natural produce. From that tribute the Spartiate paid over to his communal mess the amount required to maintain his full citizen status.

By law helots were property of 'the Spartan commonwealth' rather than individual Spartiates and, unlike chattel slaves, were allowed to reproduce themselves through family relations.[43] From a fragment of Ephoros' lost work we learn that helots were 'judged slaves on fixed conditions, their master permitted to neither manumit them nor sell them beyond the frontier'.[44] It seems, therefore, that the helot was very much akin to the mediaeval serf, who was intimately linked with demesne tenure, as he and his family were the property of the state because they were tied to the land they worked, the relationship between helot and Spartiate being set by custom. So in practice, much like a mediaeval serf, a helot cultivated land he had no right over – could not sell, exchange or bequeath it – and owed his lord and master substantial fixed payments out of the produce of the land he farmed. As Plato says, 'of all the Greek institutions it is perhaps the Spartan system of helots which gives rise to the greatest doubts and disagreements, with some people considering it a good thing and others not'.[45] The Greeks themselves were not at all precise as we would like them to have been with regards to the actual status of helots. For example, if we look at the terms of the Peace of Nikias drawn up between Sparta and Athens in 421 BC we notice that the helots are classified as 'the slave population'.[46]

Actual figures for helots are unavailable. Herodotos implies an unacceptably high seven-to-one ratio, and Xenophon confirms they outnumbered their masters by some way.[47] The relationship between Spartan and helot was one of deep-seated suspicion verging on paranoia on the former's part and outright hostility of the latter. Thucydides, for instance, records how the Athenian *stratêgos* Demosthenes suggested the taking of Pylos (425 BC) so as to take advantage of Spartan fears about helots, and in fact the historian points out that the Spartans were more than anxious once Pylos had been seized and fortified.[48] Indeed, a large body of evidence leaves little doubt that the citizen body of Sparta was constantly on the alert. Thucydides, again, reckons that 'as far as the helots are concerned, most Spartan institutions have always been designed with a view to security',[49] and Aristotle says that the helots 'are like someone sitting in wait for disasters to strike the Spartans'.[50] The Spartans distrusted their helot attendants so much that, while on campaign, they never went anywhere without their spears, and stayed near their arms and armour even 'when answering the call of nature'.[51] Kritias, of strong aristocratic descent, he of the Thirty Tyrants, refers to Lakedaimon as a land where there 'are to be found those who are the most enslaved and those who are the most free', a dramatic point obviously used to contrast helot and Spartiate. Another fragment from the pen of Kritias, who wrote on the Spartan system in prose and verse, highlights how far the distrust of helots went; so much so that 'a Spartiate at home removes the armband from his shield'.[52]

We also have to come to grips with Spartan brutality towards the helots, the worse being legalized in that sinister institution known as the *krypteia* ('time of hiding'). Keeping the helots in control appears to have been none too difficult for a régime that was prepared to work by terror and assassination for its own ends. The *krypteia* was a tradition by which young Spartans, eighteen- and nineteen-year-olds brutally fresh from the *agôgê*, set out at the dead of night with the minimum of clothing and supplies to ruthlessly hunt down and eliminate helots, particularly the few dangerous individuals, we can suppose, who were judged capable of becoming nuclei of dis-content.[53] There was also the annual declaration of war on the helots by the ephors, a legitimization of any acts of violence upon helots by individuals or the state.[54] Apologists for Sparta may dispute these facts out of hand, but on the other hand, if we take them on board we must realize their chilling implications. It is futile to attempt to show that helot-Spartan relations were basically good. To understand this, we can do no better than read Thucydides' horror story, if it is believable, of those 2,000 or so 'warlike helots' who vanished without trace.[55] Spartans at times were quite prepared to drown in blood any resistance to their dominance. To scratch a Spartan was to find something unspeakably barbarous. But then, even today there are very few societies that bear much scratching.

It is interesting to notice the pained horror of some scholars at belief in the *krypteia*, in view of their casual treatment of Sparta's visible brutality towards the helot population. Thucydides' horror story is just one side of the helot-Spartan coin. Xenophon tells us of another story, equally repulsive but showing the flip side of that coin. In it he describes a conspiracy that took place in 397 BC, which was led by 'a young man called Kinadon, strong, healthy and with plenty of courage, but not one of the *homoioi*', this being revealed by a former associate who turned state's evidence and informed on him to the ephors. In the same breath the informer says he was taken down to the agora by Kinadon and asked by him 'to count how many *Spartiâtai* were there'. The point of the exercise was to highlight the fact that the Spartiates were heavily outnumbered by 'all the others in the agora'.[56] At this critical point, Xenophon presents his readers an informative list of these other people, 'helots, *neodamôdeis*, *hupomeiones*, and *perioikoi*', the only detailed account on Spartan social structure, and Kinadon claims that all these different groups are the potential support for the conspiracy against the Spartiates, people who 'would be glad to eat them up raw'.[57] And so the plan was armed revolution against the masters, the Spartiates, a would-be *stasis* but nipped in the bud. But what can we say about the undercurrents of all these goings on?

The disgruntled Kinadon, after being arrested and broken under torture, confessed all. Revealing the names of his co-conspirators, he stated that his aim was 'to be less than no one in Lakedaimon'.[58] The inferiors, *hupomeiones*, were once Spartiates or descendants of Spartiates who had declined in status as a result of a failure to pay the *telos*, the dues owed to their communal mess. What we are witnessing here is an economically disadvantaged subgroup within the free Spartan population who no longer owed sufficient property to be able to maintain themselves as full blown citizens. Surely equally true of helots, but other components are involved as well, for Kinadon expressed his terms in a very characteristic Greek manner, namely a loss of status and the desire to be equal with the citizen body. Tensions of a social and economic nature underline this conspiracy.

Clearly Xenophon illustrates here an example of a potential *stasis* that was, accord-ing to him, a potential union of aims amongst four differing status groups, which included free men and slaves, with ex–citizens and half–citizens involved too. This highlights the problem of talking about class struggles in the ancient world, which is that the ancients had no sense of 'class', status. Thus, a free man who was poor would see no connection between himself and a slave, there being no sense of shared disadvantage or oppression. Yet Kinadon's conspiracy might suggest otherwise. The dominance of the Spartiates was deeply resented by those below them in the pyramid, and Kinadon and his associates obviously envisaged a working union between these different status groups in an armed conflict. In this respect Kinadon's conspiracy was rather unusual. As for Kinadon, the régime needed to discredit him before silencing him. So he received exemplary and typically roughshod punishment, being dragged through the streets of Sparta shackled and haltered until presumably his body was broken. Such are the cruelty and violence of a class whose position has been threatened. We know of no more conspiracies.

All in all, then, the full–blown citizens of Sparta, the *Spartiãtai*, were swamped in a sea of lesser citizens of various shades and colours: a passage in Xenophon suggests that in the early years of the fourth century BC they formed less than 2 per cent of the adult male population.[59] Of course, this is a questionable calculation, but it is probably the best we will get. Still, it was the strict code of the *agôgê* that not only equipped them with the mental or physical equipment for the rough test of war, but also assured their military supremacy over the subordinate population. We shall come to the *agôgê* presently.

Few numbers, yes, but numbers so highly trained, so finely disciplined, so mobile and so adaptable that they could stand and face with supreme confidence the more massive phalanxes of their enemies, each thick with spikes like some horrendous animal. Each Spartan was taught to consider himself a craftsman with a craftsman's self–respect and pride. He was made to understand the need for drill and exercises, and not merely to perform them laboriously. He was made healthy and was made strong. He was encouraged by the raw spirit of competition. Naturally, Sparta revealed by such customs – a morbid, violent, cruel, corporeal, complicated Sparta – did not fit into the picture of the civilized, philosophical cosmos the Athenians wanted to show the world. Sparta, in their eyes, was bred for war and for war only. No wonder it was so feared. But how did this come about?

Chapter 1

A Land of Orderliness

Mountains and sea

Greece proper with the Aegean basin is part of the great mountain zone running from the Alps to the Himalayas. For some seventy million years the great landmass of Africa has been burrowing irresistibly under Europe.[1] This titanic force has displaced, shattered, crumpled, and stretched the rocks, creating mountain ranges, ocean trenches, gorges, and upland basins. Mountain building continues, as shown by frequent earthquakes in ancient and modern Greece, and the land is 75 per cent mountainous, culminating in Mount Olympus, 2,917 metres high. The mountains themselves are primarily hard folded limestone ridges, piling up one behind the other, running from the north-west to the south-east and right down to the sea. Many of them are more than 2,000 metres in altitude. Xenophon, writing in the first half of the fourth century BC, noted the following about his homeland of Attica, the territory of the Athenians: 'High mountains with steep and narrow passes barricade our land ... and the interior is also circled with steep mountains'.[2] Indeed, Athens is set in a bowl of mountains, with the sea and its port of Peiraeus to the south-west.[3] The other crucial element in the Greek topographical equation is of course the sea, with its coastline and islands, and no one place in Greece is more than a hundred or so kilometres from the sea. Greece has about 2,000 islands, roughly 200 of which are inhabited, and almost 15,000 kilometres of indented coastline.[4]

Despite its small area, Greece has startling regional variations in climate, and the mountains everywhere generate their own microclimates. Visitors tend to forget that most of the country lies between the latitudes of 35° to 41° north, roughly the same distance from the equator as Japan or California. It is the lowlands of the Peloponnese and Attica that enjoy a true Mediterranean climate. Mild and minimally wet winters precede long, hot summers. The prehistoric climate, as inferred from pollen cores, had been less arid that today's.[5] How far climate differed in classical antiquity is uncertain. The wonderful beauty and diversity of Greece were seldom fully appreciated by ancient Greeks (to whom it was commonplace). Greece has a rich flora and fauna, the former often riotous at middle attitudes, with many species peculiar to that country, or to one mountain or island (especially Crete). In pre-Neolithic times Greece was more wooded than now. The date and nature of deforestation are controversial, but there is no good evidence that classical Greece was more wooded than today (e.g. Athens had to import timber from Macedonia for its navy).[6] Plato, writing at the beginning of the fourth century BC, noted that by his day Attica had suffered from soil erosion and tree loss: 'But in the old days when the land was intact, its mountains were covered with earth ... and the now rocky plains were covered with rich soil and there were plentiful forests on the mountains'.[7] Natural vegetation, much influenced by man of course, is a marvellous mix of North African, west Asian and south European, and consists chiefly of *garriga* (dwarf shrubs, e.g. thyme, Jerusalem sage), *maquis* (low scrub), savannah (scattered trees), and woodland (oak, pine, fir, beech, cypress, sweet chestnut).[8] The first three were valuable pastureland.

It must never be forgotten that New World crops (potato, tomato, tobacco, maize, etc.) were totally unknown in classical antiquity. Originating in India, the date of the establishment of citrus (an important cash crop for Greece today) in the Mediterranean is disputed. So the ancient Greek diet looked somewhat different from that of modern Greece, and revolved around the Mediterranean triad of cereal, olive and vine.[9] Traditionally Greek agriculture, now very much in decline, involved seasonal hard work – ploughing, sowing, picking olives, and tending vines – a hurried harvest, and long periods of relative leisure, that is, what we know as subsistence farming with daily life played out in a village setting. The productivity of Mediterranean agriculture was significantly increased because trees were often inter-cropped with cereals and legumes, increasing total yields per unit area. But we are too inclined to think of Mediterranean life as *la dolce vita*, effortlessly easy. Human labour was not relieved by the sunny climate: all the heavy work was always to be done when the sun was at its fiercest, and the resulting harvest crop was all too often meagre. Hesiod's advice in summer was to 'strip to sow, and strip to plough, and strip to reap'.[10] Hesiod (*fl.* 700 BC) tells of the endless toil of the Boiotian peasant, tied physically and mentally to his small patch of dirt and rock, worn down by bitter quarrels with his neighbours, his family, and the local magnates, resigned to being the nightingale 'gripped fast in the talons of the hawk'.[11]

The peasant's life was hard and insecure; indeed his very existence was precarious. He made a miserable living, at the mercy of the seasons, by primitive farming, and at times could hardly provide enough even for himself and his family. Even at the best of times, he lived frugally. He brought very few luxuries. He won the necessities of life by long toil from his little plot of ground. Bad weather, crop failures or worse still the peasant's absence at war (the campaign season was summer) was always uppermost in men's minds, as Aristophanes makes clear:

> *We will pray to the gods*
> *to grant the Greeks wealth,*
> *that we may all harvest*
> *barley in plenty, and plenty of wine*
> *and figs to devour,*
> *that our wives may give birth,*
> *that we may gather again*
> *the blessings we've lost*
> *and that red war may end.*[12]

It is fairly true to say that wars force men everywhere to kill each other when they want to be left at peace. Yet peace for the Greeks was not easy, being as they were confined by the mountains and the sea, the lowlands, for lack of space, confined to a few coastal strips and pockets of arable land. Thucydides postulates that the under-lying cause of Greek colonisation was the need for land; cultivable land is precious while bare rocks are so plentiful, and it is of the former that he speaks.[13] Their population was greater than their means of subsistence and so they sought fresh lands, sometimes at others' expense. It must be stressed that if food crises were common in antiquity, famine itself, on the other hand, was rare.[14] Finally, animal husbandry on a small scale probably had a place on all but the smallest properties.[15] Larger flocks and herds were moved to mountain pastures in the summer (i.e. transhumance). The value of manuring was appreciated and organic wastes were collected conscientiously from settlements and applied especially to trees and vines.

The human landscape

Greece in our period of study resembled modern Greece in little except its physical geography. Modern Greece, or the Hellenic Republic, is a European democracy ruled by a central government whose authority is active, readily obeyed and uniformly powerful over the length and breadth of the country. In classical antiquity this large mass of disciplined and highly organized humanity did not exist.

The *polis* (pl. *poleis*), or the 'city state', was the characteristic form of ancient Greek urban life. Its main features were small size, political autonomy, publicly funded institutions, social homogeneity, and a real sense of community and respect for law. Moreover, it was the members of the *polis* that turned out to meet the enemy; every citizen was a soldier as it were. Yet the tumultuous and autonomous Greek *polis* was not really a city, nor was it simply a town as its population was distributed over a rural territory that might include many agrarian villages and hamlets. It also emphasized people, the citizens, rather than territory. It was, as Aristotle so neatly expressed it, 'an association of several villages that achieve almost complete self-sufficiency'.[16] No 'city' in the modern sense was created, for the association established a new and overriding citizenship in which the political independence of the ancestral villages was submerged evermore. For Aristotle man was pre-eminently 'by nature a political animal',[17] being designed by his nature to realize his full potential through living the good life within, and only within, the framework of the self-governing *polis*, the key signifier of civilization. Just as the crowning of an acorn is the fully mature oak tree, by extension the crowing of all human social life and organization was for Aristotle the Greek *polis*. Appropriately, he defined the citizen, *politês* (pl. *politai*), as the man who shares in political judgement and rule.[18]

So a Greek *polis* was not just a physical space, it always had human dimensions, and could be crossed on foot. Most *poleis* had fewer than a thousand citizens. The distinctive sense of the *polis* was, therefore, a 'citizen state' rather than a 'city state', where 'the Spartans' or 'the Athenians' were the *polis*, as it was. So ancient Greece was divided up into many political units of small proportions, conceivable in the absence of large-scale territorial states, which always have gargantuan appetites for conquest. We tend to feel that progress is continuous, a journey from the cave to the cosmos, and that every age improves on what went before. There is such a strange power in the word 'modern'.

While the *polis* was always defined in terms of its members (e.g. the Spartans not Sparta, the Athenians not Athens), rather than geographically or through bricks and marble, its development was also a process of urbanization and the walled city, for instance, is common in Homer. Undeniably the archaeological remains of Bronze Age

Greece reveal fortifications of great strength and complexity, of huge, barely squared-off boulders, as at Mycenae, Tiryns and Gla, yet these Mycenaean citadels are the counterparts of mediaeval castles rather than of walled cities. But when the residential fortress ceases to be the citadel and becomes the *polis*, fortifications now protect the citizen body and not merely the ruler and his household. Greek *poleis*, to quote Winter, 'were much more than fortresses, they were complete social, political and economic units to a degree never achieved by their modern successors'.[19]

Because it was an agrarian-based society, the *polis* itself controlled and exploited a territory, the *chôra*, which was farmed by the citizens and their households. Around ten acres devoted to grain, olive trees, and vines could feed a peasant family of five or six (rather than provide a mount for a single aristocrat). As the *chôra* was delimited geographically by mountains or sea, or by proximity to another *polis*, parochial border wars were common. Thus, its citizens were residents of a *chôra* rather than the city itself, which was only one element in the state, though an important one, of course, since everyone made use of its agora as a centre for socialising, its acropolis as a place of refuge, and its temples and shrines to honour the gods. Politically, however, the *astu*, as it was called, was a piece with the surrounding *chôra*. The *polis* was, in essence, a community of warrior farmers, males of military age who would necessarily fight for it, in which the military power of the community controlled the political and institutional life (magistracies, council, assembly), and the reader is warned to remember at all times that, in the Greek view, the political and military spheres were totally indivisible.

There is some truth in the ancient claim that Greek *poleis* squabbled over 'paltry boundaries and strips of land not so remarkably good'.[20] It seems Greeks could not live together in peace, and the nearest and most powerful neighbour was the natural enemy. Border wars were thus common, as were inter-*polis* agreements and attempts to establish territorial rights over disputed areas. In a land of scant natural resources, autonomy was jealously guarded, but the necessities of collaboration made for a proliferation of extramural alliances, leagues of small communities, usually ethnically related, and hegemonies. There was also constant interchange and competition between *poleis*, so that despite their separate identities a common culture was always maintained. In brief, a good social definition of the *polis* might run as follows: a form of state based on a given territory whose central authority did not rest upon monarchy but with a group of agrarian citizens sharing notionally equal political powers.

A modern nation is a mass of people sharing customs, traditions, interests and culture, conscious of its identity and of the distinction between it and the rest of the world. Moreover, for a modern nation to exist it is necessary for the majority of its members to consider the preservation of its independence a matter of supreme importance. National feeling is a product of disciplined and centrally governed nations. 'Hellas', as the Greeks did and continue to refer to their land, was not a nation in classical antiquity, but rather a land where hundreds of independent *poleis*, most of them very small, jostled each other. Both the inhospitable nature of much of the terrain, and the inherent tribalism of the people had ensured Hellas had no principle of unity. In this situation war became a continuous possibility, and it was not the brief passage of an invading foreigner that had to be feared, but the constant hostility of the neighbouring *poleis*. The Greek *polis* with its walled *astu* was as fit to tyrannize over and protect its weak neighbours as a Mycenaean chieftain in his rocky citadel. Inter-state war was the natural disease of Hellas.

The citizens of these *poleis* all spoke Greek, but the Greek of each *polis* was at least slightly different from the Greek speech of other *poleis*. Athenian speech, for example, differed from that of neighbouring Boiotia, and Spartan speech differed from both of these and also from that of neighbouring Arcadia. It seemed natural to the Greeks that the people of different *poleis* had different accents. Every Greek, however, could understand every other Greek regardless of dialect, though there were of course one or two impenetrable dialects in the back country. Throughout classical antiquity the Greeks arose from three main roots: Doric, Ionic, and Aeolic. Modern scholars accept the ancient classification, but add a fourth linguistic grouping, the Arcado–Cypriote, a dialect spoken over much of the Peloponnese before the arrival there of the Dorians. Rhetorically, at least, Dorians and Ionians were eternal enemies and, much like us today, the Greeks developed, used and responded to distinct stereotypes of Dorians and Ionians. Dorians (and primarily the Spartans) were thought to be rough, hardy folk in habits – brave fighters to be sure, but rural, conservative, and a little slow. In speech they were spare, pithy, and blunt. Ionians (and primarily Athenians), on the other hand, were cultivated in manner and glib in language – clever, commercial, and adventurous.

The Spartans become Spartan

The *polis* that we all know as Sparta lay in the northern part of the Eurotas valley in the region of the south-east Peloponnese called Lakedaimon.[21] The valley is still well watered and productive, but relatively narrow and broken by small hills and ridges. Homer called the wealthy and fertile domain of Menelaos 'Lakedaimon's hollows deep with gorges',[22] and the epithet was well chosen as a description of the valley, set between the steep mountain barriers of Párnon (1,934 metres at its peak, Megáli Túrla) to the east and of Taïygettos (2,404 metres at its peak, Profítis Ilías) to the west, both running unbroken more or less north-south down two of the three prongs of land that terminate the Peloponnese, the first to stormy Cape Malea, the second to the tip of gloomy Cape Tainaron.

'The *polis* was neither consolidated nor does it possess lavish temples and buildings, but consists of village settlements of the antique Greek type'.[23] This description by Thucydides at the time of the Peloponnesian War is borne out by such archaeological evidence as can be gained from an area where a modern town occupies much of the original site. Even the location of the agora is not known. So Sparta itself was never amalgamated as a *polis*, the political process the Greeks called *synoikismos*, but remained just an odd conglomerate of four un-walled village settlements (Pitana, Limnae, Mesoa, and Kynosoura),[24] known as *obai*, with a fifth *oba* (Amyklai) having been added on at a later date, perhaps during the eighth century BC. Its citizens liked to boast that they needed no fortification walls,[25] remoteness allowing Sparta to remain without an encircling wall until the second century BC. Of course, being Spartans, they affected to regard fortification walls as effeminate, and they were proud to rely on their own self-defence purely on the masculine strength of their own militarily superb bodies. It was not an idle claim.

Yet Sparta was not only renowned for the skill and courage of its professional army, but also for the stability and excellence of its political constitution. Both, so most Greeks thought, it owed to the genius of one man, the lawgiver Lykourgos, which meant they tended to view, with a jaundiced eye it must be said, the 'Lykourgan' system as a means to an end. The principal sources on Sparta emphasize that he alone brought about *eunomia*, which means 'good order'.[26] In Sparta Tyrtaios sung the praises of *eunomia* (and who wouldn't), while another poet, Terpander of Lesbos, singled out Spartan law for special praise: 'The spear-points of young men blossom there . . . / along with the clear-sounding Muse / and Justice is in the wide streets'.[27] Nonetheless, clearly not all the elements of the Spartan socio-political apparatus can be neatly pinned down to the apparent reforms of Lykourgos (it may be significant that Tyrtaios does not mention him at all), especially as there are certain aspects of it that are very primitive. Herodotos believes that *eunomia* started in the ninth century BC, while Aristotle, whom Plutarch used as a source, claims that it was closely associated with the reign of the eighth-century BC king, Charilaos. Likewise, Thucydides also dates the *eunomia* to the early eighth century BC. It is known that Sparta's dual monarchy was instituted in the early eighth century BC. By studying the genealogy of the two royal families, that of the Agiadai, known as the senior house, appears to be correct, while that of the Eurypontidai show discrepancies before the reign of King Charilaos.[28] Perhaps the records were tampered with later to give the Eurypontidai equal footing with the Agiadai, viz. in the upper reaches of the Eurypontidai line, there are signs that surgery may have been applied.[29] If so, it can be deduced that Charilaos was one of the first kings of Sparta and, furthermore, was responsible for laying down the socio-political foundations of the future Spartan state.[30]

It does not really matter whether Lykourgos existed or not, and even the Spartans themselves were unclear about his status, for it was its special political institutions that made Sparta and the Spartans what they were. Though not a historian Plutarch had read much history and thoroughly enjoyed it. Therefore, in all probability drawing directly upon a now lost account of the Spartan constitution, the *Lakedaimoniôn politeia* by Aristotle, Plutarch quotes in full a document that purports to provide information about these special political institutions of Sparta.[31] In a commentary on it he says that the document was an oracular response brought from Delphi by Lykourgos and that it was called the *rhêtra* by the Spartans. The word *rhêtra* means, properly, any kind of pronouncement – from bargain or contract, through an oracle to a law – and it is probable that the *rhêtra* quoted by Plutarch was in origin a Spartan decree, later interpreted as an oracular response, and it should come as no surprise therefore to find the constitution of Sparta was ascribed piously to Apollo of Delphi. Xenophon, in his essay on the Spartan constitution and way of life, likewise called the *Lakedaimoniôn politeia*, calls them 'Delphic-oracle-given'.[32] Apollo Loxias was the Greek title of respect for Apollo the Crabwise, whose oracles emerged ever elusive and oblique. Much like oracular language, Sparta and its singular constitution can be construed in a number of different ways.

The *rhêtra*, which is the earliest surviving European constitutional document, provided Sparta with a means of establishing a new cult of Zeus Sullanios and Athena Sullania. It also advised the division of the people into tribes (*phylai*) and villages (*obai*, but the term *oba* is not attested outside the Spartan state), after which the people (Doric, *dâmos*) were to set up a council of elders (*gerousia*) consisting of thirty men including the two kings (*archagetai*, 'leaders'). They were also to hold assemblies (*apellai*) 'from season to season' through which the *dâmos* were sovereign to decide motions put forward by the elders and the kings. In his commentary on the text, Plutarch says that later the kings Theopompos (who had led Sparta to victory over the Messenians in about 710 BC) and Polydoros, who could have reigned together at the beginning of the seventh century BC, added a further clause: 'But if the *dâmos* make crooked utterance, let the elders and the kings decline it'.[33] This 'additional clause' to the main provisions either represents a concession to opposition at the time of the original document, or is a serious modification of the main point of the reform. The *rhêtra*, like any anthology of laws and human rights, is a grand vague statement of good intentions, but it is by no means complete. People seldom understand their own laws exactly; they have a sound idea of what is right and wrong, and a fairly vague notion of what they may and may not do. However, I am not entirely sure that this was the case with our Spartans as each was given a place in their society, hence the relative order in Sparta down to the social reforms of Agis v (r. 244–240 BC).

Whatever the date assumed for Lykourgos, the truth of the matter is that Sparta received a stable constitution relatively early, and retained it for a long period with surprisingly little modification and an almost lack of the violent change endemic in Greek politics. In all likelihood the *rhêtra* embodies the resolution of a major domestic crisis. In Tyrtaios' poem the two joint kings Theopompos and Polydoros come first and get star billing, which is what we would expect in a conservative society that had decided to retain hereditary kingship – or rather a hereditary dual kingship. In the *rhêtra*, however, the kings are downgraded to being mere members of the *gerousia*. The unique, and perhaps very novel, compromise achieved by it was to have a formative influence of the character of the Spartan state in the long term. The kings' sovereignty had presumably been under a severe threat. Now the *rhêtra* safeguarded their position by allowing them to retain their ancestral privileges, but at the cost of diminished authority. Thus the people, meeting in their assembly at regular intervals, gain the formal right to make the final decision on all matters of state. Political initiative, however, is skilfully reserved for the *gerousia*, which, of course, includes the two kings. They alone can lay business before the *apella*, and according to the supplement are even empowered to overrule any unacceptable decision by the *apella*. As the Theban lyric poet Pindar was to put it in the early fifth century BC, 'The councils of old men / Are pre-eminent there . . .'[34] This would certainly suggest that the *apella* did not have effective decisional power. Nonetheless, a *stasis* or civil disorder was worked out through the system by reforms, and one possible way of viewing the *rhêtra* is as a summary of these reforms.

One final change was the introduction of the ephorate, the office being absent from the *rhêtra*. According to Plutarch the first ephors were appointed 130 years after the time of the lawgiver (Herodotos has them concurrent), during the reign of Theopompos (*c*. 720–675 BC).[35] Aristotle too talks of Theopompos in the charming story of how the said king's wife lambasted him for diminishing the power of the kingship by giving it to the ephors. The beleaguered Theopompos snaps back 'but it will last'.[36] If the *rhêtra* is rightly dated to the era of Tyrtaios (viz. mid-seventh century BC),[37] the ephorate must have begun between this time and the first mention of the activity of the ephors in the historical record, about one hundred years later. Our sources, however, do agree on one important issue, namely that there was a gradual increase of ephors' powers, always at the expense of those of the kings.

In theory, at least, the Spartans placed a check on excessive oligarchic power by the institution of the ephorate. Nonetheless, the essence of oligarchical rule is the persistence of a certain world view and a certain way of life, imposed by the dead on the living. Whatever the virtues or defects of the political system that evolved at Sparta, at least there was a system, in the sense that a balance had been struck between opposing forces in the state. This balance seems to have eluded the majority of Greek *poleis*, including Athens, for many years.

Already in the fifth century BC Greek political theorists acquired the idea that a balance between different elements in a state would ensure stability and peace. It was a short step from there to the belief that Sparta's model stability rested on this principle of balance. Thus Aristotle's definition of the Spartan constitution says 'it partakes of oligarchy and of monarchy and of democracy ... the kingship is monarchy, the authority of the *gerousia* is oligarchy, but the authority of the ephors amounts to democracy, since they are of the *dâmos*'.[38] In other words, Aristotle speaks of Sparta as having a 'mixed constitution'.[39] Clearly for Aristotle, with his great liking for the 'mixed constitution' of Sparta, for all the *poleis* of Greece it was Sparta that held for him more promising features than any other – even if these had been imperfectly realized. The Spartan constitution seems to offer an excellent balance.

Balanced or not, Sparta was unique in its retention of the kingship as a living force; unique also in the institution of double kingship, that is, the Spartans had not one but two kings. Indeed, the most peculiar fact about the Spartan state was its dual monarchy, a phenomenon that has never been satisfactory explained. Herodotos claims that the two royal families of Agiadai and Eurypontidai shared a common ancestor, both of them proud to trace their lineage back to the tribal hero Herakles.[40] A less fanciful modern suggestion is that the two kings stem from a time when there were two tribes, each headed by a tribal chieftain. Eventually these tribes combine and the two chieftains share the leadership. We have in Pausanias an interesting story about the quarrel that arose between pairs of *obai*. He suggests that Pitana and Mesoa paired off against Kynosoura and Limnae, the rivalry resulting in bloodshed but solved through ritualizing the feud at the shrine of Artemis Orthia, Upright Artemis.

Anyway, peculiar or not, if the principal function of the old Greek kings, much like those found in Homer, were those of a war leader, chief representative of the people before the gods, and magistrate, we shall see that the Spartan kings fulfilled all these functions, but especially that of a war leader. The most extensive description of the rights and duties of the Spartan kings are given by Herodotos. He tells us that both kings shared equal powers, privileges and duties, and were the commanders-in-chief of the army for life.[41] In other words Sparta's dual kingship was a form of hereditary but non-monarchic military leadership, what Aristotle describes as 'a sort of pleni-potentiary generalship (*stratêgia*), irresponsible and perpetual'.[42]

Likewise the Spartan political constitution was tribal in its makeup, with a warrior assembly, *apella*, and a council of elders, *gerousia*. By the time of Aristotle the latter consisted of the two coequal kings and twenty-eight members, *gerontes*, who were elected for life from those Spartiates who were no longer eligible for military service, viz. more than sixty years of age, drawn *de facto* from the leading Spartiate families.[43] So there was a tight restriction to enrolment into this political body, namely one of birth. This restriction was obviously in the interests of those Spartans who accepted their system because the *gerousia* for them was the ultimate prize for *aretê*, what we usually translate as 'virtue', but it is much broader than the narrower, strictly moral English word and also encompassed the idea of nobility, which meant in reality it was a potent melange of moral and political senses of the word. Aristotle, like Plato before him, manages to bamboozle his readers into accepting such right-wing sentiments by flipping from the moral sense to the political one.[44] Like all seductions, the Aristotlean one proceeds by small, inconspicuous steps, which all together take us to a place we could never have imagined before. Many fastidious philosophers approved of Sparta's constitution because of its efficiency, without pausing to think of the quality of life resulting from it. We shall briefly touch upon this subject in the next chapter.

Unfortunately, though he tells us a great deal about Sparta and its constitutional process, we are bitterly disappointed as Aristotle does not assign the *gerousia* with a definite political function within the Spartan system. We can assume that the *gerontes* themselves represented a survival from the days of true monarchic power, when they would have been appointed by the kings, but little is known about the duties of the *gerousia* during our period of study. Herodotos does infer that the *gerontes* (he does not use the term *gerousia*) could act as a tribunal to hear capital cases, while Aristotle adds that the *gerousia* (the term he does use) had control over resolutions introduced before the *apella*, which implies one of its main functions was the all-important supervision of laws and customs.[45]

The *apella* was the main assembly comprising all adult male Spartan warrior citizens who had reached the age of thirty years; those who were of legitimate Spartan birth, who had been through the *agôgê*, who had been elected into one of the communal messes, and were in good standing. Collectively, they made up the *dâmos* (cf. Athenian *dêmos*). With the concurrence of the *gerousia* and under the presidency of an ephor, it had the right to vote on laws, decide on peace or war and the conclusion of treaties. In short, the *apella* had the ultimate sanction on matters of legislation and policy. Its other functions not only included electing members for the *gerousia*, but the election of another political body, that which was made up of the ephors. The usual mode of voting was by acclamation, not the counting of individual votes, which even Aristotle considers a childish game show – we would perhaps consider the whole process either cockamamie or crooked – even though Thucydides hints that this was not always the case.[46]

Indeed, the maturity attained by Spartan political institutions by the fifth century BC makes it is difficult to believe that the citizen body, when formally assembled, had no greater voice than had been possessed by the warrior host in the *Iliad*, which shouted its approval or disapproval when appealed to by the kings, princes and chieftains. On one crucial occasion Thucydides describes the procedure of the *apella*, and, as his choice of words shows, he at any rate thought that an actual debate had taken place. It fell to the *apella* in 432 BC to decide whether to go to war with Athens. First representatives from Megara and other *poleis* addressed the Spartan citizens, then those from Corinth, Sparta's chief ally, then an Athenian delegation, the enemy party. While the Megarians were the angriest participants, the Corinthians proved to be the most effective. They tried to persuade the Spartans that their traditional policy of discretion and disinclination to fight was disastrous in the face of the dynamic power of Athens. The Athenians were not at all conciliatory but conveyed a message of strength, confidence and determination. Thucydides says:

> They wanted to make clear the power of their *polis* to offer a reminder to the older men of what they already knew and to the younger men the things of which they were ignorant, thinking that because of their arguments the Spartans would incline to peace instead of war.[47]

Thucydides continues:

> When the Spartans had heard the accusations made by their allies against the Athenians, and the Athenians' reply, they excluded all [non-citizens] and deliberated among themselves about the present situation. The majority were of one opinion, namely the Athenians were already in the wrong and that war should be declared immediately.[48]

We certainly gain the impression from Thucydides' account that it does not seem credible that ephors, kings, and *gerontes* discussed the matter in the citizens' presence, while the citizens remained silent. The likelihood of such a proceeding seems to be excluded, in any case, by the remainder of Thucydides' narrative. After mentioning the majority view, he records the speech of the cautious old king Archidamos (against the declaration of war) and that of the fiery ephor Sthenelaidas (in favour of war).

The king's speech was balanced, measured, and relatively lengthy: Athens' power, he insisted, was greater than Sparta had been accustomed to facing, and of a different kind, and he feared, he told them, 'that we may leave this war as a legacy to our children'.[49] The ephor's rejoinder was a classic of laconic brevity and offensive bluntness: the Athenians are guilty of breaking the thirty-year treaty (of 445 BC), he stormed, 'so vote for war, Spartans, as the honour of Sparta demands'.[50] After he had made his bellicose tirade, Sthenelaidas assumes the character of a presiding magistrate and poses the question, directing the citizens to divide, instead of following their usual practice of voting by acclamation.[51] It would undoubtedly have made for a fairer debate if the citizens had been allowed to have their say after, instead of before, the ephor's speech, but Thucydides explains this too, saying that Sthenelaidas was so eager for war that he wanted an unequivocal demonstration in support of his policy. It is, therefore, not hard to understand why Sthenelaidas exploited his privileged position and posed the question without permitting further debate. Sparta was now nearer to war than peace, and the truth dawned upon Greece that the morrow would obliterate the plans of today.

The Spartan citizens elected a board of five ephors (*ephoroi*, 'overseers') annually (with no formal restrictions on eligibility but no re-election possible) at the end of the autumn and the senior ephor gave his name to the year. Aristotle alleges they were 'chosen from the people',[52] but we should not get carried away by this. Their powers were enormous. Combining executive, judicial and disciplinary powers (even over the kings), and unconstrained by written laws, they dominated both domestic and foreign affairs, including convoking the meetings of the *apella* (it usually met once a month, about the time of the full moon) and one of their number presiding,[53] receiving foreign ambassadors, declaring war, mobilizing and dispatching the army, and transmitting orders to its commanders once in the field.[54] When the ephors acted as judges, they arbitrated in civil disputes and also determined criminal cases. It is clear that their criminal jurisdiction comprised both magisterial powers and what we would recognize as the province of the police: 'The ephors are empowered to fine anyone they choose and to exact payment on the spot. They have the authority to deprive magistrates of their office and bring them to trial on a capital charge ... If they notice anyone breaking the law, they proceed to immediate punishment'.[55] If the ephors had such sanction against their fellow citizens, it is not surprising that their powers in respect of non-citizens were even more extensive: foreigners they banished from the state on their own authority, at the instance of a king,[56] and outlanders at Sparta they could condemn to death without trial.[57]

A very important reason for their preponderance arose from the fact that ephors messed together during their term of office, and so met daily; by contrast the *gerousia* was convened only at set times. Their origin, however, is wholly obscure, as they are not mentioned in the *rhêtra*, and the debate continues to this day. Certainly by the time of Xenophon Spartan constitutional theory held the kings were subject to the ephors. Xenophon informs us that all Spartans rose when the kings entered except the ephors, and that every month, in a stargazing ritual, the ephors and the kings exchanged oaths, each to uphold the position of the other, which was a mark of the constitutional restraints on the kings.[58] It suggests that in the distant, tribal past the ephors had functioned as shaman-type figures. One tradition has us believe that the first ephor 'to have given the magistracy notable strength and scope' went by the name of Asteropos, Starfaced.[59] Another tradition implies that the first notable ephor was Chilon (eponymous ephor *c.* 556/5 BC), who was the 'first man to yoke the ephors beside the kings'.[60] Usually this is read as Chilon being the first man to place the ephors on the same level as the kings, which certainly makes sense.

Thucydides says that the ephors had the power to arrest and imprison the kings, though not to judge and condemn,[61] and Herodotos demonstrates how far the ephors could indeed persuade the kings. Here he tells the story of Anaxandridas and his wife, who fails to produce a male heir. The ephors, along with the *gerontes*, go to the king and tell him to divorce her and marry another.[62] Together, it suggests that the kings would bow to the combined will of the ephors and the *gerontes*. Perhaps when complaints arose against the kings, the ephors served as mere complainants and the *gerontes* as judges. After the turn of the fifth century BC two ephors accompanied the kings on a campaign,[63] and it is not surprising that one of the central themes of Spartan history is the conflict between kings and ephors. The office itself could only be held once in a lifetime, but former ephors were likely to become members of the *gerousia*, and Aristotle considered it the most important of the Spartan state.[64] Nevertheless, we should not lose sight of the simple fact that individual kings were very powerful figures in their day through the force of their personality. In a society devoted to the art of war and so duteous of warriorlike prowess, a king with a good record of success in war would gain great glory and would be the focal point of his fellow warriors' esteem. What is more, the Spartans firmly believed that the blood of the gods ran through their kings' veins. Kings such as Kleomenes and Agesilaos, for instance, could and did transcend the Aristotlean notion that they were mere 'hereditary generals for life'.

The lion king

This may be a good moment to pause and look at one of the kings of Sparta, one, in fact, we have already met. Leonidas (r. 489–480 BC), son of Anaxandridas, was probably born in the early five-forties, born to his father's first wife (name unknown), but only after his father had a legitimate son, Kleomenes, with a second – apparently bigamous – wife (again, name unknown). Herodotos wrote that Anaxandridas' bigamy was 'an unheard of thing in Sparta',[65] but it certainly did not prevent Kleomenes, as the firstborn son, assuming the throne on his father's death. After Kleomenes' birth Anaxandridas achieved, finally, successful conception with his original wife – hence, first, Dorieus, and then two further sons, Leonidas and Kleombrotos. Obviously Anaxandridas did not abandon his first wife all together; in fact, he flatly refused to divorce her. Thus Leonidas was one of four sons of Anaxandridas, the second born to his first wife, the third overall.

Leonidas suddenly sprang into public prominence in 489 BC, nine years before he faced the Persians at Thermopylai. He became king rather unexpectedly, succeeding as the Agiadai king of Sparta after the sinister death of his elder half-brother Kleomenes, whose heiress daughter, Gorgo, he had married.[66] The official line was that Kleomenes, having turned stark raving mad, was put in chains where at last he took his own life by a nasty process of slicing himself into pieces from the feet up, or so Herodotos was told. 'Look to the end' is a popular Greek maxim meaning never judge the success of a man's life until you see how he meets his maker. Those whom the gods wish to destroy they first make mad, or so a character in a play of Euripides had once said. Most Greeks believed that it was for sacrilege that he was punished by his madness: regarding the celestial sphere with the eye of a diplomat, no one used or abused religion so much as Kleomenes. The Spartans disagreed – his sticky end was brought about because his brain had been befuddled by drinking great quantities of wine unmixed with water, a particularly nasty habit he had learned from Scythian envoys who came all the way from the northern shores of the Black Sea to propose a joint invasion of Anatolia after the misguided Persian expedition against them in 514 BC. Their plan was rejected but the habit stuck and eventually went to his head. Kleomenes became a demented alcoholic and died, unpleasantly, his brain desiccated by folly.

This is not the place to launch a disquisition on wine, but a few words may be in order. Wine for us is generally associated with mirth and merriment, but for the Greeks it was a deeply symbolic substance, and it was almost never taken neat. As such it was normally cut with water and served from a mixing bowl, *kratêr*, the proportion of wine to water noted by ancient authors being 3:1, 5:3 and, at its strongest, 3:2. So by regularly taking his wine 'in the Scythian fashion', if that is what he did, Kleomenes was no better than the most barbarous of barbarians. It was well known that the Scythians imbibed immoderately and when inebriated were capable of any excess.[67]

Yet the Spartans were notoriously abstemious and controlled wine drinkers, and the cult of Dionysos was certainly not ascribed to by them, a staple of religious expression elsewhere in the Greek world, for both men and women. The Spartans knew the true nature of the ambiguous god of wine and death, and a verse fragment of Kritias preserves a contrast between Spartan drinking habits and others:

Spartan young men drink enough to bring joyful hope to the mind of all, and friendship and restrained gaiety to their conversation. Such drinking is good for the body, good for the mind, and not harmful to the purse ... The Spartan way brings food and drink enough for thinking and working, but no excess; they have no day set aside for overindulgence and drunkenness.[68]

There were many sayings in the ancient world that wine was the keyhole into the mind, and the one we are all familiar with of course is *in vino veritas* of the Romans. But wine can also be seen as having hallucinogenic effects. The cult of Dionysos shows many traits that lead in this direction, perhaps best seen in the *Bacchae* of Euripides where feminine ecstasy culminates in ritually accelerated murder. The god of drunk, disorderly release was the very opposite of masculine Spartan control. Indeed, the only people in Sparta who were allowed – or rather were compelled – to really embrace wine and get rip-roaring drunk were helots, and this Dionysiac condition was forced on them as a deliberate demonstration by the adult Spartans to the upcoming generation of how a Spartan should not behave.

So did Kleomenes jump – or was he pushed? It would be unwise to believe everything written about Kleomenes; he had many enemies. Of course we will never know for sure, but it seems more likely that Kleomenes' reign was cut short by murder, arranged, and hushed up, on the orders of the man who succeeded him on the Agiadai throne. It is possible that when Leonidas led out his small army to Thermopylai, he had something on his conscience to expiate. Should we choose to follow the Greek idea of natural vengeance lurking at the heart of things, which is to say, if you disturb the balance of the universe, the pendulum will come back and hit you on the head? If Leonidas did indeed have his half-brother killed in the royal tradition of assassination, and so inevitably got his comeuppance, then the manner of his death was not, perhaps, entirely inappropriate.

So it was while Sparta was *en fête*, the rest of the Spartans being prevented by their overriding obligation to celebrate their most important annual festival, the Karneia in honour of Apollo Karneios, that Leonidas marched north with the Three Hundred, all 'men who had sons living'.[69] Of commands held by Leonidas previous to this one, which turned out to be his finest hour, we know nothing. As he was now beyond military age – the upper limit being sixty years of age – Leonidas could well have had experience of war stretching back to the five-twenties, but it could only have been in 'small wars', that is to say, against fellow Greeks such as the Athenians and the Argives.

As we know well, the Spartan king fell, pierced by Persian spears, while bravely leading a failed counterattack on the third day at Thermopylai. Some forty years later what were deemed to be his remains were brought back to Sparta for ceremonial reburial, and a hero-shrine was later established in his honour. As for the Three Hundred, their verse epitaph, composed by the most admired poet of the day, Simonides of Keos, and carved on a stone where they fell, is perhaps the most famous of all such inscriptions: 'Stranger, go tell the Lakedaimonians that here we lie, obedient to their laws'.[70] This lapidary and suitably laconic couplet reminded all Greeks for generations to come of the debt owed to the Spartans. The same message of pride and defiance was conveyed by the stone lion marker erected at the site, since the king of the animal kingdom symbolized martial prowess. This monument was also a nice echo of Leonidas' own name, 'descendant of Leon', since *leôn* was the Greek for our word lion.

Chapter 2

Love and War Among the Spartans

A thought-provoking feature of most ancient cultures is the predominant role played by women in the history and management of tribal affairs. Historiographies often seem to minimize the early, strongly matriarchal aspects of man's social units. The frequently myopic views of chauvinistic chroniclers of later ages (when they are mentioned at all) tend largely to either denigrate the role of women in the military history of early civilizations or ignore it entirely. Men, by a stretch of imagination, can probably picture themselves as emperors, heroes, prophets, conquerors, but not as women. Ancient sagas, archaeological discoveries, and the painstaking work of anthropologists, however, indicate widespread participation by women in tribal life in pre- and proto-historical times, from the misty lands of northern Europe to the sun-kissed cultures of the Mediterranean basin, in both the Celtic peoples and ancient Sparta, not to mention the footloose folk roaming the Eurasian steppes or, of course, the clan cultures of China.

The long shadow cast by ancient matriarchal influence, even if it continues to be ignored, can no longer be doubted. But what historical reality lies behind a time when men were stronger and braver, women more beautiful and powerful, so far removed from the peasant's misogyny of the poet Hesiod? In explaining the reasons for mankind's life of drudgery and pain, Hesiod tells two stories. Both start with the supreme god Zeus, angry with Prometheus for stealing fire and giving it to man, ordering the gods of Olympus to create another gift, a woman of great beauty and balefulness, from whom womankind is descended. In Hesiod's first version, however, she is herself enough to explain mankind's woeful lot on earth.[1] In the second version, on the other hand, she is called Pandora ('all giving') and, failing to contain her curiosity, opens a jar (the word 'box' comes from an early translation error) from which disasters, sicknesses and evils escape, leaving only hope caught within the lid.[2] Men are often brought into a situation where hope is the only thing left. How beautiful is that word 'hope', from that three leafed clover, which exalts men above the chaos of existence: faith, hope, charity. Anyway, the general meaning of this antifeminist fable is clear as it attributes the origins of all misfortune in the world to a woman, the lovely Pandora with her unblushing nature being the Greeks' equivalent of the biblical Eve, both regarded as a curse sent by a supreme being.

A woman's place

We can, of course, speculate that the tale of Pandora may have been fabricated by the Greeks to help keep their own women in line. Myths were powerful tools in Greek society, accepted as fact and used to justify societal conventions as well as to explain natural phenomena and the meaning of life. Or at least that was how myths were supposed to work. As we would have gathered by now, the Greek citizen, in the full, active and participatory sense, was always by definition an adult male. Women need not apply. Women were excluded from participating in politics or public life, and in many cases, their education, if any, was confined to the domestic arts, and not only their minds but their bodies were neglected, as they were forbidden to exercise. Even in Athens, the much heralded cradle of democracy, women were accorded the legal status of minors and depended on the protection and patronage of their husbands or a male guardian for everything from shelter to respectability. In truth, she was set apart and kept as much as practically possible out of the public eye. Not only was this a man's world, but it was one in which the inferior status of women was neither concealed nor idealized.

But when we turn to that bastion of he-man military aggression, Sparta, it seems that women were regarded as something special. As Homer sings 'I'm off to Sparta, where the women are a wonder'.[3] After all, wasn't Helen herself Spartan? Indeed, the reputation of Spartan women for eye-catching physical beauty starts with her, whose awesome charm and divine beauty captivated an unwelcome visitor to Sparta, Paris prince of Troy in Asia, overlooking the straits of the Hellespont (today's Dardanelles). This was the glorious but shameless woman whose misconduct in abandoning her husband, Menelaos, had caused countless woes for the Greeks, or so said the male poets.[4] But that is another story. As early as the seventh century BC the clairvoyant priestess of the fortune telling Apollo at Delphi issued, on the behalf of her lord and master, the following prophetic utterance: 'The best of all the land is the Pelasgian plain: best are the horses of Thessaly, / the women of Sparta, and the men who drink the water of fair Arethusa'.[5]

A similar sentiment comes from the pen of the Spartan lyric poet Alkman (*fl.* 630 BC) when he sings of 'honey-voiced maidens' and regrets his limbs will no longer carry him.[6] The lines form an apologetic prologue to an actual maiden-song or *partheneion*. The charming lyrics – meaning literally songs sung to the lyre – of Alkman remind us nicely that in his day Sparta was not all blood and thunder, and that the Spartans themselves were not all boorish, arrogant, austere, and rather anti-intellectual. In him we see nothing of the preoccupation with warfare and politics that pervades Tyrtaios' poetry. 'For in place of iron comes the beauty of the lyre',[7] and his women move like racehorses. They are compared with precious metals; their hair is long and flowing.[8] For Alkman nature made, not the reed for a boy's bedding, but flowers for a garland, and girls were girls, not battery-hens to produce Spartan warriors. Of course, as Sir Walter Scott the novelist once said, the wilder the society the more violent the impulse received from poetry and music. In this chapter we will discover how and why Spartan women were accorded more liberty and respect than their more genteel Athenian sisters.

Although a woman could not become a citizen herself, women being excluded from the *agôgê* and from the communal messes, she could inherit and manage property, including landed property, in her own right under Spartan law, probably without the necessary legal intervention of a male guardian. This was certainly true of daughters whose fathers lacked sons. Heiresses in Sparta were called *patrouchoi*, quite literally 'holders of the patrimony'.[9] This was certainly not the case in Athens, where the property went to the nearest surviving male relative and the women went with it (hence the Athenian term *epiklêros*, which means 'going with the allotment'). Athenian *epiklêroi* served merely as a vehicle for transmitting the paternal inheritance to the next male heir and owner, namely to their oldest son, their father's grandson, so on and so forth, whereas Spartan *patrouchoi* inherited in their own right.[10] Such women were highly-prized commodities, much sort after by eligible bachelors, since they could be married to any *homoios*, not only to the nearest paternal male kin. In the circumstances, it is easy to twist the facts and paint a picture of a world upside down. 'When the female rules the male', so began a Delphic oracle, meaning when everything is at sixes and sevens.

Indeed, the non-Spartan Aristotle identifies the status of Spartan women as one of the prime defects in the Spartan system, which not only led to women owning two-fifths of the land but also Sparta's decline.[11] In Aristotle's chilly world women, even free women, sat uncomfortably close to slaves. With regards to Sparta, therefore, he obviously felt affronted by the great freedom enjoyed by the women there, in contrast with their subjection in other *poleis*. All of us today, in theory at least, have the right to act as independent agents and thus enjoy the right to initiate actions of law, but not so with the women of ancient Greece. They could not carry out any legal transaction in their own name and hence the *kyrios*, a male kinsman who looked after such matters. So a daughter until married would come under the protection of the head of the household, and when married she passed into the *kyrieia* of her husband. If her husband passed away, then the eldest son assumed this role. This speaks very eloquently for the position of women in a society in which the unmarried woman had no role and no place.[12]

A woman's power

Another important factor was the *proix*, the dowry. This was the practice whereby the family of the bride would have to furnish a dowry by law, with well-to-do families including property as well as the basic provision of a trousseau. This is also significant as it was one of the chief means by which land changed hands in ancient Greece, but it is also significant for the female as it formed the basis for her eligibility for marriage, personal charms being very rarely on public display. How important, however, the dowry was lower down the social ladder is another question of course. At that level perhaps it mattered less, but even in modern Greece at the humbler levels of society there is a feeling of pride in the fact that a bride can be provided for in terms of a dowry.

'Dowry power' of course represents women's two-edged historical significance in ancient Greece. On the one hand, it demonstrates the vulnerability of women as pawns in a fundamentally masculine game of political and social chess. Yet on the other hand it was one of the ways in which women could exert a considerable amount of influence, the danger of marrying a woman who was richer than the man. Plutarch, for instance, talks of 'dowry slaves and not husbands'.[13] The husband may have untrammelled rights over his wife's dowry, but if he divorced her – a relatively easy procedure without any resulting moral stigma – the law was very clear, namely he had to return the dowry intact back to her family. If nothing else, such 'dowry power', especially in well-to-do circles, meant the husband of a rich wife had to exercise a considerable amount of moderate behaviour towards his wife. In Sparta, as we may well have guessed at this point, things were rather different, for there it looks as though the dowry was the legal property of the wife, if indeed Aristotle's reasoning for Spartan women owning so much land in Sparta was because of the 'many heiresses' and 'large dowries'.[14]

Aristotle did not like the women of Sparta. He argued with perfect symmetry that the women of Sparta, whose men were superior to other Greeks in war, were inferior to other Greek women, 'no use at all', in the face of an enemy (viz. Theban) invasion.[15] When Aristotle says that Spartan women were not trained to hardihood commensurate with their freedom and that in consequence they became licentious and dissolute, he seems to be in conflict with other authorities, which speak of the obligation imposed on women to participate in gymnastic exercise.[16] Aristotle himself adopts a pedantic, not to say the absolutely orthodox male (chauvinist), view of the matter, and his shock and horror is therefore palpable when he bursts out that the men of Sparta are *gunaikokratoumenoi*, 'ruled by their women'.[17] Some modification at least of the latter testosterone-fuelled view is required.

Amazons of Sparta

In truth, adolescent girls underwent an upbringing similar to the boys, far less brutal, of course, but centred on dancing and gymnastics, the latter pursuit involving running, wrestling, javelin and discus throwing. They also mixed freely with boys and like them, according to Plutarch and depicted as such in the art of early Sparta, exercised either completely naked or partially nude in full public view.[18] Little wonder such disregard of the normal sexual inhibitions shocked outside observers. The derogatory epithet 'thigh-flashers' was coined just for them by Ibykos, though ultimately such 'exhibitionism' was done so as to attract suitors.[19] The sexual powers of women could disturb the world of men, and Greek men were frightened of this, even if only subconsciously.

It could be argued that the Spartan marriage ceremony expressed the subordination of the woman to male society. This took the form of a ritual seizure of the woman from her family home. At the marital home the bride's hair was cropped back to her scalp by a bridesmaid, and she was dressed as a man to await the bridegroom in a darkened room, who came late at night and stayed only long enough to perform reproductive duty before returning to his communal mess.[20] The couple's subsequent amorous encounters would equally be swift and furtive, and always nocturnal, each one quick, violent – more like military skirmishes than love. Indeed, marriage was expected to be a clandestine affair. Not until the age of thirty was the man allowed the right to set up his own household and even then he was still expected to sup and sleep in his communal mess, lying with his wife by stealth.[21] Likewise the aspect of transvestism probably represented the bridegroom's *rites de passage* out of the exclusively masculine world of the communal mess, while the ritual seizure can be witnessed in many tribal societies where marriages by capture was the rule. Despite its apparent archaisms marriage was encouraged at Sparta as the most desirable basis for procreation, which the state encouraged by alleviating the burden of taxation on citizens who had more than a certain number of sons, while bachelors were publicly ridiculed by women and suffered legal disabilities. However, not all succumbed to the abuse. The notable and distinguished Spartiate, Derkylidas, remained a bachelor.[22]

That woman needed man, as man a woman, was considered self-evident in Sparta. When Leonidas was about to depart for Thermopylai and his death, his wife, the loveable Gorgo, the daughter of one king and now the wife to another, inquired if he had any last-minute instructions for her. In reply, the king merely said: 'To marry good men and bear good children'.[23] Bearing children (*teknopoiia*, 'children-making') was the most important function of Spartan women, since the state was constantly at war, as much as with the enemy within, the helots, as enemies without, and the production of warriors was of highest priority. Thus, the motivation behind the freedom of life permitted to Spartan women was purely eugenic and not humanitarian, as was the tradition to allow Spartan girls to marry in their late teens and not straight after puberty. It is this custom that has the Athenian oligarchic leader Kritias waxing philosophically in his work on contemporary Sparta: 'I will begin with the birth of a man; how would one produce the best and strongest physique? If the father exercises energetically, eats well and tests his endurance to the limit, and the mother of the potential child is strong and takes exercise herself'.[24] Plutarch observes a similar phenomenon when he says that:

> [The Spartans] took particular care about the women as the men ... [they] toughened the girls physically by making them run and wrestle and throw the discus and javelin. Thereby their children in embryo would make a strong start in strong bodies and would develop better, while the women themselves would also bear their pregnancies with vigour and would meet the challenge of childbirth in a successful, relaxed way.[25]

Tough, strong mothers were believed to produce tough, strong warriors. This is related, of course, to the greater need of the Spartan state with regards to its army.

It is for this reason that the state encouraged wife sharing. According to Xenophon and Plutarch it was perfectly honourable for a Spartan to share the begetting of children with worthy citizens. Thus if an elderly man had a young wife, he might introduce her to a younger man of whom he approved and adopt any offspring of their union. Again, a citizen might admire another man's wife for the splendid children she bore her husband and for her own wifely virtues. Thus if he gained the husband's consent, he could beget children upon her.[26] Jealousy was despised, and both Xenophon and Polybios concur that brothers could possess a wife in common.[27] We can imagine there were Spartans who did not know their genetic fathers. Sparta had always been obsessed with the fear that the number of *homoioi* would diminish, and citizens incapable of begetting sons had their wives impregnated by a famous warrior to ensure strong, robust progeny for themselves and, above all, for the state.

This brings us to a strange tale. The Greeks, feeling a need for land, had looked for it in colonies beyond the sea, and accordingly, beginning in the eighth century BC, they had taken to their agile boats and began to plant colonies around the Mediterranean basin. Some of these overseas ventures were state-sponsored, while others were purely private affairs. Either way, the new settlement was always essentially independent. The founding state was owed respect and ritual recognition, but did not exercise direct imperial control over the colony. Anyway, Greek expansion to the west and Greek trade with the east marked the beginning of four hundred years of overseas involvement, which would reach its climax with the meteoric conquests of Alexander the Great. The Spartans, however, had not taken to their boats but had sought that desired land just beyond their own frontiers – they would also miss out on that amazing and terrible Greek adventure under Alexander, but that is to anticipate. Anyway, a long, gruelling war, later known as the First Messenian War (*c.* 730–710 BC), had resulted in the subjugation of Messenia, the south-western quarter of the Peloponnese. One colony they did send out to Taras on the instep of Italy (Roman Tarentum, modern Taranto), but this was a special case.

The motives underlying Greek colonization were, indeed, very similar to those that led to colonization in more recent times: overpopulation at home and a desire to escape crowded conditions; sheer adventurism and brigandage; political intolerance and social discrimination. According to historical tradition, Taras was founded in 706 BC, and archaeological evidence indicates that such a date cannot be far wrong. The earliest and simplest reason for its foundation is given by Aristotle as an instance of the divisions that may arise in a state when the aristocracy assigns all the political privileges to itself, 'for example the so-called *Partheniai*, whom the Spartans detected in a conspiracy and sent away to be the founders of Taras'.[28]

The name *Partheniai* is not adequately explained by Aristotle. In other authors it is constantly associated with the word *parthenos*, 'virgin', and the most straightforward explanation is that is a term of contempt used by one political faction of their 'virginal' opponents. According to a contemporary of Aristotle, the historian Ephoros (in a passage quoted by Strabo), the *Partheniai* were the sons of unmarried mothers born during the First Messenian War. Spartan women left at home for the duration of the war, which turned out to be a long-drawn-out affair, wanted to avoid the risk of a future shortage of men. Hence they sent a delegation to their husbands to point out that they were fighting on unequal terms, that is, the Messenians were staying at home and fathering children while the Spartans had left their wives virtually as widows. Incidentally, the men had sworn not to return home until victorious, but yielded to the arguments of their women and sent home from the army some youngsters with orders to bed all the virgins of childbearing age in Sparta. How-ever, when the Spartan warriors at long last won the war and marched home, they repudiated the offspring of these illicit unions and denied them the rights accorded to other citizens because of their illegitimacy. Their subordinate status provoked them into rebellion, which was put down.

Whether we choose to believe or not that these dissidents were bastard born, it is typical of any nascent society to exclude for whatever reason dubious members at the point when new benefits are being apportioned. Anyway, it was decided to send Phalanthos, the leader of the dissidents, to consult Apollo's oracle at Delphi, who gave the following response: 'I give you Satyrion, both to settle the rich land of Taras and to be the scourge of the Iapygii'.[29] The oracle, probably *post eventum*, thus defines the focal points of the territory of the colony: the urban centre and its eastern outpost, and also the mention of the Iapygii anticipates the struggle against the indigenous population that Taras will have to face throughout its history. Paradoxically, Sparta's one and only overseas adventure was to become renowned as a byword for extravagance and degenerate luxury.[30] Allowing for an element of exaggeration, it is clear that in time Taras became a most prosperous *polis*, where the wealthy lived a life of great luxury.

A king's daughter

Women were definitely not allowed to complete in the Olympics, a strictly men-only affair, but this did not prevent them from participating by proxy. As owners of horses, they could not be prevented from entering their teams in the chariot events, which were held in a separate hippodrome, and several women are known to have done this at Olympia. The first and most famous of all was Kyniska,[31] daughter of King Archidamos and full sister of King Agesilaos. Plutarch, probably following Xenophon, says her brother persuaded her to enter a chariot team in one of the races, in order to prove that victory in equestrian events was purely a matter of wealth and not of skill (as in battle, of course).[32] But, according to Pausanias, Kyniska had always had one great ambition – to win an Olympic victory. This she achieved in 396 BC with a four-horse chariot team. In 392 BC she competed, and won, again. Kyniska was certainly no wallflower, and in celebration of one of these victories, probably the first, she set up two bronze monuments representing chariots, a small one in the antechamber of the temple of Zeus, and a larger one in the sacred grove known as the Altis. Part of the inscribed base of the larger monument survives and indicates that it included a statue of her. An ancient source recorded the full wording of the inscription:

> *Sparta's kings were fathers and brothers of mine,*
> *But since with my chariot and storming horses I, Kyniska,*
> *Have won the prize, I place my effigy here*
> *And proudly proclaim*
> *That of all Grecian women*
> *I first bore the crown.*[33]

Generally speaking Greek *poleis* took great pride in the achievements of their citizens, and individual citizens could convert their Olympic prestige into political power. But what if that individual happened to be a woman?

Whether or not her glorious brother tried to diminish her Olympian achievements, upon her death Kyniska was to be awarded a heroine's shrine in Sparta. Many Greek men, including Spartans, would have given their eyeteeth for that. The Spartans were fully immersed in feminine influences, both real and symbolic. This was only fitting, since goddesses were the traditional guardians of intuition, empathy, and creativity, the boons that helped the Spartans develop beyond the limitations of their solely masculine upbringing – a feature that they share with the cultures of many other heroic warrior societies. Sparta may have been an odd community isolated from surrounding fashions, yet life was not quite as grim as Plutarch paints it, and the Spartans were certainly not all soulless shells of bronze and iron. Pindar, the Theban lyric poet, wrote of Sparta that the 'dances, music, and exuberant joy flourished alongside councils of old men and the spears of young men'.[34] Turning, inevitably, back to warfare.

Mothers' sons

War for the Greeks was by gender and definition men's work. This is because the quality of courage, bravery, or pugnacity that was required to stand fast in the hoplite phalanx was in their vocabulary *andreia*, manliness. It was therefore, strictly speaking, impossible for a Greek woman to be brave in the relevant martial sense, that is to say, courageous on the red field of hoplite battle. After all, the entire male baggage of war, in the pithy phrase of the visionary Herakleitos of Ephesos (*fl*. 500 BC), was 'the father of all, the king of all'.[35]

Our two chief literary sources for Spartan society are Xenophon's *Lakedaimoniôn politeia*, an uncritical eulogy, and Plutarch's *Lykourgos*, much of whose basis is the narrative of Xenophon into which has been fitted a plethora of antiquarian facts, some bona fide others fabricated. From these two works we gather that the full citizen of Sparta, the Spartiate, was wholly at the service of the state. In order to enable the Spartiate to overcome any mental impasse precipitated by man's natural fear of death, he had to be trained to think of himself as a man whose life was not his own. Hence, the Spartiate had to be always prepared for a sudden and violent end. This conditioning began in infancy.

At birth the elders of the tribe, *gerontes*, decided on grounds of health if a newborn child should be reared, the grim alternative being exposure on the mountainside. This was the terrible law of Sparta: no male child who was deformed, and so could not become a warrior, was allowed to live.[36] The boys who passed inspection were deliberately toughened from an early age, by bathing them in wine, feeding them with plain fare and getting them accustomed to harsh conditions.[37] Then from the age of seven years (Plutarch) or fourteen (Xenophon) there began a state-organized upbringing, the *agôgê* ('raising', as of cattle), aimed at preparing them for their future role as warriors. The boys were organized into 'packs' (*agelai*, the same term that was used in Crete) under pack-leaders, whose orders the boys had to obey, who in turn were supervised closely by magistrates. An important magistrate, the *paidonomos* or Warden of the Boys, was appointed to take charge of the *agôgê*, and his authority over the boys was no less than that of a general over an army. He was assisted in the enforcement of discipline by a number of citizens called whip-bearers, and we may assume that this title was no empty one.[38]

The boys were brutally initiated into communal living, providing, for example, their bedding from reeds torn by their own hands from the banks of the shallow, sandy Eurotas. They were also prohibited everyday luxuries such as footwear, allowed only one cloak to wear throughout the year, and survived on a diet that was deliberately inadequate. The latter hardship promoted the stealing of food as an adventurous duty, to develop ingenuity in war, which in turn led to severe beatings if a boy was caught in the act. Physical pain had to be endured without betraying the slightest emotion. Formal education was kept to a minimum, but did include music, gymnastics, and fierce games embracing the principles of warfare.[39] They were also 'taught to express themselves in a style, which was at once sharp, yet at the same time attractive and suited to concise exposition of a variety of points'.[40] By the fourth century BC this spare style of speaking had acquired a name for itself, 'laconic'.[41]

Many definitions of the term education have been advanced by scholars, both past and present. All of these definitions may be conveniently reduced to two major attitudes. The first is active and embraces all those definitions that refer to education as an intellectual search for and within new or expanding fields of knowledge. The second is passive and embraces all those definitions that consider education as training in the mastery of various skills. The former type of education (therefore, of knowledge) embraces the entire range or as many aspects as possible of humanity's reality, thus becoming an independent inquiry into the unanswered dilemma its reality proposes at almost every turn. The latter type of education concentrates mainly upon a few, supposedly known and established aspects of that existence which it reiterates and reconfirms. One reaches out into the unknown and in every possible direction, while the other revolves around the familiar and, therefore, moves in one direction alone. In this context, it will be understood that the *agôgê*, by its very nature and emphasis upon producing warriors who based their very existence upon the regularity and rigid discipline of military life, concentrated upon the second type of education, which it defined, quite conservatively, as the repetition of orderly and expected patterns of thought and behaviour, according to a precise sequence leaving little or no room for improvisation. Spartan education was the most thorough system in the Greek world, but it was designed to produce cogs for a machine.

And so it was for the next fourteen years of his life that a boy worked his lonely way up through the increasingly brutal and brutalising pedagogy, an elementary education that was entirely determined by the purpose of inuring him to bear hardships, training him to endure an exacting discipline, and instilling into his heart, a sentiment of devotion to Sparta. Failure, of course, meant utter disgrace, for it often entailed (in characteristically Spartan fashion) social ostracism. Even in his day, Thucydides could compare the easy living to be had by the Athenians to the laborious life of the Spartans 'from their very cradles'.[42] And, like most peoples in most ages, the Athenian assumed that a culture different from his own must be inferior. The militaristic Spartan in turn was equally prejudiced; proud of his own culture and heritage, he had no doubt that it was superior to that of the decadent, soft-living democratic Athenian. He proudly belonged to a military caste, in which the individual was rigidly subordinated to the *polis*. He was a soldier, and his education, marriage, and the details of his daily life were all strictly regulated with a view to the maintenance of professional military efficiency.

A brave new order

As professional soldiers the Spartans showed themselves to be fearless and haughtily contemptuous of the pothering of amateurs. They made some errors of calculation and failed to make the most of their singular society, but they were not moonstruck. The madness in Leonidas at Thermopylai, for instance, was not a hysterical crazy, into-the-brink, to-the-fore madness. Rather, he was insanely calm. He never sweated beads of pearly fear. He was a seasoned Spartan soldier, a combat veteran, an ideal leader of men in the field. It was that kind of madness, the perfect guardian for the Platonic Republic. This is not to say that Leonidas did the work of the tyrant. But it was in his manner, and he cultivated it. He walked with an easy, silent, fearless stride. Leonidas was not a fanatic. He was not gung-ho; he was not a man in search of a fight. It was an Aristotlean ethic that Leonidas practised: making war is a necessary and natural profession. It is natural, but it is only a profession. And, like Aristotle after him, Leonidas believed in and practised the virtue of moderation, so he did what was necessary for a king and commander in war, and no more nor less. At least, so it appeared.

The rigid subordination of the individual, his elementary education and his private life to the ends of the state has always given the Spartan system a fascination to all who value order and conformity above freedom, to revolutionaries of the left and reactionaries of the right. Even today, when government by the people has long lost its novelty, there is no shortage of men, or women for that matter, who find democratic process contemptible, power seekers looking for obedience not debate. For Plato the Spartan model was very important indeed, and remains central to European thought to this day, whether the political thinker has elected to admire (as Machiavelli, Rousseau and Hitler all did in their different ways), or to feel repelled. Turning his back on the Athenian democracy that had executed Sokrates, Plato tries to imagine a new world in which every generation will possess and honour the equivalents of Sokrates – the people he calls philosophers.[43] Sokrates and Plato were not political thinkers but idealists: their quarry was that timid and elusive creature, the human soul, that divine spark incarcerated only briefly in the world of men.[44]

Through Sokrates, who is the main speaker of the *Republic*, Plato based his ideal *polis* in this dialogue on a critical interpretation of Spartan institutions, and Sparta plays a prominent role in his last and longest work, the *Laws*.[45] Aristotle too, erstwhile pupil of Plato, thought Sparta the most important historical model for an ideal *polis*. Both men agreed that what was wrong with the Spartan system was not its methods but its aim. Sparta aimed to produce citizens with the merits of discipline, respect for law, and excel in courage, and that was not enough. Moreover, they were stupid, greedy, and brutal to their less privileged social classes. Plato may to some extent have shared the admiration often felt by other Greeks for Sparta, but he was well aware of Spartan limitations. Implicit in his doctrines are his concern with a rational moral philosophy, his intellectual pursuit of the true scale of virtue, his vision of the soul. In short, for Plato all citizens should be trained by Spartan methods to excel in all virtues.

With the genial irony that was his trademark, Sokrates, in Plato's *Republic*, adumbrates an imaginary *polis* in which the citizens will be grouped in three classes. The highest class will comprise the guardians, who are the effective rulers of the state. Then come the auxiliaries, who are charged with the state's defence and the suppression of malefactors, 'to enforce the decisions of the rulers'.[46] These two classes, really subdivisions of a single class, share the same way of life, and are put through the same elaborate system of training and promotion. Finally there will be all the rest, the artisans, who will satisfy all practical needs, viz. farmers, manufacturers, traders. All work in harmony, guided by the expert understanding of the guardians, who, unlike the others, grasp what is in the common interest. Everyone in the ideal *polis* – men *and* women – is exposed to the same elementary education system.[47] The better one does, the higher one rises in the hierarchy of the *polis*, from artisan to auxiliary to guardian. Yet Sokrates attaches the greatest possible importance to the genetic selection, education, and training of the class of guardians, and, as we have become familiar within this chapter, his proposals resemble the institutions of Lykourgan Sparta in many details.

As we watch the gradual unfolding of Sokrates' ideal *polis* in the third, fourth, and fifth books of the *Republic*, we keep catching hints of Sparta – even though the name 'Sparta' is hardly ever mentioned. An important part of the guardians' training consists of a flexible kind of gymnastics, which not only produces a sound and healthy constitution but also prepares them for war and the endurance of pain and hardship. Furthermore, their diet must be frugal, and their lives free from sexual irregularities.[48] The same goes for the Spartiates, of course, and a further resemblance to Sparta is seen in the injunction to the guardians to expose children who are born with defects – whether they are physical, mental, or moral.[49] Like the Spartiates, the guardians are to eat in communal messes and live together like soldiers on a campaign. In addition, they are to have no truck with those contaminants, gold or silver.[50] The guardians may not journey abroad on their own occasions, any more than the citizens of Sparta are allowed to do.[51] Just as the citizenship of unworthy Spartiates could be rescinded, so a guardian might be removed into one of the other classes; the guardians should possess wives, children and property in common; the unity and harmony of the *polis* are paramount, and each individual contributes to its welfare in the manner dictated by his own nature; the *polis*, once established, is to be a highly conservative one, with the guardians taking care to prevent innovations in gymnastics or in music.[52] The young must be silent and respectful in the presence of their elders, rising when they enter or leave.[53] The women among the guardians (just like the daughters of Spartiates) are to follow the men's example and engage in gymnastic exercise lightly clothed.[54]

Plato dislikes the distraction of family affections, but he has other reasons as well. He starts from the principle of the equality of the sexes. This does not make Plato a feminist, not by a long chalk. Rather, by this he means that, though men and women have different functions in the process of reproduction, they should, apart from that difference, follow the same careers, share the same education and have the same opportunities. Women may not always be able to do quite such arduous or active work as men, the obvious example being war, but within the limitations imposed by their physique equality is to be absolute. It follows logically that they must be exempted as far as possible from family responsibilities. With complete logic therefore he removes those responsibilities by abolishing the family and substituting for it a system of state nurseries. Which brings us back to Sparta.

Absolutely typical of the Spartan system is Sokrates' provision that a soldier who deserts the ranks or throws away his weapons or commits similar cowardly acts should be demoted from the class of guardians to that of artisans.[55] The armies of Greece were citizen militias, while that of Sparta was professional, and that may, in part, have suggested to Plato that his guardians, who first appear as a military group, should be specialists in war.

It is difficult to know how seriously we should take the writings of Plato when he promotes the idea that the rule of a benevolent monarch or autocrat who is also a philosopher is a far better alternative to democracy.[56] Still, in promulgating (through the mouth of his hero Sokrates – or at any rate his representation of 'Sokrates')[57] a society that has so many points of contact with Sparta, Plato, of course, shows his political bias. He was, relevantly, a relative of Kritias, a pupil of Sokrates, and a leading light of the Thirty Tyrants, the thirty-man Spartan-backed junta that had tyrannized Athens in 404/3 BC, and what appealed to him most about Sparta was that the individual had no right to a life of his own: his interests were identified completely with the interests of the *polis*. Expert knowledge gives its possessors the right to enforce on others what the experts see to be in their true interests, just as the patient must defer to the doctor and the crew to the ship's captain. It was the denial of this healthy principle (in Plato's eyes) that led to radical democracy, which Plato disgustedly regarded as tantamount to anarchy – 'every individual is free to do as he likes'.[58] He lamented that there was a constant evolutionary trend towards egalitarianism and inclusion in Athens, and felt that the logical evolution of democracy had no end. Indeed, all hierarchies of merit would disappear like puffs of smoke as even deckhands would see themselves as captains, with a birthright to take their turn at the tiller whether or not they knew anything about seamanship. Even the animals at Athens, he jested, would eventually question why they, too, were not equal under an ideology whose aim was to lower all to a common level. The answer was simple. Renouncing seapower altogether would be preferable to having to deal with 'helmsmen, pursers, rowers, and all sorts of quite disreputable people'.[59] Some of us would undoubtedly consider Plato narrow-minded and illogical.[60] Seapower was *de rigueur* for those who wanted to play on the international stage. It is none too surprising, therefore, to find Plato's pupil, the worldly minded Aristotle, suggesting that the presence of such people was a necessary evil, which could be contained by excluding them from political rights.[61]

A dysfunctional society

In landlubbing Sparta Plato saw two major iniquities: the iniquity of a split community in which one section, a military aristocracy, exploits and holds down the remainder by force, and the iniquity of the lack of intelligence. The Spartan may have many good qualities but he simply had not the intellectual capacity to understand what he was doing; indeed he mistrusted the intellect and everything to do with it. The Spartans had the contempt for toil and economy usual in a warrior class. Under the Lykourgan system they had chained the helots to the soil, and thereafter hoped that the land, thus stocked, would support them with no further attention on their part. It all sounds simple enough in outline, but land tenure in Sparta is a complex problem. The importance of its basic understanding lies in the fundamental fact that the primary criterion for being a Spartiate was the ability to give the payment in kind, *telos*, to his communal mess. As this was tallied in so many measures of barley, of olive oil, of wine, and so forth, a Spartiate needed land.

Most of us have in the backs of our minds the notion that land was assigned to a Spartiate at birth, especially if we have read Plutarch when he promotes the tradition that Lykourgos was responsible for this.[62] In truth, again according to Plutarch, this is only part of the story, for Lykourgos sought to place the Spartiates on a footing of complete equality by dividing the territory of Lakedaimon in equal allotments or estates (Ionic *klêroi*, Doric *klâroi*), which amounted to 9,000 in number. We are assuming, of course, that the equality was by way of productivity and not size, there being rich land and poor, wet land and dry, stony land and alluvial, et cetera. Anyway, another tradition, as Plutarch points out in the same paragraph, has the division as 6,000 to Lykourgos and 3,000 to Polydoros, and yet another that half the 9,000 were allotted by Lykourgos, and half by Polydoros.[63] Whatever the truth, if indeed it is the truth, 9,000 appears to be the key figure, which we shall return to a little latter.

Both these views are certainly myths, the second probably created by the attempted social and economic revolution of Agis V, the short-lived king of the mid third century BC who wanted to carry out a land redistribution in Sparta, parcelling up certain parts for the *perioikoi* and other parts for the *déclassé* Spartans with the sole intention of increasing the number of *Spartiãtai*, who, after all, were warriors totally committed to the state. Plutarch mentions a figure of 4,500 *klêroi*,[64] which, according to some,[65] is half of that magic figure of 9,000 simply because Sparta no longer occupied Messenia, it having been removed from its control after the Spartans went down fighting to the Thebans at Leuktra (371 BC). It is pertinent to note that Herodotos tosses out remarks about Spartans who belonged to the noblest families, much like any other Greek *polis* of his day, and in his account of Lykourgos he fails to mention any radical programme of land reform.[66] Again, in Thucydides we read that the Spartans were the first Greeks to take up the habit by which the rich dress modestly, in this way 'doing their best to assimilate their way of life to that of the common people',[67] a view enhanced by Aristotle when he says that certain families were only eligible for membership of the *gerousia*.[68] All in all, we have here a clear implication that the ownership of wealth (and hence landed property) varied widely within the ranks of the Spartiates. So, though the Spartiates were in theory considered 'similars', in practice there were differences in birth and wealth. In truth, the first mention that each and every Spartiate owned only a single allotment of equal productivity is contained in a passage by Polybios. In this he talks of the dissimilarity of the Spartan constitution to that of Crete, referring to, amongst other matters, 'the land laws according to which no one [Spartan] citizen may own more land than another, but all are to possess an equal share of the state land'.[69]

By arming themselves with this Polybian statement, there are those who would argue for the existence of two types of land in Sparta, namely private land and state land. Each Spartiate, so the argument runs, would have inherited any amount of the first and owned an equal lot of the second, which was known as the *archaia moira*, 'ancient portion'. One morsel of evidence in support of this notion comes from a curious fragment of a work by Herakleides Lembos who was apparently quoting from the lost *Lakedaimoniôn politeia* of Aristotle. The fragment consists of just a few words: 'To sell land was considered disgraceful by Spartans, but to sell part of the ancient portion was not possible'.[70] A second morsel comes from Plutarch, who writes 'it was possible for foreigners to become Spartan citizens by going through the *agôgê*, but it was not possible to sell part of the portion assigned of old'.[71] Finally, Plutarch again, who says at the time of Agis V 'there were no more than 700 Spartiates left, of whom perhaps one hundred owned land in addition to their lot'.[72]

All the same, we can dispose of this argument for two types of land by looking closely at the evidence upon which it rests, taking each in turn, in reverse order. Plutarch's passage comes from a notorious chapter riddled with peculiar utterances, the implication being that the author was rather muddled here. It is fairly clear that Herakleides Lembos is talking of land but we do not know the context of the whole matter. In the final analysis we suspect the term 'ancient portion' may be an age-old term, but what does it really mean? Some scholars have proposed this 'ancient portion' was not the land itself but the produce from the land itself, and it was this produce that a Spartiate was not allowed to sell.[73] The best piece of evidence to support this, admittedly just as enigmatically confusing as those pooh-poohed above, is reflected in a fragment of the lost *Messenian Affairs* written during the third century BC (and thus after the liberation of Messenia) by Myron of Priene: 'And on handing the land (over to them), they [the Spartiates] set them [the helots] a portion (of produce) which they were constantly to hand over to them'.[74] So the land was the Spartiate's and he could do as he pleased with it (as implied by Aristotle). However, it was disgraceful for him to sell or buy land, even though he could (as implied by Herakleides Lembos).

Thus, a Spartiate could inherit, bequeath, buy or sell land but he could not do the same with the produce of that land. Evidence to back this comes from Plutarch, who says: 'Helots worked the land for them, bring to them the rent laid down of old, and there was a curse to anyone trying to get more',[75] that is to say, the rent was the 'ancient portion' and the curse stopped the master from extracting more than was set by custom. The reason being, we may hazard, is that the economy of the *klâroi* was arranged largely to supply the Spartiates' material needs. Apart from this, Sparta was much like any other Greek *polis* in so far as there was an intimate connection between land tenure and citizenship, and the land was exploited for subsistence farming and not for profit-seeking agriculture. On the other hand, the crucial difference between Sparta and the rest was of course the fact that the land was worked by helots.

Elsewhere Plutarch says that 'every father still bequeathed his lot of land to his son',[76] meaning in Sparta a Spartiate acquired land through inheritance, and of course there were not allotments of equal proportions. Two examples will suffice to dismiss the idea that equality of allotments between Spartiates had ever existed during historical times. Xenophon talks of Agesilaos, on becoming the Eurypontidai king, bequeathing half of his property to his mother's kinsfolk 'because he saw that they were in want'.[77] This indicates that normal land laws existed in Sparta. It is also an indication that property could be disposed off as one thought fit. In practice, this equality was illusory, as is shown not merely in the hints in our sources that some individuals were more equal than others while some families were more influential than others, a common feature of an aristocratic society, but also in the wide disparity of wealth. Finally, Aristotle does not mention any sort of state system for distributing land in Sparta. What he does stress, as we well know, is the acute problem of land inheritance, especially with land passing to women through the death of male heirs. By his day two-fifths of land was owned by Spartan women, and modern demographic studies suggest that if a male heir inherits one unit of land to a female's half a unit of land, then after a number of years women will own 40 per cent of all the land available. So, where did all the Spartan men go?

To answer this question, let us return to that key figure of 9,000 mentioned earlier. The only way of assessing the accuracy of this number is to observe how many hoplites were actually mustered for war. As we know, all full citizens, *Spartiãtai* or *homoioi*, from twenty to sixty years of age were liable for military service. At Plataia (479 BC) Sparta put 10,000 hoplites into the field of which 5,000 were Spartiates,[78] and we are assuming here that those were Spartiates in the prime of life (between thirty and fifty-five years of age) and that at such a crisis the main strength of Spartan manhood would have been mobilized. If these assumptions are correct, and if about 3,000 are added for the reserve and for citizens past military age, we might consider the total number of Spartiates at that time to have been roughly 8,000, a figure that Herodotos actually offers for all the adult males for the year 480 BC[79] and this corresponds fairly well with Plutarch's 9,000 *klêroi*. Thucydides informs us that only 120 of the 292 Lakedaimonians captured on Sphakteria (425 BC) were Spartiates,[80] and as these, as he tells us also, were chosen by lot from the twelve *lochoi*,[81] it can be calculated that there were about 3,500 Spartiates in total. This figure, if correct, indicates a dramatic 64 per cent decline since Plataia, though at First Mantineia (418 BC) it can be argued that the number mustered for battle was some 4,000,[82] thereby lowering the decline to 50 per cent. Still, by Leuktra (371 BC) the battle strength stood at only 700 of which 400 fell that fateful day,[83] so we assume there were only 1,100 or 1,200 Spartiates in total. So we have another dramatic decline since Sphakteria. In a passage highlighting the defects of the Spartan system, Aristotle, contrasting the theory underlying the 'Lykourgan' distribution of equal estates with the actual practice of his day, says:

> Although the country could support 1,500 horsemen and 30,000 hoplites, they do not even number one thousand. The defects of Spartan arrangements in this respect have been clearly displayed by their own experience; for the *polis* was not able to withstand a single stroke but perished on account of its small population.[84]

The 'single stroke' to which Aristotle refers is the Theban attack, which led to the demolition of the Spartan army at Leuktra.

Even before Leuktra, the Spartans had been forced to reject an appeal for help from Polydamas of Pharsalos for lack of manpower.[85] There is enough evidence to indicate that Aristotle was right in his analysis. There are three main reasons.

First, many Spartiates simply got themselves killed either in battle or through mishaps of one sort of another. However, most modern demographic studies demonstrate that losses in war are speedily replaced.

Second, there is the economic cause, that is to say, as Aristotle makes clear, the population declined through the Spartan habit of encouraging citizens to rear as many children as possible, 'hence the law which exempts fathers of three sons from military service, and fathers of four from tax'.[86] This resulted in the land being doled out between more and more offspring, which included daughters, as Aristotle bluntly points out when he says no less than 40 per cent of the land was held by women, 'partly because so many women inherit it as heiresses and partly because of the practice of giving large dowries'.[87] Of course, we must not forget the intimate connection between land tenure and citizenship.

Third, this Aristotlean thesis may well be the solution, but into this economic pot Cartledge throws in 'the greed of the wealthy'. This idea can be sharpened up slightly if we take into account the following: a point was surely reached in the fifth century BC when the full horrors of *oliganthrôpia* suddenly hit home. At the time the majority of Spartiates probably owned an estate that enabled them to live quite comfortably and fulfil their obligations as a full citizen. However, at the time they surely knew that their tidy piece of land would be divided through the generations until a point of no return was reached. It would be wise of us to remember that there are two antagonistic ideals at work here: the self-sufficient citizen 'farmer' versus the prolific citizen 'soldier'. In the hundred or so years between Plataia and Leuktra there was a point of no return.

Naturally warfare was a constant event in those hundred or so years, but if modern demographics are anything to go by, this should not have been the cause. All the same, if we consider that a Spartiate was attended by at least one helot, this meant there were at least 5,000 at Plataia,[88] and thus for that summer 5,000 helots were up in Boiotia on campaign and not down in Lakedaimon or Messenia on the land. The following decade saw a helot revolt when large tracts of Messenia around Mount Ithome were in the rebels hands, thus those Spartiates whose estates lay round here were not producing for their masters, and this lasted for at least five years. When the rebellion was finally over Sparta allowed those helots to go free, thus a number of Spartiates lost out and probably never recovered from this. Next we witness fourteen years of intermittent warfare with Athens, the first Peloponnesian war, followed by fifteen years of peace until the next conflict between Athens and Sparta, the great Peloponnesian War. During this titanic struggle we witness the freeing of helots for service in the Spartan army, and this practice was continued during Sparta's campaigns in Asia and the Corinthian War, which soon followed. The helot system was the weak part of Sparta's world.

Chapter 3

Of Matters Spiritual

War, too, involved spiritual values, a question of sacred as well as strategic considerations. The rigidity of the Spartans in such affairs was beyond doubt. Like all fighting people the Spartans were incredibly superstitious and invariably self-dramatic, and so when on campaign, they were accompanied by notoriously large herds of sheep and goats for sacrifice.[1] Still, for victory in open battle their austere thanks offering was just a single cock to Ares, worth less than an *obolos*, not because they were mean or disrespected the gods, but because they held them in awe and deemed it dishonourable to over express their mortal joy in a god-given triumph.[2]

Preparations for the slaughter of mankind have always been made in the name of some supposed higher being that men have devised and created in their own imagination. The Spartans, the keenest of sky-watchers amongst the Greeks, were particularly keen on military divination and would, before marching to war and obliterating their enemies with fire and sword, solicit the favour of the gods. According to Xenophon these initial sacrifices were made 'to Zeus the Leader and to the gods associated with him'.[3] The sacrifice to Zeus the Leader was not merely a sacrifice to the father of the gods, but also to a god who was specifically a war god, under a name traditional at Sparta. The gods associated with him were probably the Dioskouri, Castor and Polydeukes (better known under his Roman name, Pollux), twin brothers of Helen and Klytemnestra, since they were the tutelary war gods of Sparta.[4]

Before going to war the Spartans would also consult Delphic Apollo, each king having within his entourage two of four *Pythioi* – envoys despatched to the oracle on their behalf.[5] On reaching the battlefield, according to Plutarch, the king made an initial sacrifice 'to the Muses, thereby apparently reminding his men of their training and their trials, so that they should be ready to face the dangers ahead, and should perform memorable feats in the fighting'.[6] At the next sacrifice, Plutarch has 'the king sacrificing the customary she-goat'.[7] Xenophon says that this second sacrifice is performed in sight of the enemy, though for him it is a year-old male goat that has its throat slit, and done so in honour of Artemis Agrotera, the Huntress, 'as is their custom'.[8] With regards to the sex of the beast given up to Artemis, Xenophon is certainly to be favoured in this context. Not only would he have witnessed firsthand a Spartan *sphagia*, but solely for reasons of a practical nature, it was commonly the male of species that was slaughtered, the female being far too useful to 'waste'.

Artemis was one of the most esteemed of the Olympus-dwelling gods, the goddess of chastity, childbirth, hunting and the moon. Both in poetry and in painting she was celebrated above all as the mistress of wild animals, a virgin huntress armed with a bow and arrows who tracks her prey in lonely places. She typifies both the vivifying and the destructive aspects of untamed nature: she presides over the crucial transition from girlhood and virginity to marriage and motherhood but, like her twin brother, Phoibos Far Darter,[9] Apollo himself, she also slew men and beasts by means of her keen arrows, usually victims of revenge. Presumably, therefore, the battlefield sacrifice was a form of sympathetic magic designed to ensure that the same fate overtook their enemies.[10] Such was the Spartan way.

Gods of war

Hand in hand with the idealistic portrayal of war and warriors is grim realism, with the result that ritual and superstition become interlocked with the pursuit of war. Thus, most warring societies developed gods specifically devoted to war. Still, the ancient Greeks had no single and exclusive God of Battles. The Spartans, as we have just witnessed, were performing battlefield sacrifices to Artemis just before the point of contact with the opposition.

We are accustomed to thinking of bloodthirsty Ares (or Enyalios) in this role, and it is certainly true that as early as Homer he is supposed to have inspired combatants, as well as the weapons they wield, in the cut and thrust of battle.[11] 'Ares the violent' is fierce, fast and furious, he eagerly laps mortal man's blood and stands proud upon the field of the slain, armed in panoply *cap-à-pied*: the ultimate personification of the lust for battle.[12] Indeed, one would call the straight-limbed, impetuous god invincible, believing that he alone has the exclusive right to be called upon by one side or the other. Yet the truth is far from otherwise. Demonic Ares backed the wrong warhorse in that titanic struggle between the Greeks and the Trojans, and his actual perform-ance on the battlefield was far from impressive. At one point, Ares was thrashed twice in the fray by his half sister Athena, and even the mortal Diomedes managed to wound him on one occasion.[13] Certainly not very awe-inspiring for a so-called god of war.

Ares was at times invoked by the warrior,[14] though it was the *paean* that particularly belonged to Apollo as the giver of joy or the averter of calamities, no less dreadful upon the field of battle were Zeus the Saviour, or Zeus of the Rout, Athena, Poseidon, Aphrodite, or even the demi-god Herakles. Solon's temple and another – to be found in the Athenian Agora – are the only historical edifices we have to date that are definitively dedicated to Ares.[15] Pausanias does mention another two possible candidates on his travels through Greece: one in the Argolid outside Troizen, the other down in Lakedaimon at Geronthrai.[16] He also notes that he saw three altars and two roadside sanctuaries, which were dedicated to the god.[17] In addition, according to Plutarch, there is evidence that the Argives set up a shrine to Enyalios. This was in memory of their valiant women who stood in defence of Argos when the *polis* was attacked by the Spartan king, Kleomenes.[18] All in all, this contrasts with Rome where, next to Jupiter, Mars was the chief deity with major festivals in March and October, wherein he was regarded as the principal god of war and was therefore a far more Olympian figure than his Greek counterpart Ares, Butcher of Men.[19]

Ares was the son of Zeus and his queen and consort Hera, but unlike his strategically gifted half-sister Athena, who also often busied herself with warfare, Ares was a hooligan, a violent and aggressive character who loved the pungent, sickly-sweet scent of blood for its own sake and contributed next to nothing to the develop-ment of humanity. Once, his father told him bluntly that he hated him most of all Olympian gods and that the only reason he tolerated his presence at home was that he was his and Hera's son. Fearsome and savage, but not particularly bright, Ares did not marry but conducted many extramarital affairs, the most famous being that with Aphrodite, who nursed a perverse passion for him. The progeny of this amour of opposites were Harmonia (future wife of Kadmos, the founder of Thebes) and the twin sons, Deimos ('terror') and Phobos ('fear'). So much for Ares.

Before we continue, it is important for us to bear in mind two key aspects of Greek religion. First, Greeks had no religious texts comparable to the Bible or the Koran. Homer is sometimes called the Bible of the Greeks. Insofar as the Hebrew Bible was a national epic for the Jews, the comparison has some validity. But the significance of Homer for the Greeks, as for us, is rather of a cultural icon. In his epics, the *Iliad* and the *Odyssey*, all human – and inhuman and superhuman – life was to be found. So, if you wanted to know how to be a politician, a general, a father, or a lover, there was a passage or scene or book of Homer that could teach you, if you only knew where and how to look. Anyway, religion for the Greeks centred around ritual practice rather than doctrine: participation in communal activities was at the heart and soul of Greek religion, while belief was less important. The Greeks were matter-of-fact in their supplications as their notion of the gods. It was not for any mystic blessing that they begged the gods, but for tangible benefits such as rain, prosperity, victory in battle. Nor did they do it demurely. So long as the gods were receptive, and the petitioner guaranteed an adequate *quid pro quo* by way of offerings, he or she saw no reason to be denied satisfaction. Second, all Greek religious actions were, to some measure, exclusive: some religious cults were restricted to kinship groups, while others were open to those citizens of a particular *polis*. Such exclusive religious rituals included the three major Apolline festivals of Sparta, the Karneia, Gymnopaidiai and Hyakinthia.

Militant Apollo

Apollo, the son of Zeus and Leto, has been considered the 'most Greek of gods'. In art, for example, we gaze upon him as the ideal youth, that commanding yet graceful Apollo, who stands as the central figure in the west pediment of the temple of Zeus at Olympia, his arm raised to bring order out of the chaos of the battle that rages around him, or seated with his tortoiseshell lyre and pouring a libation to himself on the white *kylix* by the Pistoxenos Painter.[20] His divine functions, particularly in classical times, we see as connected with music (the lyre was especially associated with him), archery, prophecy, medicine (he was the father of Asklepios) and the guardianship of flocks and herds. Apollo is also associated with the loftier developments of Greek civilization, such as the drawing up of legal codes,[21] high moral and religious principles and favouring philosophy.[22] He is also the leader of the Nine Muses, the tutelary deities of the arts and sciences. Politically, he is especially prominent in suggesting or approving colonial adventures, with a famous oracular shrine at Delphi, in central Greece. In fact, Apollo's cult was certainly more than just panhellenic; it was truly international.

Yet as well as the bearer of enlightenment, Apollo could also spread diseases with his arrows. During the Trojan War, Apollo was the most fanatical and feared divine supporter of the Trojans. He caused an epidemic among the Greeks when they kidnapped the daughter of a priest of Apollo. According to some traditions, Apollo was responsible for the death of Achilles, who lost his near-immortal life when one of Paris' arrows hit him in the only vulnerable part of his body, his right heel.[23] It would have been the Far Darter himself, however, who would have ensured that the mediocre archer Paris would hit the fatal target.[24] This dual nature was reflected in the fact that he was the guardian deity of shepherds while at the same time being identified with their archenemy that superb hunting machine and occasional man-eater, the wolf, *lykos*, if indeed that is really the meaning of his cult epithet Lykeios.[25]

The representation of Apollo as a war god is nothing new and also not exceptional. In particular, he is presented by Homer as a nasty, petulant, violent and quick tempered god,[26] and the blind bard even goes so far as to have 'Phoibos Apollo, lord of the golden sword' lead the Trojans in battle and dash the Greek stockade pro-tecting their beachhead,[27] while the Archaic divinity has been occasionally portrayed as an armed warrior. According to Plutarch, for example, a Megarian statue of the early fifth century BC depicts Apollo with a spear. It was dedicated at Delphi by the Megarians to commemorate their victory over the Athenians not long after the Persian Wars.[28] More tangible evidence, fortunately, does exist.

The colossal statue of Apollo at Amyklai was, by all accounts, a brazen pillar thirty cubits high with hands, feet and a head. The Amyklaian Apollo, as it is known, depicted the god wearing a helmet and wielding not only the traditional bow, in the left hand, but also a spear in the right.[29] This warlike image of the Amyklaian Apollo was later to be portrayed upon the reverse of both Hellenistic Spartan *tetradrachms* and Roman bronze coins from the reign of Commodus.[30] According to Philostratos, it was reckoned among the oldest cult statues in Greece, while Pausanias hypothesized it was a primitive statue that marked the transition from the aniconic period.[31] Modern scholarship dates it to the end of the seventh century BC on account of its size. At Thornax, a mountain to the north-east of Sparta and overlooking the Eurotas valley, there was, according to Herodotos, to be found an identical colossus of Apollo,[32] although Amyklai was considered to be the most sacred of all the Lakonian sanctuaries. 'The place called Amyklai', said Polybios, 'is the best wooded and the most fertile of any in Lakedaimon, and it is twenty stades distant from Sparta. The precinct of Apollo, which is to be found there, is just about the most famous of the shrines of Lakedaimon'.[33] The towering cult statue, raised still higher by the platform upon which it was set, would have faced the setting sun. Its metallic sheen and aniconic shape, spear and bow, must have made it an awe-inspiring apparition, belonging to a different world from that of the classical sculptures of Apollo, which accentuated his compassion and beauty.

It is Plutarch, priest of Apollo, who tells us that all Spartan statues of gods are equipped with weapons so that the young men of Sparta 'may not pray to the god unarmed'.[34] Indeed, he expands upon this particular topic by explaining that the Spartans worship Aphrodite in her full panoply, while their statues of all the other deities carry spears so as to indicate that 'all the gods have valour which war demands'.[35]

Dorian Apollo
Apollo was the god who of all the Olympians was mostly associated with the Dorian peoples. In fact, all three major Spartan religious festivals were in honour of one or

other Apollo, rather than the *polis'* patron Athena. The Karneia, sacred to Apollo represented with the attributes of a ram, was a specifically Dorian festival and marked the vintage. This took place in the month Karneios (equivalent to our August–September), celebrated under the moon in bright summer evenings of the second month of the year (beginning at the first new moon after the summer solstice). Still in the late fifth century BC it was considered sacred to all Dorians and so strictly observed, and not only by the Spartans but by other Dorians within the Peloponnese too, normally abstaining from warfare.[36] But the Karneia had an aspect that was typically Spartan. According to Demetrios of Skepsis, the festival represented Sparta's military. During the time of their participation in the month-long Karneia, the young men lived like soldiers on campaign, eating in communal messes and performing the rites to words of command.[37] There is evidence too that dances involving armed men took place sometime during the festivities.[38] It was because of their overriding obligations to celebrate the Karneia properly, or so the Spartans claimed, that they could not send a full levy with Leonidas to Thermopylai.

We shall come back to the martial aspects of Apollo in a moment, after a brief digression. Ten years previously the Athenians had approached the Spartans for assistance to face the Persians. Before Athens had despatched its citizen army to meet the Persians where they had landed, at Marathon, it sent a professional long-distance runner, Philippides,[39] to Sparta so as to enlist its help. He ran the 230 kilometres to Sparta in thirty-six hours, only to be told that the Spartans would help, but could not march until 'the moon was full'.[40] Apparently it was the ninth day of the month of Karneios, during which time Dorians customarily did not go to war, as mentioned above. The Greeks told time by the cycles of the moon, and their lunar calendars had months determined by phases of the moon, namely divided into three parts for the purpose of reckoning dates. For the first third of the month, days were generally reckoned as 'rising', for the second third as 'being in their middle' or else 'after the ten', and in the last third as 'declining' or 'departing'. So the Spartans were waiting until the full moon in the second third. The week leading up to the full moon 'when the moon rides high the whole night long',[41] as Euripides says, was naturally the most sacred part of the sacred month, which covered the seventh to the fifteenth of the month. In due course, therefore, a contingent of 2,000 Spartans finally marched, to arrive in Attica on the third day out from Sparta, only a little under double the time Philippides had taken to cover the distance. An impressive achievement to say the least, and gives the lie to those cynics who believe the Spartans really did not want to aid the Athenians, but by the time they did arrive the issue at Marathon had been decided. The Spartans went there anyway, viewed the Persian corpses, 'praised the Athenians on their good work, and returned home'.[42]

The engagement at Marathon was important though hardly the triumph it was later trumpeted, and, apart from Persian court circles, the result of the battle probably raised barely a ripple. It was considered a famous victory by the Athenians, won un-expectedly perhaps, but remembered ever after for its symbolic value and those who fought at the battle were honoured in their lifetime. Indeed, Herodotos' day Marathon had already taken on the quality of legend. There was the story of Philippides' meeting with 'goat-footed Pan of Arcady' as he breasted Mount Parthenion, above Tegea, *en route* to Sparta,[43] and of Epizelos the son of Kouphagoras blinded in battle by a vision of a huge warrior, a mountain of a man, his beard covering his shield, who went for his comrade standing alongside him.[44] Later came the inevitable embroidery and transfiguration. For instance, Philippides had to return to take part in the battle, and to bring the glad news to Athens, only to die as he uttered a single exultant cry,[45] and there was the man of rustic appearance who had suddenly appeared in the thick of things, killed a number of barbarians with a ploughshare, and then vanished without trace after the battle. On enquiring whom he was, the Athenians were told to worship the hero Echetlaos.[46] And so the Athenians soon surrounded their victory at Marathon with an enduring mythology about the triumph of Greek freedom over Asian despotism. It ranked alongside such feats as defeating the Amazons and sacking Troy.[47] If the Persians regarded Marathon as a 'trivial skirmish',[48] the Athenians made it an Athenian epic.

But I digress. Another major Apolline festival at Sparta was the Gymnopaidiai, and thereby hangs an interesting etymological tale. Traditionally, the name has been translated as the Festival of the Naked Youths, deriving the title from *gumnos* and *paides*, but the central action of the festival involved a contest between three age-graded choruses singing of deeds of bravery, past, present and future – old men beyond military age, warriors of military age, and pre-military age youths – not just youths alone.[49] A more plausible etymology, therefore, takes *gumnos* to mean not naked but unarmed, and the *paidiai* bit to be derived from the Greek word for dancing. So in the Gymnopaidiai we are probably dealing with a Festival of Unarmed Dancing. The Gymnopaidiai was celebrated at the hottest time of the year in the hottest place in Greece for its height above sea-level (about 200 metres), and gave a characteristically Spartan calisthenic spin to this joyous occasion. The Gymnopaidiai also involved a number of sporting events lasting for several days, the prime aim being the conditioning of Spartiate manhood to arduous pursuits. Hooker associates this feast of sweat and muscle with 'a solemn thank-offering to Apollo for the success of Spartan arms'.[50]

A third major Apolline festival was the Hyakinthia. Hyakinthos was one of Apollo's male conquests. He was a Spartan prince, the son of King Amyklas, who was very dashing and very athletic. The inseparable lovers were practising the discus one after-noon when Hyakinthos was struck in the skull by one blown off course by the West Wind, Zephyros, who was insanely jealous of Apollo and had taken a fancy to the young prince as well. All of Apollo's healing powers were of no avail. Hyakinthos was dead. The distraught Apollo had a flower sprout from Hyakinthos' blood – not the flower known as the hyacinth, but a type of iris – and on the petals he wrote *Ai! Ai!*, the Greek cry of grief, and in grief at his loss appointed a day of sacrifice for the Spartans.[51] A pretty tale of no great depth, and one that conforms to a pattern of amour between the high gods and lesser beings. The Hyakinthia was thus one of mourning for the dead Hyakinthos and praise for the living Apollo.[52] According to Pausanias the base of the Amyklaian Apollo took 'the form of an altar, and it is said that Hyakinthos is buried in it'.[53] In fact, Hyakinthos is a pre-Hellenic deity,[54] a very ancient vegetation god who was at some point brought into association with Apollo but not obliterated by him. He represents death and the mourning for the dead, matters utterly repugnant to Apollo, who embodies a much more advanced concept. Yet death and its consequences cannot be ignored, and so both the dead and the living are given their due of honour. The Hyakinthia usually took place in the early summer.[55]

In retrospect

That rough edge of battle, combat, is the most important drama in any soldier's life, past or present. It occupies only a short time. Nonetheless, these vivid moments acquire extraordinary importance, since it is within the arena of the bloody battlefield that he witnesses the greatest violence in war. For him it is a wildly unstable physical and emotion environment; a world of boredom and bewilderment (which makes up the great part of the ordinary soldier's experience), of depression and delirium, of triumph and terror, of anger and angst, of courage and cowardice. Hence the solicitation of the supernatural. For Onasander writes:

> ... soldiers are far more courageous when they believe they are facing dangers with the good will of the gods; for they themselves are on the alert, everyman, and they watch closely for omens of sight and sound, and an auspicious sacrifice for the whole army encourages even those who have private misgivings.[56]

Chapter 4

Tyrants, Tremble

Sparta's first major conquest appears to be that of Messenia, the neighbouring region just west of the Taïygettos mountains, during the so-called First Messenian War (*c*. 735–715 BC or *c*. 730–710 BC). This was essentially a full-dress war of conquest and annexation as it enabled the Spartans to secure the south-west Peloponnese, at least doubling their territory and providing them with desperately needed land without the necessity of settling colonies overseas. This is best illustrated by the seventh-century BC Spartan poet, Tyrtaios, who says in a hymn in praise of Eurypontidai king Theopompos, 'through whom we took wide Messene, / Messenia, excellent for ploughing and excellent for planting'.[1] As we can see from Tyrtaios' verse, Messenia was an outstandingly fertile region, the utterly flat, alluvial land of the olive tree. Having crossed the high Taïygettos mountain range into Messenia and conquered it, this rich land of the Messenians was divided among the Spartans. Already their society was showing the exclusiveness and ability to engender subordinate status to those 'taken by the Dorian spear', to use Aischylos' fine phrase. In short, the rape of Messenia was undertaken because it was safe to do so, and it conformed with the ultimate Spartan aim.

Yet the Messenians were conquered so brutally and exploited so ruthlessly that a rebellion seemed likely at any moment. Somewhere about 660 BC then, and believably a consequence of Sparta's recent defeat at Hysiai, there was a second war against them (Second Messenian War, *c*. 660–640 BC), and tradition records that this conflict was a revolt against Spartan rule. The war itself was neither short nor easy, and Tyrtaios, who probably took an active part in the conflict, composed his propaganda poems with the idea of urging his fellow Spartans on to victory during these extremely difficult years.[2] Whether he was a native Spartan or, as some traditions have it, he came to Sparta from Athens or another *polis*,[3] in his war poems Tyrtaios associated himself wholeheartedly with the political interests and the territorial ambitions of the Spartan kings. Sparta at this time was an embattled *polis*, having for twenty years made relentless war upon its Messenian neighbours to the west. It faced other problems too. Jealousy and hostility on the part of other neighbouring states increased, especially from a tough Dorian rival in Argos to the north-east, resulting in fierce clashes.

The jealous rival

Scattered bits of information allow us the luxury to argue that Pheidon of Argos (r. *c*. 680–660 BC), who exceeded the traditional bounds of monarchical power and made himself a tyrant,[4] was a very successful military leader. Regarding himself as a direct descendant of the Herakleidai, as did the kings of Sparta, the Dorian Pheidon used his divine ancestry to justify the Argive expansion upon which he embarked, and his rule does appear to coincide with the height of Argive power. It is known that the men of Argos, during the contest for the control of the Thyreatis border-lands, the fertile plain lying to the west of the Argolic Gulf, won a convincing victory over the Spartans in a pitched battle near Hysiai in the hollow of the mountains on the road that leads up from the Argolid coast to Tegea in Arcadia. Pausanias, the Greek traveller from Roman Asia Minor, reports that he came across the graves of the Argive fallen on this road and places the event in the fourth year of the twenty-eighth Olympiad (viz. 669 BC).[5] The simple fact of the matter that the location of Hysiai lies beyond Spartan home territory tells us that Sparta had been the aggressor on this particular occasion. Little wonder, therefore, the away defeat left a lasting and deep wound – a score to be settled.

On the other hand, all that Herodotos recalls of Pheidon is that the king was responsible for establishing a system of weights and measures,[6] which by virtue of the fact that it was then adopted throughout the Peloponnese shows that the dynamic Argive was a ruler of no small influence, but he lived too early to have struck silver coins in Greece, as Ephoros supposes.[7] Herodotos continues, saying that Pheidon was also responsible for turning out the Eleians whose duty it was to manage the Olympic games and then proceeded to manage them himself – 'the wickedest and most arrogant thing ever done by a Greek'.[8] And so armed with the evidence of Pausanias and Herodotos, it is feasible for us to postulate that Pheidon defeated the Spartans in 669 BC and then marched right across the Peloponnese the following year in order to celebrate the Olympics of 668 BC under his own presidency.[9] In doing so, Pheidon seemingly made attacks on the places that had been captured by Herakles, and claimed the right to direct the festivals Herakles had founded, which explains his celebration of the aforementioned games. It has also been suggested that Pheidon created the first hoplite army, and through its use not only dominated his own *polis* but also large areas of the northern Peloponnese. It would have also enabled him to defeat the Spartans, who have yet to adopt the hoplite phalanx with its singular tactical doctrine. In this context, it is interesting to note that Ephoros, says Pheidon, 'had deprived them [the Spartans] of the hegemony over the Peloponnese, which they formerly held'.[10]

The development of the hoplite style of fighting has been the subject of much scholarly debate, for it represented a different form of mass warfare from any that proceeded it. The age of razor-lipped heroes with their dissyllabic, round, sonorous names, defeating armies singlehandedly (admittedly with superhuman strength and divine helpers) had always been more nostalgic Homeric myth than hard reality. After all, history has proved with depressing regularity that battles were usually won by using nameless masses of soldiery in the most advantageous manner, and aggressively too. Thus, in western military doctrine, the big battalions routinely win. Quality is thus smothered by quantity, which reminds us of that old axiom that runs something like this: soldiering is the coward's way of attacking mercilessly when you are strong and keeping out of harm's way when you are weak. These words, both witty and wise, define the essence of Western strategy. It all starts with the Greeks and the advent of hoplite warfare.

Two basic theoretical approaches have been taken to explain the rise of hoplite warfare. The first and older view is that it is the product of a technical innovation – the introduction of the hoplite shield, the *aspis*, with its revolutionary method of holding it. The nature of the new shield led directly to the development of the phalanx as the *aspis* had obvious disadvantages compared with the traditional forms outside of such a mutually supportive formation. The other view, now probably held by a majority of scholars, is that the phalanx is the product of a relatively long period of experimentation. The individual items of equipment were adopted initially by aristocratic warriors because they were technically superior as single items. These adoptions predated the phalanx. The change in tactics came later in this model. But the crucial problem is the *aspis*. Though arguments can and have been made for its use by individuals, it is clearly less functional when used by an isolated warrior than the shield types it replaced. The importance of the *aspis* will be stressed later, but for the time being it is sufficient to note that what comes out clearly in the ancient literature is the collective nature of hoplite warfare and the crucial place of the *aspis* in it. The most plausible model is that the *apsis* was adopted at the same time as the phalanx. One was dependent on the other. In the same way the Corinthian helmet with its limited field of vision and restricted range of hearing also seems geared specifically for use in a phalanx rather than by independent warriors. Which brings us back to that Dorian strongman, Pheidon.

The earliest post-Bronze Age body armour was recovered from a Late Geometric warrior's grave at Argos, commonly known as the Argos cuirass (*c*. 725 BC). This bell-shaped bronze corselet is generally recognized as the oldest and most complete example of hoplite body armour. It certainly has the telltale feature of being hinged down one side and fastened at the other and on the shoulders, decorated with incised outlines of chest and stomach muscles, as well as carefully moulded to fit the wearer, and curving outwards at the waist to give freedom of movement.[11] Also, the *aspis* was commonly referred to as the Argive shield. And then there is that prophetic utterance whereby Apollo explains exactly which parts of Greece had the best land, the best horses, the best women, the best men and the second-best men: 'The best of all the land is the Pelasgian plain: best are the horses of Thrace, / the women of Sparta, and the men who drink the water of fair Arethusa. / But better still than these are the dwellers between Tiryns and Arcadia of the many sheep, the linen-corseleted Argives, the goads of war'.[12] This Delphic oracle is certainly early, for from the sixth century BC onwards the Spartan army was preeminent, but here Spartan women are praised and the army of another state, namely Dorian Argos. If the Argives were the first to adopt hoplite tactics, then it gave them a temporary advantage that Pheidon exploited in this the last flowering of Argive power. With the death of Pheidon Argive energy declined. In the next century Sparta took the lead, and Argos never recovered it.

Sparta gains its spurs

The term 'Peloponnesian League' is a modern one and contrary to ancient usage. In reality, to paraphrase Voltaire, it was neither Peloponnesian nor a league. It never embraced all the states of the Peloponnese, Argos of course being most conspicuous by its absence, and it included from early on states that were not geographically within the Peloponnese, such as Megara. It was not a league in the modern sense, because the allies were not all allied to each other but rather all were allied individually to Sparta, and allied so on a basis of inequality. The entire alliance met only when the Spartans chose, and we hear of few such gatherings. Allies were expected to contribute a certain number or proportion of their troops to a league army, and Sparta provided the officers both to levy and command the contingents stipulated.[13] To the ancient writers the Peloponnesian League was commonly described as 'the Lakedaimonians and their allies' or 'the Peloponnesians'. It was a multi-state military alliance in which Sparta was the *hêgemôn* or leader, and the allies were *summachoi* or assistants, the former taking upon itself only defensive duties, the latter, on the other hand, always supporting all Sparta's campaigns and adventures, both defensive and offensive. In other words, Sparta demanded that their allies must always and everywhere follow the leader, a condition neatly encapsulated in the clause 'to have the same friends and allies as the Lakedaimonians'.

By the turn of the sixth century BC Sparta had extinguished entirely the political identity of Messenia, which henceforth for the best part of three centuries became part of the Spartan state, and now sought to expand northwards into Arcadia; the aim was yet more land. However, under kings Leon and Agesikles (*c*. 580–560 BC) Sparta was soundly beaten by Tegea, the first major *polis* of Arcadia that a traveller would reach travelling north from Lakedaimon. In one battle against the Tegeans, the Spartan army was defeated and the survivors taken as prisoners of war. We learn from Herodotos that the Spartans had marched out bearing measuring rods so as to parcel out the land they thought they would soon be acquiring, and chains to fetter their new Arcadian helots who would work that land for them. But they were defeated, and Herodotos adds the picturesque embroidery that 'those who were taken as prisoners were forced to wear on their own legs the chains they had brought, and to measure out the line the plain of Tegea as labourers'.[14] Under the next kings, Anaxandrides and Ariston (*c*. 560–520 BC), a very different policy emerged, perhaps to be associated with the name of Chilon, eponymous ephor in circa 556/5 BC. On advice from Delphi, the Spartans acquired by stealth from Tegea the 'bones of Orestes' and gave them a public burial in Sparta. 'And ever since that day the Lakedaimonians in any trial of strength had by far the better of it.'[15] Bones that were superstitiously regarded as those of an ancestral hero could well serve the cause of propaganda, if produced at an appropriate moment.

The hero Orestes was the son of Agamemnon, lord of Mycenae and legendary ruler of all Greece, who had avenged the death of his father at the hands of his mother, Klytemnestra, by killing her. The legend goes that Orestes was then pursued by the Furies, tried and acquitted in Athens, becoming one of the last kings of the Peloponnese before the so-called Dorian invasion. Apparently, the Spartans were laying claim to the leadership of the Peloponnese,[16] a position that had once belonged to Agamemnon. If true, then the Spartans were asserting a right to Achaian leadership and subordinating their Dorian origins. And so, in the following generation, we witness Kleomenes (r. *c*. 520–490 BC) claiming that he was an Achaian (cf. Homer's *Achaiwoí*) and not a Dorian when ordered to leave the Parthenon by the priestess because no Dorians were permitted to enter the house of Athena, the foremost goddess worshipped on the Athenian Acropolis: 'Back, Spartan stranger, do not enter the temple, it is unlawful for a Dorian to pass in here'. He said, 'I am not a Dorian, lady, but an Achaian'.[17] Here we seem to have a distinction sometimes, but by no means always, made between the Herakleidai (who were of course Achaians) and the Dorians who came with them into the Peloponnese. At such a tense moment it was natural for Kleomenes, endowed with the gift of snappy repartee noticed by Plutarch, to dwell on his 'Achaian' lineage from the Herakleidai and to overlook the Dorian component in his ancestry. Nonetheless, there was a substantial body of opposition to this Achaian policy. The naming of Kleomenes' oldest half-brother, Dorieus ('the Dorian'), may perhaps be seen as a riposte, and Herodotos relates the problems that their father, King Anaxandrides, had over his first spouse.[18]

Arcadia lies snug and safe in the centre of the Peloponnese. Though not an exact counterpart of the pastoral paintings of Poussin or the poetic fiction that made it the home of innocence and happiness, this upcountry region still preserves the way of life and physical type of it inhabitants. The rocky wilderness for long remained inaccessible to strangers. Whether or not Sparta had acquired maturer wisdom or had gained great respect for the rugged independence of the Arcadian highlanders, Sparta did not impose upon them the brutal conditions with which it had visited the Messenians. Indeed, the claim to the Achaian leaderships appears to mark the beginning of Sparta's shift from pursuing a policy of conquest and enslavement to one of seeking alliances. Tegea was to be Sparta's first ally and, as such, its people did not suffer the terrible fate of Messenians who were turned into helots and thereby reduced to dependent status. All the same, these alliances clearly marked out one ally as master. Much later on Sparta would impose on newly-acquired members of its alliance an unequal treaty of the original by adding a clause that bound them to 'follow wherever the Spartans might lead', but there is no evidence for the sixth-century BC procedure apart from Herodotos' vague remark that at the time (*c.* 547/6 BC) of Croesus' request for a Lydian-Spartan alliance against Cyrus of Persia 'the greater part of the Peloponnese had been made subject to the Spartans'.[19] This certainly suggests a certain element of inequality, but such things do not demand formal acknowledgement. Besides, the ability to accommodate new members without restriction, and without the imposition of tribute,[20] was one of Sparta's great strengths as it advanced to political, as well as military, pre-eminence in Greece.

Tyrant slayers

In later times the Spartans were to acquire a reputation for expelling tyrants of all sorts, the *eunomia* of which they were so proud about being exported overseas. Actually, their tyrant-toppling record was not quite as consistent, or principled, as the reputation made it seem. In 556 BC Sparta expelled the last tyrant of Sikyon, and although Plutarch has left us with a whole list of tyrants who suffered the same fate, they are little more than attempts to fill out the tradition that he is reflecting.[21] Nevertheless, tyranny was fast disappearing from the Peloponnese during the sixth century BC. It was being replaced by a collection of *poleis* banded together in order to safeguard their hoplite constitutions. The rise of tyrants, *tyrannoi*, in a number of Greek *poleis* during the seventh and sixth centuries BC represented a development absolutely contrary to that of the Spartan state. However, it would be rather simple-minded of us to suppose that the Spartans tried to put down tyranny out of sheer hatred of absolute rule. Although their motives may have varied slightly from case to case, their principal aim was that of fomenting unrest in other states. It goes without saying that this unrest they turned to their own advantage, and so extended their influence. Such aims appear most clearly in Spartan operations against Samos and Athens late in the sixth century BC, and Herodotos very rightly observed that Kleomenes' counsel to the Plataians that they should seek an alliance with Athens instead of with Sparta was given not so much out of good will towards the Plataians as from a desire to antagonize the Thebans against the Athenians.[22] The Thebans shared a long border with the Athenians, and in the event of war they wanted to possess Plataia, a small *polis* with fewer than a thousand citizens, but one that presented both a danger and an opportunity. The *polis*, less than thirteen kilometres from Thebes, flanked the best route from Thebes to Athens. In Athenian hands Plataia could serve as a base of operations on Thebes and Boiotia and as a threat to any Theban army attempting to enter Attica. The Thebans had long sought to unify and dominate all Boiotia.[23] Plataia was Boiotian by geography and ethnicity and its allegiance was therefore claimed by Thebes, the greatest Boiotian power of that and subsequent times. We shall meet the Thebans again in due course.

Argos was the only *polis* to remain aloof from the Peloponnesian League, Sparta quarrelling with it for the control of the borderland of Thyreatis in the eastern Peloponnese. The final showdown of this grudge match took place in 546 BC, Herodotos' celebrated Battle of the Champions, whereby the two armies left the field, after agreeing the issue should be decided by a combat between three hundred selected champions from either side. So much is plausible, but what follows in Herodotos' account is harder to believe. After a particularly violent trial of strength, Herodotos says that all the champions were killed, save for two on the Argive side and one on the Spartan. The Argives returned to their *polis*, thinking they had won the victory. However, the solitary Spartan took spoils from the enemy dead and carried them back to his army as tokens of his victory. Thus the issue was still in doubt, and it had after all to be resolved by a general engagement. This led to a great Spartan victory,[24] which was thereafter celebrated in the Gymnopaidiai by the carrying of the wreaths known as 'Thyreatic'. Moreover, they now controlled Thyreatis and indeed incorporated it within Lakedaimon. Hysiai had been avenged.

The sophist Hippias of Elis (b. *c.* 460 BC) noted that Homer was not familiar with the term *tyrannos*, and he tells us that it was first brought into the Greek language 'in the time of Archilochos'.[25] Hippias was a learned man and had the complete literature available to him, unlike us today, so he should be right about the fact. Anyway, Hippias is doubtless referring to the poem of Archilochos of Paros (*fl. c.* 650 BC) in which the speaker uses the term *tyrannos* to describe Gyges, king of the inventors of coinage and much else besides, the Lydians. Now Gyges was a usurper, who in Archilochos' lifetime had killed the legitimate king and taken the throne for himself,[26] and in the four lines that remain of this particular lyric the speaker says:

> *I care not for the things of Gyges;*
> *I am not seized by jealously;*
> *I do not gaze in envy at godlike works;*

> *nor do I long for a great tyranny (tyrannis);*
> *for it is far from my eyes.*[27]

Archilochos' speaker suggests that *tyrannis* describes the kingdom of Gyges, and it is possible that the word itself was Lydian. It might be argued that the noun *tyrannos* in the Greek meant 'usurper', but its use in later poets makes it more likely that the meaning was more neutral,[28] in fact that Archilochos used it as a synonym for king, *basileios*. Thus, it did not carry the same odium or negative connotations as our own modern word, even though of course the latter is derived from the former. Just let us consider, for a moment, the West's (mis) understanding of world leaders such as Saddam Hussein and Colonel Gaddafi, respectively erstwhile former presidents of Iraq and Libya and members of that rogue sextet labelled the 'axis of evil'.[29]

The ancient Greeks used the term *tyrannos* for rulers who had no hereditary or legal claim to rule in their *poleis*, the only exception of this phenomenon being the hereditary king of Argos, Pheidon, whom we have briefly met. The rule of these early tyrants was not necessarily oppressive or unpopular, some being remembered for their beneficial acts and popular laws (e.g. Peisistratos of Athens). Indeed, in its time tyranny had served as a useful solvent in Greek states, breaking the power of exclusive aristocracies and paving the way for more flexible societies. Thus, the term 'tyrant' could be used as a neutral term for 'monarch'. In the poems Pindar wrote for Hieron of Syracuse (r. 478–467 BC) he three times calls him 'king',[30] but once also 'tyrant',[31] and on this occasion he does not mean to be less polite. One final point, worth mentioning if only to be dismissed, is the definition of the aforementioned scholar Hippias of Elis for the word 'tyrant': 'They say that the tyrant derived his name from the Tyrrhenians. For they became troublesome as pirates'.[32]

With the conclusion of the Arcadian alliance and the victory over Argos, Sparta was now the most powerful *polis* in the Peloponnese. With that the way lay open for the direct intervention by Sparta in the affairs of states outside the Peloponnese. In 525 BC Sparta, with triremes (viz. wooden warships of a highly sophisticated design with three banks of oars) willingly lent by its ally Corinth,[33] despatched an expedition over the sea to overthrow the tyrant of Samos, Polykrates, and put his opponents in power.[34] The tyranny of Polykrates lasted for sixteen years from about the year 532 BC, and he was the most magnificent of tyrants – there was no one to compare with him. It was a time of lavish expenditure on public works,[35] courtly hospitality to poets and artists, and the establishment of the most considerable naval power in the eastern Aegean.[36]

According to Herodotos the Spartans bore Polykrates a grudge for having seized, in successive years, precious diplomatic gifts passing between Sparta and the rulers of Egypt and Lydia.[37] Herodotos, who had spent his youth on Samos only a generation after the death of Polykrates, describes the tyrant as an indiscriminate pirate who said 'that his friends were more pleased when he returned their goods than if he had never seized them in the first place'.[38] But this is an epigram rather than a serious statement of policy. Like Herodotos, we all love the villain of the piece who turns and winks at us at intervals as he sets about his villainy. Samos was no backward pirate state but a fully developed commercial *polis* where trade cannot have been merely insecure, and Polykrates' high-seas seizures are to be connected with the wars that he waged for most of his reign. Herodotos himself gives hints that larger matters of policy were in question than resentment over the bronze bowl and the linen corselet to have been taken by a couple of Polykrates' warships. The large and wealthy island of Samos lies very close to the mainland of Anatolia, and this was, as Herodotos emphasizes, the first time that Dorian Greeks had taken their arms so close to the land mass of Asia.[39] They came in great force and attacked Polykrates' *astu* from both the seaward and the landward side, but, despite individual acts of valour, they were beaten off. They then resorted to siege, but this came to nothing, and after forty days they sailed back to mainland Greece.

So the first overseas enterprise was a complete fiasco, but that mounted soon after against Lygdamis of Naxos, puppet of Polykrates and confederate of Peisistratos of Athens, was a complete success.[40] Sparta was to gain a reputation for hating tyranny.[41] This reputation was undeserved, for such adventures were based on an inflated idea of the power of Sparta in relation to that of the kings of the east, an illusion fostered by their advances to it as an equal. The limits of that power and the tensions underlying Spartan society were demonstrated in the reign of the greatest king, Kleomenes. Belittled by Spartan oral tradition, which claimed that he 'verged upon madness' and 'did not rule for very long',[42] Kleomenes, whose long reign was as distinguished as the political history of sixth-century BC Sparta, was best forgotten because he came close to achieving personal tyranny, possibly comparable to that of Pheidon of Argos, and even ended by trying to raise a helot revolt. If Machiavelli had known Kleomenes, he would have found in him the qualities he later describes in his *Prince* as necessary to the ideal ruler of a modern state, cynical use of religion and, above all, unscrupulous devotion to the single end of successful government. In particular, Machiavelli would have admired the cunning and breach of faith with which Kleomenes crushed the Argives at Sepeia. But it is one episode in particular that demonstrates the extent of Kleomenes' power in Sparta, namely the overthrow of the Peisistratid tyranny at Athens. It also reveals some important truths about that anti-tyranny reputation of Sparta.

The liberator

If it is in the nature of absolute government to react narrowly and oppressively in the long run, Hippias and Hipparchos, unlike their father Peisistratos, proved orthodox. When Hipparchos was assassinated in the name of liberty, or so Athenian tradition claims,[43] Hippias understandably treated this as a plot against himself and, according to the same handed-down tradition, he shocked Athens with a reign of terror.[44] He also disarmed the Athenians and began courting Persian aid.[45] Now the Peisistratidai had always kept on good terms with Sparta, so the Spartans had no deep-seated aversion to tyrants as such, but Kleomenes, in obedience to the command of the Delphic oracle to 'liberate Athens',[46] expelled the last of the Peisistratid tyrants in 510 BC. With Hippias ejected, along with his Thracian and Scythian mercenaries, two aristocratic factions returned to haunt the political scene of Athens, *hoi paraloi* ('the men of the shore') headed by the Alkmaionidai, and *hoi ek tou pediou* ('the men of the plain') led by a certain Isagoras, son of Teisandros. Not surprisingly, we find that the followers of the hated Peisistratidai, *hoi hyperakrioi* ('the men from beyond the hills'), had suffered an eclipse. According to Aristotle, the naming of these political cabals was derived from 'the district where they tilled the soil'.[47] In other words, they are derived from districts of Attica. If this is true, it would make these factions local in composition, each consisting of one or two powerful families who headed a multitude of dependant families.

Bitter rivalry soon developed between a leading member of the Alkmaionidai, Kleisthenes, son of Megakles, and Isagoras, with the latter leader gaining the upper hand. In desperation the blue-blooded Kleisthenes riposted by turning to the people of Athens, the *dêmos*, seeking their support, by promising them in effect the vote.[48] Whether or not he himself realized in full, the implications of this drastic action, by it he did neatly turn the tables on his rival. Isagoras responded by appealing to the Spartan king, Kleomenes, who responded by demanding the immediate expulsion of Kleisthenes and all the members and followers of the Alkmaionidai who, were, in the words of Herodotos, 'the Accursed'.[49] The Alkmaionidai stood accused of having cold-bloodedly butchered Kylon and his partisans when they had promised them their lives after an abortive *coup d'état* way back in 652 BC.[50] Kleisthenes, in the face of the attack, prudently withdrew abroad and waited.

Sure enough, Isagoras and his cronies were to overplay their hand. Their champion Kleomenes came, with a bodyguard, to support a friendly government in the restoration of good order, which meant the overturning of a lawfully constituted government by force. They also proclaimed the banishment of 700 Athenian families, including all the Alkmaionidai. The banishment was to be for ever. It was at this point that the *dêmos* rose, whereupon Kleomenes, Isagoras and their men took possession of the Acropolis of Athens. And there they held out for just two days, Kleomenes and his men departing under a truce, along with a badly frightened Isagoras, whose partisans were condemned to death and in due course 'died in prison'.[51] Never had a Spartan king been so humiliated – on leaving the Acropolis the Spartans had surrendered their arms – but Kleomenes was a cold-hearted realist.[52] In the spring of 506 BC Kleomenes led out all the power of the Peloponnesian League to crush the nascent democracy. His object, we are told by Herodotos, was to install his *protégé*, the wretched Isagoras, as tyrant of Athens.[53] In the meantime, to make final and over-whelming the victory yet more certain, the Chalcidians and Boiotians invaded Attica, at the prompting of Kleomenes, from the north-east and north-west. The Athenians looked doomed. However, if there are such things as miracles, then one happened for them. At Eleusis the grand army of Kleomenes melted away.

The Peloponnesian allies, it appears, had not been informed of Kleomenes' true intentions. By their individual treaties with Sparta they had pledged to follow where they were led, but they were not slaves of the Spartans, and when the objective did become clear, the Corinthians, old friends of Athens against Aegina and Megara, cried foul and marched home. Then Demaratos (r. *c.* 515–491 BC), the other king of Sparta, 'who had not been opposed to Kleomenes previously',[54] took the lead among the doubters. Having 'seen off' the main threat, the Athenians turned about and marched north-east against the Chalcidians. The Boiotians in turn marched east to the rescue of their Euboian allies. The Athenians then changed direction suddenly and fell upon the Boiotians first, routing them with great slaughter and the loss of 700 prisoners, who were held for ransom. Meanwhile, the Chalcidians had got away home across the water to Euboia, but the fired up Athenians crossed after them, fought a second battle on the same day, and routed them too. It was a shattering defeat for Chalcis, and the Athenians annexed a vast slice of their territory, distributing it in allotments to some 4,000 poor Athenians. The colonist kept their status as citizens of democratic Athens.[55]

Kleomenes' next move was to convoke a congress of the Peloponnesian League at which he presented the allies with the exiled tyrant Hippias, and acknowledged the mistake in removing him and proposed his restoration. Once again the Corinthians threw a spanner in the works by opposing intervention, and they were supported by the other allies. The plan therefore came to nothing. This is the earliest recorded occasion when a congress of the allies was convoked to decide a matter of high policy. Once bitten, twice shy, as the popular proverb articulates, and perhaps Kleomenes' aim was to avoid a repetition of the fiasco at Eleusis, by ensuring Sparta would never embark on any foreign escapade without having first secured the sworn allegiance of its allies. Better, he may have reasoned, to lose an argument in assembly than to be deserted on the battlefield and so exposed to danger and ridicule. The history of Spartan intervention in Athens demonstrates the dominance of Kleomenes over Spartan foreign policy, but it shows too how great were the limitations in practice upon the exercise of his powers as a king. Incidentally, Kleisthenes now passes in silence from the stage, and we hear no more of him. A later tradition has it that he was hoisted by his own petard, the very first victim of one his own ingenious laws to protect democracy, ostracism no less.[56] That eccentric genius Kleomenes, on the other hand, was still very much at large, and we shall hear from him again.

Chapter 5

The Power of the Dorian Spear

When Aristagoras, the Persian-sponsored tyrant of Miletos, came calling at the door of Kleomenes, king of Sparta, he had with him a map of the world, as he knew it, engraved on a bronze plaque. So armed, he then launches into an eloquent speech, which paints a vivid picture of the Great King's vast material wealth and the lack of valour displayed by his subjects. A nice tale, plausibly told. Of course, the artful Aristagoras had good political reasons for doing so; he wanted Kleomenes to lend his support to a planned revolt of Asian Greeks from their overlord, Dareios. But Kleomenes refuses to commit Spartan hoplites to a campaign against the Persian empire that might take them as much as three months' march inland from the familiar Aegean Sea, and, prompted by his eight-year-old daughter Gorgo, who is supposed to have been especially blessed with the gift of the Spartan gab, orders the Milesian out of Sparta before sundown. Aristagoras takes himself off to Athens where he has much better luck, for the Athenians agree to send twenty ships to help their Ionian cousins, to which their island neighbours, the Eretrians of Euboia, contribute five ships. Needless to say, this puny naval force was hopelessly insufficient to turn the scales decisively against the awesome might of Dareios, but it did have the effect of irritating him greatly. Anyway, that is another story. Despite the boisterous tone of his two speeches, Aristagoras did touch upon two relevant facts about the Persian methods of warfare when he summed up their equipment as 'bows and short spears, trousers and turbans', and remarked that they had 'neither hoplite shield nor hoplite spear'.[1]

Yet the Persians were deemed invincible in the field by most people and, according to Herodotos, the Greeks had never yet stood their ground against a Persian army. During the Ionian revolt (499–494 BC) the Persians were to fight five land battles that we definitely know of and, interestingly, of those five they won four. Unfortunately, the corresponding details are rather scarce in Herodotos. Of three (Ephesos, White Pillars, Labraunda) he offers no tactical information at all, one, in which the Persians 'were cut to pieces',[2] was a night ambush on the road to Pedasos in Caria, and the final battle was the encounter at Malêne, near Atarnaios, on the mainland immediately opposite the island of Lesbos. What little Herodotos says about this battle is intriguing, for while the Persian infantry were locked in combat the late arrival of the Persian cavalry tipped the balance and the 'Greeks fled'.[3] Indeed, Herodotos later emphasizes the confidence of the Persians at Marathon in his remark that they thought the Athenians simply mad to risk an attack 'with no support from either cavalry or archers'.[4] The Persians were bowmen first and close-quarter fighters second, relying on the power of the bow to initially soften up the opposition before they closed in to finish them off with short spear and dagger. Indeed, those who stood against the

Persians were commonly beaten by the arrow shower, thus achieving the primary purpose of combat: the opponent's subjugation.

Making war is not subject to scientific analysis. It is a 'practical art', a 'skill', a 'trade', which properly learned and with some genius can be advanced to a high art. Ultimately, however, when the art of war is reduced to its simplest elements, we find that there are only two methods by which an enemy can be overthrown on the field of battle. Either shock or the missile must be employed against him. In the former, victory is secured through the face-to-face hand-to-hand struggle, in the latter, via a constant and deadly sleet of missiles that aim to destroy or drive away the enemy before it can come to close quarters. And so battlefield weapons took on the characteristics that still define them: shock weapons like the stabbing spear, sword or axe, and projectile weapons such as stone, bow and arrow or throwing spear. Thermopylai, as we have seen, was a contest between two military systems, the close quarter fighter (Greek hoplite) versus the long-range fighter (Persian bowmen).

Missile weapons can aid infantry battle but in themselves cannot send an enemy into defeat and decide a war:

> Fire and fire only is hopeless if the enemy ever makes contact. Weapons of shock are the crushers and pincers which are held in the hands of the assailant. Shock weapons are the military instruments *par excellence*. They are not only employed by courageous fighters anxious to close with the enemy, deliver him a blow, and win a decision, but they are truly the deadly one. They win battles.[5]

And so for the Greeks there was a real desire for open, direct, and deadly daylight confrontation, using 'real' weapons face-to-face at close quarters. On the other hand, for the Persians there was a desire for mobility, speed, ruse, and terror, their strength lying with the horse and the bow, as was befitting a nomadic people with no agrarian *polis* traditions.

The hoplite

War, in the ancient Greek world, was the central factor of political life and the dominating element in war was the hoplite,[6] heavily armoured warriors who fought shoulder pressing against shoulder with spear and shield in a large formation known as a phalanx.[7] With that, the armies of Greek *poleis* were based on a levy of those citizens prosperous enough to equip themselves as hoplites.[8] Except for the Spartans, whose warriors were acknowledged as the 'craftsmen of war' because they devoted their entire lives to military training,[9] and a few state-sponsored units such as the famous homoerotic unit, the Theban Sacred Band, the *hieros lochos* of 300 men who were paired in dyadic relationship and *in extremis* sworn to die for their partner, these citizen levies were untrained, part-time warrior farmers, owing their strength to numbers and determination rather than to skill or battle experience. As a citizen of a *polis* it was your moral, social and, above all, political duty to fight on the behalf of your *polis* in times of war. Liable for military service at any time from the age of twenty years, citizens remained on the state muster rolls for at least forty years – desertion or cowardice could lead to a loss of citizenship – and even a dramatist such as the Athenian Aischylos stood in the phalanx, and was, in fact, to be remembered on his grave as a warrior, not as a wordsmith.[10] And so hoplites were the citizens in battle; citizens were the hoplites in assembly, men who had a permanent stake in the community.

At first sight it may seem surprising that when Greek warfare emerges into the light of history, it not only soon becomes dominated by close-packed, heavily armoured amateurs, but also continues to be so for some three centuries (*c.* 675–350 BC). It lasted so long because as time passed the system was maintained for the sake of tradition, shared values and social prejudice. Since hoplites were expected to provide their own implements of war and keep them in a state of readiness, the majority of the population in any given *polis* was necessarily excluded. But the full rights of citizenship were only accorded to those who could afford to take their place in the phalanx, so that the hoplites effectively were the 'nation in arms', and it would have been unthinkable to arm the *hoi polloí*. It was only in Athens, where the navy became important, that the poorest citizens, the *thêtes* who rowed the triremes, came to have a significant military role, and thence democracy,[11] or what Aristotle aptly called 'trireme democracy'.[12] Finally, as the events of the two Persian invasions of Greece (490 BC, 480–479 BC) were to prove, hoplites were extremely formidable.

The equipment

Normally the hoplite panoply, *panopliâ*, consisted of a large, round soup-bowl shaped shield, *aspis*, approximately one metre in diameter, a bronze helmet, a bronze back-and-breast or stiff linen corselet, and bronze greaves. Greek hoplites were small by modern standards, averaging 1.60 metres and fifty-five kilograms, and they would have carried on their slight frames over half their body weight. The whole panoply, when worn, could weigh in excess of thirty kilograms, the heaviest individual item being the *aspis*, weighing in at seven kilograms or thereabouts. This was the single, most important item of defensive equipment.

Built on a wooden core, the *aspis* was faced with an extremely thin layer of stressed bronze and backed by a leather lining.[13] The core was usually crafted from flexible wood such as poplar or willow. Because of its unusually great weight, the shield needed to be carried by an arrangement of two handles. It had a detachable armband, the *porpax*, in the centre through which the left forearm was passed up to the elbow.[14] The accompanying second element was a handgrip, the *antilabê*, normally a leather thong that ran around the periphery of the shield's rim. This clamping and clutching mechanism allowed a firmer and more rigid grip than was possible with a single central handgrip, and more importantly it distributed the weight of the *aspis* more evenly between the left elbow and the left hand. The hoplite therefore warded off weapon blows solely with his left arm, at times rested the shield's upper lip on his left shoulder to conserve vital energy. If held across the chest, the *aspis* covered the hoplite from chin to knee.

The mechanics of this shield, therefore, meant the hoplite could only protect his own left flank. For, despite the shield's great weight and size – more or less determined by the length of the bearer's forearm times two – its round shape and the simple fact that it was clamped onto the hoplite's left arm, meant the shield offered poor protection for the entire body. The hoplite had no other option but to stand firm in his place within the phalanx, shoulder pressing against shoulder and shield scratching against shield, and if the formation was well maintained, the *aspis* would offer some protection to the hoplite's left-hand neighbour's unprotected right side.[15] Moreover, in the push of phalanxes during mêlée the *aspis* would also act offensively too, for those hoplites unable to bring their spears to bear, viz. rank three and back, could easily have tucked their left shoulders into their convex-shaped shields and shunt the hoplites to their front. Here it is best for us to imagine each man thrusting the metre-wide metal bowl of his *aspis* flush against the metal or linen back of the comrade before him, seating his left shoulder beneath the upper rim, and, digging his soles and toes into the dirt for purchase, heaved and shoved with all his strength. The Greeks called the initial battlefield collision and the horrific scrummage that ensued the *ôthismos*.[16]

Above the flat broad rim of the bronze-face *aspis*, the hoplite's head was fully protected by a helmet, hammered from a single sheet of bronze, the favoured Corinthian style. It had a long life as it covered the face leaving only small openings for the eyes, nostrils and mouth, and yielded to a blow without cracking. A leather lining was fixed to the interior by the small holes pierced in the metal. Under the helmet many men wore a headband, which not only restrained the hair but also provided some support for this heavy piece of armour. Nevertheless, any hoplite wearing a padded bronze helmet in a hot climate was quite prepared to suffer considerable discomfort. Yet it is hard for us to imagine such discomfort, face dripping with sweat under a helmet made red hot by the sun's blaze. Out of battle the helmet could be cocked harmlessly back upon the brow, leaving the face uncovered. This is the position in which it most frequently appears in sculpture and vase paintings, and on coins.

A corselet, either of bronze or of linen, fully protected the hoplite's torso. The latter type of corselet was made up of many layers of linen glued together with a resin to form a stiff shirt, about half a centimetre thick. Below the waist it was cut into strips, *pteruges*, for ease of movement, with a second layer of *pteruges* being fixed behind the first, thereby covering the gaps between them and forming a kind of kilt that protected the groin. First appearing in around 525 BC, the great advantage of the linen corselet, *linothôrax*, was its comfort, as it was more flexible and much cooler than bronze under a Mediterranean sun. As far as protection goes, the main advantage of bronze was a surface that deflected glancing blows. A direct hit would punch through the metal, but it might be held up by any padding worn underneath. A linen corselet would not deflect glancing blows, but it would be as effective as bronze against any major thrust. This protection, then, was slightly less than that of bronze, but the advantages of comfort and weight overrode that consideration.

Finally, a pair of bronze greaves, *knemides*, protected the lower legs of the hoplite. Shaped to imitate the muscles of the leg, these clipped neatly round the legs by their own elasticity, thereby secured at the rear of the calf by the flex of the metal alone. Thus, the hoplite remained effectively armoured from head to foot.

As in all military history, technology and change both responded to the situations of conflict and dictated what forms future conflict would take, and with this new style of spear-shield warfare came the ubiquitous and terrifying weapon *par excellence* of the hoplite the long thrusting spear, *dóru*.[17] Fashioned out of ash wood,[18] carefully seasoned, and some two to two-and-a-half metres in length, the *dóru* was equipped with a socketed bronze or iron spearhead, often between twenty and thirty centimetres long, and a bronze butt-spike. As well as acting as a counterweight to the spearhead, the butt-spike, affectionately known as the *sauroter* ('lizard-sticker'), allowed the spear to be planted in the ground when a hoplite was ordered to ground arms (being bronze it did not rust), or to fight with if the ash of his spear shaft snapped or shattered in the mêlée.[19] The main drawback of the spear was, of course, the inherent weakness of the wooden shaft. The weapon was usually gripped strong over the right shoulder, poised for the overarm strike, the spear tip to the face of the foe, although it could be easily thrust underarm if the hoplite was charging into contact at the run. In both cases he needed to keep his elbows tucked close to the body so as not to expose the vulnerable right armpit. The primary target area for the weapon was the face, which was neither armoured nor shielded. Secondary target areas were the throat and right armpit, which were exposed, poorly armoured or shielded. Hits on all these areas were potentially crippling if not fatal. The centre of the shaft was bound in cord or leather for a secure grip.

The simple term 'spearhead', however, embraces a great range of shapes and sizes, complete with socket ferrules (either welded in a complete circle or split-sided) to enable them to be mounted on the shaft and often secured with one or two rivets and/or binding. For use as a stabbing weapon, practical experience tells us that the width of the blade was important, for a wide blade actually prevents the spearhead from being inserted into the body of an enemy too far, thus enabling the spear to be recovered quickly, ready for further use. In our period of study the most common designs were angular blades, with a diamond cross section, and leaf-shaped blades, with a biconvex cross section. The addition of a midrib gave greater longitudinal strength to a spearhead, increasing its effectiveness at piercing shields and armour during hand-to-hand spear play.

The hoplite also packed a sword, but it was very much a secondary weapon – a far cry from its former predominance in the epoch of Homeric warfare – to be used only when his spear has failed him: it was the instrument of last resort. The introduction of the phalanx undermined the previous prestige of this arm. Besides, in the crush and squeeze of a phalanx, a shorter weapon was preferable so as to be more easily handled. It may have required special skills to handle a thrusting type sword, but with a meat cleaver it was almost impossible to miss in the cut and thrust of the tightly packed phalanx. One type was the Greek *kopis*, a strong, curved, one-edged blade primarily designed for slashing with an overhand stroke, and certainly not for thrusting. The cutting edge was on the inside like a Gurkha *kukri*, while the broad back of the blade curved forward in such a way to weight the weapon towards its tip, that is to say, making it 'point-heavy' – basically a hacking instrument for delivering 'butcher's blows'. Whatever the pattern, the sword was worn suspended from a long baldric from right shoulder to left hip, the scabbard being fashioned of wood covered with leather, with the tip strengthened by a small metal cap, the chape, usually moulded to the scabbard.

The advance

It is Thucydides who informs us too that the hoplite phalanx, as it advanced to contact, had a tendency to edge to the right.[20] In a compressed paragraph he gives us the essence of the matter, explaining that the right-hand man would drift in fear of being caught on his unshielded side, and the rest of the phalanx would naturally follow suit, each hoplite trying to keep under the protection of his right-hand neighbour's shield.[21] Thus each right wing might overlap and beat the opposing left. Thucydides implies that this was a tendency over which *stratêgoi*, even in the Spartan army, had little or no control. At Thermopylai, as we have seen, this did not apply because the bare right spear-side of Leonidas' phalanx was suitably guarded by the sea, but at Mantinea, as we shall see, Agis' phalanx would employ this rightward shift to its advantage.

The practised Spartans, according to the impressed Thucydides, were noted for their slow and ordered advance, marching in step the whole way to the rhythm of flute players – obsessive and monotonous to our ears probably – and singing awe-inspiring war songs, which contrasted with that of the enemy 'full of sound and fury'.[22] It was usual for summertime soldiers to be warmed up by a general's eleventh-hour harangue or some peak of bronze-banging bravado built to by shouting, spear-waving, shield-pounding and the like. For the Spartans, on the other hand, there was no bluster and bronze banging. As they advanced into contact there were merely a few words of encouragement, the sort of words that are uttered in the din of battle, not distinguished individually but restoring confidence by the fact of being spoken.

And then, just before contact, so as to give themselves greater courage and strike fear into their opponents, they would raise, in unison, a collective war cry or a *paean*. The Greek war cry sounded something like *éleleleû*,[23] the Greek banzai, whereas the *paean* was a chant – sometimes a mere yell – associated particularly with Apollo and sung, amongst other occasions, before entering battle. The *paean* was a peculiarly Greek custom, Dorian in origin, but eventually adopted by the other Greeks. Aischylos describes it as a 'the strong cry of victory, / The shout of sacrifice familiar to all Greeks, / To inspire our men and make them fearless in the field'.[24] The shout of Greek armies, reverberating under clear cobalt blue skies, often seemed to shake the gods from their slumber and, indeed, had such a quality of invocation that a foe of lesser vocal potency might well tremble involuntarily and look around him fearfully, as if anticipating the sudden arrival of an unseen host. Imagine, if you will, what frightening power there is in a cry roared out by only a few thousand throats to the tramp of marching feet.

The Spartans also wore crowns of foliage, at least up to the point where they halted to perform – much later than anyone else, and deliberately in sight of the enemy – their propitiatory blood sacrifice.[25] Undoubtedly, this last-minute halt provided a chance to dress the ranks again. The slow march, paralysing war songs, shrill reed flutes piercing through the din of battle, and the surreal fresh garlands must have been an unnerving sight in the eyes of those looking from the wrong side of the battlefield. More like a serene advance to a ritual sacrifice than a shambling advance to hard contact. We are ready: are you? At this point it was common for the opposition to break and flee, that is, before actually coming 'within spear-thrust' (*eis dóru*) of the Spartans. The alternative to breaking and fleeing, of course, was to surrender or die.

The push

It was the hoplite shield that made the rigid phalanx formation viable. Half the *aspis* protruded beyond the left-hand side of the hoplite. If the man on the left moved in close he was protected by the shield overlap, which thus guarded his uncovered side. Hence, hoplites stood shoulder pressing against shoulder with their shoulder-to-knee shields locked. Once this formation was broken, however, the advantage of the *aspis* was lost; as Plutarch says the body armour of a hoplite may be for the individual's protection, but the hoplite's *aspis* protected the whole phalanx.[26] Nonetheless, a hoplite's armour was designed for fighting in such a compact formation, protected on each side by his comrades' shields. The phalanx itself was a deep formation, normally composed of hoplites arrayed eight to twelve shields deep, occasionally deeper.[27] In this dense mass only the front two ranks could use their 'death-dealing spears' in the mêlée, the men in ranks' three and back adding weight to the attack by pushing to their front. This was probably achieved by shoving the man in front with your *aspis*. Thucydides and Xenophon, men who surely knew far better than we can ever know, both commonly refer to the push and shove, *ôthismos*, of a hoplite mêlée.[28]

The opposing phalanxes collided head-on, and the resulting shock would have been tremendous: several authors familiar with hoplite combat mention the crash went contending phalanxes collided.[29] The two opposing lines of spears now crossed (and often snapped in the tremendous onrush), and the leading ranks were immediately thrust upon each other's weapons by the irresistible pressure from behind. In our mind's eye we can visualize the majority of front rankers in each phalanx going down in the initial crunch, 'While knees sink low in gory dust, / And spears shivered at first thrust'.[30] However, their comrades stepped forward – or were pushed from behind – over their dead and dying bodies to continue the struggle. Xenophon, in his eye-witness account of the battle of Koroneia (summer 394 BC), laconically recalls his own experience of the clash and collision of the *ôthismos* as the Spartans 'crashed into the Thebans front to front. So with shield pressed against shield (*ôthismos aspidon*) they struggled, killed and were killed'.[31] Elsewhere, in his panegyric to his princely patron, Agesilaos, he was happy to elaborate:

> There was no shouting, nor was there silence, but the strange noise that wrath and battle together will produce ... Now the fighting was at an end, a weird spectacle met the eye, as one surveyed the scene of the conflict – the earth stained with blood, friend and foe lying dead side by side, shields smashed to pieces, spears snapped in two, daggers bared of their sheaths, some on the ground, some embedded in the bodies, some yet gripped by the hand.[32]

Euripides, who as an Athenian citizen would have had firsthand experience of this sort of horror, had used similar language to describe what happened when phalanxes of Athens and Thebes finally come to grips with each other on the red field of slaughter: 'All down the lines the fronts of battle clashed: / Men slew – were slain – a thunder of wild war cries / Rang, roared, of men on cheering each his fellow'.[33]

When the masses of flesh and bronze had been for some time pushing against each other, their spears (if still intact) interlocked, matters were now held in the balance. In the dust and terror of the *ôthismos* at Delion (winter 424 BC), according to Thucydides, with terrific stubbornness the Thebans dug their heels in and eventually 'got the better of the Athenians, pushing them back (*ôthismos aspidon*) step by step at first and keeping up their pressure'.[34] Once experienced such a thing was never easily forgotten and even Aristophanes' chorus of veteran hoplites, fondly reminiscing about Marathon, is made to say:

> *At once we ran up, armed with warlike spear and shield and,*
> *drunk with the bitter wine of anger,*
> *we gave them battle, man standing to man and rage distorting our lips.*
> *A hail of arrows hid the sky.*
> *However, by the help of the gods, we pushed off the foe towards evening.*[35]

The pushing with these wide and weighty, bowl-shaped shields explains the famous plea of the Theban *stratêgos*, Epameinondas, 'for one more pace' at Leuktra (summer 371 BC).[36] Indeed, on this subject Xenophon, who was no admirer of the Thebans, minces no words, saying that the Spartan right at Leuktra was 'pushed back'.[37] Xenophon advocates that the best men should be placed in front and at the rear of a phalanx so that the worse men in the middle, namely the cowards and the like, could be 'led by the former and pushed by the latter'.[38]

The pushing itself could go on for some time. Gelatinous with fatigue, it was now time for one side to crack. The crisis point of the contest had been reached, when the decision could swing either way, depending on which side was most capable of delivering the last fearful push. Thucydides says that at the battle of Solygeia (summer 425 BC), a village some ten kilometres from Corinth, the Athenian and Karystian right wing 'with difficulty pushed the Corinthians back'.[39] However, time is master, always. Once one side finally crumbles and collapses, all is up, and *panique terreur* takes hold, the vanquished suffering the most fearful losses in the initial rout. The mass of fugitives would have been more like the mob of Argives Xenophon describes 'frighten, panic stricken, presenting their unprotected sides, no one rallying to his own defence'.[40] However, long-range pursuit stood not within the lexicon of hoplite warfare. The victors asserted control of the battlefield by attaching a set of enemy arms and armour to a stake or tree as a trophy at the spot where the opposition had been routed.[41]

In hoplite warfare, therefore, the phalanx itself was the tactic. When one *polis* engaged another, the crucial battle would usually be fought on flat land with mutually visible fronts that were not more than a kilometre or so long and often only a few hundred metres apart. Normally, after a final blood sacrifice, *sphagia*, by the *stratêgos*, the two opposing phalanxes would simply head straight for each other at a fast walk, pick up the pace of the advance into a swinging stride, break into a dogtrot for the last few metres, collide with a crash and then, blinded by the dust and their own cumbersome helmets, stab and shove till one side cracked. At this juncture, we should note that the role of the *stratêgos*, who himself fought (and often perished) in the front rank of the phalanx, was 'nearly exhausted with the choosing of a battleground to suit the phalanx'.[42] Few armies, except the Spartan, as we shall discover, had the structure needed to allow major changes after the initial dispositions on a suitable battleground had been made. Once these were made, therefore, the *stratêgos* fought in battle, often in the most dangerous and therefore honourable section of the battleline.[43] Leadership was an amalgam of one-third tactical ability and two-thirds encouragement through example. As Euripides impertinently points out, 'the *stratêgos* / – one man one spear among those thousands'.[44]

The experience

Hand-to-hand combat, close-quarter fighting, coming to grips or to blows, the Greeks, with a stygian sense of humour, called all this the 'law of hands'.[45] The mêlée itself was a toe-to-toe affair, close enough to see the foe's retina and the tone of his skin, the front two ranks of opposing phalanxes attempting to stab their spears into the exposed parts of the foe so as to bring the most unpleasant wounds, that is, the throat or groin, which lacked protection. Usually this was executed overarm driven by the full force of the right arm and shoulder across the rim of the shield. Euripides puts this danger in a broad prospective when he has Medea say: 'I would rather stand three times behind a shield than give birth once': pain in childbirth, which the gods had ordained immutable.[46] Every man was a murderer, breath coming in short gasps, teeth set, hands clenched round the grips of his spear and shield, nerves and sinews alive with life. He neither hated his foe nor wanted him dead, but he feared him.

While the opposing front ranks, their faces wholly hidden by helmets, tried to butcher each other with a primitive energy, the ranks behind would push. Picture this, if you will, once a hoplite was down, injured or not, he was unlikely ever to get up again. This short but vicious mêlée was resolved once one side had practically collapsed. There was no pursuit by the victors, and those of the vanquished who were able fled the battlefield. It was enough, as the philosophers noted, every so often to kill a small portion of the enemy in an afternoon crash, crack his morale, and send him scurrying in defeat and shame whence he came.

Close quarter fighting denied participants the ability to distance themselves from conflict the way people today can do merely by observing war from the safety of their living rooms. It is hard for us to imagine the copper-tasting fear just before hard contact and the wild cruel joy of being alive afterwards. Ancient combat would have made a profound impact on those participating in it, involving stabbing, slashing, bludgeoning and hitting the enemy directly. Even distance weapons such as bows and slings had a relatively short range so that it was possible to see their terrible effects.

The cost

There is a human dimension to warfare that is too easily overlooked. At this remove in space and time, the lives of thousands of citizen soldiers are not easily accessible to us. Yet some means must be found to grasp the human reality of the battlefields on which so many Greeks fought, suffered and died. The sanguinary warrior god of war may have spared far more men than he slaughtered, nevertheless even for the victors the sight of the wounded and near dead littering the battlefield offered one of war's most horrifying realities. Look at, for instance, Tyrtaios' gruesome snapshot of a casualty trying to starve off death 'with his entrails all bloody in his hands, a sight so foul to see and fraught with such ill to the seer, and his flesh also all naked'.[47] This sadly reminds us of the similar fate of one of Xenophon's comrades, the Arcadian Nikarchos.[48]

A spear thrust into the lower stomach and groin – a hoplite was usually un-protected in this region – was almost always fatal, converting a comrade into a corpse. Death would generally result from shock, peritonitis, or other local infections, as the contents of the intestines spilled out into the abdominal cavity and the victim shrank from blood and fluid loss. In the Hippocratic corpus we read of a man who suffered a javelin wound deep into the lower back, which resulted in peritonitis, an inflammation of the thin membrane lining the abdominal cavity. Though initially not painful, by the third day the patient was in severe agony and suffering constipation.[49] Twenty-four hours later, constantly vomiting and convulsing, the patient became dazed and dehydrated. He passed away, five days after the original wound.[50] Shakespeare was surely right when he penned the line: 'I am afeard there are few die well that / die in battle'.[51] Here it is worth us revisiting Koroneia and witnessing for ourselves the bloody aftermath of a hoplite battle through the keen eyes (and the lively pen) of Xenophon:

> Now the fighting was at an end, a weird spectacle met the eye, as one surveyed the scene of the conflict – the earth stained with blood, friend and foe lying dead side by side, shields smashed to pieces, spears snapped in two, daggers bared of their sheaths, some on the ground, some embedded in the bodies, some yet gripped by the hand.[52]

Tribal conflict, and that is what we are looking at here, can go beyond what we would like to recognize as conventional limits, can move beyond control or logic, so that the combatants lost any sense of guidance on the field and, rendered blind by dust and blood, wholly lost to reason, deaf to the inner plea for survival, and in primal fury go about slaughtering one another without a stint. They did just that on this battlefield; Spartan and Theban stood toe-to-toe and stabbed wildly with spear and sword, or locked arms and legs and teeth in total combat, prepared to hold on to one another until death.

Like Xenophon, Menander, acknowledged master of the genre of comedy, once saw fit to describe the disfigured remains of a battlefield, which included the blackened, bloated bodies that had been left to rot in the blistering sun for some three days.[53] An unending table of human corpses, fat feasts for carrion crows, nourishment for a field. Napoléon himself was so moved by the carnage left on one of his killing fields that he scribbled the following lines in a missive: 'The countryside is covered with dead and wounded. This is not the pleasant part of war. One suffers, and the soul is oppressed to see so many sufferers'.[54]

The wounded receive little attention in the Greek sources. Battle scars, such a source of pride in many warlike societies, hardly get a mention. 'A man who can cut out shafts and dress our wounds – / a good healer is worth a troop of other men', sings Homer,[55] but only two men in the entire Greek army stuck outside Troy count as specialist healers.[56] More or less the same situation prevailed in our period of study, most Greek armies lacking any sort of medical service, the Spartan army being the exception with its physicians attached to a king's staff.[57] These physicians were equipped with bags of medicinal herbs, hellebore and foxglove, euphorbia and sorrel and marjoram and pine resin, compresses of linen, bronze 'dogs' to heat and jam into puncture woods to cauterize the flesh, 'irons' to do the same for surface lacerations. And so the medical treatment that a Spartan soldier might expect for his wounds and illnesses were rudimentary but by no means nonexistent. As for the other Greeks, with their militia armies, we can well imagine that wounded soldiers were carried by either their comrades, walked if they were ambulatory, or left on the battlefield to await their painful deaths. Those with flesh wounds, simple fractures or concussions would have had a good chance of survival so long as infection could be avoided. But the more seriously injured, with deep penetration wounds or severe blows to the head, especially where internal bleeding was involved, could not expect to survive, even for the Spartans despite the rudimentary medical services provided by their professional army.

The rules

Hoplite battles had a strong ritual character; the idea was to defeat rather than to annihilate. So forget strategy and tactics. Hoplites fight a set piece battle on the flattest piece of terrain and physically push the opposition from the pitch, a point clearly made by Mardonios, son of the veteran general Gobryas and Dareios' sister, in a speech to his cousin Xerxes:

> The Greeks are pugnacious enough, and start fights on the spur of the moment without sense or judgement to justify them. When they declare war on each other, they go off together to the smoothest and flattest piece of ground they can find, and have their battle on it.[58]

It was easy for Mardonios to believe that the Greeks pursued their unique style of warfare out of ignorance and stupidity, but what he says is incontrovertible. It was easy to laugh at people who collided head-to-head, but on the other hand it was not easy to defeat people who were willing to collide head-to-head. As it turned out, Mardonios was to suffer most directly from its effects, losing both his life and his army in the process.

Living as we do in a world inured to the routine obscenities of early twenty-first century warfare, we may ask ourselves why did the hoplite style of head-to-head open-terrain fighting last so long? For a start, the fighting was taking place on the hoplites' own ancestral fields, and the Greek people had a special affinity with the soil of their native land. In addition, as time passed, the system was maintained for the sake of tradition, shared values and social prejudice. Hoplite warfare was for prestige rather than for the survival of a *polis*. Sparta, whose warriors were acknowledged as the past masters of this style of warfare, was an exception to the rule – its hoplites were permanent and essential rather than occasional and ritual. The aim of most hoplite warfare was not the destruction of the enemy but winning the possession of the field of battle. Indeed, there were implicit rules of engagement, the 'common customs', for Greeks fighting Greeks. These fixed and well-understood rules include the following: war declared before hostilities; hostilities sometimes inappropriate (e.g. religious festivals); some places are protected, and some persons (e.g. shrines, heralds); trophies are respected; the return of dead; non-combatants not a legitimate target; fight in the proper season; within the span of a single day the issue that precipitated the conflict to be decided; a limited pursuit of defeated and retreating foes. These rules did not apply to 'barbarians', non-Greek speakers, and they would break down during the Peloponnesian War,[59] a war unprecedented in scale, in duration, and in acts of unnecessary barbarity.[60] As Thucydides himself says, the war was 'the greatest disturbance in the history of the Hellenes, affecting also a large part of non-Hellenic world, and indeed, I might also say, the whole of mankind'.[61]

Of this great war between Athens and Sparta something may be said here. The Peloponnesian War began not with a formal declaration of war but with a sneak attack by a few hundred Thebans, infiltrated into the small *polis* of Plataia in the dark of a cloudy winter's night by a group of oligarchic traitors from within. The Theban-backed oligarchic coup against democratic Plataia failed, and the survivors of the attack were all put to death immediately and without a trial. Everything must have a beginning, and by the traditional touchstones of hoplite warfare the opening event of war was not the done thing, and it indicated the kind of conflict it would be. Both sides were pitiless, and there were cruel deeds and death by light and dark. It was a war waged *à outrance* with every means available. In peaceful and prosperous times both people and nations behave reasonably because the tissue of material well-being and security that separate civilization from brutal savagery has not been torn away and people reduced to brutal necessity. 'But war,' says Thucydides, 'which takes away the comfortable provisions of daily life, is a violent schoolmaster and tends to assimilate men's character to their condition'.[62]

One tragic incident will suffice to illustrate this. Thracian peltasts, according to Thucydides, were deployed for the first time in 425 BC by the Athenians at Pylos, on the west coast of Messenia.[63] Twelve years later, as the Athenians gathered reinforcements for their armada in Sicily, 1,300 Thracian peltasts arrived in Athens too late to sail with the relief force headed for Syracuse under the *stratêgos* Demosthenes.[64] As the Athenians had no wish to incur unnecessary expenditure, they were sent back. But to get some value from the returning peltasts, they appointed another of their own *stratêgoi*, Diitrephes, and 'as they were to sail through the Eupiros, he was instructed to use them in doing whatever damage he could to the enemy on their voyage along the coastline'.[65] The knife-carrying Thracians had a reputation for violence not always connected with events, following a rugged tribal code known as the 'Three Alls' – exterminate all, incinerate all, demolish all. Anyway, these particular Thracians were first used against Tanagra in a quick raid, and then against Mykalessos, both situated in Boiotia and whose inhabitants were defenceless. One morning at daybreak the latter town was captured and what followed was one of the worst atrocities of the Peloponnesian War. The cat-footed Thracians 'butchered the inhabitants sparing neither the young nor the old, but methodically killing everyone they met, women and children alike, and even farm animals and every living thing they saw'.[66] They then crowned their aimless exploits by storming a boy's school, 'the largest in the place, into which the children had just entered and killed every one of them'.[67] Certainly the ethics of war was not a subject the Thracians dwelt on, but Mykalessos was the shape of wars to come.

The Thracians may have added a new element of brutality to Greek warfare, but war, or the threat of it, is a constant theme to a majority of the plays of the contemporary Euripides. His tragedy, the *Suppliants*, produced at Athens within a year after its shattering defeat at Delion (winter 424 BC), was prompted by the barbaric Theban treatment of the Athenians left for dead on the battlefield.[68] This was obviously no escapist theatre where the audience were encouraged to leave their brains at home, and Euripides was noted for his ability to put in the mouths of his characters thinly veiled denunciations of crimes against humanity committed in the name of patriotism by those who might be sitting in the audience.[69] The length and ferocity of this 'worldwide' struggle would transform warfare from a seasonal activity to one in which at least low-level conflict lasted throughout the traditionally inactive winter months. Low-level conflict was, in fact, characteristic of most of the war, on the Athenian side, for instance, taking the form of seaborne raids on the Peloponnese. Only two set pieces of hoplite warfare were ever played out, a single battle on a single day, Delion and Mantineia.

During the Peloponnesian War such battles may have been rare, yet the Greeks had developed what has been dubbed by Hanson the 'Western Way of War'. This was a head-to-head collision of citizen soldiers on an open plain in a magnificent display of demonic courage, physical prowess, virile honour, and fair play. There was no interest in decoys, ambushes, sneak attacks, petty skirmishes or clever feints, in the flashy manoeuvring we tend to associate with Western military doctrine, though the attack that is heavy, clumsy, and in front is certainly not a thing of the past. Nor was there the involvement of non-combatants. There was also no honour for the Greeks in fighting from afar. An archer or a javelineer who launched his weapon from a great distance was not held in high esteem, because he could kill with little risk to himself. Only those who clashed with spear and shield, defying death and disdaining retreat, were deemed honourable.

The hoplites went into battle not for fear of punishment or in hopes of plunder and booty. The hoplites were the citizens of *poleis* who owned property – commonly farmsteads – and held certain political rights. They fought to defend their liberties and home and hearth. In the stench, filth and gore of battle they fought side by side with neighbours, brothers, fathers, sons, uncles and cousins. This meant that they did their utmost to demonstrate courage and self-confidence, side by side with their comrades and that they had a vested interest in the outcome – they stood to lose everything. This was the unseen glue that bound the phalanx, and the *polis*, together. Moreover, being, in the main, farmers, meant citizens were available for military service only during the slack agricultural period between the grain harvest in May and the vintage in September, or the ploughing in November at the latest.

Hoplite battle was brutal and personal; it came like a summer hailstorm, mowed down a field of grain, and was over for a year. Armed and armoured hoplites advanced in their phalanxes and fought to the death, pressed forward by those behind them into the anonymous strangers in that part of the enemy phalanx facing them. Their battlefields were scenes of furious fighting and carnage that usually consumed not more than an hour or two. Every man was pushed to the limits of his physical and psychological endurance – and then it was over, not to be repeated for a year or more.

Chapter 6

Top Dog

Pausanias (d. *c*. 470 BC), unexpectedly became the regent of Sparta in 480 BC, when his uncle Leonidas was killed in action at Thermopylai, and his father, Kleombrotos, died of (un)natural causes. Leonidas' son Pleistarchos was too young to rule. In the following year, the regent commanded the Hellenic League army at Plataia, where the Persian invasion was finally defeated. In the spring of 478 BC, he led the coalition forces of the Hellenic League army overseas to the Dorian *polis* of Byzantium.[1]

One cannot possibly believe the wilder accusations concerning Pausanias, yet he was recalled from the command of the Hellenic League because of personal jealousy about the role he was playing overseas. Yet Pausanias was to come to a bad end after he had overstepped the mark. Apparently, while Pausanias was at Byzantium, his arrogance and his adoption of Persian clothing and manners offended the coalition allies and raised suspicions of disloyalty. What is more, he soon lost authority when rumours were spread that he wanted to collaborate with the satrap of nearby Hellespontine Phrygia, Artabazos. Recalled to Sparta, he was tried and acquitted of the charge of treason but was not restored to his command.[2] When Sparta sent another commander, the league members rejected him outright and offered the leadership to Aristeides of Athens.[3] Thucydides says that the Spartans willingly let the Athenians take over the war with Persia,[4] and ergo the Delian League was forged.

In the meantime, the victor of Plataia, with a trireme but without a mandate, slipped out of Sparta and seized Byzantium.[5] Like his uncle Dorieus before him, Pausanias had decided to strike out on his own. He was eventually removed from his mini-kingdom by the Athenians, probably in 477 BC, retiring to Kolonai in the Troad, where he was alleged to have entered into a clandestine alliance with the Great King. Wishing to avoid suspicion, Pausanias returned home only to be imprisoned on suspicion of plotting to seize power in Sparta by instigating a helot uprising – apparently in collaboration with the exiled Themistokles.[6] Escaping from his confinement, Pausanias took refuge in the temple of Athena Chalkioikos, Athena of the Brazen House. The ephors ordered the temple to be walled up and so Pausanias was left to starve to death.[7] The ultimate ambitions of the hero of Plataia remain a mystery, but his aims might have infringed the wise rule of antiquity: nothing in excess. Anyway, after this macabre incident, Sparta decided to remain outside the war against Persia.

While Athens was busy establishing its maritime empire, Sparta was, in fact, in no position to intervene, not until 461 BC at least. Thucydides does speak of the matter-of-course corruption of Sparta's overseas commanders,[8] and Herodotos mentions that the victor of Mykale, King Leotychidas, was accused, perhaps in 476 BC, of accepting hefty bribes two years previously during his expedition of revenge and reprisal against those erstwhile medizers, the Thessalians of central Greece. He was brought to trial but fled from Sparta 'to Tegea and ended his life there'.[9] He died in 469 BC, to be followed on to the Eurypontidai throne by his grandson Archidamos, who was to rule for forty years (469–427 BC).[10] Leonidas' heir, Pleistarchos, was also still young, so Sparta now lacked royal leadership. Notwithstanding, Diodoros reports of a debate being convened in Sparta in 475 BC to discuss the recovery of the Aegean from Athenian control, and Herodotos and Aristotle each promotes the view that Sparta now opposed Athenian leadership.[11] Yet in reality, Sparta's military horizon was limited to its own backyard, the Peloponnese.

Troubles at home

Herodotos lists five battles, which were victories for Sparta. The first of these engagements was Plataia (479 BC), and the last was Tanagra (457 BC), both of which were against external enemies of Sparta, the Persians and the Athenians. The three victories in between were uncomfortably close to home: 'the second, near Tegea, against the Tegeans and the Argives; the third, that at Dipaees, against all the Arcadians excepting those of Mantineia; the fourth, that at the Isthmus [revised to "before Ithome"], against the Messenians'.[12] Herodotos' evidence indicates, therefore, that for a twenty-year period after Plataia Sparta was tied down because of disputes in its own backyard. Further evidence supports this, for Strabo says that soon after the Persian invasion the Arcadian *polis* of Mantineia underwent the political process the Greeks called *synoikismos*.[13] Also, Diodoros relates that in 471 BC Elis, with the aid of Argos, Sparta's most bitter and proximate rival, underwent the same democratization.[14] It is possible that Mantineia experienced its *synoikismos* at the same time as Elis. If this is correct, Sparta suddenly found itself surrounded by unfriendly neighbours, menaced by the likes of Tegea, Mantineia and Elis, while Argos, although it had been crippled at Sepeia by Kleomenes back in 494 BC,[15] kept up its dogged defiance. So Sparta, as the scattered evidence suggests *tout ensemble*, was in mighty trouble in the Peloponnese with its hitherto allies.

We have no date for Dipaees, the battle that ended Sparta's problems in Arcadia, but there is a faint suggestion that it was already embroiled at the time in the most serious helot revolt within living memory. Isokrates, not a reliable source at the best of times admittedly, says the Spartans 'stood arrayed with but a single line of soldiery' at the battle of Dipaees, a 'thin red line' *in extremis*.[16] Thucydides connects the revolt, or what we conveniently call the Fourth Messenian War, with the serious earthquake that struck Sparta sometime when Athens was at war with the islanders of Thasos in the northern Aegean, in other words around 465 BC.[17] It was disastrous even if we are not inclined to believe the later, more lurid tales of more than 20,000 dead, of only five houses left standing, of numerous boys being crushed by a collapsing stoa, and of Taïygettos being split asunder.[18] Later on the seemingly more reliable Thucydides appears to say the revolt ended after a ten-year struggle, but the problem is that he reckons the year to be 460 BC.[19] One plausible solution is to read 'four' instead of 'ten' in the surviving manuscripts: the evidence that the revolt did not last ten years is firm.

Anyway, what is important is the fact that Sparta appealed for aid in its current war against the Messenian rebels, who had taken refuge on Mount Ithome, where they had an excellent defensive position and space to produce food, and used this natural stronghold as a base for guerrilla raids deep into Spartan domains, especially the rich plain of Messenia.[20] Initially the Spartans were keen for Athenian aid, since the Athenians 'were skilled in siege operations'.[21] According to Plutarch it was difficult for the pro-Spartan Kimon to persuade the Athenians to help the Spartans, the anti-lobby arguing that Sparta was Athens' natural enemy and Athens should let Sparta's pride be trampled in the dust.[22] Kimon was intelligent, able, with con-servative ideas: he was popular in Sparta too and had gone to the lengths of calling his eldest son Lakedaimonios.[23] The Athenian assembly was finally swayed by an emotional appeal from Kimon, who finally led a substantial force of 4,000 Athenian hoplites to Sparta's aid,[24] which, in turn, sent he and them packing on the specious grounds that they were no longer needed.

Thucydides reports the true motive, saying the Spartans were afraid of 'the unorthodox habits of the Athenians', in other words their democracy, and if they stayed on in the Peloponnese they 'might listen to the people in Ithome and become the sponsors of some revolutionary policy'.[25] With this stinging rebuke we witness an element of paranoia and suspicion guiding the minds of the Spartans. Poor Kimon returned home and his authority there was immediately undermined, and within a couple of years the valorous *stratêgos*, the victor of many battles on land and at sea, had been discredited and shuffled off to the straightened circumstances of exile. His policy of cooperation and co-leadership of Greece between Athens and Sparta, 'yokefellows' in his words,[26] was in tatters. For Thucydides, the affair is heavy with significance. It was the beginning of evil between Spartans and Athenians. Whenever barbarism and civilization, or two distinct forms of the latter, meet face to face, the result must be war. And the essential act of war is destruction, not necessarily of human lives, but of the products of human labour. War, it will be seen, is a way of shattering to pieces materials that might otherwise be used to make human life that more tolerable.

The first war

What is called, for convenience sake, the first Peloponnesian war (461–446 BC) followed hard on the heels of the humiliating rebuff given to Athens by Sparta at Mount Ithome. The Athenians were naturally affronted by Sparta's attitude and they immediately responded by renouncing their alliance with Sparta against the Persians, and promptly allied themselves with Sparta's oldest enemy, Argos. At the same time 'both Argos and Athens made an alliance on exactly the same terms with the Thessalians'.[27] With this triple alliance we witness the formation of hegemony against Sparta, yet other Greeks will not have forgotten that Thessaly medized during the invasion of Xerxes and that Argos sat on the wrong side of the fence. Athens' new alliances were followed up with a further blow against Sparta; namely it received a number of the Messenian rebels and settled them at Naupaktos on the northern shore of the Gulf of Corinth, thereby demonstrating 'the ill feeling against Sparta that had already developed'.[28] At the same time the Megarians, allies of Sparta, were welcomed into the alliance after they had quarrelled with a fellow member of the Peloponnesian League, Corinth.[29] The defection of Megara meant Sparta was now unable to strike overland at Attica with ease. On the other hand, Athens gained the use of a base near to the Isthmus of Corinth, the gateway to the Peloponnese, and further tightened its grip on the Isthmus by building a long wall between Megara and its eastern port at Nisaea on the Saronic Gulf. In doing so Athens laid up a great store of hatred at Corinth.

However, if the alliance with Argos was to be any benefit to Athens, it needed land communications with the Argives. Thus, to this end, the Athenians had to acquire military bases in the Peloponnese *en route* to Argos. The upshot was the Athenian sea-borne landing at the best harbour between Athens and Argos, Halieis on the Argolic Gulf, which was successfully repulsed by the Corinthians and the Epidaurians.[30] Athens now turned its attention to Aegina, an island in the Saronic Gulf, the strategy being to clear the nearby seas of hostile navies and thus secure the maritime communications to Argos.[31] Matters went well for Athens, winning two naval engagements off Aegina, before laying siege to the island's chief town. Even when a Spartan army crossed the Gulf of Corinth and a full-scale battle at Tanagra (summer 457 BC) and, hoplite against hoplite, the Spartans won,[32] Athens' response was to invade Boiotia two months later with another army, defeat the Boiotians at Oenophyta,[33] and bring all central Greece under its control. Shortly afterwards, Aegina surrendered,[34] and the confidence of Athens was well illustrated when an Athenian fleet sailed round the Peloponnese, raiding as it went, and landing on Lakonian territory they torched the Spartan dockyard at Gytheion (summer 456 BC).[35]

In 459 BC Athens despatched 200 triremes to Cyprus, the fleet going on to Egypt in order to support the revolt against the Great King of Persia, Xerxes' successor Artaxerxes I. The Athenians sailed up the Nile and gained control of Memphis.[36] It seems Athens was expanding beyond the Aegean and into the eastern Mediterranean, forming an alliance, for example, with the Phoenician city of Doros. This was the high-water mark of Athenian imperial aspirations.

For Athens, riding high on the tide of success, the future never looked so bright. The helplessness of Sparta had been unveiled and Athens was emerging as the dominant power on the Greek mainland, while the Delian League under its leadership was keeping the Persians off the seas in the eastern Mediterranean and it looked as if it the Athenian expeditionary force operating in Egypt would soon crush the Persian forces there – or so it was then hoped. Yet the war was to drag on for another decade, until Athens found it had overreached itself. Its success was cut short by defeat in Egypt at the hands of the Persians, who had sent in a new army (summer 454 BC). Thucydides sums it all up best when he says: 'So the enterprise of the Greeks came to ruin after six years of war; and only a handful from a great force made their way through Libya and reached Kyrene safely; the majority were lost'.[37] This was not quite the end. A relieving squadron of fifty ships, Athenian and allied, sailed for Egypt. According to Thucydides they were 'in total ignorance of what had occurred', and it looks like a complete breakdown of communications between Egypt and Athens. Not expecting any opposition the relieving squadron was attacked by both land and water, and lost half their number. 'Such was the end of the great expedition of the Athenians and their allies to Egypt'.[38]

The victory of Oenophyta had broken the strong centralized Boiotian federation and, though Thebes itself was not taken, the rest of Boiotia came under Athenian control. Since the main threat to Athens was the formidable hoplite strength of a united Boiotia dominated by Thebes, the Athenians made it policy to encourage an appetite for independence in the Boiotian *poleis*, viz. democracies installed and oligarchs in exile. By 447 BC the number of Boiotian exiles had swollen considerably and they were not alone; anti-Athenian feeling had been mounting also throughout central Greece and in Euboia, the Aegean island that stretches along the flanks of Attica and Boiotia. Athens was forced to surrender control of Boiotia after the Boiotians successfully rose in revolt and crushingly defeated the Athenians at Koroneia (447 BC) – a single battle could put pay to any hegemony. News of Koroneia encouraged others, and the following year Euboia followed the path of rebellion. Worse still, with Megara succeeding and rejoining the Spartan alliance, a Peloponnesian army, commanded by King Pleistoanax, the son of Pausanias,[39] invaded Attica and ravaged the Eleusis and Thriasian plain from end to end (summer 446 BC). Athenians were slain, their farms were burned, and their livestock slaughtered.

Athens had had enough and a thirty-year truce was concluded with Sparta and both sides accepted its terms of conditions without much cause for complaint (445 BC). The Corinthians, for instance, having suffered the greatest during the war, were more than happy with treaty. Six years later the Peloponnesian League wanted to take military action against Athens over its highhanded treatment of Samos (440 BC), but the Corinthians vetoed the motion, telling their fellow Peloponnesians 'that every power has a right to punish its own allies',[40] and (apparently subsequently) the Spartans had refused to help Lesbos when it wished to revolt.[41] Athens was then free to crush the Samian rebellion.[42] A key clause of the treaty formally divided the Greek world into two camps, by forbidding the members of either alliance to change sides, as Megara had done. Neutrals however, could join either side. As for the Athenians, with the collapse of the land empire they gave up their claims to central Greece and ceased to interfere in the Peloponnese. However, they retained their iron grip on Aegina despite the island's nominal autonomy – a classic example of Athens' encroachment into the territories of neighbouring states weaker than it.[43] Above all else, Athens secured the recognition of its maritime empire and with this powerful propaganda point the first Peloponnesian war was ended. It had been an untidy affair from the Spartan side, more a series of mini-adventures than a full-blown systematic war, and although the adventures were all at the time successful they did not add to victory.

The thirty-year truce between Sparta and Athens was a treaty that did not aim at destruction of punishment but sought a guarantee of stability against the renewal of conflict. To succeed, such a peace treaty must accurately reflect the true military and political situation and must rest on a sincere desire by both parties to make it work. This peace was a compromise that contained the essential elements that should have guaranteed success, for it accurately reflected the balance of power between the two rivals and their international alliances. By recognizing Sparta's hegemony on the mainland and Athens' in the Aegean it acknowledged and accepted the two power blocs into which the Greek world had been divided and so provided hope for lasting peace. However, some Athenians favoured expansion of the empire, and some Spartans resented sharing hegemony with Athens, and the truce did not last. Athens and Sparta were too powerful and proud to live in the same world. Both had admitted grievances against each other, but the unadmitted grievances were bigger. The march of phalanxes may have been stilled all over the Greek mainland, but, in fact, the Greek world was taking its first strides towards more immense wars than ever.

Money, ships, and walls

Reading too much Aristotle is enough to make any reasonably rational person prefer Plato. Still, most of us, whether of sound mind or not, have neither read nor cared about the musings of two cranky Greek philosophers. But what Aristotle said about civil wars applies equally to all human conflicts, namely 'they are not about small matters; they may arise from small things, but they are waged about great things';[44] but this is after all a problem that is always with us. Today, as much as any other time, the causes of war are controversial subjects. The real motives for more recent conflicts were often psychological and irrational rather than economic and practical, which is to say, they derived from questions of honour and prestige. Just consider, for instance, those magnified echoes of the pistol shots in Sarajevo on 28 June 1914; a minor incident in a remote corner of Europe and the imperial war drums were suddenly deafening. It follows that the causes of the Great War must be sought as much within the boundaries of France, Germany and England, as in the boundaries of the toppling Austro-Hungarian empire. We must, therefore, be very wary of reasons why certain ancient conflicts took place.

In a sense, of course, such an enigmatic picture is historically valid; to most of those involved in these ancient wars, what was happening was often bewildering and obscure. Aristotles' teacher Plato, on the other hand, argues that men need 'couches, tables and other furniture, and fine foods, of course, and perfumes and incense, courtesans and cakes, all kinds of everything',[45] and as they 'give themselves over to unlimited acquisition of wealth', they will inevitably seek to expand at the expense of their neighbours. Plato closes this discussion with a triumphant 'We have discovered the origin of war'.[46] The historian, much like Plato and his reduction of all war to conflict over consumer durables, naturally wishes to construct, with the broad irony of hindsight, a clearer, simplified picture. There are two things that we do know, however. First, by the classical period wars were no longer fought for so-called living space as Sparta had in the First Messenian War, namely that age-old human desire to grab more territory and exploit it. There are no examples of the victor seizing territory from the vanquished, only examples of tribute exacted or garrisons planted. Second, wars were not fought in this period for reasons of economics or, as Plato puts it, dissatisfaction with simple bodily comforts and a demand for luxury. In Athens, a place noted for its conspicuous consumption, trade and industry was firmly in the hands of the *metoikoi*, the resident aliens, who by definition had no vote or voice in Athenian affairs, no hope of public office, but were still liable for taxes as well as military service.[47]

The world we live in today is led and governed by men who pretend they are creatures of morality and integrity, whereas most of them are self-seeking shams who take but a butterfly interest in the needs of those they lead and govern. They make wars, not for sentimental reasons (false 'humanitarianism', 'democracy', 'justice', 'self-defence' etc., words long emptied of their dictionary meaning) but for increased profits or increased power. They have got into the habit of thinking that they have only to conceive a desire for more in order to acquire it, and they continue with highhanded seizures and preposterous moral justifications. There are two kinds of people in our world: the predators and the sheep. And the predators always get to the top, because they are prepared to fight to get there and devour anyone and anything that get in their way. The majority of people have not the nerve, or the courage, or the hunger, or the ruthlessness. So our world is governed by the predators, who become the potentates. And the potentates are never satisfied. They must go on and on pursuing more of the currency they worship. And that currency can be profit or it can be power.

If there was a single cause for war in our period of study then it was *holos*, a state seeking to gain *hêgemonia*, hegemony, whereby the autonomy of one power can be secured through the subjugation of others, or those others preventing it. In this way Athens, for example, sought to bring smaller states into its orbit, adopting a sort of proto-Social Darwinism to justify crushing weaker states. Thucydides says it best when he puts into the mouth of an Athenian envoy at Sparta: 'And we are not the first to have acted this way, for it has always been ordained that the weaker are kept down by the stronger'.[48] The Old Oligarch, an anonymous and grouchy oligarch who wrote a ranting political pamphlet on Athens while Thucydides was collecting material for his history, promoted the advantages of hegemony, that is to say, the Athenian empire, because it provided tangible results for Athens.[49] The Old Oligarch may have had a shrewd idea of the benefits of an empire could bring to Athens, but such material things as profit were not as important as the intangible feeling of power, an imperial perspective fully appreciated by Alkibiades, one of the chief figures of the Peloponnesian War: 'It is not possible for us to calculate, like housekeepers, exactly how much empire we want to have'.[50] He was a close observer of human nature and some of his deductions were penetrating. Alkibiades' argument that an imperial power cannot be inactive would be one recognized by any modern superpower.

The Athenians would have appreciated the saying about the strong making meat of the weak,[51] and naturally hegemony created in other people the desire to be protected from the likes of Athens. Many if not all Greeks, quite rightly, wanted to run their own affairs, no matter how sanguinary, on the 'three selfs' policy of self-government, self-sufficiency, and self-defence. As the Mytilenaeans explained to the members of the Peloponnesian League gathered at Olympia why they had revolted from Athens: 'we did not become allies of the Athenians for the subjugation of the Greeks, but allies of the Greeks for their liberation from the Mede'.[52] Besides, despite Perikles' boast that Athens was 'an education to Greece',[53] most Greek states were just as sophisticated and as advanced in cultural and political affairs as it was. Even if Athens considered itself the cultural showpiece of the age, what right did the Athenians have, pickled as they were in self-satisfaction, rowing around the Aegean pedalling their radical democracy, a socio-political heresy to most Greeks? As with Western powers today, when Athenians talked about democracy overseas, what they invariably created was a political system that served their interests, and invariably did so with violence and arrogance.

After the defeat of the Persians at Salamis (autumn 480 BC) and Plataia (summer 479 BC), Athens rose to become the top *polis* in the Greek world, a *polis* so populous, whose riches were the seas and the water its walls. As the leading maritime power it made itself the strongest member of what modern commentators call the Delian League, a voluntary alliance of Greek *poleis* that had invited Athens to take the lead in continuing the war of liberation and vengeance against Persia. To the common effort the members of this league contributed ships plus crews or, if more agreeable to them, money,[54] which was kept in the shrine of Apollo on the sacred Aegean island of Delos. Sparta, unsurprisingly, was no part of this.

Under Themistokles and a succession of gifted imperialists, the alliance grew rapidly through a mixture of voluntary adherence and a use of force until it embraced nearly all the *poleis* of the islands and coasts of the Aegean. The studied Athenian policy was to encourage those members who contributed ships to substitute a monetary payment, 'and so the Athenian fleet expanded from the money that they contributed' until only the great offshore islands of Lesbos, Samos, and Chios were left with a navy and enjoyed relative autonomy.[55] First its leader, then its master, Athens gradually attained a position where it could demand virtually any dues to the league and did not have to account for the money sent to the league treasury, which was moved to Athens after the Egyptian disaster (454 BC).[56] Whether Athens had any right to do such a thing was very questionable. But Athens had the reality of power and was content with its action. Besides, no longer used solely for common defence, the Athenians spent much of what was now, in effect, imperial tribute, turning their *polis* into a cultural and architectural showpiece, which made those independent-minded Greek allies contributing the money more and more resentful.[57] This extraction of tribute, as Thucydides was to note, was one of the major differences between the Delian and Peloponnesian leagues, and the growing unpopularity of tribute was a major theme of Athens' increasingly imperialistic policies throughout the rest of the fifth century BC.

If the members of the Delian League had sought a first amongst equals to lead them, they found an imperialist bully. As a 'benign' police force of sorts for its tribute paying allies, Athenian triremes enforced as well as expanded Athens' dominion over as much of the Aegean as possible, creating satellite democracies in the process. Xenophon, who was certainly no friend of the Athenian democratic system, rightly said of the fully manned trireme, it was 'a terror to the enemy and a joy to her friends'.[58] When an Athenian was asked of his place of birth, he proudly answered: 'From where the fine triremes come'.[59] It was, it seems, the superior quality of Athenian ships was well worth boasting about. It is therefore safe to say that the foundation of Athens' might was its fleet, and at its apogee, the Athenian maritime empire ruled directly or indirectly some 150 *poleis*, the most remote of these being an eight-day voyage or some 400 kilometres from Peiraeus, the port of Athens, while Athenian power could be projected over the Mediterranean from Sicily to Egypt to the Black Sea. The knowledge that Athenian triremes might appear at any moment in the harbour was a deterrent to anti-Athenian elements, and each year, according to Plutarch, peacetime patrols were sent out.[60] They showed the Athenian flag, gave confidence to Athens' friends, and kept the sea clear of pirates.

Freedom is, above all, democratic and, as Sophokles put it, 'free men have free tongues'.[61] At home, democratic Athens stood for freedom and equality. The Athenians even had their triremes named *Dêmokratia* (*Democracy*), *Eleutheria* (*Freedom*), and *Parrhêsia* (*Free Speech*). Abroad, imperial Athens did not hesitate to use any means necessary in order to enforce its authority throughout the 'island empire' that it ruled. This was the most powerful empire yet known in Greek history, and it was their fighting navy, Themistokles' legacy, that was the weapon by which the Athenians achieved and maintained their power and prosperity. After making a stand against Xerxes in the name of freedom, Athens had discovered that in order to maintain its freedom at home, it would have to make difficult compromises abroad.

In time, a number of anxious *poleis* looked to oligarchic Sparta for leadership. In their eyes the Athenians were not Perikles' 'standard-bearers of civilization', who had developed political equality, perfected drama, built the Parthenon, and fashioned a dynamic culture based on expropriated capital, but rather an oppressive and unpredictable imperialist state, whose navy and democracy ensured turmoil for any who chose to stand in its way. Like all such myths, this particular myth of 'Periklean Athens' is true in parts. However, like many superpowers since, Athens saw no contradiction between democratic freedom at home and aggressive imperialism overseas, meddling in foreign lands and shipping democracy from place to place. Perikles' democracy and imperialism were bound together, and his hawkish influence almost lay certainly behind the increasingly ruthless treatment meted out to Athens' overseas allies in the course of the fifth century BC. The familiar imperialistic dogma was that might was right, that wolves survived where sheep went under, that security existed only in the spear and the shield. When international incidents began to occur, which could lead to a renewed war with Sparta, Perikles stiffened the Athenians against compromise or concession. When war did break out Perikles, according to Thucydides, had no illusions of the nature of Athenian control and said so to his fellow Athenians: 'For by this time your empire has become like a tyranny'.[62] In the fifth century BC the term 'tyranny' was an insult, a power exercised by someone that did not have the mandate to rule, and did so by exercising brute force and naked oppression. This is a damning admission by the Athenians, and if not them collectively, at least by Thucydides.[63]

Surviving inscriptions certainly bear the author out. Take the Erythrai Decree, for instance, which shows the oath that binds the citizens of Erythrai to the citizens of Athens: 'I shall not rebel from the People of Athenians or from the allies of the Athenians'.[64] The decree belongs to the year 453/2 BC. On the other hand, by reading the Eretrian Decree we become aware of the fact that the oath of allegiance has been slightly modified: 'I shall not rebel from the People of Athenians'.[65] What we are witnessing with these few words chiselled in stone is the clear-cut change from alliance to rule. The decree belongs to the year 446/5 BC. The validity of all these denunciations and admissions is that the allies voted with their feet and revolted whenever the opportunity arose. Quite simply, the allies loathed the Athenians and their empire. However, the picture is not as clear as all that. Many allies were still not full democracies and were, in effect, ruled by oligarchies. So, even if the majority of people wanted Athens' imperial rule, the aristocrats would have the final say; rebellion would spring out of the property class even if the people kept faith with Athens. The cause of what is conventionally called the Peloponnesian War (431–404 BC) may be controversial, but there is no good reason to doubt Thucydides' view that the fundamental cause was Sparta's irrational fear of Athens' pushy imperialism.

Unlike Herodotos' recounting of the conflict between Greek and Persian, the gods play no part in Thucydides' analysis of the causes of the Peloponnesian War. Oracles are not serious things but fit only for the superstitious.[66] When in 432 BC the Spartans had decided to go to war 'they sent to Delphi to inquire of the god whether they would fare better if they went to war, and the god, *as it is said* [emphasis added], replied that if they fought with their full strength, victory would be theirs, and he would be on their side whether they called on him or not'.[67] Thucydides, in qualifying the record with 'as it is said', seems to imply that the Spartans at home rather than Apollo at Delphi may have been responsible for this answer.

The reason why

At the beginning of his account Thucydides, displaying a subtle understanding of human motivation, provides what is now considered a celebrated analysis on the origin of the great war between Athens and Sparta.[68] He starts by distinguishing between the real reason for this war from what he calls the 'causes of complaint' and the 'specific instances where their interests clashed'.[69] The distinctions made by him are not so much between fundamental causes for the war but primarily ones between the 'truest cause (*alêthestatê prophasis*), albeit the one least publicised', that is to say, in the speeches of the various delegates, and 'each side's openly expressed complaints'.[70] In the view of Thucydides, the so-called openly expressed complaints pivoted upon Corcyra's appeal to Athens for help against Corinth,[71] and Poteidaia's revolt from Athenian control at the instigation of Corinth.[72]

But people in a crisis are also moved by the fear of future events. So it was with the Spartans. For Thucydides, as he constantly tells us,[73] what made the war between Athens and Sparta inevitable was Sparta's fear of the growing power of Athens. As we have already discussed, Sparta was continually concerned with maintaining its dominance on the mainland of Greece in order to check any incitement to rebellion of its subject peoples in Lakedaimon and Messenia. Unless Athenian imperialism was halted, it might well pose a threat to Spartan hegemony, especially in its own backyard, the Peloponnese. The deepest self-interest of the Spartans, therefore, required them to maintain the integrity of the Peloponnesian League and their own leadership of it. Yet this allegedly least publicized truest cause was least discussed because Sparta could hardly stand before the members of its alliance and pronounce that it was afraid of Athens. Notwithstanding Sparta's candid behaviour, Thucydides resolutely believes that fear of Athens was the root cause of the war. For instance, he recorded the envoys from the island of Corcyra, now called Corfu, warning the Athenians that 'Sparta is frightened of you and wants war'.[74] Again, he says the Spartans thought that war should be declared 'not so much because they were influenced by the speeches of their allies as because they were afraid of the further growth of Athenian power, seeing, as they did, that already the greater part of Hellas was under the control of Athens'.[75] There were two hegemonic systems: neither would brook a rival.

To amplify this last point Thucydides gives his celebrated, albeit brief, *Pentê-kontaëtia*,[76] the fifty-year excursus that charts the growth of Athenian power between the final retreat of the Persians in 479 BC and the outbreak of the Peloponnesian War in 431 BC. This historical précis accomplished, Thucydides then presents the final and most definite statement as to why the Spartans, though they saw what was happening, 'did little or nothing to prevent the growth of Athenian power, and for most of the time remained inactive, being traditionally slow to go to war, unless they were forced to'.[77] It needs but one foe to breed a war, not two, and in Thucydides' eyes the Spartans were not warmongers. Theirs was a traditional society, proud of its ways and conscious of its prestige: the Athenians – innovative, cocksure and greedy – represented everything they distrusted. Besides, as we have discussed above, Sparta had troubles at home and problems within its alliance. However, when an expansionist Athens, now puffed like the bullfrog in the fable, full blown with imperial success and smitten by the old arrogance that does not stop to count the opposition, started to meddle with the affairs of Sparta's staunchest and most powerful ally, namely Corinth (like Athens, a great commercial *polis*) and its maternal links with Corcyra (433 BC) and Poteidaia (432 BC), the Spartans were left with little choice but to act. This was particularly so when another important ally, Megara, added its voice to the clamour for war. Thucydides' account of the Corinthian delegate's speech to the Spartans hints that the Corinthians were threatening to leave the Peloponnesian League if Sparta refused their demand. As ill-luck would have it, the Athenians had aroused the ire of the Corinthians, for it should be mentioned that both Corcyra and Potidaia were Corinthian colonies, with the added complication of the first being so hated by the Corinthians it often drove them to the point of war,[78] and the second also being a tributary member of the Delian League from which it had just revolted with the connivance of Corinth.

The direct intervention by Athens in what Corinth could with some reason regard as its own sphere was the most important factor in bringing matters to a head in 432 BC, and, in fact, many modern commentators have regarded the hostility of Corinth to Athens as the main cause of the outbreak of war. As said before, this is not the view of Thucydides whose judgement is unambiguous. 'The truest cause ... was the growth of the power of Athens, and the alarm which this inspired in Sparta, made war inevitable'.[79] Consistently with this view he says that the Athenians made their alliance with Corcyra 'because they realised that war with the Peloponnese was bound to come'.[80] Yet a number of modern commentators still question Thucydides' conclusions concerning the inevitability of the Peloponnesian War.[81] Cornford, for example, argues that Athenian economic aggression against Corinth and Megara was the cause.[82] There is archaeological evidence that in the mid-fifth century BC, the distinctive Corinthian pottery was being replaced Athenian pottery, the celebrated Attic red figure ware we are all familiar with, in southern Italy, indicating successful Athenian commercial rivalry in the western Mediterranean, traditionally the economic sphere of Corinth. To support his thesis, Cornford makes great play upon Thucydides' statement respecting the position of Corcyra athwart the important sea route from the Gulf of Corinth to southern Italy and Sicily, stressing that Thucydides, in this passage, intended to say that the island was thus 'able to bar the passage of *commercial ships* [emphasis added] from there to the Peloponnese, and from Peloponnese to there'. However, Thucydides is thinking of warships, not merchantmen, as he clearly says here 'the passage of naval reinforcements'.[83] At times brilliant, without a doubt, but Cornford, who strives to emphasize Thucydides' tragic view, is widely speculative.

Others have summoned forth the notorious Megarian Decree, moved by Perikles, which is mentioned twice by Thucydides,[84] as sufficient motivation for the war. As such they criticize Thucydides for under emphasizing the decree and thus not treating it as a major issue in its own right. Economic embargoes are sometimes used in the modern world as diplomatic weapons, as a means of coercion short of war. Yet the Megarian Decree barred the Megarians themselves, and not their trading interests, from using the harbours of the Athenian empire and the Agora in Athens. Alternatively, according to the brilliantly stimulating but emphatically pugnacious de Ste. Croix the decree was 'religious in form',[85] all Megarians being polluted because their state had cultivated sacred land claimed by the Athenians.[86] Although parodied by Aristophanes, who uses this notion of Megarian sacrilege as a vehicle for a rather bad joke,[87] and the fact that Megarians were on the verge of starvation, the decree was not ratified by the Athenians until the high summer of 432 BC, a time when Greece was already sliding into war. Upon careful examination, however, modern theories do not bear close scrutiny, and it seems a pointless task to criticize Thucydides' 'truest cause' as too simplistic. He was, after all, a historian who lived through the events he was describing.[88]

Of course, in these days of rampant economic imperialism, it would be convenient to accept that there was an economic cause behind the Peloponnesian War. However, for those of you who wish to seek such a cause the best evidence for such a claim is to be found in the final Corinthian plea to the Peloponnesian League congress to declare war on Athens.[89] As such, it could possibly be argued those maritime powers were suffering as a result of Athenian aggression, while those who lived inland felt secure. Still, if wealthy Corinth was 'sacrificed' all Greece would have felt the effects.

The clash of titans

Every reader of Thucydides is struck by the contrast he draws between the two principal antagonists in the Peloponnesian War:

> For if the *polis* of the Spartans should be deserted, and nothing should be left of it but its temples and the foundations of its other buildings, posterity would, I think, after a long lapse of time, be very loath to believe that their power was as great as their renown ... Whereas, if Athens should suffer the same fate, its power would, I think, from what appeared of the *polis'* ruins be conjectured double what it is.[90]

Most conspicuously, the Spartans never properly urbanized their central place into a placeable *astu*, conserving as they did an older form of settlement by villages, *obai* as they called them. The remains of those, Thucydides predicted most accurately, are insubstantial and unimpressive.

As well as canny forecasting, Thucydides offered his readership messages to ponder upon, and one of the loudest and clearest of these was that the Peloponnesian War was bad news for the Greek world and the Greeks as a whole. In a speech delivered urging Sparta to go to war (summer 432 BC), a Corinthian delegate contrasts the two 'superpowers' in contemporary Greece.[91] Of course, we can easily argue that here we have the characteristics of the two sides according to Thucydides' own judgement and not that of the Corinthians. Moreover, like many abstractions of groups of people, it is a selective view. Even so, Thucydides does set up for us a vivid contrast between a land power and a sea power, an authoritarian régime and a democratic one.

Athenian character

Swift to take action	'They are quick to form a resolution and quick at carrying it out ... they never hesitate'.
Innovative and creative	'Each man cultivates his own intelligence, again with a view to doing something notable for his *polis*'.
Daring and impulsive	'Athenian daring will outrun its own resources ... they will take risks against their better judgement'.
Always abroad	'They think that the further they go, the more they will get'.
Optimistic and confident	'Suppose they fail in some undertaking ... they make good the loss immediately by setting their hopes in some other direction'.

Spartan character

Slow to take action	'You wait calmly on events relying for your defence, not on action, but on making people think that you will act ... you hang back'.
Lacking in initiative	'You never originate an idea'.
Cautious and conservative	'You do less than you could have done, mistrust your own judgement, however sound it may be'.
Parochial	'You think that any movement may endanger what you have already'.
Pessimistic	'You assume that dangers will last forever'.

Athens was democratic, individualistic, volatile, radical, commercial and sea-based. Sparta was land-based, hierarchical, oligarchically minded, stolid, above all conformist and conservative, prone to overvalue its version of the past and inclined to dismiss useful innovations such as coined money.

Thucydides also gives us a useful catalogue of resources available to Athens as it squared up to Sparta in the summer of 431 BC.[92] But though recording the number of hoplites divided between field army and home defence, he does not give any figure for the *thêtes*, the poorest citizens, those who served as oarsmen in the fleet. Eight years later, Aristophanes would claim there were at least 20,000 *thêtes*.[93]

Athenian inventory

Land forces	13,000 citizen hoplites of military age, 16,000 young, old and *metoikos* hoplites, 1,200 horsemen including 200 mounted archers, 1,600 foot archers – the allies of Athens: in central Greece only Plataia and Naupaktos; in the north-west, the islands of Corcyra and Zakynthos, and much of Akarnania; the Aegean islands (bar Melos and Thera – these islands were Dorian and their inhabitants claimed legendary connections with Sparta (e.g. Herodotos 8.48, Thucydides 5.84.2, Xenophon *Hellenika* 2.2.3), and the coastal regions of Anatolia, Thrace and the Hellespont).
Naval strength	300 triremes 'ready for active service', with overseas naval bases at Mytilene, Samos, Naupaktos, Corcyra, Zakynthos.
Finances	Reserve fund of 6,000 talents (Thucydides 2.13.3, can be reduced to 5,700 if we accept the text given by the scholia to Aristophanes *Plutus* 1193) plus a total income of 1,000 talents annually (600 from the tribute and 400 from internal revenue).

Spartan inventory

Land forces	30,000 hoplites, 2,000 horsemen – the Peloponnesian League encompassed all the states of the Peloponnese (bar Argos and Achaia), the Megarians on its north-eastern frontier, the peoples of Boiotia, Lokris (Ozolia & Opountia), and Phokis in central Greece, and also the Corinthian colonies of Ambrakia, Leukas, and Anaktorion in the north-west.
Naval strength	One hundred triremes (Corinthian, in the main).
Finances	Limited funds (anticipated financial aid from Persia – ironically, both Sparta and Athens saw foreign financial backing as the key to victory in this struggle). Perikles was justified in telling the Athenians that 'the Peloponnesians have no money, either public or private' (Thucydides 1.141.3).

It was possible for the Spartans to fight a protracted war with very limited financial resources, because they were a land power and were attempting to fight the war by land. Hoplites had to be fed on campaign, but an army could partly support itself at the expense of its enemy and normally campaigns were fairly limited both temporally and spatially. Fleets were very much more expensive. For instance, the Egestans in 415 BC brought the Athenians 'sixty talents of unminted silver, being a month's pay for sixty triremes'.[94]

Chapter 7

Train Hard, Fight Easy

Even though we must be wary of Plutarch's more lurid details, life for the Spartiate was certainly vigorous. Thucydides, who is not noted for his extravagance, has Perikles compare the 'laborious training' of the Spartan with the easier life to be had by an Athenian.[1] It is clear the Greeks themselves were well aware of the main reason for the superiority of Spartan hoplites on the red field of battle; it is what Thucydides calls, in one passage, their 'practised skill' or 'experience',[2] while Herodotos describes them as 'past masters' in warfare, and the Persians, just by way of a contrast, as 'lacking in professional skill'.[3] Unlike most Athenians, who thought the Spartans a pretty dreadful lot, Xenophon, who spoke as an eyewitness, enthusiastically admired them as 'the only true craftsmen in matters of war'.[4]

The oeuvre that later made Xenophon famous was still unwritten, but his soldierly intellect had already taken shape. Xenophon, son of Gryllos and Diadora, a younger contemporary of Thucydides was born about 428 BC into a well-to-do Athenian family from the Attic deme of Erchia. As such he duly received the conventional, decidedly athletic education heavily garnished with instruction in Homer, which was deemed appropriate for sons of the aristocracy simply because it provided these young, well-healed Athenians with 'the right stuff' for leadership.[5] Even the Old Oligarch, who had no love for democracy and made no attempt to disguise his prejudices, cynically admitted that although the Athenian people craved personally profitable magistracies, they were more than happy to leave the important matters of generalship to the most capable men, *oi kaloi k' agathoi*.[6] Soldering was not a profession as such and therefore was without a calculable career structure and the highest commands usually went to the socioeconomic élite rather than to men who had definite military prowess. Despite this however, these young Athenian aristocrats were generally noted for their blatant pro-Spartan oligarchic leanings and anti-democratic views, an attitude that found a natural home in the very masculine atmosphere of the gymnasium.

In one of his philosophical dialogues Plato points to the connection of an addiction to contact sport with Spartan sympathies and a distaste for Athenian democratic politics: the 'lads with cauliflower ears' who maintained that Perikles had made the Athenians a race of 'idlers, cowards, talkers and money-grubbers'.[7] For these pugnacious young gentlemen the Sparta of their day was partly seen as a kind of replica-Athens from 'the good old days', a bygone Athens when the Homeric and aristocratic virtues of fame, glory and honour (*kléos, kûdos, timê*) were all important.[8]

The Spartan system had many admirers in the Greek world; it had a completeness and aesthetic simplicity that appealed to the Greek mind, and made many Greeks admire it, though to be honest few would have wished to live under it. But if they admired they also criticized. Ridicule was Aristophanes' major weapon in his attack on the Spartan system. That Aristophanic character Bdelykleon, for instance, undoubtedly represents this class of rich young Athenian, for he stands accused by the chorus of 'Marathon-fighters', *Marathônomáchai*, of being an 'enemy of the people, a monarchist, a long-haired, tassel-fringed pro-Spartan, hand in glove with Brasidas'.[9] It is not for nothing that Aristophanes' audience is reminded of the fact that these fading 'old soldiers' had defended and upheld Athenian democracy through the courage and patriotism of their younger days.[10] Bdelykleon attempts to convert his staunchly pro-democratic father, Philokleon, to his own political and moral way of thinking. This comic socio-political metamorphosis is to be achieved by getting the father to adopt exotic and unpatriotic attire, instructing him how to parade himself in a gay manner, and suggesting that he talks of nothing other than the *pankration*, boar hunting, hare coursing and the torch race when in polite circles.[11]

Xenophon was a close student on Spartan matters, and such is his diagnosis of the key point in Spartan military professionalism, but he was the enemy of luxury, the admirer of bravery and military prowess and the champion of moral life, including the common bond of hunting. In quiet retirement he composed a number of instructive monologues from the point of view of an Athenian soldier-of-fortune turned Spartan gentleman farmer, in particular the noble pursuits of 'hunting, fishing and shooting'. In the *Kynegetikos* he describes the aristocratic pursuits of hare coursing, the hunting of fallow deer and red deer, boar hunting, with a brief notice of lions, leopards, lynxes, panthers, bears, and all the beasts of the chase to be found in foreign parts such as the Persian empire. On a more personal note, incidentally, Xenophon mentions the excellent hunting to be had in and around Skillous, his estate outside Olympia, and how he and his two sons would hunt boar, gazelle and stag during the local festival to Artemis.[12]

To Xenophon warfare constituted an expansion of the animal hunting techniques common to tribal warrior societies.[13] It is through the blood and bluster of the chase that 'men become good in war',[14] and therefore stresses Xenophon,[15] it should be one of the first activities a youngster should take up. In fact, Xenophon almost labours this point when he subsequently explains that those who take up the pursuit of hunting are the type of men who turn out to be 'good soldiers and *stratêgoi*'.[16]

First, men accustomed to bearing the arms of the chase will not easily tire when on a campaign, especially when burdened with the panoply of a hoplite.

Second, sleeping rough under the stars will be second nature to them. In fact, soldiers soon acquire the very useful ability to sleep at any time, in any place, in almost any circumstances.

Third, they will be familiar with the issuing and the receiving of orders.

Fourth and last, men who are acquainted with movement across difficult terrain, such as that encountered during any chase, will not blunder on the battlefield owing to difficulties in the ground.[17]

The last analytical point is especially relevant when we consider the very mechanical nature of the hoplite phalanx and its obvious limitations with respect to where it could fight. Xenophon,[18] however, did not restrict his findings to men of his own race, for he observed that the pursuit of hunting also prepared Persian nobles for the hardships of soldiering: it gave them courage to face the dangers of the battlefield; it practised them in the use of the tools of the trade, namely the spear and the bow; it acquainted them with the rigours of marching and running; and, last but not least, it meant they could endure the elements. According to Herodotos, Persians were not only taught to speak the truth but also to manage a horse and to shoot straight with the bow.[19] Cyrus the Younger, like the majority of the Persian nobility with whom Xenophon rubbed shoulders with, was a skilled horseman, well practised in use of bow and spear, and not only enjoyed hunting but also 'loved the danger incurred during the pursuit of wild animals'.[20] The inscription on the tomb of Cyrus' great-great-grandfather, Dareios the Great, without doubt says it all: 'I was a friend to my friends / as horseman and bowman I proved myself superior to all others / as hunter I prevailed / I could do everything'.[21]

Needless to say, exposing the body to regular physical exercise promotes good health and builds up moral fibre, which in turn helps to foster success, especially upon the field of battle.[22] Our author's motive for promoting this ethos is quite clear. At a time when formal military training for the citizen body was not officially recognized by the *polis*, Sparta being the notable exception of course, physical fitness and the ability to wield a weapon, according to him, were the responsibilities of the individual.[23]

Yet for all Xenophon's firsthand experience of the Spartans, it is left to that arch-rationalist Aristotle to actually lay his finger on the nub of the matter. He explains that it is not so much the methods the Spartans used to train their young men that made them superior, as the fact that they trained them at all.[24] That this was also true of the adults is the crux of a witty anecdote told by Plutarch.[25] On one occasion, having received bitter complaints from Sparta's Peloponnesian allies about the comparative scarcity of the hoplites that it had fielded, Agesilaos ordered the whole army to sit down. The Spartan king then asked first the potters, then the smiths, then the carpenters, then the builders, and so on and so forth, to stand up, until almost all the allied hoplites were on their feet, but still not a single Spartan. The point, of course, was that the contingent of the allies was composed of essentially sunshine warriors, peasant farmers in the main, but the Spartan of full-time professionals.

The Spartans were not men who had bent their backs day after day over the furrow. They were men who knew no other trade than that of war and had been brought up to regard skill in battle as an essential part of manhood. To the Spartans war was work. We can well imagine the view of those seated Spartans, namely that their whining allies were dismissed as a mere rabble of tradesmen, altogether raw and unfit for service. To manage the ashen spear, to wield the bronze faced shield, required continuous training. The Spartan was a fighting specialist. As such he was more skilful and, supreme advantage, and was not always worrying to get back to his farm and family like a citizen-under-arms. He had no time to earn his living so he was allotted land for his service to the state from which he could draw subsistence and pay his dues to his communal mess. Well might the philosopher Antisthenes say of the Thebans after Leuktra that they were 'no different from little boys strutting about because they had thrashed their tutor'.[26] But here we are in a position very much like that of someone who could operate a piece of machinery but had no idea of why or how it worked. The aim of this chapter, therefore, is to demonstrate how and why the Spartan army was the most formidable war machine in Greece.

Profession of arms

Jason of Pherai was no man to argue with; he had the backing of 6,000 professional hoplites and he had personally trained his private army 'to the highest pitch of efficiency'.[27] The proof is in the pudding, as they say, for Jason now held sway in his native land of Thessaly. Anyway, we shall pause for a moment and take note of our tyrant's views on the advantages of professionals over amateurs.

Citizen armies, Jason is quick to point out, include men who are already past their prime and others who are still immature. On top of this, few citizens actually bother keeping themselves physically in shape.[28] Jason's discipline was no doubt stricter than that of an elected citizen *stratêgos*, but the crux of his argument is simple and direct: mercenaries could be trained and then hardened through the experience of battle; they are in every sense of the word professionals. Mercenaries lived on war, and when peace was signed they had only two choices: to return home and retire, or to seek another war. Indeed, experience, like a trade, was gained by an apprenticeship, and so professionalism was fostered because bands of mercenaries that had served together on a particular campaign, instead of dispersing at its conclusion, could hold together and move off to fight another campaign under another paymaster. The fundamental problem with citizen armies, as Jason fully appreciates, was they included soldiers who were likely to be inexperienced or ill-equipped both mentally and physically for battle, the central act of war. Many were raw, unfit, untrained, true amateurs in the art of war.

A passage from Thucydides covers this fundamental problem in some detail. Herein the Syracusan *stratêgos* Hermokrates, future exile and mercenary captain, analyses his state's recent defeat at the hands of the Athenians and comes up with the following key points: one, the Syracusans were 'amateurs in the art of war'; two, the army had far too many *stratêgoi*; three, the rank and file were 'disorganized and un-disciplined'. Hermokrates' remedies for the army's problems include the suggestion that the citizens of Syracuse should undergo some form of compulsory military training. By doing so, argues Hermokrates, 'discipline would come as the result of training'.[29] The alternative, of course, which Hermokrates did not suggest, was for Syracuse to hire professionals. For Greek *poleis* in general, however, there was a major stumbling block that prevented them from hiring professionals. Such forces were more often than not made up of seasoned veterans who would serve for as long as they received pay or could reasonably expect it. But the organization of such a mercenary force in any strength and for a prolonged period of time imposed too severely a strain on the rudimentary financial mechanics of an individual Greek state: in the later words of Cicero, 'the sinews of war, unlimited money'.[30] In this way, the professional army raised by the Arcadian League literally faded away through lack of hard cash.[31] In the following century its successor, the Achaian League, would impose a tax upon members' states in order to maintain its mercenary army. No tax meant no mercenaries, and in 217 BC the current leader of the Achaian League, the elder Aratos, was forced to issue a decree so as to keep a league army in the field.[32]

The basic aim of any military training is the creation of that ephemeral quality, *esprit de corps*, a soldier's confidence and pride in himself and in his unit. Personal bravery of a single individual does not decide the issue on the actual day of battle, but the bravery of the unit as a whole, and the latter rests on the good opinion and the confidence that each individual places in the unit of which he is a member, and this was particularly so with the Spartan hoplite phalanx where maintenance of the formation was all-important. The Spartiate Aristodemos, for example, was posthumously chastened for having stepped outside the phalanx and sacrificed his life in a maddening act of heroism.[33] Again, Isidas son of Phoebidas was first honoured for his individual heroism, and then promptly fined by the ephors for daring to risk his life in combat without his armour.[34]

One of the only two gods Xenophon knew was physical training. The other, incidentally, was horsemanship. Formal military training, however, was not recognized by the *polis*, and in an anecdote Xenophon has Sokrates say to an unfit young Athenian 'the fact that our *polis* does not conduct military training at public expense is no reason for individuals to neglect it'.[35] Of course, most hoplite citizens were also peasant farmers and therefore tied to their land. Perhaps it is this fact that lies at the back of Xenophon's mind when he makes the comment that the hard manual graft of farming provides a man with physical strength, and as such is a benefit to both foot and horse soldier alike.[36] Plato vividly sketches two types of hoplite standing side by side in the phalanx, the spoiled man of leisure and the working man of the soil: 'The poor man will be lean and sunburnt, and find himself fighting next to some rich man whose sheltered life and superfluous flesh make him puff and blow and quite unable to cope'.[37] Aristotle's comment on herdsmen assumes a particular interest here, for he says they are 'particularly well trained for war by their habits, and make use of their physical strength and put up with sleeping rough'.[38] Soldiers enjoy, in common with shepherds, the privilege of being able to summon Morpheus instead of having to wait for him.[39]

Nonetheless, as a former professional soldier himself, Xenophon fully appreciated the benefits that formal military training had to offer.[40] On one level, Xenophon's *Kyroupaideia* is a handbook for training a new model army and in book two, for instance, we witness one of Cyrus' officers organizing a mock combat between soldiers. All have donned their body armour and picked up their shields, but instead of 'live' weapons, one side arm themselves with stout cudgels, while their opponents are instructed by the said officer to pick up clods of earth. Initially, those who are lobbing the clods have the upper hand, but as soon as the fighting comes down to close quarter work the cudgel wielders put their opponents to flight. The result is the same when the two sides exchange roles, viz. the cudgel wielders again overcome the clod throwers.[41] As students of Roman military matters well know, the peacetime training of the Roman army, undertaken with great realism, prompted one Jewish observer to write: 'It would not be wrong to describe their training manoeuvres as bloodless battles and their battles as sanguinary manoeuvres'.[42] Such realistic training, a concept that still strikes a chord of apprehension and gloom in the hearts of soldiers throughout the world, did serve a definite purpose for the Romans because their professional army was always in a constant state of readiness for war. In a modern army, for instance, a bad soldier is not only a liability to his unit, he is also, in action, a positive menace and danger to his comrades. A high percentage of casualties on active service, more in action, are caused by accidents that can be attributed to a low standard of training. The fictional Cyrus, being the model commander, obviously sees the advantages of exercising all of his men in tactical manoeuvres and, during the reorganization of his army, the Persians, who are conventionally bowmen and javelineers, are soon reequipped to fight as swordsmen.[43] Xenophon, being the experience soldier that he was, obviously knew the advantages the close quarter fighter (viz. the Greek hoplite) had over the long-range fighter (viz. the Persian bowman).

In reality of course, as Xenophon himself knew firsthand, such specialized and continuous military training was the preserve of Sparta and, in some cases, for those *poleis* that maintained at public expense tiny bodies of élite soldiers. Still, it must be emphasized that it was not the skill-at-arms of the individual Spartan that was important, as his upbringing and training as part of a unit, for the simplicity of hoplite warfare left little scope for a grand display of personal skills. Effectively, the specialized training of Sparta in all probability took the form of parade ground drill, which might explain that sneering remark made by Perikles about Sparta's 'laborious training'.[44] Nonetheless, it produced the right results, even for non-Spartans willing to learn. In 381 BC, for example, Agesilaos supplied money and arms to the oligarchic exiles of Phleious and instructed them to set up communal messes along Spartan lines and thereby train themselves for war. This the exiles did and the result was a large contingent of men 'in splendid condition of body, well disciplined, and extremely well armed'.[45]

By way of a direct contrast, we can do no better than recalling that valiant but vain attempt of the veteran Dionysios of Phokaia to train and prepare his fellow Greek citizens for their coming showdown with the Persians in the naval engagement off Lade.[46] On the other hand, in the review the young prince Cyrus held in honour of his companion and lover, Epyaxa of Cilicia, those Greek professionals known as the Ten Thousand demonstrated to their royal audience with roguish élan that they were a well drilled fighting unit, ably executing the crisp commands of its officers, one of whom was the young Xenophon.[47] This martial quality we can witness once more, this time off the parade ground and on the battlefield of Cunaxa, where the Ten Thousand, under threat from the enemy's scythed chariots, opened gaps for their plunging passage but still maintained the advancing battleline.[48] During the difficult skirmish with the mounted forces of Spithridates and Rhathines, we again witness their ability to execute battlefield orders with apparent ease. The Ten Thousand were ordered to keep their spears on the right shoulder until signalled to lower them for the assault, which was to be carried out at the march and not at the run. On the trumpet signal, the hoplites struck up the *paean*, raised a war cry and simultaneously couched their spears.[49] Further instances of the Ten Thousand's ability to adapt military techniques to difficult and testing conditions are pretty abundant.[50] In brief, the Ten Thousand was an excellently trained professional army by the standards of the day, and it is not surprising that the military proficiency of such soldiers was highly regarded by even a visiting Spartan panjandrum, Kleander, then the harmost of Byzantium.[51]

Come dancing

We have already mentioned that the mercenary army of Jason of Pherai was composed of soldiers who had been highly trained. It appears that the basis of this training was personal physical fitness, for Jason prided himself on his own bodily strength and would set an example to his men, both on and off the parade ground, by marching at their head in full panoply.[52] Furthermore, any man he found lacking in stamina he would instantly discharge from his army, while those who, like himself, revelled in the pain and pleasure of physical hardships and the dangers of war he would reward handsomely.[53] Xenophon himself recommended training with heavy burdens so as to be able to bear arms.[54] Hard, physical exercise still forms a major and critical part of a soldier's basic training; there is little point, for instance, in being a marksman with a rifle if you are unfit to use it after a hard day's 'yomp'. A physically fit soldier is a mentally alert soldier who will live longer in war. Professional soldiers the world over will appreciate this simple truth and recognize its timelessness. Physical fitness is still the keynote.

If we pause to consider the actual weight of the hoplite panoply, then the practice of what was called *hoplomachia* can be easily looked upon as physical training for hoplites. This was the art of fighting or dancing in full panoply and is believed to have originated in Arcadia.[55] In general, however, the casual approach towards *hoplomachia* was the norm. According to the distinguished Athenian *stratêgos* Nikias, for instance, the martial benefits of *hoplomachia* were somewhat limited to the rout and pursuit phase of hoplite battle, when one side gave way and the contending phalanxes broke up. It was at this juncture that such fancy weapon handling could be of practical use. He does concede, on the other hand, that the physical exercise derived from *hoplomachia* did increase a soldier's strength, 'since it is as good and strenuous as any physical exercise'.[56] Odd as it may seem to us, it was not until after their victory at Leuktra, which secured for them the hegemony of Greece, that the Boiotians considered training themselves in 'the craft of arms'.[57] According to Plutarch, the architect of that victory, the Theban *stratêgos* Epameinondas, advocated that a hoplite should henceforth have 'his body trained not only by athletic exercise but by military drill as well'.[58] Paradoxically, he was advocating exactly the same programme followed by the Spartans he had just beaten.

Xenophon, thinking back to one of those happier occasions from his mercenary days, offers his readership a marvellous description of a military parade in full fighting panoply:

> The Mantineians and some other Arcadians arose, arrayed in the finest arms and accoutrements they could command, and marched in time to the accompaniment of a flute playing the martial rhythm and sang the *paean* and danced, just as Arcadians do in their processions in honour of the gods.[59]

Naturally, as Xenophon hints, not all Arcadian dances were of a military nature. The *kidaris*, for example, was performed by the Arcadians in honour of the goddess Demeter in order to induce fertility.[60] Nonetheless, Athenaios does record that, according to Sokrates, the best dancers are likewise the best warriors.[61] For Sokrates, or so says his disciple Plato, gymnastics attends to the body while music does the same to the soul. With that, education (viz. training) if exclusively musical tends to produce softness and effeminacy; if exclusively gymnastic, hardness and brutality. The two combined alone produce the desired harmony of soul, and make it both brave and gentle.[62]

Athenaios, having remarked that dancing was closely akin to parade in arms and a display not just of discipline in general but also of concern for physical fitness and well-being, comes in due course to Spartan dancing, their marching songs and especially the war dance, *pyrrichê*, which among the Spartans was considered 'as a preparatory drill for war'.[63] The Spartans were famed for dancing in general and for one dance in particular, the *pyrrichê* (named in honour of Pyrrhos, better known as Neoptolemos, son of Achilles), which was a Doric war dance performed in armour to the sound of the flute, its measure being quick and light. Indeed, from Plato's description of the *pyrrichê*, we quickly gather that this particular war dance was certainly strenuous in nature by virtue of its rather energetic movements and dervish like gyrations, which apparently imitated the motions of warfare, such as 'modes of avoiding blows and missiles by dropping or giving way, or springing aside, or rising up or falling down'.[64]

Daily workout

Xenophon, throughout his oeuvre, laboriously stresses the vital importance of personal physical fitness for preparing men for the hardships of campaigning and the dangers of the battlefield, and even on active service soldiers were encouraged to undergo physical exercise in order to maintain unit excellence. On gathering his army in Ephesos, for example, Agesilaos wanted it to be in tiptop condition for the coming struggle with the Persians and so offered prizes to encourage this state of affairs. Xenophon, who was there, reports that Ephesos' gymnasia were full of 'men exercising'.[65] To Agesilaos, of course, this was just the Spartan way of doing things. The Spartans fully recognized the vital importance of regular exercise – particularly for the legs, arms and neck – and even on campaign Spartan hoplites kept their minds and bodies fit through gymnastics and games.[66] This was the certainly the case, as we well know, when a Persian mounted scout arrived in front of the Greek position at Thermopylai. On that day the Spartans happened to be stationed in sight, outside the reconstructed Phokian wall. With their arms piled near to hand, some of the soldiers were stripped and oiled for exercise, others combing their exceptionally long hair, a sign that they were preparing to risk their lives, and all paying him not the slightest attention. The scout may have been utterly astonished, but to the busy soldiers this was just the Spartan way of doing things.[67]

Like so many warlike people, the Spartans were sports enthusiasts. Physical exercises noted for their all-round benefits, as opposed to those that are violent or specialized, were probably popular with soldiers on campaign, so some of the Spartans outside the wall were probably ball-playing. One particular ball game, known as *episkyros* or common-ball, was played between opposing teams of equal number. A centre line was scratched in the dust between the two teams and a goal line behind each. The ball was set on the middle line and the team that got it first threw it over the opposition, whose task was to grab the ball while it was in motion and throw it back the other way. Although it was a ball game it involved, at least at Sparta, a lot of roughhousing such as pushing and shoving and punches. The game continued until one team had pushed the other over its goal line. The ball itself was small and hard, covered in leather and stuffed with horsehair. If indeed the Spartans were enjoying a game of *episkyros* on the eve of Thermopylai, then the result of the game is not recorded.

Among the most important truisms of war is that an army is rooted in a fragile psychology that is far more vital than either organization or technology. All professional armies form, to some extent, closed communities with their own customs and standards of behaviour. This was no less so with the Spartan army. Yet in the ancient Greek world Sparta, with its intimate relationship between social organization and military power, was the exception in this regard. Sparta was a totally militarized society, and the transformation began before puberty, when a Spartan boy was fully immersed in a disciplined environment in which only the pre-state warrior ethic was allowed to penetrate. No other Greek state appears to have put its young males through such a rigorous régime as the Spartan *agôgê*, and by and large, there was a prejudice, born from the militia ethos of the citizen farmer, against training in war.

Training for war, however, is a means to an end and the real measure of any true professional soldier is his experience of battle, the central act of war. Training transforms a raw recruit into a trained soldier, but battle (if he survives both mentally and physically) finally elevates him to veteran status. Battle is the 'baptism of fire' that will eventually turn the soldier into a finely honed fighting instrument. Plutarch, for instance, has Antalkidas complaining to Agesilaos about the string of campaigns the king has recently conducted in Boiotia, and as a result the amateur Thebans have now become worthy opponents of the professional Spartans. This is supremely ironic, for through the 'constant struggles' the Thebans, despite being part-timers, were rapidly transforming into battle-hardened veterans.[68]

Those hoplite mercenaries who returned home to Arcadia so as to sign up in the new professional army of the Arcadian League, on the other hand, were already seasoned campaigners as the catalogue of their martial exploits for the year 369 BC clearly demonstrate.[69] Four years later, the Arcadians were to prove their professional worth even against the Spartans. For at the battle of Kromnos they resisted the repeated assaults of the Lakedaimonian peltasts and horsemen, to eventually advance against them and drive them back. Despite being outnumbered, the Arcadians then went on to attack Archidamos' phalanx, which as a consequence, was also sent packing. Both sides now prepared themselves for another round, but as the Arcadians closed in for the kill one of the older Spartiates questioned the wisdom of continuing the fight and suggested a truce. Both sides willingly agreed, and the Spartans gathered up their dead and departed while the Arcadians erected a trophy so as to assert their control of the battlefield.[70] Veteran soldiers, it must be understood, are not only so because of the wealth of their experience, but also because of their ability to survive to fight another day. The simple desire not to die in vain is what probably prompted the angry outburst from of one of Agis' veterans when the Spartan king attempted to lead his phalanx against an enemy-held hill just outside Mantineia.[71] 'The great difference between a veteran and a raw recruit,' explains General William Walker, 'is that one knows how to take care of himself, and the other does not'.[72] The majority of hoplites who slogged it out at Kromnos would have been hard-core professional soldiers with long service records: the Arcadians by virtue of previous years as mercenaries, the Spartans because they had to spend at least forty years with the colours. Discipline will keep enemies face to face as long as they are able, but in the end it cannot supplant the human instinct of self-preservation and the deep sense of fear that goes with it.

Obedience and discipline

In a conflict of masses, however, success generally depends upon the subordinate self to the will of the group, upon obedience to orders, in short, upon discipline. In his *Art of War*, Sun Tzu wrote the following: 'If in training soldiers' commands are habitually enforced, the army will be well disciplined; if not, its discipline will be bad'.[73] The fundamental purpose of discipline, as Sun Tzu fully appreciated, is to make men fight in spite of themselves and, thus, it forms the very backbone of the efficiency of an army; no changes in the methods of warfare or in scientific developments will affect this simple truth. In its purest form it is an institution, a tradition, a system, and as such it cannot be created or secured in a single day. Such was the discipline that underlay the prolonged military success of the legions of Rome during the rise and dominance of its vast empire. In the world of the Greek *polis*, on the other hand, discipline was at best translated through the social duty that free men owed each other as fellow citizens. Citizen soldiers were not usually amenable to martial law and, therefore, a citizen army was invariably governed by a civilian code of discipline. We return to poor old Dionysios of Phokaia and his efforts to instil a much stricter code of discipline in his fellow citizens and thereby produce a superior organization and subordination within his precarious command, but after seven days, 'worn out by the hardness of the work and the heat of the sun, and quite unaccustomed to such fatigues ... they ceased to obey his orders'.[74] Greek citizens took unkindly to continued discipline.

Generally neglected by citizen armies, it was physical training that gave a definite edge to the Spartan, as it allowed him to survive the rigours and hazards of a long campaign. Having said that, however, it was the necessary virtue of military discipline that was to be one of two crucial elements that the Spartan hoplite added to the ancient battlefield. The other crucial element was his aggressive and warlike fighting spirit, that vital intangible quality whose roots lay in male bonding and was fostered and preserved through a definite unit identity. It was this complex chemistry that allowed the Spartan hoplite unflinchingly to face death, battle after battle. The close quarter encounter was a 'thing of fear'. During the destructive collision of phalanxes, a hoplite required these basic raw ingredients of unshakable discipline and stout physical and moral courage so as to confront a stranger toe-to-toe, chest-to-chest, face-to-face, and strike to kill or maim him without provocation or compunction. Most citizens probably did not have these martial qualities. Spartans, on the other hand, did, nurtured and hardened through the dualities of physical training and professional experience.

Chapter 8

Hellas' Veins Opened

The Peloponnesian War was neither Peloponnesian, nor a single war, nor did it just involve the Greeks. From the Peloponnesian point of view it was 'the Attic war',[1] that is to say, the war against Athens. It was not a single war but an amalgamation of two distinct wars with an interval of unstable peace. Though Thucydides saw it as a whole, by the turn of the fourth century BC the first ten years were called the 'Archidamian war', named after the Spartan king who warned against it. The last nine years were called the 'Ionian war', because there was much fighting off the coast of Ionia in these years. Finally, it involved not only the Greeks but also the likes of the Carthaginians, Italians, Thracians, and of course the Persians. The Peloponnesian War was, in truth, a 'world war'.

Athena waives the rules

The ensuing war was for the first time predominantly naval, which for the Spartans meant a lengthy and comfortless period of shifting out of their natural environment of the land and into the relatively unknown world of the sea. Initially Sparta's Peloponnesian allies, chiefly Corinth, could scratch together a fleet of sorts, but it could not compare in numbers or skill with that of Athens; in truth, it would be no more than a 'mosquito fleet'. Nor was there any real hope that it could be expanded by new ship building, Sparta having no source of revenue nor any reserves to compare with Athens, which was assured of a regular income from tribute for warlike purposes, above all for the payment of its ships' crews, and possessed a hefty fund in reserve upon which to draw in emergencies. Likewise, there was little hope of finding new allies at a distance, for instance the western Greeks, though some of them were well disposed enough, were not sufficiently concerned – not just yet, anyway. Besides, the Great King was not to be tempted to face the Athenians again and embassies that went to Susa in the early years of the war came back empty handed. That left, of course, one strategic option.

Able to invade Attica, Athens' home territory, through the Megarid, the stretch of land between the Corinthian and Saronic gulfs under Megarian control, Sparta was to do so on five occasions during the initial phase of the war,[2] leaving blackened farmsteads to mark their leisurely progress through the Athenian countryside on each occasion. The land invasion of 446 BC and its dramatic success in bringing the first Peloponnesian war to a swift end had convinced the Spartans and their allies that a similar strategy would bring about the same result. Repeated invasions of Attica by land in the early summer shortly before the grain harvest would either wear the

Athenians down, a slim chance, or provoke them into a full-scale hoplite battle and almost certain defeat. Yet the Spartans' (but not King Archidamos) self-assurance rested on old thinking, and had failed to realize that the Athenians, led by Perikles, were planning a totally novel strategy.

Perikles was a statesman deeply committed to a purely maritime empire and he saw no point in defending the outlying territory, which was at the mercy of the invader. This policy is consistent with Perikles' oft-repeated advice to his fellow citizens, which is to say, he was well aware that Athens could not furnish an army to match the Spartan hoplites. As war now threatened, he expected his fellow citizens to simply abandon their homes and fields and man the walls and fleet, and the rest of Attica (now an empty and silent land) would have to look after itself. Yet the majority of the Athenians, as Thucydides makes clear, normally lived in the countryside, and the gifted playwright Aristophanes in his *Acharnians* and elsewhere gives vivid glimpses of the deep attachment of a large section of the population to the soil of Attica.[3] These contemporary pieces of Aristophanes thus advance the popular thesis of the peasants' farmer as endowed with love for his land, resentment for its despoilers, and reserves of native savvy and physical courage. So when Perikles took the radical step of breaking the rules of agonal warfare by shifting the entire population behind the city walls, there were cries of anguish from the Attic countrymen since 'each of them felt as if he was leaving his native *polis*'.[4]

Whether they liked it or not, on Perikles' advice the Athenians did take refuge inside the fortification walls surrounding and linking Athens and Peiraeus, abandoning their beloved countryside to the Peloponnesian incursions and relying on the sea routes to supply the *polis* with grain imported both directly from the Athenian-controlled island of Lemnos and, above all, through the trade in grain from the Black Sea region. The Athenians responded to the Peloponnesian ravaging merely by minor cavalry operations, seaborne raids on the eastern Peloponnese, and an annual devastation of the neighbouring territory of Megara once the Peloponnesians had returned home after their invasion of Attica. These Athenian attacks, apart from extra-Peloponnesian Megara, were relative pinpricks, irritating but not really damaging. Sparta itself was untouched. Nonetheless, by avoiding pitched battles, the Athenians limited the effectiveness of Sparta's main military strength.

What is more, the destruction of grain crops was not all that easy a task. The grain had to be dry enough to be combustible, and the ravaging Peloponnesian troops had both to be equipped with sufficient tinder and firewood and protection from counter-attacks from the Athenians. They also had to be able to live off the land while they were doing their ravaging, to eke out the meagre food supplies they were able to bring from home. The longest stay of any Peloponnesian expedition in Attica was in fact a mere forty days. That was not enough time to ravage significantly, let alone entirely destroy, anything like all the grain crops of Attica, not to mention the grapevines and olives. The main weapon of destruction was fire, but this did not work on green vines, and besides mature olive trees are anyway virtually indestructible. The mission statement given out to the Peloponnesian troops may have said ravage, singe and burn all about and reduce the whole territory to a wilderness, but in truth these annual invasions of Attica were to prove increasingly and embarrassingly ineffective.

Trouble up North

After Perikles' untimely death (autumn 429 BC), he was carried off by the plague.[5] Athens, now dominated by Kleon, a crude demagogue possessed of great military skill, adopted a more daring, offensive strategy. One can never be assured of victory, but he quite rightly appreciated that with an inactive attitude one may be sure of defeat. No longer would the Athenians look timorously from behind their walls the destruction of their homes and fields. With that, they not only established fortified bases on the Peloponnesian coast – notably at Pylos in Messenia and on the island of Kythera, just off the south-eastern tip of Lakonia – they also attempted to knock Boiotia out of the war, the second invasion ending in a thundering defeat for them at Delion (winter 424 BC),[6] but by now the war had developed a momentum of its own.

The same year saw a small force marched to the Thraceward region, the only important area of the Athenian empire that could be reached by land. The military adventure was launched with true Lakonian hesitation, and the force was made up of 700 helots armed as hoplites and a hope of freedom together with a thousand Peloponnesian mercenaries.[7] No Spartiates were to be risked, but the commander of the expedition was certainly one, Brasidas the son of Tellis (unusually we know his mother's name too, Argileonis),[8] the most outstanding and un-Lakonian Spartan of the war – a good general, able diplomat, and all-round honest fellow, or as Thucydides emphasizes, Brasidas had imagination as well as courage, and could talk as well as fight. He was lucky – he regularly happened to be where he was most needed. He was brave, with a brilliant tactical and strategic eye and the boldness to act on what he saw. He was overconfident, yes, in his hopes of a ready welcome in Thrace but quick to adapt himself to what he actually found once there. Above all, as Thucydides says of him, perhaps with delicious irony, he was 'the first Spartan to go abroad and bring with him an impression of such general trustworthiness and reliability that men confidently expected the same virtues in those who followed him'.[9] Other commanders had less natural endowment and less moral excellence.

One example of the typical specimen Spartan abroad will suffice here. Alkidas, who led the Peloponnesian naval expedition towards Mytilene, the chief *polis* of Lesbos, so as to exploit the secession of the island from the Athenian empire, dithered hopelessly on the way and before returning slaughtered out of hand most of the prisoners he had taken, men whom he had come officially to liberate. Little surprise, therefore, the vocal complaints that if the Spartan policy of 'liberating Hellas' involved the execution of Greeks who were unwilling subjects of Athens, then that policy was more likely to attract hostility than good will in the Greek world in general. This sharp remonstrance did persuade Alkidas to free other prisoners, but he now washed his hands all together of the affairs of Asian Greeks and set sail for home, showing clearly that their liberation was only a pitiful veneer and universal sham. He was an intelligent man and an able servant of his state, but he was one of those Spartans – common, unfortunately – who should never have been allowed to set a foot abroad, one of those proper Spartans *sans peur et san reproche*.[10]

However, to return to Brasidas. His campaign in the Thraceward region totally surprised (and alarmed) Athens. He was able to win over a number of Athens' dependencies, including the vital colony of Amphipolis on the river Strymon, by a series of bloodless triumphs. His brief speech to the people of Akanthos, though it contained some threats, was on the whole couched in conciliatory terms, and the claim to be the 'liberator of Hellas' was more consistent with the fair dealing of a Brasidas than with the casual brutality of an Alkidas. It seems that with some Spartans one did see the hook sticking out of the rather stodgy bait.[11] By his mere words Brasidas won Akanthos from the Athenian empire and enrolled it among the so-called autonomous allies of Sparta.[12] Soon after Stagiros, on the coast to the north, broke away from Athens.[13] It was not long before those subject to Athens, 'hearing of the gentleness of Brasidas, felt most strongly encouraged to change their condition, and sent secret messages to him begging him to march on into their territory, and vied with each other in being the first to revolt'.[14]

Gentle or not, what the canny Brasidas had realized was Sparta's need to open up a second front to destabilize Athens' alliance from within. Already two years previously the Spartans had planted one of the very few colonies in their history, at Herakleia Trachinia, a few kilometres north-west of the pass at Thermopylai, which not only put pressure on Athens' control of Euboia but also lay *en route* to its interests in the far north, Amphipolis chief among them.[15] Founded as recently as 437 BC, Amphipolis guarded the key land route across Thrace to the Hellespont and the Bosporos, and also gave Athens access to timber and metals that were vital to the maintenance of its burgeoning navy.

It is tempting to guess that Brasidas was the instigator of the colony at Herakleia Trachinia, for it suits his temperament and vision.[16] What we can guess, however, is the dismay in Athens as Brasidas made a mockery of its control in the far north, more so when he snatched Amphipolis from them.[17] But petty mindedness and short-sightedness of a powerful faction at Sparta denied Brasidas any reinforcements from home. The principal motive, as ever, was jealousy, but concern was felt also for those Spartiates taken at Pylos and now held captive at Athens. As Thucydides says, 'because of jealousy towards him by the leading men and also because they preferred to recover the men from the island [i.e. Sphakteria] and put an end to the war'.[18] In truth, there were Spartans who were peacemakers in principle. They either believed in the glorious dual-hegemony policy of Athens-Sparta relations espoused by Kimon in an earlier generation, or were more *laissez faire* in their attitude towards the allies of the Peloponnesian League. So for whatever reason, many Spartans had conceived a desire to end the war and they saw the victories of Brasidas as a powerful inducement for the peace they now sought. Brasidas' own death, and that of Kleon, in battle fought before the walls of Amphipolis (422 BC), led to the swearing of a nonaggression pact and defensive alliance between Athens and Sparta, separately from all the allies on either side, the terms of which required each side to defend the other against attack and to regard the attackers as a common enemy, and committed the Athenians to give assistance to the Spartans in the event of a helot revolt.[19] It was to last for fifty years. Amphipolis, however, never returned to the Athenian fold, and its citizens literally worshipped the dead Brasidas as their new founder-hero, as something more than a mere mortal man whom they commemorated with annual athletic contests and sacrifices, thereby disinheriting their true founder-hero, Hagnon of Athens.[20]

War and peace

Machiavelli once commented that, 'Wars begin when you will, but they do not end when you please', and the war between Athens and Sparta was no exception to the rule. For no sooner were the raised fists folded in placidity than the Peace of Nikias, or 'hollow peace' as Thucydides so aptly calls it,[21] was in tatters when an increasing number of Athenians turned their thoughts to a more aggressive policy. Fundamentally Periklean imperialism had generated too much energy and appetite to allow the Athenian *dêmos* to settle down to a life of peace and quiet. Had there been the will, the way to permanent peace could have been found, but reason was no match for pride, prejudice and vested interests, and their spokesman was the overambitious, if somewhat ambiguous, Alkibiades, who was to exert a powerful influence on the course of Greek affairs for several years to come. His fertile mind began to contemplate a measure to bring about a day of reckoning. This he did by cobbling together what was an anti-Spartan league in the Peloponnese and taking Athens back to war.

Yet this came to nought when the coalition forces, led by an overconfident Athens and an unsteady Argos, were thrashed out of sight in little over an hour one summer's afternoon by the Spartans outside Mantineia (summer 418 BC). The battle of Mantineia was the first large-scale Spartan engagement since Tanagra almost forty years previously. The victory was a purely Spartan one, and much more impressive (in the eyes of the Peloponnesian states) than the remoter feats of Brasidas had been. They had triumphed in what the Greeks called *akoniti*, in a 'no-duster'.[22] In that single hour the disgrace of Pylos was wiped out.

The grand anti-Spartan coalition had occupied but one campaigning season. Yet the policy of building up a military alliance against Sparta in the Peloponnese in order to crush the Spartan army in the field was not one doomed to failure. In truth, Alkibiades was fully justified when he later claimed in front of his fellow citizens that he had 'united the most powerful *poleis* of the Peloponnese without involving you in any danger or expense, and compelled the Spartans to stake their all upon the issue of a single day at Mantineia'.[23] The battle was lost because Athens was not fully united and therefore did not wholeheartedly support Alkibiades' plan and because Elis objected to the confederate strategy and withdrew its considerable commitment of 3,000 hoplites.

When Alkibiades' grand design on the mainland failed his restlessness found a new outlet in pushing for an expansion of the empire by sea, which offered the maverick Athenian a larger stage and a bigger prize. So once again at his urging, Athens opened a whole new front by launching an expedition against Sicily (415 BC), specifically on the island's richest *polis*, the Corinthian colony of Syracuse, with himself, along with his political rival Nikias, as one of its three commanders. Although tremendously talented, his intelligence was matched by disdainful irreverence. The Athenians were attracted by his exciting and magnetic personality but fearful of his flamboyance and ambition. The charismatic Alkibiades was opposed, however, by the careful Nikias. He was the *stratêgos* who had negotiated the peace with Sparta and, like Perikles before him, resisted any attempts to pursue further imperialistic adventures. Perhaps it was in the hope of controlling the mercurial Alkibiades that the Athenians appointed Nikias. He was in nearly every way the opposite of Alkibiades. Older than his rival by twenty years, Nikias was particularly cautious and notoriously superstitious, much preferring comfortable insignificance in a world of glitter and menace. Whereas Alkibiades liked to dazzle the Athenian people, Nikias was careful to ascribe his success to the favour of the gods in order to avoid provoking envy.

It was, however, no secret that the real design of Athens was the conquest of the whole of Sicily, and the pursuit of this grandiose scheme eventually led to a renewal of the war between Athens and Sparta. Before the attack on Syracuse had begun, however, Alkibiades was recalled home to stand trial on a capital charge of scandalous acts of sacrilege.[24] There is an old saying about tall trees being cut down, and such a thought could have entered his mind as he travelled homeward. Thus, fearing some mockery of a trial, Alkibiades slipped away from the escorting ship and vanished. And so just three months after he had sailed from Athens with such pomp and splendour, he was a renegade, a hunted man with a price on his head. When the fugitive heard his fellow citizens had condemned his to death, he apparently remarked, 'I'll show them that I am still alive'.[25] And show them he did, for Alkibiades made his way to, of all places, Sparta, where he proceeded to make himself indispensable by terrifying the Spartans with an account of Athenian plans for total conquest of the far west. Alkibiades may have had his own eccentric notions of honour, but stainless veracity was not essential to it in practice. In dealing with people he masked his real views. He had 'a way with him'. He was an extraordinarily glamorous man, with a face we imagine as almost feminine in its delicacy and beauty, and despite a lisp, he was a good talker and a gladhander. He would arrive on the scene, and presto, the situation was his. He was a restless, amorous, ambitious man for whom sex was a relaxing intermission between meals of power. People just took to him, and he was 'hunted by many women of noble family' and 'sought after by men as well'.[26] In truth, few people, not even the stern Spartans, could resist the potent charm and charisma of this outsize character. For the Spartans it was going to be an instance of feeding the fox who will eat their chickens.

As this Athenian drama played out, the Syracusans, for their part, sent envoys to the Peloponnese asking for help, and Alkibiades supposedly advised the Spartans to send one of their own commanders, Gylippos, to conduct the defence of Syracuse. Meanwhile, while that storm-petrel Alkibiades, late *stratêgos* of Athens, dallied in Sparta, apparently going so native that he became more Spartan than the Spartans, the Athenians got bogged down outside the *astu* and the expedition ended in horror. The drama had turned into a tragedy, and at one stroke Athenian naval, financial and moral supremacy was gone.

At the beginning of the conflict between Athens and Sparta Perikles had warned the Athenians against being adventurous, strongly advising them 'to remain quiet, take care of their fleet, refrain from trying to extend their empire in wartime and thus putting their *polis* in danger'.[27] This principle was obviously sound, and had served Athens well, as long as it has adhered to it. The Sicilian venture had probably claimed at least, from Athens alone, 3,000 hoplites and 9,000 *thêtes* as well as thousands of *metoikoi*. Out of so many who left Athens, as Thucydides ruefully recorded, so few eventually returned. The Athenians probably now had 9,000 hoplites of all ages, perhaps 11,000 *thêtes*, and 3,000 *metoikoi*, fewer than half of the number available when the Peloponnesian War started. They had lost 216 triremes, of which 160 were Athenian, and only about 100, not all of which were seaworthy, remained. Of the

6,000 expendable talents available in 431 BC fewer than 500 now remained in the treasury. For Syracusans, however, the booty was immense. They were able to build a splendid treasury at the oracular sanctuary of Delphi, 'from the great Athenian disaster',[28] to store a tenth of the proceeds of this war, the standard tithe dedicated to the god Apollo, warrior and physician.

Meanwhile in Athens, when the news sank in, the citizens 'turned against the public speakers who had been in favour of the expedition, as though they themselves had not voted for it'.[29] The Athenians eventually came to their senses and appointed a board of ten older men to serve as *probouloi*, one of whom was the great tragedian Sophokles of Kolonos, to take a preliminary look at issues as they arose.[30] This was normally the job of the *boulê*, the democratic council of Five Hundred, and although that body was not abolished and despite the inclusion of a man like Sophokles, who had been associated and worked with Perikles, the very nature of the new council had an oligarchic ring. This is, indeed, the first hint of the reaction against democracy that was to bring about its overthrow the following year.

The oligarchs strike back

Despite his conservative connections, Thucydides was an ardent supporter of Perikles. He was no friend of the radical democracy, however, which had exiled him (probably unjustly) and which he viewed as irresponsible, short sighted, selfish, and fickle – in this, Thucydides agrees with the major literary men of democratic Athens, particularly Aristophanes and Plato. A rather good example of his attitude can be seen in his account of the revolt of Mytilene, the chief *polis* of Lesbos. The Athenian *dêmos*, no doubt led by the demagogue Kleon (whom, like Aristophanes, Thucydides thoroughly despises because he personifies, for him, the worse features of democracy), at first votes to kill all of the adult male population and to sell the women and children into slavery. In Thucydides' eyes such a man was no better than a tyrant. It is only a day later, at the prompting of more responsible leaders, that the Athenians are led to change their mind and exact a more reasonable punishment, despite Kleon's aggressive opposition. It should be added that the vote only went narrowly against him.[31]

Kleon may have been 'the most violent of the citizens' with a penetrating voice,[32] but he was also a shrewd judge of the interests and moods of the Athenian *dêmos*. Having once bent his fellow citizens to his will by speeches that were harsh and bullying in style, Kleon used his power to pursue private vendettas; his main weapon was the jury court, taking advantage of the compulsory examination of magistrates at the end of their year of office, or bringing charges of conspiracy against dangerous oligarchs.[33] In truth, Kleon was a radical demagogue with an in-your-face political style, unlike his predecessor, the eloquent Perikles. Moreover, Kleon was not of 'good repute' as he had not sprung out of the ranks of the aristocracy, and our sources portray him as a mediocre fellow not fit to lead the state. Aristotle lists the reasons why Kleon was so attacked. Namely, he 'corrupted the *dêmos* by his wild impulses, and he was the first man who, when on the platform, shouted, uttered abuse and made speeches with his clothes hitched up, while everyone else spoke in an orderly manner'.[34] Despite the bad press, Kleon was no common man from the lower orders. Admittedly he came from a different background to Kimon and Perikles, aristocrats of the bluest blood and sons of victorious *stratêgoi*, but his father had once paid for a play and thus had wealth, which probably came from trade or manufacturing, rather than from the traditional source, land. Nikias, his great rival, was also from the same origins as Kleon, and he had made his fortune by renting slaves to work in the silver mines of south-east Attica. Yet 'the best men' of Athens gladly accepted Nikias but not Kleon: Nikias, the long time supporter of Perikles, was pious, upright and reserved, and a gentleman; Kleon, the long-time opponent of Perikles, was an advocate of war, a demagogue, and a vulgarian.

Thucydides reports on Kleon's anti-intellectual stance, a position that did little to help the demagogue's image.[35] In truth, Kleon was attacking Sokrates and his 'right-wing flunkies', men who were later prominent as members of the oligarchic juntas that came to power in 411 BC and 404 BC. Yet such extremism on Kleon's part did unfortunately polarize Athenian politics and this was certainly the background to the overthrow of democracy in 411 BC. The defeat of the grand armada at Syracuse meant the backbone of radical democracy had been removed. Furthermore, revolts spread throughout the empire and Sparta, with Persian gold, built a navy. Athens was therefore ripe for an oligarchic *coup d'état*. It seems that the whole show was the brainchild of Alkibiades who had started his political career as a radical but had fled Athens for Sparta after the prospect of facing trial for his apparent involvement in a religious scandal. Once in Sparta he stirred up trouble, which resulted in him fleeing for a second time, this time for Persia. Again Alkibiades meddled in local politics, advocating to the Persians that the Athenians would make far-reaching changes in their constitution if Persia switched its support from Sparta to Athens.[36]

The first stage in the *coup d'état* opens in Samos where the hypnotic Alkibiades attempts to undermine the democratic feelings of the imperial navy, which was currently stationed there.[37] Meanwhile back in Athens, the plot only succeeded with the greatest of difficulty, as is evident from Thucydides, the *dêmos* having temporarily lost its political nerve. Thucydides speaks of violence and trickery being employed by the extremists who wanted to establish a régime in Athens on the lines of those found in Corinth and Thebes.[38] In these two states only citizens of the hoplite census (the *zeugitai* in Athens) and higher (viz. those who served as horsemen in war, the *hippeis* in Athens), were granted political rights and thus allowed to attend the assembly.

The new oligarchical régime in Athens only lasted a short while, mainly because the Four Hundred, as it was called, could never win over the *thêtes* of the imperial navy, radical democrats to a man, who obviously refused to surrender their well deserved political rights. Eventually, the council of Four Hundred was deposed and power handed over to the assembly of Five Thousand, citizens who could provide themselves with the full panoply of a hoplite. Obviously, this meant the *thêtes*, the oarsmen of the fleet, had been disenfranchised at a stroke. Extraordinarily, it is at this juncture that Thucydides voices a personal thought, giving us a rare glimpse into his own views on Athenian democracy:

> During the first period of this new régime the Athenians appear to have had a better government than ever before, at least in my time. There was a reasonable and moderate blending of the *few* and the *many* [emphasis mine], and it was this,

in the first place, that made it possible for the *polis* to recover from the bad state into which its affairs had fallen.[39]

A doyen of realism, Thucydides obviously believed that the perfect political balance was to be achieved in an assembly containing a select number of citizens – an assembly of citizens rather like himself. In a similar vein, Aristotle remarks that the Athenians 'seem to have been governed well at that time, for a war was in progress, and the state was in the hands of those bearing arms'.[40] The intellectual hostility to democracy may well surprise and dismay us today. But intellectuals were members of the social élite – wealthy, leisured and educated – whereas most citizens were not. Direct democracy, as opposed to our own representative version, gave to those ordinary citizens of Athens the kind of collective say in deciding their fate that we today can only wonder at or envy.[41] To most intellectuals it seemed that the collective say of the *hoi polloí* was a form of tyranny of the proletariat, exercised over – that is, against the interests of – themselves. For them democracy meant the control of the better by the worse.

It is impossible to understand the oligarchical mind till one realizes that it did not believe in progress in the modern sense. The ideal world of oligarchs was not in front of them, but behind; to restore the 'golden age' of oligarchy was their dream. To be frank, most of us tend to fashion utopia in our own relatively feeble image. The Thucydidean utopia of a moderate oligarchy, however, was a short-lived institution. The navy, which was still stationed in Samos, obstinately refused its support, and in the end the stubbornness of sailors forced the issue. Sneeringly called 'the yo-heave-hos',[42] the oarsmen of the triremes, being recruited from the poorest citizens of Athens, were resolutely committed to 'people power' and not that of the oligarchic Five Thousand. And so, on one day in the summer of 410 BC, 'the people quickly took away their control of the state', and full political rights returned to the entire citizen body.[43] The radical democracy that Athens had practised before the intro-duction of the *probouloi* had been happily restored. Or so it seemed for the present.

It was at Sparta that the desirable compromise formed a permanent feature of the political system. This opinion Thucydides expresses in speaking of the people of Chios: 'the Chians alone, next to the Spartans among the people I know of, have maintained their self-control after acquiring prosperity; and the more powerful their *polis* became, the stronger they made their government'.[44] In a much earlier passage, Thucydides speaks even more directly of the stability of the Spartan polity: 'the Spartan state received good laws at an earlier period than did any other, and it has never come under the rule of a tyrant; for four hundred years or a little more the Spartans have had the same constitution'.[45] Thucydides may place the Lykourgan reforms at too early a date, but the important point is that he traces back the stable institutions of Sparta to a remote phase of recorded history. Thucydides looks at the Lykourgan state and finds it praiseworthy: its laws, precisely regulating the life of its citizens at all points, have given Sparta a balanced order that leaves no room for out-and-out tyranny on the one hand or for ill-considered mob-rule on the other. Of course, like all brilliant minds, Thucydides has allowed the theoretical virtues of the Spartan constitution to outweigh the many practical (e.g. incoherence of Spartan policy) and psychological (e.g. hysterical fear of the helots) defects.

Like his contemporary fellow citizen Euripides, Thucydides is an intellectual product of the age of the sophists. Wherein Euripides' sophistic leanings tend to place him directly at odds with his elder rival Sophokles, Thucydides' approach to history is antithetical to that of his predecessor Herodotos. In large part, however, the difference can be attributed to differences in the two authors' subject matter and the tempers of their times. Like a Homeric bard, Herodotos grandly celebrates a glorious victory of the relatively distant past. The Greek triumph over Xerxes' forces provided ample room for comforting reflections on the superiority of the Greeks to the 'long-haired Mede', the glory of free men fighting for their gods and homeland against a countless mongrel horde of worthless Asiatics. It also seemed to provide striking evidence of the truth of Solon's view of divine justice: here was *kóros–hubris-atê* at work before our very eyes, the recognized law of Greek ethics that power begets folly, folly begets insolence, and insolence begets ruin. What is more, the entire event was far enough in the past to be safely idealised.

The case with Thucydides is very different: he is dealing with a contemporary war, not one fought two or three generations earlier, and it is a civil war fought between the Greeks themselves, not on idealistic grounds but as part of what Thucydides regards as a naked struggle for power. Moreover it is a very dirty war, as the episodes of Corcyra and Melos demonstrate.[46] To a great degree, then, Thucydides' subject differs from that of Herodotos as the Vietnam War differs from the Second World War in the popular imagination of today's citizens of the United States of America. The curious thing is the way in which the Peloponnesian War seemed to confirm so many of the sophists' teachings. It was a war in which self-interest and sheer power dominated, in which human society and humans as individuals were revealed as operating according to base *physis* and in which concerns for justice, fairness, religion, honour – all the baggage of law, *nomos* – were cast off, with no sign of retribution from any divine force. Thus, the cold analysis of imperialism and empire in the speeches of Thucydides is not out of temper of the day. There is no difficulty in believing that Perikles (as well as Kleon after him) could publicly call the Athenian empire a tyranny. Thucydides was an out-and-out genius who practically invented the genre of military history.

The war at sea

In the summer of 412 BC Hermokrates of Syracuse, the chief oligarchic *stratêgos* during the Athenian siege of his *polis*, fulfilled the hopes and fears supposedly expressed by various speakers in Athens three years previously,[47] by arriving from the west to assist the Peloponnesians with a fleet of twenty Syracusan and two Selinountine triremes.[48] The crippling failure of the expedition to Sicily meant that the enemies of Athens were at last encouraged to cross the Aegean and not only challenge its domination of the seaboard of western Anatolia but also threaten its vital lifeline to the Black Sea and thus consequently its ability to stay in the war.

Athens lived by its maritime trade, and on grain and flax imported by sea from the north shore of the Black Sea, and so its navy was responsible for the protection of seaborne commerce, particularly those passing through the vital bottleneck of the Hellespont. However, hitherto Sparta had been unable to match the might of the Athenian navy, only having the capability to despatch a motley fleet of amateurs and allies to stir up the occasional revolt within their maritime empire. Nevertheless the initiative now plainly lay with Sparta, and it was up to it to exploit a situation in which the allies of Athens were very restive and even the neutral states were inclined to embrace the Spartan cause. At the same time, we no longer hear of Sparta's mission 'to liberate Hellas', with the object of freeing the Greeks from the tyranny of Athenian imperialism. Rather, says Thucydides, the Spartans 'determined to engage in the war with all their heart, thinking that . . . if they destroyed the Athenians they would forthwith acquire the secure hegemony of the whole of Greece'.[49] Having made war under the banner of freedom, Sparta was now set to establish a fresh tyranny as soon as the old one was overthrown. To achieve this end, therefore, Sparta moved even farther away from mainland Greece, which had been its customary playground, and went out on to the high seas after the fashion of the Athenian navy and began to sail the 'blue waters' of the Aegean Sea.

At the start Sparta sent a fleet to blockade the geopolitical choke point of the Hellespont. This was a fleet that by then was very far from being just the usual puny flotilla Sparta alone could or would muster.[50] Despite this stratagem however, King Agis, who was holding the fort at Dekeleia,[51] reckoned it was a waste of time attempting to sever Athens' supply lines when he could still see the Black Sea grain fleet putting into Peiraeus – the Athenians had fortified Sounion so as to protect the shipping lane by which supplies were now brought to Athens.[52] The alternative, of course, was to engage Athens on the high seas, but in doing so Sparta was to suffer misfortune on a number of occasions. Though the focus of war had naturally shifted to the east side of the Aegean, the Spartans were still poorly adapted to sustain naval operations, lacking the necessary naval skills and naval personnel, with perhaps the most serious stumbling block being the lack of finance. For their part the Athenians, with extraordinary resilience and courage, built a new fleet and still kept some of their skill in using it. Thucydides' description is typically economic and vivid: 'When they saw that there were no longer enough ships in their docks, or money in the treasury, or trained crews for the ships . . . they determined to resist to the last, and to provide timber and money, and to equip a fleet as best as they could'.[53] And there was that Athenian deserter, the clever, energetic and unscrupulous Alkibiades.

It seems improbable that Alkibiades – Athenian *crème de la crème* as he was – would have been able to adapt himself to the cold rigidities of the Spartan system for any length of time but unfortunately he had no other options open to him at this present time. So for the time being he had to forsake vanity and luxury; he who radiated the first and had lived in the lap of the second all his life. Yet there was trouble in store for him because while Agis lay at Dekeleia, so the story goes, Alkibiades at Sparta had lain with Agis' wife and fathered a son by her. His real refuge from the rub of fortune was not in gymnastics or grooming, but in the arms of a new Spartan lover. But fear of royal retribution, if he had indeed seduced the queen in his duller days at Sparta, together with a natural distaste for Sparta's sober habits and thin diet, and perhaps, to be fair, a touch of remorse, turned his mind to Athens again. He was sent out with Sparta's first fleet to Anatolia in 412 BC and served it well enough, but contact and success with Tissaphernes the satrap of Ionia, soon turned Sparta's agent into a Persian adviser, and the advice, at first neutral – play each side off against the other and thus 'wear out both sides',[54] so that neither would be capable of meddling in Asia

– acquired a positively pro-Athenian tone when there seemed a chance of buying a return to Athens in exchange for Persian help.

It is not surprising that the sophisticated Tissaphernes may have come to feel easier in his dealings with the smooth talking Alkibiades than with the flatfooted Spartans. Thucydides says that Alkibiades became the satrap's 'advisor in everything' and that Tissaphernes 'gave his confidence' to him.[55] With his eyes always set firmly on the future, Alkibiades spoke most of the time in doubletalk. The double fugitive pretended to be in agreement with anyone he was dealing with, particularly if it happened to be someone who could further his cause and so aid him in resuming his place in the Athenian political sun. Whether for reasons of ideology or of self-interest, rhetorical eloquence is power; there is no question of that. The return was achieved, even though the help was not forthcoming, and so from 411 BC until his second exile in 407 BC Athens, not Sparta, had the benefit of Alkibiades' Olympian talents. Even with suspicious and half-hearted support from home, they were more than a match for any boneheaded naval commander that Sparta could send out against him.

Kynossema (autumn 411 BC) was a moral victory for the Athenians who, out-numbered seventy-six to eighty-six and lacking their former confidence, had been afraid of the Peloponnesian fleet with its Syracusan allies, 'but now they got rid of their feelings of inferiority and ceased to believe that the enemy was worth anything at sea'.[56] In the end, as Diodoros points out, the Athenian helmsmen, 'who were far superior in experience, contributed greatly to the victory'.[57] Soon after Kynossema, there was near to Abydos a hard-fought engagement, which turned in favour of the Athenians towards evening with the timely arrival of Alkibiades and eighteen triremes. Once again, the Athenians commanded the narrow waters of the Hellespont. Both sides now asked their home governments for more men and ships, as they prepared for the next conflict over mastery of the vital straits.

Kyzikos (spring 410 BC) was a scrambling fight along the southern shore of the Propontis (Sea of Marmara), but by the end of the day the main Peloponnesian fleet and its Spartan *nauarchos* ('ship leader') Mindaros had been eliminated, and again this was chiefly due to the energy and ability of Alkibiades. The success of Alkibiades was the reward of rashness, which, in war, sometimes supplies the place of prudent design. The gods of battle are capricious, and fortune that proverbially favour the brave certainly aided Alkibiades much in his operations at sea. Thucydides, who was particularly fascinated by the unexpected in history, saw the years following the victory of Kyzikos clearly in perspective. Between 410 BC and 406 BC Athens seemed likely to win the war. Thucydides had no allusions about Alkibiades' character. He knew his ambition, vanity, and irresponsibility, but Alkibiades also had magnetism and ability. For four years Athens went from success to success and this was largely the work of Alkibiades: as Thucydides says: 'his war leadership was unrivalled'.[58]

Anyway, Thucydides has now ceased to be our main source and his place is taken by Xenophon, who talks of a despatch, intercepted after the battle, from Hippokrates, Mindaros' second-in-command, to his home government: 'Ships sunk, Mindaros slain, men starving. Don't know what to do'.[59] Albeit written with laconic brevity, this is not the sort of message that the ephors would have been delighted to read. By the conclusion of Kyzikos the Spartans had lost between 135 and 155 triremes within the space of a few months. In Plutarch's assessment the chief result of Kyzikos was that, 'not only did the Athenians securely hold the Hellespont, they also drove the Spartans from the rest of the sea in any force'.[60] Indeed, this triumph gave Athens command of the high seas for the better part of the next three years.

The victories at Kynossema, Abydos and Kyzikos demonstrated that the Athenians retained their tactical dominance at sea. As matters now stood, however, the Persians with the limitless resources of their empire, could build the Spartans another fleet, even a bigger one. However many victories the Athenians won, they could do little to loosen the grip that Sparta was able to exert on their economy. Worse still, if the Athenians were once to lose their fleet, they would have lost the war in the space of a single day, since they could not build another. They remained desperately short of funds too, with many sources of imperial revenue still in Spartan hands, so the enemy could outbid them for the services of experienced oarsmen from the Greek world, particularly so as many Greeks appear to have made a living as itinerant oarsmen, flocking to any port that was known to be hiring.[61] Worse still, those oarsmen they did manage to hire and retain had their wages halved to three *oboloi* a day or half a *drachma*, a mere subsistence wage.[62] In a naval war that depended so largely on money, crews had to be regularly paid, and decently too, to remain afloat. It comes as little surprise, therefore, to find that the crews of Athenian ships were no longer the envy of other powers. Eventually the Athenians, resolving, on the eve of their own destruction, to deal a crushing blow at the Peloponnesian fleet and have done with it once and for all, were obliged to use inexperienced men as oarsmen. These unfortunates included peasant farmers, landed aristocrats who normally served in the cavalry corps, and even slaves, who, according to Aristophanes, were offered freedom and Athenian citizenship for their service 'in a single sea-battle'.[63]

The 'single sea-battle' was that off the islands called Arginousai (summer 406 BC), lying between Lesbos and Anatolia. There the Peloponnesian triremes, 'with their more skilful crews, were drawn up in a single line abeam so as to be able to execute the *diekplous* and the *periplous*'.[64] The Athenians, on the other hand, lacking their former confidence and inferior in seamanship, formed two lines, one behind the other, with each ship in the rear covering the gap between the ships in front, so as not to give the Peloponnesians the chance to execute the tactical manoeuvres they themselves had perfected to bring them naval supremacy. The Peloponnesians made a rash onslaught on the entire Athenian fleet and were completely routed. According to Diodoros, Arginousai was 'the greatest naval battle in the history of Greek against Greek'.[65] The Peloponnesians lost seventy-seven ships, astonishingly over 60 per cent of their fleet.[66] Kallikratidas, the Spartan *nauarchos*, fell overboard and vanished without trace, after his trireme had been rammed. Money could not make up for an apathetic admiral.

The fall of Athens

A few weeks before he fell overboard and drowned, Kallikratidas had sent a rather blunt message to Konon, his opposite number in the Athenian fleet, informing him in no uncertain terms 'that he would stop him committing adultery with the sea'.[67] On the strength of a minor naval victory at Notion (winter 407/6 BC), Lysandros received his successor in naval command, none other than Kallikratidas, with the words 'I hand over to you as ruler of the sea and as one who has conquered in battle at sea'.[68] Kallikratidas was as quick to mock that claim as he was to follow up his own short-lived success with that boast to the Athenian *stratêgos*. War is not a continuous battle. There is a series of battles, which are won or lost, or end inconclusively. But between battles there are long periods of inactivity when nothing seems to happen. But there is a constant ebb and flow. Certain elements get tired and drop out of activity. But they are constantly replenished with new, fresh elements moving into the conflict. The Peloponnese League still had reserves. These reserves were now mobilized for action, and Sparta would ultimately gain the upper hand.

In all this one man stands out, the formidable *nauarchos* Lysandros. As a commander his record may not be striking, one minor and one major naval victory against incompetent opposition, one unnecessary defeat on land, which cost him his life (he was to be cut down outside Haliartos in 395 BC while engaged in a foolish foray against the Boiotians), but as a diplomat and organizer his performance was almost flawless, unless we count arrogance, dishonesty, unscrupulousness and brutality as flaws. But as he once nonchalantly said to justify himself, 'where the lion's skin will not reach, it must be patched with the fox's'.[69] Indeed, Lysandros had the ability, unusual in a Spartan, to establish good personal relations with non-Spartans, Greek and 'barbarian' alike. During his first command, in 407 BC, he quickly won the confidence and full support of the young Persian prince Cyrus who had taken over the Persian command in western Anatolia, and the financial aid Sparta required for its fleet was secured on firmer footing. In fact, the two leaders got on splendidly, and Lysandros put his very un-laconic talents as a smooth-talking courtier, and 'by his submissive deference in conversation' won the heart of Cyrus.[70] The young prince asked how he could please his Spartan friend most, and Lysandros answered: 'If you add one *obolos* to the pay of each sailor'.[71] From that day the daily wage in the Peloponnesian fleet was increased from three to four *oboloi*. The morale of his crews was raised accordingly. What is more important, those foreign oarsmen currently serving in the Athenian fleet would be encouraged to jump ship, in a manner of speaking.

In the meantime, on the military front he had also sunk fifteen Athenian triremes at Notion,[72] the port of Kolophon, thus indirectly causing the second exile of Alkibiades from Athens (he retired to a private castle he had built on the Chersonese, that thin strip of land beside the Hellespont now known as Gallipoli, and held brilliant court here before being hunted down like a common criminal). Moreover, he had begun to build up the personal following among extreme oligarchs of the Greek *poleis* which, when they later came to power, turned the Aegean into something like a private empire. As Plutarch observes, he did them personal favours, 'planting in them the seeds of the revolutionary decarchies he would later bring into being'.[73] That loyalty was to Lysandros not to Sparta is shown clearly enough by their and Cyrus' refusal to co-operate with Kallikratidas, who, as the new commander of 406 BC, famously declared he would not kowtow to the 'barbarians for the sake of money',[74] and by the agitation that led to Lysandros' reappearance in 405 BC.

Kallikratidas may have preferred to fight a Greek war in a Greek way but his decent instincts needed success to nourish them. It needed money too, and lots of it. Having been restored to supreme command despite the illegality of appointing the same man to the position twice (officially he was not *nauarchos* but secretary and second-in-command to the nominal *nauarchos* Arakos, but everybody understood this was merely legal fiction),[75] Lysandros quickly re-established cordial relations with his Persian paymaster. He therefore obtained further subsidies from Cyrus and mustered a large fleet to confront the Athenians.

The Athenian *stratêgoi* allowed themselves to be lured into a vulnerable position. And so it was that Lysandros resoundingly defeated them at Aigospotamoi, dead across the Hellespont from Lampsakos (a *polis* of the Athenian empire) and only a few kilometres from Alkibiades' castle (summer 405 BC). Lysandros employed stealth and superior tactical skill to capture – on the open beach – almost the entire Athenian fleet when the bulk of the crews were on their way to the nearest market, which was several kilometres away.[76] Those Athenian sailors left behind with the ships received short shrift and were slain on the spot, while many others who survived the initial slaughter Lysandros had killed in cold blood and left the bodies unburied as an awful warning. Later sources place the number of Athenians executed at 3,000 or 4,000, which constituted about a tenth of the entire enemy force. Those lucky enough to survive the slaughterhouse apparently had their right hands cut off as an awful punishment.[77] This barbarously cruel deed represented a concept of total war, a determination to ensure the enemy did not fight (or row) again, which was largely alien to contemporary Greek attitudes to war amongst themselves. The navy on which Athens depended for its security and its food supply was all but annihilated. There can be few things more vulnerable than a warship on dry land, for only nine (including that of the *stratêgos* Konon) of 180 triremes survived the débâcle, and with their treasury empty, the Athenians could not afford to build another fleet.[78] As in the inexorable progress of a Greek tragedy, pride is followed by retribution, so now it happened to Athens.[79]

Doubtless some would say that Lysandros was a reckless man without conscience and without ideology, and indeed many butchers were of the type spawned by all wars, as history attests. Doubtless too there were ugly stains on Lysandros' record, but the human race, from the time it emerged from the rocky womb of Mother Earth, walking on two legs and dreaming of things it wanted, are as we have always known it, neither better nor worse. Thus from the hearts of knaves there springs latent honesty, from the depths of honest men there emerges a brutish appetite, a thirst for extermination, a desire for blood, killing for sheer sake of killing, an acquisition of the true taste for cutting throats. Lysandros' actions were questionable; his results were not.

How quickly the world spins in a day; how quickly life changes. In one brilliant coup Lysandros had destroyed the Athenian fleet. The survivors he shepherded back to Athens, there to suffer the full rigours of what the Athenians had put the Syracusans through a decade either. The following spring, with an armada of 150 ships, he was able to strangle the Athenians into submission, his thundering victory having effectively left their grain transports at the mercy of the Peloponnesian fleet.[80] Hunger lashed the war weariness and disillusion of the Athenians. Finally brought to its knees by the weapon of hunger, Athens was to have its wings brutally clipped, but its neck was not to be wrung (as desired by Thebes and Corinth). The ramshackle empire was disbanded, the fleet decommissioned, and the city walls dismantled to the music of flute girls while the liberation of Hellas was proudly proclaimed. It was perhaps now that Lysandros sent a typically laconic despatch home, saying simply

'Athens is taken', whereupon the ephors wrote back, 'taken' would have been enough.[81] True or not, the Athenians themselves were forced to swear an oath 'to follow the Spartans by land and sea, wherever they might lead',[82] which in effect turned Athenian foreign policy over to Spartan control. Their cherished democracy was then replaced by a pro-Spartan oligarchic junta backed by a Spartan garrison of 700 *neodamôdeis* to provide the necessary muscle,[83] a murderous puppet government who soon earned the soubriquet the Thirty Tyrants. There was no longer an Athenian assembly. The single devil of democracy had been swept away only to be replaced by the sevenfold devil of tyranny.

Lords of misrule

The uncertain months that followed Athens' surrender to Sparta in the early spring of 404 BC are an ugly period in Athenian history. Those extremists who had fled after the overthrow of the council of Four Hundred in 411 BC returned. Wasting no time they staged another *coup d'état*, which had been organized through the aristocratic dining clubs of Athens, the *symposia*, but this time they had the overt backing of Sparta. Lysandros helped Theramenes, a former pupil of Sokrates who was known as the *Kothornos*, the theatrical boot that fitted either foot,[84] institute the *syngrapheis*, a commission of thirty men with full powers to create a constitution based on the ancestral laws – what this meant was ambiguous but it certainly did not include any democratic laws.[85] It must never be forgotten that to revive the pre-democratic past was the oligarchic dream, and to this end the Thirty Tyrants promptly appointed sympathetic members to a new council and abolished the popular juries, but refused to carry out the mission for which they had been selected, namely to frame a new constitution.[86] Instead, they retained power in their own hands and used it to settle old scores. To destroy an old political organization is a comparatively easy task, and little besides brute force is requisite for its accomplishment, but to build up and reconstitute society requires more than brute force, more even than genius for the work, and competent agents with which to complete it.

Learning from the mistakes of the 411 BC oligarchic junta, of which Theramenes had been a leading light, the Thirty Tyrants employed savagery and duplicity in excess to coerce the *dêmos* and bring them to heel. In particular, the *ekklêsia* was restricted to 3,000 citizens who never really existed, in other words these were just names on a list, and those who voiced any form of opposition were simply done away with *tout de suite*.[87] And so, once the populace had been rendered harmless, a reign of terror commenced in Athens. The Thirty Tyrants and their supporters exiled or executed many Athenians either because of personal enmity or simply to acquire their wealth. They likewise targeted many *metoikoi* as a means of financing the *neodamôdeis* encamped on the Acropolis.[88] They ordered death like gods, and it is said that the purge resulted in the unlawful deaths of 1,500 people, citizens and *metoikoi* alike, and 5,000 were banished, while as many others fled Athens in fear of their lives. In those dark diabolical days it was true, if ever, that 'man is a wolf to man'. The laws of human civilization were suspended. The laws that men obeyed were jungle laws.

Theramenes, who lived up to his nickname, soon complained to his fellow tyrants about the excessive bloodletting. Kritias, another former pupil of Sokrates and Theramenes' closest friend, simply responded by striking his name from the list of Three Thousand. Theramenes could now be arrested and executed without trial. There ends Theramenes who, for all his lifelong political wheeler dealing, died a gallant death.[89]

There is one man who would become notable in the then still remote future entered the butchery. Anyone who reads Xenophon's narrative dealing with the bloody events at Mounychia, the acropolis of Peiraeus, quickly gains the distinct impression that he wrote as an eyewitness, but as an eyewitness on the wrong side.[90] Moreover, the reader's gut feeling is that the author was still with Kritias and his merry men when they had fled Athens for Eleusis, and was not among the seventy *hippeis* who deserted to the democratic forces of Thrasyboulos after their victory at Peiraeus.[91] Of course, it is only in bad novels that people are neatly divided into two camps and have nothing to do with each other. In real life everything gets mixed up. It is in the light of all this that we can begin to understand Xenophon's rather questionable role during the short but bloody reign of the Thirty Tyrants. During those last agonizing years of the Peloponnesian War, the young Xenophon, as a member of the Athenian cavalry corps, the *hippeis*,[92] and by the detail of his account,[93] probably saw action in Asia either under Thrasyllos or Alkibiades. If he missed those campaigns, the possibility exists for him of sailing with the fleet that was scraped together in 406 BC to rescue the Athenian forces blockaded in Mytilene. In this emergency, Xenophon tells us that even 'the *hippeis* went abroad in considerable numbers'.[94]

The social homogeneity of the *hippeis* engendered an *esprit de corps* and a sense of corporate identity, but it also created the potential for social upheaval in Athens. Not noted for their democratic leanings, these aristocratic horsemen, who were in the prime of their youth, aped Spartan habits: they not only had a tonsorial preference for long hair, but also wore crimson military cloaks and happily engaged in boxing and other contact sports. It was because of these practices that these horsemen of Athens were publically perceived as arrogant and out of step with the democratic ideal. The cavalry corps had not been collectively prominent in the oligarchic revolution of 411 BC, but the same cannot be said for the *coup d'état* of 404 BC, when the unit as a whole heavily involved itself in the régime, including involvement in its atrocities.[95]

To Xenophon the Thirty Tyrants were harsh rulers in harsh times and this probably explains why he stood by them despite the catalogue of killings done in their name. He was an unruly, ambitious young aristocrat hanging on the coattails of tyranny as he sought his way forward in life.[96] Whatever he thought during the death throes of this iniquitous tyranny he had actively supported, Xenophon, burning like a candle with the flame of his ideals and with a fixed animus against 'mob rule', could have felt no enthusiasm for staying in Athens after the restoration of democracy.[97] Indeed, for any young Athenian gentleman with a taste for war and a distaste for democracy, this was the time to be off.

A corner for ever Lakedaimon

History repeatedly shows that effective opposition to oppressive regimes relies on committed men who are prepared to hazard their lives and whose chances of success depend heavily upon their military skills. As discussed above, it is the Spartan loving-democracy-hating Xenophon who provides an eyewitness account of the military campaign of 403 BC between the Spartan forces of occupation and the expatriate Athenian democrats.[98] With death sentences mounting up and the tyranny becoming ever more oppressive – a warning of the dangers of entrusting power to those who feel that their sense of justice and order is the only one valid – a ragbag army of Athenian democrats, with Boiotian help, returned to Athens under Thrasyboulos, a *stratêgos* who had served alongside Alkibiades in the naval war. Having established themselves in Peiraeus, where the poorer people lived from whom the oarsmen came, the democrats challenged the oppressors, who in turn sought military aid from the Spartans.

Lysandros and King Pausanias led rival expeditions to the rescue, the first commanding an army of Peloponnesian mercenaries, the second of Lakedaimonian troops, and fought the Athenian democrats in a series of battles and skirmishes in and around Peiraeus. There were heavy losses on both sides, including Kritias, the leading spirit of the Thirty Tyrants. It was at this point that Pausanias used the chance to negotiate a settlement, bringing three of the five ephors around to his way of thinking, who in turn set up a commission of fifteen men authorized to sort out the political mess in Athens. True it was partly down to his rank jealousy of Lysandros, but the king was also a moderate man who held a genuine concern about the effect the notorious decarchies were having on the reputation of Sparta. He could not ignore the reality that these were Sparta's tools, reliable and dependable in their brutality and corruption. Lysandros tried to intervene, but Pausanias, like his father, Pleistoanax, before him, was in favour of détente with the Athenians. And so the bloody oligarchs fled, sweet democracy was restored, and a general amnesty proclaimed. This little episode well illustrates the complexity of the problem that Sparta's too complete victory raised.

To come back to the point, in his account Xenophon gives the names of some of the Spartiates who fell fighting in Peiraeus: 'Chairon and Thibrachos, both of them *polemarchoi*, were slain, and Lakrates, the Olympic victor, and other Lakedaimonians who lie buried in front of the gate in the Kerameikos'.[99] The ancient Kerameikos, 'the most beautiful suburb of Athens',[100] was to the north-west of the Athenian Agora and just outside the city walls. It served as the main public cemetery.

West of the Dipylon Gate, the principal entrance of Athens, stands a long narrow tomb of poros limestone blocks. It once carried an inscription naming those interned within, part of which has survived. The names Thibrachos and Chairon, mentioned by Xenophon, are inscribed in the Dorian alphabet at the right end of a marble plinth, written in small, upper-case lettering from right to left (i.e. retrograde).[101] The first two letters of LAKEDAIMONIOI (viz. ΛΑ) are preserved, also written from right to left but much larger. Presently replaced by a copy,[102] the surviving part of the inscription is at the west end of the tomb. The marble slab upon which is was inscribed was originally some eleven metres long, and thus ran the whole length of the front wall of the tomb.

The skeletons of thirteen casualties with recognizable wounds were found inside the tomb. An iron spearhead, for example, which had been thrust through the ribs of one of the skeletons, was found still in place, while the right leg of another had been pierced by two bronze arrowheads. Other than that, the tomb contained no grave goods and the only distinction made between the bodies was that three – presumably the two *polemarchoi* and the Olympic victor – had slightly more room and were laid out with their heads resting on two stones, rather than one stone as in the case of the others.[103]

There were no indiscrete body bags arriving in Sparta, for the Spartan custom was to bury the fallen in collective graves on or near the battlefield – it was considered a high honour so 'that there's some corner of a foreign field that is for ever Sparta'.[104] Thus after Plataia (479 BC) Herodotos explains that the Spartans buried their 'holy ones' in one grave,[105] the rest of the Spartiates in another, and the helots in a third.[106] The only exception to this custom was, according to Plutarch, 'they carry the bodies of their kings home'.[107] Still, it is a curious thing to find a tomb of the hated Lakedaimonian enemy standing in the sacred precincts of Athens' cemetery, and to read the names of Spartiate officers carved in an alphabet alien to Attica. Although they were slain when the Athenian oligarchs were still in power and Pausanias was still in Attica with his army, thus making their elaborate burial in the Kerameikos possible, it is still strange that their remains were not returned to Sparta after the restoration of democracy in Athens.

In Lysias' *Epitaphios*, delivered in 390 BC, we may have the answer to this riddle: 'The patriots who had returned from exile and occupied Peiraeus, not fearing the multitude of their enemies composed of Lakedaimonians and fellow citizens and having hazarded their own lives, set up a trophy of victory over their enemies, and *they furnished, as witness of their own valour, the tombs of the Lakedaimonians close to this monument*'.[108] The final trauma of the period of the Thirty Tyrants had awakened the Athenians to the benefits of their precious democracy, and this alien tomb was to serve as a vivid reminder that these prominent fighters of an invading enemy army had been cut down in combat by valiant Athenian democrats, patriots who believed the recovery of their independence no longer seemed a chimaera. It was also a pragmatic reminder to those who came after them, we included, of the right to disobedience and compulsion to rebellion in times of bad (for some, ungodly) government. Having become conscious of their own strength, they had risen up and shook themselves like a horse shaking off flies.

Chapter 9

Organized to Kill

Although the literary evidence can be somewhat confusing at times (when is it not!),[1] we must begin at the end and start with Xenophon, the contemporary historian who has provided us with the most information on the subject of the Spartan army and its tactical organization. Presumably he was drawing upon his extensive experience of fighting with the Spartans, particularly in Asia under Thibron and Derkylidas (399–397 BC), and under Agesilaos, to whom he became greatly devoted (396–394 BC). Xenophon's Spartan army was divided into six *morai* (sing. *mora*),[2] and even though he does not mention the *pentekostyes*, he does imply of their existence when acknowledging that the Spartan officers who attended a conference outside Haliartos in 395 BC,[3] or those in the plain of Lechaion in 390 BC included the *pentekosteres*.[4] So in Xenophon's Spartan army the *mora* was at least divided into *pentekostyes*.

Big and small units

This now leads us to the first big question, namely were the six *morai* divided into *lochoi* (sing. *lochos*)? Xenophon only mentions such units three times in the *Hellenika*, and all three occur after the killing field of Leuktra in 371 BC.[5] In his references to officers attending conferences and war councils the *lochagoi* are not mentioned at all. There are those who reckon that the *mora* replaced the *lochos* (van Wees). However, if we return to Xenophon he provides a list of Spartan officers in his *Lakedaimoniôn politeia* and this does include the *lochagoi*, and he mentions the *lochos* by name too.[6] Of course, Xenophon could have nodded in the references to the officers in his *Hellenika*, or *lochagoi* simply did not attend conferences of war councils, but if we look at the passages in which Xenophon does refer to *lochoi*, none really suggest that we are dealing with a brand new unit within the Spartan army. On balance, therefore, the *lochoi* were part of the army's tactical organization early on.

The second big question is how many subunits made up the *mora*? The only precise evidence comes from Xenophon's list of Spartan officers: 'Each hoplite *mora* has one *polemarchos*, four *lochagoi*, eight *pentekosteres* and sixteen *enômotarchoi*'.[7] Scholars and commentators universally accept that each *mora* contained eight *pentekostyes*, but there is some dispute over the four *lochoi* and sixteen *enômotiai*. Let us deal with the number of *lochoi* first. In his *Hellenika* Xenophon implies not four but two *lochoi* per *mora*,[8] which gives us a total of twelve *lochoi* for the Spartan army. It has been suggested that the figure of twelve *lochoi* came about because of the appalling loses suffered at Leuktra, that is to say, immediately after the *débâcle* there was a military reform by which the number of *lochoi* was halved from twenty-four to twelve, while the organizational level of *mora* was simply abolished altogether (van Wees).

True, in his *Lakedaimoniôn politeia* Xenophon does says each *mora* contained four *lochagoi*, and this clearly implies that there were four *lochoi* per *mora* not two. Others (Lazenby), however, point out that numbers are notoriously prone to corruption in ancient texts, and in this case blames a miserable mediaeval monk who may have easily read *dúo* (two) as *d'* (four).[9]

Like *lochoi*, Xenophon does not mention *enômotiai* in the *Hellenika* until Leuktra, but they surely existed throughout.[10] The *enômotiai* were crucial as they were the smallest tactical subunit of the Spartan army, and at full strength numbered forty hoplites.[11] The number forty obviously represents the forty age groups (i.e. twenty to sixty years of age), with one man from each group making up the full strength of the *enômotiai*. If we assume that the numbers given by Xenophon in his *Lakedaimoniôn politeia* are correct, then the nominal strength of a *mora* is 640 (i.e. 16 × 40), which in turn means that the entire Spartan army only amounted to 3,840 hoplites (i.e. 6 × 640) plus the 300 *hippeis*. But we will take up this conundrum in due course.

The Spartan army that Thucydides believed he knew apparently did not consist of *mora* but of *lochoi*, in each of which 'there were four *pentekostyes*, and in the *pentekostys* four *enômotiai*'.[12] So for Thucydides each *pentekostys* was formed of four *enômotiai* not two, as in the *Lakedaimoniôn politeia*. However, he does, much like Xenophon, provide us with a handy list of Spartan officers, namely the chain of command at the battle of Mantineia in 418 BC: 'he [the king] gives the word to the *polemarchoi*, they to the *lochagoi*, these to the *pentekosteres*, these again to the *enômotarchoi*, and these last to the *enômotiai*'.[13] So, much like a modern army, orders in the Spartan army were passed down the line to commanders of increasingly smaller units.

Age groups

As for citizens of other *poleis*, Spartiates were liable for military service between the ages of twenty and sixty thus making up the forty age groups,[14] which probably accounts for the nominal strength of the smallest tactical subunit, the *enômotia*. However, Xenophon speaks of 'the ten from manhood', viz. the age groups twenty to thirty, or 'the fifteen from manhood', viz. the age groups twenty to thirty-five,[15] which does suggest that for ease of mobilization the age groups were split into eight and in this way five men were drawn from each of these eight groups in order to make up the total of forty men. This certainly makes good sense if the ephors could not find, for sake of argument, a twenty–six-year-old for one of the *enômotiai*. Furthermore, if theoretically an *enômotia* deployed for battle five across and eight deep, the young men were easily detailed to the front rank, each rank thereafter containing progressively older men. We hear from Xenophon, for example, that the younger Spartiates could move like greased lightning and even catch peltasts – highly mobile javelineers unencumbered by body armour – when 'within a javelin's throw of Spartan hoplites'.[16] This organizational system, with its handy blocks of forty men, enabled the Spartans to tailor-make an army of any strength according to need. Nothing like this existed in any other Greek state. For the campaign of 418 BC, to use a convenient example, the ephors mobilized all the age groups for a march to the border, at which point the oldest and youngest were left behind to serve as a home guard, while those aged twenty-five to fifty-four years carried on and ended up fighting at Mantineia.[17] Tyrtaios' Spartan warrior 'with white hair and grey beard' was no poetic licence.[18]

The chosen ones

It is at Leuktra that we meet the 300 *hippeis* who, according to Xenophon, were selected by the three magistrates known as the *hippagretai*, each of whom chose a hundred men,[19] and in all probability each *hippagretas* and his chosen one hundred came from each of the three tribes. Conventionally, these élite Spartiates would have been in the prime of their lives, age groups twenty to thirty, and probably young worthies from certain families to boot. They were not chinless wonders, however, a crack unit despite their origins, a royal guard in truth. The *hippeis* only took the field when one of the kings did so, fighting on foot either before or beside the king.[20] The unit itself actually appears for the first time in the historical record in 479 BC, providing a splendid escort – an honour never before bestowed upon a foreigner – for Themistokles as he travelled home to Athens in 'the most beautiful chariot that could be found in Sparta'.[21]

Origins

When did all this come into being? This is once more a difficult and controversial topic. It is fair to say that many modern commentators believe that this organization belongs to the end of the fifth century BC, Thucydides being the first our authorities to let fall the term *mora*. It is for this reason that one scholar (Sekunda) put forward the argument that the occupation of Dekeleia in 413 BC brought about the *morai*, but it is likely that essentially Thucydides was talking about the same Spartan army as Xenophon when he wrote up his celebrated account of the battle of Mantineia even though he failed to mention *morai* at all.

When we read this account we see two fundamental problems with Thucydides' Spartan army. First, he reckoned the Spartan army was larger than that facing it, but if he is correct then we have a problem. The 'seven *lochoi* in the field' means the total Spartan strength at Mantineia, including the 600 *skiritai* too, only adds up to about 5,000 men.[22] Second, the command structure at Mantineia includes the *polemarchoi*, but what job did they do if they had no *morai* to lead? Some (Forrest, Lazenby, Cartledge) believe that Thucydides failed to mention the *morai* because he thought that as the *brasideioi* made up one *lochos* with their numbers then the Spartiates made up a further six *lochoi*. Others (van Wees), however, believe the largest unit was under the command of a *polemarchos*, with Thucydides using the generic Greek name of *lochos* for this unit and Xenophon using the technical Spartan term of *mora*.

What about Herodotos' Spartan army? Herodotos has Lykourgos establish, after he had arranged the laws, the warlike institutions, such as 'the sworn bands, and the troops of thirty, and the communal messes'.[23] The troops of thirty are otherwise unknown, but the *enômotiai* and *sussitia*, as we know, are quintessentially Spartan forms of military organization throughout the classical period. Anyway, originally mustered according to the three Dorian tribes,[24] the Spartan army was later re-organized on a territorial basis, for at the battle of Plataia (479 BC). One unit is referred to as 'the Pitanate *lochos*',[25] and Pitana was one of Sparta's main settlements, *obai*.[26] Intriguingly, the existence of the Pitanate *lochos* is denied by Thucydides, who explicitly says 'such a *lochos* has never existed',[27] and this surely is the Herodotean reference he had in mind. Humourless pedant, perhaps, and I am sure pedantry annoyed Herodotos. He was certainly no military analyst, he probably never served as a soldier, but he did put an herculean effort into his work, travelling extensively to seek out his sources. Anyway, one thing is for certain, *lochoi* existed at Plataia according Herodotos,[28] even if the Pitana one no longer did in the Thucydides' day. However, our author mentions the *polemarchos* too,[29] our first mention of that type of Spartan officer.

For the period between Plataia and Leuktra, both Thucydides and Xenophon describe an army of six units (though they give them different names, *lochos* and *mora*). The *mora* is first mention by Xenophon in 403 BC, and in 390 BC the strength of one *mora* is given as 'about 600'.[30] Thucydides, on the other hand, when he numbers the army at Mantineia in 418 BC, has six *lochoi* of 512, made up of four *pentekostyes*, each containing four *enômotiai*. Xenophon again, in his *Lakedaimoniôn politeia*, describes an army of six *morai*, each containing four *lochoi* composed of two *pentekostyes*, which in turn were made up of two *enômotiai*, i.e. with sixteen *enômotiai* in each *mora*.

It seems Thucydides is using the word *lochos* to describe a *mora* and has missed out one whole tier in his calculations, the real *lochos* of which there will have been two to each *mora*. The number of Lakedaimonians at Mantineia is thus increased to over 6,000, giving roughly one thousand to each *mora*. Xenophon too, or his text, must be wrong in the number of units he gives to the *mora* in the *Lakedaimoniôn politeia*, for the revised Thucydides has thirty-two not sixteen *enômotiai* to the *mora*. But it is hard to believe that Thucydides and Xenophon should both be wrong by making the same mistake about the size of the largest unit (sixteen *enômotiai* of thirty to thirty-five men) whatever name they give it, *lochos* or *mora*. It is even harder to believe that Thucydides, after all the pains he took, should have missed out one whole level of organization at Mantineia and should not have realized that this produced too small a total. Moreover, the *mora* of a thousand or more, which the theory demands, is substantially higher than any figure given by other sources. Here we need to look at Plutarch who provides us with the various strengths of the *mora* as given by earlier authors, viz. 500 (Ephoros), 700 (Kallisthenes) and 900 (Polybios), the last author probably speaking of a later period.[31]

Bucketfuls of scholarly ink have been spilled in trying to decide the truth about *lochoi* and *morai*, but that truth will never be known for certain, and it would be an idle game to try and guess why. Perhaps, when it all boils down to it, the Spartans played up to their image as portrayed by outsiders. Aristophanes calls the Spartans *Dieironóxenoi*, literary 'fond of poking fun at foreigners'.[32] In conclusion therefore all we can really say is that part of the difficulty lies in the fact that the Spartans were somewhat secretive and xenophobic. They were very conservative too, retaining old customs, which had long ceased to serve any purpose. However precisely the Spartan army was organized, and we can tamper with the literary evidence as much as we want, the crucial fact remains that it was organized. But what made the Spartan army what is was? First it is clear that it was highly efficient; the last defeat the Spartans had suffered before Leuktra had been back in the early sixth century BC at the Battle of the Fetters. So for two centuries the Spartan army ruled (and terrorized) the battlefields of Greece.

Serve to win

It is always dangerous to generalize, and one hesitates to state too dogmatically what the difference is between the Spartans and the rest. They are not, to put it tactfully as possible, the most immediately lovable people in Greece. The Spartan himself, who said nothing and asked less, is small and spare, physically robust and capable of ignoring personal discomforts. He is made of muscle, tough-as-nails. He can march, if he must, some 230 kilometres in three days, a steady, almost brutal pace, in an effort to prepare him for worse hardships to come – for battle itself. He carries a big load and war gear in which he fights. He is silent during the advance and makes no noise during the battle. He fights as well on minimum rations. He has the instinctive adroitness and flexibility of a wild animal. Ahead of him is blood and sweat, but no tears. Tried and tested in battle many times, he knows his job, thinks himself good at it, and believes that his superiors think so too. In summary, he is tougher and dourer than his fellow Greeks, and will stick it out however hard the fight. No doubt there were Spartans who were flamboyant, frivolous folk, and Sparta probably had its quota of fawning, polished sophisticates: they were in a tiny minority, that is all. Most Spartans gave off an air of such brute virility and barely contained violence, and an enemy who dare present himself on the field of battle to them was in very serious trouble.

That the Spartans were brave goes without saying, the enormous social pressures made sure of that. Herodotos recalls that the lone survivor of Thermopylai was shunned by his peers back home. More surprisingly, the lone survivor of the quasi legendary Battle of the Champions went home and hanged himself, thereby avoiding questions about how he was able to survive such a holocaust.[33] This was nothing like a criminal attempt by a pusillanimous malingerer to evade the tender mercies of the battlefront, bullets, shrapnel and suchlike.

Courage is nothing to laugh at, not if it is proper courage and exercised by men who know what they do is proper. Proper courage is wise courage. It is acting wisely, acting wisely when fear would have a man act otherwise. It is the endurance of the soul in spite of fear – wisely. Plato, in the dialogue called *Laches*, has Sokrates with pointed questions whittle down the definition of courage to a mere wise endurance.[34] For courage, according to Plato, is one of the four parts of virtue. It is there with temperance, justice, and of course, wisdom, and all parts are necessary to make the sublime human being. In fact, Plato says, men without courage are men without temperance, justice, or wisdom, just as without wisdom men are not truly courageous. Men must know what they do is courageous. They must know it is right, and that kind of knowledge is wisdom and nothing else. Men who have been out long enough to know, are both experienced and wise.

As well as wise endurance, courage is the product of self-confidence too, and this has a snowball effect. Thucydides provides a good example of this in his marvellous account of Mantineia. Herein he describes how during the pre-battle warm up that whereas the confederates were fired up by their haranguing *stratêgoi* the Spartans were 'well aware that the long training of action was of more use for saving lives than any brief verbal exhortation, though ever so well delivered'.[35] Here we have a brilliant comparison between the high-octane discipline of the Spartans and the shambling amateurism of the confederates facing them. Hardly surprising then, the Spartans trounced them soundly. Even the disaster of Lechaion may have been the product of Spartan over confidence. There are indications that the wounded of the first encounter were carried away safely by the helot attendants and that the *polemarchos* (unnamed by Xenophon) could have easily formed square and doubled out of danger. However, over confidence and brashness decided that the *polemarchos* would stick around and thrash Iphikrates. There was also the tiny Spartan cavalry force, which did what every incompetent cavalry force in history does: they lose cohesion and get overwhelmed by infantry. The horses charge at different speeds, some not at all, so they get separated. And they have no cavalry commander to speak of, no clear objective worth the trouble. And their horses were probably not battle conditioned, so when they saw a swarm of humans ahead of them, screaming and throwing javelins at them, they stop. With the horses stopped dead, the cavalry is doomed. Cavalry that is stopped is dead cavalry.

Spartans on foot, on the other hand, were famous for their discipline too. It goes without saying that the efficiency and courage of an army depends on discipline, and without discipline an army is a reed swaying in the wind. Discipline is, obviously, a virtue that applies to individuals, but it has its greatest application in the context of a group, and the military context sees the pinnacle of its relevance. Discipline in this context is in part a product of drill and training, that 'muscle memory' that kicks in when orders are shouted or contact is made with the enemy. Herodotos records that even at the climax of Plataia the Tegeans advanced without orders but the Spartans coolly awaited for Pausanias' command.[36] Earlier in the day Kallikrates, 'the hand- somest man in the Greek army', was killed by an arrow before battle was joined as he 'was sitting in his place',[37] the implication being that the Spartans simply sat down and suffered the arrow storm directed against them by the Persians. From the beginning of history, discipline is one of those basic qualities that distinguishes armies from mobs.

But discipline, or even skill or physical courage, was not the whole answer. Spartans could suffer just like their fellow Greeks. Xenophon recalls that Agesilaos once sent fire in earthenware pots to his men anaesthetized by cold atop a tempest- torn mountain.[38] Thucydides, in his account of Sphakteria, has the Spartans 'thrown into consternation',[39] and even Spartan hoplites could show their heels as at Lechaion when the shattered scraps of the *mora* broke towards the sea and hoped-for safety.[40] It does not take too much for us to imagine the rest of the Greek world being tickled by this, the rarest kind of news thus far in the story of Sparta; Spartan hoplites, to put it simply, were in full flight.

Yet individual fitness, courage, discipline or skill were not fundamentally important in hoplite clashes. As mentioned before, in one of his dialogues Plato has a young man being shown *hoplomachia*, but the *stratêgos* Nikias reckons such skills were of little use except when the phalanx cracked and then it was a case for each man for himself.[41] A frivolous example comes from Herodotos. Xerxes, having heard how brave the Spartans were challenged Demaratos to fight twenty of his men, to which the ex-king replied that it was not as individuals but as a team that Spartans are the 'best of all men'.[42] Finally, the answer does not lie in the training or skill of Spartan officers, junior and senior alike, most owing their position by dint of wealth, personal authority and social standing. One doubts these officers received any formal tactical or strategic training in the modern sense, except perhaps at the very simplest level, viz. the 'square bashing' mentioned earlier. So where does the answer lie?

Comradeship

As mentioned previously, the smallest tactical unit in the Spartan army was the *enômotia*, with a nominal strength of forty hoplites and, perhaps, a campaign strength of thirty to thirty-five. In modern terms, this was a small, nimble, platoon-size force. With such articulation it is no wonder the Spartans, albeit professionals anyway, developed the vital ingredient of *esprit de corps*. The *enômotia* itself was probably formed using the fifteen-man *sussition* as the basic subunit, the communal messes to which all adult Spartiates had to belong.[43] The *esprit de corps* would have been that much stronger as members of the same *sussition* were accustomed to eat, sleep, live and train together. In short, they were little communities or family, sticking together through thick and thin as long as they survived, so they formed the strongest of ties.

The Athenian army, by way of a good comparison, was very much simpler (and also less powerful) in its military organization.[44] The democratic reforms of Kleisthenes (508 BC) had transferred most of the military and political functions of the old tribes into ten newly created tribes and 147 so called demes (urban wards, rural districts). Athenian hoplites were now mobilized by deme and local levies combined to form ten tribal units, *taxeis*, each commanded by a *taxiarchos*, elected on an annual basis.[45] Nonetheless, the *taxis* ('formation') was a unit of some one thousand men, and even though it was divided into a small number of subunits called *lochoi*, their *lochagoi* appointed by the *taxiarchoi*, this is as complex as Athenian military organization ever became, tactical articulation stopping at this second tier and going no further.[46] In modern terms, it is as if the Athenian army was composed of ten British regiments (or ten American battalions), which were only subdivided into companies, each commanded by a major (or a captain), and no platoons and sections (or squads), no lieutenants, sergeants and corporals. And so when Thucydides, in his marvellous account of Mantineia, describes how the Spartan army was organized he remarks on the command structure, the implication is that this was surprising and even interesting for his audience.

The glue that holds armies together has a complex and variable composition, which includes not only major components such as hostility towards the enemy, but small, and often more powerful ones, ones like the bonds that link men in their units. Today we would say that no commander should ever suffer a defeat from lack of drilling and training. In assembling an army, individuals are brought into association from all walks of life. They become soldiers only when the commander unites them. He has to create such powerful bonds that all come to share the same intentions. Drilling and training ensures the soldiers are solidly bonded into what we call sections or squads, respond to commands, are fully cognisant of their duties to each other and their commander, and are capable of executing manoeuvres and engaging the enemy without panicking in the chaos and stress of combat, and chaos, we might add prophetically, is the worst thing that can happen in the field. Good armies rely on alchemy to turn their raw metal into gold, the bonds of comradeship set rock-hard to link men together in battleground households.

Bonding into squads of fifteen (viz. at paper strength) men remained the concrete foundation of Spartan military organization. In this way, the Spartans lived in close proximity, cooked their meals in these groups of fifteen and ate together, strengthening the sense of camaraderie. Moreover, the communal messes encouraged austerity by providing simple fare, precluding private indulgence, and bringing the conduct of each citizen under the scrutiny of his fellows. The institution of communal messes was not peculiar to Sparta, but the Spartiates embraced the institution in a more thorough manner than did the citizens of other states, they having to eat the main meal of the day in their *sussition* until they were sixty, and between the ages of twenty to thirty had to spend the night with their messmates also.

The Spartan army was also evidently unique in being articulated down into manageable tactical units, the smallest of which, the *enômotia* commanded by the *enômotarchos*, had a campaigning strength of no more than thirty-five men.[47] Contemporary occidental military theory, initially based on behavioural analysis of performance in the Second World War, recognizes small groups of six, seven or eight men as constituting the basic identifiable and motivational unit whose brutal atmosphere of comradeship was forged under fire – essentially validating the ancient insight. Being mutually responsible for each other, this is the foundation for combat, and 'small group cohesion', as this relationship is called, is a potent mélange of comradeship and firepower that steels the squad or section.

The 'buddy-buddy system', viz. a man fights for the man next to him, is the rawest form of this cohesion, whereby a man's natural fear of losing his reputation as a man among his immediate comrades armours him against the terrible experience of battle. It is a complex chemistry of individual and collective needs, loyalties and pressures that can urge men to go forward or stand firm even when in the face of certain death. Consider those immortal words that Shakespeare put into the mouth of Henry v in the famous Saint Crispin's Day oratory: 'We few, we happy few, we band of brothers; / For he today that sheds his blood with me / Shall be my brother'.[48] Experienced soldiers know what it is like to submit themselves to the ordeal of battle again and again more or less willingly. To do otherwise is to disgrace themselves in the front of their fellow soldiers whose esteem is the foundation of their own self-respect. Physical courage can be motivated by the fear of shame, which for some can be an even greater fear than the fear of death.

Of course, the face that is being saved, the image that is being preserved, is that of the tribal warrior of our pre-civilized past who fought for personal glory and stood a very good chance of surviving the fight:

Ah my friend, if you and I [Glaukos and Sarpedon] could escape this fray / and live forever, never a trace of age, immortal, / I would never fight on the front lines again / or command you to the field where men win fame. / But now, as it is, the fates of death await us, / thousands poised to strike, and not a man alive / can flee them or escape – so in we go for the attack! / Give our enemy glory or win it for ourselves![49]

To put it more succinctly, as First Sergeant Dan Daly apparently did when urging his fellow Marines through the infernal hell that was Belleau Wood (6 January 1918): 'For Christ's sake men – *come on*! Do you want to live forever?'[50] Clearly, the anarchic machismo of maleness found in the tribal warrior still forms part of our own modern day definition of masculinity. And so, the most important single factor that makes it possible for civilized man, if we can call him such, to fight the wars of civilization is the exploitation and manipulation of the ingrained warrior ethic. Small group cohesion is the warm spirit of camaraderie known particularly to soldiers, past and present, who have faced common hardship and danger time after time. Men will kill and be killed rather than lose face.

Being committed to fighting and dying in battle would ensure the survival not only of the individual soldier but of the entire army. In other words, on the ground of battle – soon to become a burial ground – soldiers commit to fight to the death; they will hold on to life and gain victory, whereas if they seek to stay alive, they will suffer defeat and death. Xenophon had witnessed the selfsame phenomenon:

> Those who are anxious in war to save their lives in any way they can, are the very men who usually meet with a base and shameful death; while those who have recognized that death is the common and inevitable portion of all mankind and therefore strive to meet death nobly, are precisely those who are some-how more likely to reach old age and who enjoy a happier existence while they do live.[51]

Still, it would seem to be easy to convince brave men that death comes more quickly and more surely to those who fly in disorder than to those who remain together and present a firm front to the enemy. In the grim words of an ancient Chinese proverb: 'The bodies of those who do not put their lives at stake will fertilize the fields and become carrion for the birds and beasts'.

Proverbs may be common sense, but the fundamental problem is simply that human beings fear danger and do not want to die, even for their native land. This is a normal human emotion. Of course, men will plunge recklessly on, as men do when determined to perform a thing they fear. Self-esteem is unquestionably one of the most powerful motives that moves men. On the field of life and death they do not wish to pass for cowards in the eyes of their comrades. It is fear that comradeship encourages, fear of being shunned from the all-important male group. Likewise, as well as their love for one another, the soldiers' love for their commander and com-bining the resultant positive motivation with their fear of harsh, certain punishment, a powerful well-disciplined army can be fashioned. If comradeship and leadership buttress their resolve, then discipline coerces men. The key lies in ensuing that when the battlefield fears of death and of the enemy inevitably arise, they are insignificant compared with the soldiers' terror at the thought of the punishment they will certainly suffer for cowardice. When punishments are draconian, then soldiers will regard the enemy lightly.

Punishment, of course, always threatens the soldier who will not yield to reason; 'pay well, command well, hang well' was Sir Ralph Hopton's brutal summary of the seventeenth-century general's art.[52] But no commander can afford to be too draconian, and the wise commander seeks, on the contrary, to make his men obey not because he forces them but because they so wish:

> Regard your soldiers as your children, and they will follow you into the deepest valleys, look upon them as your own beloved sons, and they will stand by you even until death. If however, you are indulgent, but unable to make your authority felt; kind-hearted, but unable to enforce your commands; and incapable, moreover, of quelling disorder: then your soldiers must be likened to spoilt children; they are useless for any practical purpose.[53]

Yet for most men, almost despite themselves, the carrot of comradeship weighs heavier than the stick of coercion. And the most effective means of attaining this state of consent is fostering among them bonds of loyalty and regard for each other too strong for even the violent strains of battle to break. Thus a good commander understands the difficulty of forcing men to enter battle and engage in combat, of compelling them to kill other men. He will consider ways to develop, manipulate, and ensure fighting spirit, what the ancient Chinese aptly called the *qi*, 'vital breath', of their soldiers and armies. This critical element is associated with will and intention; when the men are well trained, properly fed, clothed, and equipped, and if their spirits are aroused, they will fight vigorously. However, if physical or material conditions have blunted their spirit, if an imbalance exists in the relationship between the commander and his soldiers, or if for any reason the soldiers have lost their motivation, they will be defeated.

Spartan bonding

Though war was (and still is) not a normal human condition, the Spartan aggressive and warlike fighting spirit was a vital yet intangible quality whose roots lay in male bonding, which was fostered and preserved though a definite group identity. It was this complex chemistry that allowed the Spartiate unflinchingly to face death, battle after battle. But the personal bravery of a single individual does not decide the issue on the actual day of battle, but the bravery of the unit as a whole, and the latter rests on the good opinion and confidence that each individual places in the unit of which he is a member.

In the ancient Greek world the specialized and continuous military training was the preserve of Sparta and, in some cases, of those states that kept small bodies of élite troops. It must be emphasized, however, that it was not the skill-at-arms of the individual Spartiate that was important, as his training as part of a coherent unit, for the simplicity of hoplite warfare left little scope for the display of personal skills. When, for example, Xerxes quizzes Demaratos about the martial nature of his fellow Spartans, the latter admits that the Spartans fighting as individuals are as good as the next man but fighting together are the 'best of all men'.[54] Thus, at Thermopylai, only troops trained to move as one and instantaneously execute the words of command could have carried out those series of feigned retreats described by Herodotos.[55] Or at Plataia the following year Herodotos emphasizes Persian courage but they rushed out in ones, pairs or tens and fell upon the Spartans and were destroyed.[56] The Greeks were deeply imbued with the competitive spirit, and their word for competitiveness, *agônia*, has given us our word 'agony', which surly tells us a lot about the nature of Greek competitiveness. Being adjudged 'the best' therefore meant a very great deal.

The bedrock of military *esprit de corps*, comradeship in the Spartan army was extremely strong. According to Spartan tradition, the reforms of Lykourgos, the omni provident lawgiver who brought about *eunomia*, 'good order', in Sparta,[57] had been most particular in fostering it. The *agôgê* initially fostered comradeship and belonging as one of its cornerstones. Young boys were drilled in packs. Having survived the *agôgê*, a young Spartiate sought membership of one of the communal messes. This *sussition*, as it was sometimes called, comprised some fifteen members who spent considerable time with one another, even when not in training. It was here, of course, that they dined communally and ate simple food, including a black broth infamous throughout Greece for its nastiness and much-diluted wines. It was not the sort of diet that would have made us smack our lips and belch with repletion, and even among their Greek contemporaries the Spartans were noted for their ability to fight well rather than to feed well – and Spartan cuisine tested the toughest of guts.[58] Even the kings supped on black broth and barley bread, and Plutarch notes that when the social-reforming Kleomenes entertained foreign guests 'the servants brightened up the dinner a bit, not with any rich dishes or desserts, but by offering more generous portions and a more mellow wine'.[59] Even so, we should not expect boisterous celebrations and much good eating and drinking. Anyway, when in battle, the *sussition* was the hoplite's 'tent', and was undoubtedly the basic building block for the formation of the *enômotia*. In other words, the individual Spartiate ate, slept and fought side by side with comrades he had probably known since his agonizing boyhood days. His membership to a *sussition* was decided by a collective ballot of its members, who were all called *homoioi*, dressed the same, made by-and-large identical mess contributions and shared the same unappetising food.

In the *Poroi*, a political pamphlet of his dotage, Xenophon advocates that Athenian citizens should once again serve together in the ranks of the phalanx and not be lumped in with 'Lydians, Phrygians, Syrians, and barbarians of all sorts'.[60] The whole premise of the *Poroi* is how to cure his native city's economic woes, and this is obviously a rhetorical point concerning Athens' strong reliance upon such 'riffraff', but the idea is clear all the same.

As a former mercenary himself, Xenophon certainly appreciated the importance of small group cohesion. In the *Kyroupaideia*, for instance, the theme crops up time and time again. His fictitious Cyrus the Great, busy organizing and training his new model army and undoubtedly thinking of the professional army of Sparta as he does so, considered that those who messed together would be less likely to desert each other, and that there could be no stronger phalanx than one composed of comrades.[61] Again, having trained his army to a peak of perfection and fostered the idea of comradeship within each unit (called *taxis* by Xenophon), the wise Persian king realizes that the petty jealousies of his men will soon vanish like a summer mist once they are exposed to the harsh realities of the forthcoming campaign: 'For he knew that common dangers make comrades kindly disposed towards each other'.[62] The campaign, an invasion of 'Assyria', culminates in the battle of 'Thymbrara'. The king of Susa and fast ally of Cyrus, Abradatas, plunges recklessly into the fray and only his close comrades choose to follow him in death and glory. The moral of the tale is obvious as Xenophon is quick to point out:

> Now, it has been demonstrated on many occasions that there is no stronger phalanx than that which is composed of comrades that are close friends; and it was shown to be true on this occasion. For it was only the personal friends and messmates (*hetaîroi ... kaì homotrápezoi*) of Abradatas who pressed home the charge with him, while the rest of the charioteers, when they saw that the Egyptians with their dense throng withstood them, turned aside after the fleeing chariots [i.e. of the enemy] and pursued them.[63]

Again, it must be stressed that Xenophon has clearly used the professional army of Sparta as the role model for Cyrus' invincible army, and not the typical Noah's ark army of the Persian empire. Furthermore, there is little doubt that he has drawn upon his own personal experiences as a mercenary captain in order to portray not only the tactics of Cyrus' army, but also the human dynamics of soldiering within the ranks, as we shall soon see. The argument for small units, however, cannot be pressed too far when dealing with Greek citizen armies. It is the Spartans alone who broke down their citizen army into manageable tactical units, the smallest of which, as we know, the *enômotia* commanded by the *enômotarchos*, probably had a campaigning strength of no more than thirty-five men. On the other hand, there is no evidence to suggest that the Athenian or Theban armies, for instance, contained units smaller than a *lochos*, which, though the number varied from army to army and from time to time, almost always contained at least a couple of hundred men.

There was one truly professional unit outside Sparta that did exhibit this idea of small group cohesion, even to the extent that the 'buddy-buddy system' was very much in force within its rank, the Sacred Band of Thebes. The 300 members of the Sacred Band first fought as a unit at the battle of Tegyra where they played a prominent part in the defeat of two Spartan *morai*.[64] Thereafter, the Sacred Band was always deployed as a unit in its own right, and it was in this role that it truly became a crack force. Tradition has it that the Sacred Band was constituted of paired homosexual lovers and, in the words of Plutarch, 'a band that is held together by the friendship between lovers is indissoluble and not to be broken, since the lovers are ashamed to play the coward before their beloved, and the beloved before their lovers, and both stand firm in danger to protect the other'.[65] Naturally, Spartans were commonly satirized and caricatured outside Sparta by allegations that they all of them were hopelessly addicted to buggery. It is interesting to note too that the number of the Sacred Band was the same as that of the *hippeis*, the royal bodyguard of Sparta and of the selected force that went to Thermopylai with Leonidas, so probably this was a deliberate echo of a Spartan idea, a Theban clone. The Sacred Band was to remain unbeaten until its complete annihilation at Chaironeia in 338 BC, and even during this tragic final act the unit stubbornly stood its ground because all 300 members had decided to fight to the death.[66]

Here it is worth commenting on that Greek word, *enômotia*, which means, properly, a sworn band, it being derived from the noun *enomotos*, 'a man bound by oath'. Apparently, at Plataia, the Spartans swore an oath, which probably ran as follows: 'I shall not desert my *taxiarchos* or *enômotarchos*, whether he is alive or dead, and I shall not leave the battlefield unless the *hêgemones* [viz. his kings] lead us away, and I shall do whatever the *stratêgoi* may command, and I shall bury on the spot those of my fellow fighters who die, and I shall leave no one unburied'.[67] In the hierarchic Spartan army, sworn loyalty to state-appointed officers thus took precedence over personal obligations and safety. Similarly, a new member of the Theban Sacred Band was expected to make an oath to Eros, vowing to die a glorious death in preference to a dishonourable and reprehensible life, or so says Athenaios.[68] We are told by Athenaios too, albeit using second-hand evidence, the Spartans would make preliminary sacrifice to Eros in front of the battlelines 'with the belief that safety and victory lies in the love of those ranged alongside each other'.[69] We have a tendency to regard violet-eyed Eros ('sexual passion') as a wanton wild child who is only intermittently under the control of his mother Aphrodite. Still, whether or not we are prepared to accept the real possibility that sometimes the feelings of Spartans for their comrades were homosexual, though the Greeks themselves did not have a notion of a 'homosexual nature', the fact remains that the basic male bonding process is built upon mutual self-respect and a special kind of love that has nothing to do with sex,[70] or even idealism (very few men have died in battle when the moment actually arrived for 'God, Queen and County', for example, or even for their homes and families, sentiments best left to civilians). Besides, unlike the Theban Sacred Band, homosexual couples were not customarily stationed next to each other in the phalanx. If Athenaios is correct, and there is no real reason to doubt him here, it seems Spartan comrades were bound together by an obligation under Eros to stand by one another in weal or in woe regardless of their own lives. And so, if they had any choice in the matter at all, they invariably chose to die for each other and for their own vision of themselves.

In retrospect

When on campaign, the *sussition* was the Spartiate's 'military cloak and camp bed', and was undoubtedly the basic building block for the formation of the *enômotia*, the smallest tactical unit in the Spartan army with a nominal strength of forty men. Compare the Athenian army, for instance, where the *taxis*, the tribal contingent of around a thousand men, was only divided into a number of sub-tribal units, the *lochoi*, each of which almost always contained at least several hundred men. In other words, an individual Spartiate ate, slept and fought side by side with comrades he had in all probability known since his boyhood days, and it was these comrades' good opinion that counted more strongly with him than the mortal fear of the enemy. Honour is a notion that seems distinctly antediluvian to most moderns, yet it is the value of a person in his own eyes, but also in the eyes of his society, an estimation of his own worth. A sense of honour is one thing valued more than life by the majority of tribal warriors.

Chapter 10

Klearchos' Red Army

Before we start, perhaps a few words about Xenophon himself may help the modern reader understand his works. Xenophon was an Athenian-born soldier of fortune, historian and essayist, and a former disciple of Sokrates. Whereas Plato, his exact contemporary and fellow disciple, was cramped by the influence of Sokrates' theories, churning out an inflated lot of mysticism and metaphysics, Xenophon advanced and developed under them, taking the path of inductivity and commonsense as opposed to the one of extremist views and eccentric plans. With his happy facility for making the complicated simple, Xenophon is an extremely useful author, though generally much underrated as one. His extant works include accounts of the Spartan constitution (*Lakedaimoniôn politeia*) as well as his own military exploits as a mercenary with the Ten Thousand (*Anabasis*). His other extant works include a narrative history of Greece from 411 BC to 362 BC (*Hellenika*). After continuing Thucydides' history of the Peloponnesian War as far as the surrender of Athens and the tragic events of 403 BC, Xenophon left an interval of two years – later to be filled in – before proceeding with his account of Greek history more or less uninterruptedly down to 362 BC, the year of his eldest son's untimely death in a cavalry skirmish. Of significance is the fact that the author was present (accompanying his close friend and patron, Agesilaos) during several of the military campaigns he describes.

The true value of Xenophon stems from the simple fact that he himself played an important military and political role in his own times and could consequently rely on his experiences of and observations on warfare between Greeks and non-Greeks, not to mention his close acquaintance with leading personalities of the day, amongst whom were Agesilaos of Sparta. In his *Lakedaimoniôn politeia* Xenophon usefully details the members of a commanding king's staff on active service: 'The staff consists of all *homoioi* who are members of the royal communal mess, seers, doctors, flute players, commanding officers, and any volunteers who happen to be present'.[1] It is not difficult to place Xenophon in the latter category. But what was he doing prior to this?

Seeing the sea
Young and enthusiastic, Xenophon was not without the quick perception and rapid decision that fit a man for command in the moments of hazard. He was almost a youth in age, not thirty, but the mind matures rapidly on the field of battle, and he had by nature the true sentiment of a soldier that tells him it matters little whether violent death comes soon or late. Xenophon, the youth who had aided and abetted the Thirty Tyrants in the awful butchery of their fellow citizens, was still not done with his fighting.

For a pugnacious young man to harbour the simple belief that he could easily secure for himself fame and fortune by taking part in a military adventure beyond the sea is not so far fetched.[2] To the young Xenophon war was plausibly desirable for its own sake as a sport only a few degrees more serious than hunting. Nonetheless, this cocksure gentleman was soon to become a practitioner of warfare as well as a theoretician, an unquestionable technical expert in war. Experience was more important than example to Xenophon, and his *Anabasis* is the epic saga of the subsequent retreat homeward of the Ten Thousand (as this roving band of Greek mercenaries were known) from the battlefield of Cunaxa not far from Babylon, where they had fought sometime in the autumn of 401 BC. The trapped Greek hoplites had refused the terms of the Great King, Artaxerxes II Memnon, preferring to fight their way out of Persia. Even after their Spartan generalissimo Klearchos had been lured into a parley and captured, the leaderless Ten Thousand, far from being a doomed rabble, had still chosen to battle their way to safety, exterminating and despoiling as they did so.

It was to be an extraordinary journey of eighteen months and the best part of 3,500 kilometres all told, accomplished through long marches, laden with equipment and weapons, on scant rations: northwards from Mesopotamia, through the mountain fastness of the fierce Kurdish tribesmen, to the eastern frontier of Armenia, across the river Araxes flowing into the Caspian Sea, and eventually to the Greek colony of Trapezos (modern Trabzon) on the southern shore of the Black Sea. As they came over the mountain pass high above the *polis*, they let out the famous cry '*Thálatta Thálatta*' (The sea! The sea!) – the element that had become part of the Greek soul. And so ended the mercenaries' long retreat. From Trapezos the Ten Thousand were able to proceed mainly by ship to Byzantium, only to find that Sparta had no use or indeed liking for them, and another bitter winter had to be passed in the service of the Thracian sub-king, Suethes. Consequently, when the new ephors took office in the autumn of 400 BC, a policy change in Sparta found them better employment, and when the Spartans arrived in Anatolia for a 'war of liberation' the substantial remnants, Xenophon included, were promptly hired to serve under Thibron in Ionia.

Tramping forward all the time is what is called an *anabasis* in Greek, an excursion into nowhere: penetrating into unknown territory, being cut off by cunning and ruth-less enemies who, skulking on the flanks and rear, are waiting for the first convenient opportunity to skin you alive. On the long march from Cunaxa the Ten Thousand were to suffer consistent and persistent harassment by marauding bands bent on their destruction, first the Persians themselves, then the Kurds and other such natives who would melt away into the hills or disperse when pursued. What men they must have been. They were to endure the trials of arduous terrain, of climatic extremes of desert and mountain, of altitude sickness, snow blindness, frostbite, and freezing tempera-tures that were new to troops so far accustomed to campaigning in warmer seasons, indeed, weather crueller than the natives, of the never-ending problems of supply, of the discomforts of half-a-thousand camps, of quarrel and conspiracy.

In reality, the *anabasis* was a drawn out acknowledgement of defeat. The endurance shown was, indeed, extraordinary. The Ten Thousand's skill at manoeuvring, mis-leading their enemies, and covering huge distances over forbidding terrain made it an icon for later military adventurers.[3] If the *anabasis* was any kind of victory, it was a victory of sheer survival. Nonetheless, out of this survival came the transformation of the inflexible hoplite phalanx into a highly adaptable military force, employing such innovations as holding force in reserve, infantry tactics suitable for mountain warfare, infantry approach formations, and much else besides. Colonel Dodge once wrote:

> The soldier of greatest use to us preceding Alexander was unquestionably Xenophon ... it is he who has shown the world what should be the tactics of retreat, – how to command a rear-guard ... More tactical originality has come from the *Anabasis* than from any dozen other books.[4]

All in all, the Greek mercenaries' tactics were exactly suited to Near Eastern terrain and opposition, which was almost the exact opposite of the European situation. The Ten Thousand also became unquestionable experts in arts of mayhem, having seized the opportunity to better themselves materially by looting and brigandage. Many a local native was to lose his food, women and possessions to the locust army.

We have no testimony but Xenophon's to much of the events of the long march, and the evidence of a single witness will always be questioned. No doubt, when old soldiers tell their tales of old battles and skirmishes, they sometimes heighten and embellish the dramatic incidents of their glorious past, the classic poor old gallant remembering his days of greatness, yet the essential truth is there. Indeed, there is about the *Anabasis* a sobriety of tone, which gives an impression that the writer was thoroughly acquainted with his facts, and that his statements may be accepted by us lesser mortals with confidence. The liveliness of Xenophon's war reporting bears the stamp of an enthusiastic eyewitness. The comfortable reader is justified in a willing suspension of belief, but this author likes to believe that the *Anabasis* is a piece of work so original in its content (as only the truth can be) that it formed a genre of its own. Due largely to the industry and enthusiasm of Xenophon, moreover, the *Anabasis* is our only detailed eyewitness account of mercenary service in the classical Greek world. It is cracking stuff, especially for those of you who like high-grade adventure stories, and certainly an account 'striking enough to be worth the telling' (to use Thomas Hardy's phrase).

Discipline, discipline, discipline

Xenophon emerged from the Persian adventure a wiser and highly experienced soldier, and his surviving writings, the *Anabasis* paramount among them, reveal a man for whom discipline and efficiencies were paramount. There is no doubt from his remarks on military affairs that he constantly stresses the need to preserve good discipline. Xenophon certainly practised what he preached, knowing from bitter experience that 'discipline keeps men in safety, while the lack of it has brought many here now to destruction'.[5] We see him put these precepts into practice at one of the soldiers' assemblies held soon after the election of the *stratêgoi* to replace those lost to Tissaphernes. Here Xenophon stresses to the rank and file of the Ten Thousand that they should be far more disciplined in their outlook and show more obedience to their commanders. He then proposes to the assembly of soldiers that a vote is passed so that the unruly are punished not just by their officers alone, but by all. With danger within and without the army, the army was obviously missing the stern but vital leadership of Klearchos, and Xenophon ends his appeal for a stricter disciplinary

code with a catchy punch line: 'Not one Klearchos, but ten thousand'.[6] The proposal
was passed. Yet Xenophon did not know that his hour was close at hand.

At a later date we witness Xenophon himself dealing out rough and ready justice
in the fashion of Klearchos, striking soldiers there and then for flagrant breaches
of discipline – in direct contrast, the wanton assault upon a citizen was punishable
by confiscation of property or, worse, death. For instance, during a period of extreme
weather conditions Xenophon had resorted to physical violence and struck at least
one straggler because he had 'behaved like a weakling and refused to get up,
preferring to leave himself a prey to the enemy'.[7] As a result of this cruel-to-be-
kind chivvying, he found himself accused of gratuitously and arrogantly assaulting
his soldiers, and he was forced to defend himself twice.[8] Using a stick or spear to
punish soldiers was the mark of a strict disciplinarian. Klearchos had carried 'a spear
in his left hand and a stick in his right' and thrashed disobedient or slacking soldiers
with whichever of the two was appropriate.[9] It can be said of him that his spear
and his stick were close neighbours. Thus, so much for the dead Klearchos and his
legacy. We turn now to the living Klearchos – to myself the more important character
of my story.

A Spartan abroad

In the years immediately following 404 BC many Spartans had to go abroad, and even
live abroad for long periods of time to administer Sparta's newly won dominion in
Greece. Worse still, many of them were sent out as harmosts, a position that made
them a virtual tyrant of a *polis*. What could be more different from the restraints of
everyday life at home? It seems once removed from the restraints inherent in life in
Sparta, Spartans tended to fall away from 'Lykourgan' standards. Lysandros was a
flagrant example of this, as was Pausanias in the years immediately following 479 BC.
And there were others too.

It is safe to say that to most people the name of Klearchos, the son of Rhamphias,
conveys absolutely nothing. Because he was not successful and because he immediately
preceded Agesilaos into the arena, what he did and what he tried to do have been
almost overlooked by historians: to the world at large, his name is a strange one. Yet
he won immortality for himself by earning the respect of Xenophon, receiving much
more than a just passing mention in the *Anabasis*. These facts are true about
Klearchos. He was a high-ranking Spartiate who ended up an outlaw. Having seen
active service throughout the Peloponnesian War, Klearchos had scaled the traditional
ladder of success: ambassador (*proxenos*) for the Dorian *polis* of Byzantium when he
was residing in Sparta;[10] general (*stratêgos*) in Anatolia;[11] military governor (*harmostês*)
of Byzantium and Chalkedon;[12] second-in-command to the *nauarchos* Kallikratides
at the naval engagement off Arginousai;[13] harmost of Byzantium and Chalkedon for
a second term; the tyrant (*tyrannos*) of Byzantium;[14] general (*stratêgos*) of Cyrus'
Chersonesian contingent.[15]

Bold, tough, clever, unscrupulous, cruel, self-assured, and with his own grim sense
of humour, Klearchos would become the most prominent of the Greek *stratêgoi*
serving under Cyrus,[16] and represents the archetypal soldier of fortune who seeks not
only to enrich himself on the spoils of a troubled era but gaining a position of power
too. He was not one to relish the fruits of favour, nor savour the bread of idleness. He

was a hard man, even by Spartan standards, not the sort of man to mess with. Each Spartan in his degree was tough, and there were three degrees – tough, tougher, toughest – and Klearchos was the last. We have no portrait or sketch of him, but it is easy to picture Klearchos as a large, burly man with a thick neck and a coarse, humorous, brutal face.

Klearchos did, aged fifty, come to a violent and sudden end – the role of *condottiere* was simply not an occupation for a man who was nervous of his skin. In his lengthy obituary for his erstwhile commander and comrade, Xenophon paints a vivid picture of a larger-than-life character who professes to know and love war, a man of action, a man born for war:

> When he may enjoy peace without dishonour or harm, he chooses war; when he may live in idleness, he prefers toil, provided it be the toil of war; when he may keep his money without risk, he elects to diminish it by carrying on war. As for Klearchos, just as one spends upon a loved one or upon any other pleasures, so he wanted to spend upon war – such a lover of war. On the other hand, he seemed to be fitted for war in that he was fond of danger, ready by day and night to lead his troops against the enemy, and self-possessed amid terrors, as all who were with him on all occasions agreed.[17]

Or in the brief words of Diodoros, our Spartan was simply 'a man who has proved himself in deeds of war'.[18] Klearchos was a soldier to the backbone who was naturally fierce, energetic, subtle-minded, with a strong seam of cruelty in his character. Little wonder then, that we find him attempting to carve out a little kingdom, which would assure a comfortable and worry free end to his days as an elderly mercenary.

Klearchos had first been despatched by Sparta to govern the sensitive *polis* of Byzantium in 411 BC.[19] The importance of Byzantium, according to Polybios, boils down to one simple truth: it blocks the mouth of the Black Sea 'in such a manner that no one can sail in or out without the consent of the Byzantines', who, consequently, 'have complete control over the supply of all those many products furnished by the Pontus'.[20] Grain was a prime import for Athens, and Klearchos' brief was to strangle the Athenian grain supply originating from the Black Sea colonies. It is interesting to note that, according to Diodoros, a year later the citizens of Byzantium, 'hating the severity of his administration (for Klearchos was a harsh man), agreed to deliver the *polis* up to Alkibiades and his colleagues',[21] namely the Athenians. This was done on a fixed night. Obviously Klearchos had proved to be a harmost in the Spartan mould, harsh and arrogant, for in 403 BC he was despatched once again by Sparta to Byzantium, which had been recaptured two years previously, so as to 'bring order to the affairs of the *polis*'.[22] It seems a harsh and arrogant man was required, for not only was the *polis* having problems with the footloose Thracians without, but also with factional discord within. However, Byzantium's troubles were only just beginning.

Klearchos, with a liberal use of hard cash, collected around him a large body of mercenaries and promptly converted his official office of harmost into an unofficial one of tyrant. Klearchos was no stranger to the use of mercenaries, for, as well as Lakonian *perioikoi* and *neodamôdeis*, his first Byzantine garrison had included Boiotian and Megarian mercenaries; he himself was the only Spartan.[23] On that particular occasion, as Xenophon observes in a much earlier passage, Klearchos had set out for

Byzantium with fifteen troop ships 'manned by Megarians and other allies'.[24] Diodoros, on the other hand, merely says that Klearchos 'had in the *polis* many Peloponnesians and mercenaries'.[25] Both authors, however, remark upon Klearchos' reliance upon the satrapal purse of Pharnabazos for the garrison's pay.[26] In other words, a task force prepared to garrison an outpost so far from home is technically composed of professional soldiers at the very least.

As tyrant Klearchos began his real life, which, so soon was to end in both disaster and glory. Having beaten his way to his present pinnacle and seized the reins of power in Byzantium, Klearchos, according to Diodoros, then proceeded to steal a state by eliminating those who stood in his way. Excuses were easy to find, while the pickings would be rich. The chief magistrates of the *polis* and thirty leading citizens were quickly dispatched and their property appropriated, while trumped-up charges sent many wealthy citizens either into exile or to their deaths.[27] True, he had a fatally simple idea of how to put good order and rule upon Byzantium, but Klearchos knew he was engaged in a venture in which playing safe would almost certainly lead to defeat. Success depended on willingness to take great risks, though calculated ones. And so his ill-gotten gains soon enabled him to support an army of mercenaries, an army to give teeth to his decrees and thus set his tyrannical rule on a much firmer footing.[28]

Yet the tyrant requires more than brute force, plucky daring and uncanny luck to gather to himself the sort of dominion he wants. Otherwise, he rules no more than a banana republic, corrupt, vicious, brutal. Klearchos, having crushed all opposition, certainly demonstrated he had the ruthlessness of any other tyrant, but he was cursed with two fatal weaknesses: he was stubborn and he was impatient. His stubbornness was in large part due to the conceit that he could recognize and proclaim justice, for with this philosophy he would accept no compromise with those he considered wrongdoers. Likewise, the successful tyrant is patient; he may lack patience, but the lack always falls sort of an active characteristic, and if need be he will wait for his ends. Klearchos could not. He decided; he decreed. He wanted; he took. He tried; he failed.

Over the head of Klearchos a catastrophic storm was brewing. An urgent appeal from the Byzantines had jerked Sparta into action. At first an embassy was sent to Klearchos ordering him to lay down his power. He was too old a hand to panic. Expecting little mercy from his home government, he took no heed of their naked threats and, when they responded with force, Klearchos, with mercenary army and treasure chest, withdrew westward to Selymbria, a *polis* on the north shore of the Propontis that he currently controlled.

Even for a seasoned veteran like Klearchos it must have been a slightly nervous moment as he looked down from the city walls at the army gathered against him, recognizing all the familiar faces of old comrades, men with whom on occasion he had fought alongside in the bloody scrimmages of times past – and with whom he had probably also drunk in the communal messes back home. He would have reckoned instinctively the number of spear points, the bearing of hoplites, the weight of their arms, and apply for the thousandth time that sixth sense by which an old soldier can feel trouble in the breeze. No doubt too, the bitter memory of how the *polis* was delivered over to the Athenians during the first occasion he was its harmost played its part to prompt Klearchos' decision to vacate Byzantium without a fight. Nonetheless, outside Selymbria the renegade governor did offer his fellow Spartans battle, but, after losing in a long and bloody struggle, he was shut up with a few diehard companions inside its walls and besieged.

Klearchos was in the soup, full fathom five. His first freelance military adventure had ended in failure, and he was likely to have suffered from some measure of self-regret. After tasting high leadership and demonstrating an appetite for it, loss of power would never be easy for him to accept. Nonetheless, for a man with not many cards in his hand, he played his hand brilliantly. Where a lesser man might have simply thrown up his cards and forswore his game for that time and always, in his desperation perhaps seeking to secure Selymbria and hold it against the odds, Klearchos, never one to give up in any case, quietly slipped out one dark night and crossed over to Ionia, 'where', writes Diodoros, 'he became intimate with Cyrus, the brother of the Persian king and won command of his troops'.[29] Clearly Klearchos was not a man to be satisfied with a minor part in another man's ambitious schemes.

Out with the pretender

In 407 BC Cyrus the Younger, as he is known to history, had been appointed by his father, Dareios II Ochos (r. 424–405/4 BC), 'commander-in-chief of all the forces that muster in the plain of Kastolos';[30] it expressed the Great King's determination to put an end to Greeks playing one satrap against another and to bring Athens to defeat. Anyway, this command, in effect, made him lord of all but one of the satrapies of western Anatolia (Ionia, Lydia, Greater Phrygia, Cappadocia), thereby practically superseding Tissaphernes who, as the incumbent satrap, retained only the lesser satrapy of Caria and possibly part of Ionia. This was a remarkable decision, for Cyrus was not yet seventeen years old, and many more experienced princes and nobles, including his elder brother, were available. Even the devious double-dealing Tissaphernes belonged to one of the most important Persian families. His father is not known, but his grandfather was the Hydarnes who had commanded the élite corps of Immortals during Xerxes' ill-fated invasion of mainland Greece.[31] Hydarnes bore his father's name, and Hydarnes senior had been one of the seven noble Persian conspirators who killed the usurper Gaumâta and placed Xerxes' father, Dareios the Great, on the throne back in 522 BC.[32] Tissaphernes, in other words, was Persian *crème de la crème*. He was also a man whose natural environment was the labyrinthine politics that centred on personal animosities, treachery, and opportunism, the machinations of men bent on getting power or holding power.

As for Cyrus, he was the second son of Dareios and Parysatis. Passed over the succession on his father's death, he nevertheless claimed by right of porphyrogeniture instead of primogeniture, for, unlike his elder brother, Artaxerxes, he had been 'born in the purple'.[33] When his ally Lysandros, the Spartan *nauarchos*, defeated the Athenian fleet off Aigospotamoi, Cyrus was actually at the Persian court for the coronation of his elder brother Artaxerxes II Mnemon (r. 405–358 BC). Cyrus was a man whose ambitions outstripped his prospects and, supported by his (and Artaxerxes') mother, he returned to Sardis, Lydia, where he put in train preparations for a *coup d'état*, which included the recruitment of the Ten Thousand.

The adventurer does not live by the same rules others do; he accepts as temporary what others, in their staid lives, believe is permanent. For Klearchos, 401 BC was a good year and a bad year. It was a time for upward mobility through force of arms and political cunning. He was to establish himself as the commander of a professional mercenary army larger enough to engage the militia forces of any single Greek state. Towards the end of the year, however, he was dead. Klearchos little knew, as the biographers say, of this yet. But as usual the gods were fighting on his side, and so begins his last and boldest escapade of his adventurous and bloodstained life.

There was no place like the Persian empire for making a comeback, and Klearchos, now or ever, was no man to hesitate. After his disappointed experience in Byzantium, he quickly became immersed in the very different world of Persia with its overlapping layers of politics, plotting and violence. For now we find the exiled Spartan employed by Cyrus to maintain a force of hoplite mercenaries in the Chersonese. Presumably Klearchos already had with him the remnants of the mercenaries with whom he had supported his unsuccessful reign of terror in Byzantium. Now his efforts against the wild Thracian tribes earned him the gratitude and, what is more important, material contributions from the Hellespontine *poleis*. Or so says Xenophon,[34] but looking at Klearchos' track record to date could we not argue that this was a case of good old-fashioned extortion? Having already passed over the entire Byzantine incident in silence, it appears that Xenophon is once again guilty of covering up the unsavoury aspects of Klearchos' violent career.[35] Remember that Klearchos was always the man of action, with a quick and preferably drastic solution to any problem.

As retold by Froissart, the reminiscences of that mediaeval freebooter and mercenary captain, the Bascot de Mauléon, tell us that he once gained a princely sum of money through 'plunder, protection-money, and various strokes of luck',[36] the latter including the crafty stratagem of capturing a castle and then ransoming it back to its former owner at a lucrative price. Perhaps this was the sort of outlandish behaviour that the Athenian pamphleteer Isokrates was condemning when he equated mercenary service with atrocities such as brigandage, violence, extortion and general lawlessness.[37] Ironically, in 342 BC Athens sent one of its *stratêgoi*, Diopeithes was the scoundrel's name, to the Chersonese, who was assigned the task of 'safeguarding Athenian interests' there – a classic euphemism. Commanding a mercenary army, the ambitious and self-seeking Diopeithes was little more than a state-sponsored pirate who lived by extorting protection money from the merchant ships that passed through the Hellespont.[38]

Returning to Klearchos and his campaign against the Thracians in the Chersonese, it is interesting to note that Xenophon does not dwell on the actual details of the fighting, merely commenting that the Thracians were defeated in battle and Klearchos then 'plundered them in every way'.[39] Yet Polyainos relates a grim tale to illustrate that Klearchos was not interested in making peace with the Thracians, despite their desire to do so.[40] Apparently he saw Klearchos' conduct in the Chersonese as nothing more than that of an out-and-out freebooter – as indeed it was.

In the mean time, the bulk of the Ten Thousand slowly assembled at Sardis, in western Anatolia, under the Greek *stratêgoi* who had originally raised the various mercenary contingents for Cyrus. Klearchos and his contingent, on the other hand, were not to join Cyrus' army until it had reached the Phrygian city of Celaenae, a month or so after the march upcountry had begun.[41] It was not, however, until the Ten Thousand had crossed Phrygia and thereby entered Cilicia that they voiced their doubts about Cyrus' supposed punitive expedition against the unruly Pisidians.[42] The mercenaries began to suspect that they were marching against the Great King himself, and so mutinied. From this affair Klearchos emerged as the *de facto* Greek commander-in-chief, gaining the confidence, not only of the mutinous mercenaries but of Cyrus too. In doing so, he displaced Xenias of Parrhasia, who had served the prince longer and, hitherto, had been the top dog amongst the various Greek *stratêgoi*.[43] What is more, when more than 2,000 men from the commands of Xenias and Pasion the Megarian transferred to that of Klearchos, Cyrus took no steps to restore them, thus endorsing the Spartan's position.[44] His influence here, both with the prince and the mercenaries, was great and growing.

It was Klearchos' destiny to be the generalissimo, *stratêgos autokratôr*, of Cyrus' Greek mercenaries, despite rival claims to the position from the likes of Meno the Thessalian. By comparison, Meno was too young, too conceited, and totally lacking in self-control for such a high-pressure position: this much we can glean from Plato's sympathetic portrayal of Meno in his dialogue of the same name.[45] With so much at stake for Cyrus it is not surprising that the prince eventually showed the Spartan such favour that he became in effect the chief Greek *stratêgos*. Cyrus, for instance, invited Klearchos, alone of the Greeks, to take part in the treason trial of Orontas, a blue-bloodied Persian who had intended to throw in his lot with Artaxerxes.[46] Finally, at Cunaxa, not only does the Spartan hold the right wing, the position of honour, but also it was to Klearchos that the prince gave instructions for the coming battle.[47]

Various elements played their part in the eventual downfall of Meno, but his bid for the leadership of the Ten Thousand probably collapsed after his violent clash with the Spartan. Klearchos had condemned one of Meno's soldiers to be flogged after a brawl broke out among a group of mercenaries purchasing supplies at a market, and so incurred the hatred of his comrades. In the ugly quarrel that ensued, the Thessalian lost face when he and his command took fright when they suddenly realized that the Spartan was quite prepared to resort to a bloodletting in order to satisfy his grievance over almost being killed by stoning.[48] From that you can see very well that whoever strives for power usually gets a lemon, and when we read that Klearchos, after Meno's soldier had been flogged at the market, rode through the middle of Meno's camp with just a small escort in tow, we are left wondering if the cunning old dog had set up the whole episode so as to put the young pup back in his place. Thereafter, the two rivals for Cyrus' favours were kept as far as part as was possible.

If Meno was somewhat out of his depth when it came to the rough and tumble of mercenary leadership, he was, on the other hand, more at home in the arena of political intrigue. Xenophon informs us, in his damning character sketch of Meno, that the Thessalian 'prided himself upon ability to deceive, the fabrication of lies, and the mocking of friends'.[49] Meno's 'ability to deceive' certainly came to the fore when Cyrus' army reached the Euphrates. This was the moment when the prince chose to inform the Greek *stratêgoi* that he was intent on toppling his brother, the Great King. When the Ten Thousand heard that they were expected to march on Babylon they refused to go on, only doing so after Cyrus had promised them a bounty when the army had reached Babylon and their pay in full once they had returned to Sardis.[50]

Meno, however, saw this mutiny as a golden opportunity to secure for himself the objective upon which his heart was firmly set. Before it is clear what answer the Ten Thousand would give to Cyrus, Meno delivered to his soldiers an eloquent speech – he had been taught by the celebrated rhetorician and orator, Gorgias of Leontini[51] – in which he laid before them a devious plan by which Cyrus would be placed into their debt. Meno's scheme was to cross the Euphrates alone, and by doing so his contingent would be seen as true zealots for the prince's cause and thus be well rewarded. Moreover, and this was the beauty of the plan, if the others refused to go on then Meno's men could simply come back across the river and return with the rest to Sardis and look forward to a life of ease as garrison troops.[52] Naturally, Meno's men were persuaded to cross and, naturally, Cyrus was delighted that they did so. As a result the artless soldiers received rich promises, while their artful leader received rich gifts.[53] Even the strong are ruled by the weak and treacherous.

Despite losing out to Klearchos, Meno never surrendered his burning desire to command the Ten Thousand, and during the uncertain days that followed Cunaxa our young Thessalian was busy seeking ways and means to bring this about. The Greek mercenaries represented only a part of Cyrus' army, the most conspicuous part. Now it so happens that Meno was a very intimate friend of Ariaios, Cyrus' lieutenant and commander of his native troops, and it is through him that he made his bid for power. For after Cyrus' death on the field of Cunaxa and having then refused Klearchos' loaded offer of the throne of Persia, Ariaios had thrown in his lot with Tissaphernes, who was acting on the behalf of Artaxerxes during the negotiations between the Greeks and the Persians. Ever diligent, Klearchos not only suspected Meno of having clandestine meetings with Tissaphernes, but also of organizing a putsch in order to take over the army.[54] With the leadership of the Ten Thousand under his belt, Meno would stand to gain for himself any benefits resulting from a reconciliation with Persia.[55] This, of course, all came to nothing. Klearchos, wishing to secure his own position and pursue his own schemes, agreed to Tissaphernes' proposal that the Greek *stratêgoi* should meet with him so as to discuss the future. And so the Spartan and the Thessalian, along with three other *stratêgoi*, went to their untimely deaths, Meno, retorts Xenophon, meeting the 'death of a scoundrel'.[56] Perhaps punishment for Meno was first unbearable torture, then swift execution. A bitter irony. As an old saying goes, he that is born to be hanged will never be drowned.

Inside the mind

Klearchos had a reputation for brutality, but it was a sort of calculated brutality contrived to create the maximum fear and therefore the minimum resistance to his will. Thus, in the role of commander, he was commonly a harsh disciplinarian: he thought that an undisciplined army was good for nothing, and was reported even to have said, just as Frederick the Great would later say, that 'the soldier should fear his officer more than the enemy'.[57] It looks as if Klearchos failed, or more probably did not wish to develop the 'common touch' of command: the ability to empathize with his men, to take stock of their condition and mood, and then structure his plans accordingly without the threat of brute force. Yet it is that quality of leadership that Xenophon has in mind when he explains that commanders should be just in their dealings with their soldiers,[58] a leadership quality that Sun Tzu, the brilliant military theorist and one of the ablest commanders of ancient China (*fl.* 500 BC), had a century or so earlier postulated in his *Art of War* that 'soldiers must be treated in the first instance with humanity, but kept under control by means of iron discipline. This is the certain road to victory'.[59] On the other hand, Klearchos probably believed that it was not the business of soldiers to like him. They just did what he ordered them to do. Klearchos therefore vigorously wielded the stick, the coercive aspects of morale, without the offered carrot, its persuasive aspects. Obviously, he was a defiant champion of single-minded, hard-boiled militarism.

The Spartan had a very mediocre opinion of humanity as a whole and, having been a professional soldier for the best part of his life, in all likelihood only tolerated the camaraderie of fellow hard men who also, like him, loved the adventure of this type of soldiering where survival not so much depended on rigid routine and formal training as well as on the ready acceptance of a necessary discipline, observed willingly by all. The latter condition was certainly the case when Klearchos was in command of the Ten Thousand, for the soldiers 'yielded to him implicit obedience', while 'their fear of punishment at his hands kept them in a fine state of discipline'.[60] And just in case there were any slackers within the ranks, Klearchos had to hand a stout stick, which he would readily apply to their backs.[61]

Klearchos may not have had the gift of gaining the affection of his soldiers nor that of the enforcement of a salutary discipline save by acts of extreme severity, but none of this alters the fact that in his smooth handling of the mutiny the hard man showed that, when harshness failed, he could drop his gruff, offensive manner and dissimulate, coax, and use honeyed words as cleverly, though not so elegantly, as any silver-tongued Athenian orator. A 50 per cent increase in pay was no doubt what most of the mercenaries really desired – pay, as Klearchos knew well enough, being a crucial issue in any mercenary force – but they were also given assurances that they were only marching against Abrokomas, the satrap of Syria and Phoenicia. But at Thapsakos on the Euphrates, as we know, it was necessary to come clean and so Cyrus called all his commanders and announced his real purpose. Xenophon says that Klearchos was the only Greek who had known from the very first.[62] In response the *stratêgoi* summoned a soldier assembly, and again the army, after a ready display of anger, was persuaded through the usual promises of more money and gratuities. It is worth pointing out here that the Ten Thousand enjoyed a liberality of association, as they held spirited and boisterous assemblies, voted on proposals, and enjoyed a familiarity with their betters unknown to the Persians, a sort of nationhood of men-at-arms. Greeks were accustomed to discussing public affairs with a liberty of speech and action, and it was difficult to cure them of the habit – most dangerous in camp – of expressing their opinions about public acts and events. Such discussions were often fatal to the safety of an army, and thus, the habits of freedom, while they added to the courage of the citizen, may also diminish the fortitude unlicensed speech too often shakes.

On the field of Cunaxa there was no hint of disunity among the Greek mercenaries. We find the mercenary army well tuned and running smoothly with Klearchos at the throttle, the mercenaries acting as one under his leadership.[63] But he refused to comply with Cyrus' battle plan,[64] and his own tactics proved quite unadapted to the different conditions of a hoplite army in foreign service outside Greece. He smashed the enemy left in true Spartan style, clearing the field of slipper-wearing Persians. It was a bravura performance but when he found himself outflanked, he simply retired, casual, cocky and with no more than one casualty to show for his military adventure. Consequently, Klearchos discovered the next day that his Persian boss had perished in the fray. This left the rebellion without a pretender, Ariaios having refused the throne of Persia, which Klearchos had quickly offered him.[65]

It cannot be said of Klearchos that he ever lost his head. Quick wits and initiative are required to seize the fleeting opportunities of the game of making and breaking kings. For during this critical period, he confirmed his authority, not merely through his Spartan professionalism and stern discipline, but by force of example. Conviction breeds conviction. 'Henceforth he commanded and they obeyed,' writes the eye-witness Xenophon, 'not that they had chosen him, but because they saw that he alone possessed the wisdom which a commander should have, while the rest were without experience'.[66] Undoubtedly, Klearchos had many enemies, both between the soldiers and the *stratêgoi*, but few could deny his capacities in the art of violence – and violent were the days ahead. Significantly, Klearchos had never waited for the action or trouble to come to him. Klearchos really started to make things hum, and in him the rank and file saw they had as a commander one who could fight, and one who would punish friend and foe alike. They were looking at a real soldier, many of them for the first time, and they all knew he would sort them out in his stiff unfriendliness. The development of these all-important instruments of command would serve Klearchos well. When Persian heralds came to discuss a truce, for example, his laconic reply of 'no truce without breakfast' procured both a truce and full stomachs for his men.[67] Similarly, when Klearchos had earlier been offered a truce if the mercenaries stayed put, or war if they advanced or retreated, he brutally replied in a tone which was a proof in itself: 'A truce if we remain; if we retire or advance, war',[68] and so with this say-nothing answer he concealed his true intentions. We can easily imagine Klearchos' way of speaking, clipped and soldierly, missing out every word that well could be missed out from a notion that words were precious and ought not to be wasted.

Left to their own guidance, the Ten Thousand stood on the defensive and resisted Artaxerxes' persistent demands to disarm. As Proxenos, Xenophon's good friend from Thebes, wittily said on one of these tense occasions:

> I wonder if the King is asking for our arms on the assumption that he is victorious, or simply as gifts, on the assumption that we are his friends. For if he asks for them as victor, why need he ask for them, instead of coming and taking them?[69]

It shows what men can do when they have a commander with a determined purpose and a resolution that never flags. Their short-term position was remarkably good. Though not the largest, they were the best organized and best armed force anywhere within the Persian empire. Some of the mercenaries however, in an obvious moment of weakness (or was it idleness – a dangerous situation for any body of men), did offer themselves for service with Persia against Egypt, which was in revolt yet again.[70] Nonetheless, the Great King was probably every bit as eager to get the Greeks off his hands as quick as possible, he, no doubt remembering how they had handled themselves at Cunaxa, saw plentiful reasons for concern in the Greeks' self-sufficiency and battle worthiness. He was anxious to avoid a fight with the well-equipped foreigners. Finally, the deadlock was broken by Tissaphernes, a man with the iron cunning and cruelty of the crocodile, who appeared and announced that he had persuaded Artaxerxes to let him lead them back to Greece.[71]

Actually, Tissaphernes led them across the Tigris so as to have the mercenaries isolated and at the Great King's mercy. Klearchos, in a personal interview with Tissaphernes, renewed an earlier offer of service against Egypt, and hinted besides that the satrap might fill Cyrus' shoes as their leader and thereby use the mercenaries in his satrapy with a view to toppling Artaxerxes at a later date.[72] Manifestly, Klearchos still believed he had a strong position from which to negotiate. He certainly used all the right words, the way he always did, and that what made him so dangerous. So Tissaphernes, with the elaborate courtesy of a well-bred Persian, feigned to regard this as an honour, and without delay invited the *stratêgoi* to come and show to him their newly discovered loyalty. Obviously Klearchos had an unquenchable belief in his own abilities, which helped Tissaphernes to play him like a fish, letting out enough line to encourage him to get the hook ever more deeply embedded in his jaws as he sought his rendezvous with history. Moreover, by exploiting the rivalries and the vanities of the Greek commanders, the sharp satrap was able to capture not only Klearchos but four of his fellow *stratêgoi* too, being bundled off 'to the king and were beheaded'.[73] Klearchos had made the classic mistake that was fatal to so many mercenary leaders, the mistake of separating himself physically from his men. Besides, though he believed himself to be worldly wise, he was a mere infant when he opposed such men as the adroit Tissaphernes.

Wise or not, Klearchos was one tough cookie who lived (and died) for soldiering. The Spartan also enjoyed the hardships and the dangers that went with such a mercenary adventure as that put together by Cyrus: soldiering and action were synonymous for him. More important, Klearchos was cool in any crisis and was certainly well versed in all the tricks and stratagems of campaigning *outre-mer*. He certainly had what the French military call *le cran*, 'guts', for in the depths of danger his men 'were ready to obey him implicitly and would choose no other to command them'.[74] No commander can offer a soldier sufficient payment for his life. But a good commander can inspire a soldier to give it to him.

The good (mercenary) commander

A comparison. It has been said of the French commander in chief, the moustached and paunchy *Généralissime* (later *Maréchal*) Joseph Jacques Césaire 'Papa' Joffre, that while his dusty sweating columns fell back along the baking poplar-lined *pavé* of northen France towards the capital, he stopped work at noon exactly, took his seat at a table laid with gleaming crisp cloth, silver and crystal outside his headquarters and spent the next two hours fortifying the inner man. For the professional Spartan, at least, the good *stratêgos* needed to have a definite presence on (and off) the battlefield, like Klearchos or even Agesilaos, who toiled alongside his men in simple attire and thereby gained not only 'their obedience and their affection' but also their grudging respect.[75] Joffre's sedentary role would have deeply puzzled Agesilaos. The Spartan king would have noted that the French general failed all together to show himself to the enemy, and that he probably saw not a single German throughout August 1914, unless the German was a high-ranking prisoner-of-war.

Although Xenophon very rightly observes the fact that personal leadership in battle demands heroism, he was also shrewd (and experienced) enough to realize that other qualities were needed in the exercise of command. In this respect, Xenophon's hagiography of Agesilaos sets out to define the model professional general. His Spartan simplicity of dress, his moderate consumption of food and drink, his indifference to the elements and the needs of sleep, and his delight in toils made the king his men's equal, but he was also their trusted commander by surpassing them in endurance and inspiring his army as a whole through personal bravery. Above all, by keeping close to the daily existence of the rank and file, Agesilaos was the embodiment of the 'soldiers' general'. Sokrates, it has been told, was a brave soldier, and his description of a good general is as good as any, indeed better than most, and is in fact the one we are going to use here for Agesilaos: 'He must be inventive, active and attentive, persevering and brilliant, both friendly and harsh, both straightforward and subtle, a good protector and a good thief, lavish and rapacious, generous and grasping, steady and aggressive'.[76] If Xenophon fully recognized that the basis of leadership was the ability to care for one's command, he also fully understood that the bedrock of man management was discipline, especially in a mercenary army. Discipline depends to a large extent on long service under respected and responsible commanders. The hard man Klearchos built morale on strict discipline.[77]

Long before Napoléon, du Picq, or Foch, Xenophon had fully appreciated that morale counted for more than mere numbers: 'For you understand, I am sure, that it is neither numbers nor strength which wins victories in wars; but whichever of the two sides it be whose troops, by the blessing of the gods, advance to the attack with stouter hearts, against those troops their adversaries generally refuse to stand'.[78] Speaking to an assembly of officers, Xenophon continues, explaining that he had experienced this phenomenon firsthand. What he had experienced and understood is fighting spirit. Now war naturally generates a sense of unity, of pride, of identity, of excitement. But war also generates a human cost, and such costs are measured in death, disease, wounds and profound personal suffering. The fear of war's price tag is the soldier's universal lot, but it is fighting spirit that enables him to cope with the very harrowing business of battle and thereby sustain his will to fight. Training, experience and discipline – the physical components of professional soldiering – all play their respective part in its creation, but, as Xenophon has pointed out to us, it is morale that is the single deciding factor in war.

With an emphasis on equity rather than efficiency, the morale of a citizen army was determined too much by the feelings of each individual hoplite, and a *stratêgos'* power of punishing breaches of discipline, for instance, was limited to say the least, especially as he was subject to political and judicial control.[79] According to Aristotle, Athenian *stratêgoi* could either imprison, exile or fine a citizen soldier for breaches of discipline, but we gain the distinct impression that to do so a *stratêgos* would have to present the charges in the law courts.[80] In reality, the citizen general dare not make himself unpopular by his strictness.[81]

When we turn to Sparta, we are of course in a rather different world. Here the Spartan kings did not suffer from such political hindrances. In the very professional army of Sparta the cure for insubordination, for example, was to make the offender stand on guard duty carrying his shield.[82] According to Frontinus, Lysandros had a soldier flogged for leaving the ranks while on the march. When the soldier protested, saying he had not left for the purpose of pillage, Lysandros supposedly retorted: 'I won't have you look as if you were going to pillage'.[83] Unfortunately we are not told if Lysandros' soldier was a fellow Spartan or one from an allied contingent, but, as Thucydides makes clear, in an army that 'was composed of officers commanding other officers',[84] discipline would have been generally tight for Spartan and non-Spartan alike.

Similarly, mercenary commanders tended to emancipate themselves from the socio-political framework of the *polis*. Therefore in a mercenary army, provided of course its commander could ensure his men's pay, his authority could be absolute. Moreover, a successful mercenary captain could wield his powers beneficially and thus foster a corporate spirit as well as keep a tight rein upon discipline within the mercenary ranks. Theoretically of course, mercenary captains would need to hit a paternalistic mean between the excessive severity of Klearchos and the excessive leniency of Xenophon's comrade-in-arms and *stratêgos*, Proxenos the Boiotian. But there was much more to success as a commander than simple popularity and charm. Soldiers generally preferred a hard man who knew what he was doing to a genial incompetent. The greater a man's charm, the less he is capable of action. The very opposite of such men as Klearchos, who was odious to all those who served him. Besides, it is not a soldier's business to like a general. He just does what he tells him. In practice, therefore, a balancing act was not generally feasible when commanding an army of hard-bitten rogues, guttersnipes and scoundrels, and perhaps Klearchos was correct in believing, especially in wartime, the nearer one came to the enemy the more the soldiers should be kept in a state of fear.

Whatever else one may say, aside from Klearchos himself, Cyrus' Greek *stratêgoi* fell well short of the mark when measured against the Xenophonic canons of leadership, the skills that were required if a mercenary captain was to handle a professional army to any degree of success. Klearchos had his faults. He, for instance, set a high standard of discipline for his men and applied the same rigid standard for himself. The net effect of this was to make him aloof and unapproachable, serious and unlovely. Of course, this unchanging attitude towards his men meant they knew exactly where they stood with him at all times. On the other hand, Klearchos was not shackled by lofty idealism as was Proxenos,[85] and although he sought fame and fortune, he did not single-mindedly lust after the sensuality of power as Meno obviously did, and power, as Henry Kissinger once observed, is for some an aphrodisiac.[86] Not one to simply worship power for its own sake, Klearchos was, in a sense, the archetypal military adventurer, comfortably playing the role of kingmaker-cum-soldier. He was remorseless, he was relentless, and he fitted in with his environment. So long as anywhere in the world kings were being made and unmade, men like him were doing it. Though they hardly ever die in their beds, such men hope to carve out for themselves a pocket-sized kingdom for the support and pleasure of their old age.

A parallel life

Robert Denard, born Gilbert Bourgeaud (7 April 1929), was a classic Gallic soldier-of-fortune, what the French call a *baroudeur*, a battler, physically large, colourfully dressed, moustachioed, and a Gascon. Aged twenty-two, son of a Bordeaux peasant farmer, the marine NCO Denard had fought in and survived the colonial mess that was French Indochina. He later served as a *gendarme* in the security forces in Morocco, which led to his involvement in shadowy right-wing activities, the most notorious being the 1954 attempt to liquidate Prime Minister Pierre Mendès France, a Jewish intellectual and member of the Radical Socialist Party who was negotiating the end of the Indochina War and withdrawal from Morocco. The plot's eventual failure was to cost Denard a fourteen-month sojourn in prison.[87]

Robert Denard first pops up as a mercenary during the summer of 1960 fighting for Moïse-Kapenda Tshombé, the president of the mineral-rich Katanga province (later Shaba province) in the south-east of Congo, bordering Northern Rhodesia (now Zimbabwe) and Angola. Tshombé, with covert military and technical assistance from Belgium, which included 500 mercenaries to lead his army, had taken advantage of an armed mutiny by the *ANC* (*Armée Nationale Congolaise*)[88] to announce the secession of his province from the newly independent Congo Republic (formally the Belgian Congo, scion of the Congo Free State, later Zaire and now renamed the Democratic Republic of Congo).[89] Alongside other white mercenaries, Denard initially served under Roger Faulques, a French Foreign Legion intelligence officer from the recently disbanded *1er REP* (*Régiment Étranger de Parachutistes*).[90] Two years later, Faulques having left Katanga, Denard took command of the remaining thirty or so white mercenaries for a last-ditch stand, alongside remnants of the Katangese *Gendarmerie*, against a UN peacekeeping force spearheaded by Indian and British-trained Nepalese Gurkha soldiers.[91]

It was here, at the battle of Kolwezi (12–15 January 1963), that Denard was to earn a reputation for personal bravery and loyalty that his later activities were to do little to justify. Incidentally, 'Colonel Bob' was too flamboyant a character for the English-speaking mercenaries to take seriously, and was viewed by the Belgians with a mixture of uneasy admiration and deep suspicion. Although defeated at Kolwezi and finally forced to retreat into neighbouring Angola – the Portuguese denying that any mercenaries had so much as set foot on their soil – Denard was not to remain idle for long. With a handful of Frenchmen, he followed his former chief, Faulques, to North Yemen in order to help train the Saudi-Jordanian-backed royalist troops of Imam Mohammed al-Badr, which were currently fighting against the Egyptian-backed communists in that country's civil war. Denard was a devout anticommunist.

Katanga was reintegrated into the Congo Republic and the UN eventually withdrew their forces. Tshombé was to take a much-needed vacation in Spain before returning home later. He did so 'by the big door' in June 1964, to assume the post of Congo's prime minister. However, prior to Tshombé's triumphant return a fresh rebellion had arisen, this time in Kwilu province, east of Léopoldville (now Kinshasa). The *Simbas* ('lions' in Kiswahili), as the separatists styled themselves, were anointed with *Mai Mulélé*, 'Mulélé Water', which was supposed to turn bullets to water – in fact narcotics such as hemp or *dagga* were the main reason for their seeming immortality.[92] This time, with its own army in a state of abject terror and the deserting troops, true to form, carrying out massacres and robberies as the *Simbas*, a tough and merciless foe albeit poorly armed and badly trained, swept through the country, it was the central government that hired white mercenaries.

By March 1964 Denard was back in the turbulent Congo and commanding the French-speaking *1er choc*. According to a fellow mercenary, Irish-born Major 'Mad' Mike Hoare, Denard was 'a soldier of some ability and a well respected leader'.[93] A year later he was leading the parent unit, 6 Commando, after the commander-in-chief of the *ANC*, Général Joseph-Désiré Mobutu, had seized the reins of power in Léopoldville with the covert encouragement of the United States. The *coup d'état* of 25 November 1965 had turned out to be a bloodless event, and Mobutu was subsequently able to dismiss all the white mercenary captains hired by the old régime.[94] Nonetheless, the following summer Denard's loyalty to Mobutu was sorely tested when some one thousand of Tshombé's former Katanga *gendarmes*, who were officered by non-Congolese, mutinied. Unlike some of his fellow white mercenaries, Denard sat on the fence, and in a short African nightmare of treachery, bloodshed, massacre and sudden death the rebellion collapsed. Radio Léopoldville announced at the time: 'Most of the mercenaries grouped around Colonel Bob Denard at Stan [Stanleyville, now Kisangani] have remained loyal to the Republic'. In December 1966, however, Denard took leave in order to visit his dying mother in France: it was later rumoured that he also took the liberty to meet secretly with Tshombé, once again exiled in Madrid. What was to follow was to become known worldwide as the 'mercenaries' revolt'.

On 3 July 1967 Mobutu, his country seething with plots and counterplots, ordered Denard to disarm 10 Commando. Jean 'Black Jack' Schramme led this mercenary unit, a Flemish Belgian plantation owner turned mercenary captain of whom Mobutu was particularly suspicious. Alongside Mobutu's role of feudal overlord, Schramme played the semi-independent vassal. Denard, for his part, made no move to follow his orders. Either suspecting his command, 6 Commando, was next for disarmament, or fearing the dilemma where he had to take up arms against a fellow white mercenary, Denard helped to organize a revolt against his black paymaster. It is highly probable that he was also involved in a French-sponsored conspiracy for the return of Tshombé, who represented a real threat to the Mobutu régime, given his fortune, his European connections, and his private army of mercenaries and *gendarmes*, some of whom had returned to Angola to help the Portuguese fight the national liberation movement.[95]

The mutiny began at six o'clock on the morning of 5 July. Although initially successful, the rebellion was faltering by early August. Schramme was cornered and finally bottled up in the eastern border town of Bakuvu and, despite Denard's gallant attempt to open up a 'second front' via his bicycle borne invasion of Katanga from Angola, was forced to retreat into Rwanda. Here, on 13 November, Schramme and his men were promptly disarmed and interned. Unbeknown to Schramme and Denard, the fatal blow had been struck when the cause lost its figurehead. Tshombé, with rumours of his impending return to the Congo rife, was kidnapped on 30 June 1967 and taken to Algeria. Tshombé was to remain under house arrest near Algiers, and two years later he died of a 'heart attack'.[96]

During the next decade, in a flurry of mercenary activity, Bob Denard turned up, leading his own band of mercenaries, in various parts of Black Africa. The early summer of 1975 found him operating in the Indian Ocean, more of which later. The following year he was active in Angola and in Cabinda, the Portuguese enclave at the mouth of the Congo River. The Angolan contract casts a little light upon Denard's nebulous connections with the netherworld, for he secured the contract after clandestine talks with the CIA (Central Intelligence Agency) and the *SDECE* (*Service de Documentation Extérieure et de Contre-Espionnage*), the French intelligence service, both of whom wanted Denard to train the *UNITA* forces of Dr Jonas Malheiro Savimbi.[97] Apparently, the CIA gave Denard US $350,000 so he could recruit twenty Frenchmen on a contract for five months.[98] Later in the same year Denard was in the pay of President Omar Bongo of Gabon, as one of a select team of 'military advisers'. His contract was twofold. First, to help train the élite presidential guard and, second, to liquidate some of Bongo's more troublesome opponents. In January 1977 with the Gabon behind him, Denard arrived in another former French colony, in this case Benin. Here he was to lead an unsuccessful *coup d'etat* against the Marxist régime of President Mathieu Kérékou.[99]

Now came the crescendo of Denard's mercenary career, for his next adventure turned out to be a runaway success. In May 1978 Denard fulfilled the dream of mercenary captains throughout history; he took over a country for himself, the tiny Comoro Islands. Few people had ever heard of the Comoros, fewer yet would be able to lay a finger on the map and proclaim with total confidence *et voilà!* Nevertheless, the four dots that make up this Indian Ocean archipelago have always been strategic. Situated as they are between Madagascar and Mozambique at the northern end of the Mozambique Channel, in the era of the so-called 'warring sultans' the Comoros were a nest of slave-trading Arab, Persian, and Malay pirates, and pirates have always had a weather eye for strategic locations. Inescapably, a major European power was eventually lured to this strategic prize, and in 1843 France annexed the tiniest dot of the four, Île de Mayotte.[100]

Denard had already been involved in the islands' politics in August 1975, having aided in the coup, which began just weeks after independence, which overthrew its president, the Comoran nobleman and French senator, Ahmed Abdallah Abderamane. The way was now paved for the rise of Ali Soilih, the justice minister who was an easy-going intellectual steeped in the traditions of the May 1968 Paris students' revolt. The Comoros was soon to become the only state in the world where the extravagant ideas of May 1968 were actually put into practice.

Naturally, although technically independent of its rule, France shuddered. The pot-smoking Ali Soilih had gone too far, too fast, and too wildly: he put teenagers in charge, abolished history and legalized cannabis. So, on the night of 12 May 1978, Denard was back. Leading a group of forty-three mercenaries he landed on the picture-postcard beach of Itsandra, Grande Comore (now Njazidja), three kilometres from Moroni the capital city, captured the president and swept away his government before dawn. Ten days later Ahmed Abdallah Abderamane, the former president ousted by Denard, flew in from Paris to be welcomed by cheering Comorans. Within a week, it was reported that Ali Soilih had been, yes you've guessed it, 'shot while trying to escape'.[101]

The Comoros are in the back of beyond, difficult to reach, and, more important, free of journalists. It took some time for it to be realized the Colonel Hadji Said Mustafa M'hadju, minister of defence for the fledgling government, was none other than Bob Denard himself. Having taken Comoran citizenship, he was to be seen in white robes and a turban claiming to have been converted to Islam, even making the pilgrimage to Mecca. True or not, Denard acted as if the Comoros were his own personal fiefdom. And so, in a way, they were. His forty-odd mercenaries, in the main, also stayed. They formed the new presidential guard, the only armed force on the islands. Yet for Denard himself, it was a little too good to be true. The OAU (Organization of African Unity), outraged, refused to allow the Comoros back into its ranks while a notorious mercenary loomed large in its government, and on 28 September 1978 Colonel Hadji Said Mustafa M'hadju was seen off at Moroni airport by President Abdallah and his former cabinet colleagues. At a tearful farewell ceremony on the tarmac the president called the colonel a 'hero' who had saved the Comoros, its people, the Moslem religion and 'all that is humane in this country'.[102]

Despite the obvious blow to his fortunes this was not to be the end of Denard or his intimate association with the Comoros. The mercenary leader was fast approaching fifty years of age and looking for a quiet spot for his retirement. As he had said on French television, in one of his very rare interviews: 'I hate the traffic jams of Paris but I adore the smell of *ylang-ylang*'.[103] Denard was soon, much more discreetly this time, back in the Comoros, where he established a meat-importing company that held the lucrative monopoly on meat imports from apartheid South Africa. Likewise, many of his mercenaries also eased themselves into Comoran society and became 'men of affairs', reorganizing the islands' administration from street cleaning upwards.[104] And they stayed, confidently controlling the 500-strong presidential guard and the islands' security forces, and holding the monopolies of various trades with sanctioned strapped South Africa.[105] For ten years it was a mercenaries' dream, a lush and comfortable existence in a tropical paradise. By November 1989, however, the dream had turned sour and, naturally, the colonel had turned against the president; Abdallah was found murdered in his palace. Subsequent unrest drew French military intervention and Denard fled the country.

On 5 April 1993, Bob Denard had a five-year jail sentence quashed by a Parisian law court. He stood accused of taking part in the attempted *coup d'etat* in Benin. This failed adventure had resulted in the deaths of at least seven people and Denard had been condemned to death *in absentia* by the authorities in Benin. Charges of involvement in the murder of President Ahmed Abdallah Abderamane, Comoran patrician and French senator, were also dropped at the same trial; although Denard was in the president's office at the time of the assassination, he claims a panicking soldier fired the fatal shots.[106] Still, despite the favourable verdict, the assassination of the president would yet again haunt the colonel. For on 4 May 1999 Denard, now aged seventy, stood again in a Parisian law court charged with murdering the president of the Comoros ten years previously. Facing life imprisonment if found guilty Denard strenuously denied the charge, once more claiming the president was killed accidentally by a trigger-happy Comoran bodyguard. Denard was finally acquitted, despite the prosecution's compelling evidence that demonstrated Ahmed Abdallah was hit by bullets from several guns.[107]

Ancient and modern

But why, you ask, the Plutarchan parallel lives?

First, the obvious answers to this question. Both Klearchos and Denard were soldiers by nature as well as by trade. What is more, they were both charismatic commanders, which in turn led to the establishment of personal dictatorships. Both men easily played the adventurer's role of kingmaker. Both men were exiled from their homelands; Klearchos was sentenced to death *in absentia*, and Denard was under a *mandat d'arrêt*.

Second, and more important, both mercenary captains received some form of covert but nonetheless official backing for their respective adventures. The Spartans conveniently overlooked Klearchos' appointment as Cyrus' Greek generalissimo and even gave the prince a modicum of deniable military aid in the guise of 700 hoplites under the command of the Spartiate, Cheirisophos.[108] If we are to believe Diodoros, and there is no reason not to in this context, the despatching of Cheirisophos and his expeditionary force (he puts its figure at 800) was done 'with the consent of the ephors; the Lakedaimonians had not yet openly entered upon war [with Artaxerxes], but were concealing their purpose, awaiting the turn of the war'.[109] Likewise, France turned a Nelsonian eye to Denard's flamboyant activities in the Comoros, which certainly could not have succeeded without the sedentary support of the nearby French authorities, namely the naval base and the garrison of *légionnaires* maintained on Île de Mayotte, the fourth island of the Comoros. At his 1993 trial Denard was hailed as a true patriot by both the prosecution and the defence. Moreover, a string of French officials even stood up and 'testified that he had always acted with France in mind even if the state could not publicly condone his actions'.[110] I am not too sure that the ephors in Sparta would have done the same courtroom service for Klearchos, yet in both instances ancient Sparta and modern France were putting their foreign affairs in order without getting their hands grubby. Can it all be true? Well, yes actually.

On the night of 27 September 1995, Denard, leading twenty-seven mercenaries and 350 rebel Comorans, attempted to re-establish his island kingdom. His fourth Comoran coup lasted one day short of a week. Shortly before the Colonel surrendered to French troops a journalist asked him: 'Will we see you here on the next one?' '*Inshallah*', replied that Moslem convert and mercenary captain now in his sixty-seventh year.[111] In the strict sense of the definition, a soldier of fortune is a man who for pay, or for pure love of adventure, fights under the flag of any country. In a broader sense, he is the kind of man in any walk of life who wishes to make his own fortune; who, when he sees it coming, leaps to meet it, and turns it to his advantage. In brief, what Klearchos and Denard both craved was power, not the semblance of power. Such men will shake kingdoms.

But after all that, Colonel Robert Denard was perhaps wise enough to remember the words of one of his predecessors, fellow Gascon and one of the leaders of the mercenary Free Companies that terrorized France at the end of the first phase of the Hundred Years' War, the Bascot de Mauléon. 'I know of very few [companions], except myself,' the Bascot told Jean Froissart, the fascinated mediaeval chronicler, 'who were not killed in battle'.[112] 'I confirm that he has died' his sister told Reuters on 14 October 2007.[113] 'Colonel Bob' had died peacefully in his bed; not in his combat boots.

Chapter 11

Dressed to Kill

There are three distinct elements to the challenge of creating a professional army, what modern theorists term the components of fighting power. The first is physical, involving the weapons and equipment used. The second, so closely related, is conceptual, and concerns the evolution of military doctrine. The third is human, and centres on the myriad of complex factors that make men fight.

For us sceptical and cynical moderns, myths are made to give solace to those who find reality distasteful, and, if some find such fantasy comforting, so be it. However, myth and symbolism are but two sides of the same coin, and an essential component of the Lykourgan system was Sparta's deliberate manipulation of the visual. The warriors of Sparta decorated their clothes and weapons with ornaments: they wore their hair long and plaited it intricately before going into battle wreathed with flowers. Beauty breeds valour. Awe-inspiring, Spartan uniformity had a deep psychological impact upon the minds of those watching from the wrong side of the battlefield. When a Spartan phalanx stood upon the field of battle, even alongside its Peloponnesian allies, it was important to draw attention to it so as to let Sparta's reputation do its work. The crimson cloak and crimson tunic that were worn by a Spartan hoplite, along with his polished brazen-panoply, proved distinctive and memorable. The celebrated long hair was meant to be conspicuous and intimidating, and collectively the Spartans took great pride in the knowledge that their army gave the brilliant effect of consisting entirely of bronze and crimson. The uniformity of the Spartans spoke of reassuring discipline and obedience, but the long hair and the crimson hue also evoked the more primitive, tribal world of hunting and death. Intrinsically, a Spartan may have been part of an army rigidly controlled by law and order, but as an individual he was a professional killer.

At the battle of Koroneia (summer 394 BC) in the confederate army were contingents from Boiotia, Euboia, Athens, Argos, Corinth, and other *poleis*. The hoplites of Agesilaos were drawn from a still wider area of the Greek world, and even from some places outside it. The Spartiates serving with his army made up a very small proportion; the majority consisted of *neodamôdeis*, *perioikoi*, allies, mercenaries, and men from Ionia and the Hellespont. Still, they had fought together in Anatolia and had followed together the long march back; they were, furthermore, well motivated, well led, and well equipped. The Athenian Xenophon – himself amongst its ranks – describes this excellent army of Agesilaos made not so much of flesh and blood but as 'one solid mass of bronze and crimson'.[1] Xenophon aside,[2] there is a considerable body of evidence to suggest that the equipment and dress of the Spartan army were remarkably uniform. In this chapter we will look into Sparta's deliberate manipulation of what can be summed up as 'the fear of the known'.

Spartan battle dress

Small–group cohesion, upon which a soldier's fighting spirit depends, can be inculcated in a number of ways. The one that concerns us here, however, is the issue of a uniform, a distinctive dress with deep psychological symbolism all of its own. Military uniform helps to create a unit's identity and to strengthen the all-important bonds of comradeship between the unit's members. Even today, the badges of rank that accompany a military uniform emphasize the hierarchical structure of armies and encourage deference and due respect. Today, however armies of almost all nations dress for war in combinations of brown, green and yellow, whereas before soldiers went to war wearing a rainbow assortment of bright colours, ornamented with gold and silver, surmounted with plumes and feathers, trimmed with furs and leathers. For centuries uniforms also included features clearly designed to make the wearer look broader (hence epaulettes and brandenburgs), taller (high shakos and bearskin caps), fiercer (whiskers and long hair) or more virile (codpieces and sporrans), and to promote the soldier's status in the eyes of comrades, civilians and enemy alike.

But let's return to that evocative phrase of Xenophon, 'one solid mass of bronze and crimson'. By this date hoplites had long abandoned the bronze bell-shaped corselet commonly worn by their ancestors, and wore instead the lighter more flexible linen corselet.[3] All the same, the term 'bronze' (*chalkós*) could refer to the bronze helmet, or bronze greaves, or the bronze facing of the hoplite shield or, as seems more likely, the overall effect produced by these bronze accoutrements when the Spartan phalanx was viewed as a whole from the other side of the battlefield. This effect would have been particularly striking as prior to battle the Spartans, as was their custom, would habitually burnish their arms and armour to its most brilliant sheen.[4] Shields, in particular, flashing like mirrors must have been enough to unsettle if not strike terror into the enemy, and Euripides, in one of his plays, likened the flashing of bronze accoutrements to 'lightning flashes in a storm'.[5] The term 'crimson' (*phoiníkeos*), on the other hand, undoubtedly refers to the colour of the Spartan tunic and military cloak, although the latter garment was most probably discarded before battle commenced. In the words of Xenophon, who stood alongside Agesilaos at Koroneia, the king 'prided himself on the simplicity of his own dress and the splendid equipment of his army'.[6] Obviously these professionals, like all professional killers before and after them, kept their weaponry and equipment well tended and ready for action.

While uniform, in the sense of a national military costume principally fashioned from cloth and codified according to regulations, is a comparatively modern concept, warriors have, since the earliest beginnings of warfare, worn costumes that identify them as such, thereby differentiating them, as a group, from their enemies. Since such aims were uniform so, to an extent, might their dress be described. Yet for Sparta, with its intimate relationship between social organisation and military power, the adoption of a uniform went beyond the mere idea of looking different from one's foes. For the strength of Sparta's army lay not only in its professionalism but also in its formidable appearance, which was intentionally designed to strike terror into the hearts of Sparta's enemies.

According to Xenophon, the mysterious lawgiver Lykourgos had ordered the Spartiates to wear a crimson cloak and carry a bronze faced shield since the first least resembled women's clothing and was most warlike, while the second could be polished quickly but tarnished slowly.[7] As one would expect, Plutarch expands upon Xenophon's laconic explanation, saying that the blood-coloured tunic aroused terror in the inexperienced opponent and helped to disguise battle wounds.[8] Though Aelian repeats Plutarch almost verbatim, he does add that the colour had something superior about it.[9]

As to how far back the custom of wearing crimson clothing for military service actually went cannot be established for certain, although it could have been an early practice if the late Protocorinthian *olpe* known as the Chigi Vase, dated to around 650 BC or a little later, does indeed depict Spartan hoplites.[10] It has been suggested that because the left-hand phalanx includes in its ranks a flute player, a feature of Spartan armies down to at least as late as the time of Agesilaos,[11] the artist has depicted one of the opposing armies in his battle scene as Spartan.[12] If this is so, and only the Spartan army is definitely known to have used flute players in battle,[13] we have here one of the earliest representations of Spartan hoplites in colour. Of the four Spartan warriors shown in full (i.e. in the left-hand phalanx), two wear no tunic under their bell-shaped corselet, while the other two wear crimson tunics. So it is possible that the crimson tunic had become standard in the Spartan army even by this early date.

Tunic

The basic item of uniform was the tunic or *chitôn*. In the archaic period tunics were relatively thick woollen garments, but by the classical period they generally became lighter, and sometimes linen replaced wool. During the fifth century BC a new type of tunic, called the *exomis*, came into widespread use. Originally a garment typically worn by labourers to allow free movement of the right arm, it appears the Spartans adopted the *exomis* for warfare. This tunic was two-sleeved, but a happy feature of it was that the right-hand sleeve could be let down so as to leave the right shoulder and arm free to handle weapons in combat, as Plutarch describes when he has Kleomenes III of Sparta (r. 235–222 BC) put on his tunic and loosens the seam from his right shoulder.[14] The seam was presumably pinned back in place when the wearer wished to wear the *exomis* with the sleeve covering the right shoulder. This light and serviceable garment, so suitable for the cut and thrust activities of the wearer, reflected also the professionalism of the Spartans.

Cloak

The Greeks distinguished between two types of cloak, the *himation* and the *chlamys*. Both were rectangular, but the *himation* was much longer and was worn wrapped around the body, whereas the *chlamys* was draped over the left shoulder and secured by a pin over the right shoulder. The *himation* had been much favoured in the archaic period, but was largely replaced in the classical period by the *chlamys*, which, being much looser, was more suitable for travelling, hunting and other outdoor activities that required greater freedom of movement.

The Spartans, on the other hand, retained their traditional form of the *himation* throughout the classical period, and it was never replaced by the *chlamys*. The Spartan *himation* was called a *tribôn*, and is often described as 'mean', *phaulos*, that is to say, thin as oppose to short.[15] When the prestigious Agesilaos landed in Egypt for what, would be the last campaign of his long career, the Egyptians flocked to see him with high expectations of Spartan splendour and spectacle. To their utter amusement they found instead 'nothing but a little old man with a deformed body wearing a cloak that was coarse and mean'.[16] It was a habit of a lifetime. Spartan boys under training had to wear the same cloak in summer and winter in order to become accustomed to the cold.[17] Indeed, austerity was the keynote to the Spartan lifestyle, and Spartiates would visually emphasize their toughness by making use of a single military cloak, summer and winter, allowed to wear thin and never laundered. This item of the uniform was not normally worn in battle, but, like the tunic, it was dyed crimson. According to a parody by Aristophanes, when the earthquake of 465 BC killed a large number of Spartans and the helots were threatening to revolt as a consequence, Sparta sent Perikleidas to solicit for help in Athens, where he sat 'as pale as death in his crimson cloak'.[18]

Along with other distinctive items of Spartan dress, individuals who admired the Spartans and aped their lifestyle, adopted the *tribôn* abroad. Aristophanes ridicules Lakonian-mad young men as 'long-haired, hungry, unwashed, Sokrates-like, carrying sticks'.[19] The label 'Sokrates-like' obviously refers to the philosopher's habit, as described by Xenophon, of wearing nothing but a thin cloak 'winter and summer alike'.[20] Sokrates (469–399 BC) was a impecunious, pug-nosed, incorrigible old worrier of complacent authority and scourge of dishonest thinking, a voluble and unsparing critic of the democracy of his day. The motive force of his life was a burning desire to get at the truth, tearing aside all pretence and sophistry by a relentless process of question and answer. It is said that, in his attempts to get people to think about universal principles, he went about the workplaces of artisans and traders, as well as the haunts of sophists and youths, subjecting them all to the same procedure. No doubt he did so in his threadbare, unwashed cloak.

By donning the *tribôn*, in the eyes of the Athenian politician, Demosthenes, you were acting the Spartan.[21] For a Spartiate, on the other hand, this particular article of his uniform was treasured above all else, so much so, if we are to believe Plutarch, he would be buried without grave goods, but wrapped in his crimson cloak and crowned with an olive wreath.[22] On the same Spartan ritual Aelian is somewhat more discerning, explaining that a Spartiate was buried with an olive wreath if he died after fighting in a good manner, in his crimson cloak only if he had performed deeds of outstanding bravery.[23] If either or both commentators are correct, and there seems little reason to doubt them here, then the point of burying the fallen warrior in his crimson cloak was surely that he had valued no possession more highly than his membership of the Spartan army.

Hairstyle

Male hair is potently symbolic stuff. As discussed earlier, Spartans signalled their virility and belligerence by growing theirs and went into battle with it all braided and be-wreathed with flowers. In this way, no less than a uniform and no less of a distinctly Spartan trait was the long hair grown specifically for its military function. As to the origins of this Spartan custom we can turn to Herodotos, who reckons the legislation enjoining the Spartiates to grow their hair proudly and terrifyingly long, contrary to previous practice, had first been instituted after the victory over the Argives at the Battle of the Champions.[24] The reality of the Battle of the Champions has been doubted by some scholars, and that is understandable, but it seems that at least in the fifth century BC it was taken as historical. Still, whether or not we chose to believe in the historical truth of this battle is irrelevant here. The point of Herodotos' story is that the Spartans, at some point in their history, adopted the idea of wearing the hair long as a symbol of militaristic pride, and this is certainly the view later promoted by Xenophon.[25] According to Aristotle, on the other hand, the Spartans thought long hair noble because it was the mark of a free man, since it was difficult to perform servile tasks with long hair.[26]

It has been suggested, therefore, that the Spartans wore their hair long because in archaic times long hair was the mark of an aristocrat throughout the Greek world. In other words, the retention of this fashion was a symptom of the increasing conservatism of Spartan society from the middle of the sixth century BC onwards. Certainly in fifth-century BC Athens, long hair became the sign of those with Lakonian sympathies. Take, for example, Plutarch's picture of Alkibiades' chameleon-like adaptation to Spartan long hair, cold baths and black broth, his bearing Spartan beyond Spartan.[27] However, this hypothesis only goes part way to answer the question why Spartans wore their hair long. More important, it was a symbolic reminder of belligerent arrogance, almost inverted snobbery. As Xenophon says, men who had just entered manhood were not only permitted to don the highly-prized crimson military cloak, but also to wear their hair long in the belief that it made them look taller, more dignified and more terrifying.[28] According to a later tradition, Plutarch to be precise, wearing the hair long made handsome Spartiates more beautiful and ugly Spartiates more terrible.[29] As adornment, of course, it was also free.

This argument is strengthened by a couple of anecdotes that are set in the arena of battle. One we have encountered already, but it is well worth repeating here. It is that well-known story of Herodotos where the Spartans, calmly awaiting the Persian onslaught at Thermopylai, are passing their time in taking exercise and combing their hair.[30] Questioned about this, so Herodotos' tale continues, the deposed Spartan king, Demaratos, is said to have told Xerxes that combing their hair was a sign that the Spartans were preparing for battle.[31] Similarly, Xenophon reports young men would enter battle with their hair immaculately groomed and oiled, 'looking cheerful and impressive'.[32] If this was so, an indispensable piece of equipment for any self-respecting Spartiate was his comb. When Klearchos, the Spartan generalissimo who commanded the Ten Thousand under Cyrus the Younger, was unexpectedly captured he was hastily shuffled off to the Persian court loaded with chains. There he begged a comb from the Greek court physician, Ktesias of Knidos in Caria; he was so pleased at being able to dress his hair that he 'gave Ktesias his ring as a token of friendship which he might show to his kindred and friends in Sparta'.[33]

Despite the conservative nature of the Spartans, their coiffure did change somewhat over time. On warrior statuettes of the sixth century BC all the locks are swept to the back under the helmet. In the early fifth century BC, hair is normally dressed in four locks falling to the front, two on either shoulder, and four to the back. The beard is short and pointed and the upper lip is normally shaven. Plutarch, quoting Aristotle's lost *Lakedaimoniôn politeia*, informs us that every year upon entering office the ephors would order the Spartiates to 'cut their moustaches and obey the law'.[34] In the late fifth century BC, it seems that the hair continued to be dressed in two locks to the front on either shoulder, and the upper lip continued to be shaved, but the beard was generally longer. Plutarch appears to confirm this when he describes the statue of Lysandros in the treasury of the Akanthians at Delphi as having very long hair and beard 'in the old style'.[35] Again, Plutarch preserves a saying of a Spartan who, upon being asked why he wore his beard so very long, replied: 'So I can see my grey hairs and never do anything unworthy of them'.[36]

And now for an interesting parallel. The archaic gorgon is the most terrifying manifestation of Greek art; her protruding tongue, fangs bared, and snakes instead of hair witnesses the belief in her petrifying power, described by Pindar and later poets. The bronze *kratêr* (in effect a large bowl for mixing wine with water, a vessel most essential for the Greek symposium) from Vix near Châtillon-sur-Seine (Côte-d'Or), was made in Sparta or a Lakonian workshop in southern Italy and is dated to the end of the sixth century BC. This enormous *kratêr*, the largest (and finest) ever found (1.64 metres high, 208 kilograms in weight, 1,100 litres capacity), is equipped with two elaborate volute-handles, the lower part being formed by the head and bust of a gorgon from which, instead of legs, two snakes branch out, and a pair of snakes writhe upwards from behind her arms. Interestingly, her hair (not snakes) is shown dressed with four locks falling to the front, two that fall on either shoulder, and two that fall to the back, exactly like the hairstyle of our Spartiate warrior. For many a Greek, a gorgon freak or Spartan fighter were equally petrifying.

Blazon

Initially, in common with the rest of the Greek world, the shield of a Spartan hoplite was decorated with the owner's individual shield device. In a rather witty anecdote, as retold by Plutarch, we hear of a Spartan who had an actual-size image of a fly as a blazon on his shield. When taunted that he only wanted to escape notice, he replied that on the contrary he got so close to his enemies that his emblem was seen at its true size.[37] Also, we can surmise, the fly is the bravest of the brave because it keeps coming back however often it is shooed away by a man many times its size. At some point, possibly at the outbreak of the Peloponnesian War, Sparta began to use a uniform state shield device. In the lexicon of Photios, under the entry for the Greek letter *lambda*, we are informed that the Spartans painted this letter on their shields. Photios, a ninth-century Byzantine bishop and scholar, mentions as his source Eupolis, an Athenian comic poet born in 446 BC. His last known comedy drama was staged in 412 BC, and he died 'in the Hellespont', probably at the naval engagement off Kynossema of the following year. Therefore it is certain that the *lambda* device was in use before 412 BC, and it is generally thought that this fragment of Eupolis comes from a comedy dealing with Kleon's campaign of 422 BC.[38] The use of the proud *lambda*, incidentally, continued into third century BC, when we are told that Messenian soldiers managed to seize Elis by chicanery, having painted Spartan blazons onto their shields.[39]

The letter was presumably painted on to the bronze face of the shield in the uniform crimson colour, and it soon became, like the cloak and coiffure of the Spartan, a weapon of terror. Eupolis, in the fragment cited above, makes light of Kleon's fear of

1. It is commonly said that 'old soldiers never die: they simply fade away'. This was not so in ancient Sparta. On the field of Mantineia, to cite a single example, you would have found in the Spartan phalanx men in their fifties each, like their younger comrades, in full panoply and fully prepared for the coming struggle. A Spartan hoplite with 'white hair and grey beard' was no poetic licence. In this colour plate, prepared from an original painting by the Irish artist Seán Ó'Brógáin, we are presented with one such Spartan greybeard at the time of Mantineia. Whether or not we agree with their atheistic wisdom and heroic philosophy, this superb reconstruction surely captures for us the very essence of the Spartan way. (*Artwork courtesy of Seán Ó'Brógáin*)

2. The fertile Eurotas valley, looking northwest from the archaic structure known as the Menaleion (sanctuary of Menelaus and Helen) from ancient Therapnae to the southeast of Sparta – Greek writers emphasise the fact that this dysfunctional couple were worshipped, along with Helen's divine brothers the Dioskouri, not as heroes but as gods. Sparta traces its origins in a group of village settlements dotted along the banks of the river Eurotas in the southeastern Peloponnese. It grew by subjugating or enslaving its immediate neighbours in Lakedaimon, who thus became *perioikoi*, personally free but subject to Spartan control, or helots, standing somewhere between serfdom and slavery. (*Author's collection*)

3. View looking north across modern Sparta (founded 1834). The slight, wooded rise on the edge of the modern town, seen here in the middle background, once served as the acropolis of ancient Sparta. The Athenian historian Thucydides rightly said: 'For if the *polis* of the Spartans should be deserted, and nothing should be left of it but its temples and the foundations of its other buildings, posterity would, I think, after a long lapse of time, be very loath to believe that their power was as great as their renown' (1.10.2). Most Greek *poleis* possessed an acropolis, a walled citadel occupying an elevated position, which gave refuge to the populace in time of war, and which enshrined the temple of the presiding deity. The Spartan acropolis did not by any means conform to the usual type. (*Author's collection*)

4. This ivory plaque (Athens, National Archaeological Museum, inv. 15362), from the sanctuary of Artemis Orthia in Sparta, dated to the second half of seventh century BC, depicts a warship in low relief with her prow to the right ready to depart. As the ship is being made ready to make sail, five hoplites have already taken their places next to the gunwale, while two deckhands unfurl the sail. Another is fishing from the prow, while yet another is squatting on the ram of the ship relieving himself. A female figure standing on the gangplank in a trailing garment grasps the hand of a naked man standing in the stern, touching his shoulder with her left hand. The Spartans were notorious landlubbers, so the scene could illustrate a celebrated myth such as the abduction, or seduction, of Helen of Sparta, a woman of peerless grace, charm and beauty (the face that launched a thousand ships) by Paris, prince of Troy in Asia. (*Author's collection*)

5 (*left*). Early sixth-century BC terracotta metope (Sparta, Museum of Archaeology) depicting Spartan hoplites. Every picture tells a story. A Spartiate, all caparisoned for battle, slowly advancing to contact spoke of reassuring discipline and obedience. But the blood-coloured tunic and oiled tresses, a terrifyingly beautiful sight in its own right, also evoked a more primitive world of hunting and death. In his right hand he held a spear, a well-loved object, big and sinister. (*Author's collection*)

6 (*right*). This sixth-century BC *pithos* (Sparta, Museum of Archaeology), with mould-made applied decoration in relief, was excavated in the centre of ancient Sparta. Here we see a close-up of a Spartan warrior. The Corinthian helmet, especially when burnished, presented quite a terrifying sight to the enemy. To add to the effect, Spartans would let their hair fall below their helmets. Once the universal custom, the wearing of longhair was now exclusive to Sparta. In that well-known yarn of Herodotos (7.208) the Spartans at Thermopylai, completely naked and calmly awaiting the Persian onslaught, passed their time in taking exercise and combing their hair. For the Spartans, the culture of vestments was a psychological weapon. (*Author's collection*)

7. This finely worked marble torso of a hoplite (Sparta, Museum of Archaeology, inv. 440), of more than life-size, was unearthed to the south of Athena's temple on the acropolis of Sparta (1925). Unsurprisingly, he was immediately dubbed 'Leonidas'. The hoplite wears a Corinthian helmet (the crest of which is restored) with cheek pieces shaped like rams' heads, and the hint-of-a-smile face has the typical shaven upper lip of a Spartan. Firmly dated to the first quarter of the fifth century BC, the torso has been considered by many scholars to have formed part of the memorial that was erected on the acropolis to honour Leonidas on his reburial. The probability is strong, particularly as the Spartans at the time would have considered only one of their warriors worthy to stand on their acropolis; and that man is Leonidas, son of Anaxandridas of the race of lion-slaying Herakles. Of course, the tenacious defence of Thermopylai has been made especially memorable by Leonidas' legendary reply of 'Come and take them' to a Persian surrender demand. (*Author's collection*)

8. It is said that Herakles, his skin fused horribly to a poisoned cloak, plunged headlong into the nearest stream. But these waters increased the poison's burning power, and they have run scalding-hot forever after and gave their name to the nearby narrow pass, the Hot Gates – Thermopylai in ancient Greek. The curative waters (43°C) are said to be an excellent remedy for sciatica. Here we see the Middle Gate from the mound of the last stand, looking west towards the Persian position and the thermal springs – the white building is a popular spa and restaurant. To the left the mountain wall of Kallidromos towers stark and sheer over Thermopylai, a defensive wall nearly a thousand metres high upon which Leonidas anchored his left flank, while the ancient coastline would have been just to the right of the what was, until fairly recently, the Athens-Thessalonika National Highway. Standing today on the battlefield one is struck about the advantages for defence. (*Author's collection*)

9. The hillock of Kolonos has been identified as the site of the final tooth-and-nail struggle. The sandy mound was excavated in 1939 by the Greek archaeologist Spyridon Marinatos (1901–74) and hundreds of Persian arrowheads were discovered. Even at the very end, rather than close in for the kill, the Persians relied on aerial bombardment to finish the decimated Greeks. Here, on the summit of the mound of the last stand, can be seen a modern replica of the original plaque, upon which is inscribed Simonides' famous 'Stranger, go tell the Lakedaimonians ...' epigram. The original has long perished, but Herodotos copied it when he visited the site, and the work of his pen has been more lasting than stone. (*Author's collection*)

10. The biggest misconception of Thermopylai must be the common belief that the Spartans made their last stand alone on that fateful, final afternoon. Posterity commemorates the Three Hundred, but how many of us recall the 'Seven Hundred' who perished the same day. Indeed, it is a remarkable fact that Thespiai willingly sent all the adult males who qualified for hoplite service to fight at Thermopylai. As far as we can tell, this tiny Boiotian state had no obligations to Sparta or even Athens, although, like next-door Plataia, there was a tendency for its citizens to gravitate towards the latter out of hostility towards the neighbourhood bully, Thebes. All the same, in a few short hours an entire generation of citizen farmers was obliterated. Still, justice was finally seen to be done when, in 1996, a bronze sculpture was set up and unveiled at the site of Thermopylai to commemorate the gallant citizen soldiers of Thespiai who volunteered to fight and die with Leonidas and the Three Hundred.
Under the statue – a headless, broken-winged Eros – the simple inscription reads: 'In memory of the seven hundred Thespians'.
(*Author's collection*)

11. Attic stele (Eleusis, Museum of Archaeology, inv. 5101) from the period of the great war between Athens and Sparta (431–404 BC), depicting a fight between Athenian horsemen and Spartan hoplites. Sparta was justly famed for its professional hoplites, but not so for its amateur horsemen. The crack Spartan formation known as the *hippeis*, despite their title, fought on foot, an élite body of 300 handpicked young men who served as a guard to the kings. (*Author's collection*)

12. In the summer of 425 BC the Athenians accepted the surrender of 292 Lakedaimonians, 120 of them full-blown Spartan citizens, on the islet of Sphakteria just offshore of Pylos in western Messenia and just within Sparta's territory. They were held as hostages in Athens for four years. This was, in the words of the contemporary soldier historian Thucydides, 'the event that caused surprise among the Greeks than anything else that had happened in the war' (4.40.1). The Athenians installed a garrison at Pylos, and a number of Messenians used it for making raids upon Lakonian territory. Here we see a general view of Sphakteria islet, looking west from the mainland at Neó Kastró. The low shoreline on the left is the location of the 'Santa Rosa Landing', whilst that in the centre is that of the 'Panagia Landing'. The high point on the right is Profitis Elias. (*Author's collection*)

13. The disaster that befell the Spartan *mora* garrisoned at Lechaion, the Corinthian port on the Gulf of Corinth, in the summer of 390 BC was totally unexpected. Nonetheless, the action re-mphasised what had already been established (e.g. Sphakteria), and that was that under the right conditions a force of missile-armed troops could wear down and render unfit a force of hoplites, even Spartan ones. Panoramic view north from the Acrocorinth over the Gulf of Corinth to Perachora. The site of Lechaion is in the centre of the shot, while the battle site itself is on the extreme left, and it was here that the struggle between the Spartan *mora* and the peltasts of Iphikrates would have been played out. (*Author's collection*)

14. At Leuktra, not only were Spartan casualties heavy, but also politically the effects of the Boiotian victory were immense. Sparta lost much prestige by simply showing that its army could be beaten on the field of battle. Xenophon, in his description of the Spartan catastrophe, implies (*Hellenika* 6.4.8) King Kleombrotos and his men were more than a little tipsy on the wine they had drunk at high noon, perhaps strong and undiluted. General view of the battlefield looking northeast. The Spartans would have been arrayed on the right, the Boiotians on the left, while the level ground between was where the two clashed. (*Author's collection*)

15. A work of art generates its own momentum. Art gives shape to amorphous themes and bullies dry facts into submission. When facts get in the way of art, it is the facts that lose credibility. When Napoléon saw *Léonidas aux Thermopyles* (Paris, musée du Louvre), he asked Jacques-Louis David why he had bothered to paint the defeated. The artist, however, considered this work his masterpiece, asking at the very end of his life 'I suppose you know that no one but David could have painted Leonidas'. (*Photograph courtesy of Esther Carré*)

the 'dreaded *lambdas*'. But an incident recorded by Xenophon is especially revealing. A Spartan cavalry officer, seeing some hoplites from Sparta's ally, Sikyon, reeling back from an Argive attack, dismounted his men, ordering them to tie their horses to trees, and, taking the shields from the Sikyonians, boldly advanced against the enemy. Meanwhile, the Argives, seeing the *sigmas* on the advancing shields, 'feared nothing from them as though they were Sikyonians'.[40] The implication is clear: the Argives would have felt very differently had the shields borne the dreaded *lambdas*. It had been a different story at Mantineia in 418 BC. For the Argives had hardly waited to cross spears with the Spartans, but had promptly broken, some of them even being trampled underfoot by their own comrades in the rush to escape the battlefield during the routine hysteria of routine routs.[41] It would be a mistake to say that the Argive resistance collapsed; none was ever offered. The mere sight of an advancing phalanx of Spartan hoplites had been enough to break the nerve of their Argive opponents, even before the shock of arms. Their own fear of death had defeated them.

Helmet

When Spartan tactics started to develop in the fifth century BC, the Corinthian helmet, which completely enclosed the wearer's head, was replaced. Good vision and hearing in the Spartan phalanx were becoming more important as increasingly complex manoeuvres were executed, thus making the wearing of a Corinthian helmet a mix blessing. Consequently, a new type of helmet offering far less facial protection, the *pilos*, was adopted by Spartan hoplites. The word *pilos* literally means 'felt', and is applied to a number of articles made of that material. Felt caps were called *piloi*, and they came in a number of regional variants, distinguished by shape.[42] Arrian and Pollux mention Lakonian *piloi*.[43] They were conical in shape and slightly rounded at the point – of the type commonly worn by the Spartan heroes, the heavenly twins Castor and Pollux.

The *pilos*-helmet repeated the shape of the felt *pilos* cap in bronze. Once adopted by the Spartan army, it became as much a Spartan symbol as the crimson *exomis*, and was copied by many states both inside and outside its alliance, what is often called nowadays the Peloponnesian League. An intriguing passage from Thucydides has provoked considerable discussion with regards to the *pilos*-helmet. It tells us that the Spartan garrison on Sphakteria suffered greatly against Athenian archers, 'for their *piloi* did not keep out the arrows'.[44] Thucydides may be suggesting that the Spartans were wearing felt *piloi*, but it is more probable that by this time the word *pilos* was also used to refer to bronze helmets of that type.

Sword

There was nothing unusual in Spartan swords until the fifth century BC, when they began to get shorter and straighter. By the Peloponnesian War they had become exceedingly short, like daggers, as is clear from the representational evidence depicting Spartan hoplites. When one Athenian politician mocked that Spartan swords were so short conjurors could swallow them, Agis III (r. 338–331 BC) briskly replied: 'All the same, the Spartans do reach the enemy with their swords'.[45] Antalkidas (*fl.* 390–360 BC), when asked why the Spartan swords were so short, is reputed to have said: 'Because we fight close to the enemy'.[46] Plutarch attributes a very similar statement to an unidentified Spartan, who says that they could get to close quarters thanks to their short swords.[47] Conversely, a Spartan mother, when her son complained that his sword was too small, advised him to 'extend it by a stride'.[48]

It is significant that in these passages the use of the short sword is clearly regarded as a Spartan practice. It is also significant that in these passages the Spartan short sword is called an *encheiridion*, literally a 'dagger'. No actual examples survive, but Attic reliefs showing Spartans often depict a short sword less than a foot long and with a wide leaf- or diamond-shaped blade. The sword was probably shortened to make it handier in the crush, which ensued when two phalanxes collided. As mentioned earlier, the Greek sword was normally a medium-sized, one-edged slashing weapon, the *kopis*. When the spear was splintered, it would be employed overhand to hack and slash at the head and shoulders of the opponent. In Sparta, however, the sword was shortened in order to encourage the Spartan hoplite to get nice and close and employ a more effective underarm thrust against the vulnerable groin region of his opponent.

Striking a pose

Sparta's unique system of training its young males – through military drill, athletic contests, and mock battles – was clearly designed to produce tough and disciplined soldiers. At the age of twenty, having survived the *agôgê*, the Spartiate now sought induction into one of communal mess units around which the lives of all Spartiates were organized. The mess unit, which, according to Plutarch contained some fifteen men,[49] was the bedrock of the organization of the army.[50] A Spartiate fought beside, lived with, and ate with his fellow messmates, and this conformity of lifestyles would have produced a magnificent *esprit de corps*, a truly ephemeral quality that gave a soldier confidence in himself and his unit. Plutarch adds that the members of a mess had to be congenial comrades, and that they possessed the power of blackballing unacceptable applicants. Obviously, failure to secure election to any communal mess was tantamount to exclusion from the Spartan citizen body and, perhaps, the army. Xenophon mentions a further important effect of the communal messes, namely that they brought together in close contact citizens of various ages, a fact that both produced an illusion of equality and enabled the young to learn from the older warriors.[51] As we know, it is the old man's experience that allows an ignorant and presumptuous young one to become a man worthy of his name.

In Sparta the process of military training was designed as much to instil the group cohesion and solidarity upon which the individual Spartiate's fighting spirit depended, as it was to produce an adequate level of fitness or tactical expertise. In modern Western armies bonding is fostered early through a number of ritualistic mechanisms.

First, there is oath taking, a ritual that goes back at least to the *sacramentum*, the Roman military oath.

Second, individuality can be assailed by a haircut, which today is at best short and at worst – like the French Foreign Legion's *boule-à-zéro* – totally comprehensive. Although such *coiffures* are often defended on the grounds they promote hygiene, their prime justification is that they create a uniformity of appearance. But the fashion for establishing this identity by cropping hair close to the scalp is comparatively recent. For many centuries long hair, elaborately arranged, was the hallmark of the warrior. Eighteenth-century European soldiers, for example, squinted under the strain of having their hair caught back in pigtails. For the Spartiates, in conjunction with their ritual of pre-battle grooming, the wearing of long hair made them appear more terrifying to their foes.

Third, there is the issue of uniform, a dress with symbolism all of its own. The egalitarian effect of wearing a uniform is well illustrated by Xenophon, who has Cyrus, on having standardized the equipment of his army, explain to his soldiers: 'In this armour, then, how could any one of us have the advantage over one another except in courage'.[52] Even today, the identity of appearance that a disruptive pattern material uniform helps to create the bonding process. Likewise, as mentioned before, the badges of rank that still accompany it, albeit of a less ornate character than they once were, emphasize the age-old hierarchical structure of armies and encourage deference and due respect. The bronze warrior statuette of the late sixth century BC identified as a Spartiate – as is suggested by the warrior's long hair arrange in locks and his military cloak – wears a Corinthian helmet with an unusual transverse crest.[53] This positioning of the crest may be a badge of rank and thus probably denotes its wearer as a Spartan officer. The figure once held a stick, now lost.

Down through the centuries uniform has included a variety of features clearly designed to make its wearer look broader or taller, or to promote the warrior's status in the eyes of comrades and the enemy alike. This was no less so with Sparta. It clearly recognized the symbolic, indeed magical power of uniformity, which not only promoted group identity by assisting in strengthening the bonds of comradeship between individual Spartiates, but also instilled a special feeling of elitism amongst them as a group. Even before the clash of arms, the Spartiates would have radiated an unmistakable aura of solidarity and superiority. Imagine, if you will, the Spartans on the field of battle, with their closed-ordered shields each emblazoned with the *lambda*, which must have appeared as an array of serrated teeth, the unbroken wall of crimson-clad warriors striding forward in measured lockstep to the shrill music of double flute players. Surreal to other Greek eyes, an advancing Spartan phalanx presented a theatre of terror. The message was clear – resistance is futile – these men are hard-headed professional killers.

Fear of the known

Although the wearing of a crimson uniform was sneered at by Aristophanes,[54] the Athenians, amongst many others, undoubtedly feared meeting the Spartans in the arena of war. Kleon, commanding the Athenians in their defeat at Amphipolis in 422 BC, we are told, took off at a run as soon as he saw the 'dreaded *lambdas*' on the Spartan shields flashing across the plain.[55] Once the Persians made their way around the pass at Thermopylai they had to be assured the Greek pickets there were not really Spartan hoplites – so great had the fear of those soldiers become to them.[56] Just as frightening was the sound of Spartan pipes, which signalled to the enemy across the battlefield the onset of their slow, dreadful advance.[57] 'It was a sight at once awesome and terrifying', Plutarch remarks, 'as the Spartans marched in step to the double flute, leaving no gap in their line of battle and with no confusion in their hearts, calmly and cheerfully advancing into danger'.[58] Compare, for instance, the splendid climax of the imperial Indian army's review in Kipling's 'His Majesty's Servants':

> The line grew and grew till it was three-quarters of a mile long – one solid wall of men, horses, and guns. Then it came on straight towards the Viceroy and the Emir ... Unless you had been there, you cannot imagine what a frightening effect this steady comedown of troops had on the spectators, even when they know it is only a review.

We can easily picture the scene, the Indian force advancing, swiftly and in handsome order, the sunlight flashing from its arms. But here, of course, 'the advance stopped dead' before the concerned Emir had done more than 'picked up the reins on his horse's neck and looked behind him'.[59] Discipline and order among soldiers wins battles, a simple truth that stands the test of time despite changes in the methods of warfare or in scientific developments. In one of his Socratic dialogues Xenophon has Perikles explain to Sokrates that in the army order, discipline, and obedience are most necessary, yet the Athenians 'pay no attention to these things'.[60] When 10,000 Athenian troops landed on Sphakteria in order to clear the island of its garrison, which numbered just 420 hoplites, Thucydides says they advanced with 'their spirits crushed by the idea that they had to face Spartans'.[61] This is a striking tribute to the fear Spartan hoplites inspired. Lysias' Mantitheos, in a speech after the Athenian defeat at the Nemea in 394 BC, sums up the general feeling when he openly admits that he is not the kind of man who 'does not consider it a terrible thing to fight the Spartans'.[62] This is why the Boiotians, who stood alongside the Athenians at the Nemea, had refused to fight when stationed on the confederate left and thus opposite the Spartans but happily 'declared that the sacrifices had turned out favourable and sent round orders to make ready for battle' when stood on the confederate right and thus faced by the Achaians.[63]

Colour crimson

As previously discussed, the Spartan uniform was dyed crimson because the colour was manly, magical and disguised bloodstains.[64] But a case can be made that it was also this colour because of the availability of the dye. Red and blue were the cheapest and most widely available dyes at the time, and their dyeing process also just involved one stage. In fact, madder and the two major sources of blue pigment, indigo and woad, were the most important dye plants until the development of synthetic aniline dyes in the nineteenth century.

The herbaceous perennial madder (*Rubia tinctorum L.*), is a dye plant common to Southern Europe and the Near East. Either in wild or domesticated form, the plant's long fleshy root was the principal source of various fast, brilliant red dye pigments until the artificial production of alizarin, the colour principle of madder. Greek writers commonly knew the plant as 'the root',[65] while the elder Pliny stresses its importance for dyeing those two basic clothing materials, woollens and leather.[66] Herodotos tells us in his day 'madder was used to brighten the cloaks of Libyan women', while Theophrastos says 'its red roots are used to dye wool and leather red'. But madder was not the only red dye available in the ancient world.

Kermes (Greek *kókkos*, Latin *coccus*, 'berry') was a brilliant red dye extracted from the dried body of a female scale-insect (*Kermococcus vermilio*), which infests the evergreen leaves of the kermes-oak (*Quercus coccifera L.*), a native of the Mediterranean coast and the Near East. The females, after laying their eggs, were gathered and killed in vinegar and the bodies pounded and treated with urine to extract the red dye, and with alum as the mordant to set the colour. Although the elder Pliny,[67] as do other Graeco-Roman authors,[68] identifies kermes with a gall of vegetable origin, he does mention that the dye's colour would range from dark rose, into Tyrian purple, double-dyed purple and Lakonian purple.[69] The use of this dye goes back into prehistory,[70] and it is interesting to note that, unlike their Greek and Roman successors, the people of the ancient Near East were aware of the animal origin of kermes. Etymologists trace the word 'kermes' from the Sanskrit *krmija*, literally 'worm begotten', hence Old Persian *íirmizí* and Arabic *qîrmizi*, 'red of the worm', and fourteenth-century Spanish *cremesin*, whence our word crimson.

Chapter 12

Follow the Leader

Back in the summer of 430 BC, following the winter in which Perikles had delivered his very famous *epitaphios logos*, Funeral Oration,[1] a devastating plague struck over-crowded Athens. In the wake of the physical suffering caused by the disease, which Thucydides carefully described with clinical interest and had symptoms similar to those of pneumonic plague, measles, and typhoid, but fit no known illness precisely, came the beginnings of a moral and social revolution.[2] What the plague was to Athens for a few years, the Peloponnesian War was to Greece as a whole for a generation. Thucydides, who was a firsthand witness of the conflict, describes it like a disease, worsening by stages and ending in the collapse of the cultural ideas that he ascribes to his hero Perikles. Nowhere does he make this view clearer than when he describes the incredibly bloody internal struggle, *stasis*, which took place between the democrats and the oligarchs on the island of Corcyra in 427 BC, where slaughter was a daily pastime and no man's life safe for a moment.[3]

The physical upheaval in Greece during the Peloponnesian War, which is implicit in Thucydides, becomes explicit in the greatest of Athenian dramas of the time. Sophokles' *Oedipus Tyrannus*, produced in 429 BC, portrays a masterful ruler who enters the scene as a renowned riddle-solver, ferociously intellectual, flushed with confidence from previous success, optimistic, seemingly in firm control of his world but, significantly enough, faced with an inscrutable plague in his city. At the end of the play he is blinded, powerless and an outcast, comprehending too late the nature of great forces of which he was not the master. How the mighty has fallen! The Greek *poleis* and the political factions within them were being drawn, through their quest for *holos*, into the cycle of *kóros-hubris-atê*, which they themselves had seen in the undoing of the Persians.[4] Sophokles, pious and traditional by nature, seems bothered in *Oedipus Tyrannus* not by the blindness or irrationality of fate but by the blindness and inherent arrogance of the 'man is the measure' philosophy.[5] The pride of the 'hymn to man' in the *Antigone*,[6] written and performed in the four-forties, had turned to deep anxiety by the four-twenties. In the realm of human affairs, it seems that man's actions are still to a large extent controlled by the powers above. The gods still punish *hubris* but they are also jealous of prosperity and success. Imperialism, in fact, turned out to be the curse of Athens, its only fruits being hatred, wars, and an empty treasury.

In a letter he wrote to assembly back home while his command slowly rotted outside Syracuse, Nikias complained bitterly of the decline of the crews and the acute shortage of experienced personnel to man the fleet.[7] Athens resorted to hiring mercenary crews, yet with crucial financial backing from Persia the Spartans were often able to outbid the Athenian recruiting officers and thus produce a navy that was not only as large but also as technically competent as the Athenian. Likewise, Persian gold enabled them to float new fleets and hire new crews when battles were lost. It was, therefore, by sea, paradoxically for the normally landlubbing Spartans, that the thrice-nine-year war with the seagoing Athenians had been brought to a crunching end.

Having read Thucydides and Xenophon, the whole colossal fraud of Spartan foreign policy falls away to the bare bones of undisguised imperialism. The last Spartan ultimatum to Athens prior to the start of the Peloponnesian War stresses that they are willing to climb down if the Athenians let the Greeks be autonomous.[8] Later, Brasidas, campaigning in Macedonia and Thrace during the summer of 424 BC, reassures the Akanthians that Sparta is 'going to war with Athens in order to liberate Hellas'.[9] In other words, the Athenians have to relinquish their empire. When he describes the pulling down of Athens' walls in 404 BC, Xenophon remarks how it was 'thought that this day was the beginning of freedom for Hellas'.[10] Greece again was at peace, but by no means at ease. Having won the long, hard struggle against Athens and its empire, Sparta then proceeded to dominate the Aegean Greek world – thanks principally, it is clear, to Lysandros. Under him, the naked fact appeared, which had been hidden under the banner of liberation, that Sparta in the last resort regarded the Aegean Greek world as its demesne.

New suit, worse policies

By the high summer of 404 BC Lysandros had become the strongest man in the strongest state and, by wit, trickery and sheer brawny prowess, made certain Sparta's writ ran throughout the Aegean Greek world. After his victory at Aigospotamoi, he had gone from *polis* to *polis* in the rapidly crumbling Athenian empire, imposing peace and installing Spartan governors, *harmostês* or harmosts ('fixers'), and in some places oligarchic juntas of just ten men, decarchies, made up of those personally close to him.[11] At the same time tribute was extracted from the *poleis*, just as it had been by the Athenians.[12] Sparta, who began the war in order 'to liberate Hellas',[13] which meant the destruction of the Athenian empire and the liberation of the *poleis* it ruled, now helped itself to the revenues that came to it from the maritime states of the Aegean. It was a neat little slogan that packed a world of lies in three words, and the emptiness of this war cry of liberation was so obviously demonstrated when a victorious Sparta slipped neatly into the imperialistic role wrested from Athens. But the new shoes were a size larger than those that Sparta comfortably and usually fitted.

The cerebral Aristotle gave the proper verdict: 'the Spartans always prevailed in war but were destroyed by empire simply because they did not know how to use the leisure they had won, because they had practised no more fundamental skill than skill in war'.[14] The very completeness of that victory caused it serious constitutional problems. Having 'liberated' the Greeks only to bring them more fully into subjection, the Spartans found that their state lacked the political, administrative, ideological and economic machinery for running such a widespread empire. Profoundly conservative, the Spartans were stuck mentally in the era in which it had conquered Messenia and turned its erstwhile citizens into helots. Hence Lysandros' makeshift expedient of entrusting power to decarchies, and whether or not these provided an efficient mode of government by proxy was neither here nor there. It was much easier to govern through a small determined minority who knew what they wanted and were prepared to be ruthless to get it, than through a broadly based government of reasonable men. Lysandros' puppet oligarchs were tied to Sparta far more firmly than any of its so-called allies had been tied to Athens, and it was through them that Sparta was hated too. Then excessive power bred fears, fear of Sparta among its stronger and more independent allies, fear even of Lysandros in Sparta itself. Plutarch put it nicely when he compared the actuality of Sparta's hegemony, notwithstanding its claim to having freed the subjects of Athens, to the pouring of vinegar into the sweet wine of liberty.[15]

Though the Spartans lusted for empire as the Athenians of old, unlike Athens, Sparta was totalitarian in the sense that its ideology was based on the premise that the state is everything, the individual nothing. Let us be critical and take our reasoning a stage further. Fascism is a difficult word to handle because it comes with an iconography that touches the Nazi nerve. Today it is abused as propaganda against the West's official enemies and to promote its foreign adventures with a moral vocabulary written in the struggle against Hitler. And yet fascism and imperialism are twins. And not only that, for in the prosecution of its aims imperialism always needs to create a monster, a sinister enemy that it can demonize; exaggerating its crimes and atrocities in order to justify the perpetration of its own, even greater crimes. The Spartan empire was the old Athenian one, but a more extreme imperialistic version. The Spartans too extracted tribute, imposed governments and garrisons, and maintained a navy, but whereas the Athenians' empire had been conceived and largely maintained as anti-Persian and pro-democratic, the version hammered out by Lysandros was anti-democratic and pro-despotic, showing how hollow the talk of liberation had been.

Psychologically too, the Spartans lacked the makeup to be successful empire builders. The occasional episodes of stick-wielding Spartans in our literary sources say it all. In 411 BC, at the height of the naval war, a Spartan by the name of Astyochos was nearly lynched when he raised his stick, the Spartan *bakteriâ*, against Dorieus, a high-ranking Rhodian exile who was speaking up for his own men, sailors who were owed arrears of pay, 'free men' as Thucydides is at pains to point out.[16] Again, after Athens was defeated, the Spartan harmost Kallibios holds sway from the sacred heights of the Athenian Acropolis. This arrogant brute raised his *bakteriâ* to strike Autolykos, an Athenian wrestler, but the champion threw Kallibios to the ground. His boss, Lysandros, showed no sympathy with Kallibios' rage at this, but reprimanded him and said 'you do not know how to govern free men'.[17] Like his fellow Spartan Astyochos, Kallibios had made the mistake of treating free Greeks as if they were helots. This lack of discrimination and self-control partly explains why Spartan liberation was both a sham and stillborn in practice.

When they founded their colony at Herakleia Trachinia in 426 BC, excluding all Ionians and Achaians (viz. actual and potential enemies), people flocked in from all over Greece.[18] But the colonists were rapidly disappointed and the colony was a flop, because the Spartan harmosts treated them 'harshly and sometimes positively unjustly'.[19] In this respect, it is worth considering the following lines from Euripides, written around the same time:

> *You conquer other men and you rule over them in crime.*
> *Your government – betrayal.*
> *Principles – a lie.*
> *All snares, deceit no trace of honesty.*
> *They hate you more than anyone alive.*
> *What evil has not found its home among you?*
> *Murders, avariciousness.*
> *Famous for your lies.*
> *Well known for saying one thing with your lips and*
> *knowing you deny it in your hearts!*[20]

Granted it was written and staged during the great war between Athens and Sparta when anti-Spartan feeling was higher than usual, and that the dramatic context is very hostile to Sparta, nonetheless it probably represents, in extreme form, feelings that were widely held in Greece at large. After all, was it not the normally gentle Herodotos who made the cutting remark that the Athenians (allies at the time) 'understood Spartan ways of thinking – how they thought one thing and said another'.[21] Spartans were not suited to a role on the wider Greek stage.

By the fourth century BC it is difficult to praise the virtues and successes of the Spartan system when we consider in 378 BC the Spartan harmost of Thespiai, Sphodrias, orchestrated a treacherous and abortive attempt to seize Peiraeus. He made a night march into Attica, claiming that he intended to to surprise the Athenians and capture Peiraeus before daybreak. In fact, it was a two-day slog from Thespiai to Peiraeus, and dawn found him just east of Eleusis; he withdrew after rifling a few farmsteads. Sphodrias was tried and acquitted, and the part of King Agesilaos in the process was not remotely honourable.[22] And this was not an isolated case. Back in 382 BC the Spartan Phoebidas seized the Kadmeia, the acropolis of Thebes, in an act of gross treachery and in broad daylight too.[23] The ephors recalled him and punished him, but the Spartans kept the Kadmeia. Though he was fined,[24] Agesilaos insisted that he be judged by the criterion of Spartan interests, and so we find Phoebidas re-employed as harmost of Thespiai.[25] As Plutarch tartly observed, the Spartans 'punished the offender but approved the offence'.[26] This annexation was a more blatant piece of aggrandizement, what the Greeks recognized as *holos*, than anything Sparta had yet done. Its previous acquisitions had been preceded by some kind of justification: this had none. Worse still, the anti-Spartan leader in Thebes, Ismenias, was arrested, brought to trial, and convicted on charges of accepting bribes from and conspiring with Persia. His execution on these charges,[27] given Sparta's own record of having collaborating with the 'long-haired Mede' and having accepted subsidies in the war against Athens struck many contemporaries as stark hypocrisy. Even Xenophon, otherwise a biased champion of Sparta, could not refrain from condemnation of this 'evil doing'.[28]

For Diodoros, looking back over all those centuries, 380 BC was the climax of Spartan power, which seemed invincible: Thebes was garrisoned, the Corinthians and Argives were cowed, and the Athenians were still unpopular because, Diodoros revealingly says, of their previous policy of installing military colonies in the territory of so-called allies.[29] Though his observation is made with the luxury of hindsight, it is reflected in the following anecdote. The congress of the Peloponnesian League still met and took decisions but there is a marked difference of tone between the meeting of 432 BC where allied voices still mattered and that of 382 BC (before the attack on Olynthos) where, Xenophon says, 'most supported an expedition but mainly because they wanted to please the Spartans'.[30] A despotism, if it seeks to regulate what men think and say, expects them to say and think things that are pleasing to it. The despotism of Sparta was the swan song of its greatness.

The second Agamemnon

There is a story that Agesilaos was accused of medizing. 'Not at all', he replied, 'it is the Medes who are lakonising'.[31] And so indeed they were. So-called 'medizers', of course, were those individuals or communities who collaborated with the Persians. Anyway, good King Agesilaos may have had a sense of humour but he could not for long permit men of rival brilliance to flourish near him. Lysandros was rather too big a man to be allowed in the same land as Agesilaos. His premature death outside Haliartos in 395 BC plausibly forestalled a violent showdown between the two rivals.

The actors at the centre of the stage changed placed. Agesilaos, the man whom Lysandros manoeuvred on to the throne to be his pliant collaborator, turned out to be as much of an imperialist as was Lysandros himself. Like Lysandros, Agesilaos had a vaulting ambition for an Aegean-wide as well as mainland Greece empire, though he had his own agenda. Moreover, Agesilaos did not care to be a puppet and so was irked by the kingmaker's pretensions, and more than once had to remind him who was king, and who was commoner. The king regarded the commoner neither as an enemy nor as a friend, but as an extremely able citizen who sometimes had to be taught his place. He would receive Lysandros, his kingmaker, cheerfully and condescendingly, graciously forgiving him for his posturing. And, as the old saying goes, no one can be his superior, no one can be his associate, one can only be his subordinate. One of the strongest and ablest of Sparta's kings, Agesilaos was a shrewd, devious but a decisive politician, an excellent general and astute strategist, holding Sparta to more or less a consistent policy with surprisingly little indecision or self-contradiction until his death, as a very old warrior, in 359 BC. That policy, in essence, was to barter the Greeks of Asia once more to Persia – the slogan of 'liberation' had been forgotten for them back in 412 BC – in exchange for Persian support for Spartan rule in mainland Greece.

Crown princes in each royal house were, uniquely, exempt from the otherwise universal requirement imposed on all Spartans to go through the *agôgê* as a condition of citizenship. This exemption, we may guess, was granted for pragmatic reasons, in case a crown prince should prove not to be up to coping with the physical and psychological demands of the *agôgê*. However, it was surely for symbolic reasons, to emphasize how extraordinary Spartan kings, as 'seed of the demi-god son of Zeus',[32] Herakles, really were. On the other hand, Agesilaos as the son of Archidamos' second marriage was not expected to succeed to the Eurypontidai throne and therefore was not exempted from the *agôgê*, as crown prince Agis (future Agis II) had been. In fact, it was something of a surprise that Agesilaos was able even to go through the usual manhood trials and tests of an ordinary Spartan: he had been born lame. This imperfection should have qualified him only for a trip to the mountainside as an infant and a premature death, and yet despite his lameness he performed all the demanding physical tasks set by the *agôgê* with triumphant success. Agesilaos, since he was not heir-apparent, seems to have seized his chance to pass through the pitiless training régime with flying colours. He therefore embodied all the characteristic Spartan virtues – and vices.

And so it came about that in 399 BC a new opportunity arose for our man without moderation, Lysandros, to exert himself once more at the forefront of Spartan affairs. By then his personal friend Cyrus the Younger was dead, having got himself eliminated in a rash attempt to usurp the Persian throne from his older brother Artaxerxes II Memnon, and Sparta was again at war with Persia (which was now ably assisted by an Athenian *stratêgos* and naval crews). He did, however, have another close friend nearer to home, his former lover Agesilaos. At the death of Agesilaos' older half-brother, Agis, Lysandros had the notion of becoming a kingmaker and *éminence grise*. He was able to persuade those that mattered that the dire consequences for Sparta of a lame kingship prophesied by some oracle would not come from appointing the physically lame Agesilaos as king but from appointing his rival Leotychidas son of Agis, whose legitimacy was seriously in question – Alkibiades' intrigue with Agis' wife still had mileage and one rumour was that Leotychidas was actually the love child of Alkibiades.[33] Rumour can become the sweet breath of truth before turning sour.

Agesilaos had a lot going for him, in that he had been successfully through the *agôgê*, was a citizen of proven Spartan valour, and had shown himself utterly devoted to Lykourgan values. Yet Agesilaos displayed on occasion a certain *folie des grandeurs*, which cannot be concealed even by Xenophon, his great apologist. Agamemnon, in the days of legend, had set out from the Boiotian port of Aulis on his departure to Troy. On his departure for Asia, Agesilaos thought of himself as a second Agamemnon setting out for Troy, so he thought it appropriate for him to do the same. He sailed to Aulis, which witnessed the sacrifice of Iphigeneia, with a single trireme, and was in the act of offering sacrifice to Artemis when horsemen sent by the leaders of the Boiotian League, of which Thebes was the head, forcibly prevented him from continuing and threw down the victims from the altar.[34] That a Spartan king, and a powerful one at that, should be so insulted (an insult Agesilaos never forgot nor forgave) on friendly soil clearly indicates the strength of feeling against Sparta in some quarters of Greece. Sparta had become adept at the gentle art of making enemies.

Changing partners

Incidents such as these (some of which may seem trivial in themselves) may highlight the widening gap between Sparta and its three most powerful allies, Corinth, Thebes, and a passably revived Athens. How was it then that Corinth and Thebes, who had been Sparta's most steadfast allies during the Peloponnesian War and in 404 BC had both pressed for Athens to be erased from sight, slaking it with Athenian blood, and the like,[35] turned against Sparta eight years later? At first glance it seems Sparta was faced with a problem common to any superpower in its position. How do you reward and bind to you former neutrals and enemies who submit now that you are victorious, without simultaneously alienating those who have fought for you and thus made victory possible? It is expedient to show most favour to those whose loyalty is doubtful and needs to be bought, rather than to those whose loyalty is already certain. But to act thus, as Sparta did, looks very much like gross ingratitude. In encouraging waverers and newfound friends Sparta seemed to be neglecting those who had fought a long and bitter war for it and who despised those who suddenly offer their friendship to the victor once victory was won. Surely such 'new friends' deserved punishment rather than reward? Whether or not revenge and not pardon was seen as the order of the day, one plausible explanation may stem from its tyrannical behaviour towards its old friends. It is claimed that a Theban spokesman aired the current complaints against Sparta, such as it had refused its faithful friends a share in war booty and in the government of conquered territories, and in short had behaved like a master towards his helots.[36] Corinthian and Theban pride would naturally resent such a highhanded attitude, and by alienating Corinth and Thebes, the two chief allies who had helped it to power, Sparta gave another proof that it was not fit to wield that power. Something had to be done about this.

Corinth and Thebes were only half of the ant–Spartan coalition; the other half were those old-timers, Athens and Argos. During the Peloponnesian War Corinth had been one of the most active and persistent of the opponents of Athens, but it was to join Thebes, Athens, and Argos to challenge the Spartan domination of Greece. The war that broke out in 395 BC, and which lasted for eight years, is known to us as the Corinthian War, and it was apparently brought about through the exploitation of Corinthian and Theban fears over Sparta. Athens, for obvious historical reasons, cherished no love for Thebes or Corinth, but sought an excuse to escape its humiliating position imposed by the Spartan victory of 404 BC, that is 'to follow Sparta by land and sea'.[37] Moreover, we must not put out of mind Athens' former role as an imperial power; it may have been down and out at present, but Athens was only too keen to have its empire back.[38] Naturally, Argos lacked no excuse; it had fought the 'old enemy' for at least three centuries and, as such, had most to fear from Sparta's hegemony.

The fear of Sparta goes some way to justify the conflict, but it does not explain why these two *poleis* howled for Athens' complete destruction one minute and in the next are aiding Athenian democrats in exile. True, Thebes saw the obliteration of its hated neighbour Athens preferable to it becoming a Spartan satellite housing a Spartan harmost and a Spartan garrison.[39] On the other hand, Lysandros, the victor of Aigospotamoi, argued that Athens' destruction would have left Thebes in a position of power in central and northern Greece. Once Athens' destruction had been ruled out, both Corinth and Thebes preferred a nominally free Athens that was not under Sparta's thumb. In this respect, we can understand why both *poleis* pointedly boycotted Pausanias' intervention after the fall of the Thirty Tyrants in 403 BC.[40] This was the first open sign of post-war disaffection within the ranks of the Peloponnesian League, and one that the Spartans were later to hold against the Thebans at least.[41]

Corinth also feared Spartan actions against the Messenian enclave set up by Athens at Naupaktos after the Fourth Messenian War.[42] If the Messenians were forcibly replaced by a Spartan harmost and garrison, Sparta could easily close the Gulf of Corinth and thus Corinth's access to the west. In the west, Corinth also feared further Spartan intrusions into Sicily and southern Italy, particularly as Corinth had extremely close, and in some cases maternal, ties with the Greek *poleis* of this region. During the Sicilian expedition Sparta had despatched Gylippos to command the Syracusan forces resisting the Athenians.[43] Around the same time we hear too, of a certain 'Dexippos the Lakedaimonian who had been put in charge of Gela by the Syracusans'.[44] Dexippos, as we shall discover, had a notorious career in Sicily. In 396 BC thirty triremes, under the *nauarchos* Pharax, were ordered west to aid Syracuse in its struggle against Carthage.[45] The result of all these Spartan actions set in the saddle those Corinthians whose fear of Sparta was greater than their hatred of Athens.

Before we move on to Thebes, first a few words of caution concerning 'wealthy Corinth'.[46] We are constantly reminded that Corinth was a 'great industrial' *polis* much like Athens. Still, it is easy to over emphasize the aspects of Corinthian trade and commerce; they are Lilliputian when compared with modern standards. Moreover, much credence is given to the so-called tension between those who practised commerce and the old aristocracies of Corinth; the ancient sources tend to suggest that the vast majority of Corinthian citizens were, as elsewhere, peasant farmers. Also, there is a trend to over play Corinth's geographical position with the Isthmus (land narrows) of Corinth controlling both east–west and north–south trade routes. East–west trade was not entirely directed across the Isthmus, even after the construction of the *díolkos*, the artificial limestone track across which ships' cargoes (not merchantmen) were hauled from one gulf to the other. As for north-south trade, it was extremely costly to transport goods over land, which thus made trade by way of the sea the norm. The real importance of Corinth was its tradesmen and craftsmen, who were highly skilled from the sixth century BC onwards, and this is what made the *polis* wealthy. Herodotos rightly notes that tradesmen and craftsmen were generally frowned upon, but less so in Corinth.[47] With its two ports, Lechaion and Kenchreai, Corinth was also famously cosmopolitan, being as it was a centre for prostitution of two sorts, sacred and secular. The first is a link with the East, plausibly Cyprus,[48] while the second gave rise to the Aristophanic term *Korinthiazomai*, 'I act the Corinthian',[49] which is supposed to have meant either to be a prostitute or to pimp or to procure. The celebrated courtesan Neaira, the subject of Demosthenes' forensic speech *Against Neaira*, started her career as a young sex worker in Corinth.[50] Finally, it would be greatly mistaken of us to assume that Corinth's trading and luxury interests influenced its foreign policy. On the contrary, Corinth was very rich in agricultural land, and there was an age-old squabble between Corinth and Megara about borderlands.

Thebes had much more to worry about than Corinth; it was within striking distance of a number of Spartan garrisons and states friendly towards Sparta. As we have already discussed, after the surrender of Athens the Spartans, under Lysandros' direction, had installed garrisons and established pro-Spartan oligarchies throughout Greece. The first of these garrisons had actually been established as a colony during the early years of the Peloponnesian War. This was the one at Herakleia Trachinia not far from the pass of Thermopylai, which therefore controlled the southern approaches to Thessaly.[51] On the eve of the Corinthian War in Thessaly proper, Spartan troops were stationed in Pharsalos, the tyrant of that *polis*, Lykophron having recently allied himself to Sparta.[52] To the south-east of Thessaly was Opountia Lokris, and the Opountian Lokrians, having attacked their near-neighbours to the west, the Phokians, had prodded Sparta into helping the Phokians, which in turn had forced the Opountian Lokrians to call upon Thebes for help. Lysandros, who was also instructed to 'induce the people of Orchomenos to revolt from Thebes, commanded the army Sparta despatched to Phokis'.[53]

Alternatively, Hornblower argues that Sparta's meddling in Anatolia, to secure the Asiatic Greek *poleis* at the very edge of the pale of Persian civilization, was the 'true cause' of fear.[54] A Spartan expeditionary force under Agesilaos was having disturbing successes in Anatolia 'liberating' from the Persians those very same Greek *poleis* that Lysandros had earlier sold in return for financial support in the great war against Athens.[55] Even though Agesilaos was immediately recalled from Anatolia once the war broke out and his victory at Koroneia (summer 394 BC) restored Spartan power on land once more,[56] it is rather easy to overplay this idea, particularly by advocating that whoever controlled the western seaboard of Anatolia could thus control the mainland of Greece just across the Aegean Sea. In the past both Persia and Athens had dominated this seaboard and both, in their turn, had failed to dominate mainland Greece. Nor does it seem very likely that Spartan commanders crossing burning African deserts far beyond the Nile delta to consult oracular shrines would make Greece bow before Sparta, as Hornblower also suggests.[57] Conceivably, Sparta's widespread influence, both politically and militarily, could have given rise to a certain amount of alarm in Greece.

Chaos in Corinth

Unlike Athens, which had heard the din of battle amidst its houses, Corinth had escaped political upheavals until the three-nineties. It was then that two Corinthians, Timolaos and Polyanthes, the leaders of an anti-Spartan faction, accepted Persian gold to stir up trouble for Sparta in the Peloponnese.[58] Corinth, like many *poleis* of the time, had those who favoured Sparta and those who favoured the coalition of Athens, Argos and Thebes. Polyanthes, who had led the Corinthian navy to victory over the Athenians off Naupaktos in 413 BC,[59] resented the arrogance of Sparta in refusing to share with its allies the spoils of the Peloponnesian War. Subsequently, he and Timolaos advised the allies to attack Sparta before it grew too powerful.[60] Although the reverse at the Nemea (summer 394 BC) led to a partial eclipse of the anti-Spartan faction in Corinth, two months after the battle the group was up and fighting again. Two years on and the Corinthian War was extracting a heavy price from Corinthians, for their agricultural land was 'laid waste in front of their eyes',[61] and the anti-Spartan faction now feared the growing pressure for peace. With troops brought in from Athens, Argos and Thebes, they then arranged for the sudden slaughter of the pro-Spartan faction during the last days of the festival in honour of Artemis Eukleia, 'because they thought that on that day they would catch and kill the greatest number of people in the agora'.[62] Xenophon provides no figures, but Diodoros mentions 120 murdered and 500 exiled.[63]

At the time of the massacre an experiment in dual-citizenship was taking place in Corinth, with reciprocal rights between Corinthian and Argive, a common policy of the later Hellenistic world known as *isopolitai*. Xenophon bitterly complains that 'their fatherland was now called Argos instead of Corinth, and while they were forced to enjoy the rights of Argive citizenship, which they did not want, they had less influence in their own *polis* than did the resident aliens'.[64] However, we must not forget Xenophon's Spartan bias, and the intention of this democratic social experiment was clearly to strengthen the alliance against Sparta. Even after the King's Peace (387/6 BC) Corinth refused to surrender its *isopolitai* with Argos, not doing so until Sparta threatened violence.[65] The King's Peace also sees the flight of the anti-Spartan faction to Argos and the Corinthians returning to their traditional loyalties.[66] After Sparta's crushing defeat at Leuktra (summer 371 BC) the faction returns to Corinth, but its members are promptly massacred and friendly relations resume with Sparta.

The old struggle between Sparta and Athens had been sufficiently grim, but at least a principle had been at stake. The new contest, involving former allies and Athens, was not less grim and was dignified by no principle whatever. It was a crude struggle for power and survival. If we look at Corinth's stance on interstate affairs, we instinctively jump to the conclusion that it was responsible for the Peloponnesian War. This is unfortunate and even Thucydides reckons the war was the fault of Sparta, but it is not at all clear why Corinth took the path it did in the four-thirties. Modern commentators reckon that Corcyra was a commercial problem, but Thucydides sees it as a critical military one.[67] Thus the problem boils down to Corinthian anger over Athenian intrusion in north-western Greece, traditionally a Corinthian sphere of influence.[68] Apart from this episode, Corinth had always and continued to be the voice of moderation in the arena of Greek interstate affairs. That it sided with Athens over Samos when the Peloponnesian League congress was debating the possibility of going to war in 440 BC is typical of its behaviour.[69] Likewise, in 366 BC it took the initiative and played the role of peacemaker in the continuing conflict between Sparta and Thebes,[70] a common sense policy it adhered to until the three-forties when it sided with Athens against Philip II of Macedon, thereby finally coming to grief on the field of Chaironeia (summer 338 BC).

The Persian factor

A small country, if we can call ancient Greece as such, which survives under the shadow of a heavyweight champion, becomes quite naturally suspicious, sensitive, and fiercely jealous in regard to its neighbour. It fears him, but cannot help imitating him, and being drawn to him. Invariably, the larger inevitably attracts the smaller. And from its position of superiority it is natural that Persia should tend to overlook its tiny neighbour, and take Greece very much for granted. Indeed, to Persia, Greece was an appendage. Yet it must not be thought from this that the Persians underrated the Greeks. Far from it. They may have forgotten or ignored Greece from time to time, but when the Greeks came to their attention, they reserved a higher respect than they showed to anyone else. They recognized the Greeks as formidable, and were secretly just a little frightened of them, especially so after the events of Xerxes' grand adventure in the Greek homeland.

After 479 BC Persian policy towards Greece based itself consistently on the age-old principle of 'divide and rule'. However, Greek leaders were learning that the same policy could be easily applied to the Persians themselves. For instance, more than 10,000 Greek hoplite mercenaries, Xenophon included (the subject of his splendid *Anabasis*), supported the rival claims of Cyrus the Younger to the Persian throne on the death of his father, Dareios II. There is evidence to suggest that Sparta, now free from its preoccupation of the last three decades, the war with Athens, 'unofficially' backed Cyrus' rebellion against his elder brother, Artaxerxes.[71] During the third decade of the Peloponnesian War, like a pair of shipwrecked sailors clinging to the same piece of driftwood, the Persians and the Spartans had been constantly in touch with each other, sometimes directly, sometimes through intermediaries, otherwise by observation. Shared antipathy to Athenian imperialism had held them together. With Athens defeated, as we have already noticed, Sparta was quick to assume the mantle of Athenian imperialism and the former subjects of Athens found themselves under a harsher hand. While discontent against it was brewing in Greece, Sparta entered into hostilities with its previous paymaster, Persia, over the fate of the Asian Greeks: Aeolians, Ionians, and Dorians who once again found themselves inhabiting the fringe of the Persian empire. We should never lose sight of the fact that the over-riding aim of Persian policy was to recover and keep the Greek *poleis* of Asia. Thus, while the rest of the Greek world played at war, the Persians sat comfortably on the sidelines and happily fed money to keep the Greeks tearing each other apart in what the Persians basically saw as a tribal war.

The Oxyrhynchos Historian, on the other hand, is at pains to deny that the Corinthian War was the result of Persian money,[72] with which it was bribing the enemies of Sparta. For him the internal and parochial differences of Greek *poleis* was the underlying cause.[73] This could be true, but the mission of Demainetos would have reminded individuals from Athens, Corinth, Thebes and Argos that others thought similarly as they did. Again, such a mission would also have reminded them that Persia was also a potential enemy of Sparta. Moreover, we must remember too that the internal politics of these *poleis* did revolve around pro- and anti-Spartan factions, especially in Athens and Thebes. In this respect the Oxyrhynchos Historian is right to say that Persian money was accepted at Athens, for example, but equally right to say that hostility to Sparta in Greece was longstanding.[74]

Finally, the cause of this war, much like any other human conflict throughout history, involved a certain amount of bluffing, saying one thing and doing another. For example, look at Hitler and his attack on Poland in September 1939. Britain and France had already swallowed his excuses for attacking Czechoslovakia the year before, so why not those offered for Poland as well. Likewise, Athens had hoped to get away with attacking Sparta's allies during the four-sixties without Sparta responding militarily. Again, in 432 BC who would have thought that Sparta would be forced into war over Corcyra. In this respect it is worth looking at the Spartan ultimatum to Athens; there is no mention of Corcyra whatsoever.[75] As we all learn sooner than expected in our lives, there is seldom such a thing as outright settlement in human affairs; there are adjustment and compromise, and a semblance or promise of solution, but at best all that can be hoped is life will go on without too much disturbance, and immediate crises are avoided. Unfortunately for Greece, it was not to be this time around.

Persian peace

Normally a peace treaty was hammered out between individual states. However, 'common peace', *koinê eirênê*, involved all states, and the first example was the so-called King's Peace (or Peace of Antalkidas) of 387/6 BC. The germ for this idea had existed five years earlier when, at Sardis, the satrap Tiribazos and the Spartan Antalkidas conferred, the latter explicating how it would be in Persia's best interests to support Sparta.[76] Antalkidas, by all accounts, was one smooth operator.

In Xenophon's account of the conference a number of other states had delegates present, including those from Athens, Corinth and Argos, and there is a hint that Persia should sponsor peace and threaten those who refuse to participate.[77] Moreover, according to Xenophon, there was also an attempt to solve the general problems of the Greek world.[78] Nevertheless, it is important to stress that even though Sparta was not to push its claim over the Greek *poleis* of Asia, who were to become 'autonomous', there was no talk, or even notion, of disbanding the Peloponnesian League, the Athenian empire, or the Boiotian League. Later the talk of autonomy provoked one delegate to enquire about the status of the *perioikoi*. However, in 392 BC, as far as Sparta was concerned, the *perioikoi* were to be regarded as an integral part of its state. We must therefore take the talk of freedom and autonomy with a large 'pinch of salt'.

Xenophon says that these peace talks came to nothing.[79] However, another contemporary source mentions that a further conference was soon held in Sparta. The Athenian orator Andokides, who first coined the term 'common peace', explains that at this second conference certain concessions were made. Namely, Athens did not have to surrender its control of Samos, Chios and Lesbos as long as it relinquished its other alliances.[80] Needless to say, all these peace talks of 392 BC floundered. Persia finally decided to throw its weight behind Sparta, Xenophon giving the reason as Athens' failure to comply with the peace that 'the king [Artaxerxes II] was dictating'.[81]

Xenophon states that to entice Athens to the negotiating table a concession was made, which allowed it to retain possession of the islands of Lemnos, Imbros, and Skyros,[82] which were essential for Athens' importation of grain from the Black Sea region. Soon after, further peace talks were agreed upon and Greek delegates poured into Sardis for this, the third conference. There were heavy hints that failure to come to agreement would result in Persia pouring its famed golden darics, *dareikoi*, into Sparta's hungry war chest.[83] This would not be a peace by agreement but a peace at the behest of Persia, and it underwrote the hegemony of Sparta. The King's Peace was ratified by oath at Sardis, only the Thebans objecting since they claimed the right to swear on the behalf of all Boiotia. There was a danger of war: long haggling and heated words were of no avail, and then Sparta flexed its muscles and the Thebans backed down. During those initial peace talks at Sardis back in 392 BC the Thebans had been worried by the proposal made by the Spartan delegates that all the Boiotian *poleis* were to have autonomy.[84] Now, five years on, as Xenophon gleefully points out, the ratification of the peace forced the Thebans into granting independence to these *poleis*, and thus the Boiotian League, the source of Theban strength, came to an end.[85]

It is interesting that Corinth at first refused to disband the Argive garrison on the Acrocorinth – an interesting experiment in dual citizenship – but swiftly did so when Sparta made bellicose noises,[86] and Corinth was forced once more to rejoin the

Peloponnesian League. Naturally, as the leading power in Greece Sparta retained its own alliances. In the years that followed Athens and Sparta adhered to the terms of the King's Peace, which meant that they had bargained away the Asiatic Greek *poleis* to the Persians.[87] Sparta had more reasons than Athens not to break the treaty, especially as Persia supported it financially. Still, on at least one occasion we do witness Sparta meddling into Persian politics: the Persian rebel Glôs in Ionia is supported by Sparta, and as it had lost face by allowing Persia to regain Ionia in the first place, it is difficult for us to doubt Diodoros here.[88]

The King's Peace was the first but not the last common peace. During the next two decades the Greeks fell over themselves to make such Persian-sponsored treaties. For instance, there were three others before 360 BC. In 375/4 BC Xenophon suggests that Athens took the initiative,[89] but Diodoros makes Persia the sponsor, especially as Athens and Sparta were at war and Persia wanted to recruit mercenaries from Greece to fight in Egypt.[90]

Wars of liberation were a perennial problem for Persia, occurring as they did chiefly in Egypt and Cyprus, but once alight these revolts tended to spill over into adjacent areas. In 478 BC the Spartan regent Pausanias 'liberated' Cyprus, and subsequently Athens despatched two powerful seaborne expeditions to the island during the following two decades. The apogee of independent Cyprus was during the early years of the fourth century BC when Evagoras of Salamis held sway. Initially he ruled as a loyal subject of the Great King, a common and circumspect policy of the empire, and we see him aiding the Athenian *condottiere* Konon to sweep the Spartans from the high seas just off Knidos and allow the Persians to regain control of Ionia (summer 394 BC). The following year, however, it is clear from Xenophon's testimony that Evagoras had revolted from Persian rule.[91] For the next ten years Evagoras held out, even managing to extend his rule over the Aegean eastwards to the Levant, the important Phoenician city of Tyre included. Evagoras commanded a powerful army and navy, who included 12,000 hoplites, numerous mercenaries and at least ninety triremes. He also held many alliances that included one with Egypt and a secret treaty with the satrap of Caria, the native king Hekatomnos. In the end he fell under the sway of Persia again, but only after insisting on being recognized as the king of Salamis.[92]

For the Great King Egypt was the more serious problem, a running sore in the side of his far-flung empire, its one real weakness. It proved again and again more trouble than it was worth. The satrapy was extremely wealthy, supplying the empire with grain and gold, and potentially was a very powerful state. Much later, under the Ptolemaic dynasty, it was to be just that. The first revolt after the reconquest of 485 BC occurred on the death of Xerxes – he was assassinated in his bedchamber during a palace coup – and by 460 BC an Athenian fleet was aiding the Libyan king, Inaros.[93] Unfortunately for Inaros the Athenian fleet was destroyed (454 BC), but Artaxerxes I (r. 465–424 BC) was happy to allow his son to retain the throne and rule Egypt as a puppet king.[94] Ten years later Egypt revolted again, Athens despatching sixty triremes from its fleet operating off Cyprus to aid Amyrtaios, 'the king in the marshes'.[95] Persian omnipotence triumphed once more, but again Artaxerxes allowed a rebel's son to hold the satrapy. Persia was well aware of the effort required to crush Egypt totally and so chose the lesser of the two evils by exercising nominal sovereignty over Egypt. In 445 BC the Egyptian satrap was shipping grain to Athens as a gift,[96] which does suggest that the satrapy had once again broken away from the empire. This was certainly the scenario in 400 BC, for Diodoros mentions the flight of the rebel satrap of Ionia into Egypt.[97] Despite Persia's repeated attempts to recover Egypt, the rebellion was to last until 343 BC. All told, the rebellions of Egypt point to one glaring fact, namely the weakness of the empire's military forces. It is for this reason that Persia came to rely heavily upon mercenaries, which were, in the main, hoplites from Greece. One of the tragic consequences was that Greek often fought Greek. In 362 BC, for example, there were Greek mercenary hoplites serving both sides in Egypt, the aged Agesilaos of Sparta amongst them, more of which later. Egypt was a waste of effort, the great error of Persian policy, but that was all.

The Persian tiger
Some *poleis* came to feel more bitter against each other than against their common enemy, the Persian empire, and did not scruple to court the favour and use of the aid of the Great King in their selfish rivalries and war. Yet other *poleis* came to realize the need for common peace, especially as warfare was now a chronic disease in the Greek world. Also, although the longest period any common peace survived was eleven years (i.e. the King's Peace of 387/6 BC), these treaties had no time limit. Conjugated with this was the growing reality that many Greeks now considered 'Hellas to be their common fatherland',[98] and for them these peace accords were seen as brave attempts to cure the disease of hegemony, thereby putting an end to the parochial feuds that were tearing Greece to pieces and exhausting its vitality. Unfortunately, these treaties of peace invariably floundered upon the incapacity of the Greek *polis* either to surrender any degree of its autonomy in the interest of a national unity or to leave inviolate the autonomy of other *poleis*, particularly the weaker ones. Athens had held for a time the place of supremacy only to provoke by aggression general hatred and rebellion. Now it was the turn of Sparta, and all talk of freedom and autonomy – the catchwords of Greek politics – by the Spartans was in truth a cloak to hide their attempts to break the power of a resurgent Athens and a rising Thebes. It was not until after the disastrous battle of Leuktra that it became the fate of Sparta to be the prey instead of the terror of its fellow Greeks.

Whether Persia was interested in the right of each Greek *polis* to be free and independent, it is hard to say. Artaxerxes II was well aware of the political issues of mainland Greece, and he would also find it easier in his dealings with the Greeks if their states were autonomous. It is in this light that we can view Persia as the keeper of the peace. For example, in 367 BC it started to back Thebes; before that it had been Sparta who had replaced Athens. The trouble with being peacekeeper however, is the need to maintain peace through the threat of force, and here we can take the more familiar example of the United Nations' peacekeepers deployed to the country formerly known as Yugoslavia. Thus, what is required is a resolute and powerful policeman who would deal swiftly and ruthlessly with peace breakers. Yet the problem with this is the certitude that it contradicts the principle of autonomy. So, although an interesting concept, in reality there are too many incompatibles to make it all work effectively.

Persian involvement can be considered as remarkable, a tremendous triumph for Persia after the resounding defeats it experienced in 480/79 BC. In effect, it was able to dictate to individual Greek states and this raises the question of whether there was a 'mailed foot' inside the 'silk slipper'. Apart from furnishing the Athenian *stratêgos* turned *condottiere* Konon with a fleet (398 BC),[99] Persia did not physically involve herself with the Greek mainland, so the threat from it was an indirect one. The worse that could befall a peace breaker was to see its enemy's war coffers stuffed with Persian gold: if Persia spent money, Greeks spent blood. Persia even admitted its weakness on occasions, Artaxerxes' call for peace so that he could recruit Greek mercenaries being the most notable example of this.[100]

Persian service

By the time of the Great Satrap Revolt the imperial armies of Persia relied heavily upon the services of mercenaries from the Greek world.[101] Even though Ionians had fought alongside the Persians at Marathon and similarly Boiotians at Plataia they did so as subject allies, and besides the Great King's armies at the time were mainly composed of imperial soldiery, the Persians, Medes, and Sakai being the finest of these. Yet, by the last quarter of the fifth century BC we constantly hear of Greek hoplites, especially Arcadians, serving under Persian satraps, usually as bodyguards, *dóruphoroi* ('spear bearers'). Pissouthnes, for instance, in the summer of 427 BC hired out to the Samian oligarchs fighting Athens the Arcadians on his pay role.[102] Some four years later the satrap revolted, and at some point Lykon the Athenian actually helped Pissouthnes with mercenaries.[103] Pissouthnes' bastard son Amorges carried on both traditions, and when he was finally captured by the Spartans and handed over to Tissaphernes, his Arcadians nonchalantly entered the service of Sparta.[104]

The first great mercenary army (cf. the Free Companies of fourteenth-century Europe) was of course the Greek one that served Cyrus the Younger in 401 BC. Xenophon, himself one of the mercenaries, provides the figures for the size of this army: 11,000 hoplites and 2,000 peltasts.[105] As we know, the renegade Spartan Klearchos, who, on the behalf of Cyrus' propaganda campaign, said he was hiring troops for the Greek *poleis* of the Chersonese, recruited part of Cyrus' Greek army. Another contact of Cyrus' was a Thessalian, Aristippos, a dynast of Larissa, and another a Boiotian, Proxenos of Thebes. In fact, Xenophon provides a marvellous role call for the mercenary army when he describes the parade Cyrus held in honour of his mistress, the queen of Cilicia: Arcadians, Achaians, Athenians, Spartans, Syracusans, Cretans, Thracians, to name but a few.[106] In the spring of 401 BC he led his army of imperial natives and Greek mercenaries into the heartland of the empire, thus taking full advantage of the problems faced by the Persians in Egypt, which was once again slipping from their control. His polyglot army finally reached northern Babylonia where a battle was fought at Cunaxa, a town that lay on the Euphrates.

The battle is a puzzling affair. According to Xenophon the Greeks, led by Klearchos, were on Cyrus' right wing and, when they advanced, the 'barbarians' facing them fled without even coming to blows.[107] The Greeks thereupon pursued them for thirty stades, or about six kilometres,[108] that is for nearly an hour, without losing a man.[109] Despite the Greek heroics, however, Cyrus lost his life while leading a rash attempt to snuff out his brother, the Great King.[110] In one blow the rebellion had lost its figurehead, which thus left the Greek mercenaries, albeit undefeated, high and dry and stranded deep within hostile territory. They had also lost their generalissimo Klearchos who, along with four other *stratêgoi*, had been invited to a roundtable conference at the Persian camp by Tissaphernes only to be seized on the satrap's orders.[111] Tissaphernes, remember, had been a major player in the latter stages of the Peloponnesian War, and was regarded by the Greeks as a prime example of Persian perfidy, changing sides whenever it seemed to suit him. But it should be remembered too that his loyalty was not to Sparta or to Athens, but to the Great King in Susa. Tissaphernes himself, as satrap of Lydia, was to die six years after Cunaxa by royal command. At any rate, it is at Cunaxa that we read of the Greek mercenaries yelling their war cry and banging their spears against shields as they confidently ran into battle, and how they calmly opened their ranks to allow the Persian scythe-armed chariots harmlessly through the phalanx.[112] Little wonder that the Persians wanted to hire such professional soldiers in large numbers.

In the fourth century BC Greek mercenaries were much in demand. As already noted, in 375/4 BC Artaxerxes brought about common peace, the third to date, so that he could, as Diodoros stresses, employ out of work Greeks to recapture out of control Egypt.[113] Likewise, the Egyptian rebels also hired Greek mercenaries and, though Greek fought Greek, they were loyal to their paymasters as long as they were paid for their services. A good example of this loyalty to one's paymaster is given by Diodoros when he relates how a garrison of Egyptian-employed Greeks held out against the Persian-employed Greeks (Thebans mainly) besieging them. It was not until the Egyptian ruler had fled into the interior that the courageous garrison capitulated and made terms with the Theban commander, who then protected them from the clutches of his Persian employers.[114]

In retrospect

It is obvious that Greek intellectuals, such as the Athenian pamphleteer Isokrates, were well aware of the fact that Persia had supported Sparta during the second half of the Peloponnesian War. They were also well aware that Persia had switched its support to Athens, furnishing it with a fleet in 398 BC. However, the empire had dictated terms to the Greeks in 387/6 BC and as late as 355 BC Artaxerxes III (r. 358–338 BC) had sent an ultimatum to Athens concerning its buccaneering *stratêgos* Chares, who had no mind for moral scruples and was meddling in Egyptian affairs. Athens bowed to his wishes.

On the other hand, such goings on hardly prove that Persia was a danger to Greece, quite the opposite in all honesty. The last substantial military intervention by Persia had been the fleet operating under the command of the Athenian *condottiere* Konon, and when we consider Xerxes' grand invasion we cannot but have the feeling that the military threat from the empire during the fourth century BC was all smoke and mirrors. Isokrates, writing in the three-eighties, is himself in two minds on this question. On the one hand he considers the empire a paper tiger, while on the other hand he affirms that Artaxerxes II is busy plotting against Greece and consequently is a positive menace to the security of the Greeks. Still, in essence Isokrates is hammering home that it is a positive disgrace to allow the 'barbarian' to rule over Greek states.[115] Nevertheless, Isokrates' high talk does ring hollow when we read he also advocates the merciless exploitation of Anatolia.[116]

When, at the age of fifty-six, Isokrates wrote the first great effort of his career, the *Panegyrikos* (written for the one-hundredth four-yearly Olympiad in 380 BC), he urged that the leadership of a crusade against Persia be granted to Athens, possibly in conjunction with Sparta on the condition it must suffer a change of heart. But he became disillusioned with his fellow Athenians,[117] and the Spartans continued to abuse their power. In 356 BC Isokrates wrote a letter to the young Archidamos of Sparta in which he urges the king to emulate his father, Agesilaos, and lead a united Greece against Persia. The following year he wrote his political pamphlet *On the Peace*, which called for a universal peace among all men. Isokrates appears to have surrendered his sentimental panhellenism, namely to thoughts of Greeks in accord and united in a war against the 'barbarians'. However, nine years later, Isokrates turned to Philip II of Macedon as a man capable of carrying out so great an enterprise. At the age of ninety-seven, a year before his death,[118] Isokrates published the *Panathenaikos*, and though one of the most ambitious of his discourses, in it we see a disappointed nonagenarian man who has lost hope in the voluntary federation of free *poleis* with a common purpose and a chosen leadership. Aggression – the selfish passion to dominate – he regarded as the disease of Greek foreign policy.

Chapter 13

Bare Essentials

Man was given teeth to chew with and a demanding, hungry stomach. No great surprise, therefore, to find that men who go warring afield are ever looking to the next hope of food and of drink. Indeed, how to feed and water the men (and their animals) was probably the most important initial requirement on campaign, and one that found its way down to the humblest command. There is that Athenian communiqué to their *stratêgos* Iphikrates, for instance, who was unsure whether he should intercept and plunder a valuable dedication in transit to Apollo at Delphi: 'No need for theological inquiries; just make sure you feed your soldiers'.[1] Again, a certain Koiratadas of Thebes very briefly became the leader of the Ten Thousand purely on the strength of his ability to provide them with food – and they left him high and dry at once when his supplies 'fell far short of amounting to a day's food for each of the soldiers'.[2] Feeding the soldiery was a constant in every military plan, and remains so to this day.

Daily bread

One cereal or another has formed the staple basis of the human diet in every corner of the world since agriculture first began. In the ancient Mediterranean world barley and wheat were the two main grains – oats were viewed as a weed and thus considered fit only for animals, but given how well they grew in cold climates, they were popular among Celtic and Germanic peoples, while rye, the closest relative of wheat, was a 'northern' grain. Barley did better, and still does, in the dry and rocky areas of central and southern Greece, hence the proverbial pronouncement 'plant wheat in mud, but barley plant in dust'.[3] So much more reliable than wheat, barley has been crucial to food and survival in all periods of mankind's history.[4] It must not be forgotten, moreover, that maize, along with tomatoes, potatoes and tobacco were completely alien to the ancient world. English, French and Spanish adventurers not only plundered the New World of gold and silver, but also brought back to early modern Europe tobacco and other products such as maize and the potato. Yet barley, unlike wheat, is normally husked, which means it cannot be freed from its cover-glumes by ordinary threshing. It is therefore roasted, or parched prior to use. Unfortunately, this process destroys the gluten content of the grain – this determines the baking qualities of flour – thereby making it unsuitable for leavened bread. Still, as yeast was to make its debut, 'bread' in our period was really unleavened crust and would have looked somewhat like modern pitta and is an ancestor of the pizza.

Barley was generally known as 'fodder for slaves',[5] and was considered far less nourishing than wheat,[6] so much so that by the fourth century BC the preference for wheat and the bread made from it, in wealthy circles at least, had ousted barley from its prominent position in the Mediterranean diet. Thus wheat became the 'corn' or staple cereal of Greece, as in other parts of the Mediterranean basin, and barley the cheaper but not so popular alternative.[7] Thus in the Bible we read 'a *choinix* of wheat for a *denarius*, and three *choinikes* of barley for a *denarius*',[8] the measure of wheat being sufficient for a man for one day at a price equivalent to a labourer's daily wage. In the Roman army, for example, soldiers were fed on barley instead of wheat as a means of punishment.[9]

The mercenary Archilochos of Paros once sang that barley bread was the regular staple of his diet,[10] and a gentle browse through Xenophon's *Anabasis* will reveal that food figured largely in men's minds and he and his fellow mercenaries dined a great deal of the time on barley meal.[11] In fact, our mercenary-cum-versifier is fairly specific and describes his daily bread as a 'kneaded thing of barley'.[12] Made for the occasion, Archilochos' bread had been made of barley grain that had been milled to produce barley meal, and soldiers (or their servants if they could afford to maintain one) had to convert their daily ration of grain into flour themselves. Thus, hand mills were to be found amongst the mundane equipment necessary for an army simply because they were, as Xenophon explains, 'the least heavy amongst implements used for grinding grain'.[13] This meant that the soldiers could carry unmilled grain and thus reduce the risk of spoilage, as well as allowing them to take advantage of grain collected on the march. Most soldiers, if not all, were accustomed to seeing the daily supply of grain being milled by hand on the stone quern at home.

Thus, a soldier's barley ration was ordinarily eaten in the form of *mâza*, for having roasted and milled his barley grain, the soldier took his flour and kneaded it up with a little water, maybe olive oil and sour wine too, using a square of sheepskin as a kneading-trough, to produce a simple form of bread.[14] The fresh dough was rolled into wafer thin strips then baked quickly. The soldier would usually do this by twisting a strip around a stick and baking it the hot ashes of his campfire, which he then ate to comfort his stomach. Here we can cite the Attic comic poet Pherekrates, a contemporary of Aristophanes, who provides us with an idiot's guide for the making of *mâza*:

> *And now you must pile up your barley corns,*
> *and hull 'em and parch 'em and boil.*
> *Pound 'em, bolt 'em, water 'em, work 'em,*
> *and serve at the end of your toil.*[15]

It would have been consumed hot, otherwise, being unleavened, it would have gone rock-hard. The quality of the bread itself tended to be poor. Indeed, it would have contained substantial traces of abrasive mineral (feldspar, mica, sandstone, etc.), introduced into the flour as it was laboriously ground on the coarse stone of a quern. Over a period of time this grit wore down the enamel of teeth, causing some discomfort and pain at best, and at worst, serious abscesses and infections, which could prove fatal.

Wine and cheese

Good bread, solidly made, was a welcome friend, yet despite Xenophon's claim that when he was truly famished even barley bread tasted toothsome,[16] it was usually helped down with a little local wine and a wedge of cheese,[17] with onions, garlic, olives and anchovies as likely accompaniments, and an appetite to match.[18] However, the 'good old days' of soldiering, even for part-timers, was no picnic to those who had to endure them. Aristophanes' chorus of citizen soldiers rejoice at the return of peace, which brought with it freedom from helmet, cheese and onions.[19] These rough rations were commonly carried in a knapsack 'that only smells of onions, vinegar and bad breath'.[20] It seems that the whiff of war was not of black powder, but of raw onions. Homer sang of raw onions as a snack with wine,[21] a surprising snack – raw onion being somewhat overpowering. Three hundred years after Homer, our soldier scholar Xenophon writes: 'Homer said somewhere, "And onion as a savoury for their drink". So if someone provides an onion, you can have this benefit, at least, immediately: you will enjoy your drinking more'.[22]

Sour wine (surely a much better description than 'vinegar') of course, as opposed to vintage wine, was the drink of the ordinary soldier as proffered in an act of mercy to Christ on the cross,[23] and could be mixed with water to make the time-honoured tipple of the proletariat, what the Romans called *posca*.[24] In some cases, flavouring herbs, honey or eggs were also mixed. Popular with travellers too, *posca* was a refreshing drink on the road. Like soldiers, they carried the sour wine in a flask, ready to dilute when they found water. Its acidity not only meant it took longer to spoil but it also killed harmful bacteria, a bonus when the only available water came from a dubious source.[25] As Xenophon very rightly pointed out, 'only those without water really appreciate how many are its uses'.[26] Admirers of Spartan military professionalism pointed to the characteristic drinking cup of Sparta, the *kôthôn*, which made drinking from rivers and the like less unpleasant, since its lip filtered out impurities and its dark colour disguised the murkiness of the water.[27]

However, we return once more to sour wine. As well as purifying water, wounds could be washed clean with it, as the Good Samaritan did to those of the robbed traveller.[28] Sour wine seems to have served as a kind of 'cure-all', and the elder Pliny gives a long list of applications, including its use as an eye salve and for the treatment of diarrhoea.[29] Obviously, inadequate hygiene made diarrhoea a frequent comrade on campaign; soldiers no doubt often ate with their hands but they were not always able to observe the nicety of washing their hands before and after every meal.

Finding food

So on active service a soldier, professional or part-timer, shifted mainly on those ubiquitous staple commodities, bread, cheese and wine. He would normally serve as his own quartermaster, providing his own provisions at his own expense, hence, for example, 'report with rations for three days' was the standing order in Athens.[30] If a campaign dragged on it may have been impossible to provide a regular supply of rations for the soldiers to purchase, either from markets organized by vendors and victuallers who always tagged along with them or from local markets discovered on the way, so they were expected to forage for their food, that is to say, make the full use of local resources by living off the land in the truest sense of the word, which was easier said than done. In the wake of the Sicilian expedition, for example, there was a whole flotilla of merchant vessels following the Athenian armada 'voluntarily for purposes of trade'.[31] It is not surprising, therefore, to find Athenian soldiers destined for Sicily taking cash with them 'for the purpose of exchange'.[32] Two years later, at the disastrous conclusion of the Sicilian adventure, the 6,000 soldiers serving under Demosthenes still carried enough small change between them to fill the hollows of four hoplite shields.[33] Such 'travel money', *ephodion*, was as much as they could spare or scrounge. We hear from Lysias of two Athenian hoplites who felt able to join the levy only after a wealthy neighbour gave them each thirty *drachmae* in travel money,[34] which was probably enough cash to buy provisions for a month or two, a large amount for an expedition that was just hopping over the border into Boiotia.

However, having said all that, pushy pedlars, happy to sell the soldiers what they needed, frequently did so at inflated prices since demand was high and supply limited. At one point, the Ten Thousand ran out of grain, and none could be had locally and the only supply available was that to be found with the Lydian traders travelling with Cyrus' native army. Now these sharp sutlers were asking the equivalent of thirty Attic *oboloi* for a *capithê* of barley meal or wheat flour, about forty times the normal price at Athens.[35] Naturally, the Greeks refused to buy at such steep prices and shifted by dining on boiled meat. Similarly, some of the local market clerks who dealt with the mercenary army also had the nasty habit of bumping up the prices, and, occasionally, the disgruntled soldiers would retaliate by taking matters into their own hands.[36] Addressing his fellow officers, Xenophon sums it all up by saying 'small measures for large prices, when we have no money left, either'.[37] Because they need civilians, soldiers were open to exploitation by them. On the other hand, because civilians needed the profit derived from filling the soldier's belly, slaking his thirst and satisfying his lusts, they were exposed to his unruly behaviour. Campaigning Greek armies were very much like travelling circuses. A sluggish caravan of women and children followed them from one spot to the next, peddling merchandise as well as themselves.[38] These camp followers could be as numerous as the fighting force itself, and it was a standing joke even among the *laissez-faire* Athenians that their unsoldierly cousins, the Ionians, took their wives and children, and therefore bathtubs, with them on campaign.[39]

The Spartan army, as we would expect, was not encumbered by the presence of large numbers of women, children, and vendors, for not only was it better disciplined but it was also better served when it came to logistics. For unlike other Greek armies, it did not have to rely on rudimentary, largely private and informal supply systems, but had the benefit of an organized commissariat with a pukka baggage train complete with its own crew and officers, the latter being senior enough to be part of a king's war council. The train included levied craftsmen, as well as a convoy of donkeys, mules, wagons and carts carrying essential supplies provided by the state. On the rare occasions when an enemy broke through the Spartan line, he ran into a regular vehicle park guarded by hoplite sentries, rather than the usual drove of personal servants, prostitutes and pack animals.[40] But even the professional Spartans did not always manage to get the matter of logistics quite right. On one occasion they invaded Attica too early, 'while the grain was too green, so there was a general shortage of provisions',[41] and as a result had to return home after a mere fifteen days. Even so, the longest campaign by a Spartan army in Attica ended after only forty days.[42]

Professional generals such as Agesilaos of Sparta recognized the value of a hot meal. On hearing that a detachment bivouacked on top of a tempest-swept mountain was suffering, the king promptly dispatched fire enclosed in earthenware pots so that the men could keep warm and cook their supper.[43] He enjoyed the affection of his men because he was alive to their everyday needs and was not in the habit of neglecting anyone. Without a shadow of doubt, a lack of food constitutes the single biggest assault upon a soldier's morale. Xenophon himself stresses that good rations and adequate billeting were of supreme importance in the exercise of command.[44] In particular, at one of the soldiers' assemblies held by the Ten Thousand, Xenophon turns to his fellow mercenaries and says: 'Well then, it is better to fight today, with our breakfast already eaten, than tomorrow breakfastless'.[45] Like Napoléon, he knew what his army marched on.

A soldier's diet

One principle does emerge as a consistent rule of thumb throughout our period: the ancient Mediterranean world was largely a cereal-eating culture, deriving its proteins from pulses and dairy produce from sheep or goats.[46] This picture had some variants. Mountain people lacked the olive,[47] while those that dwell by the sea had access to its fruits. The diet was therefore relatively deficient in proteins by modern standards, and fish and meat was rare, and if eaten they were done so as a relish.[48] Still, it must not be forgotten that to most ancient Greeks the lack of meat in their diet was an acceptable fact of daily life, but a shortage of grain was a great hardship. Modern research has advocated the following estimates for the ancient Greek diet: 65 to 70 per cent cereals; 20 to 25 per cent fruits, pulses, and vegetables; 5 to 15 per cent oils, meat and wine.[49] During the closing stages of their march to Cunaxa, the Ten Thousand ran out of grain and, as mentioned before, could only obtain barley meal and wheat flour at impossibly high prices from the Lydian sutlers who accompanied Cyrus' native army. As a consequence, the Greek mercenaries slaughtered some of their pack animals and pulled through on a diet of boiled meat.[50] Once again, immediately after Cunaxa, the mercenaries had to shift for themselves as best they could by 'slaughtering oxen and asses of the baggage train'.[51]

'Grainless rations', the matter-of-fact phrase of Aineias Taktikos, leaves us to imagine forlorn conditions.[52] Campaigning soldiers were glad to be given meat when it was a supplement to the barley ration, not a substitute for it. Thus, they would survive on a basic ration of barley or wheat, while sharp pungent, salty foods, such as dried fish or meat, which kept well, were to be carried as appetizers or relishes.[53] From the list of foodstuffs the Spartan citizen was required to make as a regular contribution to his communal mess we know that their mess meal was fundamentally one of barley meal, cheese, wine and a few figs, while relishes – if any – included fish and meat (donations of money or hunting secured these items), while wheaten bread, if it ever graced the mess table, was considered a definite luxury and eaten as a dainty.[54] This was not a scene of a cornucopia. After commanding to victory at Plataia (479 BC) the largest Greek army ever yet assembled, Pausanias, the Agiadai regent of Sparta, indulged in a grand theatrical gesture while still on the field of battle. He ordered the helots to prepare a very ordinary Spartan mess meal, so that his men could see how its bare-bones functionality differed sharply from the bloated magnificence of the banquet prepared in Mardonios' captured tent.

Camp life

An army, said Napoléon, or so we are reliably informed, marches on its stomach. There are no truer words in the annals of military affairs than these. At Tarsus Klearchos, for instance, had reminded the Ten Thousand that 'without provisions neither *stratêgos* nor common soldier is of any use'.[55] Even so, an army also needs its sleep and our campaigning hoplite was no exception. As the Presocratic philosopher Demokritos once said, 'mercenary service teaches self-sufficiency in life; for bread and a straw mattress are the sweetest cures for hunger and exhaustion'.[56] When available, tents – usually of hides – were used to house the troops in the field.[57] On the other hand, Xenophon and Aristotle both imply that sleeping rough under the stars was the norm.[58] Indeed, Chionides, another Attic comic poet, sees fit to remind an effeminate Athenian youth of the example of those hoplites who 'sleep on reed mats'.[59] We also hear from our literary sources of hoplites bedding down for the night on mattresses of straw, rushes or leaves.[60] For a warmer and more comfortable night's sleep a hoplite (or his attendant) could easily opt to carry a blanket-roll or *strômata*,[61] and this could be housed in a linen sack when not in use.[62]

As we would expect in a world where men went from civilian to military mode in a jiffy, a Greek camp was a rather jerry-built affair, a miscellany of tents, improvised bivouacs, and men huddled together sleeping in the open air, a place to be abandoned rather than defended. A commander may behave as if he has total control of a camp, a foolish pose in truth, for the setting up of a camp and discipline within it was a matter very much for the soldiers themselves. Many of them cut down trees and gathered other materials to construct what must have been semi-permanent shelters, flimsy shacks even.[63] Others still appear to have used simple ridgepoles covered with animal skins as very basic one-man bivouacs.[64] Or failing that, they simply slept around their campfires.

Life in camp was anarchic by modern military standards, with soldiers going to bed, rising, and breakfasting pretty much as they pleased. Xenophon describes such a camp scene – the young Xenophon himself was likely present at the time – involving the cavalry of Athens. Even with the enemy close at hand, some horsemen were still slumbering in their beds while their comrades were already taking up their battle stations and the grooms were up and about currying the horses.[65] In the Greek camp depicted in his play, the *Aspis*, Menander has it populated with hard-drinking mercenaries who are busy celebrating after having looted the local neighbourhood. During the night the drunken campers, which, incidentally, is without defences, fall prey to a surprise enemy attack.[66] Such dramatic incidents, however, were not just confined to comic theatre, and examples of its efficiency are plenty. Polybios records how the Achaian Xenoitas lost his army after the forces of the satrap of Media mounted an attack, brutally swift, against his camp at first light. Xenoitas' mercenaries had feasted heavily and drunk to excess the night before and, as a result, most of them were caught unawares after the night of celebration and so slaughtered in their beds.[67] The so-called battles of Pallene (546 BC), and Sepeia (494 BC), were in truth little more than surprise attacks upon open camps where the enemy was still taking breakfast and unable to offer any organized resistance;[68] the Spartan attack at Sepeia is said to have left 6,000 Argives dead.[69] As Xenophon advises his cavalry commander, 'sometimes it is proper to tackle the enemy while his troops are at breakfast or supper or when they are turning out of bed. For at all these moments soldiers are without arms, infantry for shorter and cavalry for a longer period'.[70] Soldiers in the field, professionals and part-timers alike, can be as lazy and careless and stupid as civilians at home.

The Spartans, as ever, formed at least partial exceptions. As we well appreciate, here the mess groups were a permanent feature of social life, and this organization remained in place on campaign. On a number of occasions Xenophon refers to 'tent-fellowship',[71] which suggests the members of a communal mess shared a tent while on campaign. A Spartan camp, moreover, was usually circular in shape, within which each *mora* had its own space. But, like other Greek camps, it often lacked defences of ditch and palisade, and other facilities were primitive in the extreme too, lacking any form of sanitation, beyond a rule that soldiers should relieve themselves at a spot sufficiently remote 'so as not to cause one another distress'.[72] The soldiers themselves, as we would expect, found their time in camp much more regimented, with heralds announcing the time for morning and evening meals, which were both preceded by compulsory training sessions, and probably also the times to rise and retire. But in a Spartan camp, as elsewhere, soldiers were free to idle the rest of the day in amusements and siestas as they saw fit.[73]

We should now briefly return to Archilochos and the second fragment. In these three lines he has ingeniously provided a concise vignette for us, which vividly illustrates the basic everyday requirements of a campaigning hoplite. Not only are the essential elements of food, drink and rest portrayed, but we also see the thrusting spear, the weapon *par excellence* of the hoplite, and the kneaded barley bread, the regular staple of his diet. It is easily to visualize Archilochos with a hunk of camp bread in his left hand, the right hand holding up his leathern bag of wine to his sun cracked lips, while leaning on his spear, which is caught in the crook of his right elbow. The weapon thus becomes more than a weapon. It is a part of Archilochos' life and his mental makeup. In short, his spear is like an old, trusted friend who helps to keep him upright. For there is the distinct impression that Archilochos was the sort of old sweat who drinks to get drunk, and goes straight from upright and thirsty to horizontal and silent: no unseemly shouting or brawling. Indeed, Archilochos has already taken the trouble to tell us the label of the wine he prefers, and Ismaric is not your *vin ordinaire*; it is a vintage wine powerful enough to knock out a man-eating one-eyed giant. For this is 'the ruddy, irresistible wine' that Odysseus once used to get Polyphemos blind drunk, thereby effecting his escape.[74]

Whatever his reasons for becoming a mercenary, Archilochos' priorities are often very similar to most other soldiers once he has settled in to the new way of life. Generally they are concerned with problems of finding food, shelter, a dry bed, alcohol and women, and with staying alive until another day has passed. Soldiering brings out many things in a man, but above all it makes him measurelessly down-to-earth. In fact we should leave the last words on the subject of food and sleep to Xenophon, now graduated from tyro horsemen to a hard-boiled soldier of fortune: 'It was a little before sunset and they found the enemy at the fortification either bathing, or cooking, or kneading bread, or making their beds'.[75]

Chapter 14

Fall of Giants

It may be a statement of the obvious, but no one ever seizes power with the intention of relinquishing it. Power is not a means to a further end, but it is an end itself: the end is not wealth or luxury or respect or long life or happiness, only power, pure power. Still, it is a well-documented fact of history that absolute monarchs and dictators in the end succumb to a form of madness. When somebody comes to believe that they are all powerful, the line between what is real and what is fantasy becomes blurred. 'Power tends to corrupt, and absolute power corrupts absolutely', as Lord Acton famously said.[1] Wise words forsooth.

The secret of rulership, of hegemony, of control, whatever you want to call it, is to combine a firm belief in one's own infallibility with the power to learn from past mistakes. All past oligarchies, empires, totalitarians, have fallen from power because they ossified, became stupid and arrogant, failed to adjust themselves to changing circumstances, and were overthrown. Pride goes before a fall. All flesh is as grass and all the glory of man as the flower of grass. Ikaros burnt his wings. Man would like to be a giant – and he is nothing but a gnat. Discretion is the better part of valour and nothing is more harmful than excess. That is the law of the gods, and this law operates even more surely in the history of empires than in the lives of individuals. The mills of the gods grind slowly, but they grind surely. Nineveh was reduced to ruin. Carthage fell, as did its nemesis, Rome. It all goes bad in the end. Fate is even handed, after a fashion. All had tried in their search for hegemony to turn destiny their own way with the help of loaded dice, but fate had taken its revenge. We are but specks upon a speck in space.

The liberators

Soon after the Peloponnesian War, the Spartans 'held the hegemony over all the Greeks',[2] but to pursue its lust for more Sparta needed to address a perennial problem: the chronic shortage of its military manpower. At the beginning of that war, when the Athenians had the leadership of Greece, the Greek world had looked to the Spartans as liberators.[3] Some scholars may argue that the Peloponnesian War started as a war of liberation war, with the Spartans marching in full panoply to the rescue of the stricken subjects of the Athenian empire. But even they cannot deny that, if this was indeed the case, in the war's course its liberation colours wore thin. Whatever else was true about the Spartans, and posing as liberators was not one of these truths, two things were understandable. First, they were human with all ordinary hungers and wants, including that of always wanting more than they had, what the Greeks called *pleonexia*, 'greed for more'.[4] Second, they were very much aware that they were too few to risk the rest of Greece realizing how their sheer lack of numbers made them vulnerable. Spartan culture might help to weed out weaklings but equally it created a population crisis, and would eventually bring into being the means for their own overthrow.

Self-control – the disposition to live and let live, to cherish freedom for oneself and respect freedom in others – is not a virtue of empires, and so the Spartans, few as they were in numbers, needed others to do their own foreign work for them.

When we talk of the Spartan army, we naturally talk of the Spartans, but in truth they only formed a part of it. The rest of the army was usually made up of *perioikoi*,[5] allied contingents from the Peloponnesian League, hoplite mercenaries (Arcadians in the main) and, from 424 BC onwards, *neodamôdeis*, helots equipped as hoplites.[6] One compensatory method employed by the Spartans was to tap its abundant reserves of helots, whereby a member of this servile population was liberated purely for military purposes – normally overseas – and not incorporated into the social and political fabric of Sparta. As a solution, it was as good as any.[7]

We first witness the *neodamôdeis*, some 700 of them, serving as hoplites with Brasidas during his Thracian campaigns of 424–422 BC.[8] Technically these hoplites were still helots, since the survivors were only freed after loyal military service in Thrace – to be precise, the first attested *neodamôdeis* were those with whom the surviving *brasideioi* or 'Brasidas' men', as these ex-helot veterans unofficially became known, were settled at Lepreion just inside the territory of Elis in 421 BC.[9] Nevertheless, these helots, freed or not, were initially armed by Sparta solely for the purpose of providing troops for its military ventures overseas, with the promise of freedom and some status in the community in return. In the spring of 399 BC Thibron took with him 1,000 *neodamôdeis*,[10] and these were taken over by Derkylidas when he assumed the same Asian command in the following year after Thibron was recalled home, condemned and exiled by the ephors for allowing his army to plunder Sparta's allies in Anatolia.[11] Not that Sparta's Ionian allies always proved to be particularly disciplined, particularly on the field of battle. Two years later, when Agesilaos himself arrived in Anatolia, he had with him as part of his reinforcements no fewer than 2,000 *neodamôdeis*.[12]

Although the partially enfranchised hoplite helot could be a substitute for the hired soldier – he was probably much cheaper to maintain – Sparta still found a need to recruit hoplite mercenaries for its overseas campaigns. Indeed, both the Thracian and Asian expeditionary forces had mercenaries serving alongside the *neodamôdeis*.

First, Brasidas not only hired a large contingent of Thracian peltasts,[13] but he also raised, much closer to home, a contingent of a thousand Peloponnesian hoplites through 'the inducement of pay'.[14]

Second, on the first occasion that Klearchos had been despatched to the strategically important *polis* of Byzantium, the force that was to serve as its garrison not only included a small number of *neodamôdeis* and *perioikoi*, but also a contingent each of Megarian and Boiotian hoplite mercenaries who served under their own mercenary captains.[15]

Third, Thibron took over the remnants of the Ten Thousand *tout ensemble* (we shall now call them the Cyreians) and they remained in Spartan service until Agesilaos had completed his adventure in Anatolia and indeed thereafter,[16] since they fought under him at Koroneia.[17]

They were a hard bunch, the Cyreians, some no more than common thugs and broken men available for service wherever the pay was promised, and a causal remark in Polyainos suggests that some of them were still in Spartan service and operating on their behalf in the territory of Corinth several years later.[18] Isokrates, admittedly no fan of mercenaries and master of the sweeping argument, described the Cyreians disparagingly as men 'too base to be able to make a living in their *poleis*',[19] a view that their conduct, once they got clear of the perils of Persia, must have made widely shared. Having served first under Klearchos and then Cheirisophos, as hard headed as Spartans can come, the Cyreians were probably better disciplined than other mercenary armies, but they were not a whit behind in ransack and rape. Certainly, for most people today, it is the pecuniary aspect of mercenarism that immediately springs to mind as the profession's most morally problematic characteristic.

Xenophon, of course, would have none of it. According to him the motives of 'the majority of the soldiers' were far from base.[20] He certainly makes it very plain to his audience that he himself did not join their ranks as a mercenary.[21] Yet despite the apologia, Xenophon knew full well that the Cyreians typified the new, hard, practical spirit in warfare. They formed a highly professionalized, mercenary army, and it is very clear that these men, or at least a significant number of them, were not purely motivated by financial gain, but rather by paid adventurism. Of course money is relevant here, for someone who fought for free can be defined in modern parlance as a war junkie, not a mercenary that served for foreign money. Needless to say, deploying mercenaries, particularly as garrison troops, does have major drawbacks, a couple of which spring readily to one's mind.

First, mercenaries are too expensive for such a passive role, and Klearchos, as harmost of Byzantium, was in fact relying upon Pharnabazos' rather roomy satrapal purse so as to pay the freelance force he commanded there.[22]

Second, mercenaries tend to make a wretched nuisance of themselves in no time through sheer boredom (the archenemy of all soldiers), and when boredom blossoms among the *sacré mercenariat*, villainy and drunkenness are not far behind.[23] Take, for example, the case of Captain Luigi da Porto, who, after hearing the news that he was soon to be posted to the north-eastern border region of Friuli by his current employer, the Republic of Venice, scornfully replied that it was 'a theatre where there are few troops, most of them in garrison and thus, I fear, given up to greed, idleness and self-indulgence, the mortal enemies of the martial spirit'.[24]

Yet, despite these obvious drawbacks, Sparta found it a necessary evil to hire and deploy mercenaries and in 374 BC, for instance, when Mnasippos led his expedition to Corcyra, his landing party was made up of some 1,500 hoplite mercenaries together with a number of *neodamôdeis* and Lakonian *perioikoi*,[25] and by this date Sparta was even employing mercenaries on the Greek mainland.[26] The turning point was probably 383 BC when Sparta allowed the discontented members of the Peloponnesian League to commute men for cash as their stipulated contribution for the league's forces.[27] With the cash Sparta could now hire mercenaries, and these were later used in the Chalkidike against Olynthos and in Boiotia against Thebes.[28] In the campaign against Olynthos, Sparta also deployed a 2,000 strong expeditionary force made up of *neodamôdeis*, *perioikoi* and *skiritai*.[29] Finally, it is important to note that apart from those Spartiate officers who customarily made up a Spartan commander's coterie – Agesilaos had thirty Spartiates who formed his staff, and one of their number, Herippidas, was actually put in charge of the Cyreians[30] – other Spartiates do not appear to have served in these overseas armies or garrisons. Xenophon's comment that peoples everywhere obey 'even a single Lakedaimonian',[31] and the remark Thucydides puts into the mouth of Alkibiades that he considers 'even more important than the troops, a Spartiate as commanding officer to discipline the forces already on foot and to compel shirkers to serve',[32] shows how common it was for Spartan forces to contain a solitary full-blown citizen.

Sparta's foreign legion

Sparta ruled an empire out of proportion to its resources of manpower, and to illustrate its use of mercenaries as a military means to project foreign policy we can do no better than to look at its relationship with Cyrus the Younger during his bid for the throne of the Persian empire. Cyrus, with the necessary wealth to finance an armed adventure, had requested Sparta to aid him in his recruiting drive for hoplite mercenaries. Although in the *Anabasis* Xenophon is somewhat vague about this particular point,[33] in the *Hellenika* he comes right out with it and actually says Cyrus had asked the Spartans 'to show themselves good friends to him as he had been to them in their war against the Athenians'.[34]

In fact, Cyrus was calling in a debt owed to him by Sparta. For Sparta, while posing as a liberator of the Greeks from Athenian tyranny, had been obliged to rely on generous monetary handouts from Persia, and the man most responsible for securing and channelling this decisive Persian gold into Sparta's hollow war chest had been none other than Cyrus himself.[35] According to Andokides, the Persian treasury gave the Spartans no fewer than 5,000 talents for the war against Athens.[36] Furthermore, it is highly likely that the Spartans knew the actual motive for Cyrus' recruitment of hoplite mercenaries, that is to say, they would be used to unseat the Great King, his brother Artaxerxes, in accordance with the ancient and famous principle of displacing the superior to make room for the inferior. Indeed, if Diodoros is to be believed, Cyrus' whole operation had the full blessing of the ephors, who were shrewdly 'concealing their purpose, awaiting the turn of the war'.[37]

Sparta's shrewdness in fact extended as far as giving Cyrus a modicum of military aid. The ephors despatched the Spartiate Cheirisophos and 700 Peloponnesian hoplite mercenaries, and the *nauarchos* Pythagoras was ordered up with thirty-five triremes. They also conveniently overlooked Klearchos' recruitment of mercenaries and subsequent adventures in the Hellespont. Though formerly high up in the Spartan political hierarchy Klearchos was now a renegade with a price on his head for behaving despotically as harmost of Byzantium. To put it brusquely, Sparta, who still proudly wore the mantle of 'champion of Hellas', was not only paying off its debt to Cyrus at minimum cost, both in terms of hard cash and citizen manpower, but was also conducting a war against the Great King, Artaxerxes, by proxy.[38] If the whole enterprise turned sour, Sparta could simply turn away with little more than a temporary loss of face, but if things went right, then so much the better. High risk stakes, indeed, but at little cost and small risk. Sparta was having its cake and eating it.

As in chess, when a major piece falls there are winners and losers. But there is chess and there is a game of chess. Cyrus' death at Cunaxa removed a key piece from the board',[39] and thus, to judge by Anaxibios' hostile reception of the Cyreians when they arrived at Chrysopolis – a Greek *polis* directly opposite Byzantium, on the Asian shore of the Bosporos – the ephors, keeping a firm grip on the essentials, had in probability adopted a more conciliatory policy towards Artaxerxes. The Spartan *nauarchos* clearly wanted the Cyreians out of Anatolia and, at first, promised the soldiers regular pay, *misthophorán*, upon the condition that they cross over to Byzantium.[40] Once across the Bosporos, however, Anaxibios quickly renounced the deal and proclaimed that the Cyreians should quit Byzantium with all possible speed.[41] When questioned by Xenophon and the Spartan harmost of Byzantium, Kleander, Anaxibios simply replied that his orders stood and there would be serious repercussions if they were not carried out.[42]

In the final analysis, as the ephors in Sparta came to realize, the reasons for Cyrus' defeat were primarily political. Contrary to the assertions found in Xenophon's apologetic *Anabasis*,[43] he failed to gain the adherence of the Persian nobility and the empire's ruling élite, who remained largely loyal to Artaxerxes. Dynastic games were an old sport in Persia, and the revolt of Cyrus should be seen as a domestic wrangle – the struggle of one younger member of the royal blood to deprive the hated older brother of the throne. The essence of it was the single combat on the field of Cunaxa. Other than that, the revolt divided Persian sympathies as it divided the terrible royal women,[44] but the unity of the empire against outside attack was, save for the year of Cunaxa alone, unimpaired.

It is funny how some things do not change. For us moderns, if you have lived as a mercenary, often an outlaw, you are at best regarded as a soldier for hire, at worst a paid killer. Kleander's official position in this affair is somewhat equivocal and a timely reminder that mercenaries hang about the fringes of civil society in the twilight region between legality and illegality. Initially, he too had been hostile towards the Cyreians and even threatened to have them outlawed as common enemies of Greece. However, after being impressed by their smart turnout and good discipline, he eagerly offered himself as their commander in order to lead them back to Greece.[45] They must have looked good to him – tough, wiry, hardened by the spare life of their *anabasis*. On the other hand, Anaxibios had more definite plans concerning the immediate fate of the Cyreians. Once the mercenary army had decamped from Byzantium and its gates firmly closed behind it, the *nauarchos* issued a further set of instructions to the *stratêgoi* and *lochagoi*. The Cyreians were to secure their own supplies from the Thracian settlements nearby and then proceed to the Chersonese where Kyniskos, the local Spartan commander who was currently engaged in a bush war against the Thracian tribes, would take them 'into his pay'.[46]

The soldiers decided otherwise. Exasperated by Sparta's highhanded treatment of them, the mercenaries took matters into their own hands and promptly forced their way back into Byzantium. Meanwhile, Anaxibios made good his escape to the citadel and, its garrison being too small to cope with the worsening situation, immediately sent for reinforcements from nearby Chalkedon.[47] Left to their own devices, the angry mercenaries would have surely sacked the *astu*, which now lay at their mercy. Oddly enough, however, Xenophon claims that he managed to rally the men and then pacify them with a sympathetic speech. It also seems, from the general tone of his rhetoric, that the Athenian's political sympathies lay with Sparta.[48] Sparta, on the other hand, was now finding the continued existence of the Cyreians a political liability.

For their part, the Cyreians were in a desperate need of an adequate Greek employer – it was at this juncture that a wandering *stratêgos*, Koiratadas of Thebes, had made his unsuccessful bid for the army's leadership – and it was this pressing matter that now divided the *stratêgoi*.[49] Anaxibios, having once again rid Byzantium of the Cyreians and made the proclamation that any mercenary left within its walls could be sold as a slave, eagerly awaited the breakup of the mercenary army.[50] But he and Kleander were both relieved of their commands by the ephors back home. In 389 BC Anaxibios was to return to Anatolia as the harmost of Abydos. The ephors despatched him overseas with three triremes and 'money enough for a thousand mercenaries'.[51] Two years earlier and just after the death of Thibron, the ephors had sent out Diphridas to Anatolia with orders to take over whatever was of Thibron's command and then 'to raise another army from all possible sources',[52] that is, by hiring mercenaries. Nevertheless, their successors continued the antagonistic policy towards the Cyreians and, in particular, Aristarchos, the new harmost of Byzantium, lost no time in following Anaxibios' example and sold at least 400 of them into slavery.[53] Furthermore, Aristarchos made it known that he was quite prepared to use force in order to keep the Cyreians out of Anatolia and, again, the idea was to shuffle them off to the Chersonese.[54] They had little choice now but to hire themselves to Seuthes, a local Odrysian prince.

Finally, in the late autumn of 400 BC, a decisive initiative was announced that would mark a definite weather change for the Cyreians. The new ephors had undertaken to fight both Tissaphernes and Pharnabazos so as to secure the 'autonomy' of the Asian Greeks and, as a consequence, Thibron was ordered east armed with a mandate to hire the remnants of the Ten Thousand.[55] As the French say: *'Plus ça change, plus c'est la même chose'*: The more things change, the more they stay the same. So the war against Persia continued. But unlike the Cyrus episode, which was essentially a backroom operation supported by a few of Cyrus' friends in Sparta, the Asian expedition of 399 BC was a major enterprise of the Spartan state. The decision saved the Cyreians and in good time destroyed Sparta's empire, the benefit of hindsight telling us that this was the greatest error of foreign policy ever made by Sparta.

Grand politics aside, Sparta's imperialistic interests were also to be covertly served through two of the men who in turn held the overall leadership of the Ten Thousand. Although Cheirisophos was not, as one would initially expect, the chief Greek *stratêgos* under Cyrus, the job was to be given in effect to another Spartan, a hard man who believed in executing first and asking questions later, Klearchos. However, although this appointment was largely achieved through his own political cunning and soldierly skills, Klearchos' prominent position, as the generalissimo of Cyrus' Greek mercenaries, still required Spartan compliance. Although an exile, Klearchos was also under a sentence of death for running amok as the harmost of Byzantium. Hence his position was utterly different from that of another Spartan exile, Drakonitos, who had been exiled as a boy for the manslaughter of another boy and, therefore, had joined Cyrus as a common soldier of fortune,[56] as had another Spartan by the name of Leonymos.[57] Moreover, Cheirisophos, no less than the other *stratêgoi*, recognized him as the *de facto* leader. It was he, for example, who acted as one of Klearchos' ambassadors entrusted with the delicate mission of offering the throne of Persia to Cyrus' lieutenant, Ariaios.[58]

After Tissaphernes' treachery had cost the Greeks Klearchos, Cheirisophos, however, soon acquired a similar pre-eminence as their generalissimo. He took charge of the meeting of all the surviving officers, presided over the subsequent meeting of the whole mercenary army, and acted as the spokesman for all the *stratêgoi* to the Great King's envoys.[59] Thereafter, in the third and fourth books of the *Anabasis*, he is almost the only *stratêgos* named, apart from Xenophon himself, of course. In other words, just as his fellow Spartiate Klearchos had done before him, Cheirisophos naturally took charge of the mercenary army, but not just in any capacity, as Diodoros would like us to believe – that was to come later.[60] More to the point, Xenophon actually proposes to the soldiers' assembly that Cheirisophos 'takes the lead' since he is a Spartan, that the two oldest *stratêgoi*, Kleanor and Sophainetos, take charge of the two flanks, while Timasion and he, the two youngest *stratêgoi*, should command the rear. The motion was carried.[61]

Although Xenophon plays a prominent part in his own account, there are the occasional hints that he had, along with the other three *stratêgoi*, accepted a subordinate role under Cheirisophos. After the encounter with Mithridates, for example, Cheirisophos and Kleanor found fault with Xenophon for leaving the main body of the army in hot pursuit of an enemy that he could do little harm to.[62] During a later engagement, we actually witness Cheirisophos summoning Xenophon from the rear and, despite the lively tone of the conversation that ensued between them, the younger man did grudgingly recognize the Spartiate as the *primus inter pares*.[63] It was only after Cheirisophos' departure in order to secure ships from his friend, the Spartan *nauarchos* Anaxibios, that Xenophon appears to take charge of the affairs of the mercenary army.[64] Eventually, at Sinope, Cheirisophos having been absent for more than two months, the soldiers felt that a single commander-in-chief should be appointed. Xenophon was to be the army's first choice, but he promptly refused, and so Cheirisophos, now returned from his mission, was duly appointed by the soldiers' assembly.[65]

Cheirisophos' formal period of sole command was to be short lived; he did not pander to the soldiers' wishes, that is, to extort and plunder Greeks and natives alike, and apparently fell into a deep depression, besides having contracted an illness from which he soon died.[66] Cheirisophos' contingent, namely the 700 Peloponnesian hoplite mercenaries officially sent by Sparta, now fell under the command of his Messenian *hypostratêgos*, Neon of Asine.[67] It is interesting to note that during his *stratêgos*' absence, Neon had stirred up trouble for Xenophon in a blatant attempt to undermine the latter's growing influence within the army.[68]

Neon, although only a *perioikos*, was most desirous of becoming assimilated into the Spartan military establishment (e.g. the Spartan fleet operating in the eastern waters of the Aegean during the summer of 411 BC was commanded by Diniadas, a *perioikos*) and therefore had aspirations to becoming the mercenary army's next leader.[69] He certainly had high hopes of the Spartan authorities and thus was more than keen to see that the mercenaries obey Sparta's wishes by marching off to the Chersonese.[70] But that was not to be, and Neon, along with 800 other men, was to remain with the Spartans when the rest of the mercenary army, which for the very first time was now out of hand and beyond the reach of Sparta's normally long arm, joined Seuthes.[71] It was in fact through his negotiations with the Odrysian prince that Xenophon was to eventually emerge as the third unofficial leader of the Cyreians.[72] Equally, the Spartan officials in Byzantium certainly regarded the Athenian as holding the prime influence within the troublesome mercenary army,[73] and he was to maintain this position until Thibron finally took over the Cyreians.

Spartans for hire

As well as employing mercenaries for achieving its own hegemonic goals, Sparta had a tradition of contracting its own military personnel out to foreign powers too. A foreign commission of this type usually allowed the Spartan officer in question to act as a mercenary captain for a friendly power. On some occasions, however, it also gave him much wider operational scope, thereby enabling the officer to act in an advisory capacity, or even assume a supreme commander's role. A befitting modern parallel is the British officer or non-commissioned officer who is seconded to or contracted to (but in both cases paid by) the Arab Gulf States. In 1958, for example, Colonel David Smiley was offered the command of the armed forces of the sultan of Muscat and Oman. He accepted and held this position for four years while still a serving member of the British Army. After quitting the sultan's service in 1961, Smiley was offered command of all three Special Air Service regiments but chose to leave the British Army instead. He was soon recruited for the Saudis, his former enemies from the Omani days, by an old Special Operations Executive friend to act as an adviser to the royalist forces in Yemen. Smiley later was given command of all the mercenaries in Yemen, including a small number of Frenchmen under a certain Robert Denard, whom we discussed earlier.

Colonel Smiley (as was Colonel Denard) was a state mercenary, and it is into this category that we could place the first attested Spartan mercenary captain, the *mothax* Gylippos, who, in 415 BC, was seconded to the embattled Syracusans by the ephors with explicit instructions 'to act as their commander-in-chief'.[74] And so, once he has joined forces with the Syracusans, he immediately takes on the role of their supreme commander and organizes the defence of their *astu*.[75] Later, Sparta was to despatch to Syracuse a 600–strong hoplite force made up 'of helots ... and *neodamôdeis*'.[76]

Next up we have Dexippos, not a Spartan but a Lakonian *perioikos*.[77] He first appears in 406 BC at the siege of Akragas commanding 1,500 mercenaries in the fight to keep the eastern portion of Sicily Greek in the face of a massive Carthaginian thrust from the west that had begun three years previously. Diodoros, quoting Timaios of Tauromenion, relates that before his appointment by the Akragantines Dexippos had been residing at Gela and was in high repute because of his Lakedaimonian origins.[78] Unfortunately, Diodoros does not inform us as to how and why Dexippos had come to Gela in the first place. According to Parke, 'he was merely an adventurer'.[79] Cartledge, on the other hand, reasons that Dexippos' presence in Gela was part of an official Spartan policy of providing limited military aid to the Sicilian Greeks with a view to receiving reciprocal support in their war against Athens. Cartledge backs his argument by pointing out that it was somewhat odd that Dionysios, who was busy setting himself as master of Syracuse, sent Dexippos packing back to Greece in case the Lakonian should frustrate his plans rather than simply liquidate him on the spot.[80]

In 404 BC, Sparta certainly sent official aid to Dionysios to prop up his tottering tyranny in the person of Aristos,[81] and other Spartan 'advisers' were to follow, such as Aristoteles in 396 BC,[82] and Aristomenes sometime after 397 BC.[83] In 398 BC, the Spartans even granted Dionysios' recruiting agents permission 'to enlist as many mercenaries from them as they had need'.[84] Fortunately for the struggling Spartans, Dionysios was to prove a longstanding ally for, in 369 BC and 368 BC, the tyrant was to reciprocate their earlier support of his régime by despatching to them much needed military aid in the form of two large contingents of mercenaries. The first contingent, according to Xenophon, was large enough to fill twenty triremes and was made up of Celts and Iberians.[85] Diodoros places the number of troops in this batch at 2,000, and the author adds that their wages had been paid for the next five months,[86] which is to say, Sparta was receiving their services *gratis*. The composition and size of the second contingent are not specified by our sources.

As for Dexippos, he next pops up in Anatolia among the survivors of the Ten Thousand,[87] which does, at the very least, adds support to the opinion that Sparta readily exported its military expertise overseas. There is no sense in forming an opinion when there is no evidence to form it on, evidence being the bones of an opinion. For Dexippos, like his fellow *perioikos* Neon of Asine, was undoubtedly a member of Cheirisophos' coterie that headed Sparta's official contribution of 700 hoplite mercenaries to Cyrus' adventure.[88]

Back in 431 BC, when Sparta still had an adequate unpaid citizen army, King Archidamos had made much of the cost of war and of Sparta's lack of state funds; in the fourth century BC when mercenaries had become an almost necessary part of warfare, poverty spelled failure – or a policy of peace. Sparta's imperial sun had well and truly set during the aftermath of Leuktra, and to mend poverty (in booty if nothing else) Spartans from time to time would use the mercenary market to their advantage and even Spartan kings appear in foreign service. There is something sympathetic in the image of a Spartan king earning his livelihood – and how else was he capable of earning it?

The most notable example of a Spartan king being hired out by the Spartan authorities to a foreign power and thereby 'rending the service of a hired captain of mercenaries',[89] is that of Agesilaos. The term 'soldier of fortune' implies swash-buckling, quixotic danger, incredible achievement, all executed by a roaring, magnificent freelancer. Cranky, old and battered, but still active (and dangerous), an aura of past powers and glories seems to cling to Agesilaos and, despite Xenophon's sad attempt to represent this final episode of his hero's long military career as another dubious example of Agesilaos' panhellenic quest to liberate the Asian Greeks,[90] the truth is very much more mercenary. The motivation for despatching the elderly king to act as a mercenary captain for Tachôs of Egypt was materialistic rather than imperialistic as Sparta sorely needed to acquire a pile of cash quickly – 230 talents of silver were to be Agesilaos' Egyptian bounty – in order to refill Sparta's depleted war chest. Solvency secured, Sparta was to augment its shrinking military strength with mercenaries,[91] though it could be easily argued that the master plan was to use these mercenaries in the struggle to recover Messenia.

When he sailed to Egypt, Agesilaos took with him a thousand hoplites, along with thirty Spartiates to act as his staff officers, *sumboúloi*, as on his earlier Asian venture.[92] Diodoros provides no clue as to the actual identity of the hoplites, but the presence of the Spartiate officers does indicate the gravity with which the ephors viewed Agesilaos' mission.[93] It was clear from the start, that the elderly Spartan king and the rebel Egyptian pharaoh were not going to see eye to eye. Local rulers, however hard-pressed, rarely like outsiders to come and tell them how to run their wars of liberation. On his arrival in Egypt, Agesilaos probably made noises that he, Agesilaos, would be running the show. But he was to be bitterly disappointed when he learned that he was not to act as the pharaoh's commander-in-chief, but was required to subordinate himself to Tachôs as *stratêgos* to the 10,000 Greek mercenaries that had been recruited for the occasion.[94] Moreover, his advice to Tachôs that the Egyptian army should wait and meet Artaxerxes' forces on Egyptian soil fell on deaf ears. Hence, in the spirit of a true *condottiere*, Agesilaos set his eye to the main chance and treacherously went over with his mercenaries to Nektanebis, a cousin of Tachôs who commanded part of the army and had set his sights on the Egyptian throne.[95] Tachôs threw himself at the feet of Artaxerxes, while Agesilaos and his new boss hurried back to Egypt where another claimant to the Egyptian throne had arisen. This pretender, confusingly called Nektanebis too, tried to persuade Agesilaos once more to desert his paymaster. But this time the Spartan proved unyielding, and under his skilful leadership the pretender and his Egyptian supporters were sent packing by the Greek mercenaries.[96]

The campaigning season for 361 BC was now over, and Nektanebis tried to persuade Agesilaos to stay in his services for the coming spring campaign. But the old warhorse wished to return home and help Sparta with the money earned by his work as a mercenary. It was not to be. Agesilaos was to die on his way back home at a site known as the Harbour of Menelaos in what is now Libya. The name of the death place was apt enough for a Spartan king, but the manner of his being there marked a very sorry end to a reign that had begun four decades ago when Sparta seemingly occupied a pinnacle of power and success both at home and abroad.

Agesilaos was not the last Spartan officially to serve as a mercenary captain in the defence of Egypt's independence from Persia: Gastron and Lamias were to follow in his kingly footsteps.[97] Nor was he the last Spartan to act as a mercenary commander in the service of a foreign power: the Spartiate Xanthippos, generalissimo of the Carthaginians for a brief period during the First Punic War (264–241 BC), surely ranks as one of the most celebrated of Agesilaos' *condottieri* successors. It was he who, with a mix-bag of Carthaginian citizens and Greek mercenaries, demolished a Roman consular army at the battle of Tunis (spring 255 BC).[98] But his ace in the hole was the elephant. Xanthippos used nearly a hundred of them in a hell for leather charge to open proceedings (at full tilt an elephant can reach a speed of some forty kilometres per hour). Our Spartan *condottiere* was not one to suffer the penalty that is usually exacted from generals who fail to keep abreast of technical developments. As a graduate of the Hellenistic school of warfare, he doubtless knew the proper use of the pachyderm.[99]

But Sparta's days of imperial expansion had long gone and Agesilaos' service abroad was a definite sign of the times that set a precedent for future Spartan kings.

Indeed, his son and successor, Archidamos III (r. 360—338 BC), was not like many sons of famous fathers, a peanut personality. Striving doggedly to restore Sparta's direct rule of Messenia and its hegemony in the Peloponnese and beyond, Archidamos was to end his reign in the same manner as that of his father. Having backed the wrong horse during the Third Sacred War and with that emptied Sparta's coffers, Archidamos took the opportunity to restore Sparta's bankrupt finances overseas. After pausing to rescue the supposedly Spartan colony of Lyktos on Crete from the mercenaries employed by neighbouring Knossos,[100] he made his way to southern Italy to fight as a mercenary captain in the pay of Sparta's only true overseas colony, Taras, against the native Lucanians and their allies.[101] By a piece of historical irony, Archidamos supposedly met his death in battle against the Messapii near Mandorium on the very day that Chaironeia (summer 338 BC) was fought in Greece.[102]

Chapter 15

Masters of the Red Field

The Spartans struck an excellent, grim fighting form in the field of battle, and knew well that they were the only hoplites in Greece who, when their phalanx was broken, could reform and fight just as well at the side of a stranger. They were trained to perform the commonplace under uncommon conditions, and not for themselves alone, as Achilles or the solo champions of yore, but do it for one's brothers-in-arms. That was the Spartan way. It should come as no surprise, therefore, to find that the Spartan army does not appear to have suffered any significant defeat in pitched battle between the disastrous fight against the Tegeans early in the sixth century BC, where the Spartans ended up as prisoners of war wearing their own chains,[1] and Leuktra in 371 BC, the battle that marked the end of Spartan hegemony in the Aegean Greek world.[2] Sparta, the unconquerable, was conquered.

Plataia, summer 479 BC

The watery epic at Salamis certainly did not end the war with Xerxes, though in their euphoria the Greeks may have thought it did, making dedications for victory, and trying to decide who was to receive prizes for their part in it. But the Persian army, now swelled by the medizing Greeks of Thessaly and Boiotia, still remained undefeated. So Xerxes probably left the bulk of his land forces behind, threatening Attica and the Peloponnese beyond, under his very able cousin Mardonios. He had been the leading hawk at court, a prime advocate of the grand invasion.

Yet Mardonios was more than a hardline general; he was a strategist and a diplomat. Wintering in Thessaly, Mardonios, in his capacity as satrap-designate of Greece, tried by diplomatic means to woo Athens to his side, and when this failed, marched south again in the early summer of 479 BC, compelling the re-evacuation of Attica for Salamis. A second embassy, this time to Salamis, failed to win the Athenians over, but Spartan procrastination almost succeeded where Persian diplomacy had failed, and at one point Athens actually threatened to make peace with the Persians. In the end the Spartans realized their defences across the Isthmus of Corinth, a rugged neck of land that narrows to a width of about eight kilometres, would not save them if the Athenian navy passed under Persian control. It might be another Thermopylai. So they mobilized their army, not under the command of King Kleombrotos, for he had recently passed away, but under Pausanias, his son, who held the regency for his cousin Pleistarchos, the son of Leonidas.

According to Herodotos, Mardonios had decided to quit Attica because it was not good cavalry country and the exits out of it were dangerously narrow.[3] Before doing so, however, he decided to pounce upon the thousand Lakedaimonian hoplites that had reached Eleusis and destroy them. The attempt failed. Herodotos tells us that this was the farthest west that any Persians ever came,[4] the Mongol's Krakow if you like.[5] Mardonios then beat his retreat by way of Dekeleia and over the mountains into Boiotia. Just south of Thebes hard by the river Asopos he ordered the construction of a palisaded camp 'approximately ten stades square'.[6] Meanwhile, the Peloponnesians had moved from the Isthmus of Corinth to Eleusis, where they were joined by the Athenians under the command of Aristeides. From Eleusis the Hellenic League army marched to Erythrai and deployed along the foothills of Kithairon.[7]

Mardonios did not want to fight a battle; he was more concerned with conducting a war of diplomacy and therefore hoped to break up the Hellenic League. However, Herodotos did not believe any of this; for him Artabazos 'the cautious' was the one who did not want to fight, and he has Mardonios 'the fire-eater' pursue a belligerent policy right up to the very end. This idea can be dismissed. Herodotos' two reasons for Mardonios quitting Attica are untrue as they stand because, first, Attica did have good cavalry country (e.g. in 512 BC Hippias' Thessalians had bowled over the Spartans at Phaleron),[8] and second, the three exits out of Attica (i.e. via Marathon, Dekeleia, and Phyle) were good if not better than those to be found out of Boiotia (e.g. lake Kopaïs was smack in the middle of Boiotia). So Herodotos' reasoning is wrong but his facts are right.

Mardonios retreated because he did not want to engage the Greeks. The facts speak for themselves. He made no attempt to harass the Greeks as they debouched into the Boiotian hinterland down from the Kithairon heights. Moreover, his position along the Asopos, admittedly no Rhine and in truth no more than a muddy ditch, was one of defence. Having failed in his attempt to bully Athens into quitting the Hellenic League with his occupation of Attica, Mardonios had withdrawn northwards into friendly territory so as to wait for the Hellenic League army to break up and its petty contingents to return to their respective homes. The veteran Persian general had formulated a sound strategy based firmly upon the realities of the situation. Round one had been lost, but he was still very much in the game.

Herodotos opens his battle account with Masistios' cavalry attack on the Greek position on the foothills of Kithairon.[9] The Greeks successfully repelled all attacks, and Masistios was one of the casualties. Having defeated the Persian cavalry, horse archers and javelineers in the main, the Greeks under the Spartan regent Pausanias, and eventually some 38,700 hoplites strong, moved down to a position along the Asopos 'near the spring called Gargaphia'.[10] It seems Mardonios had wanted to give the Greeks such an experience of what his massed cavalry was capable of even under adverse conditions,[11] that they would take fright and withdraw. In any case, the Greeks responded by moving off the foothills of Kithairon and down into the plain. Their ultimate aim was obviously to bring the Persians to battle and conclude the campaign quickly, even the Peloponnesians sought this, otherwise we see no reason why they were there in the first place. As for the Persian aim, Mardonios had no intention of engaging the Greeks in pitched battle and, despite Herodotos thrice inferring that he was eager to fight,[12] he was prepared to play a waiting game, in the hope that the Hellenic League army would melt away.

Herodotos now dishes up for us a wonderful story concerning who is to take up what flank, and then provides us with dispositions and numbers. It will be noticed that he gives us 800 too many lightly armed troops – are these the Athenian archers? They certainly feature in the battle; an arrow from one Athenian brought down Masistios.[13] Anyway, we suspect that Herodotos cannot be accused of poor mathematics but has used two sources. As for those dispositions, the Spartans had the Greek right wing, the post of highest honour, while the Athenians and Tegeans quarrelled over who would have the left wing, the second most honourable post. Herodotos says the Athenians won it in a debate decided by a vote of the army's officers. It all sounds very democratic and typically Athenian. Having described all this, Herodotos now provides an account of the Persian dispositions and numbers. As for the latter, he says the Asiatic troops numbered 300,000 foot and guesses there were 50,000 Greek foot in addition – he gives no numbers for horse.[14] These figures are obviously inflated, and a very rough estimate may be provided by the size of the palisaded camp. If it was square with sides ten stades long, comparisons with Roman camps suggest it could have held 60–70,000 men, including 10,000 cavalry. As for the medizing Greeks, it is doubted that there were more than 20,000 of them including cavalry.[15]

Herodotos next tells a curious story of 'a Theban named Timagenides, the son of Herpys', and his advice to Mardonios, namely 'to watch the passes of Kithairon'.[16] This is a typical tale to provide that special Herodotean dramatic effect. He then explains that eight days of inactivity passed before Mardonios unleashed his horsemen towards those passes.[17] Mayhem and slaughter followed as a wagon train pulled by 500 draught animals was cut off and sliced up. 'The Persian horsemen showed no mercy,' says Herodotos, 'sparing none, neither man nor beast'.[18] This harassing of Greek supply lines from the Isthmus of Corinth was yet another attempt to send the Hellenic League army packing. Two more days passed during which the Persian cavalry harassed the Greeks across the Asopos. The horse soldiers rode up and down the Greek lines and, as Herodotos evocatively says, 'proceeded to show what stuff they were made of'.[19] We can imagine the Persian shooting bows, whooping and yelping, hurling javelins, and taunting the Greeks and calling them women. Matters were going Mardonios' way.

There now followed a council of war in which Artabazos advised Mardonios to withdraw back to Thebes where the Persians would find plenty of food and fodder. He also suggested the use of bribery so as to break up the Greek alliance,[20] but Mardonios argued, as Herodotos says, for a general engagement.[21] The big question of course is how did Herodotos know what was actually said? The best suggestion is that he gleaned the information from one or more relatives of either Mardonios or Artabazos or both. The second best suggestion is a contemporary Greek source, but there again the question arises of how did Greeks get to know what Persian generals discussed in confidence prior to the battle. We suspect a combination of the second coupled with Herodotos' own reconstruction. It is hard to press any of the details of this war council, yet that such arguments were being aired by the Persian high command seems a logical guess. As for the lack of food and fodder, this is rather odd as Thebes was only five kilometres to the rear and the Persians were no amateurs when it came to logistical matters.[22]

That very night Alexander of Macedon galloped into the Greek lines to warn the Athenians of the intention of Mardonios to attack at first light. He also advised them to stick it out even if no attack came, for the Persians were running short of supplies. On learning this, Pausanias proposed that the Athenians and Spartans swop wings.

Herodotos says that his idea was to have the Athenians fight the Persians while the Spartans faced the Boiotians and Thessalians, because the Athenians had beaten the Persians at Marathon, while the Spartans had no experience of them, but plenty of their fellow Greeks. The shifting of positions was spotted by the Boiotians, who reported it to Mardonios, who in turn shifted his Persians to face the Spartans again. Pausanias then returned his Spartans to their original post, and Mardonios followed suit. Absolutely bizarre, and one is reminded of that royal and incapable commander, the grand old Duke of York. Even Plutarch regarded the whole episode as preposterous.[23] Whatever the truth of the matter, and one may suspect it was an Athenian *canard*, no attack came. Instead Mardonios launched his horsemen at the Greek positions and they succeeded to choke the Gargaphian spring.[24] Obviously the Persian horse soldiers, 'flinging their javelins and firing arrows',[25] had managed to work their way behind the Spartan position and into their rear area.[26]

The result was that the other Greek *stratêgoi* went to Pausanias to complain about the lack of provisions, now that the supplies from the Peloponnese were no longer getting through. After deliberation, Pausanias suggests that the army retreats to a place called 'the Island'. Here the Greeks hoped to find plenty of potable water and better protection from the Persian horse soldiers. The suggested refuge was ten stades away, in front of Plataia and formed by two tributaries of the Oëroë – an impossible task to locate today as there is a myriad of such streams running off Kithairon.[27] Pausanias' plan was to move 'at the second watch of the night',[28] to avoid harassment from the Persian cavalry. When they reached 'the Island', one half of the army was to hold the position while the other half was to take up a position up on the lower slopes of Kithairon, in this way releasing the wagon trains entrapped there by the aggressive activities of the Persian cavalry.[29] However, panic prevails, the centre contingents hightailing it for Plataia some twenty stades away and once there grounding their arms at the temple of Hera just outside the walls. According to Herodotos, 'they had no intention of making for the Island'.[30] Bias on Herodotos' part, or is it all part of the original plan? We must remember that Greek armies were not homogeneous creations, and in this case we are dealing with citizen hoplites from more than twenty different *poleis*. What is more, the retreat was carried out during the night, and there was a lack of knowledge concerning the terrain over which they were meant to retreat. Perhaps panic was indeed what motivated the centre contingents.

At the same time, the '*lochagos* of the Pitanate *lochos*',[31] the obstinate Amompharetos, refused to retreat and argued his case all through the night. This episode is not at all clear, and it reads more like a scene from an *opéra bouffe*. But before we dismiss it as a Herodotean cock-and-bull story, we should read Thucydides' account of Mantineia to see similar pigheadedness from Spartan officers.[32] Whatever the truth of the matter, as they were fully aware of these nocturnal Lakonian shenanigans, the Athenians decided to stay put and await events. Dawn thus found the Spartans and Tegeans and the Athenians and Plataians were still in their old positions, but Pausanias finally ordered the retreat and moved off keeping 'to the higher ground'; the Athenians followed suit but 'took the lower road across level country'.[33] Amompharetos, seeing himself abandoned, followed the main Spartan body, which decided to wait ten stades away 'near the river Moloëis and a place called Argiopion, where there is a temple dedicated to Demeter of Eleusis'.[34] The Persian cavalry followed in hot pursuit.[35]

Not far from their tails the Persian infantry followed 'in the chase as fast as their legs would carry them'.[36] Mardonios, having only seen the Spartan and Tegean contingents and therefore plausibly thinking it was too good an opportunity to miss, had led his foot soldiers at the double across the Asopos, 'on the track of the apparently fleeing Greeks'.[37] Battle was joined and Mardonios was killed.

Unfortunately, Herodotos provided far too few details with regard to the tactics employed by either side. The Spartans, we are told, just sat in their ranks and endured an arrow storm while the *mantis* performed the necessary sacrifices, which were late in coming.[38] Sceptics of course can dismiss all these pious observances as religious mumbo jumbo, a deliberate play on Pausanias' part in order to keep his men in check until the right moment. However, we must not forget that it is quite clear that the ancients took all this seriously, and even a cynic like Thucydides reports that the Spartans responded to the omens sent to them from the Olympian gods. Whatever else one may say, the Tegeans finally took matters into their own hands and leapt to their feet and attacked ahead of everyone.[39] The omens then came right for Pausanias and the Spartans stepped forward to do their bit.[40] The Persians had planted a hedge of wicker shields, behind which they had let loose volley after volley of arrows. But the clash that followed 'when the shields fell', according to Herodotos, was a slaughter, with no tactical detail apart from the fact that the Persians 'in courage and strength were as good as their adversaries, but they were deficient in armour, untrained, and greatly inferior in skill'.[41] Having laid aside their bows, they flung themselves upon the Spartan phalanx in penny packets and were skewered wholesale. We can see three fundamental reasons for this.

First, the Persians were armed with the composite bow and were obviously highly skilled in its use. Thus, their inferiority in skill was in comparison with the Spartans in particular and not the Greeks in general.

Second, and more important, Persian inferiority in skill lay precisely in their rushing headlong against the Spartan phalanx, 'sometimes singly, sometimes in groups of ten men, sometimes in smaller or larger groups'.[42]

Third, the Persians' ruin, as Herodotos rightly emphasizes, was their 'lack of armour',[43] fighting, as they were, against hoplites.

Individual courage and strength are all very well, but this was no way to fight hoplites, Spartan or otherwise. The engagement on the right wing was a massacre; the Persians went down before the Spartans as skittles do before a ball.

Meanwhile, in a separate engagement, which was long and stubborn, the Athenians managed to successfully fight off the Boiotians on the Persian side, the Thebans losing 300 men for their troubles,[44] though they at least prevented the Athenians from joining Pausanias.[45] The Theban cavalry caught 'the Megarians, Phleiasians and others by the level route through the plain',[46] in other words, as they were crossing the level ground by the shortest route to join Pausanias, and this tragic episode is a telling example of what can happen to hoplites if caught out of formation by horsemen. As for the Corinthians and those associated with them, Herodotos says that they set off along the foothills of Kithairon 'straight for the temple of Demeter',[47] but he does not tell us whether they actually took part in the fighting.

The 'Dorian spear' had soundly beaten the Persian 'bridle and bow', and the death of Mardonios, conspicuous on his white charger and 'surrounded by his thousand

Persian troops, the flower of the army',[48] had decided the issue once and for all. Apparently, the brave Mardonios was killed by Aeimnêstos, 'a distinguished Spartiate',[49] and there is a later tradition that says that the Persian noble fell with his skull broken by a stone hurled by the Spartan.[50] It has been objected of course that an eminent Spartiate would stoop to throw stones, but to strike down the enemy chief, as large as life upon his warhorse, any weapon that was effective would be best. If it is more palatable to those historians who are scandalized, let us contend that it was not Aeimnêstos himself who threw the stone that killed Mardonios, but his attendant helot who, for the sake of this argument, was armed with a bag of river pebbles and a slingshot.

When the rout began, a large body of Persian troops commanded by Artabazos withdrew straightaway to Phokis, bypassing Thebes all together.[51] Naturally, the Thebans retreated to their own *astu*.[52] In the meantime, those Persians who were lucky enough to extricate themselves from the grinding phalanxes of the Spartans and Tegeans, fled as fast as they were able back across the Asopos to the apparent safety of their palisaded camp. Those who made it managed to resist all the efforts of the Spartans to break in, since they allegedly 'never mastered the art of attacking defensive works', but 'with the arrival of the Athenians, the fight for the palisade was long and violent, until at last, by courage and perseverance, they forced their way up and made a breach'.[53] Of those who had defended the camp, Herodotos says, not 3,000 survived, while the Spartan losses in battle were ninety-one killed, the Tegeans sixteen and the Athenians fifty-two.[54]

Mardonios, as he had probably been scheming for all along, had got the enemy on the run, and should have been content with a moral victory, which might have brought about the disintegration of the fragile Greek alliance. But whether because he lost control of over-enthusiastic men and was thus dragged into a rash offensive, or because he thought he saw a chance to annihilate the Spartans (and Tegeans), who, being on higher ground, were the only enemy in view, he made the fatal mistake of blundering into a confrontation that suited hoplites far better than his own more mobile, missile-armed troops and was thus routed. The struggle on the field of Plataia thus ended up as a soldier's battle rather than one directed by generals, and Mardonios lost both his army and his life.

As Herodotos says, Pausanias 'won the most splendid victory of all those we know'.[55] But we may ask ourselves why did he wait once he had come down off Kithairon, which after all offered his army a good defensive position? The move off the high ground certainly suggests an aggressive stance on Pausanias' part, and one possibility for his inaction down in the plain was that he was waiting for more troops.[56] Alternatively, Pausanias did not want to attack over the Asopos. Though little more than a sloughy stream, perhaps even a dry ditch in the high summer, it was still a linear obstacle capable of disrupting a hoplite phalanx. This is an interesting speculation, but unfortunately cannot be more.

This, then, was the battle of Plataia. It was a brave but untidy victory, won as even the Athenians conceded 'by the Dorian spear',[57] but with no great display of Dorian brains, which only reinforced the image of the Spartans both as tongue-tied primitives and as repositories of archaic nobility. Yet no Greek, Spartan or otherwise, had ever commanded an army as large as the one Pausanias commanded at Plataia, or one drawn from so many different *poleis*. Moreover, Pausanias, as far as we know, had never before commanded an army in war. We should also recognize that Pausanias' position was a presidency over a loose alliance of more than twenty sovereign states, many of them mutually hostile in normal times, with the whole alliance bound together by oaths of allegiance and not by the force of a central government, for no such force existed.

Pylos, summer 425 BC

The early years of the Peloponnesian War were spent in peripheral campaigns apart from routine annual invasions of Attica by the Peloponnesians, which did not alter the balance of power. However, in 425 BC the Pylos campaign gave Athens the chance of striking a war-winning blow at Sparta.

The scene of the campaign was the bay of Pylos in the south-west Peloponnese, which is now the bay of Navarino and the largest safe anchorage in that part of the world.[58] The bay is some five kilometres long and three kilometres broad. It is protected from the west by the rocky island of Sphakteria, but is open to the south-west by an entrance a kilometre or so wide. The northern end of Sphakteria is separated from the cape of the mainland by a channel only navigable for small boats.

At the start of the year the Athenians sent a fleet of forty triremes out from Peiraeus. The fleet was commanded by two of the ten *stratêgoi* for the year, Sophokles and Eurymedon, and accompanying it was one of the *stratêgoi* (now out of office and thus a private citizen without command) from the previous year, Demosthenes.[59] Demosthenes the son of Alkisthenes was an energetic *stratêgos* with experience of both land and sea operations. After a disastrously impetuous foray into darkest Aitolia the previous year,[60] Demosthenes, who was in his first term as *stratêgos*, had redeemed himself by saving the Athenian naval base at Naupaktos, and then by defeating the Peloponnesian army that had invaded Akarnania. Demosthenes was one of those soldiers who could profit from his mistakes, and, as we shall shortly discover, he would use what he had learned from his experiences to good advantage in the future.

The orders for the fleet were somewhat contradictory. It was supposed to be making its way to Sicily, but before reaching its destination it was meant to call in on Corcyra so as to aid the island's democratic faction currently involved in a very vicious civil war with the Corcyraean oligarchs. To cap it all, Demosthenes, though holding no official position, had been granted authority by the Athenian Assembly 'to use the fleet, if he wished, upon the coast of the Peloponnese'.[61]

In the meantime, Sparta had despatched a Peloponnesian fleet of sixty triremes to Corcyra so as to try to take the island, and Sophokles and Eurymedon were anxious to overrule Demosthenes, and press on to engage them. At that point fortune played its hand. The Athenian fleet was forced into Pylos by bad weather, and Demosthenes, surely the most imaginative of Athenian *stratêgoi*, was able to put his plan into operation.

Once at sea he had been free to reveal to his colleagues the details of the plan he could not explain in the Athenian Assembly for fear it would reach the enemy. He meant to land at a place the Spartans called Koryphasion, the site of Homer's Pylos, and once there the objective was to build an *epiteichismos*, or permanent fort, and maintain it. The position could be readily supplied by sea, and it was in Messenian territory. It had every natural benefit as a permanent base where Messenian enemies of Sparta might be inserted, both to ravage the land of Messenia. What is more important, as the Messenians were unwilling subjects of the Spartans, a centre of helot revolt would have far-reaching consequences for Sparta, which was only 'about four hundred *stadia* distant',[62] that is, seventy kilometres away as the crow flies. Demosthenes was right to believe that 'this place had advantages over any other'.[63] He, we assume, must have taken note of the area on a previous voyage and consulted with his Messenian acquaintances (Messenians from Naupaktos had taken part in his Akarnanian expedition) about it.

Demosthenes' plan was straightforward enough: to occupy the deserted promontory of Pylos, fortify it and hold it. The plan was accordingly put into operation, the place fortified in six days, which was not such a difficult task as the promontory was mostly a natural fortification with plenty of timber available nearby, and Demosthenes left with a small garrison, and five triremes. His garrison was augmented by a thirty-oared Messenian privateer and a pinnace who joined him. The total force under his command will have been in the order of 1,100 men: 50 Athenian hoplite marines, 20 Athenian archers, 930 oarsmen with improvised weapons and wicker shields,[64] 40 Messenian hoplites, and 50 Messenian oarsmen with improvised arms.[65]

Everything seemed to confirm that Demosthenes intended to dig himself in and hunker down for a long time in the position he had won, and the Spartan response was immediate. The main Peloponnesian army in Attica was hastily recalled, and the entire weight of Sparta's land forces was diverted to dislodge the bantam Athenian landing force. Thucydides provides no numbers for us here, but it is conceivable that Diodoros' total of 12,000 is about right.[66] Furthermore, the fleet sent to aid the oligarchic faction on Corcyra was hurriedly recalled, slipped past the Athenian fleet sailing north, and so arrived to blockade Pylos. The two entrances to the bay of Pylos were blocked by the fleet, and the long, narrow island of Sphakteria, which shielded the bay from the sea, was occupied by a force of Spartans, 420 strong, 'drafted by lot from all the *lochoi*',[67] along with a number of helots to service and support them. The occupation of Sphakteria was clearly to deny the use of the island to the Athenians. Even, therefore, if the Spartans failed to take the fortified promontory by direct assault, they could expect to hold it besieged and keep any relief force the Athenians might care to send at bay. The major weakness in this plan was the impossibility of closing off the southern entrance to the bay, a kilometre or so across and about seventy metres deep.

Demosthenes, meanwhile, had managed to send out secretly two of his precious triremes (thereby losing 340 oarsmen from his command, the marines and archers would have stayed) to intercept Sophokles and Eurymedon,[68] which they did at Zakynthos. His three other triremes he beached and palisaded to protect them from enemy vessels. He positioned most of his troops behind the rough and ready fortifications facing inland, while he himself, with sixty hoplites and a handful of archers, took on the more difficult task of defending the section of the rocky promontory that was most vulnerable to an enemy landing, the south-western tip of the promontory. He then shared with his tiny force a simple truth about amphibious warfare: 'It is impossible to force a landing from ships against an enemy on shore, if the latter but stand their ground and do not give way through fear of the splashing oars and of the awe-inspiring sight of ships bearing down upon them'.[69]

The Spartans, with forty-three of their triremes, attacked precisely where Demosthenes expected, urged on by the conspicuous bravery of Brasidas, who on this occasion was serving as a *triêrarchos* on one of the Peloponnesian triremes. As he attempted to get ashore, he was overcome by his many wounds and lost his shield in the sea. The shield, 'being carried ashore, was picked up by the Athenians, who afterward used it for the trophy, which they set up in commemoration of this attack'.[70] For the naval assault each Peloponnesian ship had been modified and equipped with an *apobathra*, a temporary gangway fixed at the forward end of the outrigger down which soldiers (acting as marines) could assault the shore.[71] But the Athenians stood their ground, and the Spartans withdrew after two days of fighting. On the third day after the abortive amphibious assault, Sophokles and Eurymedon sailed in from Zakynthos with a fleet that had grown to fifty triremes by the addition of four Chian triremes and several from the naval base at Naupaktos.[72] The Spartans waited inside the bay, preparing their ships for the expected hot engagement. And came it did, with an Athenian victory and a humiliation for the Spartans, whose courage was spent mainly in wading into the surf in full armour after abandoned triremes and preventing the Athenians from towing them away.[73] The Athenians erected a trophy of victory and sailed freely around the Spartan hoplites, who were cut off and imprisoned on the island of Sphakteria.

When the Spartans realized that their men could not be rescued they decided immediately to ask for a truce at Pylos, during which they would negotiate a general peace treaty and recover the force on Sphakteria. We may marvel that a fierce warrior nation like Sparta should have even considered, let alone should have been willing, to seek peace merely to recover 420 men. But this group of hostages probably represented one-tenth of the manpower of Sparta, at least 180 of who were Spartiates. They thus formed a bargaining counter of immense importance.

The truce allowed the Athenians to continue their blockade of Sphakteria but not to attack it, and they were to allow the delivery of specific rations to the men trapped there but under their supervision. In return the Spartans promised neither to attack the Athenian fort at Pylos nor to send any vessels surreptitiously to the island, and also agreed to surrender more than sixty triremes as surety. An Athenian trireme carried Spartan envoys to Athens for peace talks; the truce would last until their return, when the Athenians were to restore the Spartan ships in the same condition they received them. Any violation of these terms would end the truce, which gave the Athenians carte blanche to claim some breach and thus retain the sixty triremes. The Spartans, on the other hand, were in no position to refuse the conditions, even with such an unpropitious loophole.

Conceding the Athenians had the upper hand but reminding them that their victory was not a result of a fundamental shift in the balance of power, the Spartan envoys offered an offensive defensive alliance with Athens in exchange for the 420 hostages. The Spartan speech to the Athenian Assembly revealed that Sparta continued to believe that Athenian ascendancy was the result of circumstances that could be reversed at any time. 'We have not been brought to this misfortune by any decay in our power, or through having our heads turned by aggrandisement; no, our resources are what they have always been, and our error has been an error of judge-ment, to which all are equally liable'.[74]

The Athenians must have understood that, after regaining its hostages, Sparta could resume hostilities any time it pleased, and they recognized that as long as the men on the barren island remained in their grasp they had a virtual guarantee of peace. But, Thucydides says, 'they grasped at something further',[75] by which he means greed, ambition, and the extension of empire were motivating the Athenians.

Anyway, the failure of the negotiations at Athens meant that the truce was at an end; the Athenians alleging certain breaches of the truce, refused to hand back the Peloponnesian triremes. They now had the task of blockading Sphakteria so as to prevent the Spartans there being supplied, and so starving them into submission. This turned out to be a far more difficult problem than had been anticipated, how-ever, as the Spartans displayed surprising ingenuity in the face of this challenge, offering large rewards to free men and freedom to any helots who would run the blockade with supplies for the trapped men. Many risked danger and death and took advantage of wind and darkness to reach the island. When there was a strong breeze off the sea the Athenian blockaders had to take refuge inside the bay, while the Spartans had people who were willing to run small boats ashore on the harbourless seaward side of Sphakteria, wrecking the boats but getting supplies through, while others crossed the channel underwater 'towing after them by a cord, skins filled with poppyseed mixed with honey and bruised linseed'.[76] These heroic efforts kept the men on the island alive long after the time they were expected to surrender.

In consequence the summer wore on and the Athenians were no nearer to success. If the stalemate dragged on until winter, the Spartans could expect an opportunity to withdraw their men from the island without the Athenians being able to prevent them doing so. There was thus an urgent need for them to mount an assault on Sphakteria. Such an assault was being planned by Demosthenes, and, remembering his bitter experiences of the previous year, the main strength of his attacking force was also made up of lightly armed troops.

Meanwhile, back in Athens, Kleon, in the course of a full-blooded attack on the *stratêgoi* in the Athenian Assembly, boasted that if he were in command he would bring back home the Spartans alive to Athens within twenty days or kill them on the spot. The command was thrust upon him, and the few reinforcements he chose to take with him were all lightly armed troops, *psiloi* from the east Aegean islands of Lemnos and Imbros, peltasts from Thrace, and 'four hundred foot archers from other places'.[77]

The Spartan dispositions on Sphakteria were as follows. Since the island was rocky and landing places were few, the main body of Spartans under their commander Epitades was concentrated in the centre of the island, guarding its only water supply,[78] with a small outpost at the southern end and another one near the northern tip. The island had been densely wooded, which had made Demosthenes more reluctant to assault, as he had suffered that heavy defeat in Aitolia at the hands of lightly armed troops in wooded country. However, once again fortune favoured the bold. Because of the cramped conditions at Pylos and the fact 'there was only one spring, high up on the acropolis',[79] some of the Athenian crews had been in the habit of landing in secluded places to cook meals, and one of these crews had accidentally started a forest fire.[80] Before long most of the woods had been burnt off. This made Demosthenes more confident in planning his assault, although he now saw that the enemy numbers on the island were larger than he had thought. When Kleon arrived with his reinforcements, Demosthenes was ready to put to use the valuable lessons he had learned the hard way in Aitolia.

Demosthenes' plan called for an initial assault on the outpost at the southern end of the island just before dawn by the hoplites available, 800 all told.[81] These men were landed from a small flotilla of triremes, an operation that went unnoticed by the Spartans because they mistook it for one of the regular blockade moves routinely made by the Athenians. The small Spartan garrison at this point of the island, about thirty hoplites,[82] was surprised and outnumbered. The men were immediately overwhelmed while still in their beds. With the landing place secured, the main Athenian force quickly landed. It is a measure of the moral superiority that Spartan professionals enjoyed that although the Athenians had already landed twice their opponent's numbers in hoplites, they followed up with about 10,000 other troops, of which 800 foot archers and at least the same number of Thracian peltasts and Greek *psiloi* were to be the spearhead of the attack. The majority of the Athenian force was made up of the oarsmen of somewhat more than seventy triremes, less those of the lowest level of a trireme, the *thalamioi*, or hold-rowers, armed as best as they could be, primarily with javelins and daggers.[83] We have to imagine that, as the morning limped along, getting hotter and hotter, a weary, under-rationed Spartan band stood and faced the overwhelmingly superior Athenian host; it was cooked by the weather, running short of victuals, and almost out of time.

The Athenian hoplites accordingly formed up to face their Spartan opposite numbers in the centre of the island. But when the Spartans advanced to engage, 'wishing to come to close quarters with them',[84] the Athenian hoplites refused to meet them, and stood off and watched while the lightly armed troops, who had been split into penny packets of about 200, fell on their flanks and rear with missiles. The key to Demosthenes' tactics was the use of lightly armed troops:

> In short, they were the most difficult to fight, since they fought at a distance with arrows, javelins, stones and slings. It was not possible to attack them, for even as they fled they held the advantage, and when their pursuers turned, they were upon them again. Such was the plan with which Demosthenes first conceived the landing, and in practice that is how he arranged his forces.[85]

The Spartans tried to charge their tormentors, who easily retreated to safety on high, rough ground. When the lightly armed troops realized the enemy was physically worn down by repeated vain pursuits they in turn charged at the Spartans, shouting and firing missiles as they came. The Spartans were disconcerted by the clouds of dust from the recently burnt vegetation, the constant rain of missiles, and the hue and cry of the darting enemy, which prevented them from hearing the orders of their officers. Thucydides also adds an intriguing detail that 'their felt caps (*piloi*) afforded no protection against the arrows, and the points of javelins broke off and clung there when the men were struck'.[86] In the end, unable to reply effectively, steadily losing men, the Spartans retired in relatively good order to the northern end of the island. Here there was an old fortification, rubble built, which was held by a small detachment of their own men, perhaps thirty hoplites strong.[87] In the fort they were able to keep their flanks and rear secure, and obtained relative security from the enemy missiles.

A deadlock ensued, until one of Demosthenes subordinates, Komon the commander of the Messenians,[88] volunteered to find a way round the rear of the Spartan position, and taking some of the archers and peltasts, succeeded in working his way up a precipitous cliff from the shoreline and into a position commanding the Spartan rear.[89] With no further retreat possible and their position compromised, the stunned Spartans faced total destruction. Interestingly, Thucydides likens their predicament to the Three Hundred at Thermopylai; 'for there they had perished when the Persians got in the rear by the path, and here they were caught in the same way'.[90] But the comparison ends there, for the Athenians hastened to propose terms, realizing that live prisoners were worth more than dead bodies. Despite his men being scorched, famished and run through, the ranking Spartan, Styphon – Epitades, had been killed, and his second-in-command, Hippagretas, badly wounded – refused to take the responsibility for capitulation, so he sent a herald to get orders from Sparta. There, the authorities likewise tried to avoid accountability, sending the message: ' "The Lakedaimonians bid you decide your case yourselves, but do nothing dishonourable". So they took counsel with one another and then surrendered themselves and their arms'.[91]

And so Kleon fulfilled his boast, and 292 prisoners were taken under guard to Athens, including 120 Spartiates. The Athenian casualties were few. 'Mad as the promise of Kleon was,' Thucydides remarks, 'he fulfilled it'.[92] Clearly Kleon was neither braggart nor fool. Since it had been Demosthenes' plan to attack at once, now that the necessary lightly armed troops were at hand, a quick decision was inevitable: Kleon was certainly in close communication with Demosthenes and knew of his plans to assail Sphakteria. In *Knights* it is said that Kleon had 'one foot in Pylos and the other in the Athenian Assembly',[93] and, for all the sheer venom of Aristophanes' hatred, unmatched in any of his works, Kleon was both an accomplished orator and a *stratêgos* who had led an army to victory against the dreaded Spartans. The Pylos campaign swung the balance of war in Athens' favour.

First, it provided the Athenians with a very valuable bargaining counter to use against Sparta, as the threat of killing their hostages was a strong deterrent against any vigorous offensive upon Attica by the enemy.

Second, Pylos itself was permanently garrisoned by Messenians from Naupaktos and used as a base for raiding and subversion into Messenia. The helots began to desert.

Third, and more important, it illustrated the lesson that Greek commanders were starting to learn, namely under proper circumstances and conditions, a small body of lightly armed troops could be far more use than a plodding phalanx of hoplites.

The outcome certainly shocked the Greek world. 'Nothing that happened in the war surprised the Hellenes so much as this. It was the general opinion that no force or famine could make the Spartans give up their arms, but they would fight on as they could, and die with them in their hands.'[94] The stunned Spartans sent emissary after emissary to negotiate for the return of Pylos and for the release of the prisoners, but to no avail. Anyway, to end here on a lighter note, the Spartans may have lost the battle, but they did not lose their laconic sense of humour, judging by the following anecdote as retold by Thucydides: 'people could scarcely believe that those who had surrendered were the same stuff as the fallen; and an Athenian ally, who some time after insultingly asked one of the prisoners from the island if those who had fallen were the best and bravest (*kaloi k' agathoi*), received for an answer that the 'spindle' (*atrakos*) – that is, the arrow – would be worth a great deal if it could pick out the best and bravest men from the rest'.[95]

Amphipolis, 422 BC

To recover Amphipolis, the Athenians sent thirty triremes, 1,200 hoplites, 300 horsemen, and a large force of those excellent *psiloi* from the islands of Lemnos and Imbros.[96] Kleon, elected one of the ten *stratêgoi* for the year and still basking in the glory of Pylos, gladly assumed command of the expedition on the behalf of the Athenian *dêmos*.

Kleon initially did very well, making a feint at Skione, the obvious target, but attacking Torone instead, the principal Spartan base in the region. At the time Brasidas was away, and the garrison was no match for the Athenians. Kleon arranged a rare combined operation from land and sea that drew the defenders to his assault on the curtain walls, while his triremes assailed the unguarded shore. The Spartan commander fell for the trap, and by the time he had disengaged from Kleon and fled for Torone he found the Athenian fleet had taken the *astu*, and he himself was captured. Kleon sent Torone's adult males to Athens and sold the women and children into slavery. Brasidas' relief force was less than six kilometres from Torone when it fell. From Torone, Kleon went to Eïon to establish a base for the attack on Amphipolis.

Kleon planned to wait in Eïon until the arrival of forces from Perdikkas of Macedon and Polles, chieftain of the Thracian Odomantians,[97] which would thus enable him to lock Brasidas up in Amphipolis and then take it. Brasidas, however, anticipated the threat, and it was probably then that he moved his army 'across the river [Strymon] not far from Amphipolis' to the hill called Kerdylion to the south-west of Amphipolis in the territory of the Argilians, leaving Klearidas in charge of Amphipolis itself. From this hill he had 'a good view in all directions', and could track Kleon's movements with ease.[98]

Kleon soon moved his army to a hill north-east of Amphipolis, a decision Thucydides dismisses as having had no military purpose but rather a response to the grumbling of the Athenian troops, whom he characterizes as annoyed by their inactivity and distrustful of the leadership of the *stratêgos*, contrasting his incompetence and cowardice with the experience and effrontery of Brasidas. But even critics of Kleon would hardly have charged him with those particular shortcomings, and Thucydides himself portrays him as too overconfident and optimistic. Brasidas, in fact, expected him to be rash enough to attack without waiting for his allies, and he had fulfilled his mad promise to take Sphakteria and had shown himself to be shrewd, skilful and successful at Torone.

A better explanation for Kleon's move is that he meant to wait until his allies came, encircle Amphipolis and then take it by storm. To accomplish this, he needed to have an accurate assessment of the size, shape, the height and strength of its walls, and the lie of the land immediately outside it. That obviously required a reconnaissance in force, which is exactly what Thucydides describes Kleon as making: 'Accordingly he went and posted his force on a strong hill (*lóphos karterós*) before Amphipolis, and was himself surveying the marshy part of the Strymon and the situation of the *astu* in respect to the surrounding Thracian country'.[99]

When Kleon reached the hill, he saw no forces manning the fortifications and no troops rushing out of the gates to cut him up. Thucydides says that Kleon believed he had made a mistake not to have brought siege equipment with him, for he realized he could have used it to take the *astu* with the force he had at hand, but how he was able to know Kleon's intentions are unclear. Kleon died in battle, and the Athenians who might have served as Thucydides' informants almost two decades later when he wrote up his account of the battle were not likely to have been party to Kleon's private thoughts. There is no evidence that Kleon underestimated the Peloponnesian force and foolishly endangered his army. In fact, when Brasidas saw Kleon marching northwards from Eïon, and having come down from Kerdylion and joined up with Klearidas in Amphipolis, he did not dare to make an attack, judging his own force to be inferior in quality if not actual numbers. Kleon had every reason to conclude that he could make his reconnaissance and return to Eïon in safety.

Brasidas, however, wanted to decide the issue then and there, for without financial and material support from home his position grew weaker each day, while Kleon would soon be greatly strengthened by Macedonian and Thracian troops. Leaving his army with Klearidas and picking out 150 hoplites to accompany him, 'he determined to make a sudden attack before the Athenians withdrew, thinking that he could not again cut them off thus isolated once reinforcements should reach them'.[100] As part of a scheme to deceive Kleon and lead him into a trap, he began with a great show of making the sacrifices that habitually preceded battle and sent the forces of Klearidas to the northernmost, or Thracian, gate of the *astu*. By threatening to attack Kleon from that particular gate, he would force him to move southward towards the safety of his base at Eïon, past the eastern circuit of Amphipolis. Marching in the shadow of the *astu* the Athenian army would be no longer be able to see movements within, and would believe they were now safe from attack. Brasidas, however, planned to attack them with his select band, which he had posted on the southernmost gate of the *astu*, what Thucydides describes as 'the first gate of the long wall'.[101] The surprised Athenians, assuming the entire army had followed them from the northern to the southern gate, would concentrate fully on defeating the men before them. Meanwhile, Klearidas would advance with the main force from the Thracian gate and take the Athenians in the flank.[102]

It appears Kleon took a small force to scout the terrain north or north-east of Amphipolis. When he learned that the enemy army was gathered at the Thracian gate, while most of the Athenians were south of that position, he judged it prudent and safe to order a withdrawal to Eïon, for he had never planned to fight a pitched battle without reinforcements. Thucydides reports that before any attack was launched, Kleon, judging that there was sufficient time to get away, gave orders for the withdrawal. A complicated manoeuvre by the left wing was required to guarantee the safety of the retreating column, but this operation took some time to execute. Like a good commander, Kleon posted himself at the most exposed position on the right wing and wheeled it around to march left, leaving its unshielded right side highly vulnerable. This movement, or the failure to coordinate it with the movement of the left wing, caused confusion and a breach of order.

Brasidas allowed the Athenian left wing to advance and took this tactical misstep as an opportunity to attack. He burst from the southern gate at the run and struck the Athenian centre, which was taken wholly by surprise. The Athenians, 'amazed by his audacity, as well as panic-stricken because of their own disorder, turned and ran'.[103] At just the right moment Klearidas, as he had been ordered, burst from the Thracian gate, catching the Athenians on the flank and throwing them into further disarray.

Being out of reach and well on their way south, the men on the left wing hastened to Eïon. The now outnumbered men on the right wing, where Kleon was in stationed, stood their ground bravely. As for Kleon himself, who had never intended to stand and fight, Thucydides tells us that he 'fled at once', and was overtaken and dispatched by the javelin of a Myrkinian peltast.[104] However, coward or not, and we have only Thucydides' accusation for such, his contemporaries believed that Kleon served bravely at Amphipolis,[105] and, along with those who fought with him, he was buried in the Kerameikos, where the honoured war dead was entombed in the Demosion Sema, the State Burial Ground. In Sparta, as we know, those who died in battle were buried where they fell but, during the early fifth century BC, the Athenians began the practice of bringing home their war dead, honouring them with a state funeral and burying them here. Thucydides explains the practice of funerary orations and describes the celebrated oration of Perikles on the dead of the first year of the Peloponnesian War.[106] So Kleon was interned alongside the tyrannicides Harmodios and Aristogeiton, and other important figures, including his old political rival, Perikles himself.

In spite of Kleon's death his men stood their ground and struggled bravely. They had rallied at 'their first position on the hill [viz. the *lóphos karterós*], twice or thrice repulsed the attack of Klearidas', and they were not routed until assailed by the Myrkinian javelineers and Chalcidian horsemen, 'who surrounded and hurled javelins at them'.[107] The Athenian cavalry seems to have been left behind at Eïon, since no battle had been intended or expected, a grave mistake in truth. About 600 Athenians fell, while only seven Spartans fell, among whom was Brasidas, who was carried from the field still breathing, but like Nelson, he lived long enough to learn he had won his final battle. According to Plutarch, a spear had penetrated through his shield, which prompted Brasidas to exclaim: 'My shield betrayed me'.[108] Brasidas does not seem to have had much luck with his shields, having lost one in the sea at Pylos and another, his last, split asunder outside Amphipolis.

Brasidas and Kleon, the pestles of war, as Aristophanes mockingly called them,[109] 'the men on each side most opposed to peace', as Thucydides said,[110] were dead. After almost a decade of war the words that spring to mind are Macbeth's. 'It is a tale / Told by an idiot, full of sound and fury, / Signifying nothing'.[111]

Mantineia, summer 418 BC

In 419 BC the Argives opened a campaign against their old homegrown enemies, the Epidaurians, so as to secure themselves any offensive moves originating by way of Corinth and to allow their new allies, the Athenians, easier access into the Argolid from the island of Aegina. The Spartans garrisoned Epidauros in response. Finally, in the next year, the Spartans under their young king Agis launched a major expedition against Argos, calling up the Corinthians and Boiotians in support. A showy series of evolutions and manoeuvres resulted in the Argive army being trapped between converging columns of Spartans and their allies while deployed at Nemea. Instead of crushing the Argives, Agis concluded a truce. Presumably this was done in the hope that Agis' oligarchic friends could win Argos over. The king was wrong. The Argives were persuaded by Alkibiades to dig in and resume the war. It was at this point that Orchomenos in Arcadia was captured by the forces of the confederation against Sparta – Argos, Athens, Mantineia and Elis. Sparta's northern allies, Sikyon, Corinth, Boiotia, Phokis and Lokris were now hampered in their attempts to join the Spartans in their campaign in the Argolid.

This event marked the total failure of Agis' policy of a rapprochement, and went some way to explain the reaction of the ephors towards him on his return. In their anger they resolved to demolish his house as a symbol of disgrace and fine him 100,000 *drachmae* (*c.* 23 Aiginetan talents), but his promise to avenge the disgrace when he next took the field stayed their hand for the time being. The confederates, prompted by the Mantineians, decided to advance on Tegea, Mantineia's ancient foe and Sparta's staunchest ally, in opposition to the Eleians, who wanted to move against Lepreion, a Spartan stronghold on their border with Messenia.[112] The Eleians took offence and voted with their feet by withdrawing their contingent of at least 3,000 hoplites. This created a numerical disparity between the two sides.

The threat to Tegea was both external and internal and the Spartans reacted with unaccustomed speed, mobilizing 'the Lakedaimonians themselves and of the helots in full force'.[113] This speed shows the perceived magnitude of the threat to Sparta's position in the Peloponnese as well as to its borders. Sparta was to be left undefended.

The choice of Agis to command the Spartan army heading north, despite the anger against him, must have been due to the discrediting of the other king, Pleistoanax, who had favoured an alliance with Athens. Agis' past record must be a factor in assessing his conduct on this campaign. He had shown himself to be both unlucky and unskilled in a Spartan king's chief function, the conduct of war. His two invasions of Attica had been unsuccessful, and neither campaign had given him any experience in battle, and both were attended by bad luck. To this must be added the failure of his earlier expedition against Argos. Twice he had turned back from the frontier, allegedly because of unfavourable omens, and when he finally had the chance to fight an outnumbered and surrounded Argive army, as we have just discussed, he had rejected it. Little surprise, therefore, to find that this dissatisfaction with Agis' recent conduct meant ten advisors, *sumboúloi*, were selected and appointed to accompany him on this campaign. But their actual role is far from clear. In Thucydides' account the advisors do not play any role at all as a group. They must have exercised some general oversight over the campaign strategy, while the battlefield tactics were probably left to the king to avoid a division of command. Their appointment is unparalleled on a campaign conducted by a Spartan king. Anyway, Mantineia was Agis' last opportunity to prove himself; success would bring salvation, but failure would mean shame.

Agis and his army marched up the Eurotas valley towards the north-west, a route that assured an easier passage for the commissariat and its wagons, and facilitated a meeting with the Arcadian allies. The choice of Orestheion in Mainalia as a stopping point on the border with Arcadian facilitated his juncture with them. The united army then crossed the south-east corner of the plain of that *polis*. It must have been here that the king received the welcome news that the Eleians were not going to play. This meant he would now have a numerical advantage and this allowed him to send one-sixth of his army back to defend Sparta while still keeping his superiority in numbers. Thucydides says this 'included the older and younger men',[114] and Lazenby reckons that this sixth part consisted of eighteen- and nineteen-year-olds and the last five age classes, thereby leaving the age classes from twenty to fifty-four inclusive.[115]

The best modern estimates are about 10,000 to 11,000 hoplites on the Spartan side opposed by 9,000 to 10,000 on the confederate side. Three unusual units feature in this battle. To prepare for war, Argos had trained at state expense 1,000 young men who were 'strongest in body and in wealth' as an élite band capable of fighting the Spartans at their own game,[116] or so it was hoped. The *brasideioi* were the veteran survivors of those who had campaigned with Brasidas in Thrace and were enfranchised helots who had been rewarded for their military service. They had been brought back home by Klearidas, and were still fighting in a separate unit, not mixed with the Spartans proper, hence their unit moniker. Agis also had some *neodamôdeis*, helots who had yet to earn their freedom through military service. Finally, there was the *skiritai*, frontiersmen from the uplands north-west of Sparta, Arcadians rather than Lakedaimonians perhaps, who usually served as scouts or operated alongside cavalry.[117]

There are a number of topographical puzzles in Thucydides' account. It may be that he had never personally visited the battle site. The Herakleion, which was a sanctuary dedicated to Herakles and was the appropriate location of the Spartan camp, *tò stratópedon*,[118] was probably in the eastern side of the Mantiniki, at the foot of what the ancients called Mount Alesion, today's Mount Barbéri (1,030 metres), and it was on the lower slopes of this same mountain that the confederates originally encamped, in what Thucydides describes as 'a strong position, which was difficult to approach'.[119] By now the Eleians had been asked to rejoin their allies and were on their way, and a thousand hoplite reinforcements from Athens were also en route, With the Eleians and the extra Athenians the confederates would have a superiority in numbers and could choose the moment to fight, so long as the battle took place before Sparta's northern allies could appear. Until reinforcements reached them, the confederates had every reason to sit tight and avoid battle, unless Agis was foolhardy enough to come to them.

This is exactly what Agis attempted to do, charging his men up the lower slopes of Mount Alesion. It was a reckless act of a desperate man, for even with a small numerical advantage an uphill slog against waiting hoplites was doomed. The Spartans came 'within a stone's throw or a javelin's cast' when the advance suddenly halted. 'One of the older men', gauging the impossibility of the situation, called out to Agis that what he had in mind was 'to cure one wrong with another',[120] alluding to the king's alleged failure earlier that summer to crush the Argive army. The wise elder was perhaps one of the *sumboúloi*, who understood that with this madcap action, the young king was attempting to erase the memory of his behaviour in the Argolid. Heeding the warning Agis ordered a rapid retreat without making contact with the enemy, and only the unwillingness of the confederates to pursue him prevented a disaster. The idea had been insane, and it had been a blunder of the highest magnitude.

It appears that, when he gave up his abortive attack on the confederates, Agis decided that the only way to bring his opponents down from the heights to give battle was to divert into the Mantiniki what Thucydides calls 'the stream of water', and says was a source of friction between Mantineia and Tegea. Agis' plan was to force the Mantineians to come down off their hill to prevent the flooding of their territory, and so bring about a battle on the plain.[121] Since the Mantiniki slopes down slightly towards its northern end where Mantineia stood, the planned hydraulic operation would be a too difficult undertaking. Probably what was diverted were the contents of a major watercourse in the southern part of the Mantiniki near Tegea, the stream now called the Sarandapotamos, into another stream, the Zanovistas, which flowed north into Mantineian territory, thereby inundating that area when the more copious waters of the former had raised the water level of the latter. Presumably there already existed a channel that connected the two streams. This would explain the speed of the operation, which took less than a day to complete. Moreover, as all the streams and mountain torrents of the Mantiniki emptied into sinkholes in the limestone beneath the soil, selected sinkholes could be stopped up and with the onset of the autumnal rains, which were due in a matter of weeks, Mantineian territory would be totally swamped. As these hydraulic fun and games were going on, Agis sent a message to Sparta asking that the men he had sent back earlier rejoin him at Tegea.

Agis' plan, the best gamble available to a desperate man, assumed that the Mantineians would force their allies to seek a battle the confederates as a whole wanted to delay. After the day spent in the territory of Tegea he marched again toward the Mantineian Herakleion, keen to put his army in battle order so as to fight and await the confederate advance off the lower slopes of Mount Alesion and down into the plain. But Agis never reached his old camping ground at the Herakleion. Instead the stuff of Greek alliances, political suspicion and distrust, played directly into his hands.

After the sudden withdrawal of the Spartan army from Mount Alesion the confederate forces were astonished, and the Argives in particular began to complain of their *stratêgoi* inaction: 'On a previous occasion the Lakedaimonians, when fairly caught near Argos, had been allowed to escape, and now when they were on the run no one bothered to pursue them; on the contrary, the enemy were quietly making good their safety, while they themselves were being betrayed'.[122] The last word Thucydides' uses is revealing, for he puts into the mouths of the malcontent soldiers the charge of treason and not, as we would expect, cowardice. It is possible that the accused *stratêgoi* were those from the thousand picked men of the Argives, and as Agis' earlier approaches to the oligarchs of that *polis* must have made them suspect among the democrats of Argos as well as the democratic members of the confederacy, the Athenians and the Mantineians. The intensification of such suspicions now compelled them to descend the heights into the plain and prepare for battle.

As Agis' army advanced in a column of march northwards he was flabbergasted to find the confederate army close by, well away from Mount Alesion and in full battle order.[123] The confederates had camped in the plain over night, and their pickets must have informed the confederate *stratêgoi* of Agis' approach. As a consequence they were able to deploy and wait in a line of battle of their own choosing. Some would say that Agis had blundered into a trap, and they are probably correct. Nonetheless, we have to understand those Greek armies, even the Spartan one, did not behave as modern armies are meant to do, and would therefore have screened its advance with patrols to feel the way. Besides, even modern armies have been taken by surprise.

The king's first urgency of course was to deploy his army for battle before the enemy could exploit its temporary disarray and attack. Here the unrivalled discipline, training and organization of the Spartan army came into its own, for Agis only needed to give his orders to the *polemarchoi* of the six Spartan *lochoi*, as Thucydides continually calls them,[124] and the chain of command did the rest. Unlike other Greek armies, the Spartan army, in the notable words of Thucydides, 'was composed of officers commanding other officers, for the responsibility of carrying out orders is shared by many'.[125] All the same, Agis had an uncommon stroke of luck as the confederate *stratêgoi* chose not to strike before his army could form into line of battle, though pressed by their soldiers' disgruntlement they obviously looked determined to decide the issue that very day. The Spartans were able to deploy for battle, and even had time to encourage each other with their war songs and reminders of their martial prowess while the confederate *stratêgoi* encouraged their men with appropriate harangues.[126]

It has been suggested that the deployment of the confederate army reveals careful planning, with the right wing being ordered to take the offensive and fight the decisive part of the battle while the left wing was ordered to stand fast in a holding operation.[127] But this is not the case. The placing of the Mantineians on the right wing, along with their Arcadian allies, was not because they were the best of the bunch but because they were fighting on their home ground and thus expected the position of honour in the battleline. Alongside the Arcadians stood the thousand picked men of the Argives, and this élite unit was surely the best of the bunch and if there had indeed been a battle plan they would have been placed on the right wing so as to deliver the killing blow. As we can see this was not the case, and next in line stood the older hoplites of Argos, and beside them the hoplites of Orneai and Kleonai. On the left wing were the Athenians supported by their own horsemen, being placed there because they were the only contingent that had cavalry and this by convention was placed on a wing. Apart from the number for the élite Argives, Thucydides gives no figures for the confederate side, though we can infer from an earlier reference to a thousand Athenian hoplites and 300 horsemen.[128] For the other contingents we can only guess: the Mantineians may have numbered about 3,000 hoplites,[129] the older Argives 5,000, the other Arcadians and Argolids perhaps a thousand in all.[130]

Likewise, it has been suggested that the Spartan line of battle indicates no particular plan of battle, but it is more probable that it was largely dictated by convention rather than confusion. For the *skiritai*, 600 in number, held their customary position on the left wing.[131] Next came the *brasideioi*, those veteran ex-helots who had earned their freedom fighting under Brasidas in Thrace, along with a number of new fighting helots, *neodamôdeis*, together numbering 512 hoplites according to Thucydides.[132] The Spartans themselves held the centre, as Thucydides says 'ranging their *lochoi* one after another', and next to them stood their Arcadian allies from Heraia and Mainalia. Though the battle was not being fought in their territory but next door, the Tegeans took up the position of honour on the right wing, supported by 'a few of the Lakedaimonians' who held the extreme right of the battleline, perhaps to stiffen the Arcadians. Thucydides gives us no numbers for these Arcadian hoplites. The force of cavalry was split between both flanks, numbers and composition unknown.[133]

The confederate army of 10,000 hoplites stretched across a front that extended about a kilometre, while the Spartan army of about 11,000 hoplites formed a battle-line about a hundred metres longer.[134] The Tegeans and the small contingent of Lakedaimonians with them on the right wing extended beyond the Athenians opposite them on the confederate left, but the slightly outnumbered confederates did not try to compensate for that deficit by sending forces there. On the contrary, they extended their own right far beyond the *skiritai* on the enemy left. The Spartans advanced at their customary slow pace, keeping time to the measured rhythm of the many flute players who played to preserve the order of the phalanx, but the confederates 'advancing eagerly and impetuously'.[135] Plainly the confederate *stratêgoi* meant to turn the enemy left before their own left or centre collapsed.

On learning that his left wing was in danger of being turned, Agis ordered the *skiritai* and the *brasideioi* and *neodamôdeis* next to them to shift further left to match the Mantineians opposite them. Because this created a dangerous gap in the Spartan array, he therefore ordered the *polemarchoi* Hipponoïdas and Aristokles to take their *lochoi*, as Thucydides calls them, from the right end of the Spartan centre to plug it.[136] There is no parallel to this extraordinary manoeuvre in the annals of hoplite warfare. To change the battleline while two armies were on the verge of contact, to open a second gap to fill the first, all of these tactics are unheard of. In fact, the shift to the right that alarmed Agis was typical of all hoplite armies because of, as Thucydides points out, the natural tendency of hoplite phalanxes to move crablike towards their unshielded side,[137] and should have been anticipated by him, but once again he probably acted out of inexperience, this being his first battle.

We shall never know if Agis' manoeuvre might have worked. The commanders of the *skiritai* and *brasideioi* moved leftwards as ordered, opening a yawning gap between themselves and the Spartans in the centre, but the two *polemarchoi* simply refused to carry the command to fill that gap. Such insubordination meant Hipponoïdas and Aristokles were later condemned as *trésantes*, 'tremblers', and exiled for their so-called cowardice.[138] But these two hard-bitten veterans were hardly cowards. They kept their *lochoi* (as Thucydides calls them) in their original position in the Spartan centre, and they did not flee or seek sanctuary afterwards but returned to Sparta for trial. It is possible that they lacked confidence in their king, with their experienced eyes viewing him as an amateurish nincompoop unfit for high command. Since first encountering the enemy, he had led his men in a reckless and abortive uphill charge, taken them back down after coming within a spear's cast of the enemy, and, finally, allowed the enemy to surprise him with a battle on a ground and in a formation of their own choosing. We can imagine that old war-worn *polemarchoi* were hardheaded, practical men. They did not easily believe in the ability of ignorant youth to plan campaigns and command armies.

In the end the Spartans were victorious even though the two *polemarchoi* disobeyed the king's orders – and perhaps because of their refusal. Because they stood their ground there was no gap on the right side of the Spartan centre, and it was the centre where the victory was won. When Agis realized that his orders were disobeyed he ordered the left wing to close up the battleline again, but it was too late. The Mantineians were upon the *skiritai* and the *brasideioi* and *neodamôdeis*, and then, aided by the thousand picked men of the Argives, who ploughed into the gap between the Spartan left and centre, completed their discomfiture. As a result the Spartan left wing was swept from the field.[139]

For the Mantineians and their allies this was the decisive moment in the battle and the great chance for triumph. If they had ignored the fleeing Spartan left wing and turned their phalanx left against the flank and rear of the Spartan centre, they would surely have gained the victory, for the Spartan centre was still advancing to contact with its opposite number. Instead they made the easy and natural decision and hared after the soft target, needlessly pursuing the fleeing *skiritai*, *brasideioi* and *neodamôdeis* across the killing field as far as the wagons in the rear, doubtless preferring to kill the wounded and violate the dead than take on those dreaded masters of the trade of war.

Elsewhere on the grim stage of war it was a very different story, for Agis and the Spartan centre saw off the mediocre forces before them, the older hoplites of Argos and their Argolic allies. In fact, mediocre is too kind a word, for 'most of them did not even stand and fight but fled as the Spartans approached; some were even trampled in their hurry to get away before the enemy reached them', and the rout was particularly marked in the dead centre where Agis himself was, and around him the three hundred *hippeis*.[140] It seems that the Argive hoplites were in a demoralized condition of superstitious terror; they had probably become satisfied that the Spartans were in league with Ares himself. By reason of this, a good deal of their courage had oozed out and evaporated. The long ingrained fear of the Spartans came upon them at Mantineia, and without stopping to analyze the matter they simply turned and fled in a panic at the mere sight of them at hand.

By now the Spartan right wing was beginning to encircle the outflanked Athenians on the confederate left. In Thucydides' opinion the Athenian cavalry prevented a rout,[141] but though they retreated in good order disaster still loomed, for the failure of the confederates on the right to exploit that gap had decided the issue.

Once the tide of battle had turned, Agis rapped out a couple of orders that determined the nature of the victory. Instead of allowing his right wing to deliver the *coup de grâce* to the Athenians who were backpedalling before it, he commanded his centre and right to wheel left, which allowed the Athenians and the older Argives to escape safely but left the Mantineians and the élite Argives at his mercy. The élite Argives got away relatively unscathed, the majority escaping, whereas the Mantineians were attacked on their unshielded side as they tried to run past. Diodoros has a rather interesting story to tell at this juncture. He claimed that Pharax, one of the *sumboúloi* of Agis, directed the king to allow the thousand picked men of the Argives to escape, rather than trap them and force them to sell their lives dearly.[142] Scholars fall into two camps on this issue. There are those who argue that Agis spared the picked Argives for political reasons, that is, if the political élite of Argos were allowed to return home they could possibly gain control of the *polis* and bring it into a Spartan alliance.[143] Others, on the other hand, reckon Diodoros' story is not worth considering as it can hardly stand against Thucydides' silence on this particular matter.[144]

The losses on the confederate side were 700 of the Argives, Orneatai and Kleonaians, 200 Mantineians and 200 Athenians, including both Athenian *stratêgoi*, Laches and Nikostratos. On the Spartan side the losses among their allies were said to be hardly worth mentioning – small solace to their grieving relatives – and their own were said to be about 300, though Thucydides admits that 'it was difficult to learn the truth'.[145] There is one monument of the battle that survives in the form of an inscription recording the death 'in war at Mantineia' of one Eualkes, perhaps a *perioikos* from Geronthrai serving as a volunteer with the king's entourage.[146]

The reinforcements from Elis and Athens, 4,000 hoplites in total, finally arrived at Mantineia after the battle was concluded, but if they had arrived in time to strengthen the confederate array, it may have ended differently. Anyway, in the autumn Argos threw in the towel and renounced its alliance with the democratic league of Athens, Mantineia and Elis and accepted a Spartan treaty. As Thucydides points out, 'after the battle the friends of the Spartans found it much easier to persuade the many to make an agreement with Sparta'.[147] The Mantineians also reached an accommodation with Sparta at about this time.[148]

Though Thucydides was critical of the 'skill' displayed by the Spartans,[149] Mantineia is a good example of a battle won in the communal messes of Sparta. The great anti-Spartan confederacy numbers and confidence proved no match for Spartan professionalism, with its small group cohesion and discipline. As Thucydides also remarks, the victory at Mantineia had wiped out the disgrace of Sphakteria and dispelled any notion that the Spartans had gone soft: 'they might seem to have been worsted by fortune, but in spirit they were still the same'.[150] The battle is also a very good illustration for the employment of hoplite tactics. The real failure of the confederates was their inability to exploit the gap opened in the Spartan battleline by Agis' novel tactics. Though there is some lack of clarity here, it seems that the Spartan right curled round the confederate left and would have taken the confederates on that side in the flank, if Agis had not decided to come to the aid of his defeated left. This wheeling manoeuvre appears to have developed accidentally in this battle. But the Spartans perceived its effect and would learn to use it to defeat their enemies on the field of battle and, as we shall soon discover, were to brilliantly exploit it at the battle we know as the Nemea.

The Nemea, summer 394 BC

The Corinthian War had opened with an internal revolution and a massacre in Corinth; as a result the surviving pro-Spartan oligarchs were exiled. The confederate forces of Athens, Argos, Boiotia and the Corinthian democrats then combined at Corinth, which dominated the entrance of the Isthmus of Corinth and thus denied Spartan forces easy access into Attica and Boiotia. Sparta, in the meantime, acted by sending an army up to Corinthian territory via Sikyon, gathering allies on the way. Xenophon says that 'since Agesipolis was still a boy, the state commanded Aristodemos, who was of the royal family and the boy's guardian, to lead the army'.[151] The confederates moved westward along the southern shore of the Gulf of Corinth to meet the Spartans, and did so in the vicinity of the Nemea river, the boundary between the *chôra* of Sikyon and that of Corinth.[152]

The confederates had a large superiority in numbers, having 7,000 hoplites from Argos, 6,000 from Athens, 5,000 from Boiotia (but not the Orchomenians), 3,000 from Corinth, and 3,000 from Euboia, making a total of 24,000 hoplites. There were also 800 Boiotian horsemen, 600 Athenian, a hundred from Euboian Chalcis, and fifty from Ozolia Lokris. Xenophon also says 'there was a great number' of lightly armed troops, mainly allies of the Corinthians from Ozolia Lokris and Akarnania.[153]

The Spartans mustered at least 13,500 hoplites if not more, of whom 6,000 were Lakedaimonian and the rest Peloponnesian allies.[154] They also had 600 Lakedaimonian cavalry, 300 Cretan archers, probably mercenaries, and no fewer than 400 slingers from the borders of Elis, while the confederates had a proportional superiority in these arms. However, our primary source Xenophon leaves us wanting as to their actual participation in the ensuing battle.

The Spartans themselves occupied the right of their battle array, with the Tegeans next to them, while on the left wing were the Achaians opposite the Boiotians,[155] mostly Sikyonians but with some hoplites at least from Pellene – they are found later battling it out with those from Thespiai.[156] This would leave the 3,000 hoplites from Elis, the 3,000 hoplites from Epidauros and other *poleis* in the Argolid, and possibly 2,000 or so hoplites from Mantineia, to occupy the rest of the Spartan battleline. Xenophon does not say how deep this array was, but we can guess between eight shields deep, as they had done at Mantineia,[157] and twelve shields deep, as they would do at Leuktra.[158]

The confederates had a long dispute between those who wanted to use their superior numbers to make the phalanx as deep as possible, to avoid being broken, and those who wanted as long a battleline as possible. A sixteen-shield deep formation was finally agreed upon.[159] The instigators of the deep formation approach were the Thebans.

According to Xenophon, no lover of the Thebans, the Boiotians unashamedly waited until it was someone else's turn in the days prior to the battle to face the seemingly invincible Spartans, and then announced that the omens were favourable and that the engagement would be fought. They then led off the deployment, and not only disregarded the agreed sixteen shields deep formation and 'made their phalanx really deep',[160] perhaps twenty-five shields deep, but also led off well to the right, ensuring their deep phalanx would handsomely outflank their opponents, the Peloponnesian allies of the Spartans. It was to be the fate of the Athenians to face the dreaded Spartans. Xenophon implies cowardice on the Boiotians' part, but we must remember that when their *stratêgos* took his turn as the confederate generalissimo he did seize the opportunity to engage the enemy.

The upshot of all this Boiotian roguery was that the unlucky Athenians were bound to be outflanked by the Spartan phalanx. This unhappy state of affairs would have happened anyway without the Spartans (as they did) leading off well to the right so as to ensure that their phalanx would handsomely outflank their opponents too. It is clear that the Spartans and the Boiotians were capitalizing on the 'rightward drift' phenomenon of a hoplite phalanx. The Spartans did not at first see the enemy advance, 'for the place was thickly overgrown; but when the latter struck up the *paean*, then at length they knew, and immediately gave orders in their turn that all should make ready for battle'.[161] The two armies closed until they were less than a *stade* (less than 200 metres) apart, then the Spartans sacrificed a goat to Artemis Agrotera, the Huntress, and continued the advance, 'wheeling round their overlapping wing to encircle the enemy'.[162] The result of the battle was the right wings of both armies were easily victorious, and the confederate centre drove back the Spartan centre. But the disciplined Spartans kept their phalanx well in hand, while each of the victorious confederate contingents merely sauntered back across the field towards the camp after defeating its opposite numbers. The professional Spartans therefore swung smartly across the battlefield, catching each returning contingent on its unshielded flank, rolling it up, and with that vanquishing it. The first victims were the Argives, and Xenophon says that 'as the first *polemarchos* was about to engage them head-on someone is said to have shouted to let the front ranks go by',[163] and so the *polemarchos* in question, presumably the commander of the first *mora* situated on the extreme right of the Spartan line, stopped his wheel so as to hit the right, unshielded side of the Argives as they went by. The same misery was inflicted upon the Corinthians and Boiotians as the relentless Spartan phalanx strode on.

According to Xenophon, the Spartans later claimed that only eight of their own men were killed, compared with 'very many' of the enemy, though they admitted that 'not a few' of their allies had fallen.[164] The Nemea was to be the last clear-cut victory won by the Spartan army. Before we leave this battle there are two rather important points for us to digest.

First, the rolling-up of the enemy line by the Spartans was deliberate in comparison with what happened at Mantineia, as was the shift to the right that brought it about.

Second, the Spartans were now quite prepared to sacrifice their own left wing, which only involved their allied troops.

Koroneia, summer 394 BC

While the Nemea was being fought and won, the Spartan king Agesilaos was marching home from his inglorious military escapade in Anatolia. As he entered Boiotia, a partial solar eclipse came to pass.[165] He was also met on the road by a messenger bearing bad news: the Peloponnesian fleet had been shattered in a great battle off Knidos, and with that terminated their maritime empire in the eastern Aegean. We can well imagine the mood of the king.

Unfortunately, none of our sources gives totals for either army in the battle that followed. Agesilaos had with him a *mora* and a half of Spartans, the full *mora* under the *polemarchos* Gylis having been sent to join him, probably after the Nemea, the half *mora* having had garrisoned in Orchomenos since the previous year.[166] In addition, he had the *neodamôdeis* he had commanded in Anatolia, originally 2,000 in number,[167] those that remained of the Ten Thousand, including Xenophon himself, and now commanded by the Spartiate, Herippidas,[168] and contingents from some of the Asiatic Greek *poleis*, as well as those from Phokis and Orchomenos, which joined him en route.[169] In all Agesilaos may have commanded some 15,000 hoplites.

Xenophon lists the opposing forces as consisting of Boiotians, Athenians, Argives, Corinthians, Ainianians, Euboians, and both Opountian and Ozolian Lokrians,[170] but again without giving any numbers. We can, however, probably assume that the Boiotians were in greater strength than at the Nemea, since they were in their home territory, perhaps 6,000 rather than 5,000, and their near neighbours, the Athenians and Euboians, who had escaped relatively unscathed from the Nemea, fielded about the same number, viz. 6,000 and 3,000 respectively. Yet it seems unlikely that the Argives and the Corinthians had sent as many as 7,000 and 3,000 respectively, in view of their heavy losses at the Nemea and the danger of their own territories from the victorious Spartan army. The presence of contingents from both Lokrian peoples might have compensated to some extent, though it would be wrong of us to assume they were very numerous, while the contingent of Ainianians were presumably lightly armed troops. All in all, then, the confederates probably had something like 20,000 hoplites.[171]

Xenophon also says little about the dispositions on either side. Agesilaos himself commanded the Spartan right, as was customary, and presumably had the Spartan *mora* and a half under his direct command, perhaps also the *neodamôdeis*, while the contingent from Orchomenos was on the left of his line.[172] On the confederate side, the Thebans were on the right, facing the Orchomenians, while the Argives had the unenviable task of facing the Spartans. The encounter took place, according to Xenophon, 'in the plain of Koroneia',[173] with Agesilaos and his army coming from the Kephisos river and his opponents down from the northern slopes of Helikon,[174] and this has been interpreted to mean that the battlelines faced respectively north and south. We cannot be certain.

Xenophon, who was an eyewitness, mentions the deep silence in which the two sides approached each other, but when they were about a stade apart, the Thebans broke into a double, raising a war cry,[175] and when the battlelines had closed to within three *plethra* (i.e. half a stade, or some hundred metres), the Cyreians, followed by the Asiatic Greeks from the centre of Agesilaos' line, ran forward in turn,[176] and soon after the two armies had closed to spear thrust distance. On the Spartan right, the Argives 'fled towards Helikon without awaiting the attack of Agesilaos', or so said Xenophon in both of his accounts of the battle.[177] Those next to them in the confederate line, now left in the lurch, were quickly overwhelmed by Agesilaos' centre. But as some of the Cyreians were garlanding the king, someone brought the news that the Thebans had cut their way through their fellow Boiotians, the Orchomenians, and were now busy amongst the baggage train.[178] As this undoubtedly contained Agesilaos' loot from his Asian adventures, it needed to be rescued.

Immediately, Agesilaos, in Xenophon's words, 'countermarched his phalanx and led it against the Thebans'.[179] The Thebans, despite being separated from the rest of their allies, did not waver one moment, but 'wishing to break through to them,' says Xenophon, 'formed up in close order and came on resolutely'.[180] At this point of his eyewitness account Xenophon offers an opinion, saying Agesilaos 'certainly did not adopt the safest plan' by meeting the Thebans head on instead of letting them go by and then falling on their rear.[181] It was probably the fact that in the ensuing clash, the two sides were facing in the opposite direction to the way they had faced at the beginning of the battle, which led Xenophon to describe it in both of his accounts as 'like no other battle fought in our time'.[182] Be that as it may, it was this final clash between hated rivals that left an impression of unusual ferocity upon Xenophon, who, after all, had experienced a number of full-blown battles and many a skirmish: '[Agesilaos] crashed into the Thebans front to front. So with shield pressed against shield they struggled, killed and were killed'.[183] In his other account, Xenophon adds that there 'was no shouting, nor was there silence, but the strange noise that wrath and battle together will produce'.[184] In the end, some of the Thebans broke through to the slopes of Helikon, 'but many others were killed on their way there'.[185] Agesilaos himself was dragged wounded from the field of the slain.

Plutarch alleges that the fiercest fighting involved what he calls the 'fifty volunteers' who acted as the king's bodyguard, and it was 'these men's courage and the ardent rivalry that they showed in defending their king, which apparently saved his life',[186] and this is highly plausible. He also claims:

> In the end it proved too difficult to break the Theban front, and the Spartans were obliged to carry out the manoeuvre that they had rejected at the beginning. They parted their ranks and allowed the enemy to pass through, and then, when the Thebans had passed beyond them and were moving in looser formation, the Spartans followed, broke into a run, and attacked them from the flanks. But they failed to put them to rout. The Thebans withdrew in good order to Mount Helikon, proud of their achievement in keeping their own contingent undefeated.[187]

Presumably that rejected manoeuvre was the same one Xenophon says Agesilaos had originally decide not to do. Though Plutarch was a Boiotian, and it could be claimed he was indulging a little bit of patriotism here, may well be right. On the other hand, Xenophon, despite being an eyewitness to the day's bloody events, was also given to bias when it concerned his hero Agesilaos, and this double battle, a sort of knockout championship between hated rivals (viz. Thebans versus Orchomenians, Spartans versus Argives, Spartans versus Thebans), was in his eyes one of his hero's finest hours, and therefore remains silent on how the Thebans got through. Anyway, about eighty Thebans, who apparently got left behind, took refuge in a nearby temple, but Agesilaos ordered his men to let them go.[188]

Afterwards, Xenophon describes the battlefield:

> Now the fighting was at an end, a weird spectacle met the eye, as one surveyed the scene of the conflict – the earth stained with blood, friend and foe lying dead side by side, shields smashed to pieces, spears snapped in two, daggers bared of their sheaths, some on the ground, some embedded in the bodies, some yet gripped by the hand.[189]

According to Diodoros, more than 600 of the confederates fell, for only 350 on the Spartan side,[190] but although the wounded Agesilaos claimed the victory, ordering a trophy to be erected next day and a parade of his army, garlanded 'in honour of the god', with flute players playing, and although the undefeated Thebans recognized the fact by sending heralds to ask that they might bury their dead under a truce,[191] the wounded king made no effort to follow up his victory. With the confederates holding a strong position on the slopes of Helikon, he made his way home by way of Delphi, without venturing further into Boiotia. Koroneia had been a victory, but a fruitless one. As Lazenby sagely says, 'the Spartans should have taken more note, one feels, of the effects of a charge of close-packed Theban hoplites in depth'.[192]

Lechaion, summer 390 BC

The main theatre of the Corinthian War, following the initial clash at the Nemea and Agesilaos' pyrrhic victory at Koroneia as he led his army from Anatolia through Boiotia, remained in the neighbourhood of Corinth. Corinth itself was held by the confederates, with the exiled oligarchs of Corinth and a Spartan garrison in Lechaion, the port of Corinth on the Gulf of Corinth, north-west of the *astu*. The land route across the Isthmus of Corinth to Attica and Boiotia was now open to Sparta. In the meantime, the young Athenian Iphikrates had been staging destructive raids and ambushes against Sparta's Peloponnesian allies with almost invariable success, although his peltasts had suffered one reverse when they were countercharged and caught by Spartan hoplites before they could evade.[193] This made the Spartans confident that peltasts could be defeated by a resolute and sudden countercharge, 'running out' tactics that had not been possible at Sphakteria, thirty-five years before, because of the nature of the terrain.

In consequence, the Spartan *polemarchos* in charge of the garrison at Lechaion did not anticipate danger from Iphikrates and his peltasts. The action itself occurred when the main Spartan force was raiding north of the Isthmus, and the Lechaion garrison had been ordered to provide an escort for the men of Amyklai, 'who invariably go back home to the festival of the Hyakinthia for the *paean* to Apollo, whether they chance to be on campaign or away from home for any other reason'.[194] The Lechaion garrison, a *mora* of 600 hoplites and a *mora* of Lakedaimonian horsemen, possibly 120 troopers strong,[195] accordingly set off with the homecoming troops along the coast towards Sikyon.

Their route led them past the Athenian held walls of Corinth, and Iphikrates with his peltasts and the Athenian *stratêgos* Kallias with a force of Athenian hoplites (we have no definite numbers for either),[196] considered this as a possible target. When the *polemarchos* left the convoy in the care of the *mora* of horsemen and began to tramp back to Lechaion, the sight of a column of Spartan hoplites exposing their unshielded sides, and unaccompanied by supporting troops, proved too tempting for the Athenian commanders. As the experienced Xenophon points out, the 'peltasts, the nimblest of all troops, could easily escape the hoplites'.[197]

Out from Corinth came Iphikrates' hungry peltasts, who rapidly set on the Spartan column peppering it with their javelins, while Kallias' hoplites moved up in close support. It was going to be a rerun of Sphakteria. The Spartans found to their astonishment that the peltasts, skilfully handled on this occasion, could in fact evade before they could be caught, even on level ground, and they could do nothing to avoid being shot down one after the other. Xenophon describes how the *polemarchos* 'ordered the first ten year-classes to drive off their assailants', but the peltasts easily evaded these young hoplites to return probing, relentless and mean, and so 'the *polemarchos* again ordered the first fifteen year-classes to pursue'. This did no better, and more Spartans were picked off with javelins.[198]

The return of the Lakedaimonian cavalry ought to have saved the situation for the poor *polemarchos*, who, incidently, remains unmistakably anonymous in Xenophon's narrative. But the commander of the cavalry, the *hipparmostes*, badly mishandled it, keeping strict formation with the hoplites when they sortied, and so failing even with his superior speed and mobility to contact the peltasts let alone run them down at a full gallop. As the Spartans became fewer and fainter of heart, their tormentors became bolder and more bent on destroying them. 'Therefore in desperation they gathered on a small hill, distant from the sea about two *stadia*, and from Lechaion about sixteen or seventeen *stadia*'.[199] At the same time their comrades in Lechaion launched a rescue bid, coasting along in small boats until they were opposite the hill. Now in total despair, and with the Athenian hoplites now preparing to close in for the final kill, the Spartan survivors broke and fled towards the sea with the exulted peltasts in hot pursuit. The pathetic cavalry had already made itself scarce, escaping to Lechaion with a lucky few hoplites hanging on for dear life to the horses' tails, but of the luckless rest, few made it alive to the waiting boats. Xenophon says it all when he says before the collapse the shield bearers, *hypaspistai*, as he calls the helot attendants of the Spartiates, had been detailed to take up the wounded and carry them back to Lechaion; 'these were the only men in the *mora* who were really saved'.[200] Some 250 members of the doomed *mora* were left as corpses.

Leuktra, summer 371 BC

Seven years after the swearing of the King's Peace (387/6 BC), Greece was to witnesses the Theban patriots, Epameinondas and Pelopidas amongst them, liberating their *polis* from Spartan domination.[201] They also revived the old Boiotian League under the new brand name of Commonwealth of Boiotia (*Koinon*). The new confederation only had seven *Boiotarchoi* to serve as *stratêgoi* in the federal army. This does suggest that there were only seven instead of the original eleven federal districts now, and as Orchomenos and Thespiai still housed Spartan garrisons they were in all likelihood abolished. However, its decision-making body was a federal assembly and not the federal councils as before. This new federal assembly convened in Thebes and, as of old, the Thebans still retained the right to provide four *Boiotarchoi* (viz. two on the behalf of the *polis* itself and two on the behalf of the Plataians, those staunch supporters of the Athenians). Likewise, as the army numbered 7,000 hoplites and 700 horsemen, the old levy of 1,000 and 100 respectively from each federal district was still in place. At this time Thebes also raised the Sacred Band, an élite hoplite unit formed by Gorgidas after the liberation of Thebes from Spartan occupation (379/8 BC) and comprising 150 pairs of homosexual lovers maintained at state expense. The original plan was to deploy them as a unit only in limited operations, usually forming the front rank of a Theban phalanx, but Pelopidas' victory at Tegyra (375 BC) led to their deployment together on all occasions. This made for a crucial rôle at Leuktra (371 BC) and their complete annihilation at Chaironeia (338 BC).

It was the first of those aforementioned fights, the pitched battle on the plain of Leuktra in Boiotia, which marked the end of Spartan hegemony in Greece. The Spartan army was led by one of the kings, Kleombrotos, that of the Boiotians by the Theban Epameinondas.[202] The ancient sources are in disagreement about numbers beyond the fact the Spartans and their allies outnumbered the Boiotians. Xenophon says nothing except that there were four Spartan *morai*,[203] and that the *enômotiai* were formed up in three files of not more than twelve men each.[204] Xenophon mentions other troops, such as mercenary hoplites and Phokian peltasts.[205] Pausanias says Arcadians fought at the battle – mercenaries probably – and there were probably hoplites from Phleious and Herakleia Trachinia too.[206] Anyway, neither army will have exceeded 10,000 men, of whom most were hoplites, and perhaps 1,000 horsemen on either side. The figures generally accepted would give the Spartan army a total of 9,000 to 10,000 hoplites and between 800 and 1,000 horsemen.[207] The Lakedaimonians supplied between a quarter and half of the hoplites. The Boiotian army, which included no allied contingents, was composed of about 6,000 to 7,000 hoplites, 4,000 of whom were Thebans, and 700 horsemen.[208]

According Xenophon the Thebans were keen to engage, 'since many of them had been in exile before, they estimated that it was better to die fighting than to be in exile again'.[209] On the other hand, both Diodoros and Frontinus stress the fact that the Thebans were reluctant to engage in battle.[210] All the sources agree, however, about the various omens of victory and disaster that were manifested to either side, some even going so far as to suggest that some or all were deliberately manufactured by Epameinondas and Pelopidas.[211] The most amusing, and perhaps the most likely to be authentic because the most unusual, is the story told by Frontinus:

> When ... Epameinondas was about to open battle against the Spartans, the chair on which he had sat down gave way beneath him, whereat all the soldiers, greatly troubled, interpreted this as an unlucky omen. But Epameinondas exclaimed: 'Not at all; we are simply forbidden to sit'.[212]

Xenophon has an interesting tale to tell too. Pointing out that in the coming battle the Boiotians had all the luck, while for the Spartans everything turned out for the bad 'For it was after the morning meal that Kleombrotos held his last council over the battle, and drinking a little, as they did, at the middle of the day, it was said that the wine helped somewhat to excite them'.[213] If Xenophon is correct in his analysis and not just searching around for a suitable excuse for the looming disaster, then it is possible that the Spartans were more than slightly sottish prior to the clash, and thus instead of stealing their nerves for the upcoming head-to-head with the Thebans, the drink had probably endangered their chances of success due to alcohol–induced recklessness. Xenophon does give the impression that there was some initial Spartan confusion in the battle, which began an entire succession of fatal blunders.

The disposition of the contending armies was to some extent similar on both sides, with the cavalry posted opposite each other in front of their respective battlelines, right wing for the Spartans and left wing for the Boiotians.[214] The terrain was a level, small valley between low, gentle hills. The Spartan battleline was twelve shields deep, Xenophon being very precise with his details here by telling us that the Spartans had 'led each *enômotia* three files abreast, and that this resulted in the phalanx being not more than twelve deep',[215] which also tells us that each *enômotia* on this occasion was some thirty-six hoplites strong. Xenophon implies that Kleombrotos and the *hippeis* were on the Spartan right,[216] and presumably the right half of the Spartan array was composed of the four *morai*, the king and his bodyguard perhaps stationed between the second and third *morai* counting from the right.[217] The left would have been composed of the mercenaries and allies.

On the other side, it is clear that the Thebans were on the left wing of the Boiotian array, and 'were not less than fifty shields deep',[218] following their preference for the deep phalanx, though to a lesser degree, in other battles over the last fifty or so years.[219] What appears to be a new departure is that the remainder of the Boiotian battleline was echeloned away so that the main clash of the Theban phalanx under Epameinondas would occur before the other Boiotians got stuck in. Epameinondas, as a *stratêgos*, was something new. He intended that the mass on the left would meet the Spartans at the point where Kleombrotos was and break the Spartan line before it had a chance to encircle his left. If we can believe Plutarch, and there is no real reason to doubt him here, the élite Sacred Band formed the cutting edge of the Theban phalanx,[220] perhaps its first three or four ranks. Their current commander was of course Epameinondas' very good friend Pelopidas.[221]

The battle opened around midday, after Kleombrotos and his men perhaps had one or two too many, as noted above. Boiotian cavalry was greatly superior to the Lakedaimonian, but there is little surprise there, the latter being recruited from nominees provided by wealthy Spartiates who supplied the mounts and the equipment. Since the best Lakedaimonians wished to serve as hoplites, and since the nominee first encountered his horse and tack on mobilization, standards were not good. As Xenophon says, these nominees were least strong of body and least ambitious too.[222] The result was that the cavalry clash, which took place while the armies were still drawing up, was swiftly over, with the Lakedaimonian horsemen being driven back in disarray. Xenophon, himself a noted horseman, praises the Boiotian horsemen for being well trained and battle ready,[223] and here we witness Xenophon the professional soldier as opposed to Xenophon the pro-Spartan historian. Indeed, the Boiotians had a long tradition as horsemen, consciously maintained by constant riding and mounted training. In contrast to his assessment of the Boiotian cavalry, Xenophon heavily criticizes the poor quality of the Lakedaimonian cavalry since they lack training and experience.[224]

The victorious Boiotian horsemen were rapidly followed up by Epameinondas, and the result was the fleeing Lakedaimonian horsemen shoved their way through their own phalanx, disorganized it, and it was still disorganized when the Theban phalanx, in effect a steamroller, hit it square on and eventually broke it. In the words of Diodoros, 'the heavy phalanx led by Epameinondas bore down upon the Lakedaimonians, and at first by sheer force caused the line of the enemy to buckle somewhat'.[225] Supposedly, Epameinondas then asked his Thebans for 'one step forward to please me'.[226] The Theban resistless charge caught the Spartans in confusion, caused partly by their cavalry, partly by whatever tactical evolution they were attempting at the time – either a transfer of men from the left *mora* to the right *mora* to increase the depth of their phalanx there, or a turn to the right and so overlap the enemy line – and to make matters worse, Kleombrotos begun to advance 'at first before the army with him so much realized that he was advancing'.[227] If true, it demonstrates how badly the Spartans had been caught napping. In came the Thebans and down went the king – the first to fall in battle since Leonidas. Xenophon says the Spartans were able to carry Kleombrotos, still breathing, from the field. But the fall of the king and the death of many of those around him, including the *polemarchos* Deinon, one of the king's tent companions, Sphodrias, along with the latter's son, Kleonymos, must have added to the confusion and eventual collapse. Xenophon claims that even then discipline was maintained, the surviving Spartans having crossed 'the trench that chanced to be in front of their camp they grounded their arms at the spot from which they had set forth'.[228] So for Xenophon, the Spartans fought like the Spartans; when that is said, there is no more to say. On the other hand, Diodoros and Plutarch suggest a larger element of *sauve qui peur*.[229]

Spartan losses were severe in this, the first defeat in memory of a Spartan army in a pitched hoplite battle. According to Xenophon, of 700 Spartiates present, 400 fell, along with 1,000 other Lakedaimonians.[230] Diodoros reckons 'not less than 4,000 Lakedaimonians' fell to only 300 Boiotians (all Thebans, probably),[231] which is surely better than Pausanias' paltry 47 Boiotian dead.[232] Diodoros' figure for the Spartan army probably includes the allies and mercenaries too. Returning to Xenophon's figures, if correct, we can guess of the 400 Spartiates who fell, 300 of these were the *hippeis*, wiped out during the furious struggle to struggle the mortally wounded Kleombrotos.

What was unprecedented about Leuktra was Epameinondas had formed an irresistible phalanx with which he won the battle before his hoplites of the centre and right could lose it. The traditional Spartan tactic of rolling up the line from their right to left had been refuted at a single stroke, forcefully and surprisingly. Xenophon may have written, 'wise generalship consists in attacking where the enemy is weakest, even if the point be some way distant',[233] but Epameinondas is an instance of the exception. The best illustration of this notion is the story Polyainos recounts of how Epameinondas caught a snake, and by crushing its head, showed his men how useless the rest of it was,[234] and even Xenophon hints as much when he says the Thebans 'calculated that, if they proved superior in that part of the field where the king was, all the rest would be easy'.[235]

First, Epameinondas enlarged upon and developed certain features that were traditional elements in hoplite warfare in combination with a peculiarity of Theban hoplite tactics, namely their habit of arraying their hoplites in an unusually deep formation.

Second, Epameinondas made use of in a purposeful manner a normal characteristic of hoplite warfare, namely the decision to concentrate efforts on one wing, usually the right.

Third, Epameinondas' tactics were purposely contrived to overcome the Spartans themselves on their right, where they had been accustomed to winning their battles, as at Mantineia (by chance) and the Nemea (by design), and by refusing his left to deny the enemy any chance of retrieving the situation there.

Ought we judge battles by the numbers killed and the ruin wreaked? Or should we not rather judge them by the results that flowed from them? Truly, one will say that a battle is only truly great or small according to its results. Judging by results, Leuktra was more than great, it was epoch making. Many empires have been lost through a series of battles, a process of battles, a weary tale of wasting conflicts stretching over years, but Sparta reached that point in a single afternoon and by a single battle; at Leuktra Sparta had 'cut the hair of its glory'.[236]

If the myth of Spartan invincibility on the field of battle was forged at Thermopylai, then it was shattered at Leuktra where Kleombrotos, several of his highborn companions, and the Spartiate element in his army were obliterated by Theban hoplites, which in the end was decisive. This was not so much because the Spartan army had been destroyed, or even because this defeat put an end to its victories – there were Spartan victories to come – but because it revealed that Sparta's position as the great hegemonic superpower of the Aegean Greek world had long rested on what amounted to a big bluff, since its manpower resources, in terms of actual citizen soldiers, had never really been sufficient to sustain that position. But behind that bluff there had always remained, in the last resort, the hard reality of the Spartan army, and its defeat at Leuktra was a symbol of the passing of a great power: it would have been a bagatelle if Sparta had had manpower fitted to its hegemonic policy. But Sparta was beggared.

Chapter 16

Sackers of Cities

Effective tactics and techniques for siege warfare were developed by large territorial Near eastern monarchies that possessed and were able to mobilize the necessary resources. Of these techniques, the use of siege mounds was the simplest, and promised the fastest results if conditions were ideal. The Assyrians employed them with ruthless skill, as did the Lydians and Persians. Herodotos says Alyattes of Lydia took Smyrna (c. 600 BC), and the discovery there of a huge ramp of earth and felled trees, as well as stones, mud-bricks and timbers from nearby houses, strongly suggests that this was the method by which the Lydians stormed the Greek *astu*.[1] According to archaeological evidence, the ensuing action was essentially one fought with long-range weapons; some 125 bronze arrowheads both leaf-shape and of the triangular 'Scythian' form, peppered the *astu* and the siege mound itself.[2] A century on, the Persians under Harpagos easily carried the Ionian *asteôs* by direct assault, using the siege mound to get men up and over the walls.[3]

Having described in great detail the battle of Salamis, which took place on land and at sea, Herodotos then glosses over the Persian re-conquest of Cyprus in the winter of 498/7 BC. He says, 'of the besieged *asteôs*, Soli held out the longest; it fell in the fifth month after the Persians had undermined its walls'.[4] One of the anonymous 'besieged *asteôs*' was Palaipaphos (today's Kouklia) and the siege mound erected by the Persians has been identified (in fact, its remains are still very much visible to this day). Located near the Northeast Gate on what is now known as the Marcello Hill, excavations in and around the siege mound have revealed the buried remains of one historical event; the elaborate siege and counter siege works during the early part of the Ionian revolt. The siege mound itself was constructed out of the wreckage from a nearby sanctuary, together with earth and timber to fill the fosse and raise a seven-metre high ramp against the defences. Archaeological finds included some 500 bronze and iron arrowheads and spearheads, 422 sling stones, and a well-preserved Corinthian helmet securely dated to around 500 BC, which represents the only hoplite helmet found so far in a battle context.[5]

The distribution of missiles through the siege mound reveals the tactics of both sides. Three-winged arrowheads of an Eastern type, made to a standard pattern, were concentrated in particular areas of the siege mound, notably in the re-entrant between the curtain-wall and north-western bastion of the Northeast Gate. These were the standardized weapons of professional archers, who provided covering fire during the operation and concentrated firepower for the final assault. In contrast, four-sided javelin heads, crudely made, were scattered widely over the siege mound. They obviously belonged to the defence, able with the advantage of height to hurl javelins in a pattern of continual harassment. Stone balls of varying weight from 2.7 to

21.8 kilograms were found not concentrated, but scattered mainly along the base of the fortifications. They probably belong to the defence rather than the attack, and represent attempts to crush – heads would have offered no more resistance than rotten apples to these descending stones – the attackers in the final, desperate stages of the siege. The impression is on the attacking side of a thoroughly professional body with a well-established technique of siege warfare, which relied not on artillery (yet to be invented) to take the *astu* but on the siege mound, built doubtless by impressed local labour and protected by Persian archery.

Nevertheless, it appears the Persians did not gain Palaipaphos without a fierce struggle for the siege mound had been undermined from within the *enceinte* in two different ways. First, by a passage dug through the berm and, second, by four tunnels cut through the bedrock underneath the fortifications (likewise still very evident), the wooden pit props of Tunnel 1 and Tunnel 3 having been fired on completion by means of some inflammable substance (sulphur and pitch?) carried in large bronze cauldrons. Once taken, however, Palaipaphos was without doubt delivered to the tortures of the peeved Persian soldiery.

Besides the siege mound the Persians were also quite familiar with mining and the use of siege machines,[6] and doubtless had inherited a considerable skill in the use of siege machines from their Assyrian and Babylonian predecessors. The Greeks themselves, although lacking in skill when it came to taking fortified positions by siege, also employed the siege mound. As we shall discuss in good time, the Peloponnesians built such a ramp, using local timber to form latticework, which was then packed with earth and stone, during their siege operations against Plataia in 430/29 BC.[7] Also, during the latter half of the fifth century BC, the Greeks certainly used 'engines of war', which at least included battering rams and tortoises.

But it remains true that until the last decade of the fifth century BC no Greek *astu* of any size was taken by direct assault, a notable exception being the successful assault on Mykalessos by the Athenian *stratêgos* Diitrephes, commanding a hundred Thracian mercenaries, in the spring of 413 BC. Arguably these 'barbarian' mercenaries were expendable. At any rate, as Thucydides clearly points out, 'the inhabitants were caught off their guard, since they never expected that anyone would come so far from the sea to attack them'.[8] In the same passage he also notes the dilapidated state of the fortifications of Mykalessos. Inevitably, the Thracians 'burst into Mykalessos, sacked the houses and temples, and butchered the inhabitants, sparing neither the young nor the old, but methodically killing everyone they met, women and children alike, and even farm animals and every living thing they saw'. Despite his Thracian connections, Thucydides then betrays his prejudices by ascribing the ferocity of the attack to the natural savagery of 'bloodthirsty barbarians'.[9]

Plato judges that one facet of virtue is to be found in the traditional contest of hoplites facing each other in open battle. The use of walls as protection is therefore 'unnatural' and can only lead to the deterioration of the moral character of the citizen of his state.[10] The wall made a psychological difference, unfavourably so in Plato's considered opinion. The ideal *polis* therefore must be un-walled like Sparta, so that the citizens will not be tempted to cower behind their walls like the Athenians had done in the Peloponnesian War. Plato was particularly averse to *astu*-based defence. He reviled Themistokles, Kimon and Perikles for having 'glutted Athens with harbours and dockyards and walls and tribute and rubbish of that sort'.[11] This conservative view that the strength of a *polis* consists not in the walls that gird an *astu*, but in the quality of its citizenship, is a warning to be found in other writers of the period too, for instance Xenophon and Isokrates.[12] Even Thucydides, despite his enthusiastic support for Perikles' *astu*-based system of defence,[13] has Nikias say, 'men make the *polis* and not walls'.[14] Clearly, the *polis* was meant to put its citizen manhood into the field.

In this way, cities surrounded by walls and crowned by towers do not have a place in that central moment of Greek warfare, the clash of opposing phalanxes. The ethic of hoplite warfare and the practical restrictions imposed by the heavy panoply meant the hoplite was ill equipped to deal with the difficulties of cracking fortified positions except under exceptionally favourable circumstances such as surprise and treachery. These factors favoured set-piece battles in open country. The equation between hoplite status and citizenship also made the rate of casualties a significant political consideration and the relatively small citizen populations of many of the *poleis* magnified this factor. Since the hazardous adventure of a direct assault generally imposed the greatest number of losses, there was a tendency to shun such operations unless unavoidable. Cities stated to have been taken by storm, *katà krátos*, were insignificant or un-walled.[15]

What the citizens of a *polis* had to fear most from their fellow Greeks was not siege and sack but rather the reduction by starvation or their betrayal to the enemy from within. Although Perikles is credited with the use of siege devices against Samos,[16] the *astu* held out for eight months and then capitulated,[17] which suggests that it was reduced by blockade, by starvation or the fear of starvation, rather than by direct assault. Plataia, after ingenious attacks, which seem to have been the acme of contemporary Greek siege craft was, in the end, left to fall to the long drawn pressure of starvation after two years of close drawn circumvallation.[18] Actually this siege highlights the real weakness of Greek siege craft, and is a clear indication of the difficulties that still stood in the way of capturing a fortified position during the Peloponnesian War even with the latest techniques available.

Thucydides describes how the Boiotians used a remarkable flame-throwing contraption to incinerate the wooden fortifications, and many of its defenders, hastily erected in three days by the Athenians at the sanctuary of Apollo at Delion (winter 424 BC), what was in effect an *epiteichismos* planted on Boiotian soil just across the Attic border. To construct this enormous flamethrower, an ingenious but an anonymous Boiotian engineer arranged for a wooden beam to be split in two and hollowed out. The two-halves were then rejoined and sheathed with iron. A large iron cauldron was suspended from the business end by means of a chain, and an iron tube was inserted through the length of the device. This tube curved down into the cauldron, which was filled with lighted coals, sulphur and pitch. The device was strapped to carts and wheeled right up to the stockade while covering fire was given to its operators. At that point the Boiotians attached large bellows to their end of the device and pumped great blasts of air through the tube to direct the chemical fire in the cauldron at the stockade.[19] And thus was Delion captured.

The Athenians had some reputation for siege craft,[20] but Potidaia held out against them for nearly three years and then surrendered only on terms, and these too were grudgingly given, although it was important for Athenian prestige to bring the siege to an end as quickly and decisively as possible.[21] When Mytilene revolted against Athens the *astu* could not be taken until the beginning of starvation led to its surrender. In fact, capitulation only came about when the mass of the citizens was armed and were able to get their way against the more determined aristocrats who had been responsible for bringing about the rebellion in the first place.[22] Likewise, some form of a *coup de main*, helped by local treachery, captured the Long Walls at Megara.[23] The Athenians had no hope of taking Syracuse except by circumvallation or a movement for surrender within the *astu* itself.

For the Athenians the prolonged encirclement and starvation of the trapped populace may have been the keys to victory, but mounting a formal siege was a ruinously expensive undertaking. The siege of Samos had cost the treasurers of Athena more than 1,400 talents,[24] while that of Potidaia was an even greater financial drain, costing no less than 2,000 talents or two-fifths of the reserves of Athens.[25] But it was the siege of Mytilene that strained Athenian fiscal resources almost to the breaking point. The Athenians, needing money for the siege, decided on a desperate solution and 'raised among themselves for the first time a property tax of two-hundred talents'.[26]

During the latter half of the fifth century BC, the Greeks certainly used siege mounds and deployed *mêchanaîs*, 'devices', as siege machines were called. This un-qualified term is entirely indefinite, but almost certainly included the scaling ladder, battering ram, tortoise and shed, although not the catapult. The absence of artillery from the detailed military narrative of Thucydides is one of the strongest arguments for thinking that it had not been invented before the turn of the fourth century BC.

Engines of war

Samos	440 BC	Plutarch *Perikles* 27.3	*Mêchanaîs*
		Diodoros 12.28.3	*Mêchanaîs*, battering rams (*krioùs*) and tortoises (*chelônas*)
Oinoe	431 BC	Thucydides 2.18.1	*Mêchanaîs*, possibly battering rams
Poteidaia	430 BC	Thucydides 2.58.1	*Mêchanaîs*
	423/2 BC	Diodoros 12.46.2	*Mêchanaîs*, possibly battering rams and sheds/tortoises
		Thucydides 4.135.1	*Mêchanaîs*, possibly scaling ladders
Plataia	430/29 BC	Thucydides 2.76.4	Battering rams (*mêchanaîs*)
Minoa	427 BC	Thucydides 3.51.3	*Mêchanaîs*, possibly scaling ladders
Pylos	425 BC	Thucydides 4.13.1	*Mêchanaîs*, possibly scaling ladders
Peiraeus	403 BC	Xenophon *Hellenika* 2.4.27	*Mêchanopoios*, possibly battering rams
Egyptian Larisa	399 BC	Xenophon *Hellenika* 3.1.7	Sheds/tortoises (*chelônas*)

The non-torsion catapult was first pioneered and deployed, in the form of a simple 'belly-shooter', *gastraphetês*, by Dionysios I of Syracuse during his siege of Motya, the Carthaginian island fortress at the westernmost end of Sicily, in 398/7 BC.[27] In essence an overlarge crossbow, it acquired this seemingly homely and unthreatening name because of a concavity at the rear of a two-part wooden stock, which could be placed against the belly. This concavity had two handles. The operator pushed the sliding part of the stock as far forward as possible, until the trigger on the topside of the sliding part of the stock engaged the bowstring. He then placed his belly in the concavity, and seizing the handles, he pressed all his weight on the end of the belly-shooter, with the end of the sliding part of the stock on the ground or against a wall. The sliding part of the stock including the trigger thus drew string to its maximum extension, and a ratchet kept it from moving forward again. The operator, having fully cocked his belly-shooter, could now lay a missile bolt in the groove on the top-side of the sliding part of the stock. The belly-shooter was now ready to fire.[28]

Whilst powerful and accurate, the belly-shooter was quite impractical for use in the field. However, the revolutionary development of this mechanical propulsive device, which essentially accumulated and stored human strength, would, when modified with the addition of a stand and a winch, eventually threaten fortifications by the sheer amount of force it could produce. Catapults would come to epitomize the acme of ancient military technology. Archidamos, the son of Agesilaos, made a telling comment when he saw for the first time a missile bolt shot from a catapult: 'By Herakles! A man's valour is dead'.[29]

But in the first half of the fourth century BC the full effect of siege machines was yet to be realized. In his treatise *Poliorkêtika* (*How to Survive under Siege*), the soldier of fortune Aineias Taktikos (*fl.* 350 BC) writes from the point of view of personal experience.[30] Despite the beginnings of the mechanisation of siege craft – and here the techniques of defence he discusses are almost wholly non-mechanical, mentioning artillery only once[31] – the major preoccupation of Aineias remains the threat of betrayal, and it is clear from his obsessive writing that he was haunted by the spectre of some faction or another within opening the gates to the enemy without.[32] Catapults may have horrified Archidamos as a detestable symbol of unheroic war, but symbols to some extent they remained. They were gradually influencing siege warfare and the art of fortification; they inflicted unexpected casualties and introduced a new atmosphere of uncertainty and fear into warfare, but they won no battles as yet and took surprisingly few cities.

Siege of Plataia, 429–427 BC

Fearing infection from the plague, the Spartans decided to avoid Attica and attack Plataia instead, a small Boiotian *polis* at the north foot of Mount Kithairon (summer 429 BC). The decision to attack Athens' oldest ally had been initiated by the Thebans, who were eager to use the Peloponnesian army led by King Archidamos for their own purposes. Thucydides cuts through the hypocrisy to explain the true nature of Spartan motives: 'The hostile attitude of the Spartans in the whole matter of Plataia was chiefly on account of the Thebans, for the Spartans thought that the Thebans would be useful to them in the war just then beginning'.[33] It seems that the Spartans were preparing for a long haul in which Boiotian support would be a more critical factor than a reputation for justice and decency.

Plataia had been the only *polis* to send its army to help the Athenians drive off the Persians at Marathon (490 BC). Eleven years later, after the battle of Plataia, the Spartans had administered an oath to all the Greeks who had taken part in it by which they restored to the Plataians 'their *astu* and *chôra*, and declared it independent and inviolate against aggression or conquest'.[34] The Spartan attack on Plataia, therefore, was not only an embarrassment but filled with brutal irony.

Archidamos gave the Plataians the option of exercising their freedom by joining in the fight against Athens, or at the very least, of remaining neutral. Neutrality was out of the question, however, for the Plataians could not receive both sides as friends when the Thebans waited to pounce and Plataia's women and children were in Athens. Archidamos then invited the Plataians to evacuate their *astu* and *chôra* for the duration of the war. Assurances came from the Spartans that they would hold their land and property in trust, paying rent for its use, and restore it intact after the war ended. This offer, too, was a charade, for once Plataia was in Spartan hands the Thebans would never permit its restoration. The Plataians finally countered by requesting a truce to ask permission of the Athenians to surrender. Assurances from the Athenians that they would not abandon the Plataians 'but would aid them with all their power' convinced those still inside the *astu* to hold out come what may.[35] Their plight illustrates the helplessness of small states caught between great powers. Independence, so highly cherished by humanity, is illusory in a world of political alliances and bankable deals.

Initially, the besiegers erected a surrounding palisade to keep any defenders from escaping. Next they began building a siege mound, using local timber to form lattice-work, which was then packed with earth and stone. As the siege mound neared the defences, the besieged responded by erecting a wooden scaffold, and inside these men raised the wall facing the growing ramp by using mud bricks procured from nearby houses. The timbers were covered in rawhide, 'so that the workmen and woodwork might be safe and shielded from incendiary arrows'.[36]

Once the siege mound reached the wall, a feat apparently taking seventy days and nights, the Plataians tunnelled through and attempted to undermine it. The besiegers countered by using reed wattles packed with clay to provide a tough facing to the ramp. They then deployed battering rams against the raised wall but the Plataians responded by lowering nooses and hoisting up the rams. They also used cranes to drop heavy beams on the rams so as to snap their heads off. Despite these counter-measures, however, sections of the raised wall collapsed under the battering. Wisely the defenders had earlier constructed a second semicircular wall within the *astu* (viz. a lunette), so that when the attackers broke in they found themselves in a walled enclosure.

In reply the besiegers filled the enclosure with bundles of wood and fired them using liberal quantities of pine resin and in a bold innovation, sulphur. The combination of sulphur and pitch 'produced such a conflagration as had never been seen before, greater than any fire produced by human agency'.[37] This chemically enhanced fire almost destroyed the Plataians for, along with the bright blue sulphur flames and the acrid stench, the fumes would have been deadly since the combustion of sulphur creates sulphur dioxide. A good part of the lunette was destroyed, but then the wind changed and a chance rainstorm doused this toxic-conflagration.[38] After this final failure, Archidamos sent many of his troops home to attend the harvest, while having the remainder build a double wall of circumvallation with a view to starving the Plataians into submission (autumn 429 BC). Some 2,000 Spartan and Boiotian troops remained on guard duty through the winter. Plataia lay in the strangling grip of the Spartans and their allies.

Most of the Plataians had escaped before the siege began, and only a garrison of 480 men, eighty of them Athenian, and 110 women 'to make bread',[39] remained in the beleaguered *astu*. The small garrison and wise stockpiling of provisions meant that the defenders were in no immediate danger of starvation. In fact they held out for two years. Half the garrison managed to escape in the last months of the siege by negotiating the circumvallation one stormy, moonless night in midwinter, and then eluding a large pursuing force, but the remainder held out in the pathetic belief that the Athenians would relieve them. In the end, facing starvation, they surrendered (summer 427 BC). Under pressure from Thebes, Plataia's hereditary enemy, and after some specious legal proceedings, the Spartans executed all 225 male survivors, which included some twenty-five Athenians, and sold the surviving women into slavery. They then turned the Plataian territory over to the Thebans, and a year later the *astu* itself was levelled with the ground, the rubble being converted into a temple of Hera with an adjoining two-storey hostel for visitors.[40] The Athenians, no doubt feeling embarrassment, even shame, at the fate of its comrade in arms at Marathon and fast ally ever since, granted the surviving Plataians the rare privilege of Athenian citizenship, but it was hardly adequate compensation for the loss of their native land.

The outbreak of the current conflict between Athens and Sparta had seen the cold-bloodied murder by the Plataians of 180 Theban prisoners who had surrendered with a promise of safe conduct. The Athenians were not directly involved but their memories were long enough to offer immediate, if unsubstantial support to their only allies at the battle of Marathon almost sixty years ago, one of the defining moments in Athenian history. Sadly, much like the history of more recent conflicts all over the world, there was never a lack of an atrocity to fuel the cheap and hypocritical outrage of those whose consciences go into hibernation the moment a conflict breaks out.

Siege of Mantineia, 385 BC

The existence of Mantineia was important because the security of its curtain walls encouraged Mantineian autonomy in foreign policy and the development of an independent democratic political system that was hostile to Sparta.[41] It was shortly after the Persian Wars, according to Strabo,[42] that the Mantineians left their five village settlements, known as *kômai*, and united as one *polis*, an event that can be linked with the establishment of democracy in Mantineia.[43] If political and physical union, the process Greeks knew as *synoikismos*, 'joining together', led to the adoption of a democratic constitution, then life in village settlements fostered oligarchic rule that encouraged loyalty to Sparta's own interests.[44]

Although they bowed to Sparta's orders as to the dispositions of their military forces as members of the Peloponnesian League, the Arcadians maintained their collective independence and never became Sparta's obedient allies during the fifth and fourth centuries BC. Being an artificial foundation, Mantineia lacked an acropolis. Thus, albeit with some natural protection from a small river, the Mantineians built their *astu* on what was, for Arcadia, practically level ground. Situated in eastern Arcadia, the *chôra* of the Mantineians was a bare upland plain (629 metres), known as the Mantiniki, enclosed by an amphitheatre of barren mountains and grudgingly shared with their hated neighbours, the Tegeans. The Mantiniki, Arcadia's largest plain, was directly linked with the Eurotas valley through the northern Lakonian hills by at least two major routes. Other routes out of this upland plain gave access to the Megalopolis plain to the southwest and thence Messenia, to Hysiai and Argos to the east, and to Orchomenos to the north. It was desirable, therefore, for Sparta to have the *poleis* of Mantineia and Tegea subservient to its interests.

These were the two leading Arcadian *poleis* that, unless policed, could often establish hegemony over the smaller and weaker Arcadian settlements, which would, in turn, threaten Sparta's vital domination of the Peloponnesian League.[45] Hence the Mantiniki, whose terrain and location made it a convenient meeting place for invading armies moving up from the south or down from the north, often became the cockpit in which pro- and anti-Spartan alliances settled their differences, as in 418 BC, 370/69 BC and 362 BC, and both sides regarded Mantineia as of immense strategic importance. Moreover, the existence of Mantineia was important because the security of its walls encouraged Mantineian autonomy in foreign policy and the development of an independent democratic political system.[46]

Nonetheless it should be stressed that though Arcadia became a strategic thorough-fare during several campaigns, the land routes to and from its upland plains traversed difficult terrain and were often snowbound from late autumn to mid-spring. For example, Philip v of Macedon, when he marched through Arcadia, encountered heavy snowstorms and his army suffered 'many hardships' as a consequence.[47] Likewise, Pausanias recalls how the Tegeans once beat the Spartans because of the bitter and unforgiving Arcadian weather conditions. It seems the Spartans were in rotten condition too, and as ' it was snowing, they were chilled, and thus distressed by their armour'. The Spartans then ditched their armour, while the Tegeans 'untroubled by the cold donned, they say, their armour, went out against the Lakedaimonians, and had the better of the engagement'.[48] It was Arcadia's most famous son, Polybios, who wrote that the harshness of the Arcadian character was the direct result of 'the cold and gloomy atmospheric conditions' that prevail in Arcadia.[49] It could be so terrifically cold that birds dropped dead on the wing, wine froze in the flask and spittle before it reached the ground, and when the thermometer notched up a couple of degrees, the fog, cloud and mists were such that it could be said when the sun shone, even the dogs barked in fear.

It was to this outlandish part of the Peloponnese that Agesipolis of Sparta (r. 395–380 BC) came in 385 BC so as to punish to the Mantineians. Accused of disloyal leanings during the Corinthian War, they had been ordered by Sparta to tear down their walls, which were constructed of sun-dried mud-brick resting on a low stone socle.[50] On their refusal, Agesipolis led a Peloponnesian army to ravage the northern half of the Mantiniki and invest Mantineia.[51] Interfering with water by diverting rivers was an environmental ploy that was capable of wrecking great havoc. Pausanias, in his description of the ensuing siege of Mantineia mounted by Agesipolis, pinpoints the mechanical strength of mud-brick fortifications:

> Against the blows of engines brick brings greater security than fortifications built of stone. For stones break and are dislodged from their fittings; brick however, does not suffer so much from engines, but it crumbles under the action of water just as wax is melted by the sun.[52]

Then again, Agesipolis' conquest of Mantineia also highlights the structural weakness of brickwork and the destructive potential of water.

Normally the Spartans did not take kindly to sieges. They were essentially, as we well know, denizens of the battleground, delighting in trial of combat, agitated with the dull recurrent routine of a blockade. Nonetheless, after laying waste to the surrounding countryside, Agesipolis detailed half his troops to dig a trench and erect a palisade around Mantineia, thereby sealing it off from the outside world. The Mantineians, however, opted to resist as they had taken the precaution of stockpiling a large reserve of grain within their curtain walls. Not wishing to commit his Peloponnesian allies to a long and drawn out siege, Agesipolis decided to mount an aquatic assault against Mantineia. This was accomplished by diverting the Ophis, the river that flowed through the *astu*, by means of a makeshift dam. The heavy rains of the previous winter meant that the river was in full spate, and the diverted water rapidly rose above the stone socle of the circuit. The water was on the besiegers' side, so at this point Agesipolis broke off his attack to let it do their work for them. As the rising water begun to affect the lower courses of mud-brick, the upper ones also weakened. At first cracks appeared in the brickwork and then signs of collapse.

Despite the Mantineians valiantly shoring up their crumbling defences with timber baulks, total collapse was imminent, and so it was decided that the best course of action was to surrender themselves to Agesipolis. The walls of Mantineia were levelled with the ground, an oligarchic government with strong pro-Spartan leanings was placed in power, and the *astu* dissolved by dispersing the Mantineians back to their ancestral villages.[53] It had, in the event, been quite easy.

It is a matter of curiosity that Pausanias, in his version of the siege of Mantineia, concludes with the following statement:

> Agesipolis did not discover this method of demolishing the fortifications of the Mantineians. It was a stratagem invented at an earlier date by Kimon, the son of Miltiades, when he was besieging Boges and other Persians who were holding Eïon on the Strymon.[54]

However, although Herodotos, Thucydides, Plutarch, Polyainos, and a singular little document known as the *Oxyrhynchos Papyri*, all cite Kimon's attack on Eïon (476 BC), none of them mention that he flooded the *astu* by damning up the Strymon.[55] The capture of Eïon was celebrated in verse on three herms in Athens and the inscriptions, quoted by Aischines and Plutarch,[56] support the above sources. But the division of the river, the cunning trick ascribed to Kimon by Pausanias, is probably a later invention to explain these 'Eïon epigrams'.

And what of the fates of Agesipolis and Mantineia? The Spartan king was to die of a fever outside Olynthos, where he was conducting another siege. As for Mantineia, following the spectacular defeat of the Spartans at Leuktra (371 BC) by the Theban *stratêgos* Epameinondas, the scattered Mantineians, with Theban aid, were able to re-establish their *astu*,[57] and very quickly it was girdled with massive walls with towers at intervals along the ramparts. As well as raising these extensive fortifications whose ruins we see today, they also rearranged the course of the Ophis so that it became a defence instead of a danger. The Mantineians were obviously concerned with avoiding a repetition of the disaster of 385 BC, when this river was damned and the rising waters caused a stretch of the mud-brick fortifications to collapse. Although still employing mud-brick in the construction of their new curtain walls, the Mantineians took the wise precaution of altering the channel of the Ophis so that it now flowed around, instead of through the *astu*, and in this way the base of the new walls was lapped by the river. Promoted by Epameinondas, the leading soldier of the day, new Mantineia probably incorporated in its defensive system all the most up-to-date ideas in such a way so as to raise fortifications to take any kind of punishment a besieger can throw at it. In itself, the use of the Ophis as a wet moat encircling the *astu* was a stroke of genius.

Epilogue:
Between History and Legend

Those who remember the past are doomed to repeat it too, or so an old history joke has it. True or not, the war against Xerxes had its moments of selfishness, error and muddle much like any other war, and Greeks and Persians sometimes distinguished themselves, and occasionally disgraced themselves. But it was in a battle against the odds that the heroism hides the faults, namely the unhappy but glorious attempt to hold the pass at Thermopylai. To poach those immortal words of Churchill: 'in the field of human conflict never was so much owed by so many to so few'.[1] History, which is largely a matter of reputations and monuments, rarely favours losers, yet it is difficult to have anything but respect and awe for those Spartans who stood to the bitter end and died courageously at Thermopylai. Even from the grave these men exert a powerful influence. As for their fellow Greeks, in the immediate post-war years they were still under the spell of emotions that most stupendous, most disastrous, yet most glorious of battles had unleashed. It had been grand and heroic, from whichever side you looked at it. Not even after a distance of years were the Greeks able to free themselves from this obsession and to view it critically and dispassionately.[2] We still read of Western battles when men stood their ground against all odds. Unnecessarily. We celebrate such stubbornness.

Dead men tell no tales

It is worthwhile remembering the past – for comparison. All the same, the black-and-white picture of events that become conventional wisdom afterwards should be shaded in grey. Thus, splendid though it may be, we cannot press Herodotos' dramatic account of the last stand at Thermopylai too closely, since we are bound to ask how he learned the details if all the Greeks were killed. Dead men, as we all know, tell no tales of their own glory, do they? Of course it is possible that some of the Thebans who survived were still near enough to see what happened. Intriguingly, Herodotos says of the Thebans that as they were surrendering they were shouting to the Persians they had 'come to Thermopylai against their will'.[3] There is no reason to doubt that at least some of the Thebans, having decided that they had done enough in the aid of a cause that was clearly hopeless, opted to surrender and survive rather than to face a certain death.

Yet there is a strong element of bias – probably derived from an Athenian source – in Herodotos' remarks about the Thebans both here and elsewhere in his account of the battle.[4] For instance, he says that Leonidas was particularly anxious to pick up the continent from Thebes he took with him to Thermopylai, because of serious accusations of medisim against the Thebans.[5] In reality it is possible that the Spartans were still confident that the Thebans would support them, though they presumably hoped for more than the 400 hoplites they got as Thebes was the principal *polis* of Boiotia. It seems this modest contingent of Thebans with Leonidas represented those in Thebes who were inclined to resist the Persians. As Diodoros, indeed, says they were 'of the other party',[6] namely political opponents of the current government in Thebes. If this was so, then we can understand a little better why the surviving Thebans surrendered to Xerxes at the very end, for with the mark of the Great King upon them they were safe from their political enemies back home. At the time most of the Thebans back home, namely those who were inclined not to resist the Persians, were preparing to ingratiate themselves with Xerxes. Indeed, after Thermopylai, all the Boiotians except Thespiai (an enemy of Thebes) and Plataia (an ally of Athens) medized, so that the reputation of all the Thebans, pro- and anti-Persian, was especially blackened when the Persians were eventually beaten back in the following year. The 400 Thebans who turned out to fight at Thermopylai deserve all honour, even if they represented a tiny anti-Persian faction, which had nothing to lose and everything to gain. Of course, we would like to believe that Herodotos' story of their surrender at the end is untrue, more so when we consider it deeply tainted by prejudice. Posterity would immortalize the Three Hundred and them alone.

Exposing the myths

Myths are ecumenical and eternal stories that reflect and shape our lives – even today, in our increasingly cynical world; they explore our desires, our fears, and our longings and provide narratives that remind us what it means to be human. All nations have their myths. Britain stood alone in 1940 – according to Churchill. Someone with a thought for the Commonwealth added 'alone, the whole 500 million of us', not to mention plucky little Greece (modern, that is) too. But the myth has won, not perniciously. And so the Thermopylai legend, the legend of a glorious defeat, was not slow to be born. Thus by Herodotos' time the exploits of Leonidas and the Three Hundred had already passed from legend into myth, the eternal story of a small band of heroes selling their lives dearly for the salvation of Greece. Herodotos himself, the inimitable storyteller, was proud to relate that he had learned the names of the Three Hundred.[7]

As expected, therefore, Herodotos only mentions the helot attendants of these heroic Spartans to say one of them pointed his blind master in the direction of battle, and then shamefully 'took to his heels'.[8] Yet in the aftermath of battle passing reference is made of helot corpses lying on the battlefield,[9] from which it seems fair to suggest that many of the 300 helots had fought alongside the Spartan hoplites as lightly armed troops. This was certainly the case with the helots who served at Plataia the following year, for Herodotos says they were in some fashion 'armed for war'.[10] It seems that an enslaved helot workforce provided its Spartan masters with more than the economic basis of their unique lifestyle, as they also accompanied them on campaign where helots not only carried equipment and provisions, but pitched tents, fetched water, prepared food, and, armed with a bundle of javelins or alternatively a couple of slings, even fought. Helots ranked for ancient theorists, too, as people 'between slave and free'. The rhetorician and sophist Alkidamas of Elaia, who had been schooled by Gorgias, said that 'God (*? theós*) has left all men free; nature (*phusis*) made no man a slave',[11] which obviously implies that all slavery was purely a human convention without divine warrant and therefore unwarranted. This occurred in a speech to the Spartans recommending them to emancipate the Messenians. For Alkidamas the helot system of the Spartans was the most controversial slave system in all Greece, mainly because the helots were fellow Greeks, not non-Greek 'barbarians' like most of the unfree in the Greek world.

The impact of Thermopylai was mainly ideological, a fight between a fistful of free citizens of autonomous states defending their own soil and an invading horde of slaves thick as locusts. The Persians were the national enemy, the barbarians, a subservient pantalooned race ruled by an arrogant and cruel court. And so was born the leitmotif that the Greeks in general and the Spartans in particular, fought of their own free will but in obedience to their laws or customs.[12] As spearmen they seek open battle, which they will fight hand-to-hand. The Persians, on the other hand, were subject to the whims of a single man and only fought coerced by the whip.[13] They are servile cowards, because as bowmen they seek to avoid close quarter combat and will only fight under the lash. In Persia the Great King is the state, while in Greece the hoplites form the state. Separating stereotypical myth from labyrinthine reality is difficult, particularly in the case of this legendary battle.

It should be noted at this juncture that all the Greek writers were fascinated by the wealth and power of the Persian rulers, so they often recount stories of court intrigue and the moral decadence that comes from indulging in unlimited luxury. In such anecdotes, the Great King appears as an essentially weak, lustful figure, prey to the machinations of powerful women and sinister eunuchs. This is an inversion of Greek social and political norms, with which we, as Westerners, have usually identified and still do so to this day – the binary oppositions of 'us' and 'them' so apparent during the current conflict in Afghanistan, just as it was in the recent one in Iraq too. As such, the fundamentally flawed images of the cowardly, effeminate Persian monarch have exercised a strong influence through the centuries, making the Persian empire into a powerful 'other' in Western orientalism, contrasted with 'Western' bravery and masculinity.

The Seven Hundred

So whilst Western posterity remembers the Three Hundred who gave their lives willingly at Thermopylai, few will recall that over twice that number of Thespians died on the same day. The contingent of 700 Thespians, with their *stratêgos* who bore the Dionysiac name of Dithyrambos, probably comprised all the adult males of Thespiai who qualified for hoplite service. It was an extraordinary muster that emptied the *polis* of its property-holding citizenry. Various explanations have been offered for their remarkable courage, ranging from the fatalistic notion that nothing remained for them in a medizing Boiotia dominated by their hated rival Thebes, to a genuine belief that their gallantry might give valuable time for their own women and children to evacuate knowing well that their *astu* would be soon destroyed. People are capable of great things, but only when great circumstances call on them. They cannot live at that pitch all the time, and most circumstances are not great. In daily life people are tempted by comfort and peace; they are a little slothful, a little greedy, a little cowardly, a little lustful, a little vain, a little cranky, and a little envious. In times of crisis people are forced to do great things.

Yet the Thespians do seem to have been endowed with stubborn courage, and later, seeing that all was up for them upon the field of Delion (winter 424 BC), chose to stand firm and face destruction, and those 'who perished were cut down fighting hand-to-hand'.[14] In fact, their losses that day were so great that the Thebans were able to annex them and destroy their fortifications. Whatever, of the 1,400 Greeks who stayed behind with Leonidas, the Thespian dead represents at least 50 per cent of those annihilated, a remarkable percentage when we remember that they comprised only about 10 per cent of the original Greek force of 7,000 hoplites.[15] The following year 1,800 Thespians turned out for Plataia, but without arms,[16] strongly suggesting that all the hoplite manpower of Thespiai had fallen at Thermopylai. Lest we forget, therefore, the gallant citizen soldiers of Thespiai who volunteered to fight with a spear, then a sword, then a fist, then with their teeth, and then finally die with the Three Hundred.

Two kings

So it was an expensive business for both sides, in lives lost. Xerxes certainly did not forget Leonidas. Herodotos says the Great King had the body of the Spartan king identified, and ordered the head to be hacked off and stuck on a pole for all to see and to give sport to the crows and ravens.[17] It is certainly possible that Xerxes had this dastardly deed done, *pour encourager les grecs*; he was perfectly capable of it and his patience must have been tested almost to the limit. At the same time, apparently, the other Greek dead, including helot corpses, were collected and left lying in heaps until sightseeing parties from the fleet had a chance to view the battered heads, the glazed eyes, the chopped and slashed bodies and limbs. However, Xerxes' attempt to conceal his own losses – he had hastily buried all but a thousand of the 20,000 killed – fooled no one, as Herodotos points out.[18] The Persian losses were not as high as 20,000, which is almost certainly an overestimation, and cannot be checked, but they were certainly higher than a thousand.[19] The Persian juggernaut had been badly bashed. A humiliation for one king, Thermopylai, had been another king's finest hour.

Like Leonidas, the Great King was not a stupid man, but unlike Leonidas, he had long been surrounded by a camarilla of yes-men who, for reasons of their own survival, never contradicted him and reinforced his sense of omnipotence and invulnerability. At Thermopylai, by offering their royal general-in-chief guarded phrases, colourless and noncommittal, the Persian high command had committed the cardinal sin of underestimating the enemy.

Ripping yarns

The struggle between good and evil is just one of those staple features of Western storytelling that the masses never seem to get bored with. Little surprise, therefore, that the eternal fascination with Thermopylai is not only due to the tragic events of those three high summer days, but also to the inextricable tangle of history and myth that surround it. Having inspired writers of all times, good, bad and ugly alike, since Simonides and Herodotos, Thermopylai is a golden story that has been often told and retold and remodelled. Thus, we have Diodoros' cockamamie yarn of the commando-style raid, staged during the small dark hours prior to the final day at Thermopylai, behind enemy lines to try and liquidate Xerxes, culminating, apparently, in the annihilation of Leonidas and his swashbuckling band in the Persian camp itself.[20] This story flatly contradicts Herodotos, and it is from Herodotos in the first place that we form our best impression of Thermopylai. In more recent times there has been the full-length comic book adaptation of the powerful Hollywood film *The Three Hundred Spartans* (1962), published as *Lion of Sparta* (1963), a sterile hackwork, while the five-part *Three Hundred* (1998) is rather a mixed bag. And then there is the more recent *300* (2007), the comic book film about Thermopylai, the 'Hoo-ah!' retelling of this story. We shall leave it there, for the moment.

Fortunately for us moderns, there is Steven Pressfield's *Gates of Fire* (1998), a stupendous larger-than-life novel crammed full of some of the best historical drama you are likely to read. Rather than present the battle in an epic, heroic light, Pressfield tilts more towards the tragic. The scenes of carnage and horror that accompany the clash of battle are matter-of-factly described, and are made all the more horrifying for it – just cast your mind back to the opening battle sequence of *Saving Private Ryan* (1998). War, as Pressfield's narrator tells it, is not glamorous nor is it heroic. More than that, he conveys so poignantly as he tells his story not only the ugliness of war but the utter futility of anything connected with it. Yet in the blood-sweat-urine stench of infantry combat, men are capable of incredible acts of valour and earn for themselves that priceless reward – undying fame.

Celluloid heroes

And now for something completely different! There is a popular belief that where history is concerned, Hollywood always gets it wrong, and in view of some of the monstrosities that have been put on the screen, sometimes it does – we need only take, for instance, that truly diabolical film of 1955 with a young Richard Burton conquering the known world in the name of Alexander the Great. However, what is overlooked is the astonishing amount of history Hollywood has got right. So, history according to Hollywood, is not a bad thing after all. In fact, many of us get our first real taste of the ancient world via the silver screen, and I gladly include myself in this category. Of course, many academics shook their heads or wrung their hands after having viewed an ancient epic 'with a cast of thousands' such as *Troy*, *Alexander* or *300*, muttering dark words about historical inaccuracies and the like. Presentation of the past in the present is so often a controversial topic, and you can appreciate their point of view, namely that once Hollywood has seized a historical theme, past-fact is usurped by present-fantasy. Gore Vidal once famously said: 'In the end, he who screens the history makes the history'. Okay, Hollywood is not a school for teaching history but spicing it up. Hollywood is a dream factory that stirs our imagination and makes monstrous amounts of money in the process. *Panem et circenses.*

True, these epic films can shape modern perspectives on the ancient world, but in a grey world ruled by grey men uttering grey words, they can also act as a visual panacea to a disillusioned populace. With the end of public freedoms eloquence has disappeared, logically enough, since there is no audience to convince by clever stratagems or the power of the word. Besides, our grey men have the minds of lawyers and bankers rather than of classically trained statesmen, and even though they can calculate political moves like lawyers and bankers, they neither see far ahead nor look behind. So it is heartening to think that heroes of old, such as Achilles, Alexander and Leonidas, are still worthy of the Hollywood treatment. Let me explain.

To catch the popular imagination, a historical epic should furnish the impression, atmosphere, and feeling of history, not the sort of accuracy demanded from an academic dealing with the same historical topic. Yet the ancient sources are readily available in translation, and thus easy to check, and often more dramatic and entertaining than the modern script. Plutarch himself, for instance, would have made an ace Hollywood screenwriter. Whereas *Troy* attempts to rationalize the supernatural world of Homer by banishing the gods off stage, and *Alexander* busies itself with the seamier side of Alexander's private life, one of the major appeals of the *300* is that somebody had obviously picked up a copy of Plutarch and read it well. For the film effectively portrays the 'Lykourgan' system, peculiar to Sparta and framed with the specific purpose of making its warriors deadly efficient in war. Still, when compared with that more effective epic, *The Three Hundred Spartans*, it has a good deal more gore than glory.

However, Leonidas and all his Greeks embodied valour, real heroes and not those fictional ones that dissolve at the end of a book or film reel. At the root of the psychology of war is the myth of glory, first introduced into occidental thought by the ancient Greeks and sustained by almost all national and religious authorities of every nation state ever since. Even today, where modern technology has usurped the traditional role of the individual soldier, the myth that wars provide an opportunity for unique virtue remains. Each soldier, with his blood, will fertilize the vast fields of glory of the régime he serves. With fearless courage, despising his life, he will charge forward under the bullet-ridden ensign of his regiment through the smoke and powder of the hurricane fire of the foe towards new glories and new victories. No army, to my knowledge, has yet abandoned the custom of awarding battle decorations. In the British Army, for instance, a regiment's colours are embodiments of its martial pride and sacred traditions. They are embroidered with battle honours, hung with battle streamers, and given an almost religious reverence. They were traditionally blessed when presented, and are stilled accorded dignified treatment even though their use as a rallying point upon the field of slaughter has long gone. What is more, military institutions remain cluttered with a vast array of trophies from past conflicts and the promise that the brave acts of soldiers will live on in the collective memories of the people remains, especially for the young, as seductive as ever. In reality, the closer you get to the frontline, the fewer abstract nouns you are likely to hear. War is a horrible trade, where men fight like beasts and hideous things are done. War, that devourer of men, is to be condemned, as Wilfred Owen once said, as 'The old Lie: Dulce et decorum est / Pro patria mori'.[21] When you are down to your last bullet, do you still need flyblown patriotism?

Victory in defeat

Lykourgos the miracle worker may have been one of many things, a god, a hero, or a myth, but it was for his radical laws that the Spartans who perished at Thermopylai gave their lives so willingly. Indeed, if he was a myth, he was a useful one, since the Spartans believed in the truth of it and it provided a very strong social bond, for the Lykourgan system was framed with the specific purpose of making them deadly efficient in war. With its emphasis on rigorous training, physical fitness, and competence in hoplite warfare, courage and obedience were the supreme virtues of the Spartan warrior. The catastrophic losses the Spartans suffered on the plain of Leuktra tend to cloud the issue of the ferocious display of valour on their part as they fought it out to the death in the desperate struggle to rescue Kleombrotos, their mortally wounded king,[22] much as they had done at Thermopylai for the corpse of Leonidas. The second virtue comes to the fore in that famous epitaph composed by Simonides on Leonidas and the Three Hundred. Taking a leaf from the Spartan book, in just a few, spare words, he came up with the best remembered of epitaphs: 'Stranger, report to the Lakedaimonians that here we lie, obedient to their commands'.[23] Even we moderns, both men and women, young and old, still praise the Spartan defeat at Thermopylai as grander than any victory. The battle may have been only an episode in a long campaign but it left a permanent mark on history.

In this book we have followed the fortunes of the Spartan army, first in the struggle to gain local and regional supremacy, then in the two conflicts between Sparta and its erstwhile ally of the great war with Persia, Athens, and then in the one that came after those, namely the conflict between Sparta and its erstwhile allies, Corinth and Thebes, who, perhaps unsurprisingly, were now supported by their onetime foe, Athens. In this book we have met those universal rhythms of rise, flowering and decline. Xerxes' grand army sets out in the pride of power, and goes back broken and beaten; so will the brave armada that the Athenians send in their folly to Sicily; and the Spartans, who arrogantly seize the acropolis of Thebes and impose a junta every bit as unpopular as the one they had imposed on an earlier victim, will be overwhelmed from that very quarter. Pride, folly, arrogance: three apocalyptic imperialists who, booted and spurred, are still very much at large in the freewheeling sovereign state of today. If there is one lesson to be learnt from the history of Sparta, it is that peoples must work out their destinies in terms of hard realities, not of unrealizable theories.

Appendix 1

The Size of Greek States

Aristotle once suggested, man was 'by nature a political animal',[1] but modern sociologists reckon that *Homo sapiens* can only cope with a certain number of very intensive face-to-face interactions. Where no communities number more than 100 to 150 individuals, there is little differentiation and the basic social relationship is that of the household. Above this size of community, where groups number in the order of 150 to 350, it is harder to handle all the social relationships at a personal level, and subgroups of a higher level than the household appear. These 'mediating structures' now allow individuals to relate to a wider range of people in a less intensive fashion. Within this society rank is achieved through a man's own efforts.

In permanent settlements of 500 people or more, constituted offices begin to emerge, with access restricted by birth. An agrarian community starts to take on the features common to a peasant society, including the division into socially stratified groups. Aristotle also said 'the political community must consist only of those who possess hoplite arms and armour'.[2] Greek states were tiny by our standards. The Greeks did not keep population statistics, and their historians displayed a corresponding disinterest in anything like the precision a modern historian would ideally demand. But there are figures preserved in the works they wrote, and by glancing at the figures in the literary sources (given in brackets) for the hoplite numbers deployed at various battles, we can quickly gain a rough, albeit arbitrary, impression how small Greek states were by the standards of a modern city, let alone a modern state:

Athens	490 BC = 10,000 (Justin 2.9)
	479 BC = 8,000 (Herodotos 9.28.7)
	431 BC = 13,000 (Thucydides 2.13.6, cf. 8.65.3)
	394 BC = 6,000 (Xenophon *Hellenika* 4.2.17)
	362 BC = 6,000 (Diodoros 15.84.2)
Sparta	480 BC = 8,000 (Herodotos 7.234.2)
	479 BC = 5,000 (Herodotos 9.10.1, 11.3, 28.2)
	371 BC = 1,100 (estimated, cf. Aristotle *Politics* 1270a)
Argos	418 BC = 6,000 (estimated)
	394 BC = 7,000 (Xenophon *Hellenika* 4.2.17)
Corinth	479 BC = 5,000 (Herodotos 9.28.4)
	394 BC = 3,000 (Xenophon *Hellenika* 4.2.17)

Thebes	447 BC = 4,000 (Oxyrhynchos Historian 16.3.4) 394 BC = 4,000 (estimated) 371 BC = 4,000 (Diodoros 15.53.2, 3)
Mantineia	480 BC = 500 (Herodotos 7.202) 418 BC = 3,000 (Diodoros 12.78.4, Lysias 34.7)
Sikyon	479 BC = 3,000 (Herodotos 9.28.5) 394 BC = 1,500 (Xenophon *Hellenika* 4.2.17)
Megara	479 BC = 3,000 (Herodotos 9.28.6)
Tegea	480 BC = 500 (Herodotos 7.202) 479 BC = 1,500 (Herodotos 9.28.3)
Plataia	490 BC = 1,000 (Justin 2.9) 479 BC = 600 (Herodotos 9.28.6)
Phleious	479 BC = 1,000 (Herodotos 9.28.5)
Troizen	479 BC = 1,000 (Herodotos 9.28.5)
Epidauros	479 BC = 800 (Herodotos 9.28.5)
Thespiai	480 BC = 700 (Herodotos 7.202)
Orchomenos (Arcadia)	480 BC = 120 (Herodotos 7.202)
Aegina	479 BC = 600 (Herodotos 9.28.5)
Chalcis	479 BC = 400 (Herodotos 9.28.5)
Hermione	479 BC = 300 (Herodotos 9.28.5)
Lepreion	479 BC = 200 (Herodotos 9.28.5)
Pale (Kephallenia)	479 BC = 200 (Herodotos 9.28.6)
Mycenae	480 BC = 80 (Herodotos 7.202)
Epidauros, Troizen, Hermione & Halieis	394 BC = 3,000 (Xenophon *Hellenika* 4.2.16)
Eretria & Styreion	479 BC = 600 (Herodotos 9.28.5)
Mycenae & Tiryns	479 BC = 400 (Herodotos 9.28.5)

Apart from Athens, which was by Greek standards large, it is clear that the other *poleis* in our list have fewer than 10,000 citizens (viz. males eighteen years of age and above, capable of bearing arms), while the greater majority of them have citizen populations of less than 5,000. In a far-reaching study the German historian

Ruschenbusch has counted some 750 *poleis* in the core area of the Greek world alone. This is a fantastic figure, one that is reflected in the work of Aristotle, who painstakingly classifies no fewer than 158 possible political constitutions. Most of our evidence for the *polis* of course comes from Athens and Sparta, and Ruschenbusch asks the pertinent question, namely how typical are these two giants. He calculates that 'a typical *polis*' has a territory of only 25–100 square kilometres and an adult male citizen membership of no more than 133–800.[3] Athens, on the other hand, has an adult male citizen population averaging 40,000 who control a territory of 2,400 square kilometres, while its rival Sparta, at its height, has an adult male citizen population of 8,000 controlling a territory of at least 8,400 square kilometres. Here it would be pertinent of us to remind ourselves that Athens and Sparta seemed to have swelled up in our modern minds, like Tweedledum and Tweedledee, until they blocked out the whole political landscape of ancient Greece, which was not just limited to the Balkan mainland. Athens and Sparta were atypical *poleis*, monsters in truth.

Appendix 2

The Median Host at Thermopylai

There is little doubt that the Persian empire of Xerxes was bulging with manpower. Indeed, according to the epitaph for the Peloponnesians who fell at Thermopylai, they had bravery stood against 'three hundred myriads'.[1] Three million Persians at Thermopylai is an alluring idea to which it is very tempting to subscribe. But one starts to think of logistics (to use a relatively new term to describe an age-old practice) and organization, and one cannot prevent a doubt forming. From this doubt springs the thought, even if only from the advantage of plain, common sense, that Xerxes' Asian army, almost continuously on the march, and for the most part depending on its own resources, could maintain its coherence only as long as it was able to support itself logistically. If food and fodder were not being provided by the pre-prepared supply dumps along the line of march, they would have to be acquired locally and by force. And then there is water – 'Or was there a river, except those of unusual size, which sufficed for his troops to drink?'[2] It is very hard to believe that an army bigger than 100,000 fighting personnel could support itself in such conditions, and in a hostile environment. In any army at any time, logistics is the boss.

In the autumn of 481 BC Xerxes, who was to lead the invasion in person, moved his grand army to Sardis in order to spend the winter there in training. Herodotos provides us with a whole battery of figures concerning Xerxes' invasion, including those for the fighting personnel of both arms, army and navy, as well as non-combatants, camp followers and concubines. For instance, we have the grand total figure of 5,283,220,[3] the 2,317,610 combatants of the combined land and sea forces,[4] the 1.7 million infantrymen,[5] the 80,000 horsemen,[6] the 20,000 camels and chariots,[7] not to mention the 300,000 medizing Thracians and Greeks who were picked up *en route*.[8] But what can we make of all this?

The estimation of numbers in war is always a snare for the historian as he or she seeks to counterbalance the exaggerations of contemporary hearsay and propaganda. But all is not lost. There are three ways of thinking of Xerxes' army: first, there is the total force available to the Great King, viz. if he stripped his empire bare of soldiery; second, Xerxes' army operating in the field, viz. its operational strength during the invasion of Greece; and third, Xerxes' army in a particular battle, viz. at Thermopylai. Herodotos may not be a reliable guide, but what he is probably giving us here is the paper strength of the absolute manpower resources available to Xerxes from his empire, and not the operational strength of his invasion force. But figures are one thing, logistic realities another. Though they could be mobilized in theory, in practice it was often difficult to get these human masses to a distant theatre of operation, and once there they were not easy to feed and water.

The strength of any military expedition is limited to the number of troops that can be 'delivered' on a fighting front in the right place at the right time, and fed and watered there, not the number that can be recruited back home. In other words, no matter how sophisticated the logistical organization, and Xerxes had organized his route well with supply dumps and garrisons at key strategic points, there are limits to how many men it can feed and supply, and that number decreases geometrically with the distance over which supplies must be humped. The soldiers Thucydides and Xenophon knew this, the historian Herodotos, perhaps not. To give him his due, he does put explicit discussions of the dangers of a logistical breakdown into a conversation between Xerxes and his 'wise and cautious' uncle, Artabanos (reminiscent of Nestor in the *Iliad*), who is then sent packing. Xerxes' answer was that his grand army was carrying provisions with it and might expect to find more in Greece, since, as he believed (wrongly, in fact), he was invading a cultivated land.[9] Nonetheless, after the grand review at Doriskos, Xerxes did divide the army into three columns,[10] presumably for reasons of logistics. As Thucydides was to say, the underlying cause for the earlier Greeks taking to their boats to plant colonies around the Mediterranean was the need for land; cultivable land was precious while bare rocks were (and still are) so plentiful in the craggy countryside of Greece.[11]

Thucydides, who could have met him, a fellow exile, puts into the mouth of Hermokrates of Syracuse a speech that warns his fellow citizens of the forthcoming Athenian invasion, but stresses that the great size of their expedition might be their undoing as logistical difficulties alone may defeat them, without Syracusan effort:

> Few indeed have been the large armament, either Hellenic or barbarian [viz. Persian], which have gone far from home and was successful. They cannot be more numerous than the people of the country and their neighbours, whom fear unites, and if they fail for want of supplies in a foreign land, to those against whom their plans were laid nonetheless leave renown, though they may themselves have been the main cause of their own discomfort.[12]

We can take for granted that Hermokrates himself did not believe that Xerxes' army had run into the millions.

Herodotos has a story that at Doriskos, the fort built by Dareios at the mouth of the Hebros, the foot soldiers were herded by their officers into pens – we can almost hear the soldiers crying baa, baa, baa, as they shuffled into them – built to hold 10,000 and counted batch by batch. By this method they were found to number 1.7 million. It was at this point, says Herodotos, Xerxes' grand army was divided into twenty-nine commands (he actually says 'divided by nations').[13] It has been suggested (e.g. Maurice, Burn) that the Iranians (including what Herodotos calls the Immortals) may have been of myriad strength, while the rest, counting as 'expendable barbarians', were smaller units, useful but tokens, if you wish. We can, therefore, sensibly settle upon 80,000 as a sober estimate of Xerxes' land forces. This figure, naturally, would have shrunk speedily during the campaign, if only through sickness. Anyway, keeping this figure in mind, let us return to the key question of logistics.

A number of the Persepolis Fortification Texts are Persian records dealing with individuals and groups of people travelling on functionary business across the empire (ambassadors, caravan leaders, fast messengers, etc.). An official chit allowed them to receive a daily amount of food for themselves and fodder for their animals from the royal supply stations for the duration of their journey. Many of these documents mention a daily travel ration of flour equivalent in volume to either 1.71 litres or 2.28.litres per adult male (women and children received less).[14] Of course, these are peacetime rations for royal agents on the Great King's business. It seems that his soldiers had to tighten their belts and shift on less.

Herodotos reckons the Persian troops were receiving a daily ration of one *choinix* (1.08 kilograms) of cereal per man.[15] It was the Roman practice in the second century BC, according to the contemporary testimony of Polybios, to issue a monthly ration of cereal equal to two-thirds of an Attic *medimnos* (34.56 kilograms) to each legionary,[16] which is more or less equivalent to the daily allowance of one *choinix* Xerxes' campaigning soldiers were receiving some three centuries before. In a similar but a comic vein, Aristophanes suggests 'for one giant loaf, use just one *choinix*',[17] which was regarded as a slave's ration by well-fed stay-at-home aristocrats.[18] Just by way of a comparison, the chain-gang of the elder Cato consumed four to five Roman pounds (1.31 to 1.64 kilograms) of bread per day, but they consumed little else.[19] Similarly, the Athenians allowed the Spartans trapped on Sphakteria a daily ration of two *choinikes* (2.16 kilograms) of barley meal, two *kotylai* (0.57 litres) of wine, and a little meat, and for each helot attendant half as much.[20] Nevertheless, apart from the wine and meat, there is no mention of other dietary supplements being supplied to these stranded soldiers by the Athenians, which plausibly explains why they were receiving what was probably a double ration of barley meal. Herodotos says that Spartan kings were given double portions at public banquets or private dinners and, when they did not attend such gastronomic galas, they were allowed two *choinikes* of barley meal and a *kotylê* (0.29 litres) of wine.[21] At the other extreme, we have the tragic example of the Athenian prisoners of war in the Syracusan quarries who were surviving on a daily ration of only a *kotylê* of water and one-half *choinix* of grain.[22] All in all, the evidence safely allows us to believe Herodotos' testimony that a soldier of Xerxes' army was receiving each day one *choinix* of cereal, more or less. So, to put this into some sort of perspective, 80,000 Persian troops would have required 86,400 kilograms of cereal each and every day as they tramped through the Balkan peninsula.

And then there are the camels, just to mention one of the more exotic baggage animals Xerxes brought with him.[23] While an average camel (*Camelus dromedarius*) can carry 136 kilograms of supplies for extended periods, it needs 4.54 kilograms of grain and 11.35 kilograms of straw per day, and, despite popular belief, it ought to be watered daily and will guzzle 45.6 litres of the stuff. These figures are based on the statistics of Major A.G. Leonard, a colonial soldier who knew his camels.[24]

Of course, when all is said and done, we can play with the figures until we end up chasing our own tails. There are just too many imponderables and not enough hard facts. Besides, statistics are just as much a fantasy in their meliorated modern version as in their original Herodotean version. However, our consolation for these uncertainties is that at least they allow our imaginations full play. After all, is this not one of the main attractions of studying Thermopylai?

Appendix 3

The Literary Evidence for the Spartan Army

For those who wish to solve the enigma that is the Spartan army, particularly with regards to its numerical size and unit organization, not to mention that rather ticklish topic of *lochoi* and *morai*, the following chart will be of some use in that quest.

Xenophon *Hellenika*

6.1.1, 4.17	Six *morai* in total circa three-seventies
6.4.12, 17	Strength of each *enômotia* at Leuktra (i.e. three files by twelve deep), and at full strength (i.e. forty age groups, twenty- to sixty-years of age)
4.5.12	Strength of *mora* near Lechaion in 390 BC (*c.* 600 men)
4.5.14	'Ten from manhood' (i.e. twenty- to thirty-years of age) dash out against Iphikrates' peltasts
4.5.16	'The fifteen from manhood' (i.e. twenty- to thirty-five years of age) dash out against Iphikrates' peltasts
5.4.13, 6.4.17	Liability for military service up to 'forty years from manhood' (i.e. sixty-years of age)
7.1.30, 4.20, 5.10	The only references to *lochoi* in *Hellenika*
3.5.22, 4.5.7	*Enômotarchoi* and *pentekosteres* at councils of war
6.4.14	*Hippeis* (i.e. Royal Guard) who surround the king at Leuktra in 371 BC

Xenophon *Lakedaimoniôn politeia*

11.4	Each *mora* contains one *polemarchos*, four *lochagoi*, eight *pentekosteres*, sixteen *enômotarchoi*
4.3	Selection process of the *hippeis*

Thucydides

5.64.3, 66.2, 67.1, 68.3, 72.3	Organization of Spartan army at Mantineia in 418 BC
4.8.9, 31.2, 38.5	Organization of Spartan army at the time of Sphakteria in 425 BC
5.72.4	*Hippeis* who surround the king at Mantineia in 418 BC

Herodotos

1.65.5, 7.173.2, 9.53.2, 57.1, 72, 85	Organization of Spartan army in his day (viz. early to mid fifth century BC)
6.56, cf. 1.67.5, 8.124.3	*Hippeis* – note Herodotos says that when on a campaign the kings were attended by a bodyguard of one hundred picked men, but it is not known why he gives this number. He may be thinking of the strength of the contingent supplied by each of the three tribes of Sparta rather than the overall total, since he does give the correct figure elsewhere. We know from a number of allusions that the *hippeis* was composed of 300 picked Spartiates at full strength (e.g. Thucydides 5.72.4, Strabo 10.4.18). Originally, the *hippeis* were probably mounted warriors – they may have been the horsemen that Pausanias (4.7.5, 8.12) records as participants in the First Messenian War – but hoplites in the wars of the fifth and fourth centuries BC.
7.203, cf. 1.82.3, 7.202, 205.2, 9.64.2	*Hippeis* is a force of 300 men, and the Spartans, according to Herodotos (8.123), used the term *hippeis* for their royal guard. Moreover, even though the aristocracy generally owned horses, they did not normally act as the cavalry arm of a Greek state's army, mounts being ridden to and not in battle. Indeed, the ability to own and pasture horses was an outward sign of wealth.

Appendix 4

A Note on Athenian Democracy

For Herodotos the outstanding moral truth of the Greek victory in the Persian Wars was that the Greek political system, and in particular the democracy of Athens, which promoted the freedom and liberty of man, had triumphed over oriental despotism, Persian style. It is for that reason that he presents to his audience, in detail, a debate among three Persian nobles following the death of their lord and master, Kambyses.[1] The so-called Persian Debate is premised on the discovery that all forms of human government must be species of just three genera: rule by one, rule by some, rule by all. Herodotos twice assures his readers that this debate actually occurred, wherein one of the nobles, Otanes, recommended the establishment of a democracy in Persia. We may scoff of course, but whatever the truth of the matter, Herodotos' Persian vignette does proffer us a valuable insight into the democratic ideals current during the decade before the outbreak of the Greek tragedy that was the Peloponnesian War. For his part, in promoting democracy Otanes talks of 'equality under law' and the marvellous idea that 'all questions are put up for open debate';[2] in other words, the people are sovereign and thus have the right to govern themselves. Perikles confirms both these notions in his famous Funeral Oration, stressing to the Athenians that 'everybody is equal before the law' and 'the power is in the hands not of the minority, but of the whole people'.[3] Thus, it is important to remember what a democracy in Athens was like, for the Athenians never invented representative-style government; on the contrary, it had a very direct system of government, especially when compared with our form of democracy. By way of a simple comparison, Athenian democracy would be the equivalent to the United Kingdom government holding a referendum every ninth day. Imagine that.

People power

Fundamentally, in Athens the assembly of citizens, the *ekklêsia*, held sovereignty over all matters, and this fact cannot be over emphasized. The *ekklêsia* was the government of Athens. Even when the council of Five Hundred, the *boulê*, made policy it did so as an organ of the *dêmos*.[4] In no sense did Athens have a parliament akin to that of Britain, for Athenian citizens ran their affairs by perpetual plebiscite. In some respects the Athenians went beyond what even modern democracies can reach in achieving Lincoln's ideal of 'government of the people, by the people, for the people'.[5]

Such a complete system of popular control has never been known before or since. Thucydides puts the *ekklêsia* in perspective when he describes the visit to Athens of the Spartan envoys seeking the release of their hoplites taken as prisoners of war at Pylos (425 BC). The envoys wanted a committee to be appointed with whom they could discuss the matter, but Kleon stood up and demanded that if their intentions were true they should be willing to stand before the *ekklêsia* and there do business.[6] Basically, committees were not the means through which Athenians carried out policy. Again, Thucydides demonstrates the machinery of democracy when he relates the great debate in the *ekklêsia* over Pylos. Kleon stood up and attacked the *stratêgos* conducting the campaign; he, whether he liked it or not, was promptly handed the command there and then.[7]

Aristophanes poked fun at the foibles of democracy, and in *Acharnians* portrays a comic version of the *ekklêsia* and its function.[8] At the beginning of the play the hero, who is fed up with the Peloponnesian War and wants to make a private treaty with the Spartans, arrives punctually at the Pnyx hoping to discuss peace, only to find nobody has turned up. At last, the members of the presiding committee appear, jostling for the best seats, the benches fill and the meeting proceeds to business – ignoring all need for peace talks. So furious becomes our honest hero that he declares he can feel a drop of rain, a pronouncement sufficient to send everyone scampering for home.

On the more serious side however, several decrees, *probouleuma*, which were initially drawn up by the *boulê*, appear to have been passed by the *ekklêsia* without any amendment. On the other hand, many other decrees do exhibit signs of amendment by the *ekklêsia* before ratification. Other decrees suggest lengthy discussion, for example, that entitled The Foundation of an Athenian Colony at Brea contains an amendment that begins as follows: 'Phantokles made the motion. Concerning the Brean colony (let all the rest be) just as Demolkeides moved'.[9] It suggests that the whole question of the planned colony at Brea had been thrashed out by the *ekklêsia*. Another such example is the decree Athens Honours Neapolis in Thrace where whole sections of the decree had been omitted by the *boulê* so that the *ekklêsia* could discuss the matter for it was ratified.[10] The *ekklêsia* also had the power to instruct the *boulê*; this is clearly demonstrated by the decree Phrynikos' Assassins Honoured and the decree Athens Aids Eretria.[11] The *ekklêsia* did decide policy, and quite detailed policy at that. Indeed, throughout his work Thucydides always refers to the *ekklêsia* but never to the *boulê* when discussing Athenian democracy.

Democratic Athenians believed in the sovereignty of the popular will, yet even this could turn authoritarian. It is the anti-democratic Xenophon who provides for us an extreme case of democracy in action, an example of 'sheer mob-terrorism'. In his *Hellenika* the author relates a rather ugly incident, namely the trial of the *stratêgoi* in 406 BC following the naval battle of Arginousai. The eight *stratêgoi* stood charged of leaving their sailors to drown after winning a crushing victory over the Peloponnesian League fleet, and it was advocated in the *ekklêsia* that the eight should stand trial as a group without individual due process, and there should be no further debate, but only a vote on their guilt or innocence. The motion was put in the most prejudicial language, namely whether or not the eight were guilty 'for failing to rescue the men who had won the victory in the naval battle'.[12] The penalty would be death and a confiscation of property. Quite rightly there were more sober heads who declared the motion unconstitutional, and the *prytaneis* – members of the *boulê* chosen by lot and rotation to preside over the *ekklêsia* on any given day – refused to put it to a vote on the grounds that it was illegal, and called forth the *grâphe paranomon*, a relatively new procedure for defending the Athenian constitution. Their logic rested on two strong arguments: first, that to try the eight *en masse* violated the traditional practice of the *ekklêsia*; second, that the eight had not been given the time and opportunity to speak in their own defence as prescribed by law. Uproar ensued, but Kallixenos, the member of the *boulê* who had presented the charges made against the *stratêgoi* in the *ekklêsia*, retaliated by shouting 'it was unconstitutional not to allow the *dêmos* to do what it so wished'.[13] He also proposed that the same charges be levelled against the *stratêgoi* be made to include the obstreperous *prytaneis*. The *dêmos* responded with a roar of agreement. The presiding committee collapses, bar one, Sokrates,[14] and six *stratêgoi* (sensibly, two had chosen not to return home), who included the son of the great Perikles and his equally celebrated Milesian mistress Aspasia, Perikles junior, are condemned for dereliction of duty.

There was a very serious side to being an Athenian citizen. Take as one example Demosthenes, in his *On the Crown*, where he describes what happened when the news came in that Philip II of Macedon had passed through Thermopylai unopposed and was thus only a couple of days' march from Athens. With war on hand, a gathering of the *ekklêsia* was called for the following day.[15]

The mechanics

The *boulê*, although not sovereign, was extremely important. For without the preparation carried out by this council of 500 citizens the machinery of democratic government would cease to function. The *boulê* was subdivided into committees of fifty, each of which was responsible for carrying on public business during one-tenth of the year. But important as its functions were, its powers were in practice limited by the rule that it should be chosen at random from the citizen body, that membership was limited to one year, and that no citizen might hold membership more than twice. The *boulê* thus never became a continuing body with a policy of its own: the *ekklêsia* remained supreme. And so the Five Hundred were chosen by lot, fifty members from each of the ten tribes, *phylai*, and each candidate had to be thirty years of age and over. The annual selection occurred at deme level, each being allocated a number of councillors according to size. Akharnai, one of the largest demes, provided twenty-two councillors, while some small demes such as Pambotadai and Sybridai took turns to send a single councillor.

It is according to Aristotle that a citizen could serve as a member of the *boulê* twice in his lifetime,[16] there being seventeen such men known for certain during the fourth century BC. This was due to the fall in the number of citizens, for in the preceding century a citizen could only serve on the *boulê* once in his lifetime. There were always accusations of bribery linked with certain citizens being elected and this suggests a form of electoral manipulation. For example, prominent citizens did achieve councillor status during important years: Kleon in 427 BC, the year of the Mytilenaean Debate, and Demosthenes in 346 BC, the year of the Peace of Philokrates.

Hornblower hints that the *boulê* was more of a brake upon democracy than originally proposed.[17] We do have two decrees from the early fourth century BC that do not start with the usual formula 'it seemed good to the *boulê* and the People of the Athenians', but refer only to the *boulê* as having ratified them.[18] However, these can best be explained as slipshod cutting of the inscriptions. Also as evidence, Hornblower cites the passage of the Oxyrhynchos Historian on the sailing of a trireme from Athens in 395 BC under the command of a certain Demainetos to the south-eastern Aegean 'not on the instructions of the *dêmos*' but after Demainetos had unveiled his plans in secret to the *boulê*.[19] However, Hornblower fails to mention that when the plans of Demainetos were discussed in the *ekklêsia* the *dêmos* repudiated the *boulê* for its underhand actions.

The third important machine of Athenian democracy was the popular jury court system, which certainly existed by 422 BC when Aristophanes produced his comedy *Wasps*. The juries were simply subcommittees of the *ekklêsia* and, therefore, there was no appeal to a higher body as the defendant had been judged by the *dêmos*: 'We can't be held to account afterwards, as the magistrates are' Philokleon cries triumphantly to his son.[20] This was the one basic principle upon which the jury system rested. The *dêmos* ruled in the courts as they did in the *ekklêsia*, a citizen volunteering for jury service and, if we can believe Aristophanes, these volunteers were normally old men who had passed the age for military service. There were no restrictions of class or time, so any citizen was entitled to serve as a juror. The pay was two *oboloi* a day, which was increased to three *oboloi* by 425 BC – not quite a living wage, but attractive to old men (who regarded it as a sort of pension) and to the very poor. All they had to do was listen to speeches, record their verdict – guilty or not guilty – and pass a sentence. Each year the Athenians empanelled by lot a permanent pool of 6,000 citizens, from which were selected, again by lot, the juries who sat on 150 to 200 days a year to judge every conceivable public or private lawsuit. The lottery system, which went for the entire magisterial offices bar that of *stratêgos*, involved an allotment machine, the *klêroterion*, which spat out black and white balls randomly at the turn of a handle. A jury panel could number from a minimum of 201 to the full quota of 6,000 citizen jurors.

We also know that from at least 415 BC there was a supreme court that allowed one citizen to indict another because the latter had proposed a motion that was contrary to the law. In 346 BC, for example, the orator Aischines attacked his rival Demosthenes for immorality through his accomplice. The jury courts in Athens, therefore, could easily be used for political purposes.

The ideals

Athenian democracy can be summed up by two distinct words, equality and freedom (*isoetes kai eleutheria*). Aristotle, in his political pamphlet *Democratic Theory of Justice*, equates *isoetes* as equality strictly between fellow citizens who are not judged by their worth. Likewise, Isokrates exclaims that 'in the good old days' equality was unjust as it judged a man according to his worth, that is the 'best men' and the 'worst men'. And so, at the apogee of Athenian democracy magistrates were elected through the lottery system and therefore the Athenians exercised equality through luck. On this basis, all Athenian citizens were treated as equals. *Isoetes* can also include the Athenian idea of *isonomia*, equality of law. We have already mentioned that Herodotos has the Persian noble Otanes speak of *isonomia*.[21] Likewise Perikles, in his very famous speech known as the Funeral Oration, explains how the Athenians are all equal before the law of Athens.[22] The reverse of this democratic ideal is clearly demonstrated by the Thirty Tyrants and their nominal list of 3,000 citizens. Those not on the list could be executed without trial. In this case then, the law was made by the few strong men who ruled and it was for their advantage. But we should not be surprised by this.

On far too many occasions in human history the law has become what it is to suit the advantage of those who make it.

Isoetes also included the notion of *isogoria*, equality of speech (cf. our own democratic ideal of freedom of speech). In Athens there was no law of libel and thus citizens could, and certainly did, say anything that they liked. In his speech *Against Leptines* Demosthenes proudly proclaims that a man could not praise the laws of Athens in Sparta, but he could praise the laws of Sparta in Athens.[23] The Athenian idea of *isogoria* went way beyond our notion of 'freedom of speech' because everybody had the right to be heard. Aischines, for example, says that anybody who wishes to speak can do so, no matter his political clout. Again, Plato, in *Protagoras*, has Sokrates explain that no matter your station in life, be it carpenter, seaman, captain, labourer, potter, rich or poor, you had the right to advise the Athenian state.

Another paradigm of *isoetes* was that of *isomoiria*, equality of opportunity. Thucydides depicts Athenagoras, the leader of the democratic faction in Syracuse and thus pro-Athenian, as saying to his fellow Syracusans that the citizens of the same state should enjoy the same rights.[24] The Athenians, within the shocking limitations of their time (the exclusion of women, foreigners and slaves), interpreted equality more strictly than we do in our own plutocracies that masquerade as democracies.

The Athenians prided themselves on their freedom, *eleutheria*. Both Perikles and Lysias exhort the idea of Athenian freedom in their respective funeral speeches.[25] Athenians certainly interpreted an individual's freedom more liberally than we do today. Even Athens' loudest critics stated that each Athenian lived as he so desired, which was, of course, 'a bad thing' for these double-dyed reactionaries. Aristotle, for one, defined the freedom of the Athenians as the complete antithesis of slavery.

The reality

The ideals of Athenian democracy only applied to the Athenian citizen, who was – after Perikles' Citizens Decree of 451/0 BC – a male eighteen years of age and above provided that both his parents were themselves freeborn Athenians. Thucydides reports that at the beginning of the Peloponnesian War Athens could muster 29,000 citizen and *metoikos* hoplites for its army, while eight years later Aristophanes claims there were at least 20,000 *thêtes*.[26] All together, in the second quarter of the fifth century BC Athens appears to have had a population that stood at approximately 40,000 adult males or even more.[27] In the following century the number of citizens appears to have fallen. Demosthenes, for example, says there were 20,000 citizens circa 350 BC, while a census of 320 BC records a figure of 21,000 of which 9,000 were hoplites. Whatever the figures, the number of citizens was a small body compared with the total population of Athens.

We can assume that there were an equal number of women in Athens as there were citizens, thus increasing our citizen figures by factor two. As for the number of *metoikoi*, we do know that at the height of Athens' prosperity there were around 15,000 in all. As for the number of slaves in Athens, we unfortunately only have two dubious sources to hand. The lesser of two evils, the Byzantine lexicon known to us as the *Souda*, makes the claim that the Athenians owned some 150,000 slaves. We should note here that Thucydides relates how, in 413 BC, 20,000 slaves from the Attic silver mines fled to the Spartan fort at Dekeleia,[28] and he does express the opinion that Chios and Sparta contained the largest servile populations in the Greek world.[29] There are no excuses for slavery, now or then, but in the ancient world, democratic Athens included, it was an acceptable practice to own and work slaves.

In reality, population figures aside, no citizen excepting the aristocracy held the reins of leadership in Athens. Although Perikles makes great play upon the fact that poverty, *penia*, did not bar any citizen from holding office, attending the *ekklêsia*, or serving as a juror, in practice his fellow aristocrats ran Athens. Of course, the question remains how far this 'inequality' went in Athens. The ten *stratêgoi* were obviously the 'best men' but what about those who serve the *ekklêsia*, the *boulê*, or the jury courts?

Aristophanes claims that some of the jurors had pulled an oar in the fleet in their day, which is to say they are *thêtes*, while others had proudly served as hoplites.[30] Also, these old men joke about the loss of 'dinner money' if the archon does not allow the court to sit that particular day. This is hardly a jury packed with members of the Athenian aristocracy. We must always keep at the back of our minds that to its articulate opponents, men such as Plato, Isokrates and Aristotle, democracy was seen in principle as the rule of mere opinion, constitutionally as the rule of the many, and socially as the rule of the poor. Indeed, all these intellectuals gripe that the undeserving poor used the jury courts as a means to soak off the deserving rich. Indeed, to the better off Athenians it seemed that the democratic leaders' internal policy was one of exploitation of the rich for the benefit of the freewheeling masses. Likewise, we should not forget the dreadful power of the *dêmos* if things go wrong or if agitators stir them up.

In the *boulê* a *thête* was technically barred, but only if he admitted to the fact that he was of that property class. The bias, nonetheless, was towards the aristocrat who could afford to attend council meetings fairly frequently, especially so if you consider a councillor only received five *oboloi* per session for doing so. The average daily wage for a skilled worker at the end of the fifth century BC was reckoned at nine *oboloi*. Indeed, the list of 248 councillors serving the *boulê* in 366/5 BC shows that ten to eleven names belong to families that are wealthy enough to equip a trireme for the fleet.[31]

The forensic speeches of Demosthenes suggest an aristocratic bias in the *ekklêsia* as well. For instance, in the emergency meeting of the *ekklêsia* he describes in *On the Crown*, he says 'on this occasion nobody spoke, although all the *stratêgoi* and all the usual speakers were there'.[32] While everyone had a right to be heard, Demosthenes indicates that in practice certain prominent people, individuals of flair, such as the *stratêgoi* and others who made a habit of speaking, would be more likely to have something to say than any Tom, Dick or Harry (or whatever their Athenian counterparts were). Naturally with human relationships, the audience had its favourites, and was neither patient nor polite with incompetent performers. No amount of swotting or sophistry could compensate for a weak or inexpressive voice, a lack of authoritative presence, slowness on the feet in verbal repartee, and a failure to command the issues of the day (state religion, state security, food supply, etc.).

Xenophon and Plato, unswerving critics of democracy, have Sokrates speak of fullers, carpenters, blacksmiths, shoemakers, butchers and potters attending the *ekklêsia*, and not just the high and the mighty. To appreciate this fact, we only have to dip into Aristophanes' *Acharnians*, produced in 425 BC, or encounter the hero of

Knights, produced in 424 BC, who is known as Demos of the Pnyx, 'a farmer and bad-tempered to match, he's got a morbid fascination for beans'.[33] Or, finally, the savage little farmer 'covered in dust and reeking of his breakfast' who attends the *ekklêsia* in Aristophanes' *Ecclesiazusae*.[34] This last example also demonstrates that the urban population did not dominate the *ekklêsia*. In *Acharnians* the hero Dikaiopolis, whose name means 'good city state', was not from the city proper, the *astu*, but is a poor citizen farmer from the deme of Akharnai, which was some fifteen kilometres to the north-west. Also, in *Lysistrata*, we hear of Lysistrata's supporters coming as far as field as the island of Salamis. Therefore, the *ekklêsia*, the pillar of Athenian democracy, represented all classes and all geographical regions of Athens and Attica. Lest we forget the oligarchic junta of 411 BC decided to convene a meeting of the *ekklêsia* not on the Pnyx but outside the fortification walls near the Spartan camp, and then only those privileged enough to be on the list of Five Thousand could attend. Again, the Thirty Tyrants in 404 BC limited the catalogue of citizens to 3,000. Let us leave the last word to 'the laughing philosopher', Demokritos: 'Poverty in a democracy is preferable to so-called prosperity among masters (*dunástai*) to the same extent as freedom is to slavery'.[35]

Appendix 5

A Note on the Athenian Army

At first glance we would consider Athenian military arrangements as easygoing and unprofessional by comparison with those of the Spartans. To a certain extent this is true.

Service as a hoplite at Athens appears to have been based on the possession of a property rating that then led to entry of the individual's name in a list of all those persons eligible for service. Such eligibility started at the age of eighteen, when the Athenian male was registered in his deme as a citizen and was approved by the *boulê*. He was then liable for active service in times of war until the age of sixty (later, fifty-eight). Rich men, the *pentakosiomedimnoi* and *hippeis*, could serve in the Athenian cavalry corps, the *hippeis*, providing their own mount and horse tackle, while those men, the *zeugitai*, who could afford hoplite panoply made up the bulk of Athens' hoplite force. The poorest citizens, the *thêtes*, mostly manned the fleet as oarsmen, but to a lesser degree could serve in the army as lightly armed troops, *psiloi* ('nudes').

There are some scholars who dispute the actual existence of one central register, or *katálogos*, a master list that of those citizens qualified by property and age to serve as hoplites. On the other hand, there is good evidence from a number of contemporary, literary sources for the existence of muster rolls, which probably listed those liable to be called up for hoplite service.

First, Thucydides, on the mobilization of the first armada for Sicily: 'As for the land forces, they were picked from the best men who were liable for calling up.'[1]

Second, Thucydides again, this time on the size of the first armada sailing for Sicily under Nikias: 'There were 5,100 hoplites in all. These included 1,500 Athenian citizens drawn from the muster rolls and 700 *thêtes*, who served as marines on the ships'.[2]

Third, Thucydides once again, this time on the mobilization of the second armada for Sicily: 'The Athenians voted in favour of sending out another military and naval force, drawn mainly from the citizens on the muster rolls and partly from the allies'.[3]

Fourth, Thucydides for the last time, this time on the reinforcements being despatched to Sicily under Demosthenes: these include '1,200 Athenian hoplites from the muster rolls'.[4]

Fifth, Aristophanes: 'When a hoplite's name appears on the muster roll for an expedition, on that muster roll it will stay, with no chopping and changing of any kind for the benefit of the well-connected'.[5]

Sixth, Xenophon on the register drawn up by the Thirty Tyrants: 'Next day they called a meeting in the Odeion of all the hoplites and horsemen whose names were on the list'.[6]

Seventh, according to Lysias and Aristotle, the magistrate who enrols a citizen into the muster roll is known as the *katalogeús*.[7]

Thucydides gives the military strength of Athens on the outbreak of the Peloponnesian War as follows: 13,000 citizen hoplites of military age, 16,000 young men, old men and *metoikoi* 'who bore heavy arms',[8] 1,200 *hippeis* including 200 horse archers, 1,000 foot archers, and, finally, 300 seaworthy triremes.[9] The foot archers, it should be noted, were a mixture of citizen and barbarian archers, and did not include the body of 300 Scythian archers maintained as a police force by the magistrates.[10]

The generals of Athens

The democratic system of Athens was a vigorous institution. The main decision-making body was the assembly, the *ekklêsia*, to which all adult males of Athenian birth on both sides and eighteen years of age or over was eligible to attend. To help the assembly with its deliberations, there was an annually elected council of 500 citizens over the age of thirty, the *boulê*, which would prepare an agenda for the assembly. As we know, the vast majority of the executive officials who carried out the will of the *dêmos*, were not elected but annually selected by the lottery system, and could not hold the same office twice. Once in office the people retained a tight control upon their magistrates, as manifest by the narrow job descriptions and the fact that they were scrutinized before, during and after their term of office.

Yet the Athenians were intelligent enough to realize that the *dêmos* as a whole could not govern the state. They thus designed an elaborate system for electing a chairman for both the *ekklêsia* and the *boulê*. The system was geared so these chairmen, when in office, did not hold too much power, if any at all. There was, however, one exception to this sensible rule. The top officials in Athens, the ten *stratêgoi*, were unique by virtue of the fact that the candidates, invariably well-to-do if not of 'good birth', were elected annually by the *ekklêsia* from citizens aged more than thirty.[11] However, unlike other magistrates, *stratêgoi* could be re-elected as long as they held the confidence of the electorate, and in this way they might exercise great personal influence and ensure an all-important continuity of policy. Perikles, for instance, is recorded as having been elected as one of the ten *stratêgoi* for fifteen consecutive years running (443/2–429/8 BC), and from that position skilfully guided Athenian policy and affairs until his untimely death in 429 BC.[12] While this office was his constitutional base, his practical political effectiveness came from his forceful personality, his persuasiveness, his admitted foresight, his strategic talent, his recognized integrity, and the general respect he commanded. Indeed, so great was his authority that Thucydides famously declared that this meant that 'in what was nominally a democracy, power was really in the hand of the first citizen'.[13]

Typically the position of *stratêgos* combined the most important civil powers with the chief responsibility in military matters. The equation of civil and military leadership was, in part, the result of the fact that military leadership was simply a facet of overall command, in the same way that liability to service was a part of the duties of an individual citizen. As a natural consequence, therefore, the position of *stratêgos* quite quickly became the principal political prize for an ambitious Athenian. Such elections, as Aristotle pertinently points out, were undemocratic as it allowed for birth, wealth, and ability to be taken in to account.[14] Yet without direct elections one feels that any idiot could have cropped up and led Athens, especially in wartime. Even an ultra-democrat would have been loath to entrust Athenian fortunes in battle to whomsoever the lottery happened to throw up. An army of sheep led by a lion would defeat an army of lions led by a sheep, as an Arab proverb sagely urges.[15]

Ultimately, every magistrate, whether directly elected or selected randomly by lot, was kept in check by the *dêmos*. Even the 'blue-bloodied' Perikles, during his penultimate year as a *stratêgos,* was stripped of his command and fined the enormous sum of fifteen talents when the assembly decided to blame him for the plague. Yet this was mild compared with the twenty-year exile of Thucydides or the dreadful fate of the six *stratêgoi* after Arginousai, a battle they had painstakingly won for the fickle democratic assembly.

Hearing that in Athens ten men were elected annually to serve on the board of generals, Philip II of Macedon is reputed to have said that the Athenians were remarkably fortunate people because every year they found ten *stratêgoi* to elect (an incredible thing!); he himself in all his soldiering years had found only one, Parmenion.[16] Of course, Philip was a leader with *all* authority in his hands in place of a tenth of it along with nine other *stratêgoi* equipped with an equal tenth apiece. Yet the incumbent required a whole range of skills as the position took on executive duties that were more than merely military in nature. As such, the responsibilities of the *stratêgoi* were those of domestic and foreign policy subject to the control of the *ekklêsia*. Fortifications and munitions, both military and naval armaments, mustering of citizen soldiers and citizen oarsmen and the imposition of war taxes all fell within the scope of their administration. The *stratêgoi* were more than military commanders, they were in effect what we would recognize as prime ministers. Of course, though they were more than military commanders, *stratêgoi* could be appointed as commanders both in the field and at sea, taking responsibility for strategic and – up to a point – tactical decisions. However, as already alluded to, the conditions of Greek warfare placed practical limits on the nature of command exercised by a *stratêgos*, Athenian and non-Athenian alike.

The hoplites of Athens

During the Persian Wars the tribal units, *taxeis*, which made up the Athenian hoplite force had been commanded by the ten *stratêgoi*. In the course of time, as we have just discussed, the majority of the *stratêgoi* started to become the equivalent of civilian ministers of war, and only one or two would take on the military responsibility of leading out an expedition. Each *taxis*, though mustered from each of the ten tribes,[17] was now commanded by a *taxiarchos* and divided into a number of *lochoi*, each commanded by a *lochagos*. Along with the ten *stratêgoi*, the Athenians also elected the ten *taxiarchoi*, one from each tribe, and these officers commanded their fellow tribesmen and appointed their own *lochagoi*.[18]

Thus, citizens of a given tribe fought side by side in the ranks, officered by men from their own tribal group: in the surviving lists of the fallen, officers and other ranks are listed tribe by tribe, campaign by campaign. The precise strength of the *taxeis* would vary from campaign to campaign. The Athenian *dêmos*, for example, might pass a decree to despatch an army of one thousand hoplites, as for the Mantineia campaign (418 BC),[19] which meant that on this particular occasion each *taxis* was around a hundred strong, or 6,000 hoplites, as for the Nemea campaign (394 BC),[20] making each *taxis* this time 600 strong or so. For the mustering of their commands, the ten *taxiarchoi* would examine the muster rolls on which the citizens liable for hoplite service were entered by archon year.[21] They would work out up to what archon year the age classes had to be called out to meet the number required for the forthcoming campaign. Such a levy was known as an eponymous levy. An expedition involving a call-up for active service of all age classes up to the upper age limit was known as an expedition 'of the whole people'. On reaching fifty years of age, the citizen passed from the active service muster rolls to the reserve. Though occasionally those 'past military age', as Demosthenes prosaically puts it,[22] were called out for active service, in general these old men were called upon only to perform home defence.

The horsemen of Athens

The Athenians only instituted a proper cavalry corps after the Persian Wars, its members being recruited from those wealthy enough to maintain a horse. And so, by the mid-fifth century BC there was a body of some 300 horsemen, albeit with little military function,[23] having risen to 'a thousand brave men' by the start of the Peloponnesian War.[24]

Owning a horse was very costly, Aristotle remarks that 'horse breeding requires the ownership of large resources'.[25] Xenophon also stresses the need for 'ample means', and adds that such men should also have an interest in the affairs of the state.[26] The members of the cavalry corps, therefore, were drawn mainly from the second of the four property classes, the *hippeis*, comprising citizens whose land yielded between 300 and 500 *medimnoi* of grain or the equivalent in other produce.[27] According to Xenophon preparation for service in the cavalry corps began while a youth was still under the control of his legal guardian, in other words before the age of eighteen.[28]

Each of the ten tribes at Athens furnished a tribe, *phylê*, of horsemen, each with a nominal strength of a hundred and headed by a *phylarchos* ('tribal leader').[29] Within the *phylê*, every ten-man group or file was led by a *dekadarchos* ('leader of ten'), and Xenophon tells us that these formed the front rank, implying a depth of ten ranks, which is deeper than Greek horsemen normally fought.[30] He then adds that an experience trooper should be posted at the rear of each file, as 'iron has most power to cut through iron when its edge is keen and its back is reliable'.[31] The ten *phylai* of horse were under the overall command of two *hipparchoi*, each of who would command in battle a wing made up of five *phylai*,[32] and this is supported by Xenophon in his descriptions of the equestrian displays held annually in Athens.[33] The *hipparchoi* had powers that were the same as those of the *stratêgoi*, that is to say, they had disciplinary power over their men.[34] The *hipparchoi* would also maintain the cavalry muster rolls.[35] Like the *stratêgoi*, all but one of these equestrian officers would be annually elected by the *ekklêsia*, the two *hipparchoi* from the whole citizen body and the *phylarchoi* one from each tribe.[36] The *dekadarchoi*, on the other hand, were personally selected by the *phylarchoi* 'from sturdy men, who are bent of winning fame by some brilliant deed'.[37]

As service in the military was a normal duty of citizenship, the horsemen, like the hoplites, were not paid a regular wage, but unlike the hoplites they were given an allowance of one *drachma* per day for fodder in times of war.[38] On entering service with the cavalry corps the young aristocrat would also be paid an establishment grant, the *katastasis*, to cover the cost of his mount, which, along with his equipment, he provided himself. The grant was a loan, not a gift, the money being repaid to the state on leaving the corps, unless the mount had been killed or crippled during active service.[39]

To avoid the fraudulent claiming of allowances an inspection, the *dokimasia*, was performed annually by the *boulê*, following the election of the officers, which enable Xenophon to make the generalization, 'the *polis* ... has charged the *boulê* with the duty of taking a share in the management of the cavalry'.[40] And so each rider, whether a new recruit or veteran trooper, and his horse would be scrutinized for fitness for service, brands and any markings noted.[41] Mounts that failed to pass the inspection were branded on the jaw with the sign of a wheel in order to prevent them being slipped through on another occasion.[42] If passed, the riders' names would be entered on the cavalry muster rolls, which would be passed on to the ten *taxiarchoi*, the commanders of the ten tribal *taxeis*. The *taxiarchoi* would delete the names of those entered on the cavalry muster rolls from the tribal muster rolls to ensure that no one became liable for both hoplite and cavalry service.

A class apart

By virtue of their wealth and prominence in Athenian life, the *hippeis* in general, and the serving horsemen in particular, formed a distinct and readily identifiable group within Athenian society. This high public profile arose from private horse usage, collective and individual training, public equestrian displays, religious festivals and processions. The *phylarchos* in Aristophanes' *Lysistrata*, for example, remains mounted even while eating the porridge he had just purchased from an old woman's stall in the Agora.[43] Conversely, in a speech Lysias wrote for a client trying to get a disability pension restored, the speaker claims that he rides a horse around Athens 'through necessity and not through arrogance'.[44] The linking of the *hippeis* with arrogance was partly determined by their image as wealthy and aristocratic, but it was also tied in with the perception of them as an essentially youthful organisation.

Thus, the horsemen of Athens formed a largely homogeneous group whose members shared a similar outlook and a common social milieu. They were typically portrayed as wealthy, aristocratic, long-haired, and youthful section of society. This view, for instance, occurs frequently in both comedy and prose. The horsemen of Aristophanes' comedy *Knights* are identified as long-haired, aristocratic young men,[45] which are perfectly exemplified by Mantitheos of Thorikos, a litigant in the Athenian law courts.[46] Sculpture and painting also present the view that the Athenian horsemen were youthful. Only two of the horsemen on the Parthenon frieze are portrayed as bearded, the others are youths ready for adventure.[47] This pattern is repeated on grave stelae and other sculpture where bearded, and hence older horsemen, are much less common than beardless youths. This is hardly surprising, for young athletic men have the skill, strength and stamina to ride horses without saddles and stirrups in sometimes difficult equestrian manoeuvres on uneven and hazardous terrain. Besides, in the recruiting of horsemen Xenophon clearly emphasizes that physical endurance is as important as possession of wealth, and he should surely know.[48]

Appendix 6

A Note on Iphikrates and his Peltasts

Xenophon makes an interesting distinction of names when he describes javelineers who do not have shields as *psiloi*, lightly armed, whereas those with shields are *peltastai*, peltasts.[1] Of all the skirmishers used in Greek armies the peltast was the most effective. He was a javelineer who derived his name from his shield, the *pelte*, and it was a term originally used of Thracians.[2] The Thracian peltast is described by Herodotos and Xenophon as wearing the traditional costume of his cold country – a tunic underneath a long, brightly coloured, geometric patterned heavy cloak, the *zeira*, high fawn-skin boots and fox-skin cap with ear flaps.[3] He wore no armour and relied on his speed and mobility to get him out of trouble. His weapons were a bunch of javelins and a short sword or dagger. Fighting in a loose order formation, his tactic was to run in, throw the javelins and then run away before the enemy could come to grips with him.[4] Unlike the hoplite, he thus emphasises mobility over shock-power, shoot and scoot instead of stand and fight.

The *pelte* was smaller and lighter than that carried by a hoplite, lacking a rim or any kind of bronze facing. Either of simple wickerwork or of wood and covered with the skin of a sheep or goat it was of crescent shape, being held so that the tips were uppermost thus allowing the peltast unobstructed vision while casting his javelin.[5] The *pelte* could be carried with a central handgrip and could also be equipped with a carrying strap as Thracians invariably slung their shields on their backs when running away. Often the front of the *pelte* would be painted with some kind of good-luck symbol, the most popular being a stylised face. Although contemporary vase paintings suggest that the tyrant of Athens Peisistratos employed them (*c*. 540 BC) it is Thucydides whom first remarks on the presence of Thracian peltasts, and he does so in connection with the Peloponnesian War (431–404 BC).[6] More effective as skirmish troops than the standard Greek javelineer, who lacked a shield (viz. *psiloi*), though they could not hope to defeat hoplites in pitched battle, if they managed to keep their distance they could wear a hoplite phalanx down by prolonged missile fire, as at Sphakteria (425 BC) and Amphipolis (422 BC).[7]

In the fourth century BC, however, most peltasts were of Greek origin, particularly those recruited from the Thracian seaboard where there were a number of Greek *poleis*. This came about mainly because of the tactical innovations of the Athenian commander Iphikrates who had family connections in Thrace, and saw the potential of peltasts.[8] Their greatest exploit was the annihilation of a *mora* of Spartan hoplites outside Corinth at Lechaion (390 BC), when a mercenary unit of peltasts was commanded by the formidable Iphikrates.[9] He circumvented a frontal assault, and used mobility to pester and retreat, in this way harrying the enemy until they were confused and ripe for a great defeat. Iphikrates, who had a reputation as a strict and at times fierce disciplinarian, was a particular enthusiast for properly trained lightly armed troops and therefore had taken care to combine in his peltasts a high level of individual training and discipline – vital ingredients, if lightly armed troops are to be of use on the battlefield – with a strong dose of that emphemeral quality, *esprit de corps*. Indeed, if we were to find three words to sum them up, then they would be agile, mobile, hostile. Certainly, during the Corinthian War Athens' mercenary peltasts were feared 'as little children fear the bogeyman' by all except the Spartans, who 'looked down on the peltasts'.[10] If that was so, then Spartan confidence must have been severely shaken after Lechaion. The days had passed when a single arm could dominate the Greek battlefield.

Iphikrates (b. *c.* 413 BC) first won distinction in boarding an enemy ship during the engagement off Knidos (394 BC).[11] As we have just discussed, it was his destruction of a Spartan *mora* outside Corinth that earned for him everlasting fame (390 BC). Redeployed, with his peltast command, to the Hellespont by the Athenian *dêmos*, he eliminated the new Spartan harmosts of Abydos, Anaxibios, who had been sent out with enough cash for a thousand mercenaries to stir up trouble for Athens in this sensitive region (388 BC). Following the King's Peace (387/6 BC) he married the daughter of the Thracian chieftain Kotys,[12] spending the next decade in Thrace before joining an unsuccessful Persian invasion of Egypt (374 BC).[13]

Having quarrelled with the satrap Pharnabazos, who had been appointed commander of the Egyptian expeditionary force, Iphikrates returned to Athens. Elected as one of the ten *stratêgoi* for the year, he sailed to check Spartan interference on Corcyra, which prompted Sparta to negotiate for peace (371 BC). Again named *stratêgos*, he aided Sparta against Epameinondas of Thebes (369 BC). Next in the north, he secured the Macedonian throne for his adoptive brothers – including the future Philip II – but failed to recapture Amphipolis for Athens (368 BC). Recalled home in disgrace, he sided with Athens' enemies and thus aided his father-in-law, Kotys, in a war for the absolute possession of the Thracian Chersonese (365 BC). Although eventually pardoned, it was to be several years before he reappeared in Athenian service. The Embata débâcle (356 BC), when he and two of his colleagues refused to give battle during a violent storm, ruined his career, though a robust defence secured his acquittal. Afterwards, he remained in Athens or, as seems more likely, retired to his *pied à terre* in Thrace until his death in about 353 BC. In serving Athens or a foreign power, this self-made cobbler's son invariably provided for his own interests. Nevertheless, he was a commander who achieved victory and did so by using his brains and not bravery alone: his ingenuity was the subject of many later anecdotes (e.g. Polyainos, Frontinus).

Appendix 7

A Note on the Ten Thousand

It is at Cunaxa that we witness the true professionalism of the Ten Thousand, when they raise a loud war cry to Enyalios, and as they do so they dash towards the Persian battleline, some of the mercenaries even clashing their spears against their shields. Small wonder then that the Persians flinched and, 'before an arrow reached them [viz. the hoplites], the barbarians broke and fled'.[1] Diodoros' retelling of the same event provides us with one critical and complimentary detail, namely Klearchos orders the hoplites to advance slowly, *à la Spartiate*, initially so as to remain nice and fresh for the fight, but once at close range (viz. 200 to 150 metres) they are to pick up the pace and run into contact as 'the missiles shot by bows and other means' would then fly harmlessly overhead.[2] Still, to the running men the killing zone must have seemed endless. In their second encounter of the day, the hoplites, as Xenophon personally recalls, 'once again struck up the *paean* and advanced to the attack much more eagerly than before; and the barbarians once again failed to await the attack, but took to flight when at a greater distance from the Greeks than they were the first time'.[3]

Though technically the victor on the field of Cunaxa, Artaxerxes was still 'terrified by the approach of the [Greek] army'.[4] So much so at this point in time that instead of demanding their arms as he had done previously, he was now seeking a truce with the Ten Thousand.[5] In essence, the mere sight and sound of the Ten Thousand at around one stade were enough to strike fear into any sensible man's heart. This was their *tour de force*, and the ritualistic terror tactic of striking up the *paean*, raising a war cry to Enyalios, clashing spears against shields and dashing into contact – usually as the foe's missile started to fly – would be repeated again and again whenever the Ten Thousand came up against 'barbarians'.[6] In fact, this martial superiority is personally emphasized by Xenophon in an address to the officers of Proxenos' command. Here he tells them that the Greeks, in comparison to the 'barbarians', 'have bodies more capable than theirs of bearing cold and heat and toil'.[7] His message mirrors that of our own colonial attitudes; we are inherently superior to the foreigner intellectually, morally, and physically. Still, this fighting spirit of the Ten Thousand was to live on, for at Koroneia some seven years later, the charge of the Thebans was quickly answered by the countercharge of the Cyreians, as the canny survivors became known, who were the first to dash forward 'from the phalanx of Agesilaos'.[8]

But we should return once again to Cunaxa, where the Ten Thousand struck terror into the Persians both by the brilliant splendour of their panoply and by 'the skill they displayed', or so says Diodoros.[9] In the very next breath, Diodoros briefly explains how the Ten Thousand had acquired its warlike skill: the hoplites had been battle hardened through the Peloponnesian War and were therefore 'far superior in experience'.[10] Although I have argued elsewhere that over half of the Ten Thousand were from Arcadia and Achaia,[11] and as a consequence had been employed by the Persian empire for a number of years already, the essential fact remains that these professional soldiers had plenty of past experience. Indeed, a year or so later the 5,300 surviving Cyreians decided to accept a Thracian contract negotiated by Xenophon simply because 'they had become accustomed to the life of a soldier'.[12] Xenophon himself says that the Cyreians were 'now exceedingly efficient through constant service'.[13] If we return to the encounter between the Ten Thousand and the Persian force commanded by Spithridates and Rhathines discussed awhile earlier, we can see for ourselves this efficiency firsthand. The Greek mercenaries, having already completed two successful charges against the enemy, now prepared themselves for a third. 'Although they were tired', explains Xenophon, 'they nevertheless thought that they must make as stout an attack as they could upon these troops also, so that they should not be able to regain courage and get rested'.[14] Most Greek militias were incapable of a second, let alone a third, effort even after winning in their part of the field. Experience and discipline will beat battle fatigue and disarray at any time.

Warriors for a working day

At first glance the Ten Thousand appear to have been organized rather loosely into national contingents under the various *stratêgoi* who had initially raised them. We can see this rather ad hoc unit organization at the military review at Tyriaeion, for example, with 'each *stratêgos* marshalling his own men',[15] or again much later, when each *stratêgos* marshalled his men 'nation by nation'.[16] Likewise, when the mercenary army split into three contingents, we witness the ethnic solidarity of the Arcadians and the Achaians.[17] There is also the vague use by Xenophon of technical terms such as *taxis*, which can either denote a unit of horsemen, or peltasts, or hoplites, or can even be used to describe the contingent commanded by a *stratêgos*.[18] The one exception seems to be the review in Byzantium when the Ten Thousand formed up eight deep with the men acting as their own marshals.[19] This does suggest, at the very least, that each individual hoplite knew his place within the phalanx. In addition, there was a point when the Ten Thousand saw the need for a single commander, *autokrátora*, to replace the leadership by committee; the general consensus was that one head could 'handle the army better'.[20]

Irrespective of all this apparent confusion, however, there is good evidence to suggest that the army of the Ten Thousand were well organized and even articulated down into small manageable tactical units. As a consequence of this, as we shall discuss, we can argue coherently that each unit developed its own cohesive spirit. So the evidence.

First, the *lochos* under its *lochagos* remains the prime tactical unit for the Ten Thousand throughout their *anabasis*, and is the vehicle by which the majority of tactical manoeuvres were accomplished.[21]

Second, the size of the *lochos* remains, with one exception, fairly consistent throughout the *anabasis*, viz. a unit of around a hundred hoplites. For example, at one point we are told by Xenophon that the army now consisted of eighty *lochoi* of hoplites, with 'each *lochos* numbering close upon one hundred'.[22] The one notable exception to all this appears to be when Xenophon gives the combined strength of two *lochoi* from Meno's contingent as one hundred hoplites,[23] but they are detached and this is before Cunaxa not after.

Third, there are hints from Xenophon that the Ten Thousand had adopted at some point a quasi-Spartan system of unit organization with the articulation of the *lochoi* down into smaller tactical units.

An example: at one point of their *anabasis* there was a collective decision by the *stratêgoi* to reorganize their formation of march, for the hollow square first suggested by Xenophon himself was proving to be too cumbersome.[24] We are told, as a result of this tactical reorganization, that the rearguard was now formed of six *lochoi* each of a hundred men and commanded by a *lochagos*, 'adding also *pentekosteres* and *enômotarchos*'.[25] The *lochagos* also had under him a second-in-command, a *hupolochagos*,[26] and, in the rearguard at least, the *lochagoi* would rotate the position of 'officer of the day in command of the *lochagoi* of the rearguard'.[27] The addition of these junior officers to the command structure of its organization strongly suggests that each *lochos* now consisted of two *pentekostyes*, each of fifty men, with each of these consisting of two *enômotia*, each of twenty-five men.

Later on, Xenophon mentions *enômotiai* again, but this time we can actually see them in operation upon the battleground. The Ten Thousand have reached the south bank of the Kentrites, the river that separates Armenia and the land of the Kardouchians, only to find their way forward blocked by the forces of Orontas, the satrap of Armenia, and their rear under threat from the Kardouchians, a fierce and perpetually troublesome race of highlanders, notoriously hostile to foreigners and nigh impossible to govern. A mountainous region, with its harsh climate, poor soil and pastoral economy, has traditionally been the bane of many empires. Anyway, caught between the hammer and the anvil, the mercenary army is quickly divided into two divisions: Cheirisophos to take the lead with his division and attempt a crossing of the river while Xenophon and his division are to remain behind and act as the rearguard. Xenophon now orders his *lochagoi* to deploy their *lochoi* by *enômotiai*, 'moving each *enômotia* by the left into line of battle; then the *lochagoi* and the *enômotarchoi* were to face towards the Kardouchians and station file closers on the side next to the river'.[28]

It looks all very efficient and highly Spartan in its tactical concept. Indeed, once the rearguard is deployed, the Kardouchians advance to the attack, and Xenophon now orders his men to hold their charge until the 'sling stones reached them and shields rang'. When the highlanders turn to flee (the Kardouchians not being best equipped for hand-to-hand combat), Xenophon continues in the same paragraph, the trumpeter will sound the charge in order to deceive the enemy (now bent on his escape), at which time the men 'were to face about to the right, the file closers were to take the lead, and all of them were to run and cross [the river] as fast as they could with every man keeping his proper place in the line'.[29] Like Lakonian clockwork, events went according to Xenophon's plan and the rearguard safely crossed the river to rejoin the rest of the army.[30] The roots of the *enômotiai* were nourished on the long march home, and the twenty-five men of an *enômotia* who had worked and struggled together and had developed confidence in each other were not to be thrown by entry into a new tactical situation or a new hostile environment, so long as they kept their unity.

Unfortunately, there is no evidence to suggest that the other *lochoi* of the mercenary army were organized in the same quasi-Spartan manner as the six that formed its rearguard under Xenophon. Guesses remain guesses, but the fact remains that all these *lochoi*, when compared with those *lochoi* that usually made up a citizen army, such as we have witnessed with that of Athens, were small tactical units in their own right and under their own officers. In a couple of passing comments, moreover, Xenophon does indicate that the men of a *lochos* did, in fact, mess and sleep together in small groups.

First, Klearetos, a *lochagos* from an unspecified contingent, plans a night raid upon a local native stronghold with the intention of securing booty and then deserting the army. He will do this with 'his messmates'.[31]

Second, Xenophon orders a muleteer to unload his 'messmates' baggage' so that the mule can be used to transport a sick man.[32] Admittedly not much to go on, but it does appear that the unit morale of the *lochoi* that made up the Ten Thousand was strengthened through those ties of close camaraderie that we witness in the contemporary Spartan army.

Likewise, the Ten Thousand employed military icons to promote unit identity and so instil a feeling of elitism amongst unit members. As we well know, the army of Agesilaos at Koroneia also included the Cyreians and, therefore, these also formed part of that celebrated 'solid mass of bronze and crimson'.[33] In fact, Xenophon confirms that the Ten Thousand had a common uniform very much like that of the Spartans. In his description of the military review at Tyriaeion he says that 'the Greeks all had helmets of bronze, crimson tunics, and greaves, and carried their shields uncovered'.[34] In addition, there is some evidence to suggest that these hoplite mercenaries also wore a cloak, though whether or not it was the crimson military cloak in the style of the Spartans we are not told by Xenophon and have no way of knowing otherwise.[35] Nevertheless, along with their obvious display of discipline, their brilliant appearance, the comportment of these professionals from beyond the sea was enough to inflict sheer terror upon both Cyrus' native levy and innocent bystanders alike.[36] The same effect, according to Diodoros, was to be repeated for real at the battle of Cunaxa. For, as the Ten Thousand struck up the *paean* and ran into contact, the Persians facing them were immediately rattled 'by the splendour of their arms and by the skill they displayed'.[37]

Soldierly pride also played an important part in fostering and promoting a mercenary's fighting spirit. Haranguing the soldiers prior to one engagement, Xenophon asks the Ten Thousand to remember how many battles they had won 'by coming to close quarters'.[38] Here Xenophon was appealing to the pride of each individual soldier by reminding him of his soldierly superiority over that of his enemies. In the same address, Xenophon also offers each and every one of them the chance of achieving immortal glory 'though some manly and noble thing, which one may say or do today' on the coming field of battle.[39] Individual pride is also translated into collective pride – what the British Army aptly calls regimental pride – and the Ten Thousand also exhibited this vital tribal spirit, as the following episode aptly demonstrates. At one point in their *anabasis*, some of the mercenaries decide to join up with a local Mossynoecian raiding party, 'not under orders from their *stratêgoi*, but seeking plunder'.[40] Unfortunately, these free enterprising mercenaries, along with their newly found Mossynoecian associates, were put to full flight during an attempt to storm a nearby stockade, and as a consequence the rest of the Ten Thousand are exceedingly angry, not because the enemy had been heartened by their success, but because their comrades had taken to their heels, 'a thing which they had never done before in the course of the expedition'.[41] In other words, the honour of the 'regiment' had been tarnished. In an obvious attempt to play down this setback and so restore 'regimental pride', Xenophon calls a soldiers' assembly and before it analyzes the defeat: 'Those among them who took little thought of the battle formation we use and got the idea that they could accomplish the same results in company with the barbarians as they could with us, have paid the penalty, – another time they will be less likely to leave our ordered lines'.[42] Xenophon finishes his analysis by simply referring to these greedy fools as nothing but a 'disorderly mass'.[43]

In the *Anabasis*, Xenophon also implies that there existed within the mercenary army a friendly rivalry between individual *lochagoi*. Talking of four of his own *lochagoi* during a particularly difficult assault upon a Taochian stronghold, Xenophon discloses that 'all these four were rivals in valour and continually striving with one another'.[44] Such competitive and professional spirit undoubtedly permeated through-out their respective *lochoi* and the wise *stratêgos* was able to exploit the resultant unit rivalry and so put it to good effect upon the battlefield. On laying his plans for an arduous assault upon a stockade belonging to the Drilae tribe, for example, Xenophon ordered each of the *lochagoi* to deploy his *lochos* 'in the way he thought it would fight most effectively; for near one another were the *lochagoi* who had all the time been vying with one another in valour'.[45] Carrying out this order, each *lochagos* and his *hupolochagos* drew up their *lochos* in such a manner that they themselves and 'those among the men who claimed to be not inferior to them in bravery were all grouped together in the line and, moreover, watching one another'.[46]

We began by discussing how the high morale and martial skill of the Ten Thousand enabled it successfully to dominate the battlefield, and how this fighting spirit had its roots in the bonds of comradeship that existed between soldiers who faced the constant dangers and hardships of professional soldiering. Moreover, we have seen how this spirit of camaraderie derived from the concept of small group cohesion, which certainly existed within the ranks of the Ten Thousand, just as it did in that other professional army of our period of study, the Spartan army, from which the Ten Thousand drew some of its inspirations. Sparta was no longer unique in its professionalism.

Appendix 8

Herodotos and the Topography of Plataia

Herodotos: master storyteller, tireless traveller, the first 'historian', and a genius whose true worth is frequently underrated and occasionally denied. Take for instance, his survey of the customs of the Persians, which nicely reminds us that Herodotos was not only a historian.[1] As a geographer, Herodotos has his merits, too. He was the first to understand the relative size and situation of Europe, Africa and Asia. He was aware of the fact that the Caspian Sea was surrounded on all sides by land, and knew reports about the circumnavigation of Africa (this statement was generally questioned until the Portuguese navigator Bartholomew Diaz at last rounded the Cape of Good Hope in 1486). Herodotos knew that the world was tens of thousands of years old: again, many people considered this an exaggeration.

Despite the fact that his care as a topographer is largely lost to us, the physical environment should always be taken into account, and can sometimes play a vital part in the argument. The main problem for us is not the fact that we often have to make allowances for changes in the landscape, but in trying to identify the locations Herodotos mentions, prone as he was to using local toponyms. However, this ought not surprise us, since he was simply reporting what the local guides had told him, the classic Herodotean example surely being the 'Black Buttocks' rock above Thermopylai.[2] On many occasion we see how clearly Herodotos defined landmarks on the battle-field, but intriguingly his indications become riddles in their turn. The name 'Black Buttocks' no longer means anything – a great pity. Anyway, let us briefly look at Herodotos' topographical knowledge with regards to the battle of Plataia.

The Gargaphia
- 9.25.3: situated in the territory of the Plataians
- 9.52: just outside Plataia is a temple dedicated to Hera, twenty stades from the spring
- 9.49.2: Persian horsemen succeed in choking up the spring, and only the Lakedaimonians are deployed near the spring

The Gargaphia is clearly the one now called Alepotrypi either ('foxhole', presently an eight-centimetre pipe), some 500 metres south-west of Agios Ioannis, or, more likely, the one called Rhetsi, about a kilometre south-east of the chapel and below Hill 360. In this location there are two well heads, which give ready access to a plentiful supply of water, albeit somewhat stale, and are still used by local shepherds. Below the modern concrete at the water line, what appears to be four classical blocks (tooled-faced, ashlar-shape) make up the fabric of one of the well heads, while similar blocks are scattered round about. This well obviously serves the thirsty occupants of a nearby *mandra* or sheep pen. It is a fair hike from the spring up to the Asopos ridge.

Asopos river

- 9.31.1: the Greeks take up a position (i.e. the second) along the Asopos
- 9.40: the Persians harass the Greeks along the Asopos
- 9.49.3: all the Greek contingents are deployed near to the Asopos
- 9.59.1: the Persians cross the Asopos

The river can never have been very much of an obstacle during the summer months, and the ground beyond it to the north would have been, if anything, a lot more suitable for an army strong in horse and missile armed troops. Today the river is but a dried out bed marked by a distinctive line of trees and shrubs running mainly east–west. Half-a-kilometre or so to the south of what was once the Asopos runs a canalized watercourse, which was constructed in the nineteen-eighties to bring much-needed potable water to the population of Athens from the far distant mountains of Aeolia.

Greek second position

- 9.25.3: near the Gargaphian spring and the sanctuary of Androkates; it consists of slight elevations and level ground
- 9.28.2: Lakedaimonians (10,000 hoplites) and Tegeans (1,500 hoplites) on the right wing, the Athenians (8,000 hoplites) and Plataians (600 hoplites) on the left wing; the battleline would have been some 4.5 kilometres in length if the hoplites had deployed in their respective phalanxes eight shields deep (viz. paper strength of 38,700, at eight hoplites to the metre)
- 9.52: a good half of the Greek army (viz. the centre contingents) escapes from the Persian cavalry (cf. 9.69.2)
- 9.56.1: during the retreat the Lakedaimonians (and Tegeans) keep to the higher ground, while the Athenians (and Plataians) opt for the lower route across level ground but out of sight

Thucydides also mentions the sanctuary of the hero Androkates in his splendid account of the breakout of part of the Plataian garrison during the early stages of the Peloponnesian War. He appears to locate it on the right of the road from Plataia to Thebes, and not more than 1,400 metres from the former.[3] Pritchett locates the said sanctuary some 200 metres to the south-west of a ruined Byzantine chapel located less than a hundred metres south-west of the Alepotrypi spring.[4]

As Herodotos implies, both the Spartans on the Greek right and the Athenians on the left occupied relatively high ground, and it is likely that the former was on what modern commentators have termed the Asopos ridge, and the latter on what is now called Pyrgos hill. The centre contingents would then have occupied the low ground between these two features, that is, astride the ancient road from Plataia to Thebes.

The Island

- 9.51.1–2: in front of Plataia, some ten stades from the Asopos and Gargaphian spring; a river, the Oëroë, splits into two streams near its source on Kithairon; on the plain below these two streams are some three stades apart; the location has an abundant supply of water

Herodotos implies that 'the Island' was at most only some 600 metres wide. In other words, there would not have been enough room for the whole Greek army *if* it tried to form a phalanx. However, the Greeks probably did not actually envisage deploying for battle on 'the Island' – Herodotos does imply that it was to be more in the nature of a temporary refuge from the continuous harassment being meted out by the Persian horsemen.

Immediately to the north of the modern road that connects the village of Plataia with the town of Erythrai, and roughly two kilometres from the latter, there is a large hillock upon which sits the chapel of Agios Analypsis. Rising out of the plain, this natural feature is covered in relatively lush vegetation, suggesting the proximity of good water supplies. As it looks today, this natural feature would present a formidable obstacle to those operating on horses, particularly on its western flank. The course of the 'Moloëis' is still visible, being as it is clearly delineated by a line of well-established trees. However, the position itself looks somewhat cramped when we consider the numbers that made up the Greek army. There may have been more water about at the time of the battle of course, and there may well have been changes in the *flora* too. So we need to be careful in our assumptions and speculations. As a final point, however, I will say that is important to realize on all ancient battlefields, even at 'Armageddons' such as Gaugamela and Cannae, the extent of the actual killing ground to the modern eye seems extraordinarily small.

Appendix 9

A Note on the *Diekplous* and the *Periplous*

Lack of space in the hull for food and water, low freeboard, low cruising speed under oars, and limited sailing qualities, lowered the trireme's range of operations. Thus, in addition to the necessity for regular beaching to allow the crews to eat and sleep, naval engagements customarily took place near the coast, where ships could be handled in relatively calm water and there was some hope for the shipwrecked. Sails were used for fleets in transit, but when approaching the battle area the masts would be lowered and the ships rowed. The opposing fleets normally deployed in line abreast two deep.

There were two main methods of fighting, which placed contradictory demands on trireme design. The first was ramming. This called for the smallest possible ship built around the largest number of rowers. The Athenian navy with its small number of marines followed this philosophy. The other was boarding. This called for larger, heavier ships able to carry the maximum number of boarders. The Chians, for example, with their forty marines per trireme,[1] followed this philosophy. The latter view eventually prevailed, since, to ram, a vessel had to make contact, which was just what the boarders wanted. Hence the later development of large ships with full decks (the triremes of our period were only partially decked), namely the four, five and six-banked ships of the Hellenistic period, which were primarily designed as heavily armoured floating platforms to carry either catapults or marines.

In his scornful description of the sea battle of Sybota (433 BC), Thucydides says the style of fighting had been 'of the old clumsy sort'.[2] Here the triremes were carrying many hoplites and archers and the engagement 'had almost the appearance of a battle by land',[3] with both sides (apart from the small Athenian contingent) fighting 'with fury and brute strength rather than with skill'.[4] Thucydides' so-called old fashioned style of fighting was obviously a reliance on sea soldiers, of various sorts, topside repelling boarders or boarding another vessel themselves.

Whether boarding or ramming, ships had to collide, and this also limited their tactical capabilities. With the ram the trireme itself could be used as an offensive weapon, but the problem was to avoid damaging one's own ship or becoming so entangled with the enemy vessel that boarding became inevitable. Yet speed and manoeuvrability could make it possible to attack vulnerable sides and sterns. For the Athenians ramming head on had come to be considered a sign of lack of skill in a helmsman,[5] and the manoeuvre-and-ram school, in which the Athenian navy reigned supreme, relied on two tactical options, the *diekplous* and the *periplous*.

The *diekplous* was a manoeuvre involving single ships in line abeam, the standard battle formation, in which each helmsman would steer for a gap in the enemy line. He would then turn suddenly to either the port or the starboard to ram an enemy ship in the side or row clean through the line, swing round and smash into the stern of an enemy ship. The top-deck would be lined with marines and archers at the ready, but their main role was mainly defensive. The main weapon was the attacking ship's ram. Neither Herodotos, Thucydides nor Xenophon makes the details of this manoeuvre very clear, but Polybios, in his account of the sea battle of Drepana (249 BC), describes it as such: 'To sail through the enemy's line and to appear from behind, while they were already fighting others [in front], which is a most effective naval manoeuvre'.[6] Although he is writing in the second century BC about a naval engagement that was fought in the third century BC, the action was still contested by ships propelled by oars and armed with rams. Moreover, the Carthaginian ships executing this 'most effective naval manoeuvre' were well constructed and had experienced oarsmen.

The *periplous* was either a variation involving outflanking the enemy line when there was plenty of sea room, or the final stage of the *diekplous*, when the manoeuvring vessel, having cut through the line, swung round to attack from the stern. Once the enemy formation had broken up, the *periplous* would have become the most important tactical option available to the helmsman.[7] And so the *periplous* was a tactical manoeuvre that a single trireme, when skilfully handled, performed to make a ramming attack that did not involve prow-to-prow contact. Even so, it required room for its execution, and timing was of the essence. With a modest speed of nine knots each trireme, assailant and victim, would travel its own length in about six-and-a-half seconds. If the attacker arrived too soon, he could himself be struck and holed by the target vessel, too late and the speed of impact fell off rapidly and he could deliver no more than a mild bump.

Since both manoeuvres required plenty of sea room, there were two counter moves to the *diekplous* and *periplous*. One option was to occupy a position that was physically crowded; this was the case with regards to the four sea battles in the Great Harbour of Syracuse (413 BC).[8] Or, if in open water, one could form the *kuklos*, a defensive circle with rams pointing outward.[9] The alternative, especially for a large fleet, was to form up in double line abeam, as the Athenians did at Arginousai (406 BC).[10] The ships in the second line would try and pick off any enemy vessel that broke through before it could turn and ram a friendly vessel in the first line.

Glossary of Greek Terms

I give here a brief description of some basic Greek words and technical terms that are used in the book. Where applicable, plural forms appear in parentheses.

acropolis – 'high city', the original citadel of a *polis* (q.v.), typically it was the site of temples and shrines

Aeolians – those Greeks, found mainly in Boiotia (Boiotian Aeolic, e.g. Pindar), Thessaly, Lesbos (Lesbian Aeolic, e.g. Sappho) and a small part of the northern Anatolian coast, who spoke the Aeolian dialect and whose lives shared certain distinctive cultural and religious features

agôgê – 'raising', the education system to which the young males of Sparta were subjected

agora – 'marketplace', the centre for commercial, social and political activity in a *polis* (q.v.)

antilabê – handgrip of *aspis* (q.v.)

aspis – 'Argive shield', a soup-bowl shaped shield, some 80 to 100 centimetres in diameter, held via an *antilabê* (q.v.) and a *porpax* (q.v.)

astu (-eôs) – 'city', the urban centre of a *polis* (q.v.)

aulos (-oi) – wind instrument akin to a pipe

boulê – council of Five Hundred that prepared matters for consideration by the *ekklêsia* (q.v.)

capithê – dry measure equal to two Attic *choinikes* (q.v.)

Corinthian helmet – full-faced helmet formed out of a single sheet of bronze and lined with leather, the 'standard-issue' of its day

chous (-es) – liquid measure

choinix – dry measure equivalent of a man's daily grain ration (Attic *choinix* = 1.087 litres)

chôra – territory, often as opposed to the *polis* that exploited it

cubit – unit of measurement equal to the length from the elbow to the tip of the middle finger (Attic cubit = 0.45 metres, Doric cubit = 0.49 metres)

deme – the rural districts and urban wards into which Athens/Attica was divided

dêmos – 'people', the citizen body of Athens

Dorians – those Greeks, found mainly in Peloponnese (except Arcadia), Libya, Crete, Thera, Rhodes and in the Dorian colonies of Sicily and Italy, who spoke the Doric dialect and whose lives shared certain distinctive cultural and religious features

dóru – 'Dorian spear', a thrusting spear, 2 to 2.5 metres in length, armed with a spearhead (bronze or iron) and a *sauroter* (q.v.)

drachma(e) – standard weight as well as silver coin worth six *oboloi* (q.v.), average daily wage of casual labourer (Attic-Euboic *drachma* = 4.3 grams, Aiginetan *drachma* = 6.1 grams)

ekklêsia – the assembly of adult male citizens at Athens

ephors – the highest magistrates, five in number, in the Spartan state

enômotia (-iai) – 'platoon' in Penguin translations, at full strength a unit of forty men commanded by a *enômotarchos (-oi)*

gerontes – 'elders', members, twenty-eight in number, of the chief deliberation and judicial council at Sparta, the *gerousia*

harmostês – 'fixers', Spartan military governors

hêgemonia – 'leadership', a concept prominent in Greek interstate relations, viz. a *hêgemôn* controls subordinate allies without abolishing their separate identities

helots – indentured serfs who worked the land of Spartans and served as attendants and lightly armed troops in war

hippeis – 'horsemen', the Royal Guard of the Spartan kings *hippeus (-eis)* – 'horseman', member of the cavalry corps of Athens

homoio (-oi) – 'similars', term used of full-blown citizens of Sparta

hoplite – heavily-armed foot soldier accustomed to fighting shoulder to shoulder in a phalanx

Ionians – those Greeks, the Athenians believed that the Ionians had originated in Athens, who spoke the Ionic dialect and whose lives shared certain distinctive cultural and religious features. The language itself was divided into Old Ionic (e.g. Homer) and New Ionic (e.g. Herodotos); the latter includes Attic, the ordinary dialect of Athenian writers (e.g. Thucydides)

klâros (-oi) – 'land plot', Doric form of *klêros*, the estates assigned to the *homoioi* (q.v.)

knemides – greaves, bronze body armour for the lower legs

kopis – single-edged, heavy slashing-type sword shaped like a machete, the hoplite's secondary weapon

kotylê (-ai) – 'cup', dry or liquid measure equivalent to *c.* 0.25 litres, four making up a *choinix* (q.v.)

lambda – the Greek letter 'L' (Λ)

lochos (-oi) – 'regiment' in Penguin translations, at full strength a unit of 640 men commanded by a *lochagos (-oi)*; also used as a tribal unit of various sizes in other Greek armies

linothôrax – stiff linen corselet, which is lighter and more flexible (but more expensive) than the *thôrax* (q.v.)

mantis (-eis) – seer who accompanied the phalanx

medimnos (-oi) – dry measure equal to 48 Attic *choinikes* (q.v.)

metoikos (-oi) – resident alien at Athens

mora (-ai) – 'division' in Penguin translations, at full strength a unit of 1,280 men commanded by a *polemarchos (-oi)*

neodamôdeis – 'new citizens', helots freed after hoplite service in the Spartan army

oba (-ai) – the four (later five) villages that made up Sparta

obolos (-oi) – smallest unit of weight and coinage (Attic-Euboic *obolos* = 0.72 grams), six *oboloi* equalled one *drachma* (q.v.)

ôthismos – push/shove, pushing stage of hoplite battle

paean – collective war cry sung in unison, Dorian in origin but eventually adopted by other Greeks

panopliâ – 'full armour', the panoply of a hoplite (q.v.)

pentekostys (-yes) 'company' in Penguin translations, at full strength a unit of 160 men commanded by a *pentekon(s)ter(es)*

perioikos (-oi) – 'those who dwell round', these were the free inhabitants, being the original population of Lakedaimon, who enjoyed civil but not political liberty. In return for being allowed to live in their own semi-independent communities, Sparta expected the *perioikoi* to serve as hoplites in its army

phylê (-ai) – 'tribe', an ethnic subdivision either of the Greek race *in toto* or else those Greek residents in a particular place

polis (-eis) – conventionally translated as 'city state', the term actually refers to an autonomous political community of Greeks and better translates as 'citizen state'

porpax – detachable armband of *aspis* (q.v.)

pteruges – 'feathers', stiffened leather or linen fringing on corselet

sauroter – 'lizard sticker', bronze butt-spike

stadion (-ia) – unit of distance that varied from place to place, and it is for this reason that we generally consider it to be roughly equivalent to 200 metres

stasis – civil discord or disturbance, sometimes running to civil war

stratêgos (-oi) – general or commander of phalanx

sussition (-ai) – the communal messes at Sparta

thêtes – lowest property class at Athens

thôrax – bronze bell-shaped corselet, which is made up of front and back plates and flared at the waist and neck

talent – fixed weight of silver equivalent to sixty *minae* or 6,000 *drachmae* (Attic-Euboic *tálanton* = 26.2 kilograms, Aiginetan *tálanton* = 43.6 kilograms)

taxis (-eis) – tribal unit in the Athenian army, commanded by a *taxiarchos (-oi)*

trésantes – 'tremblers', term used of cowards in Sparta

triêrês (-êis) – trireme, oared ship rowed at three levels with one man to each oar, the principal warship of the period

Notes

Abbreviations

FGrHist	F. Jacoby, *Die Fragmente der griechischen Historiker* (Berlin & Leiden 1923–58)
Fornara	C.W. Fornara, *Translated Documents of Greece and Rome I: Archaic Times to the end of the Peloponnesian War*, 2nd edition (Cambridge 1983)
Harding	P. Harding, *Translated Documents of Greece and Rome 2: From the end of the Peloponnesian War to the battle of Ipsus* (Cambridge 1985)
IG	*Inscriptiones Graecae* (Berlin 1923–)
PF	R.T. Hallock, *Persepolis Fortification Tablets* (Chicago 1969)
Sage	M.M. Sage, *Warfare in Ancient Greece: A Sourcebook* (London 1996)
Tod	M.N. Todd, *A Selection of Greek Historical Inscriptions II: From 403 to 323* BC (Oxford 1948)

Maps and Plans

1. Lazenby 1985: 7–9.
2. Xenophon *Anabasis* 1.10.6.
3. E.g. ibid. *Hellenika* 4.3.18, *Kyropaideia* 8.5.15.
4. Ibid. *Lakedaimoniôn politeia* 11.8.
5. Ibid. *Agesilaos* 2.11–13, *Hellenika* 4.3.18–20. See also Lazenby 1985: 26, 144–6.
6. Ibid. *Lakedaimoniôn politeia* 11.6.
7. Ibid. *Anabasis* 1.10.9.
8. E.g. ibid. *Kyropaideia* 7.5.3.
9. E.g. Plutarch *Pelopidas* 23.1.

Prologue

1. Tyrtaios fr. 10 West.
2. Ibid. fr. 11 West.
3. Archilochos fr. 114 West.
4. Simonides fr. 9 Mackail. Simonides of Keos (b. *c.* 556 BC), the most admired poet of the day, composed the three epitaphs that were later set up on the battlefield: one recording the feat of 4,000 Peloponnesians withstanding three million of the enemy, one saying that the Spartans lie there obedient to their state's command, and one honouring the *mantis* Megistias. Earlier, he had commemorated the Athenian dead of Marathon, and in his poems on the battles of Artemision and Salamis he was to pay full tribute to the part played by Athens in the resistance to Persia. There is a tradition that he was a personal friend of Themistokles and the eclipse of the Athenian statesman may have been a factor in his going to Sicily in 476 BC, where he remained till his death in 468 BC.
5. Herodotos 7.175.2.
6. Ibid. 7.208.2–3.
7. Ibid. 7.209.3.
8. Herodotos was an Ionian historian of Doric-speaking Halikarnassos (now Bodrum in western Turkey) in Caria, on the very edge of the Persian empire, but spent much of his life in Athens. Nicknamed 'the father of History' by Cicero, Herodotos was the first to make events of the past the subject of research and verification, which is what the word *historiê* meant. His work, in truth a masterpiece, is the chief source for the events of the great conflict between west and east, between 'the Greeks and the Barbarians' (1.1.1), or what we call the Persian Wars of the early fifth century BC, with the description of Xerxes' campaign against mainland Greece forming the climax of the work, but contains much else,

including wonderful accounts of various cultures, geography, history, legends and lore of these regions. If we believe what he says, he travelled extensively in the known world to the Greeks, from the northern shores of the Black Sea to Elephantine on the First Cataract of the Nile, and from the 'heel' of Italy to western Iran. We have no means of checking most of this, but he was a terrific collector and teller of marvellous stories, *logoi* – cracking bedtime reading.

9. Xenophon *Lakedaimoniôn politeia* 11.3.
10. Ibid.13.9. The *Lakedaimoniôn politeia* preserved among the works of Xenophon has been generally accepted as genuine by scholars, and rightly so. The work itself concentrates almost solely on the education and training of a Spartan from cradle to grave, and the army such a system produced.
11. Diodoros 11.5.4–5.
12. Plutarch *Moralia* 225D.11.
13. Herodotos 7.210.1.
14. Ibid. 7.56.1.
15. Ibid. 7.211.2.
16. Xenophon *Hipparchikos* 5.9, 11.
17. Ibid. *Agesilaos* 1.17.
18. Ibid. *Lakedaimoniôn politeia* 2.6–9, cf. *Anabasis* 4.6.14–15.
19. Herodotos 7.211.3.
20. The composite bow consisted of a wooden core on to which was laminated sinew (the front) and horn (the back). The elasticity of the sinew meant that when the bow was drawn it stretched and was put under tension. By contrast, the strips of horn were compressed. By exploiting their mechanical properties, both materials thus reacted to propel the bowstring. This type of bow was very difficult to string and required the use of both legs and arms.
21. What the Greeks called a *gorytos*, was a smart combination of bow-case and quiver-holder that had been invented by the Scythians. Worn at waist level, the *gorytos* had two separate but capacious compartments: one held the composite bow and the other was a pocket for a great many diminutive arrows (of reed with bronze or iron heads) that could be tightly closed with a flap.
22. Herodotos 7.226, cf. Aristophanes *Wasps* 1084: 'So thick with arrows was the air, we couldn't see the sun'.
23. Herodotos 7.211.1.
24. Ibid. 7.212.2.
25. Ibid. 7.215.1. The Immortals (Greek *Athanatoi*, cf. Old Persian *Amrtaka* or Followers) as the Greeks called them, because they liked to believe, falsely, that their 'number was at no time either greater or less than ten thousand' (ibid. 7.83.1). According to Xenophon (*Kyroupaideia* 7.5.68) it was Cyrus the Great who ordered the unit's formation, which was done by selecting 10,000 of his best fighting men. Leastways, by Xerxes' day, if not earlier, this superbly trained unit was mostly ethnic Persian though closely related Medes from northern Iran and Elamites from southern Iran, those warlike tribes that had once exasperated Assyria and Babylon, are also known to have been members. In addition, there was an élite within an élite, the unit of foot soldiers made up of 'one thousand spearmen, the noblest and bravest of the Persians' (Herodotos 7.41.1). These formed a personal bodyguard, the handpicked warriors that followed close after the Great King. Officially known as the King's Spear-bearers' (Old Persian *Arštibara*), their short spears were distinctively knobbed with golden apples from which they gained the nickname the 'apple-bearers' (Greek *melophoroi*). As a prince of the cadet branch of the ruling Achaemenid clan, Dareios, the father of Xerxes, served in this illustrious guard of spearmen during Kambyses' Egyptian campaign (ibid. 3.139.2). It seems that the King's Spear-bearers with their famed apple-butted spears were formed from the Persian nobility, while the Immortals were from the pick of Persian, Median and Elamite commoners.
26. Strabo 9.4.28.
27. Herodotos 7.217.1.
28. Ibid. 7.219.1.
29. Ibid. 7.220.2, cf. Plutarch *Moralia* 225A.4.
30. Herodotos 2.53.
31. E.g. ibid. 2.120.
32. E.g. ibid. 3.108.
33. Ibid. 7.222.

34. Plutarch *Moralia* 865D.
35. Herodotos 7.228.3.
36. Plutarch *Moralia* 225D.13.
37. Herodotos 7.223.1.
38. Ibid. 7.223.3.
39. In Greek: *ôthismos* ... *pollôs*, ibid. 7.225.1.
40. Ibid. 7.225.2.
41. Ibid. 7.225.3.
42. Loc. cit.

Introduction

1. In Old Persian his name comes out something like *Kuraš*; Cyrus is the Latin form of the Greeks' approximation of his name, the ancient Greek language lacking, as it still does, the 'sh' sound. Herodotos, for instance, was utterly convinced that all Persian names ended in 's'.
2. Achaemenid derives from the eponymous founder of the ruling dynasty, Achaemenes; it was the name of the Persian royal clan, members of which ruled the empire for some two centuries. Its formation began around 550 BC, with the conquests of Cyrus the Great (r. 559–530 BC) and his eldest son Kambyses (r. 530–522 BC); it was brought to an end by Alexander's conquest between 334 BC and 323 BC. It was the largest and most complex empire the world had seen, spanning the territory from the blue Hellespont to the muddy Indus, including Egypt (most of the time) and extending into central Asia to the frontiers of modern Kazakhstan.
3. Herodotos 1.153.1.
4. Modern Sparta was founded in 1834 by King Otto (1815–67), he of the Bavarian Wittelsbach dynasty imposed upon the fledgling and weak Greek state of the time by the three Powers, Britain, France and Russia.
5. Thucydides 1.12.3. According to his reckoning this took place about 1100 BC.
6. Herodotos (7.204) Hyllos was believed to have given his name to one of the three Dorian tribes, Hylleis, Dymanes, Pamphylloi (e.g. Tyrtaios fr. 19.9 West, Pausanias 4.3.3).
7. E.g. *Iliad* 10.68.
8. Apollodoros *Bibliotheca* 2.4.12, cf. *Iliad* 14.323–4.
9. In Homer's version of the tale of Troy, despite the anachronisms, one basic fact is clear and consistent in his picture of the political geography of Greece. Namely, Agamemnon of Mycenae was the most powerful warrior king of Achaia, and that he wielded some sort of loose overlordship over the other independent warrior kings of Achaia, of Crete, and some of the Aegean islands. These local chieftains, in their turn, were obliged to supply him with contingents for foreign ventures like that mounted against Troy. If we are to accept Homer's tale, this geo-political unity is basic to it. The Homeric conception of Achaia as a nation under a single ruler may reflect Mycenaean reality. Here it should be noted that for Homer the term 'Achaia' is the collective name for mainland Greece, and 'Achaians' (*Achaiwoí*, e.g. *Iliad* 1.371, 3.131, 10.287 etc.) the Greeks and their allies ranged against the Trojans.
10. *Iliad* 5.738 Fagles.
11. Diodoros 4.32.2, Apollodoros *Bibliotheca* 2.6.4.
12. Plutarch *Moralia* 241F.16.
13. Ibid. 240C.
14. Thucydides 4.80.5, 5.34.1, 7.19.3, 58.3, Xenophon *Hellenika* 3.1.4, 4.2, 6.5.29.
15. Xenophon *Hellenika* 3.3.6.
16. Ibid. *Lakedaimoniôn politeia* 10.7.
17. Herodotos 7.231, Plutarch *Agesilaos* 30.2–4.
18. Xenophon *Lakedaimoniôn politeia* 9.4–6, cf. Aristotle *Politics* 1271a26, 1272a13–14.
19. In the literary sources the communal mess is variously called *sussitia*, *andreiâ* or *phidition*. It can turn up as *suskania* ('tent-fellowship') too.
20. Plutarch (*Lykourgos* 12.3) tells us that King Agis was fined after the Mantineian campaign for eating at home with his wife.
21. Phylarchos *FGrHist* 81F43.
22. Athenaios 6.271e-f.
23. Plutarch *Lysandros* 2.1.

24. Ibid. *Perikles* 22.3, cf. Thucydides 1.114.2, 2.21.1.
25. Plutarch *Perikles* 22.4, cf. *Lysandros* 16.
26. Athenaios 6.24.
27. E.g. Pausanias 6.2.1–2.
28. According to Plutarch (*Lykourgos* 12.3), each and every *homoios* was obliged to contribute to his communal mess enough to feed at least three men, and the annual income required to sustain these contributions seems to have amounted to 205 measures of produce (Hodkinson 2000: 126), and estimates of the size of the average Spartiate estate vary between fifteen to twenty hectares (ibid. 382-5), larger than those of the lowest Athenian hoplite property class (the *zeugitai*, with an annual income of at least 200 *medimnoi* of agricultural produce) because they supported helot families as well.
29. Plutarch *Lykourgos* 25.4. Paidaretos nonetheless became the harmost of Chios (Thucydides 8.32.1–33.4, 38.3–4), where he was to be killed in action in 411 BC (ibid. 55.3).
30. Strabo 8.4.11.
31. Pausanias 3.21.3.
32. Thucydides 2.56.5, 6.105.2, 7.18.3.
33. Xenophon *Hellenika* 7.2.2.
34. Pausanias 3.24.1.
35. Herodotos 9.28.2.
36. Xenophon *Hellenika* 3.5.7, 5.1.33, 6.5.21, 7.4.27.
37. Pausanias 3.21.4.
38. Xenophon *Lakedaimoniôn politeia* 14.3.
39. Theopompos *apud* Athenaios 6.272a.
40. Thucydides 1.101.2.
41. Tyrtaios frs. 6, 7 West = Fornara 12C (5).
42. Plutarch *Moralia* 239D–E.
43. Pausanias 3.20.6.
44. Ephoros *FGrHist* 70F117.
45. Plato *Laws* 776d–e.
46. Thucydides 5.23.3.
47. Herodotos 9.10.1, 29.2, Xenophon *Hellenika* 3.3.4–11. See Lazenby 1993: 227–8, Cartledge 2002: 150–1.
48. Thucydides 4.3.3, 41.2–3.
49. Ibid. 4.80.2, cf. 1.132.4–5, 5.23.3 – 'the slave population'.
50. Aristotle *Politics* 1269a.
51. Xenophon *Lakedaimoniôn politeia* 12.4.
52. Kritias fr. 88B37 Diels-Kranz.
53. Plato *Laws* 630d, Plutarch *Lykourgos* 28.2–5, 7 = Aristotle fr. 538 Rose). One suggestion is that this baleful body was in fact the *hippeis*, for in the Kinadon conspiracy they are sent out to apprehend a woman of Aulon.
54. Plutarch *Lykourgos* 28.4.
55. Thucydides 4.80.3–4, Diodoros 12.67.3–5.
56. Xenophon *Hellenika* 3.3.5.
57. Ibid. 3.3.6. This phrase is an echo of Homer *Iliad* 4.40–1 Fagles: 'and devour Priam / and Priam's sons and the Trojan armies raw'.
58. Xenophon *Hellenika* 3.3.11.
59. Ibid. 3.3.5 (two kings + five ephors + twenty-eight elders + about forty other Spartiates vs 4,000 non-Spartiates).

Chapter 1

1. A string of extinct or dormant volcanoes, including the islands of Melos and Thera, marks the busy junction of the African and European tectonic plates.
2. Xenophon *Memorabilia* 3.5.25.
3. These mountains, as Xenophon would have known them, were Hymettos (modern Imittós), Parnes (modern Párnitha), and Pentelikon (modern Pendéli).

4. Greece is the splintered south-eastern tip of the Balkan peninsula, and the rocky coastline of the mainland is equal in length to that of France, though that nation is four times larger.
5. The climate is as follows: temperature 22–32° C (summer) and 4.3–10° C (winter); rainfall October to April with drought May to September (the 'dead' season); winds July to mid-August, predominantly from the northeast, what today's Greeks call *to meltémi* but their ancestors of yore the Aetesian winds.
6. Indeed, Greece as a whole was poor in natural resources, particularly lacking in minerals, therefore tin and most of the copper for making bronze (90 per cent copper, 10 per cent tin) was imported. The following minerals were available: marble (Mount Hymettos, Mount Pentelikon, Naxos, Paros, Thasos), clay (Attica, Corinthia), silver (Attica, Siphnos), copper (Cyprus), and iron (small deposits throughout Greece).
7. Plato *Kritias* 111c.
8. The ecological zones are six in total: (1) plains; (2) cultivated hillsides on soft rocks; (3) uncultivated hillsides on harder rocks; (4) high mountains; (5) fens; (6) coasts and sea. The land typology is threefold: (1) lowland = 0–700 metres above sea level; (2) deciduous = 700–1,500 metres above sea level; (3) coniferous = 1,500–2,000 plus metres above sea level.
9. The Mediterranean triad consists of the following: cereals (barley – needs less water than wheat – oats, durum wheat); olive (not much above 600 metres, thus Arcadia and parts of Achaia lack the olive); vine. Secondary crops included: figs, apple, pear, plum, pomegranate, cherry, pistachio, walnut, almond, chestnut, carob (mainly for animal feed), pulses, and broad beans. For a survey of the staple foods of ancient Greece, see Dalby 1996: 82–92.
10. Hesiod *Works & Days* 392.
11. Ibid. 204.
12. Aristophanes *Peace* 1320–8.
13. Thucydides 1.15.1.
14. See especially, Gallant 1991: 37–9.
15. Mixed husbandry included the following: sheep and goats (milk products, textiles); pigs (meat); cattle (limited, if any); mules and donkeys (pack animals); fish (fresh, salted – imported in huge quantities, especially from the Black Sea region); beekeeping for honey (chief sweetener, preservative, medicinal).
16. Aristotle *Politics* 1252b8. The *Politics*, which he composed towards the end of his life at around 330 BC or so, is Aristotle's great work of political science and political theory within the given framework of the Greek *polis*.
17. In Greek: *zoon politikon*, ibid. 1253a9.
18. Ibid. 1275a5–8.
19. Winter 1971: xvi.
20. Herodotos 5.49, cf. 1.66–68, 82.
21. Laconia, in fact, was not a name in use among the ancient Greeks: it is a Latin coinage, appearing first in the works of elder Pliny (*Historia Naturalis* 6.34.39, 17.18.30, cf. 25.8.53). From Laconia, of course, we get the adjective laconic.
22. *Iliad* 2.573 Fagles.
23. Thucydides 1.10.2.
24. Pausanias 3.16.9, cf. Strabo 8.5.3.
25. E.g. Plutarch *Moralia* 210B.29, 217E.7.
26. E.g. Herodotos 1.65.
27. Terpander *apud* Plutarch *Lykourgos* 21.3.
28. The suspicious names amongst the Eurypontidai include Prytanis, 'president', and Eunomos, which was obviously derived from *eunomia*, 'good order'.
29. The Agiadai were named after the second king of their line, viz. Agis, and the Eurypontidai after the third, viz. Eurypon, who as eponyms should be the real founders of their respective dynasties, or so we assume.
30. Charilaos' name translates as 'joy of the people', and his grandson was Theopompos, which places Charilaos around 800 BC. Aristotle/Plutarch names Lykourgos as his uncle thus placing the lawgiver, who at the best of times appears rather shadowy in our sources, circa 800–750 BC.
31. Plutarch *Lykourgos* 6.
32. Xenophon *Lakedaimoniôn politeia* 8.5.

33. Plutarch *Lykourgos* 6.7, cf. Tyrtaios fr. 4.1–6 West. It is interesting to note that the Boiotian farmer poet Hesiod, who composed around 700 BC, warns his brother of 'crooked judgements', usually at the hands of 'bribe-swallowing princes' (*Works & Days* 250, 263–4). Obviously Hesiod knows well enough why the high and mighty are able to get away with their injustice: they have all the power.
34. Pindar *apud* Plutarch *Lykourgos* 21.
35. Plutarch *Lykourgos* 7.1.
36. Aristotle *Politics* 1313a26.
37. Such a complex written document can hardly be envisaged before 700 BC: Xenophon (*Lakedaimoniôn politeia* 10.8) places Lykourgos at the time of the sons of Herakles, which absurdly means the time of the 'Dorian invasion', Thucydides (1.18.1) places, without reason, the introduction of the Lykourgan constitutional reforms at about 804 BC, Aristotle connects the man himself with the swearing of the first Olympic truce, viz. 776 BC, while Herodotos (1.65.1) dates him to the mid-sixth century BC. It appears the lawgiving Lykourgos spooks across the Spartan stage and across the Greek centuries.
38. Aristotle *Politics* 1265b33–42.
39. For a good, albeit brief, discussion of this see Hooker 1980: 125–6.
40. Herodotos 6.52.
41. Ibid. 6.56–59.
42. Aristotle *Politics* 1285a4. The rule that only one king should accompany an army was established after the fiasco of Demaratos' jealous disagreement with Kleomenes during the invasion of Attica in 506 BC, thus reversing earlier practice (Herodotos 5.75.2). Perhaps the Spartans came to realize that too many kings, like too many cooks, may spoil the feast. Kleomenes eventually got the better of his co-king Demaratos, whose disposition he contrived with the aid of the Delphic oracle. Shortly before Xerxes' invasion Demaratos went over to the Persians and accompanied Xerxes to Greece. He must have been an acute embarrassment to Sparta, but in Herodotos' narrative he always remains a dignified figure, faithful at heart to his old motherland Sparta, but loyal to his new master Xerxes.
43. Aristotle *Politics* 1270b6–7.
44. The same implication is made again by Aristotle in *Politics* 1272a31–32 and 1294b29–31.
45. Herodotos 5.40, Aristotle *Politics* 2.8.3.
46. Aristotle *Politics* 1270b27–28, 1271a9–10, Thucydides 1.87.2.
47. Thucydides 1.72.1.
48. Ibid. 1.79.1–2.
49. Ibid. 1.81.6. Archidamos' prediction, of course, would come true, but he would have been absolutely astonished to learn that the great war between Sparta and Athens would actually end in a resounding triumph at sea in league with the very 'barbarians' his father, Leotychidas, had been so proud to have defeated at Mykale in 479 BC.
50. Thucydides 1.86.5.
51. Ibid. 1.87.1–2.
52. Aristotle *Politics* 1265b7–8.
53. Xenophon, in a debate concerning war with Elis (398 BC), uses the phrase 'it seemed good to the *ephoroi* and the *apella*' (*Hellenika* 3.2.23), which is reminiscence of the Athenians and their decrees.
54. Herodotos 3.148, 9.9–10, Thucydides 6.88.10, Xenophon *Lakedaimoniôn politeia* 8.4, *Hellenika* 2.2.12–13, 19, 3.2.23, 5.2.11.
55. Xenophon *Lakedaimoniôn politeia* 8.4.
56. Herodotos 3.148.2.
57. Isokrates *Panathenaikos* §181.
58. Xenophon *Lakedaimoniôn politeia* 15.6, 7.
59. Plutarch *Kleomenes* 10.3.
60. Diogenes Laertius 1.68.
61. Thucydides 1.131.2.
62. Herodotos 5.39.
63. Ibid. 9.76.3, Thucydides 8.11.3, cf. Aristotle *Politics* 2.6.14, 20.
64. Aristotle *Politics* 1270b.
65. Herodotos 5.37.
66. Marriages between uncles and nieces were quite common elsewhere in Greece too, and for the same reasons, basically a concern to keep the property intact within the male family line. However, it would

be wrong of us to think of Gorgo merely as a passive patrimony pawn in such a transaction. Even from the little we know of her, she had a mind, and a voice, of her own. In a frequently quoted incident, she was quizzed by an Athenian woman why Spartan women were the only women in Greece who rule their men. Gorgo replied, 'because we are the only women to give birth to (real) men' (Plutarch *Moralia* 240E.5). One way to read this is to say only men with self-confidence to accept women as equals were men at all.
67. The modern Greek word for wine, *krasi*, is derived from the ancient Greek word, *krâsis*, which meant mixing.
68. Kritias fr. 88B11 Diels-Kranz.
69. Herodotos 7.205.2.
70. Ibid. 7.228.2.

Chapter 2
1. Hesiod *Theogony* 565–619.
2. Ibid. *Works & Days* 42–105.
3. *Odyssey* 13.469 Fagles.
4. Thus, Aischylos characterizes her as Helen the Spoiler, 'spoiler of ships, spoiler of souls, spoiler of a city' (*Agamemnon* 689).
5. *Anthologia Palatina* 14.73 Drees.
6. Alkman fr. 26. Though he writes as a Spartan, Alkman may have had a Lydian origin, perhaps 'one from lofty Sardis' (fr. 16.5). His poetry certainly reflects a society of high culture open to eastern influences and fascinated by the exotic.
7. Ibid. fr. 41.
8. Ibid. fr. 1.50–56.
9. E.g. Herodotos 6.57. Of course, *patrouchos* is an Ionic corruption of the Doric word, as found in the Gortyn law code, *patraoikos*.
10. I am not sure if this is entirely relevant, but one is reminded of one of those apparent sayings of that man of mystery, Lykourgos. When asked to install democracy in Sparta, he crisply replied: 'Make your own household a democracy first' (Plutarch *Lykourgos* 19.3).
11. Aristotle *Politics* 1270a11–31, cf. Plutarch *Moralia* 228B.
12. The plight of the unmarried forms the climax of Lysistrata's dialogue with one of the ten *probouloi* (Aristophanes *Lysistrata* 591–7). Likewise, when Lysias catalogues the crimes of the Thirty Tyrants, the culminating atrocity is not that they put over a thousand citizens to death without due course to the law, but they 'prevented many men's daughters from being given in marriage' (12.21).
13. Plutarch *Moralia* 13.
14. Aristotle *Politics* 1270a23.
15. Ibid. 1269b37–39.
16. Xenophon *Lakedaimoniôn politeia* 1.3–4, Plutarch *Lykourgos* 14.2, 15.1.
17. Aristotle *Politics* 1269b7. Aristotle was not alas untypical with regards to his chauvinist philosophical view of women. Take, for instance, the Presocratic philosopher Demokritos: 'To be ruled by a woman is the final insult for a man' (fr. 68B111 Diels-Kranz).
18. Plutarch *Lykourgos* 14.4, 15.1. There are some very fine bronze figurines manufactured in Sparta in the sixth century BC depicting adolescent girls or young women in athletic poses, e.g. bronze figurine of running Spartan girl in breast-exposing tunic, circa 520–500 BC. It was found at Prizren, Serbia, was possibly made in or near Sparta, and is now at the British Museum (inv. GR 1876.5–10.1).
19. Look at Aristophanes *Lysistrata* 82 for the lewd joke about gymnastic exercises practised by Spartan women, and Euripides *Andromache* 598 where he condemns Spartan women for running around with 'bare thighs and loose clothing!' Incidentally, Aristophanes' *Lysistrata* is the first known comedy to have been named after its heroine, played of course by a male actor, in drag. It is a brilliant drollery, citizen women from both sides of the Peloponnesian War conflict revealing their ultimate strength by refusing to lay with their war-mad men. This collectivist sex strike, they trust, will bring their men kicking and screaming to the negotiating table. Their dastardly plot is ultimately successful. At first glance this play is extraordinarily modern in its concept, but the joke lies in the complete reversal of the laws and therefore impossible.

20. Plutarch *Lykourgos* 15.2, Athenaios 13.555c. In Argos (another Dorian state) the bride wore a false beard on her wedding night.
21. Xenophon *Lakedaimoniôn politeia* 1.5–6. It is interesting to note that in Hesiod's day a man married at thirty a virgin in her fifth year from puberty (*Works & Days* 695–9), rather old as fourteen to sixteen was later the common age of marriage for girls except in Sparta.
22. Plutarch *Lykourgos* 15.1.
23. Ibid. *Moralia* 225A.2.
24. Kritias fr. 88B32 Diels-Kranz.
25. Plutarch *Lykourgos* 14.2.
26. Xenophon *Lakedaimoniôn politeia* 1.7–8, Plutarch *Lykourgos* 15.6–7.
27. Xenophon *Lakedaimoniôn politeia* 1.9, Polybios 12.6.8.
28. Aristotle *Politics* 1306b2.
29. Strabo 6.3.2. Much successful colonisation was advised by the oracle at Delphi. Before embarking for pastures new, leaders of colonial adventurers would, as a matter of course, consult the Pythia, the priestess who sat in communion with Apollo. Dorieus, bitter at being ruled by his elder half-brother Kleomenes, took the earliest opportunity to leave Sparta by leading a colonising expedition to Libya. Herodotos reports it as remarkable that the Spartan leader 'neither took counsel of the oracle at Delphi as where he should go, nor observed the customary usages' (5.42.2). The oversight was reason enough, Herodotos clearly implies, for the failure of this man's first foreign venture. For the second one he did consult the oracle, asking the Pythia whether he would hold the land for which he was bound. She gave Apollo's affirmation, saying that he would hold it. So Dorieus gathered up his followers once again and sailed along the shores of Italy. After a number of adventures along the way, he finally arrived in northwest Sicily, where he was defeated and killed in battle by rival Phoenician colonists. Thus, in accordance with the oracle, he occupied that land permanently. Dorieus, if will be remembered, was the eldest son of Anaxandridas' *first* wife but conceived *after* the second wife bore one son, Kleomenes. In the eyes of many Spartans, Dorieus was the 'man who should have been king'.
30. Athenaios 12.522d–f.
31. Her name sounds like a childhood nickname, because it means (female) puppy. An ancestor of hers had been given the equivalent masculine nickname Kyniskos. The dog itself was a particular type of hound bred in Sparta, the female of the species being renowned for its ability to scent out the wild boar.
32. Plutarch *Agesilaos* 20.1.
33. *Anthologia Palatina* 13.16 Drees.
34. Pindar fr. 199 Snell.
35. Herakleitos of Ephesos fr. 22B53 Diels-Kranz.
36. Plutarch *Lykourgos* 16.1.
37. Wine was reputed to induce convulsions in weak babies while tempering the strength of healthy ones.
38. The first real mention of the term *agôgê*, however, is by Polybios (1.32.1) when he talks of Xanthippos, the Spartan *condottiere* who greatly aided Carthage during the First Punic War. It is used, rather vaguely, in another (now lost) source, Demetrios of Skepsis, but the question remains, did he write before or after Polybios? We do know for certain that the term was not used by Herodotos, Thucydides, Xenophon or Aristotle, our principal sources for this period. Nonetheless, this should not unduly worry us because the *Lakedaimoniôn politeia*, which we attribute to Xenophon, mentions many of the elements equated with the training of Spartan boys, in particular, look at *Lakedaimoniôn politeia* §§2–3, while Thucydides' Periklean Funeral Oration mentions (2.39.1) the laborious system employed in Sparta to train its boys.
39. Xenophon *Lakedaimoniôn politeia* 2–3, Plutarch *Lykourgos* 16–18.
40. Plutarch *Lykourgos* 19.1.
41. Aristotle *Rhetoric* 2.21.8.
42. Thucydides 2.39.1.
43. Today 'philosophy' and 'philosopher' are common words, even though we may still dispute their exact meaning. This was not true in Plato's day. We need only to think of Aristophanes' *Clouds* (423 BC), which satirises the sophists, *sophistes*, and especially the logic-chopping Sokrates, portraying him as the proprietor of a 'thinking shop' where the main item on the syllabus is advanced rhetorical chicanery. Sophists were travelling orators who claimed to teach the art of government and whom Plato so disliked. Philosophy for Plato consists essentially in the belief that the world possesses an intelligible

nature distinct from the sensible appearances with which we are generally acquainted. The intelligible is more real and more valuable than the sensible, and the object of any knowledge we can ever had. Philosophers understand that the objects of knowledge are only illustrated, but never understood, through their sensible representations. As a result of their education, they eventually become aware of the existence of the single intelligible essences, which underlie and give substance to the multiple, changing sensible phenomena that surround us. Plato believes that most of us are incapable of realizing that we are only seeing shadows of objects projected on the back wall of a cave, ergo we should be willing to take the advice of philosophers on what life is best for us. Philosophers, then, are distinguished as the only men who know truth and reality, and they alone, therefore, will be capable of understanding the real principles underlying the ideal *polis*.

44. Political thinking would arrive with Plato's pupil Aristotle. Here we are nicely reminded of Raphaël's masterpiece *Scuola di Atene* (1510–11), a fresco commissioned by the *papa terrible*, Julius II (1503–13), for the Apostolic Palace, Vatican. Raphaël's *chef-d'oeuvre* centres upon *maître à penser* and educatee engaged in dignified disputation. Whereas the elder giant of philosopher points heavenward to his ideal world of metaphysics, the younger one calmly gestures earthward to indicate his more materialistically grounded approach to the good life for man. Plato (actually Leonardo da Vinci) is depicted as old, grey, wise-looking and barefooted. In his left hand he holds, in book form (a fairly recent development), his *Timaios*. In contrast, Aristotle is all mature manhood, very handsome, well shod and dandily dressed; he is the focus of attention. In his left hand, again in book form, his *Nikomachaian Ethics*. Of course the fresco is anecdotal, but the tale it tells is clear. But while Plato moved in the realm of pure thought, Aristotle had the practitioner's itch to translate ideas into facts.

45. The *Republic* (c. 375 BC) was the product of Plato's early years in the Academy, the school he founded (c. 386 BC) in Athens for the education of the philosopher statesmen, a training ground for rulers. With its misleading title – in Greek it can mean indifferently 'constitution', 'state', or 'society' – the *Republic*, in short, is a statement of aims that the Academy set itself to achieve. Whether or not Plato ever thought that the *Republic* was achievable is another matter. It is notable that in his last work, the *Laws*, he stressed the importance of laws, and the government and administrative arrangements contained therein are certainly less austerely autocratic than those in the *Republic*.

46. Plato *Republic* 414b.

47. Thus it may *in Platonic principle* be true that the position assigned to women in Greek society (and indeed any other societies down to the present today) entailed a gross waste of talents 'of half of the human race' (Plato *Laws* 781).

48. Plato *Republic* 404a–e.

49. Ibid. 410a.

50. Ibid. 417a–b.

51. Ibid. 420a.

52. Ibid. 423c–424b.

53. Ibid. 425b.

54. Ibid. 452b. It is interesting to note that in Aristophanes' *Ecclesiazusae* the women, once in power, introduce a raft of measures that bear a very strong resemblance to certain ideas put forward by Plato in the *Republic*. This is probably not a coincidence, as the two men were almost certainly well acquainted and possibly close friends. Plato's *Symposium* (189a–193e) contains a convincing portrayal of the playwright. Even though the *Republic* was not publicly circulated until some years after the date of the *Ecclesiazusae* (c. 393 BC) it is likely that amongst his friends and acquaintances Plato had been working out some of his ideas for many years beforehand.

55. Plato *Republic* 468a.

56. Plato had firsthand experience of tyranny, having resided in Rhegion in 388 BC, the year it was being besieged by Dionysios I of Syracuse (Diodoros 14.108). Plato's objective at that time was to make contact with the Pythagorean philosophers of southern Italy and, according to Diodoros and Plutarch, the unpredictable Sicilian tyrant sold Plato into slavery when he captured Rhegion. Both authors relate how Dionysios told Plato that he would come to no harm for, as a slave, he was now going to live by his own doctrines. Plutarch (*Dion* 10–11) adds that in 367 BC Plato was invited back to Sicily by Dion, the brother-in-law of the tyrant, to serve as the tutor to Dionysios' son, the younger Dionysios, in an attempt to turn him into a philosopher ruler. His visit was not a success. The lessons were wasted, and as a tyrant the son proved to be a man of straw whereas his father had been a man of steel.

57. The major problem with reconstructing Sokrates' thoughts and beliefs is that, like Christ, he never wrote a word of his teachings.
58. Plato *Republic* 557b.
59. Ibid. *Laws* 707a–b, cf. *Republic* 488a–b.
60. To be fair to Plato, he does warns us in several places in the *Republic* of the difference between theory and practice (e.g. 472a–d, 592a–b), and it contains comparatively little about the detail of practical legal or constitutional arrangements (cf. 425c–e). Much closer to the Platonic idea of the philosopher king was Hermeias of Atarneios, former student of the Academy and tyrant of Assos and ruler of the Troad in northwest Anatolia (Harding 79). Of the happy dealings Plato had with this ruler we learn something in Plato's Sixth Letter. The intellectually minded Hermeias is accredited with having moderated his rule according to the strictures of Plato, going so far as to encourage one of the philosopher's former disciples, Aristotle, to live and teach in Assos. Aristotle, along with his nephew Kallisthenes, spent two years in the court of Hermeias, marrying his niece and adopted daughter Pythias, before moving on to the court of Philip II of Macedon to become tutor to the young Alexander (the later Great). Hermeias possessed a formidable naval, military, and financial power, and was virtually independent of the Persian empire. However, philosopher king or not, he did come to a rather sticky end; the Persians, who were gathering information about Philip's future intentions against them, flayed him alive (341 BC). According to Theopompos (Harding 90A), who had spent some time in Hermeias' court and later wrote a pretty cynical account of the tyrant, Hermeias was no philosopher king. On the other hand, Aristotle and Kallisthenes composed hymns honouring the tyrant's kingly virtue (Harding 90B).
61. Aristotle *Politics* 1327b7–9.
62. Plutarch *Lykourgos* 16.1.
63. Ibid. 8.3.
64. Ibid. *Agis* 8.1.
65. E.g. Cartledge 1979.
66. Herodotos 1.65.
67. Thucydides 1.6.4.
68. Aristotle *Politics* 1270b6–7.
69. Polybios 6.45.3.
70. Herakleides Lembos 373.12 Dilts.
71. Plutarch *Moralia* 238E.
72. Ibid. *Agis* 5.4.
73. E.g. Lazenby 1995, *contra* Cartledge 1979: 142–4.
74. Myron of Priene *FGrHist* 106F2 = Fornara 13A.
75. Plutarch *Moralia* 239E.
76. Ibid. *Agis* 5.1.
77. Xenophon *Agesilaos* 4.5.
78. Herodotos 9.10.1,11.3, 28.2.
79. Ibid. 7.234.2.
80. Thucydides 4.38.3.
81. Ibid. 4.8.9.
82. Ibid.5.68.3.
83. Xenophon *Hellenika* 6.4.15, 17.
84. Aristotle *Politics* 1270a29–34.
85. Xenophon *Hellenika* 6.1.17. For the decline in the number of Spartiates, see especially Cartledge 1987: 38 fig. 4.2. The total number of full citizens, the *Spartiãtai*, available to Sparta declined throughout the classical period, a process Aristotle calls *oliganthrôpia* ('fewness of men', *Politics* 1270a33).
86. Aristotle *Politics* 1270b3–4.
87. Ibid. 1270a15.
88. Herodotos' claim (9.29) for 35,000 may in fact be the figure for the total helot population of Sparta.

Chapter 3
1. Xenophon *Hellenika* 3.4.3, *Lakedaimoniôn politeia* 13.3, Pausanias 9.13.4.
2. Plutarch *Moralia* 25.

3. Xenophon *Lakedaimoniôn politeia* 13.2, cf. 15.2, Herodotos 6.56.
4. Their joint names in patronymic form claimed their father variously as Zeus (Dioskouri = Sons of Zeus) or King Tyndareos of Sparta (Tyndaridai = Sons of Tyndareos). Although Homer (*Iliad* 3.426, *Odyssey* 11.299–300), assumed that Helen alone of Leda's children was a daughter of Zeus, a later tradition claimed that Polydeukes and Helen were begotten by Zeus when, wearing his best swan-suit, he called upon Leda. Castor and Klytemnestra, on the other hand, were fathered by Tyndareos. Polydeukes and Helen were therefore immortal, but Castor and Klytemnestra were mortal (Pindar *Nemean Ode* 10.80, Apollodoros *Bibliotheca* 3.10.5–7). The present story being about the Spartans, lets us opt for the second story. The Dioskouri, who were never separated from each other in any adventure, became the pride of Sparta. Castor was an authority on war – he even instructed Herakles in military arts – and famous as a tamer of horse, Polydeukes as the best boxer of his day – the only noticeable difference between them was that his face bore the scars of his sport – winning prizes at Olympia.
5. Herodotos 6.57.2, Xenophon *Lakedaimoniôn politeia* 15.5, Cicero *De divinatione* 1.43.95.
6. Plutarch *Lykourgos* 21.3.
7. Ibid. 22.2.
8. Xenophon *Hellenika* 4.2.20, cf. 3.1.17, *Lakedaimoniôn politeia* 13.8, Herodotos 9.61.3.
9. Phoibos, *phoibos*, means 'shining', 'bright', or 'pure', while Far Darter ('the one who strikes from afar', *Homeric Hymn* 3.1) obviously refers to his use of the bow by which he makes his fatal influence felt from afar.
10. The summit shrine of Taïygettos was once dedicated to Apollo, but with the coming of Christianity it was rededicated to his descendant the Prophet Elijah (Profitis Ilías). Indeed, Taïygettos has always figured predominantly in local religion and folklore. Its original name was Taleton, a Doric word whose meaning has long since been lost. The current nomenclature stems from a certain Taygete, depending on sources either a daughter of the Titan Atlas or a member of Artemis' retinue. Taïygettos was, in fact, sacred to both Apollo and Artemis.
11. E.g. *Iliad* 16.615, 17.210.
12. Pindar *Pythian Ode* 1.10, cf. Simonides fr. 171, Archilochos fr. 48 Edmonds. For Ares as synonymous with strife, battle or war see especially, *Iliad* 5.31, 859–63, 909, 13.297–300, Pindar *Pythian Ode* 5.85, 9.36, *Olympian Ode* 9.76, *Isthmian Ode* 5.48.
13. *Iliad* 5.590–909.
14. E.g. Xenophon *Anabasis* 1.8.18, *Hellenika* 2.4.17, Archilochos fr.1 Edmonds.
15. Plutarch *Solon* 9.4, Pausanias 1.8.4. The first temple of Ares was built after Solon took Salamis. The second Athenian example – a late fifth century BC temple of the Doric order – was originally, according to Camp, erected in the deme of Akharnai. However, during the reign of Augustus it was moved from there and set up in the Athenian Agora so as to honour Caius Caesar, the emperor's eldest grandson, as the 'New Ares'. See Camp 1986: 184–5, 1990: 114–5.
16. Pausanias 2.32.9, 3.22.6, 7.
17. Ibid. 2.25.1, 3.19.7, 5.15.6, 8.32.3, 37.12.
18. Plutarch *Moralia*. 245C, cf. Herodotos 6.77.
19. Mars was invoked to protect Roman crops and to assist Roman arms in waging war beyond the margins of early Rome. Mars' dual agricultural and warlike nature is indicated by the fact that the early Romans began the year with the month of March, *mensis Martius*, which took its name from the god and marked the return of spring, plant life, and the campaigning season. Similarly, the end of the campaigning season was marked by a ceremony in honour of Mars, the *armilustrium* of 19 October, in which men assembled under their standards fully equipped and underwent ritual purification. The war gear and standards were then stored for the winter months. It appears that on this occasion captured arms were dedicated to Mars too.
20. Delphi Museum, inv. 8140.
21. Herodotos 1.65.
22. Ibid. 6.86, Aelian *De natura animalium* 3.44.
23. Ovid *Metamorphoses* 12.847–86 Martin, Apollodoros *Epitome* 5.3.
24. As depicted, for example, on a *pelike* by the Niobid Painter, *c.* 460 BC. One interpretation of his motive is that it was in revenge for Achilles' cruel murder of Troilos, the god's own son by Hekuba, chief wife of King Priam, on the very altar of the god's own sanctuary. Two different motives are suggested for

the actual murder: Achilles was in love with Troilos and cold-bloodedly killed him when he spurned his advances, or, more likely, that there was a legend that Troy could not be taken once Troilos reached the age of twenty, and thus Achilles was obliged to kill him. Homer mentions the doomed youth only once (*Iliad* 24.257) and then in passing as one of the sons Priam lost. But the ancient artistic sources, pottery iconography in the main, reveal a rich and detailed story.

25. The literature falls into three camps: (1) Aelian *De natura animalium* 10.26 offers 'the wolf-born lord of the bow' when discussing *Iliad* 4.101, cf. Lattimore translates *Apóllōn Lykêgenés* as 'Apollo the light-born, the glorious archer', whereas Fagles has 'Wolf-god, glorious Archer'; (2) Curtius (*G.Et.* 5.160) sees the meaning of the epithet as 'light-born'; (3) Sophokles (*Electra* 7) talks of Apollo as the 'the wolf-slaying god', though in the previous line, he mentions the agora in Argos which, according to our travelling author Pausanias, housed 'the most famous building' there, 'a sanctuary of Apollo Lykeios' (2.19.3, cf. Plutarch *Pyrrhos* 31.3), and the wolf was a common device on the coins of classical Argos. Of course, certain Apolline myths, especially those concerning his origin, will not support this possible link with the wolf.

26. *Iliad* 1.43–53, cf. Pindar *Paean* 6.110–21, Archilochos fr. 27 Edmonds, Sophokles *Oedipus Tyrannus* 469–70.

27. *Iliad* 15.305 Fagles.

28. Plutarch *Moralia* 402A.

29. Pausanias 3.19.1–2.

30. The *tetradrachm*: obverse = head of King Areos (r. 309–265 BC), reverse = Amyklaian Apollo wearing a crested Corinthian helmet and wielding a hoplite spear and a composite bow. See Sear 1978: 1.262 #2833. For the Roman coin see Alroth 1989: 27 fig. 9.

31. Philostratos *Life of Apollodoros* 3.14, Pausanias 3.10.8.

32. Herodotos 1.69.4.

33. Polybios 5.19.2–3.

34. Plutarch *Moralia* 232D.

35. Ibid. 239A.

36. Thucydides 3.89.1, 5.54.2–4, Pausanias 3.13.3–4.

37. Demetrios of Skepsis *apud* Athenaios 4.141e–f.

38. Kallimachos *Hymn to Apollo* 85.

39. Although the best manuscripts of Herodotos give his name as 'Pheidippides' (6.105.1, 106.1, cf. Nepos *Miltiades* 4.3), it was probably 'Philippides' as one manuscript spells it, and as Plutarch (*Moralia* 862B), Pausanias (1.28.4, 8.54.6) and Lucian (*Pro lapsu inter salutandum* 3) read it in their texts of Herodotos. Philippides is attested as an Attic name, whereas Pheidippides ('son of the sparer of horses') is not found as a proper name in Attica except as the butt of Aristophanes' play *Clouds*, where it is specifically said to be a sort of compromise between Pheidonides (the name favoured by the bearer's father) and the mother's desire for an equestrian-sounding name ending in -ippides (*Clouds* 62–7). But see Badian 1979.

40. Herodotos 6.106.3, cf. Plutarch *Moralia* 861E–F.

41. Euripides *Alkestis* 450.

42. Herodotos 6.120. Isokrates says (*Panegyrikos* §87) they covered the distance in a march of three days and three nights.

43. [Simonides] fr. 143 Diehl, Herodotos 6.105.3. Pan was a god the Greeks visualized with the horns and hooves of a goat, and the story goes that the deity hailed the runner with an ultimatum: Honour Pan and Pan would succour Athens in its crisis. As a result, a hollow in the rock was converted into a shrine for the shaggy god at the north-west corner of the Acropolis (Pausanias 1.28.4, Lucian *Bis accusatus sive tribunalia* 9), which subsequently acquired erotic associations (Euripides *Ion* 492–5, 938, Aristophanes *Lysistrata* 721, 911).

44. Herodotos 6.117.3. On the strength of this supernatural encounter, Epizelos was to earn for himself immortality by being depicted in the celebrated painting of the battle exhibited in the Stoa Poikile (Aelian *De natura animalium* 7.38).

45. Lucian *Pro lapsu inter salutandum* 3, cf. Plutarch *Moralia* 347C.

46. Pausanias 1.34.4.

47. For the linking of Amazons, Troy and Marathon, see Herodotos 9.27. Also, in his account of the Athenian Agora the travel writer Pausanias describes (1.15.1) in some detail the famous great paintings in the Stoa Poikile, and three of the four subjects were taken from the familiar repertoire of Athenian

panegyric, the battle against the Amazons, the sack of Troy, and the battle of Marathon. Painted by Polygnotos of Thasos, the greatest painter of his day, and probably commissioned by Kimon, they were titled respectively *Battle of Theseus and the Athenians against the Amazons*, the *Fall of Troy*, and the *Battle of Marathon*. Kimon had brought back what were believed to be the bones of Theseus to Athens from Skyros; his father Miltiades, hero of Marathon, was duly emphasized in the painting of the battle; and the *Fall of Troy* may have been an oblique reference to Kimon's victories over the Persians. Late in life Aischylos, the founder of tragedy, retired to Gela, Sicily, where he died in circa 456 BC. Apparently, a tortoise dropped on his head by an eagle killed him, the bird having mistaken the bald shiny pate of the venerable poet for a stone. His tomb was inscribed with the epitaph he wrote for himself: 'Aischylos, Euphorion's son / of Athens, lies under this stone / dead in Gela among the white / wheat lands; a man at need / good in fight / witness the hallowed field of Marathon, / witness the long-haired Mede' (*Vita Aeschyli* 11). The tragedian made no reference to his writings, which numbered some seventy plus plays. Aischylos obviously prided himself more on his military services to Athens – with Marathon as the supreme day of his life – than on his dramatic art, preferring to be remembered for wielding the spear rather than the stylus. Incidentally, his fellow 'Marathon-fighters', *Marathônomáchai*, appear in the comedies of Aristophanes (e.g. *Acharnians* 181, *Clouds* 986) sixty-five years and more after the battle. So the memory of Marathon early acquired its mystique. In cold fact it was as Bannockburn, as Morgarten, as the defeat of the Armada, as Valmy, leaving the invader weakened only for a moment. Nonetheless, the Athenian victory has had quite an effect upon Western intellectual psyche. In the words of Samuel Johnson (1709–84), 'man is little to be envied, whose patriotism would not gain force upon the plain of Marathon' (*A Journey to the Western Islands of Scotland:* Icolmkill 1817: 230). The Utilitarian philosopher John Stuart Mill (1806–73) once postulated that 'the battle of Marathon, even as an event in English history, is more important than the battle of Hastings'. Sir Edward Shepherd Creasy (1812–78), who opens his *Decisive Battles of the World*, with Marathon thought that the battle 'secured for mankind the intellectual treasure of Athens, the growth of free institutions, the liberal enlightenment of the Western world, and the gradual ascendancy for many ages of the great principles of European civilisation' (1851: 31). Indeed, apart from being laced with explicit references to the barbarism and wickedness of non-Europeans, the significance of five of his fifteen chosen battle, in his puritanical Eurocentric mind, was that their outcome denied Asiatic peoples access to European soil.

48. Robert Graves 'The Persian Version' line 2.
49. Plutarch *Lykourgos* 21.
50. Hooker 1980: 60.
51. The tale is told first in the *Helen* of Euripides (lines 1465–74), produced in 412 BC, later being embellished, e.g. Apollodoros *Bibliotheca* 3.10.4, Pausanias 3.1.3.
52. Athenaios 4.139d-f.
53. Pausanias 3.19.2.
54. His name is certainly not Greek in origin, as shown by its ending *-nthos* (cf. famous place names such as *Korinthos*, Corinth, or *Tirynthos*, Tiryns).
55. Pausanias 3.19.3.
56. Onasander *Stratêgikos* 10.26. For a comprehensive list of pre-battle sacrifices see especially, Pritchett 1971: 114.

Chapter 4

1. Tyrtaios fr. 5 West.
2. E.g. ibid. frs. 10–12 West.
3. Strabo 8.4.10, cf. Plutarch *Moralia* 230D.4.
4. Aristotle *Politics* 1310b.
5. Pausanias 2.24.7. Some scholars (e.g. Kelly 1970, Hall 2006: 145–54) have argued that the battle of Hysiai was a pure fiction, an invention of the Argives.
6. Herodotos 6.127.3, cf. Aristotle *Athenaiôn politeia* 1.10. It should be noted that this *Athenaiôn politeia*, which was discovered on an Egyptian papyrus and published in 1890, is the only surviving example of the 158 constitutions of Greek *poleis* complied by, or more likely under the direction of, Aristotle. It provides a concise survey of Athenian constitutional history from mythical times down to 403/2 BC, and then gives a description of the Athenian constitution at the time of its compilation, i.e. late three-thirties.

The account is not always reliable and is rather slanted towards the oligarchic tradition of Athenian history. Modern scholarship is divided in its opinion about the authorship of this work. One group of scholars (e.g. Rhodes) believe the *Athenaiôn politeia* was composed by one of Aristotle's students, mainly so on stylistic differences and historical inaccuracies. The other group (e.g. Moore) believe that Aristotle did compose the *Athenaiôn politeia*, rejecting the arguments of the other camp. As there is no real possibility of resolving this issue, the *Athenaiôn politeia* will be attributed to Aristotle throughout this work for reasons of convenience and sanity.

7. Ephoros *apud* Strabo 8.3.33. According to Herodotos (1.94.1), the Lydians were the first to strike coins at the beginning of the seventh century BC. The earliest coins of the Aegean world are indeed from Lydia, dated to *c*. 625–600 BC, and made from electrum, the alloy of gold and silver panned from the rivers of Lydia. A busy and ingenious people, Herodotos also tells us 'that they invented the games of dice and knucklebones and ball and all other forms of game except dice, which the Lydians do not claim to have discovered' (1.94.1).
8. Herodotos 6.127.3.
9. Pausanias 6.22.2.
10. Ephoros *apud* Strabo 8.3.33, cf. 6.18.
11. The corselet is of beaten sheet bronze, with the edges at the hips, neck and armholes rolled forward over iron wire so as to strengthen them. The bronze is some two millimetres thick, which is thicker than the bell-shaped corselet we are usually familiar with. Also, for added strength, there is a narrow embossed ridge parallel to each armhole and two narrow embossed ridges parallel to the lower edge. Two further narrow embossed ridges run around the midriff in imitation of a belt. On the breastplate the ridges stop 1.6 millimetres short of the edge of the shoulders, indicating that the backplate overlapped the breastplate here. A hole in the middle of each shoulder piece on the backplate slotted over a corresponding iron pin on the breastplate. This is a simple fastening, but the fastenings at the sides display a high level of technical skill. The ridges on the backplate at the sides stop four centimetres short of the front edge, again a positive indication that the breastplate overlapped the backplate. The right side of the breastplate has two hinge tubes, which are pushed through slots cut in the backplate and a hinge pin is then inserted on the inside, thus protecting it from impairment. The left side of the breastplate has a small bronze loop on the inner face of the corselet near to the lower edge, which corresponds to a matching loop on the outer face of the backplate. These loops would have been fastened together by a length of bronze wire or a rawhide thong, and the resultant join would have been covered by the breastplate. To make the join firmer, the piece of rolled over bronze on the bottom edge of the backplate on this side is opened up and lacks the iron wire core for the last couple of centimetres, so that the bottom edge of the breastplate could slide snugly into the channel thus formed. This same channel technique is employed on the lower edge of the left armhole too. For the Argos cuirass, which is on display at the Argos Museum of Archaeology, see especially, Courbin 1957, Everson 2004: 88–9.
12. *Anthologia Palatina* 14.73 Drees.
13. Thucydides 2.75.3.
14. Herodotos 1.66.4. This engagement became known as the Battle of the Fetters, and a century later Herodotos was shown what was claimed to be the very leg irons in the temple of Athena Alea at Tegea. Some six centuries later, the Greek traveller Pausanias (8.47.2) was shown allegedly the very same chains. This was one of those splendid saga-like occasions that Herodotos took advantage of to entertain his audience with a Delphic oracle given to Sparta, a real classic in hexameter verse: 'Arcady? Great is the thing you ask. I will not grant it. / In Arcady are many men, acorn eaters, / And they will keep you out. Yet, for I am not grudging, / I will give you Tegea to dance in with stamping feet / And her fair plain to measure out with the line' (1.66.2).
15. Herodotos 1.68.6. Again, Herodotos takes the opportunity to entertain us with another Delphic oracle given to Sparta: 'In Arcady lies Tegea in the level plain, / Where under strong constraint two winds are blowing; / Smiting is there and counter-smiting, woe on woe; / This earth, the giver of life, holds Agamemnon's son. / Bring him home, and you will prevail over Tegea' (1.67.4).
16. The Peloponnese forms the southern extremity of the Balkans. Joined to the Greek mainland by an insignificant six-kilometre wide neck of land, the Isthmus of Corinth, now cut by the Corinth Canal, it was known to the ancients as the Island of Pelops, whilst its mediaeval name, Morea, derives from the fact that the mulberry tree flourished here.
17. Herodotos 5.72.3, cf. Aristotle *Athenaiôn politeia* 20.3.

18. Herodotos 5.39–42.

19. Ibid. 1.68.6.

20. Thucydides 1.19. An inscription (Fornara 132), probably belonging to the four-twenties, lists some haphazard-looking contributions to the Spartan war fund, and confirms that Sparta did indeed suffer from a lack of tribute reserves that the Athenians enjoyed.

21. Plutarch *Moralia* 859C–D.

22. Herodotos 6.108.2–3.

23. From 447 BC to 386 BC all but a couple of the twenty or so Boiotian *poleis* would be united in a federal state, a confederation run on oligarchic lines and dominated by Thebes. The foundation of this oligarchic federal state followed on the liberation of Boiotia from a decade of Athenian control and democratic intervention. Its dissolution would come as a result of the King's Peace of 387/6 BC. The terms of this peace treaty were drawn up by the stylus of a Persian king, Artaxerxes, but implemented with the sword of a Spartan king, Agesilaos.

24. Herodotos 1.82.3–6.

25. Hippias of Elis *FGrHist* 6F6 = Fornara 8A.

26. Herodotos 1.8–13.

27. Archilochos fr. 19.3 West.

28. It turns up next in the poems of Solon, after his settlement of Athens' socioeconomic troubles in 594 BC. In fr. 4 (West) we read that the lawgiver was less than happy with the path Athens was declining down; he attacks the greed shown by the high and mighty. His supporters, on the other hand, expected him to take the road to tyranny but as he claims in fr. 5 (West): 'I stood holding my shield over both, / and I did not allow either to triumph unjustly.' His refusal to seize power in Athens can best be summed up by taking a line from fr. 36 (West): 'These things I did by force, / fitting together might with right.' Tyranny came to Athens in the end, in spite of Solon, and was popular under the first Peisistratid tyrant, Peisistratos.

29. The tag 'axis of evil' was first used by George W. Bush in his State of the Union Address, 29 January 2002. Bush picked out Iran, Iraq and North Korea, and said 'states like these and their terrorist allies constitute an axis of evil, arming to threaten the peace of the world'. The same year, on 6 May, the future United States UN Ambassador, John R. Bolton, delivered a speech entitled 'Beyond the Axis of Evil', and in it he added three more nations with the already mentioned 'rogue states': Libya, Syria and Cuba.

30. In Greek: *basileios*, Pindar *Olympian Ode* 1.23, *Pythian Ode* 1.60, 3.70.

31. In Greek: *tyrannos*, ibid. *Pythian Ode* 3.85.

32. Hippias *FGrHist* 6F6. In Greek: *Turrhênoi* or *Tursênoi*, the Etruscans to you and me.

33. Herodotos 3.48.1.

34. Ibid. 3.46–47, 54–56.

35. Three great 'wonders' were constructed under Polykrates' authority: a one-kilometre tunnel through a mountain to provide its *astu* with an assured and defensible water supply, a large jetty to protect its port, and a magnificent temple for its patron deity Hera. Polykrates' buildings are among Aristotles' examples of public works of the tyrants.

36. Herodotos 3.39.2.

37. Ibid. 1.70.2–3, 3.47.

38. Ibid. 3.39.4.

39. Ibid. 3.56.2.

40. Plutarch *Moralia* 859D, cf. 236D, scholia to Aischines 2.77.

41. Herodotos 5.92a.1, Thucydides 1.18.1, Aristotle *Politics* 1312b, Plutarch *Moralia* 859D.

42. Herodotos 5.42.1, 48. Kleomenes actually reigned for well-nigh three decades.

43. Herodotos 5.55, Aristotle *Athenaiôn politeia* 58.1, *IG* i^3 131.

44. Herodotos 5.62.2, Thucydides 6.59.2, Aristotle *Athenaiôn politeia* 19.1.

45. Thucydides 6.56.2, 58.2.

46. Herodotos 5.63.1.

47. Aristotle *Athenaiôn politeia* 13.5.

48. Herodotos 5.66.2, Aristotle *Athenaiôn politeia* 20.1. Herodotos (5.70) is particularly vague on the democratic reforms of Kleisthenes and only mentions the increase in the number of tribes. Fortunately, Aristotle (*Athenaiôn politeia* 21.2–6) is more forthcoming. As far back as any Athenian

could remember the Athenians had been divided into four tribes to which membership was hereditary. The four tribes would continue to exist for religious and social purposes, but now Kleisthenes introduces a new division of all citizens (adult males only, of course) into ten artificial tribes.

49. Herodotos 5.71.1.
50. Thucydides 1.126.3–11.
51. Herodotos 5.73.1.
52. A century later the chorus of Old Men in Aristophanes' *Lysistrata*, when the women conspirators have seized the Acropolis of Athens, recall, by dramatic licence, their part in the matter: 'He seized our citadel, / But didn't go scot-free; / He left with just a cloak, for he'd / Given up his arms to me' (lines 274–7).
53. Herodotos 5.74.1.
54. Ibid. 5.75.1. Both men thereafter looked for excuses to stir up hostility against each other.
55. Ibid. 5.77.
56. Aelian *De natura animalium* 13.24.3.

Chapter 5

1. Herodotos 5.49.3, 97.1.
2. Ibid. 5.121.
3. Ibid. 6.29.1.
4. Ibid. 6.112.2. Athenian cavalry at Marathon are attested only in an unreliable passage of Pausanias (1.27.1), which is contradicted by Herodotos 9.21. See Appendix 5.
5. Turney-High 1971: 12.
6. In Greek: *hoplítês* (pl. *hopíltai*). It is wrongly believed by many scholars and commentators that it was from his shield that the hoplite derived his name. The noun *hoplon*, in the singular, is in fact extremely rare in Greek in the sense of 'hoplite shield', the one example I know of being found in Diodoros 15.44.3: 'called hoplites, from the shield they carried'. In truth, the common noun for hoplite shield is *aspis*. If, therefore, hoplites had been so called because of the shield they bore, they should be *aspistai*. Now, *hopla*, in the plural, is very frequent in the sense 'arms', and so it can be reasonably assumed that *hoplítai* means 'armed men'. Indeed, the noun *tà hopla* is often employed for *hoi hoplítai* (e.g. Thucydides 4.74.3). See especially, Lazenby/Whitehead 1996.
7. In Greek: *phalanges*, literally 'stacks' or 'rows' of men.
8. The problem of trying to estimate the value of hoplite equipment in modern monetary terms of ancient currencies is a difficult one. The best that can be done is to indicate contemporary wages and prices to give the reader some idea, a labourer earning between a *drachma* and a *drachma* and a half per day in the late fifth century BC. It has been estimated that the cost of a complete bronze panoply was in the order of seventy-five to a hundred *drachmae*, the equivalent of about three months' wages (Hanson 1995: 294–301), though this does seem to be top of the range. There is an Athenian decree, which probably dates from the late sixth century BC, listing regulations for an Athenian citizen colony on Samos. It contains the following ordinance: 'Each [colonist] is to provide arms himself to the value of thirty *drachmae*' (Sage 38).
9. Xenophon *Lakedaimoniôn politeia* 13.5.
10. Aischylos' tragedy *Persai* provides our earliest literary evidence for Xerxes' invasion, a war in which the citizen playwright was a participant. Late in life Aischylos retired to Gela, Sicily, where he died circa 456 BC.
11. In Greek: *dêmokratia*, from *dêmos* (the people) and *kratei* (rule).
12. Aristotle *Politics* 1291b21, cf. 1304a8, 1321a2, Pseudo-Xenophon *Athenaiôn politeia* 1.2. It has been argued (Strauss 1996) that the experience of naval service itself fostered attitudes that were essential to the functioning of democratic politics. Working as part of a large, well-drilled team, within which everyone had an equally vital part to play, might indeed seem likely to encourage egalitarian sentiments and close cooperation among Athenian citizens. Note that the Pseudo-Xenophon *Athenaiôn politeia*, as opposed to the Aristotelean one, has come down among the works of Xenophon, but scholars now agree that it cannot be his. The work, a hard-headed analysis arguing that Athenian imperial democracy, though immoral, is effective, appears to have been written when Xenophon was still a child. Its unknown author is referred to as the Old Oligarch, although his age at the time of writing has not been determined.

13. Herodotos 5.95, Xenophon *Memorabilia* 3.9.2, Aristophanes *Wasps* 19.
14. Bacchylides 13.6, Sophokles *Ajax* 576, Euripides *Phoenissae* 1127, Aristophanes *Knights* 858, cf. 849.
15. Cf. Plutarch *Moralia* 220A.2.
16. For pushing, *ôthismos*, with body and shield in the mêlée: Thucydides 4.43.3, 96, 6.70.2, Xenophon *Hellenika* 4.3.19, *Memorabilia* 3.1.8, Polyainos 2.3.4, 3.9.27, 4.3.8, Herodotos 7.225.1, 9.62.3, Aristophanes *Wasps* 1085. See also Theokritos 24.125 (Castor, the twin brother of Pollux, advises Herakles 'to put his shoulder behind his shield'). The actual nature of what this 'push' might have entailed has been much debated. For those modern commentators in support of the (orthodox) view that the *ôthismos* was a massed shoving match between two phalanxes, see Hanson 1989: 157–9, 174–5. For those modern commentators in support of the (unorthodox) view that the *ôthismos* ultimately led to one side being figuratively rather than literally 'pushed' off the battlefield, see van Wees 2004: 184–91.
17. Archilochos fr. 2 Edmonds, Herodotos 7.89, Xenophon *Peri Hippikes* 8.10, *Hellenika* 4.3.17, *Lakedaimoniôn politeia* 11.10, Polybios 3.115.9.
18. Ash wood (as frequently mentioned in the heroic verses of Homer and Tyrtaios) was the most frequently chosen because it naturally grows straight and cleaves easily. What is more, it is both tough and elastic, which means it has the capacity to absorb repeated shocks without communicating them to the handler's hand and of withstanding a good hard knock without splintering. All in all, ash has a suitable modulus of elasticity for spear work, with enough density and weight to be thrown too, and these properties combined made it an excellent choice for crafting a spear.
19. In the tight packed phalanx the spear could be held vertically by those not able to thrust with it, the blow being delivered by bringing the point of the butt-spike straight down. Its stout design and blunt, square shape made it an effective and efficient dispatcher, which was quite capable of piercing armour and crushing bones.
20. Thucydides 5.71.1.
21. *Contra* van Wees 2004: 185–7.
22. Thucydides 5.70.
23. Aristophanes *Birds* 364.
24. Aischylos *Seven Against Thebes* 268–70. By reading one of Alkman's fragments we quickly gain the impression that the singing of the *paean* inspired comradeship and forged group cohesion: 'At feast and in the companies of the men's mess, it is well beside them that sit at meat to strike up and sing the paean' (fr. 87).
25. Xenophon *Lakedaimoniôn politeia* 13.8, *Hellenika* 4.2.18, Plutarch *Lykourgos* 22.2.
26. Plutarch *Moralia* 220A.2, 241.
27. E.g. the Athenians were eight deep at Delion (Thucydides 4.94.1), and again at Peiraeus (Xenophon *Hellenika* 2.4.34); the Spartans at Mantineia were an average of eight deep (Thucydides 5.68.3), similarly Derkylidas, in Anatolia, 'ordered the *taxiarchoi* and the *lochagoi* to form up their men in a phalanx eight shields deep' (Xenophon *Hellenika* 3.2.16) as did Mnasippos with his men on Corcyra (ibid. 6.12.20), while at Leuktra the Spartans opted for a phalanx twelve deep (ibid. 6.4.11), and Agesilaos, in Arcadia the year after, deployed his phalanx with a depth of 'nine or ten shields deep' (ibid. 6.5.19); the Confederates finally agreed on a maximum of sixteen deep at the Nemea (ibid. 4.2.13, 18); the Syracusans before Syracuse had also formed up sixteen deep (Thucydides 6.67.2). However, the Thebans stood twenty-five deep at Delion (ibid. 4.93.4), the first recorded use of a very deep phalanx, and at Leuktra their phalanx was beefed-up so as to stand 'no less than fifty shields deep' (Xenophon *Hellenika* 6.4.12). Curiously, Xenophon (*Anabasis* 1.2.15) informs us that four deep was the 'customary order' of the Ten Thousand, though much later he has them 'fallen into a phalanx eight deep' (ibid. 7.1.23). Finally, for what it is worth, the late Hellenistic Asklepiodotos (*Taktika* 2.1, cf. 7) theorizes that the depth of a hoplite phalanx could be eight, ten, twelve or sixteen, although his ideal for the depth of the perfect phalanx, whatever that was, is sixteen.
28. Thucydides 4.43.3, 96.2, 6.70.2, Xenophon *Hellenika* 4.3.19, 6.4.14.
29. Tyrtaios fr. 19.18 West, Aischylos *Seven Against Thebes* 100, 103, 106, Euripides *Herakleidai* 832, *Supplicants* 699.
30. Aischylos *Agamemnon* 66–7 Vellacott.
31. Xenophon *Hellenika* 4.3.19.
32. Ibid. *Agesilaos* 2.12, 14.
33. Euripides *Supplicants* 699–701.

34. Thucydides 4.96.4, cf. Tyrtaios fr. 11.31–32 West, Euripides *Herakleidai* 836.
35. Aristophanes *Wasps* 1081–5.
36. Polyainos 2.3.2, cf. 3.9.27, 4.3.8.
37. Xenophon *Hellenika* 6.4.14.
38. Ibid. *Memorabilia* 3.1.18.
39. Thucydides 4.43.3.
40. Xenophon *Hellenika* 4.4.12, cf. *Hipparchikos* 2.7–9.
41. Defined by the Greeks as 'those tokens of victory, which we set up are named from the turning and pursuit of the enemy' (*Etymologicum Magnum* s.v. Tropaion = Sage 151), the *tropaion* was quite literally a 'turning point marker'.
42. Snodgrass 1967: 62.
43. For *stratêgoi* who fell in mêlée, look at: Herodotos 7.224 (Leonidas & Dithyrambos at Thermopylai), Thucydides 1.63.3 (Kallias at Potidaia), 2.79 (Xenophon, Hestiodoros & Phanamachos at Spartolos), 3.109.1 (Eurylochos at Olpai), 4.44.2 (Lykophron at Solygeia), 101.2 (Hippokrates at Delion), 5.10.8–11 (Brasidas & Kleon at Amphipolis), 74.3 (Laches & Nikostratos at First Mantineia), Xenophon *Hellenika* 1.3.6 (Hippokrates at Chalkedon), 6.4.13 (Kleombrotos at Leuktra), Plutarch *Pelopidas* 32.7 (Pelopidas at Kynoskephalai), Diodoros 15.87.1 (Epameinondas at Second Mantineia).
44. Euripides *Andromache* 695–6.
45. Herodotos 8.89.1.
46. Euripides *Medea* 250–1.
47. Tyrtaios fr. 10.25 West.
48. Xenophon *Anabasis* 2.5.33.
49. Cf. *Iliad* 13.657–8 Fagles, speared him 'between the genitals and the navel – hideous wound, / the worst the god of battles deals to wretched men'.
50. Hippokrates *Epidemics* 5.61, cf. 7.33.
51. Shakespeare *King Henry V* IV.i.141–2.
52. Xenophon *Agesilaos* 2.14.
53. Menander *Aspis* 71, 109.
54. *Correspondence de Napoléon Ier* 14.11813, a letter he wrote to Josephine after his pyrrhic victory at Eylau (8 February 1807). Apparently, after viewing the dreadful butchery left on the snowy field of Eylau, with tears in his eyes he was overheard to mutter: 'What a massacre! And for what result? A spectacle well formed to inspire princes with a love of peace, the horror of war ... A father who loses his children finds no charm in victory. When the heart speaks, even glory has no more charm in victory'. As Maréchal Ney described it in a hard-hitting idiom when he rode over the killing ground the following day: '*Quel massacre! Et tout cela pour rien!*'.
55. *Iliad* 11.606–7 Fagles.
56. Ibid. 2.732, 11.833.
57. Xenophon *Lakedaimoniôn politeia* 13.7.
58. Herodotos 7.9b.1.
59. See especially, Krentz 2002.
60. Thucydides 1.50.1, 2.90.5, 3.50.1, 5.32.1, 116.4, 7.29.3–5, 87.3.
61. Ibid. 1.1.2.
62. Ibid. 3.82.2.
63. Ibid. 4.28.4.
64. Ibid. 7.27.1,cf. Aristophanes *Lysistrata* 563.
65. Thucydides 7.29.1.
66. Ibid. 7.29.4.
67. Ibid. 7.29.5.
68. Ibid. 4.97–99. Few ancient battles were more renowned in antiquity than Delion, chiefly because Sokrates fought in it as a hoplite – he was to distinguish himself in the flight of the Athenian survivors – and Alkibiades, reputedly his young lover at the time, with the cavalry (Plato *Symposium* 220e7–221c1, Plutarch *Alkibiades* 4).
69. Euripides *Suppliants* 522–7: 'I'd not set war in motion / nor did I invade the land of Kadmos with these me. / But I judge it right to bury these lifeless corpses, / I bring no harm to your *polis* nor do I bring it man-destroying strife, / but I simply follow the custom of all Greeks. Where is the wrong in this?'

Chapter 6

1. Thucydides 1.94–95.1, Diodoros 11.44, Plutarch *Aristeides* 23.2–3, Justin 2.15.13–16, cf. Herodotos 5.104, 108–115.
2. Thucydides 1.94.1–5.
3. Plutarch *Aristeides* 23.2–3.
4. Thucydides 1.95.7.
5. Ibid. 1.128.3.
6. Ibid. 1.131.1–2. Not long after the repulse of Xerxes' invasion, Themistokles was ostracized and, hounded by both the Athenians and the Spartans, sought and received honoured asylum in the Persian empire. On the royal command of Artaxerxes, the son of his great enemy Xerxes, the revenues (fifty talents) of Magnesia were assigned to him for bread, those of Myos for condiments, and those of Lampsakos for wine (ibid. 1.138.5). Treachery? Enlightened self-interest? Take your choice. His fellow Athenians treated it as the former. In 459 BC he died aged sixty-five in comfortable retirement at Magnesia. It was said that his bones were secretly transferred to Attica (Plutarch *Themistokles* 32.3).
7. Thucydides 1.134.1–3.
8. Ibid. 1.95.7.
9. Herodotos 6.72.2.
10. Diodoros 11.48.2, 12.35.4.
11. Ibid. 11.50, Herodotos 8.3, Aristotle *Athenaiôn politeia* 23.2.
12. Herodotos 9.35.2.
13. Strabo 8.3.2.
14. Diodoros 11.54.1.
15. Herodotos 6.76–79.
16. Isokrates *Archidamos* §99.
17. Thucydides 1.101.
18. Diodoros 11.63.1–2, 4, Plutarch *Kimon* 16.6–7, Polyainos 1.41.3, Pausanias 1.29.8, 4.24.5–6.
19. Thucydides 1.103.1.
20. Diodoros 11.63–64.
21. In Greek: *teichomacheîn*, Thucydides 1.102.2. The reference is presumably to the successful outcome of their recent siege of Thasos. See also Herodotos 9.70.2, 102.2–4, the Athenians successfully storming the Persian fortified camps in the aftermaths of Plataia and Mykale.
22. Plutarch *Kimon* 16.
23. Ibid. 4.10.
24. Ibid. 16.8, Thucydides 1.102.1, Diodoros 11.64.2.
25. Thucydides 1.102.3.
26. Plutarch *Kimon* 16.8.
27. Thucydides 1.102.4.
28. Ibid. 1.103.3.
29. Ibid. 1.103.4.
30. Ibid. 1.105.1.
31. Ibid. 1.105.2.
32. Ibid. 1.105.5.
33. Ibid. 1.108.3.
34. Ibid. 1.108.4.
35. Ibid. 1.108.5.
36. Fornara 77, 78.
37. Thucydides 1.110.1.
38. Ibid. 1.110.4.
39. Pleistarchos had died in 458 BC, leaving the Agiadai throne to Pausanias' son.
40. Thucydides 1.40.5.
41. Ibid. 3.2.1.
42. During the bitter eighth-month siege, the Athenians, it was said by the Samian historian and tyrant Douris (b. *c.* 340 BC), had branded their Samian prisoners with the Attic owl, the Samians had retaliated with the *samaina*, a broad warship with a turned up beak invented under the patronage of Polykrates (Douris *FGrHist* 76F66, cf. Plutarch *Perikles* 26.4, where the author has reversed the role

and made the Samians brand with the owl). Not only that, the Samian captains and marines (but not the common oarsmen) were taken to the agora at Miletos and crucified there, and, having been left hanging for ten days, Perikles gave orders that they should be taken down and their heads broken with clubs and their bodies to remain exposed without proper attention (Douris *FGrHist* 76F67, cf. Plutarch *Perikles* 28.2–3, where the pro-Athenian author rejects the story out of hand and accuses the Samian historian of slander, finding confirmation of his charge in the silence of Thucydides, Ephoros and Aristotle).

43. Thucydides 1.67. Aegina was an old enemy, and Perikles was later to label it 'the eyesore of the Peiraeus' (Aristotle *Rhetoric* 3.10.7).
44. Aristotle *Politics* 1303b17.
45. Plato *Republic* 373a.
46. Ibid. 373d, e, cf. *Phaedo* 66c.
47. A figure of 10,000 has become a common estimate for the number of *metoikoi* in Athens, though at the height of Athens' prosperity there were probably around 15,000 in all. The only firm figure comes from Thucydides when he says (2.31.2) in 431 BC no fewer than 3,000 *metoikoi* served with the Athenian hoplite field force against Megara.
48. Thucydides 1.76.2.
49. Pseudo-Xenophon *Athenaiôn politeia* 2.2–8, 11–14.
50. Thucydides 6.18.3.
51. Here we are reminded of Hesiod's cautionary tale (*Works & Days* 202–11) of the hawk and the nightingale, a "fable for princes who themselves understand".
52. Thucydides 3.10.3.
53. Ibid. 2.41.1.
54. The first assessment was apparently 'fixed at 460 talents' (Thucydides 1.96.2).
55. Ibid. 1.99.3.
56. Diodoros (12.38.2, 40.1–2) gives two variants for the very large sum of money that had accumulated in the league coffers at Delos by this date, namely 8,000 and 10,000 talents.
57. According to Thucydides 'an average revenue of 600 talents of silver was drawn from the tribute of the allies' (2.13.3).
58. Xenophon *Oikonomikos* 8.8.
59. Aristophanes *Birds* 108.
60. Plutarch *Perikles* 11.4.
61. Sophokles fr. 927a Lloyd-Jones.
62. Thucydides 2.63.2.
63. In Aristophanes' *Knights* the chorus of horsemen echoes Thucydides' language: 'O *dêmos*, a fine empire is yours when all men fear you as a tyrant' (lines 111–14).
64. *IG* i 11, 12–13A = Fornara 71.23–4.
65. Fornara 102.7–8.
66. Thucydides 2.21.3, 54.263, 5.26.3, but see 2.17.162, an interesting exception.
67. Ibid. 1.118.3.
68. Ibid. 1.23–65.
69. Ibid. 1.23.5.
70. Ibid. 1.23.6.
71. Ibid. 1.31–55.
72. Ibid. 1.56–65.
73. Ibid. 1.23.6, 33.3, 86.5, 88, 118.2–3.
74. Ibid. 1.33.3.
75. Ibid. 1.88. The term 'Hellas' encompassed not only mainland Greece but the entire area of Greek settlement, which stretched from the Pillars of Herakles in the west to the far eastern end of the Black Sea.
76. Thucydides 1.89–117.
77. Ibid. 1.118.2.
78. E.g. Herodotos 3.48–49.
79. Thucydides 1.23.6.
80. Ibid. 1.44.2.

81. For this see, especially, Kagan 1969: 357–74, who offers a somewhat neutral study.
82. Cornford 1965.
83. Thucydides 1.36.2.
84. Ibid. 1.67.4, 139.1–140.5, cf. 144.2.
85. de Ste. Croix 1972: 50–63, cf. Hornblower 2002: 108–9.
86. Thucydides 1.139.3.
87. Aristophanes *Acharnians* 517.
88. Thucydides was a young man, probably in his late twenties, when the Peloponnesian War began. Immediately, he perceived that this would be a conflict on an unprecedented scale, and he decided to become its historian. How he went about his self-assigned task we do not know, for he says very little about his methods apart from a famous brief passage on the unreliability of eyewitness testimony (cf. Herodotos). 'My narrative', he writes, 'rests both on what I saw myself and on the reports of others, after careful research aiming at the greatest possible accuracy in each case . . . my conclusions have been reached with effort because eyewitnesses disagree about the same occurrence, from imperfect memory or from bias' (1.22). He never names his informants, and on only two occasions does the author say that he was a direct participant (4.104–7, 5.26). Basically, everything – the debates in the assembly, the embassies, the behind-the-scenes-manoeuvres, the battles – was probably reconstructed from what he was told or had witnessed. This unfinished masterpiece, *History of the Peloponnesian War*, is our most important single source for the Peloponnesian War. Thucydides obviously was an eyewitness to many of the events and personalities he describes, or at least was able to gain information from reliable sources. Our problem in seeing the war through his eyes (until 411 BC, at any rate, when his account comes to an abrupt end halfway through a sentence amid the events of that year) is certainly not one of having to eliminate crude bias in favour of his own side and against the enemy, but the more subtle difficulty of escaping from his densely written narrative, which does not furnish us with alternative accounts. It is therefore sometimes easy to mistake his overall interpretation of events and their significance as an authoritative narrative. The speeches, of which there are 141 presented both in direct and indirect discourse, are an especial problem. Thucydides says (1.22.1) he wrote what he could remember of the speeches that he heard, but also wrote what seems likely to have been said on an occasion; you might imagine the problems therefore.
89. Thucydides 1.120.
90. Ibid. 1.10.2.
91. Ibid. 1.69–71.
92. Ibid. 2.9.4, 13.6–9, 31.2, cf. Diodoros 12.40.4, who gives the same total but slightly different figures of 12,000 citizen hoplites of military age and 17,000 young, old and *metoikos* hoplites.
93. Aristophanes *Wasps* 709.
94. Thucydides 6.8.1.

Chapter 7
1. Thucydides 2.39.1.
2. Ibid. 4.33.2.
3. Herodotos 7.211.3, 9.63.2.
4. Xenophon *Lakedaimoniôn politeia* 13.5.
5. Aristophanes *Clouds* 960–86, Thucydides 1.121.4, 123.1, Plato *Laches* 179c, Xenophon *Memorabilia* 1.2.4, 3.5.3, 9–11, 22, Isokrates *Areopagitikos* §45.
6. Pseudo-Xenophon *Athenaiôn politeia* 1.3, cf. Xenophon *Memorabilia* 2.6.26. The phrase *oi kaloi k'agathoi*, literally 'the best and good', referred to Greek elites, while *agathoi* also had the meaning of 'brave men'. Similarly, the word *kalos* means both 'beautiful' and 'useful'.
7. Plato *Gorgias* 515e, cf. *Protagoras* 324b.
8. Cf. Aristophanes *Clouds* 961–83, Xenophon *Memorabilia* 4.4.15–17.
9. Aristophanes *Wasps* 474–6, cf. 1069–70, *Birds* 1281–3, Lysias 16.18. *Wasps* was written and performed at a time when bellicose and anti-Spartan feelings were running high in Athens. The important Athenian colony of Amphipolis had not long been captured by Brasidas, and recent news from the northern theatre informed the Athenians that Skione had just revolted from their empire and promptly gone over to him (Thucydides 4.102–6, 120.1).
10. Aristophanes *Wasps* 1060–1101, cf. 678, 684–5, 709–11.

11. Ibid. 1168, 1196–1204.
12. Xenophon *Anabasis* 5.3.9–10.
13. Ibid. *Kynegetikos* 12, *Kyroupaideia* 1.2.10, 6.28–29, 39–41, 7.5.62–64, cf. Plato *Euthydemos* 290b–d.
14. Xenophon *Kynegetikos* 1.18, cf. *Kyroupaideia* 8.1.34–36, 6.10.
15. Ibid. *Kynegetikos* 2.1
16. Ibid. 12.1.
17. Ibid. 12.2–5, cf. *Lakedaimoniôn politeia* 4.7, Aristotle *Politics* 1303b13.
18. Xenophon *Kynegetikos* 1.2.10.
19. Herodotos 1.136.
20. Xenophon *Anabasis* 1.9.5–6, cf. 2.7.
21. Strabo 15.3.7.
22. Xenophon *Memorabilia* 3.12.4.
23. Ibid. 3.12.5
24. Aristotle *Politics* 1338b 27–30.
25. Plutarch *Agesilaos* 26.4, *Moralia* 214A.72, also found in Polyainos 2.17.
26. Plutarch *Lykourgos* 30.6, cf. *Moralia* 217E.6.
27. Xenophon *Hellenika* 6.4.28.
28. Ibid. 6.1.5.
29. Thucydides 6.72.3–4.
30. Cicero *Philippics* 5.2.5.
31. Xenophon *Hellenika* 7.4.34.
32. Polybios 5.91.4–7, cf. 4.59.2, 74.6, 5.30.6.
33. Herodotos 9.71.3–4.
34. Plutarch *Agesilaos* 34.8.
35. Xenophon *Memorabilia* 3.12.5.
36. Ibid. *Oikonomikos* 5.4, 5, cf. 14.
37. Plato *Republic* 556d.
38. Aristotle *Politics* 1319a22–24.
39. This was certainly the firm belief of later Roman writers. The elder Cato, for instance, wrote: 'From farmers the bravest men and the strongest soldiers are born' (*On Agriculture* preface 4). Likewise Vegetius: 'The rural peasantry are the best equipped for military service' (1.3).
40. Xenophon *Kyroupaideia* 8.1.37–39.
41. Ibid. 2.3.17–20. 'Unless one has trained beforehand through mock battles', wrote Roger of Hovedon, 'the art of war will not be possessed when it is necessary to put it into practice' (*Chronica* 2.166).
42. Josephus *Bellum Iudaiacum* 3.76.
43. Xenophon *Kyroupaideia* 2.1.16.
44. Thucydides 2.39.1.
45. Xenophon *Hellenika* 5.3.17.
46. Herodotos 6.11–12.
47. Xenophon *Anabasis* 1.2.17–18.
48. Ibid. 1.8.19–20, cf. Diodoros 14.24.2–3. Persia was the last major world empire to deploy chariots on the field of battle. They had reinvented the chariot by affixing scythes onto the axle ends, a lethal weapon against infantry, if caught off guard of course. Anyway, these slicing machines were designed to cut holes in the enemy battleline. The two horses were blinkered and driven by a single charioteer.
49. Xenophon *Anabasis* 6.5.25, 27.
50. E.g. ibid. 1.5.13, 4.3.20–34, 8.9–13, 6.5.9–11.
51. Ibid. 6.6.35.
52. The training programme instituted by Philip II of Macedon for his new model army included forced marches, complete with arms, rations and equipment (Polyainos 4.2.10, cf. Frontinus *Strategemata* 4.1.6). In the Roman army, according to Vegetius, raw recruits were given frequent practice in carrying loads up to sixty Roman pounds (19.8 kilograms) with which they marched along at a brisk military pace, for 'on strenuous campaigns they will be faced with the necessity of carrying their rations as other arms' (1.19, cf. Josephus *Bellum Iudaiacum* 3.95). And such matters do not change. During their Green Beret course at Lympstone, Royal Marine recruits undergo timed thirty-kilometre route marches over quaggy Dartmoor in full fighting order. Such 'laborious training', for example, enabled Royal Marine

Commandos to 'yomp' across the rock and peat of East Falkland (Falkland Islands/Malvinas) packing individual loads of thirty-six to forty-six kilograms weight and still be ready and able to slip into the trial of combat afterward. On the contrary it has been maintained how stupid it is when a soldier drags about with him all sorts of 'useless articles'. He is needlessly encumbered with them. It fatigues him unnecessarily and if he carts such a weight about with him he cannot easily fight, or so this school of thought hypothesises. In the light of cold reality, of course, individual loads for fighting operations must be a compromise between two opposing principles: minimum weight and maximum self-reliance.

53. Xenophon *Hellenika* 6.1.6.
54. Ibid. *Kyroupaideia* 2.3.14.
55. Athenaios, quoting from Hermippos' lost *Lawgivers*, states that 'regular courses of instruction in *hoplomachia* were first instituted in Mantineia' (4.154d), while Ephoros (*FGrHist* 70F54) suggests that *hoplomachia* had its origins in that Arcadian *polis* sometime in the mid sixth century BC. Polybios, an Arcadian himself, writing on the same subject, stresses the vital importance of music and dancing for the education of Arcadian youth. 'For the practice of music,' writes Polybios, 'I mean real music, is beneficial to all men, but to the Arcadians it is a necessity'. He then continues by explaining that Arcadian men up to the age of thirty were not only under an obligation regularly to study music, but also to practise 'military parades to the music of the flute and perfect themselves in dances and give annual performances in theatres, all under state supervision and at public expense' (4.20.4–12). It seems, on the basis of Polybios' evidence at least, that the martial pursuit of *hoplomachia* was taken very seriously by his fellow Arcadians.
56. Plato *Laches* 182a–d, cf. Aristotle *Athenaiôn politeia* 42.3 for the later ephebic training at Peiraeus.
57. Xenophon *Hellenika* 6.5.23, cf. 7.5.19.
58. Plutarch *Moralia* 192C, cf. D, 788A, Nepos *Epameinondas* 2.4, 5.
59. Xenophon *Anabasis* 6.1.11.
60. Athenaios 14.631d, cf. Pausanias 8.15.3. Demeter the earth-mother goddess who spent part of each year underground to be with her daughter Persephone, the very reluctant bride of Hades, stood for the powers of fertility, animal and vegetable as well as human.
61. Athenaios 14.628f.
62. Plato *Republic* 410a–e.
63. Athenaios 14.630d–631c.
64. Plato *Laws* 815a.
65. Xenophon *Hellenika* 3.4.16, cf. *Agesilaos* 1.25, *Hipparchikos* 1.26.
66. Ibid. *Lakedaimoniôn politeia* 5.8–9, 12.5–6, cf. *Kyroupaideia* 1.6.17.
67. Herodotos 7.208.2–3.
68. Plutarch *Pelopidas* 15.1.
69. Xenophon *Hellenika* 7.1.24–25.
70. Ibid. 7.4.22–25.
71. Thucydides 5.65.2, cf. 59.2–3, Sun Tzu 7.33.
72. Walker 1985: 33.
73. Sun Tzu 9.44.
74. Herodotos 6.12.2–3.

Chapter 8

1. Thucydides 5.28.2.
2. The years of invasion were 431 BC, 430 BC, 428 BC, 427 BC, 425 BC. In 429 BC there was no invasion – the siege of Plataia took precedence (Thucydides 2.71.1) – but the devastating plague, possibly a form of typhus and definitely a product of invasion conditions, was doing more harm than the Spartans ever could. Indeed, the Athenians' first reaction was to accuse the Spartans of poisoning their wells. Again, in 426 BC there was no invasion, the invasion force being turned back by earthquakes at the Isthmus of Corinth (ibid. 3.89.1).
3. Thucydides 2.14.2, Aristophanes *Acharnians* 32–3, *Knights* 40–3, *Peace* 1320–8, *Farmers* frs. 162, 163 Dindorf, *Islands* fr. 344 Dindorf.
4. Thucydides 2.16.2.
5. The effect of the plague on the Athenian moral is incalculable; what is known is that by the time it had recurred in 427 BC it had caused the total loss of 4,400 hoplites, 300 horsemen, and an untold number

of *thêtes*. Thucydides held that 'nothing else did the Athenians so much harm or reduced their strength for war' (3.87), the plague wiping out perhaps one-third of Athens' population. The Athenians, crowded into the *astu* as a result of Perikles' policy, must have been particularly vulnerable to the contagion.

6. At Delion, Thebes had given the first dim indications of the brutal power of its phalanx when deployed really deep.

7. Thucydides 4.78.1, 80.4, Diodoros 12.67.1, 3, 5.

8. Among the apophthegms attributed to Spartan women, the first is credited to Argileonis (Plutarch *Moralia* 240C).

9. Thucydides 4.81.3. Brasidas had first appeared upon the Spartan stage in 431 BC, when he rescued the perioikic settlement of Methone (now Méthoni) in Messenia from an Athenian assault by heading a charge of one hundred men directly through the surprised raiders to reinforce the hard-pressed defenders. This act of a derring-do earned for him the first official vote of thanks to a Spartiate in this war (ibid. 2.25.3), as well election to ephorate for the year 431/30 BC (Xenophon *Hellenika* 2.3.10). In 429 BC he was one of the three advisers, *sumboúloi*, sent to put some spine into Knemos before the second naval engagement against Phormio in the Gulf of Corinth (Thucydides 2.85.1, cf. 93.1), and in 427 BC he was an adviser to Alkidas in the expedition to Corcyra (ibid. 3.69.1, cf. 79.3). A *triêrarchos* at Pylos in 425 BC, he was to be severely wounded in action leading an amphibious assault against Demosthenes' shoreline fortification (ibid. 4.11.4–12.1, Diodoros 12.62.1–5).

10. The exceedingly sorry picture cut by Alkidas in Thucydides' narrative (3.32.1–2) is perhaps to be modified a little in the light of an inscribed marble stela found to the south of Sparta. The text (Fornara 132) gives a list of contributions 'for the war' from a number of sources, both private and public. Among the states named are Ephesos and Melos. This inscription possibly belongs to 427 BC, the year of Alkidas' expedition, and if it does, it both gives an insight into Spartans' method of getting money to carry on the conflict (since they had no financial reserves and did not yet exact tribute from their allies) and provides some small justification for Alkidas' poor time on his eastward voyage. His late arrival was perhaps due to a stop at Melos, and his making for Ephesos after Lesbos would be explained by the funds that had been promised from that quarter. Alternative dates for this marble stele are given as *c.* 405 BC or 396/5 BC.

11. When he addressed the Akanthians, he vowed to respect their autonomy, urged them to help liberate themselves and Hellas from Athens, and made veiled threats of what their grape harvest would suffer if they refused (Thucydides 4.85–87).

12. Akanthos, today's Ierissós on the south-eastern coast of the Chalkidike, is not far from the canal Xerxes had dug across the neck of land connecting the Mount Athos peninsula to the Chalkidike so as to avoid the danger of the violent storms prevalent off Mount Athos. During the digging of the canal, which took some three years to complete, the citizens of Akanthos willingly helped the Persian effort and offered hospitality to the Persian officials overseeing the project. Xerxes honoured the Akanthians and 'sent them as a present a Median dress' (Herodotos 7.116). It was at Akanthos that Xerxes separated from his fleet and joined his land force for the march south (ibid. 7.121.1).

13. Thucydides 4.88.2. Stagiros, today's Stágira, is the hometown of Aristotle (b. 384 BC), hence his later epithet *o Stageiritês*, the Stagirite. He trekked south to Athens aged eighteen to study for the subsequent twenty years at Plato's Academy.

14. Thucydides 4.108.3.

15. Ibid. 3.92.4.

16. E.g. the colony was to serve as Brasidas' staging post on his march to Thrace in 424 BC (ibid. 4.78.1), and by reinforcements sent to him in 422 BC (ibid. 5.12.1). Clearly, then, the colony looks forward to the possibility of sending an expeditionary force overland to Thrace.

17. Before its capture, Eukles, the Athenian commander of the garrison, sent to nearby Eïon, asking Thucydides, the historian, who as one of the ten *stratêgoi* for the year commanded the Athenian fleet in the Thraceward region, to come to the rescue. The trouble is, Thucydides was not at Eïon, less than five kilometres away at the mouth of the Strymon, but at Thasos, about half-day's sail away. Thucydides as he himself reports it: 'Thucydides at once set sail with seven triremes, which he had with him, in order, if possible, to reach Amphipolis in time to prevent its capitulation, or in any case to save Eïon' (4.104.5). He was, in fact, too late to save Amphipolis, but he did prevent the capture of Eïon. Thucydides was held responsible by his angry countrymen, brought to trial and sent into an exile that lasted for twenty years. Ancient biographers of Thucydides report that Kleon was his accuser and

that the charge was *prodosia*, treason, which, like that other favourite peculation, was an accusation often levelled against unsuccessful *stratêgoi*. Although Thucydides never directly discusses the sentence passed on him, and chooses instead an apparently objective description of the events he was involved in, his bare narrative is a most effective defence. It gives no answer to the key question – likely to have been asked by the court – namely, why was he at Thasos rather than Eïon. If we can be selfish, however, his punishment was in all probability a blessing for future generations for perhaps without his banishment he might not have written his history. It is characteristic of him that he reports this fact briefly and without comment, except to add that he was in a better position thereafter to obtain information from both sides. Thucydides' father was Oloros, a name probably Thracian and princely, and his father's ancestors certainly had property in Thrace, which enabled him to go on with his work at leisure. His exile, he claims (5.26.5), gave him opportunities for appreciating the point of view of each of the combatants. He lived through the entire war, was apparently permitted to return to Athens when it ended, and died not many years later.

18. Thucydides 4.108.7.
19. Unlike us moderns, the ancient Greeks did not sign treaties but swore them, in the name of the gods who would act as their guarantors. Thus to break a peace treaty or a treaty of alliance was an act of sacrilege liable to be punished by or in the name of the god or gods directly invoked.
20. Thucydides 5.11.1, cf. 4.102.3, 4.
21. Ibid. 5.26.2.
22. The term *akoniti* was customarily applied to wrestling, boxing and the *pankration* (a form of all-in-no-holds-barred wrestling) when a victor overthrew his opponent so swiftly that the bout had failed to raise the dust of the ring, in other words, a 'dustless' win was a victory won without a fight or competition.
23. Thucydides 6.16.6.
24. On the eve of the departure of the great armada for Sicily, the Athenians awoke one summer morning to find the Hermae (square pillars of stone bearing the head and the distinctive erect phallus of the god Hermes, protector of voyagers among other things) across Athens defaced and castrated (ibid. 6.27.1–2) and Alkibiades was implicated. As reputed ringleader of the Herm-Choppers, *Hermokopidai*, whose impious vandalism had thrown the city into such a state of frenzy, the *dêmos* issued orders recalling Alkibiades to Athens. His enemies brought forward fresh indictments, including profanation of the Eleusian Mysteries when Alkibiades and others of his aristocratic circle had donned mock-sacral garments and had amused themselves by presiding over sham initiations in irreverence of the grain-goddess Demeter and her daughter Persephone. These offences were cited not merely as outrages against the gods, meriting death on that account alone, but as evidence of their perpetrators' utter contempt for democracy itself. They were the acts of a revolutionary, a would-be tyrant who set himself above all law. Eleusis, the venue for the Mysteries, came to symbolize not only the death and resurrection of nature but also humankind's eternal preoccupation with a future life, its hope for the immortality of the soul. At a much later date, its mysteries and initiation rites attracted the most exalted foreigners: Cicero, Hadrian, Antonius Pius, Marcus Aurelius, Iulian the Apostate.
25. Plutarch *Alcibiades* 22.2.
26. Xenophon *Memorabilia* 1.2.24.
27. Thucydides 2.65.7.
28. Pausanias 10.11.4.
29. Thucydides 8.1.1.
30. Ibid. 8.1.3.
31. Ibid. 3.1–50.
32. Ibid. 3.36.6.
33. In *Wasps* (422 BC), Aristophanes has the household slave Xanthias ask the audience what they think of his master Philokleon ('in love with Kleon'), only to reject their answers one by one except for that which says that his master is 'addicted to serving on juries' (*Wasps* 87). Here Aristophanes is attacking Kleon's reliance upon the Athenian judicial system for political support. In *Knights* (424 BC), Aristophanes parodies Kleon as a slave from Paphlagonia in Anatolia. In essence, this play is nothing more than a prejudiced attack by the playwright upon Kleon, an unsavoury individual who is 'an arrant rogue, the incarnation of calumny', a sticky politician 'in love with the *dêmos*' (*philodêmos*, a term first used by Aristophanes). As well as personal, Aristophanes' hostility to Kleon was political too, because

in 426 BC Kleon had prosecuted him for slandering Athens in the presence of foreigners with his play *Babylonians*, and he had been convicted. Aristophanes had dropped broad hints in *Acharnians* (425 BC) that he would shortly take his revenge (lines 300–1, cf. 502–6), and he now does so. Kleon was again infuriated beyond measure by *Knights*, and he threatened to prosecute Aristophanes for falsely pretending to be an Athenian citizen. This accusation probably never came to trial; a passage in *Wasps* seems to suggest that Aristophanes, perhaps fearing Kleon's influence over the juries, those 'Comrades of the Order of the Three Obols' (*fráteres trióbólou*, *Knights* 255), offered some sort of apology.

34. Aristotle *Athenaiôn politeia* 28.3.
35. Thucydides 3.37.
36. Ibid. 6.89, a jolly good summary of Alkibiades' political views.
37. Ibid. 8.53.
38. Ibid. 8.65–66.
39. Ibid. 8.97.2.
40. Aristotle *Athenaiôn politeia* 33.2.
41. See Appendix 4.
42. In Greek: *tò rhuppapaî*, Aristophanes *Wasps* 909. Sometimes the oarsmen would join in a rhythmic cry, repeating it over and over, to mark time. The cries *O ôpóp, O ôpóp* and *rhuppapaî*, which mimic the rhythm of the oar stroke, are both attested for Athenian crews (ibid. *Frogs* 208, 1073, cf. 180, *Birds* 1395).
43. Aristotle *Athenaiôn politeia* 34.1.
44. Thucydides 8.24.4.
45. Ibid. 1.18.1.
46. Ibid. 3.82–83 (Corcyra), 5.84–116 (Melos).
47. Ibid. 6.6.2, 10.1, 18.1.
48. Ibid. 8.26.1.
49. Ibid. 8.2.4, cf. Diodoros 11.50.
50. There is a telling anecdote from Thucydides (6.104.3) where the Athenian *stratêgos* Nikias mistook a Spartan fleet sailing to Sicily for a private raiding party.
51. During the Peloponnesian War an innovative use of seapower was the establishment of a permanent fortified base (*epiteichismos*, 'to-plant-a-fortification-in-enemy-territory') on or off the enemy's seaboard from which troops could damage, harass, and discourage and demoralize the enemy. Such bases were planted by the Athenians at Pylos (425 BC), a headland on the west coast of Messenia, and on Kythera (424 BC), the island just off the south-eastern tip of Lakedaimon (Thucydides 4.3–5, 7.26, cf. 4.53–54). Demaratos, the ex-king of Sparta who had returned to Greece as a highly valued member of Xerxes' coterie, once wisely advised the Great King to send a strong fleet to the island of Kythera, a base from which he will be able to harry the Spartan's own homeland (Herodotos 7.235). It looks as if the Athenians were carrying out at last Demaratos' policy, for from the fortified base they established on the island they made a number of raids on coastal towns such as Asine and Helos. Indeed, the establishment of these Athenian strongholds within enemy territory did stir up trouble for the Spartans as they led to an increase in helot unrest. Yet such a scheme does not appear to be a component of the Periklean strategy, and it was in fact the Corinthians who first advocated the use of *epiteichismoi* in 432 BC (Thucydides 1.122.1). In truth, Perikles only envisages the use of *epiteichismoi* as a countermove if the Spartans attempted to establish a base in Attica (ibid. 1.142.2–4), as they eventually did, on Alkibiades' recommendation, at Dekeleia on Mount Parnes in north-eastern Attica (413 BC). Visible from the walls of Athens, this 'fort was built to threaten and control the plain and the richest parts of the *chôra*' (ibid. 7.19.2). The position was well chosen. For, in contrast to their annual ineffective invasions of Attica, the raids made by the Spartans and their allies were now unremitting. Occupied year-round, Dekeleia became the *epiteichismos par excellence* (Andokides 1.101, Lysias 14.30, Isokrates *De Bigis* §10, Oxyrhynchos Historian 12.3). 'Instead of a *polis* Athens became a garrisoned fortress' (Thucydides 7.28.1). Day and night the Athenians were forced to man their walls, winter and summer alike, were robbed of all Attica – so much so that they were no longer able to extract the silver-bearing lead at Laureion in south-east Attica – and were cut off from one of their main supply lines, the overland route to Euboia. Their cavalry went out daily to brush with the Lakedaimonians so as to keep them at bay, tiring the horsemen and laming the horses. Their slaves could desert, and their dissidents could think of revolution. It must have seemed to the hard-pressed Athenians that the tide of war had turned against them.

52. At Cape Sounion, a promontory much feared by sailors, stood a temple dedicated to Poseidon. A few crystalline marble columns still stand on an almost intact base, on a point of a rocky spearhead, presenting a very photogenic first plan on a magnificent panoramic background. From this height the 'wine dark' Aegean is beautiful, whether reflecting the midday ardour or the argent rays of the moon. Sounion is therefore the goal of day and night excursions for swarms of tourists. Unfortunately, most of them in their haste to be enchanted by the sacred architecture miss the indestructible heap of military architecture that once sealed off the promontory on its landward side.
53. Thucydides 8.1.2, 3.
54. Ibid. 8.46.4.
55. Ibid. 8.45.2, 46.5.
56. Ibid. 8.106.2.
57. Diodoros 13.39.5.
58. Thucydides 6.15.4.
59. Xenophon *Hellenika* 1.1.23.
60. Plutarch *Alkibiades* 28.6.
61. For foreigners listed among the crews of Athenian triremes, e.g. *IG* i³ 1032, Thucydides 7.63.3. For oarsmen hired from anywhere in Greece, e.g. Thucydides 1.31.1 (by Corinth), Isokrates *On the Peace* §79 (by Athens).
62. Thucydides 8.29, 45.2, Xenophon *Hellenika* 1.5.4, 7, Plutarch *Alkibiades* 35.4. According to Thucydides 'the crews of the ships were all paid at the same rate' (3.17.4); before 413 BC this rate was paid at a *drachma* a day (6.31.3), but halved to three *oboloi* in the austere days in the aftermath of the Sicilian expedition (8.45.2). Normally, as Thucydides points out, only half the rate of a *drachma* a day was actually payable to Athenian crews while on active service; the rest became due when the ship was paid off in Peiraeus (8.45.2).
63. Aristophanes *Frogs* 693, cf. Fornara 164A, Xenophon *Hellenika* 1.6.24.
64. Xenophon *Hellenika* 1.6.31. For the tactical manoeuvres *diekplous* and the *periplous*, see Appendix 9.
65. Diodoros 13.98.5.
66. Cf. Xenophon *Hellenika* 1.6.34, the Spartans nine out of their own ten ships and more than sixty of their allies', which near enough tallies with Diodoros' figure.
67. Xenophon *Hellenika* 1.6.15.
68. Ibid. 1.6.2.
69. Plutarch *Lysandros* 8.4.
70. Ibid. 4.2.
71. Xenophon *Hellenika* 1.5.6.
72. Ibid. 1.5.14, cf. Diodoros 13.71.4, who says twenty-two Athenian triremes.
73. Plutarch *Lysandros* 6.4.
74. Xenophon *Hellenika* 1.6.7.
75. The *nauarchos* enjoyed the same powers of a king on campaign, but was limited to a single year in office with no second term.
76. Xenophon *Hellenika* 2.1.22–28. Notable for mobility rather than capaciousness, little storage space was available on a tightly packed trireme. A crew of 200 needed an estimated 300 kilograms of grain and 500 litres of water per day, not to mention 'wineskins and oar-loops and jars, or garlic and olives and nets of onions, garlands and anchovies and flute girls and black eyes' (Aristophanes *Acharnians* 550–2), and there was no storage space for more than two or three days' supply. Nor was there enough space for more than a part of the crew to sleep on deck. A trireme therefore normally made land at noon for a repast, and again at dusk. Moreover, finding a location that could offer provisions for thousands of empty-bellied and dry-throated jack-tars was hard, and crews might have to wander several kilometres from their landing places to gather enough food, reach a satisfactory spring, or get to a local market willing to do business with outsiders. For the trireme, see especially Morrison/Coates 2000: 94–9, 100–20, 131–3, 210, 227–30.
77. Xenophon *Hellenika* 2.1.31–32, Plutarch *Lysandros* 13.1, *Alkibiades* 37.4, Pausanias 9.32.9, Frontinus *Strategemata* 2.1.18. It was said the Dioskouri fought alongside the Spartans at Aigospotamoi, and victors afterwards hung up two golden stars in their honour at Delphi, but these fell down and disappeared shortly before the fatal battle of Leuktra (Cicero *De divinatione* 1.34.75, 2.32.68).

78. There are slight discrepancies between our sources as to how many Athenian triremes escaped the débâcle, with figures varying from none (Frontinus *Strategemata* 2.1.18) to twelve (Lysias 21.11). Xenophon's figures (*Hellenika* 2.1.28) are as good as any.

79. What we generally translate as overreaching arrogance, the Greeks called *hubris*, a peculiarly Greek concept meaning unprovoked aggression not motivated by a desire for material gain but by a wish to humiliate the victim and deprive him of *timê*, honour.

80. Xenophon *Hellenika* 2.2.9–11.

81. Plutarch *Lysandros* 14.4.

82. Xenophon *Hellenika* 2.2.20.

83. Ibid. 2.3.14, Aristotle *Athenaiôn politeia* 37.2.

84. Xenophon *Hellenika* 2.3.31.

85. Ibid. 2.3.2.

86. Ibid. 2.3.11.

87. Ibid. 2.3.18.

88. Ibid. 2.3.21.

89. Ibid. 2.3.15–56.

90. Ibid. 2.4.10–19.

91. Ibid. 2.4.24, 25.

92. Cf. ibid. *Anabasis* 3.3.19, 4.47–49, 4.7.24, *Oikonomikos* 11.14–18. Xenophon's sons Gryllos and Diodoros, who were both trained and educated at Sparta, fought as members of the Athenian cavalry corps at Mantineia in 362 BC (Pausanias 1.3.4, Diogenes Laertius 2.54–55).

93. Xenophon *Hellenika* 1.2.7, 3.6.

94. Ibid. 1.6.24.

95. Ibid. 2.4.8, cf. 26.

96. For Xenophon's political views, see Anderson 1974: 40–5.

97. It must be stressed that Xenophon was not exiled from Athens until after his adventures with the Ten Thousand (Plutarch *Moralia* 603B, cf. Diogenes Laertius 2.53, 58, Dio Chrysostomus *Orations* 8.1, Pausanias 5.6.5). Modern commentators generally fall into two camps when discussing the actual date of his exile: either in 399 BC on a charge of medisim (cf. Xenophon *Anabasis* 3.1.5, see, for example, Anderson, 1974: 149); or in 394 BC, after Koroneia, on a charge of laconism (cf. Xenophon *Agesilaos*, see, for example, Rahn 1981).

98. Xenophon *Hellenika* 2.4.28–34.

99. Ibid. 2.4.33.

100. Thucydides 2.34.5.

101. *IG* ii 11678. Reading the inscription left to right: THIBRAKHOS POLEMARCHOS KHAIRON POLEMARCHOS. It was written in retrograde so that a traveller making his or her way to the Dipylon Gate could read it with ease as they passed by the tomb.

102. The original marble slab with its fragmentary inscription is now housed in the Oberländer Museum, which is nearby.

103. For a detailed discussion of the excavation of the tomb, see Hodkinson 2000: 249–59.

104. To paraphrase Rupert Brooke's 'Soldier' lines 2–3.

105. In Greek: *hireës*, viz. men of outstanding merit, not priests or young ones, as deemed by the survivors of the battle. See especially, Hodkinson 2000: 256–9.

106. Herodotos 9.85.1–2, cf. 71.2–72.1.

107. Plutarch *Agesilaos* 40.3.

108. Lysias *Epitaphios* §63, emphasis mine.

Chapter 9

1. See Appendix 3.

2. The term *mora* literally means 'portion'. Xenophon mentions such units three times in the *Hellenika* (2.4.3, 4.3.15, 5.12).

3. Xenophon *Hellenika* 3.5.22.

4. Ibid. 4.5.7.

5. Ibid. 7.1.30, 4.20, 5.10. The term *lochos* literally means 'band'.

6. Ibid. *Lakedaimoniôn politeia* 11.4, 10.

7. Ibid. 11.4.
8. Ibid. *Hellenika* 7.4.20, 5.10, cf. 1.30.
9. However, lest we forget that in the absence of printing, the transcription of ancient manuscripts was the only way in which our surviving sources could be preserved. Furthermore, though their peculiar contribution was the preservation and multiplication of texts, the monasteries of Europe had also helped in the revitalisation of education. Let us take, for instance, the survival of Aristotle. The writings of the Greek philosopher first reached Catholic Europe from the Moorish schools in Spain, and came, therefore, in a second-hand Arabic version. Largely because of this it was at once suspected of tending to heresy, and the Papacy at first forbade the teaching of Aristotle as a precautionary measure. It fell to the Dominicans to rescue Aristotle from official disapproval. The sack of Constantinople in 1204, dignified and justified by the title of crusade, gave the Dominicans the opportunity to obtain Latin translations of Aristotle direct from the Greek. The greatest of these Dominican scholars of course was Thomas Aquinas (1225–74), who had studied Aristotle in the Dominican schools at Paris and Cologne. His lifework was to reconcile completely the philosophy of Aristotle with Catholic doctrine, the chief product of his herculean labours being the massive *Summa Theologica*, which became a standard authority in the schools.
10. Xenophon *Hellenika* 6.4.12, 17. In his *Anabasis* Xenophon certainly features the *enômotia* as a tactical subunit of the Ten Thousand (see Appendix 7).
11. Thucydides (5.68.3, cf. 64.3) gives the size of the *enômotia* as on average thirty-two men (viz. four times eight) at Mantineia, with the rest in the role of home defence. Xenophon (*Hellenika* 6.4.12 with 17) has thirty-five men per *enômotia* at Leuktra, viz. those up to fifty-four years of age, plus an extra five mobilized for home defence in the emergency that followed, viz. those aged between fifty-five and fifty-nine years.
12. Thucydides 5.68.3.
13. Ibid. 5.66.3.
14. Xenophon *Hellenika* 5.4.13, 6.4.17, Plutarch *Agesilaos* 24.3.
15. Xenophon *Hellenika* 4.5.14, 16.
16. Ibid. 4.4.16.
17. Thucydides 5.64.2–3.
18. Tyrtaios fr. 10.19–27 West.
19. Xenophon *Lakedaimoniôn politeia* 4.3.
20. Thucydides 5.72.4.
21. Herodotos 8.124.
22. Thucydides 5.68.3.
23. In Greek: *enomotías kaì triekádas kaì sussítia*, Herodotos 1.65.5.
24. E.g. Tyrtaios fr. 19.8–9 West
25. Herodotos 9.53.2.
26. Pitana was the burial place of the Agiadai kings and Herodotos (3.55.2) claims to have visited the village where he spoke to one of the inhabitants, a certain Archias. It also contained the acropolis of Sparta and the important temple of Athena of the Brazen House. Aristotle (fr. 541 Rose) is cited as saying that Sparta had five *lochoi*, named *Edolos* or *Aidolios, Sinis, Arimas* or *Sarinas, Ploas,* and *Messoages* or *Mesoates*, the meanings of which are very much debated.
27. Thucydides 1.20.3. For the problem see Cartledge 1979: 255–6, Kelly 1981. Still, it certainly existed in the late third century AD, for one of the cohorts in Caracalla's army was called the Pitanate *lochos* (Herodian 4.8.3).
28. Herodotos 9.53, 57.
29. Ibid. 7.173.
30. Xenophon *Hellenika* 4.5.12.
31. Plutarch *Pelopidas* 17.2.
32. Aristophanes *Peace* 623.
33. Herodotos 1.82.
34. Plato *Laches* 192b–193d.
35. Thucydides 5.69.2. Before any clash, as was customary, the two opposing chiefs strode through the ranks, and are said to have made oratorical harangues to stiffen up the sinews of their own soldiers. But these pre-battle speeches, if not made up by the author, perhaps meet the eye rather mended. We can hardly suppose each could extend his eloquence, let alone his voice, to a hundred odd lines in folio.

Such speeches, as is often the case with speeches, contain some truths, some falsehoods. What probably happened was that the two chiefs strode up and down the lines before battle, speaking reassuringly to their soldiers, reminding of the basics of weapon-handling, which, like the sensible injunction to 'wait until you see the whites their eyes', might be forgotten in the heat of battlefield emotion, and telling them of the justice of their cause.

36. Herodotos 9.62.
37. Ibid. 9.72.
38. Xenophon *Hellenika* 4.5.4.
39. Thucydides 4.34.2.
40. Xenophon *Hellenika* 4.5.17.
41. Plato *Laches* 182a–d.
42. Herodotos 7.104.4, cf. 211, 9.62, Thucydides 4.33.2, Xenophon *Hellenika* 4.5.15–16.
43. Plutarch *Lykourgos* 12.2.
44. See Appendix 5.
45. Theophrastos, nephew of Aristotle, talks of that proverbial character, Cowardice, having 'his messmates' (*toùs sussítous*, 25.3) next to him in the phalanx. The craven hoplite also stands alongside his 'fellow demesmen' (*toùs demótas*, 25.4) and his 'fellow tribesmen' (*toùs pulétas*, 25.5), which does suggest that in the Athenian phalanx, at least, citizens who knew each other fought together as hoplites. The forensic speeches of Lysias provide at least four other examples of this phenomenon. The first (20.23) involves the eldest son of Polystratos, who is speaking on behalf of his father in 410 BC, when he informs the law court that his father's demesmen could testify to the number of occasions he had served on campaign without shirking military service. In the second (31.15–16), a certain Philon stands accused of not aiding the democrats in person and of failing to contribute funds to arm his fellow demesmen. In the third (16.14) Mantitheos when his fellow demesmen assembled to march to the relief of Haliartos in 395 BC, donates thirty *drachmae* each to two of his fellow demesmen so that they could buy provisions for the campaign. The fourth, during the following campaign season, Mantitheos is with the Athenian contingent at the Nemea where, he recalls for the jurors, his 'tribe had the worse fortune, and suffered the heaviest losses amongst its own men' (16.15). The earliest piece of evidence of Athenian demesmen fighting alongside each other comes from a fragment of a Corinthian helmet found at Rhamnous, the remote northernmost deme of Attica (thirty-nine kilometres north-east of Athens), and bears the inscription: 'The Rhamnousians (who were) in Lemnos dedicated (me) to Nemesis'. The helmet is probably best associated with the booty taken during Miltiades' expedition to seize the island of Lemnos in 499 BC (Herodotos 6.137–140), which was then dedicated at the temple of Nemesis on behalf of the demesmen of Rhamnous who fought and died together on this overseas campaign. For this inscription, see Petrakos 1984: no. 706, pl. 122b.
46. E.g. Thucydides 6.98.4, Xenophon *Hellenika* 4.2.19, Aristotle *Athenaiôn politeia* 42.1, Isaios 2.42, Lysias 13.79, 16.15, Diodoros 18.10.2, Plutarch *Aristides* 5, 19, Pausanias 1.32.3, *IG* i 929, 931, 943, 1085.
47. Thucydides 5.68.3, Xenophon *Hellenika* 6.4.12, 17, *Lakedaimoniôn politeia* 11.4.
48. Shakespeare *King Henry V* IV.iii.
49. *Iliad* 12.374–81 Fagles.
50. This is the version of the battle cry later told by Daly, then a sergeant major.
51. Xenophon *Anabasis* 3.1.43.
52. Sir Ralph Hopton, *Maxims for the Management of an Army*, 1643.
53. Sun Tzu 10.25–26.
54. Herodotos 7.104.4.
55. Ibid. 7.211.3.
56. Ibid. 9.63.
57. Ibid. 1.65.
58. The black broth of Sparta, *mélas zômós* (Plutarch *Moralia* 128C, *Lykourgos* 12.7, *Kleomenes* 13.5), was probably pork (including the trotters) cooked in its own blood with salt and sour wine. It is thought the sour wine was used as an emulsifier to keep the blood from clotting during the cooking process.
59. Plutarch *Kleomenes* 13.4.
60. Xenophon *Poroi* 2.3, cf. Isokrates *Panegyrikos* §115.
61. Xenophon *Kyroupaideia* 2.1.28, 7.1.30, cf. Aineios *Taktikos* 27.13. Xenophon's *Kyroupaideia*, a political and philosophical romance, describes the boyhood and training of Cyrus the Great. The work,

in truth, hardly answers to its name, being for the most part an account of the beginnings of the Persian empire – despite its moralizing tone, it thus preserves useful Achaemenid information – and of the victorious career of Cyrus its founder. The *Kyroupaideia* contains in fact the author's own ideas of training and education, as derived conjointly from the teachings of Sokrates and his favourite Spartan institutions. It is believed the work was written in opposition to the *Republic* of Plato, which, in turn, prompted a response from Plato in parts of *Laws*.

62. Xenophon *Kyroupaideia* 3.3.10, cf. 58.
63. Ibid. 7.1.30, cf. Onasander *Stratêgikos* 24.
64. Plutarch *Pelopidas* 17.2–4, 19.3, Diodoros 15.81.2.
65. Plutarch *Pelopidas* 18.2, cf. Plato *Symposium* 179e.
66. Plutarch *Pelopidas* 18.5, cf. *Alexander* 9.2, Diodoros 16.86.3. Beneath the Lion of Chaironeia, a Macedonian monument, which stands at the western end of the battle site, were later discovered 254 skeletons laid out in seven rows. Was this the final resting place for these do or die professionals of Thebes? I would like to think so.
67. Tod 204.25–31. An oath sworn by the Greeks before the battle of Plataia is mentioned in several sources (e.g. Lykourgos *Against Leokrates* §80, Diodoros 11.29.2), but this oath is recorded in a fourth-century BC inscription from Athens. However, as scholars argue, the lines quoted throw light upon the Spartans and not the Athenians in 479 BC. The reference to *stratêgoi* is of course relevant to the Athenians, whose armies were led by such. However, the proceeding clause makes no sense in an Athenian context but a Spartan one, as *hêgemones* is what Spartans called their kings (e.g. Tyrtaios fr. 19.11 West). The *enômotarchos*, moreover, is a purely Spartan figure without Athenian parallel, and Herodotos (9.53.2) mentions *taxiarchoi* in the Spartan army, although the Athenian army also had *taxiarchoi*. As unchallenged leader of the ground forces, it seems probable that Sparta dictated the bulk of the oath, with the Athenians, perhaps, adding the addendum 'I shall do whatever the *stratêgoi* may command'. See especially, van Wees 2004: 243–4.
68. Athenaios 13.561f. Eros' most famous shrine was at Thespiai, where the Boiotians worshipped him as a simple phallic pillar. This is the location for Plutarch's *Erotikos* (*Dialogue on Love*).
69. Athenaios 13.561e.
70. That is, Kipling's 'passin' the love o' women' in 'Follow Me 'Ome' 9.3, a reference to male comradeship as between David and Jonathan in the Bible (2 Samuel 1:26), or Graves' 'wet bond of blood' in 'Two Fusiliers' 3.2.

Chapter 10

1. Xenophon *Lakedaimoniôn politeia* 13.7.
2. I am not so sure nowadays, perhaps time and manners has changed all that, but it was a natural thing for a young man, spurred by a venal ardour to learn and to acquire reputation, to seek war as a roving adventure. To the adventurous spirit, a life of hardship and hazard abroad was preferable to one of idleness and comfort at home. During the Renaissance, for instance, such men were known as *voluntaires* in Tudor England, *soldati di fortuna* to the Italians, *soldats de fortune* to the French, and *adventureros* to the Spanish and were the youths of gentle or aristocratic families who were much prized by commanders for their chivalry and, above all, cheapness. At a time when formal training was rudimentary, thanks to their prior knowledge of sword and horse and the missile weapons of the hunt, and their habituation to shouting orders at their own or their fathers' tenantry, contact with an army quickly made effective soldiers of them. But campaigning was only an instant within their careers. Either they returned home when the chill rains of autumn spoiled the liveliest of play or becoming addicted, and in this category we can place Xenophon, stayed on to join the larger socially far more various sector of long-serving freelancers who served for pay and made war a long-term avocation. To these thrusting young nobles going to the wars was treated as if going to a tournament, travelling abroad at their own expense with a servant or two to quest adventure and renown. With romantic casualness, these gallant gentlemen would take themselves off to a foreign army and risk life and limb for princes and pretenders, mountebanks and monarchs.
3. In the words of Francis Bacon the long march of the Ten Thousand encouraged the Greeks 'to make invasion upon the kings of Persia, as was afterwards purposed by Jason the Thessalian, attempted by Agesilaos the Spartan, and achieved by Alexander the Macedonian' (*The Advancement of Learning* 1.7.30). Indeed, Agesilaos talked lordly in the spring of 394 BC about another *anabasis* (Xenophon

Hellenika 4.1.41), and Jason indulged in similar fine utterances some twenty years later (ibid. 6.1.12), but in spite of the big talk it was left to a young Macedonian to conqueror Asia with an army only quadruple the size of the retreating Ten Thousand.

4. Dodge 2002: 7–8.
5. Xenophon *Anabasis* 3.1.38.
6. Ibid. 3.2.31.
7. Ibid. 5.8.14.
8. Ibid. 5.7.34, 8.10–18.
9. Ibid. 2.3.11.
10. Ibid. *Hellenika* 1.1.35.
11. Thucydides 8.8.2–3, Diodoros 13.40.6, 51.1–4.
12. Thucydides 8.80.1–3, Xenophon *Hellenika* 1.1.36, 3.15–19, Diodoros 13.66.5–6.
13. Diodoros 13.98.1.
14. Ibid. 14.12.2–9, Polyainos 2.2.7, cf. Xenophon *Anabasis* 2.6.3, who glosses over this episode. Bassett (2001: 3) postulates that Klearchos would have taken part in the battle of Aigospotamoi in 405 BC, and subsequently remained with Lysandros during the latter's naval blockade of Athens.
15. Xenophon *Anabasis* 1.1.9, 2.9.
16. Ibid. 1.6.5, 8.4,12.
17. Ibid. 2.6.6–7.
18. Diodoros 13.98.1.
19. Xenophon (*Hellenika* 1.1.36) places Klearchos' appointment in 410 BC, but according to Thucydides (8.80.1–3) he had been sent out the previous year, which may confirm Diodoros' view (13.51.1, 4) that Klearchos had fought at Kyzikos, and had presumably taken refuge with Pharnabazos, the satrap of north-western Anatolia, like the other fugitives. He had probably accompanied the satrap to Antandros (cf. Xenophon *Hellenika* 1.1.25). On this see Bassett 2001: 2.
20. Polybios 4.38.1–3, cf. 44.
21. Diodoros 13.66.6. For Alkibiades' successful nocturnal seizure of Byzantium, see ibid. 13.67.3, Plutarch *Alkibiades* 30.4–5.
22. Diodoros 14.12.2, cf. Polyainos 2.2.7. For a discussion on these two passages, see Bassett 2001: 3–6. For Lysandros' recapture of Byzantium in 405 BC and his instalment of Sthenelaos as harmost, see Xenophon *Hellenika* 2.2.1–2. The Spartans were to hold the *polis* until 390 BC when it was 'liberated' by the Athenian *stratêgos* Thrasyboulos (Xenophon *Hellenika* 4.8.27).
23. Xenophon says (*Hellenika* 1.3.15) there were 'some' Lakonian *perioikoi* and a 'few' *neodamôdeis*, the bulk of Klearchos' garrison being made up of Megarian and Boiotian hoplite mercenaries under the commands of Helixos the Megarian and Koiratadas the Boiotian. Incidentally, Koiratadas turns up again in Byzantium sometime in 400 BC as a mercenary captain (ibid. *Anabasis* 7.1.33–41) and finally becomes a leading Theban politician five years later (Oxyrhynchos Historian 17.1).
24. Xenophon *Hellenika* 1.1.36.
25. Diodoros 13.66.5.
26. Xenophon *Hellenika* 1.3.17, Diodoros 13.66.6.
27. Here we are following manuscript P of Diodoros' work, which has the word 'Byzantines' here. Bassett (2001: 6), on the other hand, favours 'Boiotians' as the identity of these thirty men. However, the only Boiotians in Byzantium at this time were mercenaries, which made up part of Klearchos' command.
28. Diodoros 14.12.3.
29. Ibid. 14.12.7.
30. Xenophon *Anabasis* 1.1.2, cf. *Hellenika* 1.4.3.
31. Herodotos 7.81.
32. Ibid. 3.70.
33. Ktesias *FGrHist* 688F15. Succession had always caused problems for the empire. In 465 BC Xerxes was assassinated through the machinations of a guard commander. His son Artaxerxes, who had to fight to preserve his throne, his brothers Artabanos and Dareios losing their lives in the revolt against the royal family, succeeded him. Xerxes II followed Artaxerxes in 424 BC, only surviving for a year and being replaced by his half-brother who clung to the throne for a mere seven months. Eventually, the illegitimate son of Artaxerxes climbed the dais and, as Dareios II, reigned for twenty years, to be succeeded by his son Artaxerxes II in 405 BC. It was Artaxerxes' brother, Cyrus the Younger, who

made a bid for the throne, backed by Greek mercenaries, but this was nothing new. In 522 BC Kambyses was assassinated and usurped by a so-called pretender. Many scholars now believe that the 'false' Smerdis was of royal blood.

34. Xenophon *Anabasis* 1.1.9.
35. For a discussion of this see Bassett 2001: 7–10.
36. Froissart 1978: 289.
37. Isokrates *On the Peace* §§45–6.
38. Demosthenes 8.6, 8, 20–7, cf. Pseudo-Demosthenes 12.3.
39. Xenophon *Anabasis* 2.6.5.
40. Polyainos 2.2.8.
41. Xenophon *Anabasis* 1.2.9.
42. Ibid. 1.3.1.
43. Cf. ibid. 1.2.10.
44. Ibid. 1.3.7, 4.7, cf. 6.1.32, where Cheirisophos refers to the Ten Thousand as 'Klearchos' army'.
45. Plato *Meno* 76a, b, 80b, c, 86d. Plato regularly used real people as characters in his philosophical dramas, though of course we have to be aware that we know about them only as much as he wants or allows us to know.
46. Xenophon *Anabasis* 1.6.5.
47. Ibid. 1.8.12.
48. Ibid. 1.5.11–14.
49. Ibid. 2.6.26.
50. Ibid. 1.4.12–13.
51. Plato *Meno* 70a, 76c, cf. Xenophon *Anabasis* 2.6.16.
52. Xenophon *Anabasis* 1.4.14–15.
53. Ibid. 1.4.16–17.
54. Ibid. 2.5.28, cf. Ktesias *apud* Photios *Epitome* §64, §68.
55. It is not only in Xenophon's version of events that Meno plays the *mauvaise rôle*. In his account of the *anabasis*, Diodoros says (14.27.2) that Meno was quite prepared to betray his fellow Greeks, a view backed up by the Greek physician who spent seventeen years, from 405 BC onwards, at the Persian court, Ktesias of Knidos (*apud* Photios *Epitome* §69). So, despite the fact that Xenophon, as part of 'smear-the-dead-guy' routine, wrote about the man with a hatred that was thoroughly frightful and irreconcilable, we would not be far wrong in our appraisal of Meno if we express that he was devious, manipulative, greedy, self-seeking, and treacherous.
56. Xenophon *Anabasis* 2.6.29.
57. Ibid. 2.6.10.
58. Ibid. *Oikonomikos* 9.13–15, *Kyroupaideia* 8.2.27.
59. Sun Tzu 9.43.
60. Xenophon *Anabasis* 2.6.13, 14, cf. *Memorabilia* 3.5.5.
61. Ibid. *Anabasis* 2.3.11. No less than a uniform and no less of a distinctly Spartan trait, especially abroad, was the walking stick, *bakteriâ*, with a T-shaped crosspiece at the top, which allowed the traveller to lean on it when stationary. Spartan violence often took the form of the threat or actual use of a stick, such as in the case of the 'madness' of King Kleomenes (Herodotos 6.75.1).
62. Xenophon *Anabasis* 3.1.10. Diodoros says (14.19.9) from the outset Cyrus had informed his commanders but not the troops of his real purpose. However, we are not told if this included the Greek *stratêgoi*. Earlier, Diodoros mentions the fact that Cyrus saw Klearchos as 'an apt partner for his bold undertakings' (14.12.9), which does suggest, at the very least, that Klearchos was in the know, thus following Xenophon's view.
63. Xenophon *Anabasis* 1.8.4, 12, Diodoros 14.22.5.
64. Xenophon *Anabasis* 1.8.13, cf. Plutarch *Artaxerxes* 8.3–7.
65. Xenophon *Anabasis* 2.1.4, cf. 3.2.5.
66. Ibid. 2.2.6, cf. Diodoros 14.26.1–27.2.
67. Xenophon *Anabasis* 2.3.5.
68. Ibid. 2.1.23.
69. Ibid. 2.1.10. Obviously these words recall the famous answer that Leonidas at Thermopylai made to the same demand: *molôn labé*.

70. According to Xenophon (*Anabasis* 3.3.7, cf. 2.2.7), only twenty mercenaries and one *lochagos* deserted the Ten Thousand and went over to Artaxerxes. If true, then the vast majority stayed with the mercenary army during this difficult period of its existence.

71. According to Ktesias (*FGrHist* 688F27), who was in attendance on Artaxerxes on the battlefield of Cunaxa, Tissaphernes had been given command when the king was wounded and withdrew from the battle. This is not mentioned by Xenophon in his account.

72. Xenophon *Anabasis* 2.5.13–15, cf. 23.

73. Ibid. 2.6.1.

74. Ibid. 2.6.11.

75. Ibid. *Agesilaos* 6.4–7, cf. *Hellenika* 4.1.30.

76. Ibid. *Memorabilia* 3.1.9. For all these leadership qualities see: Xenophon *Agesilaos* 5.1–4, 6.4–7, 7.2, 8.1–4, 6–8, 9.1–2, 11 *passim*, cf. *Kyroupaideia* 1.2.1, 8.1.22–23, 34–37, *Hellenika* 3.4.18, 4.1.30, *Memorabilia* 3.1.6–7.

77. Ibid. *Anabasis* 2.6.9–14.

78. Ibid. 3.1.42, *Kyroupaideia* 3.3.19, cf. *Memorabilia* 3.3.7. Those two gems from Napoléon: 'In war morale is everything', and 'Morale is to the physical as three is to one' (*Correspondence de Napoléon Ier* 15.933, 17.14276).

79. Perhaps the most notorious example of this was the trial of the *victorious* Athenian *stratêgoi* after Arginousai (Xenophon *Hellenika* 1.7). Politics and soldering just do not mix, and in fourth-century BC Athens, for instance, we witness the advent of the *stratêgos* who is exclusively seen as a soldier and not as a politician (e.g. Isokrates *On the Peace* §54, Aristotle *Politics* 1305a10). Politics is the art of the possible. It is also the art of survival. Soldiers, on the other hand, are trained to view issues in black and white terms. Negotiation is equated with weakness, compromise and capitulation. Soldiers should be the men who execute, or die in the attempt, the ultimate decisions of politicians, no matter how stupidly, brightly or even brilliantly conceived.

80. Aristotle *Athenaiôn politeia* 61.2.

81. E.g. Herodotos 6.11–12. See especially, Aineios Taktikos 28.5 for the inherent difficulties of disciplining citizen soldiers.

82. Xenophon *Hellenika* 3.1.9.

83. Frontinus *Strategemata* 4.1.9.

84. Thucydides 5.66.4.

85. Xenophon *Anabasis* 2.6.17.

86. 'Power is the new aphrodisiac', to quote Kissenger correctly (*The New York Times*, 28 October 1973).

87. 'French mercenary Bob Denard dies', BBC, 14 October 2007.

88. Originally called the *Force Publique*, the *Armée Nationale Congolaise* was formed by the Belgians in 1886 and was recruited mainly from neighbouring territories in West Africa. In 1894 they decided to recruit only Congolese: the tribal chiefs, from among the men they wanted to be rid of, chose these recruits for the Belgian administration. Not surprisingly, there were discipline problems, and revolts erupted from time to time. At Independence (30 June 1960) the *ANC* comprised some 25,000 men, with one thousand Belgian officers and warrant officers. The highest rank held by a Congolese was that of *adjudant-chef* (sergeant major). In reality, the *ANC* existed as a brutal, undisciplined and often lawless force, whose Belgian officers were incapable of enforcing order.

89. As well as diamonds, Katanga contained most of the valuable mineral deposits of the Congo, especially copper and uranium, and these were owned and developed by a group of companies headed by the *Union Minière du Haut-Katanga* (*UMHK*) based in Brussels, of which the Belgian state and the British-Rhodesian company Tanganyika Concessions were the major shareholders. According to one of Tshombé's mercenary captains, *UMHK* was 'bankrolling the whole operation' (Hoare 1967: 11). Incidentally, the Congo Free State was the backdrop for Joseph Conrad's 1898 novella *Heart of Darkness*, in which the central character, the mysterious Mr Kurtz, sets off in search of ivory but also to 'civilize the savages', and instead he succumbs to the darkest aspects of the dark continent. Full of contempt for the rapacious traders, who ruthlessly exploit the indigenous tribes along the River Congo, the narrator of the story, Charlie Marlow, cannot deny the power of this figure of evil who calls forth from him something approaching reluctant loyalty. The novella follows closely the actual events of Conrad's Congo journey of 1890 and Francis Ford Coppola loosely adapted it for his 1979 Vietnam War film *Apocalypse Now*, starring Martin Sheen (US Army Captain Benjamin Willard, the narrator) and Marlon Brando (US Special Forces Colonel Walter E. Kurtz, the 'embodiment of evil').

90. Colonel Moké, an illiterate former *adjudant-chef* in the *Force Publique*, who was said to possess a voice that could split an eardrum at a hundred paces, was officially the commander of the Katangese *Gendarmerie* (he is probably the inspiration for Forsyth's Colonel Bobi in his 1974 novel *The Dogs of War*). Commandant Faulques was his chief-of-staff but in fact the *de facto* chief of the outfit. Roger Faulques (1924–2011) had served in the French Army in almost continuous action since he was first commissioned in the year the Second World War broke out, and recently had fought in French Indochina and been evacuated from Dien Bien Phu in the eleventh hour of that gruelling operation. All told, he had suffered twenty-two wounds, including a duelling scar that ran vividly down one cheek, in as many years service under *le drapeau tricolore*. He was the sole survivor of his year at Saint-Cyr (Hoare 1989: 79).

91. The Security Council resolution of 13 July 1960 had empowered and required the United Nations to put its forces at the disposal of the Congolese government to expel foreign elements (notably unwanted Belgians), to reduce the secession of Katanga, and to restore law and order throughout the country. For an excellent study of the first Congo crisis, see Nzongola-Ntalaja 2002: 94–120.

92. Their leader was the Chinese trained Pierre Mulélé, who said he was fighting for Congo's 'second independence' and had secured promises of support from Peking. A charismatic and calculating character, Mulélé had fired blank bullets at himself to demonstrate his invulnerability to his followers, who drank *Mai Mulélé* to make themselves immune to bullets. Other magico-religious rituals included the wearing of various fetishes, and the observation of a strict code of conduct involving sexual abnegation and certain dietary restrictions on the eve of battle. Mulélé had just returned from Peking where he had studied the guerrilla tactics of Mao Tsetung whose doctrine emphasized the necessity for fighting to be married to clear political objectives. He was soon to be aided in his liberation struggle by Ernesto 'Che' Guevara. The Argentine-born Cuban revolutionary led an élite group of 112 Cuban guerrillas, all volunteers and all black, in a clandestine operation designed to rescue the Congolese revolution after its major defeat at the hands of the US-led counterinsurgency in November 1964. Nevertheless, Che failed to make a difference as *Opération Dragon Rouge*, the combined land and air offensive that culminated with the US-Belgium airborne assault of 24 November 1964, had virtually broken the back of the Marxist-Leninist insurrection. Mobutu's generals assassinated Mulélé on 3 October 1968, after he had returned to Kinshasa (as Léopoldville had been renamed as part of Mobutu's process of 'decolonization') under a false promise of amnesty by the Congolese president.

93. Hoare 1967: 221. Like Denard, Hoare (b. 1920) was part of a 700-man force of South African, Rhodesian and European mercenaries, which did much of the fighting against the *Simbas* as 'spearheads' of élite units of the *ANC*. The latter was headed by the former commander of the colonial *Force Publique*, Colonel Frédéric Vandewalle, who had been brought in, together with a number of Belgian officers, to stiffen up the army of the Léopoldville government. The US Air Force gave critical air support to Congolese troops and white mercenaries, as did the anti-Castro Cuban pilots recruited by the CIA in Florida. By the way, Vandewalle had only just left the Congo, having served for two years as adviser to Tshombé in Katanga. See especially, Weissman 1974: 391–3.

94. Born Joseph-Désiré Mobutu, son of a cook and a former *adjudant-chef* in the *Force Publique*, he was later to reinvent himself as Maréchal Mobutu Sese Seko Kuku Ngbendu Wa Za Banga, President-Founder, Helmsman. In Kiswahili, Sese Seko Kuku Ngbendu Wa Za Banga means no more than 'the all-powerful warrior who, because of his endurance and inflexible will to win, will go from conquest to conquest leaving fire in his wake'. Another la-di-da title of Mobutu, *le seul guide du pays*, gave rise to the Zaïrois joke: 'Why are there so few tourists in Zaire?' Answer: 'Because there's only one guide' (Packham 1996: 267).

95. After gaining independence from Portugal in 1975, this nationalist movement was to splinter into three warring, tribal factions. These were the Zaire-based and US-backed *FNLA* (*Frente Naçional de Libertação de Angola*) recruited from the Bakongo in the north-west, the South African trained *UNITA* (*União de Naçional para a Indepedência Total de Angola*) recruited from the Ovimbundu from the south and centre, and the Soviet-backed and Cuban-trained *MPLA* (*Movimento Popular de Libertação de Angola*) recruited from the Mbundu in the centre of the country. In their mutually exclusive agendas to stop a left-wing Marxist-Leninist *MPLA* government, other Western countries such as Britain, from where an advance party of mercenaries arrived to beef up and reorganize the *FNLA* in 1976, backed both *UNITA* and the *FNLA*. These mercenaries, mainly ex-paratroopers, were paid for with crisp new hundred-dollar bills courtesy of the CIA. Incidentally, given the fact that Mobutu, their nemesis, also backed *UNITA* and the *FNLA*, the Katangese went over to the *MPLA*.

96. Although Tshombé's death certificate states he died of a heart attack, it has long been suspected that he was liquidated at the instigation of the CIA, whose policy was to keep Mobutu in power in order to have the Congo as an ally against the Soviet Union. Consistent with the logic of both Cold War politics and institutional racism in the United States, it was felt that a vast and multi-ethnic country such as the Congo needed a 'strongman' to keep it together and prevent chaos, and therefore communist subversion and takeover. In September 1991, for instance, one thousand French and Belgian paratroopers – doing what their fathers had done twenty-seven years before – were deployed in Zaire (as Mobutu re-baptised the Congo Republic in 1971, along with its river and its currency, a name originally given to the Congo River by the Portuguese in the fifteenth century) courtesy of the United States government. They were supposedly there to aid the evacuation of their nationals after the recent countrywide spree of looting and violence by Mobutu's unpaid and hungry soldiery. There were some 10,000 Belgian nationals in Zaire, while France had around 4,000 citizens there, including some eighty paratroopers and airmen as part of a permanent aid mission training the *31er brigade aéroportée*. This élite unit had, incidentally, recently sacked houses in the residential areas of the capital, Kinshasa. But sceptics, on the other hand, saw this military operation to cover the exodus of foreign nationals from Zaire as an attempt by the Western Troika to prop up Mobutu's failing dictatorship. See especially, Julian Nundy, 'Mitterrand capitalises on Zaire crisis', *The Independent*, 26 September 1991. The current conflict in the Democratic Republic of Congo, which began in 1998 in the aftermath of the upheavals caused by the toppling of Mobutu, had led directly and indirectly to the deaths of an estimated four million people by 2004, and many estimates suggest another million, and possibly more, may have died since (Baker 2011: 145). The Congo has reverted to the state of civil war that characterized the early post-independence period, with combatants from no less than six surrounding countries participating in this fratricidal conflict.

97. The bearded and bumptious guerrilla fighter, Jonas Savimbi (1934–2002), was to return to the Angolan capital, Luanda, for the first time in sixteen years on 29 September 1991. He was allowed to do so after having signed a peace treaty (soon to be broken) with the ruling *MPLA*, thus terminating (temporarily, as it turned out) one of Africa's longest and most intractable civil wars (it was also a proxy fight between the two Cold War superpowers, not to mention Cubans against South Africans). See, for example, 'Crowds welcome back Savimbi', *The Independent*, 30 September 1991. Although he had received his guerrilla training at the Nanking Military Academy, was an admirer of Mao Tsetung, and had counted Ernesto 'Che' Guevara as one of his closest friends, Savimbi did not want a communist doctrine either for *UNITA* or for Angola (he would pose on the international scene as a protagonist of anti-communism). Later, there was an attempt to create a government of national reconciliation, which culminated in the UN-sponsored 1994 Lusaka Peace Accord between *UNITA* and the *MPLA* despite Savimbi's absence. See, for example, Lynne Duke, 'Angolans Inching into Peace; Savimbi's Rebels Quit Bush, Straggle to Disarmament Centers', *Washington Post*, 14 February 1996. Nevertheless, following the breakdown of negotiations in December 1998, the civil war was to resume once more. On 22 March 2002, after the *MPLA* régime had come to terms with the USA, Savimba was killed in a firefight with Angolan government troops. See, for example, 'Savimba died with gun in hand', BBC News, 25 February 2002. Soon after Savimba's death, a ceasefire between the two warring factions was signed, *UNITA* giving up its armed struggle and assuming the role of major opposition party. Angola is potentially one of the richest countries in Africa with vast oil and diamond reserves. It also has good agricultural land and fisheries, and was once, under Portuguese rule, a major exporter of coffee. However, the years of war and conflict have reduced it to enormous poverty, and the plight of the ordinary Angolans remains desperate.

98. Mockler 1985: 167–8, 237.

99. 'Benin: Abortive Coup', *Africa Research Bulletin: Political and Cultural Series* 14 (January 1977), 4288–9.

100. On 31 March 2011, following the wishes of a 2009 local referendum, Mayotte became an overseas department of France (DOM, *départment d'outre-mer*), and will become an Outermost region of the European Union on 1 January 2014.

101. Numerous highly colourful accounts of the coup were published at the time. See, for example, Tony Avirgnan, 'Col Denard's Newly Won Kingdom is no Island Paradise', *The Guardian*, 19 August 1978, and, David Lamb, 'Comoros: a Path to Democracy', *Los Angeles Times*, 21 October 1978.

102. Tony Avirgnan, 'Comoros Colonel forced out', *The Guardian*, 27 September 1978.

103. This interview took place on 5 June, three weeks after the coup when French journalists had finally uncovered his new identity. The British press were somewhat slower. See, for example, Robin Smyth, 'Mercenary Hangs on to Power after Coup', *The Observer*, 25 June 1978. That tree, the *ylang-ylang*, which the colonel so adores is a Malaysian evergreen tree with highly fragrant greenish-yellow flowers.

104. Ahmed Abdallah was prepared to condone openly Denard's continue association with the islands. In an interview given to Jean-Pierre Langellier of *Le Monde* and published 25 April 1981, the president sagely said: '*Pourquoi empêcheras-je Bob de vénir ici, lui qui a libéré mon pays? Est-ce que je protéste contre la présence des Cubains à Madagascar?*'

105. Natural resources are in short supply and the islands' chief exports are vanilla, cloves, copra and perfume essence. The Comoros are potentially a holiday paradise but those troubled islands have experienced a series of more than twenty coups or attempted coups since independence in 1975 (in which four have involved our Gascon) and 2001, and the resultant political instability has done much to undermine a fragile tourist industry. See especially, Patrick J. McGowan, 2003, 'African military coups d'état, 1956–2001: frequency, trends and distribution', *The Journal of Modern African Studies* 41: 339–70. The latest coup was on 9 August 2001, with an attempted one again on 24 September 2001. See, for example, Kevin Rushby, 'Another day, another coup', *The Guardian*, 1 October 2001.

106. Christopher Burns, 'Bob, Denard, Africa's Ageing but Notorious Mercenary, Strikes Again', *Associated Press*, 28 September 1995.

107. Paul Webster, 'Mercenary tried for Comoran killing', *The Guardian*, 5 May 1999, and, Jon Henley, 'Dogs of war in nudist coup', *The Guardian*, 19 August 2000.

108. Xenophon *Anabasis* 1.4.3.

109. Diodoros 14.21.2.

110. 'Bob Denard', *The Independent*, 6 April 1993. In an interview at the time, Denard prefer to describe himself as a corsair rather than a mercenary or a pirate: 'The corsairs in France would receive written permission from the king to attack foreign ships. I didn't have such permission, but I had passports given me by the intelligent services.' English translation of the French from Marlise Simons, 'Bob Denard, Hired Gun for Coups, Is Dead at 78', *The New York Times*, 16 October 2007.

111. 'Aging Mercenary stages isles coup', *Athens News*, 29 September 1995. See also, 'Coup Leader flown to France', *Athens News*, 7 October 1995. An interim government ruled the Comoros for five months until President Taki was elected in 1996 in internationally monitored elections, which were declared free and fair. France re-established its military presence in the same year at the new president's invitation. Divisive personal, clan, ethnic, and inter-island rivalries persist.

112. Froissart 1978: 288.

113. 'French mercenary Bod Denard dies', BBC News, 14 October 2007.

Chapter 11

1. Xenophon *Agesilaos* 2.7.

2. In his own words upon his good self: 'Hereupon Xenophon arose, arrayed for war in his finest dress. For he thought that if the gods should grant victory, the finest raiment was suited for victory; and if it should be his fate to die, it was proper, he thought, that inasmuch as he had accounted his office worthy of the most beautiful attire, in this attire he should meet his death' (*Anabasis* 3.2.7). Xenophon, according to Aelian, was accustomed to wearing '*hopla kalá*' in battle (*De natura animalium* 3.24).

3. The first depiction of this type of body armour is that seen on the sculptural friezes from the east and north pediments of the Siphnian Treasury at Delphi, which was erected sometime around 525 BC. A real treasure (pun intended) for hoplite aficionados, the right-hand half (as viewed) of the east frieze is an episode taken from the Trojan War, namely Aineias and Memnon fight Achilles and Ajax (?) over the corpse of Antilochos, son of Nestor. The four contestants are depicted as hoplites in careful detail, two of which wear the newfangled *linothôrax*, the other two in the older, and heavier bronze bell-shaped corselet. The north frieze is a Gigantomachy, the battle of the Gods (new order) and the Giants (old order). The Giants are dressed and fight as hoplites. The Gods are the Gods, apart from Ares, who comes to the 'dance' dressed as a hoplite and, fittingly, one decked out with a *linothôrax*.

4. Xenophon *Lakedaimoniôn politeia* 13.8.

5. Euripides *Phoenissae* 110.

6. Xenophon *Agesilaos* 11.11.

7. Ibid. *Lakedaimoniôn politeia* 11.3.

8. Plutarch *Moralia* 238F, cf. scholia to Aristophanes *Acharnians* 320.
9. Aelian *De natura animalium* 6.6.
10. The Chigi Vase (Rome, Villa Giulia Museum, inv. 22679) by the Macmillan Painter of Corinth (*fl. c.* 660–640 BC), which was exported to Veii in Etruria (*c.* 650 BC) where it was discovered. This Protocorinthian *olpe* (round-mouthed wine jug) depicts in lively detail scenes of war and hunting. The scene around the neck shows hoplites being piped into battle. It gives a clear representation of the hoplite phalanx in action, and ranks as the first and supreme example of such we have to date. Of interest too, are the individualized blazons decorating the shields of the right-hand phalanx.
11. According to Plutarch, when Agesilaos was asked why the Spartans 'go into battle to the music of flutes', he said: 'So that, as they proceed in step to the music, both the cowards and the brave may be clearly distinguished" (*Moralia* 211A.36). Presumably the brave would step smartly; the cowards skittishly shuffle.
12. Sekunda 1998: 52–3. Spartan flute players, *aulêtai*, were members of an honoured hereditary guild, 'the sons of father who followed the same profession' as Herodotos (6.60) phrased it. As such, they were on par with the hereditary Spartan citizen heralds and ritual sacrificers. As we have seen, music in general occupied an honoured place in Spartan culture and society. Pratinas of Elis amusingly likened every Spartan to a cicada.
13. Thucydides 5.70, Plutarch *Lykourgos* 21.3, 22.2, *Moralia* 238B, Cicero *Tusculanae disputationes* 2.16.37, Valerius Maximus 2.6.2, cf. Xenophon *Lakedaimoniôn politeia* 13.7, 8.
14. Plutarch *Kleomenes* 37.2.
15. E.g. ibid. *Nikias* 19.4.
16. Ibid. *Agesilaos* 36.5, cf. *Moralia* 214.D76.
17. Xenophon *Lakedaimoniôn politeia* 2.4.
18. Aristophanes *Lysistrata* 1140.
19. Ibid. *Birds* 1281–3. The stick Aristophanes mentions here is the *skutâlê*, a Spartan despatch. When about to send a commander to the field, the ephors had two staves made of the same thickness and the same length. One of these they gave to the commander who was to take the field; the other the ephors kept. When they desired to send secret orders to the commander abroad, they wrapped a piece of white leather round the stave and then wrote on the leather. The commander on receiving it wrapped it round his stave and so read it.
20. Xenophon *Memorabilia* 1.6.2, cf. Plato *Symposium* 219b, *Protagoras* 335d.
21. Demosthenes 54.34.
22. Plutarch *Lykourgos* 27.1.
23. Aelian *De natura animalium* 6.6.
24. Herodotos 1.82.8.
25. Xenophon *Lakedaimoniôn politeia* 13.8, cf. Plutarch *Lysandros* 1.1.
26. Aristotle *Rhetoric* 1.9.26–27.
27. Plutarch *Alkibiades* 23.
28. Xenophon *Lakedaimoniôn politeia* 11.3.
29. Plutarch *Lykourgos* 22.1, *Moralia* 189E, 228F.
30. Herodotos 7.208.2–3.
31. Ibid. 7.209.
32. Xenophon *Lakedaimoniôn politeia* 13.9, cf. Plutarch *Lykourgos* 22.1.
33. Ktesias *apud* Plutarch *Artaxerxes* 18.1.
34. Plutarch *Kleomenes* 9.3.
35. Ibid. *Lysandros* 1.1.
36. Ibid. *Moralia* 232E.
37. Plutarch *Moralia* 234C–D 41.
38. Eupolis fr. 359 Kock.
39. Pausanias 4.28.5.
40. Xenophon *Hellenika* 4.4.10.
41. Thucydides 5.72.4, cf. Euripides *Bacchae* 303–4.
42. E.g. Aineios Taktikos uses the word *pilos* for a cap made of felt (11.12, 25.2–3, cf. 33.3 for the material).
43. Arrian *Taktika* 3.5, Pollux 1.149.

44. Thucydides 4.34.3.
45. Plutarch *Lykourgos* 19.2, *Moralia* 191E, 216E.1.
46. Ibid. *Moralia* 217E.8.
47. Ibid. 323E.
48. Ibid. 241F.18.
49. Ibid. *Lykourgos* 12.2.
50. Plato *Laws* 633a.
51. Xenophon *Lakedaimoniôn politeia* 5.5.
52. Ibid. *Kyroupaideia* 2.1.17.
53. Hartford, CT, Wadsworth Atheneum Museum of Art, inv. 1917.815.
54. Aristophanes *Peace* 303, 1173, cf. 1175.
55. Eupolis fr. 359 Kock.
56. Herodotos 7.218.
57. Thucydides 5.70.
58. Plutarch *Lykourgos* 22.2–3, cf. *Moralia* 211A.36.
59. Kipling, *The Jungle Book*, 1899: 272.
60. Xenophon *Memorabilia* 3.5.21.
61. Thucydides 4.34.1.
62. Lysias 16.17.
63. Xenophon *Hellenika* 4.2.18.
64. For non-Spartans in crimson tunics, see Xenophon *Anabasis* 1.2.16 (the Ten Thousand), *Kyroupaideia* 7.1.2 (Cyrus' army).
65. In Greek: *rhizion*, Strabo 13.4.14, Dioskorides 3.160.
66. Pliny *Historia Naturalis* 19.47–48.
67. Ibid. 9.65.141, 16.9.32.
68. Theophrastos *History of Plants* 3.7.3, 16.1, Dioskorides 4.48, Galen 12.32, cf. Pausanias 10.36.1.
69. Pliny *Historia Naturalis* 21.22.45.
70. It is known the Egyptians used kermes to dye leather: Middle Egyptian *dšr*, 'to redden', and the synonym for 'blood', *dšrw*, and desert, *dšr.t*.

Chapter 12

1. Thucydides 2.35–46.
2. Ibid. 2.52–54.
3. Ibid. 3.82–83.
4. A (non-mythical) theme portrayed with such brilliance in the *Persai* of Aischylos, produced in 472 BC, for which the twenty-something Perikles had acted as financial sponsor. This was Perikles' first known appearance on the public stage. Since Perikles was to follow in the wake of Themistokles so far as his naval policy and attitude to the growth of the empire were concerned, it is not entirely fanciful to read Perikles' sponsorship of the *Persai* as a youthful political statement of intent. It was Themistokles, after all, who had been the author of the great naval victory of Salamis, the crucial backdrop to the *Persai*.
5. It was the moral and political philosopher Protagoras of Abdera, good friend and political advisor to Perikles, who once said 'man is the measure of all things'. Plato wrote a critique of the idea in his *Theaetetos* (151e–179b).
6. Sophokles *Antigone* 332–68.
7. Thucydides 7.11–15 seemingly quotes this missive verbatim.
8. Ibid. 1.139.2.
9. Ibid. 4.85.1.
10. Xenophon *Hellenika* 2.2.23.
11. Diodoros 14.13.1, Plutarch *Lysandros* 13.4, cf. Xenophon *Hellenika* 3.4.2.
12. Diodoros (14.10.2) puts this tribute from Athens' former subject allies at over a thousand talents per annum.
13. Thucydides 2.8.4, cf. 1.139.3.
14. Aristotle's summary as quoted in Forest 1995: 126.
15. Plutarch *Lysandros* 13.5.

16. Thucydides 8.84.2. Incidentally, this is the only occurrence of the word *bakteriâ* in Thucydides.
17. Plutarch *Lysandros* 15.7. Xenophon makes Autolykos the principle character in his *Symposium*. Sadly, as Plutarch tells us in the same passage, the Thirty Tyrants 'soon afterwards put Autolykos to death, to please Kallibios'. As a boy, in 422 BC, Autolykos had won the *pankration* at the Greater Panathenaia of that year, the festival in honour of Athens' patron deity Athena, which was held quadrennially and open to all Greeks. The *pankration* was not for the fainthearted, for it not only involved wrestling-style holds, but punching, kicking, choking, finger breaking, and blows to the genitals were allowed too, only biting and eye gouging being prohibited (considered far too effeminate perhaps). Bouts continued until one athlete gave up or was incapacitated. Stories tell of deaths and even a posthumous victory: before he died in a stranglehold, the *pankratiast* Arrhichion is said to have broken his opponent's toe, forcing him to give up (Pausanias 8.40.1–2).
18. Thucydides 3.92.5.
19. Ibid. 3.93.2.
20. Euripides *Andromache* 445–54, cf. Thucydides 5.105.4.
21. Herodotos 9.54.1.
22. Xenophon *Hellenika* 5.4.20–24, 34, Diodoros 15.29.5–8, Plutarch *Agesilaos* 24.3–26.1. On Sphodrias' trial see de Ste. Croix 1972: 133–7.
23. Xenophon *Hellenika* 5.2.25–31. Xenophon clearly says (ibid. 5.2.29) the act was performed in the middle of a hot summer's day.
24. Diodoros 15.20.1–3, Plutarch *Pelopidas* 6.1.
25. Xenophon *Hellenika* 5.2.32, 4.41, cf. Diodoros 15.20.2, where the charge that Phoebidas had been put up by Agesilaos to the seizure of the Kadmeia is aired, along with the story that is was the same king who persuaded the Spartans to keep what they had in essence outrageous stolen. This is indeed plausible, and we can reckon Agesilaos of course disclaiming all responsibility for the dastardly plot, but no one being impressed.
26. Plutarch *Pelopidas* 6.1.
27. Xenophon *Hellenika* 5.2.35–36.
28. Ibid. 5.4.1.
29. Diodoros 15.23.3–5, cf. Xenophon *Hellenika* 5.3.27.
30. Xenophon *Hellenika* 5.2.20.
31. Plutarch *Moralia* 213B.61.
32. Thucydides 5.16.2.
33. Plutarch *Alkibiades* 23.3–4, cf. Xenophon *Hellenika* 3.3.2 who airs the rumour but refrains from actually naming Alkibiades.
34. Xenophon *Hellenika* 3.4.3–4.
35. Ibid. 2.2.19. According to Polyainos (1.45.5), there were Spartans of that way of thinking too.
36. Xenophon *Hellenika* 2.4.1, Demosthenes 15.22, Diodoros 14.6.1, Justin 5.10.
37. Xenophon *Hellenika* 2.2.20, cf. 3.2.21–3, 3.1.4.
38. Ibid. 3.5.10, Diodoros 14.39.3.
39. Xenophon *Hellenika* 2.3.13, 4.30, Polyainos 1.45.5.
40. Xenophon *Hellenika* 2.4.29–30.
41. Ibid. 3.5.5.
42. Thucydides 1.103.3.
43. Ibid. 6.93.2–3.
44. Diodoros 13.93.4.
45. Ibid. 14.63, 70.
46. By the time of Homer Corinth's natural epithet was already 'wealthy' (*Iliad* 2.570), as Thucydides noted (1.13.5).
47. Herodotos 2.167.
48. Simonides *apud* Plutarch *The Malice of Herodotos* 39.871B, Pindar fr. 107 Snell-Maehler.
49. Aristophanes fr. 354 Dindorf.
50. Attributed to Demosthenes, the speech was almost certainly written by Apollodoros son of Pasion, although he received plenty of sage advice from the great orator and politician.
51. Thucydides 3.92.4–93.2, cf. Diodoros 14.38.3–4.
52. Diodoros 14.82, cf. Xenophon *Hellenika* 6.4.24.

53. Xenophon *Hellenika* 3.5.6.
54. Hornblower 2002: 212–14.
55. Xenophon *Hellenika* 3.4.2–25, 4.1.
56. Ibid. 4.2.2, 3.12–18.
57. Hornblower 2002: 218.
58. Xenophon *Hellenika* 3.5.1–2.
59. Thucydides 7.34.
60. Xenophon *Hellenika* 4.2.11–12.
61. Ibid. 4.4.1.
62. Ibid. 4.4.2–5.
63. Diodoros 14.82.1.
64. Xenophon *Hellenika* 4.4.6.
65. Ibid. 5.1.34
66. Ibid. 5.3.27.
67. Thucydides 1.36.3–4.
68. Ibid. 1.40.4.
69. Ibid. 1.41.2.
70. Xenophon *Hellenika* 7.4.6–10.
71. E.g. ibid. 3.1.1. There was also Artaxerxes' personal hatred for the Spartans, whom the contemporary Deinon says he considered as the 'most shameless of men' (*FGrHist* 690F19). This is probably an allusion to the Spartan military assistance to Cyrus.
72. Oxyrhynchos Historian 6–7.
73. Ibid. 9–10.
74. Ibid. 10.2, *contra* Xenophon *Hellenika* 3.5.2 who says Athens did not accept Persian gold.
75. Thucydides 1.139.
76. After the death of Cyrus the Younger at Cunaxa, Tissaphernes had been reappointed as satrap in Sardis. However, the smashing Spartan victory at Sardis (395 BC) led to the satrap's downfall and death (Xenophon *Hellenika* 3.4.25). For the battle, see ibid. 3.4.21–24.
77. Xenophon *Hellenika* 4.8.13.
78. Ibid. 4.8.14.
79. Ibid. 4.8.15.
80. Andokides 3.17. The date, 392 BC, is secure from Philochoros fr.149.
81. Xenophon *Hellenika* 5.1.25.
82. Ibid. 5.1.31.
83. The obverse of the *dareikos* invariably bore an image of the Great King wielding bow and spear. Armed and dangerous, this was the picture of the Persian monarch to be seen by millions who never saw him or his likeness otherwise. First introduced by Dareios, this coin of remarkably pure gold soon became the 'dollar' of its day.
84. In Greek: *autonomia*, Xenophon *Hellenika* 4.8.15.
85. Ibid. 5.1.32–3. The Boiotian and Arcadian leagues, and the later Achaian League, which would emerge in the third century BC, involved groupings of ethnically akin peoples who all share a great deal in common both culturally and politically. As such, therefore, these federal leagues were interesting social experiments, especially when the states within a particular league looked beyond their parochial differences and endeavoured to co-operate. Thus we witness here a positive step by the Greeks of these ethnic confederations moving, in theory at least, towards the idea of forming a united nation.
86. Xenophon *Hellenika* 5.1.32–34.
87. See, for example, Harding 28, the plea by Erythrai to Athens, and Harding 31 & 35, Athens submits that nothing should contravene the King's Peace.
88. Diodoros 15.9.1. Glôs son of Tamôs, was an Egyptian who after joining the rebellion of Cyrus the Younger served Artaxerxes until his liquidation in 380/79 BC for intriguing with the Spartans (*contra* Lewis (1979: 58 n. 59) who suspects merely alleged intriguing). Aineias Taktikos says he held the rank 'admiral of the King of Persia' (31.35), which is feasible given his nationality.
89. Xenophon *Hellenika* 6.2.1.
90. Diodoros 15.38.1.
91. Xenophon *Hellenika* 4.8.24.

92. Diodoros 15.9.2. Evagoras had gained the throne not later than 411 BC, and died in 374 BC. Aristotle says (*Politics* 1311b) that the king was murdered, but Isokrates is silent with respect to manner of the death of his hero in his rhetorical eulogy entitled *Evagoras*.
93. Thucydides 1.104.2.
94. Herodotos 3.15.
95. Thucydides 1.112.3.
96. Fornara 86.
97. Diodoros 14.35.4, cf. Xenophon *Anabasis* 2.1.14.
98. Isokrates *Panegyrikos* §81.
99. Since escaping from Aigospotamoi, Konon had been a welcomed guest in the court of Evagoras of Cyprus (Isokrates *Evagoras* §52). It was the king's influence that secured for the very able Athenian the appointment of admiral in the Persian navy (Diodoros 14.39.1).
100. Diodoros 15.38.1.
101. The Great Satrap Revolt broke out in 366 BC when Timotheos of Athens, who had just expelled the Persian garrison on Samos, went to the aide of Ariobarzanes, the rebel satrap of Phrygia. Ariobarzanes was soon joined by a whole host of fellow satraps, including Mausolos of Caria, the satraps of Mysia, Cappadocia, Ionia, and Lycia, which meant he headed a major revolt against the crown (Diodoros 15.90.3). Still, it all frizzled out, being bedevilled by treachery from within at the very start, and thus the Persian empire survived yet another trauma.
102. Thucydides 3.34.2.
103. Ktesias *FGrHist* 688F15.53.
104. Thucydides 8.5.5, 28.4.
105. Xenophon *Anabasis* 1.2.9.
106. Ibid. 1.2.14–18.
107. Ibid. 1.8.17–20.
108. Ibid. 1.9.4.
109. Ibid. 1.8.20.
110. Ibid. 1.8.24–29.
111. Ibid. 2.5.27–34.
112. Ibid. 1.8.17, 20. For a discussion on the professionalism of the Ten Thousand, see Appendix 7.
113. Diodoros 15.38.1
114. Ibid. 16.49.
115. Isokrates *Panegyrikos* §117, §122.
116. Ibid. §131, §134, §187.
117. E.g. in the *Areopagitikos* Isokrates complains, 'insolence is regarded as democracy, lawlessness as liberty, impudence of speech as equality, and the licence to do whatever one likes as happiness' (§20), to be a caricature of a democracy should be. As such, Athens was, in his mind, in no position to adopt and carry out any sound principle of foreign policy let alone to manage a great military undertaking. Obviously pure democracy was no more to the liking of Isokrates as it had been to Thucydides.
118. The tradition that he committed suicide on hearing that Philip had won the battle at Chaironeia, made familiar through Milton's lines from his Tenth Sonnet: 'As that dishonest victory / At Chaeronea, fatal to liberty, / Killed with report that old man eloquent,' must be set down as fable as Isokrates' third letter to Philip was written in the autumn of 338 BC, not long *after* the Greek defeat.

Chapter 13
1. Diodoros 16.57.2.
2. Xenophon *Anabasis* 7.1.41.
3. Plutarch *Moralia* 915E.
4. For the Greeks and their use of barley, see Pliny *Historia Naturalis* 18.72–75. For the benefits of barley over wheat as the main subsistence cereal, see Garnsey 1988: 10–13.
5. Athenaios 7304b, cf. Aischylos *Agamemnon* 1041.
6. Dioskorides 2.86, Galen 6.507.
7. E.g. Aristophanes *Wasps* 715–18, *Lysistrata* 1203–15.
8. Revelations 6:6.

9. Polybios 6.38.2, Suetonius *Divus Augustus* 24.2, Plutarch *Antony* 39.7, Frontinus *Strategemata* 4.1.37, Vegetius 1.13.
10. Archilochos fr. 2: 'In my spear is my daily bread, / In my spear my Ismaric wine, / On my spear I lean and drink'. Ismaros was a *polis* on the Thracian coast not far from the island of Thasos. Its wines are referred to by Homer (*Odyssey* 9.39, 198).
11. Xenophon *Anabasis* 4.5.26, 5.3.9, 6.1.15, 2.3, 5.1, 7.1.37 etc.
12. In Greek: *mâza*, Archilochos fr. 2. See also Thucydides 4.16.1, Aristophanes *Wasps* 610, *Knights* 55, *Ecclesiazusae* 606, Antiphanes fr. 226 Edmonds = Athenaios 2.60c.
13. Xenophon *Kyroupaideia* 6.2.31.
14. Ibid. 6.2.28. Thucydides 3.49.3, Hermippos fr. 57 Kock.
15. Pherekrates *The Servant Trainer* 46a Edmonds.
16. Xenophon *Kyroupaideia* 1.2.11.
17. Cheese was the major source of protein in the ancient world, as milk would not keep in a hot climate – besides, the actual drinking of milk was seen by Greeks as a mark of pastoral 'barbarians' (e.g. Herodotos 1.216, 3.23, cf. *Odyssey* 1.240). The main source of protein for Olympic athletes was fresh feta cheese, 'straight out of the basket', as Pausanias (6.7.10) puts it. According to the elder Pliny, animals with two nipples – goats and sheep – made the best cheese and today feta is made from a combination of ewe's milk and goat's milk (usually in a ratio 7:3), salted and cured in a brine solution (based on water or whey) for several months. The result is a crumbly white brined cheese, commonly produced in blocks and stored in barrels. As well as feta cheese, other milk products today include clarified butter, and another soft cheese known as *mizithra*, which is made from the whey left after feta production (cf. *Odyssey* 1.219, 244–9). Milk is also mixed with wheat in the production of processed cereal products such as noodles or porridge. Both are made in the summer but eaten in the winter, the period when sheep and goats are not lactating.
18. Thucydides 3.49.3, 4.26.5, Aristophanes *Acharnians* 550–1, *Knights* 599, *Peace* 368, Eupolis fr. 255 Kock.
19. Aristophanes *Peace* 1126–9.
20. Ibid. 528–9.
21. *Iliad* 11.629.
22. Xenophon *Symposium* 4.8.
23. John 19:29.
24. Plautus *Miles Gloriosus* 837, *Truculentus* 610.
25. This explains why there are remarkably few references in the literary sources to soldiers actually carrying water.
26. Xenophon *Lakedaimoniôn politeia* 15.6.
27. Kritias fr. 88B34 Diels-Kranz. With its small handle, which meant it was jolly convenient for stowing away, the *kôthôn* was a popular item of kit not only among Spartan soldiers but others too (Archilochos fr. 4, Aristophanes *Knights* 600, Xenophon *Kyroupaideia* 1.2.8, Theopompos fr. 54 Edmonds, Athenaios 11.483b, *IG* ii 47.6).
28. Luke 10:34.
29. Pliny *Historia Naturalis* 23.27, cf. Celsus 4.5.2.
30. Thucydides 1.48.1, 6.31.5, Lysias 16.14, Aristophanes *Peace* 368, 1181–2, Aristotle *Rhetoric* 3.10.7 (provisions supplied by the individual), Aristophanes *Peace* 311, *Acharnians* 197, *Wasps* 243 (standard three-day ration in Athens), contra Pritchett 1971: 32–3, 34–5, 48, who assumes that provisions supplied by the state were the standard practice.
31. Thucydides 6.44.1, cf. 7.24.2.
32. Ibid. 6.31.5.
33. Ibid. 7.82.3. For local markets selling provisions to campaigning citizen armies, see Herodotos 7.176, Thucydides 1.62.1, 3.6.1, 6.44.3, 50.1, 7.39.2, Xenophon *Hellenika* 3.4.11, 5.4.48, 6.4.9, 5.12, Diodoros 14.79.2. Using the Ten Thousand as a good example: procuring their daily provisions from a market (Xenophon *Anabasis* 1.2.18, 24, 3.14, 5.6, 10, 12, 2.3.26–27, 4.5, 28, 3.1.20, 2.21, 4.8.8, 23, 5.7.13, 23, 6.2.8, 7.6.24, cf. 5.5.6, 7.33, 6.4.16); foraging for their daily provisions (ibid. 2.5.37, 3.4.18, 31, 5.1, 14, 4.1.8, 2.22, 4.2, 7, 9, 6.27, 8.19, 5.1.6, 4.27–29, 6.1.1, 5.32, 6.1).
34. Lysias 16.14.

35. In other words, the Lydians were charging 120 Attic *drachmae* per Attic *medimnos* for their barley meal or wheat flour. For a contemporary comparison, see Aristophanes *Ecclesiazusae* 547–8, which suggests a price of three Attic *drachmae* per *medimnos*.
36. Xenophon *Anabasis* 5.7.20–26.
37. Ibid. 3.2.21.
38. E.g. ibid. 4.3.19, 5.3.1, 4.33 (women), 4.1.14, 6.3, 7.4.7–10 (boys/youths).
39. Eupolis fr. 256 Kock.
40. Xenophon *Lakedaimoniôn politeia* 11.2, 13.4 (commissariat), Thucydides 5.72.3, 6.7.1, Xenophon *Hellenika* 5.4.17 (baggage train & vehicle park).
41. Thucydides 4.6.1.
42. Ibid. 2.57.2.
43. Xenophon *Hellenika* 4.5.4.
44. Ibid. 5.1.14–17, *Hipparchikos* 6.3, *Memorabilia* 3.1.6, *Kyroupaideia* 1.6.9, 12.
45. Ibid. *Anabasis* 6.5.21.
46. Plato (*Republic* 372b, c) has Sokrates and Glaukon allow the citizens of their primitive model *polis* a plain and wholesome diet consisting of bread, wine, salt, olives, cheese, onions and green vegetables. This might be followed by a simple dessert – figs, chickpeas, beans, myrtle beans and roasted acorns. Again, using the Ten Thousand as our example, in his *Anabasis* Xenophon mentions cheese (2.4.28), wine (1.5.10, 2.3.14, 4.28, 4.2.22, 4.9, 5.26, 8.23, 5.4.29, 6.1.15, 2.3, 5.1, 6.1, 74.3) dried fruit (4.4.9, 6.6.1), pulses (4.4.9, 5.26, 6.6.1), and olive oil, or the lack of it (6.6.1), and, finally, barley meal, wine, olives, garlic and onions as part of the soldier's daily diet (7.1.37). Of course, there were times when the mercenaries tightened their belts and simply went hungry (1.1.18–19, 3.1.3, 4.5.5, 8, 11, 7.1.9). Yet one more detail, the indefatigable Xenophon tells us elsewhere (*Kyroupaideia* 1.2.11) Persian nobles were quite prepared to count one day's rations as two in order to harden themselves against possible shortages of food during a campaign. Sensible fellows.
47. In the Peloponnese, according to the British Admiralty (1944–45: II.67), the upper limits above sea level for the olive is 685.8 metres in the west, and 609.6 metres in the east (the Mantiniki in eastern Arcadia, for instance, sits at an elevation of 630.9 metres above sea level). The redoubtable Colonel Leake (1830: I.3.101) claims to have seen olive trees around the village of Paviltza in south-west Arcadia; they do exist there but as the wild mountain variety. As for the cultivated olive in Arcadia, a small number are to be found, but only below the village of Karitaina (personal observation). These specimens, however, are more akin to their wild cousins, as opposed to their more solid sisters to be found in areas like the Argolid or Messenia.
48. Cheese made from ewe's or goat's milk contains fewer calories but more protein than an equivalent weight of bread, onions, garlic and olives considerably less on both accounts, pulses a similar amount of calories but more protein, olive oil many more calories but no protein. A *choinix* (the dry measure equivalent of a man's daily grain ration) of barley meal will provide 2,320 calories, but when cooked and digested as bread it only contains 1,897 usable calories and 63 grams of protein (Foxhall/Forbes 1982: Table 3). Modern medical opinion considers (for largely sedentary populations) that 1,750 to 1,950 calories and around 55 grams of protein are sufficient for a civilian male, while 3,250 calories as a reasonable minimum should sustain a soldier. However, we have to remember an ancient soldier tended to be older, smaller, and more inured to hardship than the pink-faced boys common to modern Western armies. Foxhall and Forbes point out according to United Nations Food and Agriculture Organization standards 'a man aged 20–39, weighing 62kg, would require ... only 2,853 calories per day if he were moderately active', and argue this would be the man of ancient Greece (ibid. 56). By this reckoning, therefore, our ancient soldier would derive some 66 to 67 per cent of his energy needs from consuming his daily bread. For men undertaking arduous physical work, carbohydrates (viz. bread) are obviously crucial. Fats (viz. dairy and olive products) keep out the cold, but protein, though desirable, can wait awhile.
49. Garland 1991: 68.
50. Xenophon *Anabasis* 1.5.6.
51. Ibid. 2.1.6.
52. Aineias Taktikos 40.8.
53. Xenophon *Kyroupaideia* 6.2.31, 3.4, Aristophanes *Acharnians* 54, 1100–1.

54. Plutarch *Lykourgos* 12.1–3, *Moralia* 230D.6, Xenophon *Lakedaimoniôn politeia* 5.3. Plutarch's list provides the following figures for the monthly contributions from each member: one *medimnos* of barley, eight *choes* of wine, five *minae* of cheese, and two and half *minae* of figs.
55. Xenophon *Anabasis* 1.3.12.
56. Demokritos fr. 68B246 Diels-Kranz.
57. E.g. Xenophon *Kyroupaideia* 4.2.35, 37, 5.3.46, *Anabasis* 1.5.10. At a later date, however, the Ten Thousand elected to reduce their baggage train, which included burning the army's tents (ibid. *Anabasis* 3.2.27, 3.1).
58. Ibid. *Kynegetikos* 12.2, Aristotle *Politics* 1319a22–24.
59. Chionides fr. 1 Kock.
60. Xenophon *Hellenika* 7.1.16, 2.22, Aristophanes *Peace* 348, Eupolis fr. 254 Kock, cf. Polybios 5.48.4.
61. Aristophanes *Acharnians* 1136, Xenophon *Anabasis* 5.4.13, *Kyroupaideia* 6.2.30, Aischines 2.99, Alexis fr. 115.
62. Xenophon *Anabasis* 5.4.13, Aischines 2.99.
63. Polyainos 2.1.20, Thucydides 6.75.2, Plutarch *Moralia* 177E.
64. Xenophon *Anabasis* 1.5.10.
65. Ibid. *Hellenika* 2.4.6.
66. Menander *Aspis* 45–7, 53–61, 63, 103–7.
67. Polybios 5.48.1–4.
68. Herodotos 1.63, 6.77.3–78.2.
69. Ibid. 7.148.2, cf. 6.83.1.
70. Xenophon *Hipparchikos* 7.11, cf. Aineios Taktikos 16.12. For other examples in our period of study, Thucydides 7.40 (Syracusans outside Syracuse in 413 BC), Xenophon *Hellenika* 2.1.27 (Spartans at Aigospotamoi in 405 BC), Polyainos 3.9.53 (Iphikrates, no context no date), Demosthenes 23.165 (Charidemos at Perinthos in 359 BC).
71. In Greek: *suskania*, Xenophon *Lakedaimoniôn politeia* 5.2–4, 9.4, 13.1, 7, *Hellenika* 5.3.20.
72. Ibid. *Lakedaimoniôn politeia* 12.1, 4–5.
73. Ibid. 12.5–7.
74. *Odyssey* 9.219 Fagles. According to Odysseus, Ismaric is so divinely potent that to one cup of it are mixed 'twenty cups of water' (ibid. 9.232 Fagles). A powerful wine indeed, for though the ancient Greeks habitually drank their wine diluted with water, the usual proportions of water to wine were 3:1, 5:3, or 3:2.
75. Xenophon *Hellenika* 7.2.22.

Chapter 14
1. Lord Acton, 'Letter to Bishop Mandell Creighton', 5 April 1887, published in J.N. Figgis. & R.V. Laurence (eds.), *Historical Essays and Studies* (London 1907).
2. Xenophon *Anabasis* 6.6.9.
3. Thucydides 2.8.4.
4. Though commonly found in the writings of Plato and Aristotle, *pleonexia* is also a philosophical concept to be found in the New Testament (e.g. Luke 12:13–21).
5. E.g. Herodotos 9.28.2.
6. Thucydides 4.80.5.
7. Cf. Islamic states, in order to maintain a standing army, would often use slave units. The most famous (later, infamous) of the soldier slaves were the élite corps of Janissaries (*Yeni Çeri*, 'new soldiery) who served and protected the Ottoman sultans. Initially, these regiments of pride, discipline and fanaticism were built up by an annual draft, the *devsirme*, of a tenth of all Christian children aged between seven and ten in the sultan's dominions. Once taken from their parents, they were brought up strictly in Islam, vowing to celibacy, absolute loyalty and obedience. After ten years of severe training they were drafted into the corps of Janissaries. In return the sultan provided a career, a status and a salary for life. An alternative to the erratic and disorderly levies of the sultan's vassals-in-arms-for-the-time-being, these professional soldiers with their fierce moustaches and their reputation for merciless plundering, were the sultan's most powerful single weapon, the very symbol of his far-flung rule. Their very name was feared from the banks of the Euphrates to the gates of Vienna, and it would remain so until these 'fearful fiends' of Allah lost their discipline, when they became unmanageable and often mutinous bands.

8. Thucydides 4.80.4.
9. Ibid. 5.34.1.
10. Xenophon *Hellenika* 3.1.4.
11. Ibid. 3.1.8, 23, 2.7.
12. Ibid. 3.4.2.
13. Thucydides 5.6.4.
14. Ibid. 4.80.4 with 78.1.
15. Xenophon *Hellenika* 1.3.15.
16. Ibid. *Anabasis* 7.6.1, 7.57, 8.24, *Hellenika* 3.1.6, Diodoros 14.37.1.
17. Xenophon *Hellenika* 4.3.15, 17.
18. Polyainos 3.9.45.
19. Isokrates *Panegyrikos* §146.
20. Xenophon *Anabasis* 6.4.8.
21. Ibid. 3.1.4.
22. Ibid. 1.3.17, Diodoros 13.66.6.
23. Cf. Aineios Taktikos 12.1, 13.1–4.
24. Quoted in Hale 1998: 133.
25. Xenophon *Hellenika* 6.2.5.
26. Ibid. 5.4.15, 37, 45, 6.4.9, 5.12, 17, 29, 7.1.27, 41, 5.10.
27. Ibid. 5.2.21.
28. Ibid. 5.3.10 (Olynthos), 5.4.15 (Thebes).
29. Ibid. 5.2.24, cf. 3.9, Diodoros 15.9.3, 20.3.
30. Xenophon *Hellenika* 3.4.20. For the Spartan habit of attaching military staff, *sumboúloi*, to their kings and commanders in the field, see Thucydides 2.85.1, 3.69.1, 5.60.1, 63.4, 8.39.2, 54.2, cf. 3.79.3.
31. Xenophon *Anabasis* 6.6.12.
32. Thucydides 6.91.4.
33. Xenophon *Anabasis* 1.4.2–3, cf. 2.21.
34. Ibid. *Hellenika* 3.1.1, cf. Diodoros 14.19.4.
35. Thucydides 2.65.12, Xenophon *Hellenika* 1.4.2–3, 5.3–7, 2.1.14, 3.8.
36. Andokides 3.29.
37. Diodoros 14.21.2, cf. Isokrates *On the Peace* §98, *Panhellenika* §104, Plutarch *Artaxerxes* 6.3, Justin 5.11.6–7.
38. Cyrus and money for Sparta, Thucydides 2.65.12, Xenophon *Hellenika* 1.4.2–3, 5.3–7. See also: Xenophon *Hellenika* 3.1.1, where Cyrus had asked the Spartans to 'show themselves as good friends as he was to them in the war against Athens'; Isokrates *On the Peace* §98 and *Panathenaikos* §104, where the author reckons that Sparta sanctioned Klearchos' command officially; and Plutarch *Artaxerxes* 6.3, where the author tells us that the Spartans ordered Klearchos to give Cyrus 'every assistance'.
39. Cartledge 1987: 191.
40. Xenophon *Anabasis* 7.1.3, cf. 6.1.16.
41. Ibid. 7.1.7.
42. Ibid. 7.1.11.
43. See especially ibid. 1.9.1–29.
44. Ktesias *apud* Photios *Epitome* §70.
45. Xenophon *Anabasis* 6.6.5–36, cf. 7.2.6.
46. Ibid. 7.1.14.
47. Ibid. 7.1.20.
48. Ibid. 7.1.25–31.
49. Ibid. 7.2.1–2, cf. 11.
50. Ibid. 7.2.4.
51. Ibid. *Hellenika* 4.8.33.
52. Ibid. 4.8.21.
53. Ibid. *Anabasis* 7.2.6, cf. 1.36.
54. Ibid. 7.2.12–13, 15, 3.3.
55. Ibid. *Hellenika* 3.1.3–4, cf. 2.12, 4.5, *Anabasis* 7.6.1. According to Diodoros, the ephors sent an ultimatum to Tissaphernes, which told him 'not to bear arms against the Greek *poleis*' (14.35.6).

56. Xenophon *Anabasis* 4.8.25, 6.6.30.
57. Ibid. 4.1.18.
58. Ibid. 2.1.4–5, cf. 2.1.
59. Ibid. 3.1.32–47, 2.1.3, 33, 3.3.
60. Diodoros 14.27.1.
61. Xenophon *Anabasis* 3.2.37–38.
62. Ibid. 3.3.11.
63. Ibid. 3.4.38–42, cf. 4.1.17.
64. Ibid. 5.1.5–13, 2.1, cf. 6.25.
65. Ibid. 6.1.17–19, 25, 31–32.
66. Ibid. 6.2.6, 14, 18, 4.11.
67. Ibid. 6.4.11, 23, cf. 5.6.36.
68. Ibid. 5.7.1–4, cf. 6.2.13–14.
69. Thucydides 8.22.1, cf. 6.4.
70. Xenophon *Anabasis* 7.2.2, cf. 1.13.
71. Ibid. 7.2.11, 3.2, 7, cf. 2.17, 29.
72. Ibid. 7.1.5, 2.2, 10, 2.17–3.14, cf. Diodoros 14.37.1–3.
73. Xenophon *Anabasis* 7.1.8–11, 39, 2.8.
74. Thucydides 6.93.2, cf. 91.4, 7.2.1.
75. Ibid. 7.3.1, 4, 4.2, 5.1–6.2.
76. Ibid. 7.19.3, cf. 58.3.
77. Xenophon *Anabasis* 5.1.15.
78. Diodoros 13.85.3–4.
79. Parke 1933: 64 n. 2.
80. Cartledge 1987: 320.
81. Diodoros 14.10.2–3, 70.3.
82. Ibid. 14.78.1.
83. Polyainos 2.31.1.
84. Diodoros 14.44.2, cf. 58.1. As its fortunes waned, Sparta increased its stakes in the business of supplying mercenaries. So much so, that by the end of the fourth century BC, Cape Tainaron – ideally situated for maritime traffic both east and west, its windswept dead grey rocks were fit for nothing better – became a flourishing international mercenary mart, among other things because a good source of recruits was near at hand (ibid. 17.111.1, 18.9.1, 3, 21.1, 20.104.2, cf. 16.62.3).
85. Xenophon *Hellenika* 7.1.20, cf. Justin *Epitome* 20.5.6.
86. Diodoros 15.70.1.
87. Xenophon *Anabasis* 5.1.15.
88. Ibid. 6.1.32, 6.9–33. Roy (1967: 304) lists Dexippos as a *lochagos* on the basis of his previous career in Sicily.
89. Plutarch *Agesilaos* 36.1.
90. Xenophon *Agesilaos* 2.28–31, cf. Isokrates *To Archidamos* §11.
91. Plutarch *Agesilaos* 36.2, 37.4–5, 40.1, *Moralia* 214D.76, Nepos *Agesilaos* 7.2. Compare, for instance, the case of Agesilaos' old adversary, the buccaneering Chabrias, who went to Egypt in a private capacity as Athens, and although an ally of Tachôs, had declined the pharaoh's plea for military assistance (Diodoros 15.92.3, *IG* ii^2 2.119).
92. Diodoros 15.92.2, Plutarch *Agesilaos* 36.3.
93. Parke (1933: 111) reckons that these hoplites were in fact *neodamôdeis*, while Cartledge (1987: 328) disputes this and argues for mercenaries with a smattering of *déclassé* Spartans who had been depraved of full citizenship through the loss of their estates in liberated Messenia.
94. Diodoros 15.92.2, Plutarch *Agesilaos* 37.1–2, cf. Athenaios 14.616d.
95. Plutarch *Agesilaos* 37.6, cf. Xenophon *Agesilaos* 2.28–31.
96. Plutarch *Agesilaos* 39, cf. Diodoros 15.93.
97. Polyainos 2.16, Frontinus *Strategemata* 2.3.13, Diodoros 16.48.2.
98. Polybios 1.32.1, 7, 9, 33.5–7, 34.1–6. For the battle, see Fields 2010: 42–4.
99. Lazenby (1996: 103) suggests that Xanthippos may have seen elephants in action when the 'elephant king', Pyrrhos, invaded the Peloponnese and attacked Sparta (272 BC). It is, of course, possible.

100. These mercenaries were none other than the remnants of those that had, until fairly recently, been in the employ of Phokis during the Third Sacred War, and were, in fact, still under the command of the Phokian *stratêgos*, Phalaikos. Even more of a coincidence is the fact that Knossian recruiting agents at the Malean promontory in Lakedaimon had hired Phalaikos' mercenary band. Archidamos had backed Phokis against Thebes in this war, which meant Phalaikos and his men, who had been Archidamos' allies in Phokis, now found themselves his enemies on Crete.

101. Diodoros 16.62.3.

102. Ibid. 6.62.4–63.1, 88.3, Plutarch *Agis* 3.4. Lazenby (1985: 169) expresses the feeling that Archidamos ought to have been at Chaironeia.

Chapter 15

1. Herodotos 1.66.
2. Xenophon *Hellenika* 6.4.8–15.
3. Herodotos 9.13.3.
4. Ibid. 9.14.
5. When the yak-tailed standards of the Mongols entered the Polish capital of Krakow it was deserted, and on 24 March 1241 it was burned. To this day the disaster is commemorated: every hour on the hour, a trumpeter from the city fire department sounds the call from the four corners of the cathedral tower, but the call is never finished, it splutters abruptly to an end just at the moment when a Mongol arrow struck the lookout.
6. Herodotos 9.15.2. If Herodotos is correct, and we have no real reason to doubt him here, the palisaded camp would have had sides some two kilometres long. A stade (*stadion*, pl. *stadia*, whence our word stadium) being a Greek unit of distance that varied from place to place, and it is for this reason that we generally consider it to be roughly equivalent to 200 metres.
7. Herodotos 9.19.3. Ancient Erythrai was probably some distance to the east of the modern town of the same name, perhaps a kilometre or so west of the modern village of Dhaphni near the *metóchi* (farm-priory) of the monastery of Osios Melétios (Pritchett 1965: 103–6, Fossey 1988: 101–26). Pausanias probably used the Dryoskephalai pass ('Oak-Heads', today's Kaza pass), the major access route leading north-south between the Kithairon and Parnes ranges (Pritchett 1965: 109). Anyone passing from central Greece to the Peloponnese had to come through this pass, which was known in antiquity as the 'road to Erythrai' (Thucydides 3.24.2, Xenophon *Hellenika* 5.4.14, Arrian *Anabasis* 1.7.9, Pausanias 9.1.6, 2.1–2). Erythrai itself, according to Strabo (9.2.31) and Pausanias (1.38.8–9), at times belonged to Boiotia and at times to Athens. On the other hand, Diodoros (4.2.6, 3.1), Pliny (*Historia Naturalis* 4.7.26), and Apollodoros (*Bibliotheca* 3.5.5) all refer to it as Boiotian. The status of Erythrai at any one period is by no means clear. It seems likely that the Athenians had control late in the sixth century BC, probably after they defeated the Boiotians in 506 BC (*IG* i^3 501 = Fornara 42, Herodotos 5.77, cf. 6.108, Thucydides 3.55.1). In the following century a citizen from Erythrai appears on an Athenian casualty list (*IG* i^2 943 11.96–97), but otherwise the little evidence we have suggests it was under Boiotian control. Both Herodotos (5.74.2) and Thucydides (2.18.2), for instance, recognize Oinoe – and not Erythrai – as the limit of Attica. Nowadays modern Erythrai is an enclave of Attica as the boundary line between the nome of Boiotia (Viotía) and that of Attica (Attikí) runs more or less along the course of the tiny Asopos.
8. Herodotos 5.63.3–4.
9. Ibid. 9.24.
10. Ibid. 9.25.3. Identified by Pritchett (1965: 113–15, 1985: 103) as the Rhetsi, about a kilometre south-east of Agios Ioannis, one of two chapels situated on the Asopos ridge. Of course we should take Herodotos' Gargaphia as a group of springs, not just one, particularly if large numbers of men were to draw from it. See Appendix 8.
11. According to Herodotos, they had attacked 'by squadrons' (*katà télea*, 9.20, 22.1), but when they learned of their commander's death they charged *en masse* (9.22.3, 23.1). The tactic was for each squadron to 'shoot and scoot', that is to say, for squadron after squadron to ride up to within missile range, fire its arrows or hurl its javelins, and then wheel away. The idea was to whittle away enemy resistance and morale by repeated attacks, until they broke and fled.
12. Herodotos 9.13.3, 37.1, 41.4.
13. Ibid. 9.22.1, cf. 61.

14. Ibid. 9.32.2.
15. Burn 1984: 511, Lazenby 1993: 228.
16. Herodotos 9.38.2.
17. Ibid. 9.39.1.
18. Ibid. 9.39.2.
19. Ibid. 9.40.2.
20. Ibid. 9.41.3.
21. Ibid. 9.41.4.
22. See Appendix 2.
23. Plutarch *Moralia* 872B.
24. Herodotos 9.49.2.
25. Loc. cit.
26. The Spartans on the right and the Athenians on the left occupied relatively high ground (Herodotos 9.56.2), and it is likely the former were on what modern commentators have termed the Asopos ridge, and the latter on what is now called Pyrgos hill. The central contingents would have then occupied the low ground astride the Plataia-Thebes road, and the whole position could loosely be described as 'on the Asopos' (ibid. 9.31.1).
27. Ibid. 9.51.1–2.
28. Ibid. 9.51.3.
29. Ibid. 9.51.4.
30. Ibid. 9.52.
31. Ibid. 9.53.2, cf. Thucydides 1.20.3.
32. Thucydides 5.72.1.
33. Herodotos 9.56.1.
34. Ibid. 9.57.2. It seems that we are somewhere near the modern town of Erythrai, formerly the modern village of Kriekouki, for two inscriptions (*IG* vii 1670–1) that mention Eleusian Demeter have turned up here, found in the fabric of a building.
35. Cf. Woodhouse (1898: 52–4) suggests that Amompharetos and his command was *meant* to be left behind, and that the argument had been about who was to form the *rearguard*, an idea that is supported by Lazenby (1993: 237, 240).
36. Herodotos 9.59.2.
37. Ibid. 9.59.1.
38. Ibid. 9.61.2 with 72.1.
39. Ibid. 9.62.1.
40. For the Spartans and battlefield sacrifice, see Xenophon *Hellenika* 4.2.20, cf. *Anabasis* 3.2.12, *Lakedaimoniôn politeia* 13.8.
41. Herodotos 9.62.2.
42. Ibid. 9.62.3.
43. In Greek: *gymnetes*, literally 'naked', ibid. 9.63.2.
44. Ibid. 9.67.
45. Ibid. 9.61.1.
46. Ibid. 9.69.2.
47. Ibid. 9.69.1.
48. Herodotos 9.63.1.
49. Ibid. 9.64.2. Aeimnêstos was to fall in battle, together with the 300 men (the *hippeis*, or an example of *enômotiai* chosen by lot from the twelve *lochoi*?) under his command, near Mount Ithome during the Fourth Messenian War.
50. Plutarch *Aristeides* 19.1, who calls him Arimnêstos instead of Aeimnêstos.
51. Herodotos 9.66.3. Elsewhere, Herodotos has Artabazos escaping with 'the Medes' (9.77), which would have placed him left of the centre in the original battle line (ibid. 9.31.2) between the Persians on the left and the Bactrians in the centre. Artabazos has been accused of deserting Xerxes' cousin, Mardonios, but Xerxes, who was no easygoing master, thought otherwise, considering Artabazos had done well in extricating his command intact. He was to continue his career with success, retaining the royal favour 'after the affair of Plataia' (ibid. 8.126.1). As satrap of Daskyleion in 478/7 BC he assisted in the intrigues of Pausanias that led to the Spartan regent's ruin (Thucydides 1.129.1–3). His father,

Pharnakes, who features in the Persepolis Fortification Tablets (PF 662, 665, 668, 1272, 1795, 1799, 1807, 2070) as 'Parnaka', had held the highest office at court, heading the economic administration of Persepolis and Persis. It is not surprising; he was after all the uncle of Dareios I.

52. Herodotos 9.67.

53. Ibid. 9.70.2.

54. Ibid. 9.70.5, cf. Fornara 58, quoting Plutarch *Aristeides* 19.5–6: 'Of those who struggled on the behalf of Hellas there fell in all 1,360 men. Fifty-two of these were Athenians, all of them from the tribe of Aiantis, as Kleidemos says [Kleidemos *FGrHist* 323F22], it having fought most valiantly'. Herodotos' figures do look small, and it seems, for the Athenians at least, he took the funeral monument of this single tribe to be that of all the Athenians (Hignett 1963: 341). There will certainly have been some fatalities in other tribes. The secondary sources give far larger figures; we have the 1,360 from Plutarch mentioned above, while Diodoros says (11.33.1) more than 10,000 Greeks fell. In Herodotos defence, however, the losses given here do not include the 600 from the centre contingents who were cut down by the Theban cavalry (9.69.2).

55. Herodotos 9.64.1.

56. Cf. ibid. 9.38.2, 41.1, 77.

57. Aischylos *Persai* 817.

58. It was in the waters of this bay on 20 October 1827 that the last fleet action fought between wooden sailing ships ('Heart of oak are our ships, jolly tars are our men') took place. This multinational battle, where the British, French and Russians were aligned against the Turks and Egyptians, was fought under vague orders and in extraordinary disarray, but resulted in the complete destruction of the Turco-Egyptian fleet, which greatly outnumbered that of the Allies (their weight of metal amounted to 1,962 guns against the 1,270 of the Allies). Furthermore, not one of the five nations involved was officially at war with another, and one of the governments on the winning side – the British – refused point-blank to recognize the actions of its admiral and relieved him of his command (the new prime minister, the Duke of Wellington, called the battle 'an untoward event'). All in all, from both the political and tactical point of view, the battle of Navarino presents a picture of utter confusion.

59. This was Sophokles son of Sostratides (Thucydides 3.115.5), and not Sophokles of Kolonos, the famous playwright.

60. Thucydides 3.94.3–98.4.

61. Ibid. 4.2.4.

62. Ibid. 4.3.2.

63. Ibid. 4.3.3.

64. For a similar improvisation of wicker shields by the Athenians, see Xenophon *Hellenika* 2.4.24 (Peiraeus 403 BC).

65. Thucydides 4.9.1–2. The full complement of a trireme was 200 (Herodotos 3.13.1–2, 7.184.1, 8.17, Thucydides 6.8, 8.29.2, Xenophon *Hellenika* 1.5.3–7), of whom 170 were the oarsmen. According to the Decree of Themistokles (Fornara 55), which records the measures taken by the Athenian Assembly in 481 BC to meet the threatened Persian invasion, the fighting men of an Athenian trireme included hoplites, enlisted as 'deck-soldiers (*epibatai*), ten to each ship, from men between the ages of twenty and thirty, and four foot archers (*toxotai*)' (lines 23–6). This practice appears to have continued throughout the fifth century BC (Thucydides 2.23.2, 3.94.1, 95.2). This left ten deckhands plus the sea-captain (*triêrarchos*), the helmsman (*kubernêtês*), the bow officer (*prôratês*), the shipwright (*naupêgos*), the bosun (*keleustês*, 'exhorter'), who controlled the oarsmen, and a flute player (*aulêtês*), who piped time for them (Pseudo-Xenophon *Athenaiôn politeia* 1.2, *IG* ii² 1951.94–105).

66. Diodoros 12.61.2

67. Thucydides 4.8.9. Lazenby (1985: 114) points out the plausible suggestion that this force was made up of twelve *enômotiai* of thirty-five men each, viz. individual units and not individual hoplites were chosen by lot.

68. Thucydides 4.8.3.

69. Ibid. 4.10.5.

70. Ibid. 4.12.1. Curiously, we have this little item from the traveller Pausanias: 'In the Poikile are deposited bronze shields ... others, smeared with pitch to protect them from the ravages of time and rust, are said to be the shields of the Lakedaimonians who were captured at the island of Sphakteria' (1.15.4). Excavations at the Stoa Poikile in the Athenian Agora uncovered the bronze facing of an *aspis*

upon which the crudely punched inscription: ATHENAIOI APO LAKEDAIMONIÔN EK PYLO, the Athenians [dedicate this, taken] from the Lakedaimonians from Pylos. Now in the Agora Museum (Case 36 #34), the so-called 'Shield of Brasidas' was found in a cistern that was filled up in the third century BC, and it cannot therefore have been seen by Pausanias when he visited Athens around AD 150, although it is certainly one of the same series.

71. Thucydides 4.12.1. Such *apobathrai* had been used similarly in the opposed landing at Mykale in 479 BC (Herodotos 9.98.2). The outrigger, *parexeiresia*, was an extension beyond the side of the trireme, which gave greater leverage to the oars pulled by the top-level oarsmen.

72. The origin strength of the fleet was forty triremes (Thucydides 4.2.2), of these five were left with Demosthenes at Pylos (ibid. 4.5.2), of which Demosthenes sent two to seek the main fleet (ibid. 4.8.3), which in turn gained four Chian triremes and 'some of the ships on guard at Naupaktos' (ibid. 4.13.2), viz. nine triremes (40 − 5 + 2 = 37 + 4 = 41 + 9 = 50).

73. The ram of a trireme could smash a hole in an enemy vessel and so cripple her, but could not literally sink her. Ancient sources use terms meaning 'sink', but it is evident that ships so 'sunk' could still be towed away. For instance, the Greek word *kataduein*, which is almost invariably translated as 'sink', in fact means no more than 'dip' or 'lower'. So, when triremes were holed in a sea battle, though they had become absolutely useless as fighting vessels, the combatants went to great lengths and some risk to recover the wrecks. These could be towed home as prizes; after being repaired, equipped and renamed, they became part of the navy (e.g. *IG* ii^2 1606).

74. Thucydides 4.18.2.
75. Ibid. 4.21.2.
76. Ibid. 4.26.8. Black poppyseeds were usually scattered over bread as they are today, while white poppyseeds were roasted with honey and served in pastry or cakes. Alkman fr. 55 Diehl is good evidence for the use of poppyseed and linseed as food by the Spartans: 'Seven couches and as many tables / spread with poppy cakes and linseed and / sesame, and among the wooden flagons / were honey cakes for the young.' This is a drinking bout, not a feast, the cakes and seeds serving as sweetmeats.
77. Thucydides 4.28.4.
78. Spot height 94 metres, the location of 'Grundy's Well'.
79. Thucydides 4.26.2. This is the location known locally as Palaiókastron, the site of a Frankish castle built in 1278 by Nicolas II de Saint-Omer, joint Lord of Thebes (1258–94) and Bailly of the principality of Achaia (1287–9).
80. The reference here by Thucydides is to the two triremes, which kept up a constant patrol round the island (4.23.2). As there was no good anchorage near the shore of Sphakteria on the seaward side, as Thucydides himself notes (4.8.8), at mealtimes the crew of one trireme would make a landing somewhere on the other side of the island and cook their meal, while the other trireme would be out at sea.
81. These would have been all the marines who were part of the complement of an Athenian trireme plus the forty Messenian hoplites that had joined Demosthenes earlier in the campaign (Thucydides 4.9.1), viz. the origin fifty triremes, the four from Chios, nine from Naupaktos, and the twenty with Kleon, a total of eighty-three triremes.
82. Thucydides 4.31.2. This figure probably represents one *enômotia*.
83. According to Athenian Naval Inventories there were twenty-seven oarsmen each side at the lowest level of the trireme, the *thalamîoi*, or hold-rowers. These men worked their oars through oar-ports, *thalamia*. In the middle level there were twenty-seven oarsmen each side, the *zugîoi*, or thwart-rowers. The top level of oarsmen, the *thranîtai*, or stool-rowers, thirty-one on each side, rowed through an outrigger.
84. Thucydides 4.33.1.
85. Ibid. 4.32.4.
86. Ibid. 4.34.3.
87. The scant remains of such rest upon the highest point of the island, Profitis Ilías (131 metres).
88. Pausanias 4.26.2.
89. Though the island is generally rocky to the shore line, there is a small sandy beach on the northeastern tip of the island. This location is today heavily overgrown, particularly with gorse, ilex and holly oak under which lies outcrops of difficult-to-cross rock, but we have to take into account the fact that Sphakteria has not been grazed since the late nineteen-fifties. The cliff face here is virtually sheer, but there are possible ascent routes ('Pritchett's *Skala*'?), which are certainly climbable for those familiar with the local terrain, viz. the Messenian Komon.

90. Thucydides 4.37.3.
91. Ibid. 4.38.3.
92. Ibid. 4.39.3.
93. Aristophanes *Knights* 75–6.
94. Thucydides 4.40.1.
95. Ibid. 4.40.2.
96. Ibid. 5.2.1, 8.2.
97. Ibid. 5.6.2, cf. 4.132.1.
98. Ibid. 5.6.3. Jones (1977: 81–2), following Kromayer and Gomme, reckons Kerdylion is the hill the British, fighting Germano-Bulgarian forces (1916–18), called Saint Catherine's Hill (Hill 164) and is so marked on the British Army map of 1916. However, Pritchett (1965) prefers it to be Hill 339 midway between the Hill 277 and the now abandoned village of Kato Kerdylion. Of the two, Saint Catherine's Hill certainly offers outstanding views of Amphipolis and Eïon, and therefore would have provided Brasidas an excellent position for both guarding Amphipolis and keeping a weather eye out for the Athenians.
99. Thucydides 5.7.4. Jones (1977: 90, cf. 89) reckons this hill was the one known as Hill 147, which sits just east of Amphipolis, viz. the Hill of the Macedonian Tombs, the location of two Macedonian tombs. Pritchett (1965, 1980) reckons that this hill was the one known as Hill 113, a freestanding mesa some two kilometres north-east of Amphipolis. Hill 113 was originally known as *Ennea Hodoi*, Nine Ways, for which reason, according to Herodotos (7.114), Xerxes took eighteen local children, nine boy and nine girls (viz. Thracian Edoni), and buried them alive on the spot. It was the original Athenian colonization site in 437 BC after an abortive attempt twenty-eight years earlier. The hill was fortified by Bulgarian troops in 1916–18.
100. Thucydides 5.8.4. Brasidas' army numbered 2,000 hoplites, 300 Chalcidian horse, 1,000 Myrkinian and Chalcidian peltasts, and an untold number of Amphipolians, hoplites presumably (ibid. 5.6.4, 9.7, 10.9).
101. Ibid. 5.10.6.
102. In this description of the battle we are following the topography of Jones (1977). Pritchett (1980: 308, 336), however, has Brasidas leave Amphipolis via the first gate in the northern circuit opposite a bridge across the Strymon (1,200 tree trunks and posts, which formed the foundation of a wooden bridge, were excavated at this spot by Lazarides in 1977, and Colonel Leake (III.196) mentions the existence of a wooden bridge here in 1806). Brasidas therefore strikes the Athenian column north of Klearidas' point of contact, which Pritchett argues was the rear of the left-wing or 'southern wing' (1980: 342). In other words, Pritchett has Brasidas' and Klearidas' positions in the Lakedaimonian battleline reverse. This perspective of the battle is also followed by Mitchell (1991), who also uses Pritchett's map (1980: 306).
103. Thucydides 5.10.6.
104. Ibid. 5.10.9.
105. Diodoros writes: 'Brasidas, after fighting with the greatest distinction and slaying a very large number, ended his life heroically; and when Kleon also, after displaying like valour, fell in battle, both armies were thrown in confusion because they had no leaders, but in the end the Lakedaimonians were victorious and set up a trophy' (12.74.2). Diodoros clearly did not use Thucydides as his principal source here, but probably Ephoros.
106. Thucydides 2.35–46.
107. Ibid. 5.10.9.
108. Plutarch *Moralia* 219D.2.
109. Aristophanes *Peace* 261, 281.
110. Thucydides 5.16.1.
111. Shakespeare *Macbeth* V.v.26–8.
112. Located just beyond the northern border of Messenia, Lepreion had been a tribute paying ally of Elis, but a few years previously it had won Spartan support. It was here in 421 BC the *brasideioi* along with recently raised *neodamôdeis* were settled, a hoplite colony one thousand strong (Thucydides 5.34.1 with 49.1).
113. Ibid. 5.64.2.
114. Ibid. 5.64.3.

115. Lazenby 1985: 126.
116. Diodoros 12.75.7.
117. Thucydides says (5.67.1) they always occupied the left wing of a Spartan battleline and thus implies they were hoplites rather than lightly armed troops such as peltasts, though they could as scouts or pickets (Xenophon *Lakedaimoniôn politeia* 12.3, 13.6).
118. Thucydides 5.64.5.
119. Ibid. 5.65.1. Thucydides subsequently (5.65.4, 6) refers to the position as on a hill, *lóphos*, which can be identified as the south facing slopes below spot height 830 metres near to the church of Agios Nikolaos, which serves the community of nearby Mêléa, a hamlet a kilometre or so south-east of Mantineia's walls. The actual location of the Herakleion is a matter of dispute of course, Lazenby, for example, says it was probably 'southwest of Mantineia itself' (2004: 119). However, having walked the battle site on a number of occasions, it is equally possible to place the site of the Herakleion approximately 1,500 metres down the minor road running south from Mêléa – which you please.
120. Thucydides 5.65.2.
121. Ibid. 5.65.4.
122. Ibid. 5.65.5.
123. Ibid. 5.66.2.
124. Ibid. 5.67.1, 68.3, 71.3.
125. Ibid. 5.66.4.
126. Ibid. 5.69.1–2.
127. Kagan 1981: 123, 2003: 235.
128. Thucydides 5.61.1.
129. Cf. Diodoros 12.78.4, Lysias 34.7.
130. Thucydides has the Argives deployed in 'five *lochoi*' (5.72.4), and perhaps each contained a thousand hoplites like the unit of élite Argives, making 6,000 Argives in all. At the Nemea, twenty-four years later, there were said to by 'about 7,000' (Xenophon *Hellenika* 4.2.17).
131. Thucydides, 5.68.3 (strength), 67.1 (position).
132. Lazenby (1985: 42–3, 128, 2004: 121–2) argues for double that number, and the same for the Spartans themselves, believing they had twelve *lochoi* in their line and not six as Thucydides implies.
133. Thucydides 5.67.1.
134. Assuming, of course, each hoplite occupied a front of three Greek feet (*c*. 1 metre). According to Kromayer (1926: 217) the confederate frontage was 1,025 metres long, the Spartan frontage 1,125 metres. As Thucydides said, 'the army of the Lakedaimonians appeared the larger' (5.68.1).
135. Thucydides 5.70.
136. Ibid. 5.71.3.
137. Ibid. 5.71.1.
138. Ibid. 5.72.1.
139. Ibid. 5.72.3.
140. Ibid. 5.72.4.
141. Ibid. 5.73.1.
142. Diodoros 12.79.6.
143. E.g. Kagan 1981: 131–2, 2003: 239–41.
144. E.g. Lazenby 1985: 133–4, 2004: 125.
145. Thucydides 5.74.2, cf. 68.2.
146. *IG* v[1] 1124.
147. Thucydides 5.72.6.
148. Ibid. 5.81.1.
149. In Greek: *empeiriai*, ibid. 5.72.2
150. Ibid. 5.75.3.
151. Xenophon *Hellenika* 4.2.9.
152. Strabo 8.6.25, Livy 33.15.1. Though named after the Nemea (modern Koutsomadiotikos), the battle was probably fought near the Rachiani (ancient Longopotamos), a river further to the east. The latter river is about six kilometres from the Acrocorinth, whereas the former is some thirteen to fourteen kilometres, an important consideration when we read in Xenophon that 'the defeated troops at first fled to the walls of Corinth; but afterwards, since the Corinthians shut them out, they encamped again

in their old camp' (*Hellenika* 4.2.23), which was in all probability on the east bank of the Rachiani. Xenophon himself only mentions 'the district of Nemea' (ibid. 4.2.14), while the river itself is given no name other than 'the riverbed' (ibid. 4.2.15), viz. it was a typical Greek winter torrent and therefore bone-dry at this time of the year. All the same, dry or wet, the river still presents a formidable linear obstacle, its limestone, arboreous banks rising sheer for some eight to ten metres along its length between the modern town of Perigialio and the hundred-metre escarpment. For the topography of the battle, see especially Pritchett 1969: 76–83.

153. Xenophon *Hellenika* 4.2.17. At this time Orchomenos supported Sparta (it also had a Spartan garrison of one *mora*), and thus we will find them fighting at Koroneia with Agesilaos, which was fought a little after this battle (ibid. 4.3.15). With regards to the number of Argives, Xenophon appears to show some doubt about the figure, which does seem rather high. Finally, it should be noted that all ten tribes of the Athenians were represented in this battle (ibid. 4.2.19).

154. In his list of Sparta's allied contingents Xenophon (*Hellenika* 4.2.16) omits the contingent from Tegea, which he mentions in his account of the battle (ibid. 4.2.19), possibly a contingent from Mantineia, where he says the Spartans picked up hoplites on their march to Sikyon, along with the Tegeans (ibid. 4.2.13), and possibly a further contingent from Achaia, for he mentions Achaians (other than Sikyonians) in a latter passage (ibid. 4.2.18, cf. 20). According to Diodoros, the hoplite numbers were 23,000 Spartan (14.83.1) and 15,000 confederate (14.82.10), and it is tempting to suggest that he has got his totals for the two armies the wrong way round. Thus, by using Diodoros' figures we could argue there were 15,000 hoplites on the Spartan side and 23,000 hoplites on the confederate side, which does come close to Xenophon's totals. Lazenby (1985: 136) reckons we should add about 5,000 to Xenophon's total for the Spartan army, thereby bumping it up to between 18,000 and 19,000 hoplites.

155. Xenophon *Hellenika* 4.2.18.

156. Ibid. 4.2.20.

157. Thucydides 5.68.3.

158. Xenophon *Hellenika* 6.4.12.

159. Ibid. 4.2.13, 18, cf. Diodoros 14.82.2–3.

160. Xenophon *Hellenika* 4.2.18.

161. Ibid. 4.2.19.

162. Ibid. 4.2.20.

163. Ibid. 4.2.22.

164. Ibid. 4.3.1, cf. Diodoros 14.83.2, who says 1,100 of the Lakedaimonians and their allies for 2,800 of the Boiotians and their allies

165. Xenophon *Hellenika* 4.3.10. The date of the eclipse, according to our calendar, was 14 August 394 BC.

166. Ibid 4.3.15. For Gylis, see ibid. 4.3.21, 23, *Agesilaos* 2.15.

167. Ibid. *Hellenika* 3.4.2.

168. Ibid. 4.3.15, cf. 3.4.20, *Agesilaos* 2.11, *Anabasis* 5.3.6, Plutarch *Agesilaos* 18.1. At this date the Cyreians probably numbered no more than 5,000 hoplites (cf. Xenophon *Hellenika* 4.2.5).

169. Xenophon *Hellenika* 4.3.15. The contingent from Orchomenos perhaps numbered around one thousand hoplites (cf. ibid. 4.2.17).

170. Ibid. 4.3.15, cf. 4.2.17.

171. Lazenby 1985: 144, cf. Xenophon *Hellenika* 4.2.17, the confederate numbers at the Nemea.

172. Xenophon *Agesilaos* 2.9, *Hellenika* 4.3.16.

173. Loc. cit. The acropolis of ancient Koroneia, some three kilometres south-west of the village of Mamoura, is a disappointing site apart from the remains of a Frankish tower on its north-eastern slope. The tower, with its commanding view of the Kopaic basin, belonged to the Lordship (after 1260 the Duchy) of Athens and Thebes, which had first been granted in 1205 to Othon de la Roche-sur-l'Ognon, a Burgundian knight, with the title Grand Seigneur of Athens and Thebes. The magnificence of the Athenian court under Guy I de la Roche, the first Duke, is noted by the Catalan chronicler Ramon Muntaner, while the excellence of the French spoken at Thebes was much written about by Western visitors. The Duchy, of course, was part of that strangest freak of mediaeval history, the short-lived Latin Empire of the East, which had been the sordid result of the ill-famed expedition generally called the Fourth Crusade.

174. Mount Helikon (1,750 metres) was of course sacred to the Nine Muses, and the settlement of Askra in its shadow, the home of Hesiod.
175. Xenophon *Agesilaos* 2.10.
176. Ibid. 2.11, *Hellenika* 4.3.17.
177. Loc. cit.
178. Ibid. *Hellenika* 4.3.18.
179. Loc. cit. For the Lakonian countermarch, see Plan 3.
180. Loc. cit. Close order, according to Asklepiodotos (4.1), was when men locked their shields and stood only one cubit (0.45 metres) apart between left shoulders. Normally, each hoplite had a frontage of about one metre.
181. Xenophon *Hellenika* 4.3.19.
182. Ibid. *Agesilaos* 2.9, *Hellenika* 4.3.16.
183. Ibid. *Hellenika* 4.3.19.
184. Ibid. *Agesilaos* 2.12.
185. Loc. cit.
186. Plutarch *Agesilaos* 18.3.
187. Ibid. 18.4. Frontinus (*Strategemata* 2.6.6) and Polyainos (2.1.19) also both say that the Spartans deliberately opened ranks to let the Thebans through, though they then say the Spartans attacked them from the rear and not the flanks. A minor difference, perhaps.
188. Xenophon *Hellenika* 4.3.20. Plutarch (*Agesilaos* 19.2) identifies this as the temple of Itonian Athena, which has been plausibly located by Pritchett (1969: 85–9) at the site of the present-day Agios Metamorphosis, about a kilometre east-north-east of the village of Mamoura. Again according to Plutarch (loc. cit., cf. *Perikles* 18.2–3), outside the temple stood a trophy commemorating the Boiotian victory over the Athenians at the First Koroneia in 447 BC. Incidentally, Mamoura was the site of the Panboiotia, the Boiotian general assembly.
189. Xenophon *Agesilaos* 2.14.
190. Diodoros 14.84.2.
191. Xenophon *Hellenika* 4.3.21. The god being honoured of course was Dorian Apollo.
192. Lazenby 1985: 148. It is assumed that the Thebans had formed their phalanx at least twenty-five shields deep, as at Delion in 424 BC (Thucydides 4.93.4, cf. Xenophon *Hellenika* 4.2.18).
193. Xenophon *Hellenika* 4.4.16, Polyainos 3.9.24. Iphikrates was probably born about 413 BC, and his age makes it most unlikely that he was a *stratêgos* at this time, being less than thirty years of age. Xenophon speaks of Kallias as 'the *stratêgos* of the Athenian hoplites' and Iphikrates as 'the leader of the peltasts' (*Hellenika* 4.5.13).
194. Ibid. 4.5.11.
195. Cf. ibid. 4.2.16, Lazenby 1985: 12.
196. Xenophon says that when Iphikrates left the Isthmus for the Chersonese he took with him '1,200 peltasts, the majority of whom were of those whom he had commanded in Corinth' (*Hellenika* 4.8.34).
197. Ibid. 4.5.13.
198. Ibid. 4.5.14, 16. These hoplites were the youngest fifteen year classes, each year-class including those who had reached military age (viz. twenty years of age) in the same year. According to Lazenby (1985), the Spartans in the fourth century BC organized themselves into at least eight groups of age classes by which men were divided from their twenty-first year to their sixtieth year, the oldest age group comprising men in their fifty-sixth to sixtieth years were not normally required for campaigns abroad. So in the first 'running out', *ekdromê*, the *polemarchos* sent out the men of age groups twenty to thirty years of age, and in the second *ekdromê*, men of age groups twenty to thirty-five years of age.
199. Xenophon *Hellenika* 4.5.17. In modern parlance this works out to be 370 metres and three kilometres respectively. In the modern village of Lekhaion there does exist a potential location for Xenophon's 'small hill', Hill 32, which is some three kilometres from the course of the Long Walls of ancient Corinth and some 400 metres from the Gulf of Corinth. From its northern flank it does indeed resemble a small hill, but from its southern flank it does not, having been cut by the old Corinth-Patras highway. The site now accommodates the church of Agios Konstandinos and a tavernas complete with veranda and patio. The location, despite the modern clutter, still offers a good view of the Gulf of Corinth to the north, and the sugarloaf mountain of the Acrocorinth to the south-east.
200. Xenophon *Hellenika* 4.5.14.

Notes

201. Ibid. 5.4.1–14.
202. Xenophon's account of Leuktra is somewhat wanting; Epameinondas and Pelopidas are not named and their plans and actions not explored. Some help is provided by Diodoros (15.51–56) and Plutarch's *Pelopidas* (20–23), but much is still uncertain. In his account of the battle, Diodoros fails to give any hint of the cavalry action that opened the day's events, which was probably coordinated with the rapid advance of the Theban phalanx. Plutarch, naturally, is concerned with the doings of his fellow Boiotian, and unfortunately his life of Epameinondas has not survived.
203. Xenophon *Hellenika* 6.4.17.
204. Ibid. 6.4.12.
205. Ibid. 6.4.9.
206. Pausanias 8.6.2.
207. Plutarch *Pelopidas* 20.1 gives us the figure of 10,000 hoplites and 1,000 horsemen for the Spartan army, the latter being made up of Herakleots, Phleiousians and Lakedaimonians according to Xenophon *Hellenika* 6.4.9, 10.
208. Diodoros 15.53.2, 3, and Pausanias 9.13.3 give us the figures of 4,000 and 3,000 for the Theban and Boiotian hoplites respectively, while Plutarch *Pelopidas* 23.2 mentions the 300 Sacred Band. As for the horsemen, we are assuming of course that each of the seven federal divisions that made up the Boiotian League provided a hundred horse, which meant 400 of them would have been Theban.
209. Xenophon *Hellenika* 6.4.6.
210. Diodoros 15.33.3–4, Frontinus *Strategemata* 1.11.16.
211. Cf. Diodoros 15.53.4–6, Plutarch *Pelopidas* 20.3–4, Frontinus *Strategemata* 1.11.16, Polyainos 2.3.8.
212. Frontinus *Strategemata* 1.12.7.
213. Xenophon *Hellenika* 6.4.8.
214. Major Bellenden's remarks on Sir James Turner spring to mind: 'He wants to draw up the cavalry in front of a stand of pikes, instead of being upon the wings. Sure am I, if we had done so at Kilsyth [15 August 1645], instead of having our handful of horse upon the flanks, the first discharge would have sent them back among our Highlanders' (quoted in Sir Walter Scott *Old Mortality*, note VII).
215. Xenophon *Hellenika* 6.4.12.
216. Ibid. 6.4.14.
217. *Contra* Buckler 1980: 63.
218. Xenophon *Hellenika* 6.4.12.
219. At Delion in 424 BC the Thebans on the Boiotian right had been massed twenty-five shields (Thucydides 4.93.4); at the Nemea in 394 BC, the Boiotians had 'made their phalanx really deep' (Xenophon *Hellenika* 4.2.18), and certainly deeper than sixteen shields deep.
220. Plutarch *Pelopidas* 23.2.
221. Ibid. 20.2, cf. 23.4. With 4,000 Theban hoplites massed fifty deep, the phalanx would only have had a frontage of eighty shields.
222. Xenophon *Hellenika* 6.4.11. A force of 400 cavalry had first been instituted by Sparta after the Athenian occupation of Kythera in 424 BC (Thucydides 4.55.2).
223. Xenophon *Hellenika* 6.4.10.
224. As we saw outside Lechaion nineteen years previously, the Lakedaimonian cavalry put up a very poor showing (Xenophon *Hellenika* 4.5.16).
225. Diodoros 15.56.1.
226. Polyainos 2.3.3.
227. Xenophon *Hellenika* 6.4.13.
228. Ibid. 6.4.14. The Spartan camp overlooked the plain of Leuktra, probably just south of the level ground between the fork in the modern Livadhóstrata-Thespiai road and the Epameinondas *tropaion*. Livadhóstrata on the Gulf of Corinth is the site of ancient Kreusis, where Kleombrotos captured twelve Theban triremes (ibid. 6.4.3 – ten according to Diodoros 15.53.1). The Boiotians, for their part, probably had their camp directly opposite to the north on Hill 371. See especially Pritchett 1965: 57–9. The Epameinondas *tropaion* sits to the east of the battle site, and has been reconstructed. The sculptured shields are originals bar one – this was later found and left at the foot of the monument – and are full-size stone replicas of the *aspis*. On 7 August 1991 (a memorable day) the Boiotian Survey Team B (Cambridge University) located a large worked block of marble, which was soon

identified as one of the circular triglyphs and metopes belonging to the monument. The find was some four kilometres from the battle site, sitting in a cotton field just south of ancient Thespiai. As reconstructed, the monument is a circular plinth of triglyphs and metopes with a dome-shaped roof of nine hoplite shields sculptured in high relief.
229. Diodoros 15.56.2, Plutarch *Pelopidas* 23.4.
230. Xenophon *Hellenika* 6.4.15.
231. Diodoros 15.56.4.
232. Pausanias 9.13.12.
233. Xenophon *Hipparchikos* 4.4.14.
234. Polyainos 2.3.15.
235. Xenophon *Hellenika* 6.4.12.
236. Pausanias 9.15.4. This was actually one of the verse lines of the epitaph inscribed upon the tomb of Epameinondas at Thebes. Fitting words, for he was of course Sparta's chief nemesis.

Chapter 16

1. Herodotos 1.16.2.
2. Cook 1958–1959: 24.
3. Herodotos 1.162.2.
4. Ibid. 5.115.2.
5. For the Corinthian helmet, see Hellström 1984.
6. E.g. Herodotos 4.200.2 (mining), 6.18 ('making use of every known device').
7. Thucydides 2.75.2–3.
8. Ibid. 7.29.3.
9. Ibid. 7.29.4.
10. Plato *Laws* 778d4–779a7.
11. Ibid. *Gorgias* 519a.
12. Xenophon *Oikonomikos* 5.4–5, 6.6–7, 10, Isokrates *Areopagitikos* §13, cf. *On the Peace* §77, §84.
13. Thucydides 1.143.5, cf. Pseudo-Xenophon *Athenaiôn politeia* 2.14–16.
14. Thucydides 7.77.7, cf. Alkaios frs. 28, 29 Page.
15. Thucydides 2.30.1 (Astakos), 3.97.2 (Aigition), 5.6.1 (Galepsos), 8.62.2 (Lampsakos), Diodoros 14.36.2–3 (Magnesia), Xenophon *Hellenika* 7.1.28 (Karyai), 4.20 (Kromnos).
16. Diodoros 12.28.3–4.
17. Thucydides 1.117.3.
18. Ibid. 2.75–78, 3.52.1–2.
19. Ibid. 4.100.2–4.
20. Ibid. 1.102.2, cf. Herodotos 9.70.2, 102.2–4.
21. Thucydides 2.70.1–3, Diodoros 12.46.4–6.
22. Thucydides 3.27–28.
23. Ibid. 4.66–68.
24. *IG* i³ 363.19 = Fornara 113, cf. Nepos *Timotheos* 1.2, Isokrates *Antidosis* §111, Diodoros 12.28.3, who give 1,200 talents.
25. Thucydides 2.70.2, Diodoros 12.46.4, cf. Isokrates *Antidosis* §113, who gives 2,400 talents.
26. Thucydides 3.19.1, cf. 1.141.5.
27. Diodoros 14.50.4, cf. 41.4.
28. Heron *Belopoïika* §§75–81.
29. Plutarch *Moralia* 191E.
30. It is conceivable that this military gentleman was none other than Aineias of Stymphalos, not merely a contemporary of Xenophon's but actually mentioned by him as a '*stratêgos* of the Arcadians' (*Hellenika* 7.3.1). For a summary of the arguments one way or the other, see Whitehead 2001: 10–13. Stymphalos was an Arcadian *polis* north of the Mantiniki and controlled the surrounding area, which included the *poleis* of Oligyrton and Alea. Interestingly, Stymphalos at this time produced another soldier scholar, Sophainetos of Stymphalos, one of the original *stratêgoi* of Cyrus' Greeks (Xenophon *Anabasis* 1.1.11, 2.3, 2.5.37, 4.4.19, 5.3.1, 8.1, 6.5.13) and thus not only a contemporary of Xenophon's but a comrade in arms too. He also compiled an account of the adventures of the Ten Thousand but, unfortunately, we

have only four extant fragments of his work (*FGrHist* 109F523). And who was it that said Arcadians were artless analphabetic acorn eaters?

31. Aineias Taktikos 32.8.
32. Ibid. 1.3–7, 11.1–2, 18–20.
33. Thucydides 3.68.4.
34. Ibid. 2.71.2.
35. Ibid. 2.73.3.
36. Ibid. 2.75.5
37. Ibid. 2.77.4.
38. Four years later, as already mentioned, the Boiotians built their primitive flamethrower, which got around the problems encountered by the Spartans by containment and by creating a manmade wind.
39. In Greek *sitopoioí*, Thucydides 2.78.3. This is one of the few references by Thucydides to women, and not a particularly glorious role for them either.
40. Ibid. 3.20–24, 52–68.
41. Xenophon *Hellenika* 5.2.1–2, cf. Thucydides 5.29.1.
42. Strabo 8.3.2.
43. Aristotle *Politics* 1318b4–5.
44. Pausanias 8.8.9, 10, Xenophon *Hellenika* 5.2.7, 6.4.18, cf. 5.3–5.
45. Thucydides 4.134.1–2, 5.28.3–29.2, 33.1–3, 81.1.
46. Xenophon *Hellenika* 5.2.1–2, cf. Thucydides 5.29.1.
47. Polybios 4.68.5, 70.1.
48. Pausanias 8.53.10.
49. Polybios 4.21.1.
50. Completion in mud-brick unquestionably saved a great deal of time and money. The bricks could be made rapidly with little apparatus and by unskilled labour. Nor were speed and cheapness the only advantages brick offered. Mud-brick is fireproof and practically indestructible to the weather when the surface is properly protected. Also, a brick construction is not affected by minor earthquake shocks.
51. Xenophon *Hellenika* 5.2.1–3.
52. Pausanias 8.8.7–8, cf. Apollodoros *Poliorkêtika* 157.1–158.3.
53. Xenophon *Hellenika* 5.2.4–5, cf. Diodoros 15.12.1.
54. Pausanias 8.8.9.
55. Herodotos 7.107.1, Thucydides 1.98.1, Plutarch *Kimon* 7, Polyainos 7.24, *Oxyrhynchos Papyri FGrHist* 13.1610 F 6 = Fornara 61B (2).
56. Aischines 3.183–185, Plutarch *Kimon* 7.3
57. Xenophon *Hellenika* 6.5.3.

Epilogue

1. Sir Winston Churchill, Speech in the House of Commons, 20 August 1940.
2. E.g. Isokrates comments (*Panathenaikos* §§185–187) that because the gods are careless and their vast neglect often permits the just to lose and the unjust to win, men should esteem a just defeat over an unjust victory, precisely as men praise the Spartan defeat at Thermopylai.
3. Herodotos 7.233.1.
4. The Boiotians in general and the Thebans in particular had a poor reputation in Greece as boorish anti-intellectual pork-eating gluttons, but that was largely a smear spread by their stuck-up neighbours in Athens. After all, Hesiod (by adoption), Pindar and Plutarch, not to mention the philosopher *stratêgos* Epameinondas, were Boiotians.
5. Herodotos 7.205.3.
6. Diodoros 11.4.7.
7. Herodotos 7.224.1.
8. Ibid. 7.229.1.
9. Ibid. 8.25.1.
10. Ibid. 9.28.
11. Alkidamas *apud* scholia to Aristotle *Rhetoric* 2.2.1373b18–19, cf. *Politics* 1253b20.
12. Herodotos 7.104.4.
13. Ibid. 7.103.4, 223.3.

14. Thucydides 4.96.3.
15. See especially Hanson 1999.
16. Herodotos 9.30.
17. Ibid. 7.238.1.
18. Ibid. 8.24.1.
19. Lazenby 1993: 148.
20. Diodoros 11.10.1–4.
21. Wilfred Owen 'Dulce et Decorum Est' lines 27–8. This famous Latin tag is Horace's old do-or-die aphorism, and was just epitaph for the thoroughgoing insane: 'The glorious and the decent way of dying/Is for one's country.'(*Odes* III. ii. 13–14). The first three books of Horace's *Odes* were published in 23 BC. And then there is John Owen's commonsense response to Horace's claim: '*Pro patria mori dulce et/Decorum est* / But for both you and your country / To live is best.'
22. Xenophon *Hellenika* 6.4.13–15.
23. Herodotos 7.228.

Appendix 1

1. Aristotle *Politics* 1253a9.
2. Ibid. 1297b1–2.
3. Ruschenbusch 1984: 55–7, 1985: 253–63.

Appendix 2

1. Herodotos 7.228.1. A myriad is ten thousand. However, when we hear of the Persian 'myriad' (Gr. *murias*) it commonly stands for 'countless numbers' in the Greek sources much as we use loosely millions, billions or trillions.
2. Ibid. 7.21.
3. Ibid. 7.186.2.
4. Ibid. 7.185.1.
5. Ibid. 7.60.1, 185.1.
6. Ibid. 7.87.1, 185.1.
7. Ibid. 7.185.1.
8. Ibid. 7.185.2.
9. Ibid. 7.50.4.
10. Ibid. 7.121.2–3.
11. Thucydides 1.15.1.
12. Ibid. 6.33.5.
13. Herodotos 7.60.2.
14. E.g. PF 1285, PF 1318, PF 1404.
15. Herodotos 7.187.2.
16. Polybios 6.39.13.
17. Aristophanes *Lysistrata* 1207.
18. Athenaios 6.272b.
19. Cato *On Agriculture* 56.
20. Thucydides 4.16.1.
21. Herodotos 6.57.
22. Thucydides 7.87.2.
23. Herodotos 7.125.
24. Leonard 1894: 134, 153–4,187–206.

Appendix 4

1. Herodotos 3.79–83.
2. Ibid. 3.82.
3. Thucydides 2.37.1.
4. It should be noted that the Greek term *dêmos*, though commonly translated as 'people', does not mean 'people' in any sense with which we are familiar.
5. The Gettysburg Address, delivered by the president at Gettysburg, Pennsylvania, 19 November 1863.
6. Thucydides 4.22.1–2.

7. Ibid. 4.27–28, cf. Demosthenes 19.19–23, Aischines 2.47–53.
8. Aristophanes in *Acharnians* 1–173.
9. Fornara 100B.34–5.
10. Ibid. 156.
11. Ibid. 155, Harding 66.
12. Xenophon *Hellenika* 1.7.9.
13. Ibid. 1.7.12.
14. Plato *Apology* 32b–c, Xenophon *Memorabilia* 1.1.18.
15. Demosthenes 18.168–177.
16. Aristotle *Athenaiôn politeia* 62.3.
17. Hornblower 2002: 138.
18. Harding 20, 38.
19. Oxyrhynchos Historian 9.1.
20. Aristophanes *Wasps* 587.
21. Herodotos 3.82.
22. Thucydides 2.37.1.
23. Demosthenes 20.106.
24. Thucydides 6.38.5.
25. Ibid. 2.37–39, Lysias 2.14.
26. Thucydides 2.13.6, Aristophanes *Wasps* 709.
27. See especially Hansen 1982: 173.
28. Thucydides 7.27.5.
29. Ibid. 8.40.2.
30. Aristophanes *Wasps* 231,
31. In Athens the state paid for the ship and its crew, whereas the equipment and repairs were paid for by a rich citizen as one of the liturgies, the *triêrarchia*. According to the Decree of Themistokles the 'qualifications are the possession of land and a house in Attica, children born in wedlock, age not over fifty' (Fornara 55.20–3). We do have a figure for the total of those wealthy enough to qualify for this public honour at the time of the Peloponnese War, the 400 mentioned by the Old Oligarch (Pseudo-Xenophon *Athenaiôn politeia* 3.4). The *triêrarchia* was a brilliant Athenian notion, which shamed the richest citizens into spending their wealth on the state, without the need for taxation – the Athenians, like most Greeks, found direct taxes of any kind objectionable. This carefully organized and legally sanctioned system allowed the citizen to serve, for one year, as the *triêrarchos* of the vessel he had thus sponsored. The position bought honour, but it also entailed much trouble, risk of life, and often-exorbitant financial demands, an aggregation felt to be particularly onerous during the distressing final years of the Peloponnesian War. The amounts involved were indeed considerable. For a complete set of equipment *triêrarchoi* were required to pay 2,169 *drachmae* if it included an ordinary, 'heavy' sail (*IG* ii² 1629.667–673), or 2,299 *drachmae* if it included a finer, 'lighter' sail (*IG* ii² 1629.577–584). Other gear included 170 working oars plus thirty spares, two steering-oars, two ladders, three poles, as well as various bits of tackle and ropes of various thickness and length. Replacement of a hull meant payment of 5,000 *drachmae* (*IG* ii² 1628.353–368), which thus puts the replacement of an entire ship at 7,169 or 7,299 *drachmae*. Towards the end of our period, the value of trireme gear had risen to about 4,100 *drachmae* (*IG* ii² 1631.446–448, 462–466). Little wonder then to see the orator Lysias pinning on the triremes the epithet 'gluttonous' (fr. 39 Talheim). He, in another forensic speech (19.29, 42), speaks of a man who had been a *triêrarchos* for three consecutive years and spent 8,000 *drachmae* (an annual average of 2,666 *drachmae*). There were large costs involved in keeping a trireme afloat.
32. Demosthenes 18.173.
33. Aristophanes *Knights* 41. The Pnyx was a rocky hill near the Acropolis, and it was here, forty or so regular meetings a year, the *ekklêsia* was held.
34. Aristophanes *Ecclesiazusae* 292.
35. Demokritos fr. 68B251 Diehl-Kranz.

Appendix 5
1. Thucydides 6.31.3, cf. 26.2 Lysias 15.11.
2. Thucydides 6.43.

3. Ibid. 7.16.1.
4. Ibid. 7.20.2.
5. Aristophanes *Knights* 1369–71.
6. Xenophon *Hellenika* 2.4.9.
7. Lysias 20.13, Aristotle *Athenaiôn politeia* 49.2.
8. Hansen (1981) reckons that the oldest and youngest men are not just of the *zeugitai*, the third property class, but the oldest and youngest from all four property classes. This explains, he says, why the 'home guard' outnumbers the field army. True or not, in times of hostilities it was these hoplites who occupied the border forts and manned the walls of Athens and Peiraeus.
9. Thucydides 2.13.6–8. For what it is worth, the same figure for the triremes is given by Aristophanes *(Acharnians* 545).
10. For citizen archers, see Herodotos 9.22, 60 (Plataia), Thucydides 3.98.1 (Aitolia), 4.9.2, 32.2, 4, 34.2 (Sphakteria), 5.84.1 (Melos), 6.43, 94.4 (Sicily). See also, Thucydides 3.98.1, *IG* i² 79.7, *toxárchos* ('leader of archers'), and Fornara 78, the Athenian casualty list of the Erechtheid tribe (460/59 BC), which includes four citizen archers (lines 67–70). For the Scythian police force, see Aristophanes *Acharnians* 54, Plato *Protagoras* 319c, cf. Thucydides 8.98.1.
11. Aristotle *Athenaiôn politeia* 61.1. Most importantly, Aristotle says here, 'the ten *stratêgoi*, who once were elected one from each tribe, *phylê*, but are now elected from the whole citizen body'. In other words, the ten *stratêgoi* were in origin the ten tribal commanders, because the pre-democratic Athenian army was commanded by the *polemarchos*, the third archon of Athens after the eponymous and king archons. Kleisthenes' democratic reforms of 508 BC had included the election of the *stratêgoi* 'by tribes, one from each tribe, while the whole army was under the command of the *polemarchos*' (ibid. 22.2). From 487 BC onwards, however, the appointment of the archons, including the *polemarchos*, was done by lot. Now, though the *polemarchos* retained the sacrificial duties connected with war and the judicial competence over visiting foreigners and resident aliens (viz. *metoikoi*), the office had now lost its military importance (ibid. 22.5, 58.1–3, cf. Herodotos 6.109).
12. Plutarch *Perikles* 16.3.
13. Thucydides 2.65.9.
14. Aristotle *Politics* 1273a26–27.
15. This slice of Arabian wisdom was later accredited to George Washington, who ostensibly said: 'It is better for an army of donkeys to be led by a lion than an army of lions to be led by a donkey'.
16. Plutarch *Moralia* 177C.
17. E.g. Xenophon *Hellenika* 4.2.19, Diodoros 18.10.2.
18. Aristotle *Athenaiôn politeia* 60.3. Although Aristotle wrote the *Athenaiôn politeia* during the three-twenties, there is much earlier confirmation that the *taxiarchoi* and *lochagoi* served under the *stratêgoi*. Xenophon (*Memorabilia* 3.1.5, cf. 4.1, Aristophanes *Peace* 1172–4) mentions one Nikomachides who had served both as a *lochagos* and *taxiarchos*. At an earlier date, Aristophanes (*Acharnians* 575, 1074, cf. Plutarch *Moralia* 186F) twice refers to the *lochoi* of Lamachos in passages that are otherwise completely uninformative. Slightly later, Xenophon (*Hellenika* 1.2.3) refers to two *lochoi* of hoplites during his account of the campaign of Thrasyllos in 409 BC.
19. Thucydides 5.61.1.
20. Xenophon *Hellenika* 4.2.17.
21. Note, as discussed above, some scholars (e.g. Hansen) dispute the existence of a central register, the *katálogos*.
22. Demosthenes 3.14.
23. Andokides 3.5, cf. Aischines 2.173.
24. Aristophanes *Knights* 225, cf. Thucydides 2.13.8, Philochoros fr. 39, Andokides 3.7, Aischines 2.174, Aristotle *Athenaiôn politeia* 24.3. The Athenian cavalry corps was expanded to a thousand-strong during the archonship of Diphilos in 442/1 BC, probably as a result of a law moved by Perikles. For a discussion on the number of Athenian horsemen, see Burgh 1988: 39–52, Spence 1995: 97–102.
25. Aristotle *Politics* 1321a11, cf. 1289b33–36.
26. Xenophon *Peri Hippikes* 2.1. For wealth as one of the characteristics of the *hippeis*, see Spence 1995: 191–3.
27. Aristotle *Athenaiôn politeia* 7.3–4.
28. Xenophon *Hipparchikos* 1.11.

29. Ibid. 2.2.
30. See Arrian *Taktika* 16.6–11 for a discussion on the relative merits of tetragonal and wedged-shape cavalry formations.
31. Xenophon *Hipparchikos* 2.3.
32. Aristotle *Athenaiôn politeia* 61.4.
33. Xenophon *Hipparchikos* 3.6, 11.
34. Aristotle *Athenaiôn politeia* 60.4.
35. Lysias 15.11, 16.13.
36. Aristotle *Athenaiôn politeia* 1.3, 61.4–5, Demosthenes 4.26.
37. Xenophon *Hipparchikos* 2.2.
38. Thucydides 5.47.6, Demosthenes 4.29, scholia to Aristophanes *Knights* 225–6, scholia to Aristophanes *Acharnians* 6, cf. Fornara 154.13: '[monthly] allowance for grain for horses was paid'. Anderson (1961: 138) reckons the sixteen and a half talents spent by the Treasurers of Athena in 410/9 BC was more than adequate to feed a thousand cavalry mounts.
39. Lysias 16.6–7.
40. Xenophon *Hipparchikos* 1.8.
41. Found in the Athenian Agora were thin lead tablets, either rolled or folded, inscribed with a man's name in the genitive case on the outside, and the colour of his horse, a description of the horse's brand, and a price in hundreds of *drachmae* on the inside face: e.g. 'Of Arkesos, black, with a snake, 700 *drachmae*' (Kroll 1977: no. 36), or 'Of Konon, a chestnut, with a centaur, 700 *drachmae*' (Kroll 1977: no. 69). These documents are no other than part of the archives of the Athenian cavalry corps and were used for record keeping and reimbursement by the state should a horse be lost in battle. Twenty-six of them date to 350–340 BC, another eighty-five to around 250 BC, while several hundred of these lead tablets, dated to the third century BC, were also found in a well in the courtyard of the Dipylon Gate, some 400 metres to the north-west of the Agora. In the fourth-century BC sample values range from 100 to 700 *drachmae*, with the median (the middle price in the total range) and the mode (the most frequently paid price) both at 500 *drachmae*. The maximum price assessment for a horse is given as 1,200 *drachmae*. Although these tablets belong to the cavalry archives of the fourth and third centuries BC, the first extant reference to the *katastasis* is contained in two lines from a comic play by Eupolis entitled *Philoi* whose production date is between 429 BC and 425 BC. The lines translate 'You have not shown good sense, old man, by rashly accepting the *katastasis* before learning to horsemanship' (Eupolis fr. 293 Kassel-Austin). For the arguments about when the *katastasis* was actually instituted in Athens, see Kroll: 1977: 99, Bugh 1982: 309–11.
42. Aristotle *Athenaiôn politeia* 49.1–2.
43. Aristophanes *Lysistrata* 561–2.
44. Lysias 24.11.
45. Aristophanes *Knights* 580, 731, 1121, cf. *Lysistrata* 561, *Clouds* 14.
46. Lysias, *In Defence of Mantitheos*, is a speech dated between 393 BC and 389 BC. At the examination subsequent to his election to the *boulê*, Mantitheos' opponents demanded that he be barred from that body on the ground that he had served as a member of the cavalry corps under the bloody Thirty Tyrants.
47. West frieze, slab IV figure 8, slab VIII figure 15. Martin (1886: 149–50) notes direct statements of cavalry involvement in specific festivals are rare, however, Xenophon lists among the civic duties of the *hipparchos* state festivals 'worth seeing' (*Hipparchikos* 3.1, cf. Demosthenes 4.26, Plutarch *Phokion* 37.1). Spence (1995: 267–71) justly criticizes the theories that the mounted participants are the heroized dead from Marathon or mounted *epheboi*.
48. Xenophon *Hipparchikos* 1.9, cf. Aristotle *Athenaiôn politeia* 49.2.

Appendix 6
1. Xenophon *Hellenika* 2.4.12.
2. E.g. Euripides *Alkestis* 498, Xenophon *Memorabilia* 3.9.2.
3. Herodotos 7.75.1, Xenophon *Anabasis* 7.4.4.
4. E.g. Thucydides 7.30.2, Xenophon *Anabasis* 7.4.17.
5. Aristotle fr. 498 Rose, cf. Herodotos 7.75, 89, Aristophanes *Lysistrata* 563, Euripides *Rhesus* 305, Aineias Taktikos 29.6. Although Aristotle implies that the shield was round, in art it is depicted as crescent shaped with a segment being cut out of the top edge. It also appears as such in Scythian art.

6. E.g. Thucydides 2.29.5, 4.28.4, 111.1, 5.6.4, 7.27.1.

7. Ibid. 4.34.2–3, 5.10.9.

8. For the so-called (and rather dubious) reforms of Iphikrates, see Nepos *Iphikrates* 1.3–4, Diodoros 15.44.2–4, cf. Xenophon *Memorabilia* 3.5.27.

9. Xenophon *Hellenika* 4.5.11–17. Its ethnic composition cannot be determined. It apparently numbered about 1,200 peltasts (ibid. 4.8.34). The mercenary unit is first heard of two years before, when it held the right of the confederate line against the Spartans in the battle within the Long Walls of Corinth (ibid. 4.4.9). The celebrated Athenian admiral Konon, who was in Persian service at the time, first raised it (Androtion *FGrHist* 324F48, cf. Xenophon *Hellenika* 4.8.7), apparently being disbanded at the end of the Corinthian War.

10. Xenophon *Hellenika* 4.4.17.

11. Plutarch *Moralia* 187A.

12. Anaxandridas fr. 151 Kock.

13. There is some confusion in our sources as to whom did Iphikrates serve in Thrace: Nepos says (*Iphikrates* 11.2.1) Seuthes; Demosthenes says (23.129) Kotys. Now, Seuthes was Kotys father, and thus it can be argued that Iphikrates served both, father and son, in a war against their overlord, Hebryzelmis, king of the Odrysai (cf. Polyainos 3.9.60). However, one's enemies are sometimes members of one's own household, and it was not unusual for Thracian families to feud amongst themselves.

Appendix 7

1. Xenophon *Anabasis* 1.8.19.

2. Diodoros 14.23.1, cf. Polyainos 2.2.3 for a similar account.

3. Xenophon *Anabasis* 1.10.10–11.

4. Ibid. 2.2.18.

5. Ibid. 2.3.1–7, cf. 1.8.

6. Ibid. 4.3.19, 5.18, 5.2.14, 6.5.27, 29, cf. 3.2.16. Herodotos (6.112.2) reckons it was the Athenians and their allies the Plataians at Marathon (490 BC) who were the first hoplites to charge at the run, the Persian arrows overshooting as the Greeks suddenly accelerated forward. See Xenophon *Anabasis* 4.1.18 where an arrow pierces Leonymos the Lakonian through his shield and corselet, while his comrade, Basias the Arcadian, is shot clean through the head.

7. Xenophon *Anabasis* 3.1.23, cf. 1.73.

8. Ibid. *Hellenika* 4.3.17, cf. *Agesilaos* 2.11.

9. Diodoros 14.23.3. Xenophon (*Hellenika* 3.2.18) casually informs his audience that Tissaphernes still remembered with dread the skill of the Ten Thousand at Cunaxa four years after the day.

10. Diodoros 14.23.4.

11. Fields 2001.

12. Diodoros 14.37.1, cf. 31.4. See Roy 1967: 320 with notes 133 & 134, and Stronk 1995: 21. Cf. Xenophon *Anabasis* 7.7.23 where the figure is given as a round 6,000.

13. Xenophon *Anabasis* 5.6.15.

14. Ibid. 6.5.30.

15. Ibid. 1.2.15.

16. Ibid. 5.5.5.

17. Ibid. 6.2.16.

18. Ibid. 1.5.14, 4.3.22, 4.8, 5.23, 7.2, 7.3.15. The latter can be described also as a *strageúma* (ibid. 4.1.6), or as a *hamphì tiná* (ibid. 4.3.21, 22).

19. Ibid. 7.1.23.

20. Ibid. 6.1.18.

21. Ibid. 4.2.11, 13, 16, 6.6, 7, 8.14, 5.2.11, 4.22.

22. Ibid. 4.8.15, cf. 3.1.33, the first assembly of *stratêgoi* and *lochagoi* after Cunaxa where we are told by Xenophon these officers numbered around one hundred.

23. Ibid. 1.2.25. Cf. ibid. 4.7.8–9, where the combat strength of the *lochos* of Kallimachos of Parrhasia is given as some seventy hoplites. However, battle losses and the like might easily account for this figure. Elsewhere, the size of a *lochos* would vary considerably, e.g. Xenophon himself mentions a *lochos* of only twenty-four men (*Kyroupaideia* 6.3.21).

24. Ibid. *Anabasis* 3.4.19–20, cf. 2.36, Thucydides 4.125 (Brasidas in Thrace), 6.67.1 (Athenians in Sicily).
25. Xenophon *Anabasis* 3.4.21.
26. Ibid. 5.2.13.
27. Ibid. 4.7.8.
28. Ibid. 4.3.26.
29. Ibid. 4.3.29.
30. Ibid. 4.3.30–34.
31. Ibid. 5.7.15.
32. Ibid. 5.8.6.
33. Ibid. *Agesilaos* 2.7 with 11.
34. Ibid. *Anabasis* 1.2.16. Off the battlefield, a campaigning hoplite, either part-time or professional, would protect his bronze faced shield with a leather covering.
35. Ibid. 4.3.17, 4.12, 5.19, cf. 7.4.4.
36. Ibid. 1.2.19.
37. Diodoros 14.23.3, cf. Xenophon *Anabasis* 1.8.18–19.
38. Xenophon *Anabasis* 6.5.23.
39. Ibid. 6.5.24.
40. Ibid. 5.4.16.
41. Ibid. 5.4.18.
42. Ibid. 5.4.20.
43. Ibid. 5.4.21, cf. *Hipparchikos* 2.7–9.
44. Ibid. 4.7.12. Here we are reminded of two of Caesar's centurions, the celebrated rivals in courageousness Lucius Vorenus and Titus Pullo (Caesar *Bellum Gallicum* 5.44.1).
45. Xenophon *Anabasis* 5.2.11.
46. Ibid. 5.2.13.

Appendix 8

1. Herodotos 1.131–140.
2. In Greek: *Melampygus*, ibid. 7.216.
3. Thucydides 3.24.1–2.
4. Pritchett 1965: 112.

Appendix 9

1. Herodotos 6.15.2.
2. Thucydides 1.49.1.
3. In Greek: *pezomachia*, ibid. 1.49.2.
4. Ibid. 1.49.3.
5. Ibid. 7.36.5.
6. Polybios 1.51.8.
7. Thucydides 7.36.3, 4, Xenophon *Hellenika* 1.6.31.
8. Thucydides 7.36.1–38.1.
9. Ibid. 2.83.5, 3.78.1.
10. Xenophon *Hellenika* 1.6.28.

Bibliography

Admiralty, 1944–45. *Greece*, vols. I–III. London: Naval Intelligence Division Geographical Handbook Series

Alroth, B., 1989. *Greek Gods and Figurines. Aspects of the Anthropomorphic Dedications*. Uppsala: Almqvist & Wiksell (Boreas, Uppsala Studies in Ancient Mediterranean and Near Eastern Civilizations, 18)

Anderson, J.K., 1961. *Ancient Greek Horsemanship*. Berkeley & Los Angeles: University of California Press

Anderson, J.K., 1965. 'Kleon's orders at Amphipolis'. *Journal of Hellenic Studies* 85: 1–4

Anderson, J.K., 1970. *Military Theory and Practice in the Age of Xenophon*. Berkeley & Los Angeles: University of California Press

Anderson, J.K., 1974. *Xenophon*. London: Duckworth

Austin, M.M. & Vidal-Naquet, P., 1977. *Economic and Social History of Ancient Greece: An Introduction*. London: Batsford

Badian, E., 1979. 'The name of the runner'. *American Journal of Ancient History* 4: 163–6

Bagnall, N., 2004. *The Peloponnesian War: Athens, Sparta and the Struggle for Greece*. London: Pimlico

Barker, D-P., 2011. *Just Warriors, Inc. The Ethics of Privatized Force*. London: Continuum

Bassett, S.R., 1999. 'The death of Cyrus the Younger'. *Classical Quarterly* 49: 473–83

Bassett, S.R., 2001. 'The enigma of Clearchus the Spartan'. *Ancient History Bulletin* 15: 1–13

Bassett, S.R., 2002. 'Innocent victims or perjurers betrayed? The arrest of the generals in Xenophon's *Anabasis*'. *Classical Quarterly* 52: 447–61

Best, J.G.P., 1969. *Thracian Peltasts and their Influence on Greek Warfare*. Groningen: Wolters-Noordhoff

Blundell, S., 1995. *Women in Ancient Greece*. Cambridge, MA: Harvard University Press

Blyth, P.H., 1977. *The Effectiveness of Greek Armour Against Arrows in the Persia War (490–479 BC)*: An Interdisciplinary Study. Reading: University of Reading (Diss.)

Blyth, P.H., 1982. 'The structure of a hoplite shield in the Museo Gregoriano Etrusco'. *Bollentino dei Musei e Gallerie Pontifice* 3: 5–21

Bradford, E., 1980. *Thermopylai: The Battle for the West*. New York: De Capo Press

Braudel, F., 1998. *Les Mémoires de la Méditerranée*. Paris: Éditions de Fallois

Briant, P., (trans. P.T. Daniels) 2002. *From Kyros to Alexander: A History of the Persian Empire*. Warsaw, IN: Eisenbrauns

Brosius, M., 2000. *The Persian Empire from Cyrus II to Artaxerxes I*. London: London Association of Classical Teachers (LACTOR 16)

Buckler, J., 1980. *The Theban Hegemony, 371–362 BC*. Cambridge, MA: Harvard University Press

Buckley, T., 1996. *Aspects of Greek History 750–323 BC: A Source-Based Approach*. London: Routledge

Bugh, G.R., 1988. *The Horsemen of Athens*. Princeton, MA: Princeton University Press

Burn, A.R., 1984 (2nd edition). *Persia and the Greeks: The Defence of the West, c. 546–478 BC*. London: Duckworth

Cameron, A. & Kuhrt, A. (eds.), 1993 (rev. ed.). *Images of Women in Classical Antiquity*. London: Routledge

Camp II, J.M., 1986. *The Athenian Agora – Excavations in the Heart of Classical Athens*. London: Thames & Hudson

Camp II, J.M., 1990 (4th edition). *The Athenian Agora (Guide)*. Athens: American School of Classical Studies

Camp II, J.M., 1991. 'Notes on the towers and borders of classical Boiotia'. *American Journal of Archaeology* 95: 193–202

Camp II, J.M., 2001. *The Archaeology of Athens*. London: Yale University Press

Cartledge, P.A., 1977. 'Hoplites and heroes: Sparta's contribution to the technique of ancient warfare'. *Journal of Hellenic Studies* 97: 11–27

Cartledge, P.A., 1979. *Sparta and Lakonia: A Regional History, 1300–362 BC*. London: Duckworth

Cartledge, P.A., 1981. 'Spartan wives: liberation or licence?' *Classical Quarterly* 31: 84–105

Cartledge, P.A., 1987. *Agesilaos and the Crisis of Sparta*. London: Duckworth

Cartledge, P.A., 2000. *The Greeks: Crucible of Civilization*. New York: TV Books

Cartledge, P.A., 2001. *Spartan Reflections*. London: Duckworth

Cartledge, P.A., 2003 (2nd edition). *The Spartans: An Epic History*. London: Channel 4 Books

Cartledge, P.A., 2006. *Thermopylae: The Battle that Changed the World*. Woodstock, NY: Overlook Press

Cassin-Scott, J., 1977. *The Greek and Persian Wars, 500–323 BC*. Oxford: Osprey (Men-at-Arms 69)

Cawkwell, G.L., 1989. 'Orthodoxy and hoplites'. *Classical Quarterly* 39: 375–89

Cook, J.M., 1958–1959. 'Old Smyrna, 1948–1951'. *The Annual of the British School at Athens* 53–54: 1–34

Cook, J.M., 1983. *The Persian Empire*. London: Dent

Cornford, F.M., 1907, 1965. *Thucydides Mythistoricus*. London: Routledge & Keegan Paul

Coulton, J.J., 1995. *Ancient Greek Architects at Work: Problems of Structure and Design*. Oxford: Oxbow Books

Courbin, P., 1957. 'Une tombe géométrique d' Argos'. *Bulletin de Correspondance Hellénique* 81: 322–86

Curtis, J., 1990. *Ancient Persia*. Cambridge, MA: Harvard University Press

Curtis, J. & Tallis, N. (eds.), 2005. *Forgotten Empire: The World of Ancient Persia*. Berkeley & Los Angeles: University of California Press

Dalby, A., 1992. 'Greeks abroad: social organization and food among the Ten Thousand'. *Journal of Hellenic Studies* 112: 16–30

Dalby, A., 1996. *Siren Feasts: A History of Food and Gastronomy in Greece*. London: Routledge

Dawson, D., 1996. *The Origins of Western Warfare: Militarism and Morality in the Ancient Greek World*. Boulder, CO: Westview Press

Dayton, J.C., 2006. *The Athletes of War: An Evaluation of the Agonistic Elements in Greek Warfare*. Toronto: Edgar Kent

Dinter, E., 1985. *Hero or Coward: Pressures Facing the Soldier in Battle*. London: Frank Cass

Dodge, T.A., 1889, 2002. *The Great Captains*. Stevenage: Strong Oak Press

Drews, R., 1988. *The Coming of the Greeks*. Princeton, NJ: Princeton University Press

Dubin, M.S. & Cullen, M., 1993. *Trekking in Greece*. Hawthorn, Vic: Lonely Planet Publications

Ducat, J., Stafford, E. & Shaw, P-J., 2006. *Spartan Education; Youth and Society in the Classical Period*. Swansea: Classical Press of Wales

Ducrey, P., 1985. *Guerre et guerriers dans la Grèce antique*. Paris: Éditions Payot

Engels, D.W., 1978, 1980. *Alexander the Great and the Logistics of the Macedonian Army*. Berkeley & Los Angeles: University of California Press

Epps, P.H., 1933. 'Fear in Spartan character'. *Classical Philology* 28: 12–29

Everson, T., 2004. *Warfare in Ancient Greece: Arms and Armour from the Heroes of Homer to Alexander the Great*. Stroud: Sutton

Fagan, G.G. & Trundle, M. (eds.), 2010. *New Perspectives on Ancient Warfare*. Leiden: E.J. Brill

Fantham, E. *et al.*, 1994. *Women in the Classical World: Image and Text*. New York: Oxford University Press

Farrokh, K., 2007. *Shadows in the Desert: Ancient Persia at War*. Oxford: Osprey

Fields, N., 1994. *Anatomy of a Mercenary: From Archilochos to Alexander*. Newcastle-upon-Tyne: University of Newcastle (Diss.)

Fields, N., 1995. 'A soldier's diet'. *Ad familiares* 8: 13–14

Fields, N., 2001. '*Et ex Arcadia ego*'. *Ancient History Bulletin* 15: 102–30

Fields, N., 2003. 'Dexileos of Thorikos: a brief life'. *Ancient History Bulletin* 17: 108–26

Fields, N., 2006. *Ancient Greek Fortifications, 500–300 BC*. Oxford: Osprey (Fortress 40)

Fields, N., 2007. *Ancient Greek Warship, 500–322 BC*. Oxford: Osprey (New Vanguard 132)

Fields, N., 2007. *Thermopylae 480 BC: Last Stand of the 300*. Oxford: Osprey (Campaign 188)

Fields, N., 2008. *Syracuse 415–413 BC: Destruction of the Athenian Imperial Fleet*. Oxford: Osprey (Campaign 195)

Fields, N., 2010. *Roman Conquests: North Africa*. Barnsley: Pen & Sword

Foley, H.P. (ed.), 1982. *Reflections of Women in Antiquity*. London: Routledge

Forbes, H.A., 1976. 'The 'Thrice-Ploughed Field': cultivation techniques in ancient and modern Greece'. *Expedition* 19: 5–11

Forbes, R.J., 1964. *Studies in Ancient Technology*, vol. IV. Leiden: E.J. Brill

Forrest, W.G., 1963. 'The date of the Lycourgan reforms in Sparta'. *Phoenix* 17: 157–79

Forrest, W.G., 1995 (3rd edition). *A History of Sparta*. Bristol: Bristol Classical Press

Forde, S., 1989. *The Ambition to Rule: Alcibiades and the Politics of Imperialism in Thucydides*. Ithaca, NY: Cornell University Press

Fossey, J.M., 1988. *Topography and Population of Ancient Boiotia*. Chicago: University of Chicago Press

Foxhall, L., 1986. 'Greece ancient and modern: subsistence and survival'. *History Today* 36: 35–43

Foxhall, L. & Forbes, H.A., 1982. '*Sitometreia*: the role of grain as a staple food in classical antiquity'. *Chiron* 12: 41–90

Frazer, A.D., 1942. 'The myth of the phalanx scrimmage'. *Classical Weekly* 36: 15–16

Froissart, J., 1978. *Chronicles*. London: Penguin Classics

Frye, R.N., 1962. *The History of Persia*. London: Weidenfeld & Nicholson

Gabriel, R.A., 1990. *The Culture of War, Invention and Early Development*. London: Greenwood Press

Gabriel, R.A., 1991. *From Sumer to Rome: The Military Capabilities of Ancient Armies*. London: Greenwood Press

Gallant, T.W., 1991. *Risk and Survival in Ancient Greece: Reconstructing the Rural Domestic Economy*. Cambridge: Polity

Garlan, Y., 1976. *War in the Ancient World: A Social History*. London: Chatto & Windus

Garnsey, P.D.A., 1988. *Famine and Food Supply in the Graeco-Roman World: Responses to Risk and Crisis*. Cambridge: Cambridge University Press

Goldsworthy, A.K., 1997. 'The *ôthismos*, myths and heresies: the nature of hoplite battle'. *War in History* 4: 1–26

Gomme, A.W. *et al.*, 1945–1981. *A Historical Commentary on Thucydides* (5 vols.). Oxford: Clarendon Press

Grant, J.R., 1961. 'Leonidas' last stand'. *Phoenix* 15: 14–27

Green, P., 1996. *The Greco-Persian Wars*. Berkeley & Los Angeles: University of California Press

Griffith, G.T., 1935, 1985. *The Mercenaries of the Hellenistic World*. Chicago: Ares

Grundy, G.B., 1901. *The Great Persian War and its Preliminaries: A Study of the Evidence, Literary and Topographical*. London: John Murray

Guevara, E., (trans. P. Camiller) 2000. *The African Dream: The Diaries of the Revolutionary War in the Congo*. London: Harvill Press

Gwynn, A., 1918. 'The character of Greek colonisation'. *Journal of Hellenic Studies* 38: 88–123

Hale, J.R., 1985, 1998. *War and Society in Renaissance Europe 1450–1620*. Stroud: Sutton

Hall, J.M., 2006. *A History of the Archaic Greek World, ca. 1200–479 BCE*. Malden, MA: Blackwell

Hamel, D., 1998. *Athenian Generals: Military Authority in the Classical Period*. Leiden: E.J. Brill

Hamilton, C.D., 1979. *Sparta's Bitter Victories*. Ithaca, NY: Cornell University Press

Hansen, M.H., 1981. 'The number of Athenian hoplites in 431 BC'. *Symbolae Osloenses* 56: 19–32

Hansen, M.H., 1982. 'Demographic reflections on the number of Athenian citizens 451–309 BC'. *American Journal of Ancient History* 7: 172–89

Hanson V.D., 1983. *Warfare and Agriculture in Classical Greece*. Pisa: Giardini Editori

Hanson, V.D., 1989. *The Western Way of War: Infantry Battle in Classical Greece*. London: Hodder & Stoughton

Hanson, V.D. (ed.), 1991. *Hoplites: The Classical Greek Battle Experience*. London: Routledge

Hanson, V.D., 1999. *The Wars of the Ancient Greeks*. London: Cassell

Hanson, V.D., 1999. 'Hoplite obliteration: the case of the town of Thespiai', in J. Carman & A.F. Harding (eds.), *Ancient Warfare: Archaeological Perspectives*. Stroud: Sutton, 203–17

Harding, P., 1988. 'Athenian defensive strategy in the fourth century'. *Phoenix* 42: 61–71

Hellström, P., 1984. 'A Corinthian bronze helmet'. *Bulletin Medelhausmuseet* 19: 49–56

Higgins, W.E., 1977. *Xenophon the Athenian: The Problem of the Individual and the Society of the polis*. Albany, NY: State University of New York Press

Hignett, C., 1963. *Xerxes' Invasion of Greece*. Oxford: Oxford University Press

Hoare, M., 1967. *Congo Mercenary*. London: Robert Hale

Hoare, M., 1989. *The Road to Kalamata: A Congo Mercenary's Personal Memoir*. Lexington, MA: Lexington Books

Hodkinson, S., 1986. 'Land tenure and inheritance in classical Sparta'. *Classical Quarterly* 80: 378–406

Hodkinson, S., 2000. *Property and Wealth in Classical Sparta*. London: David Brown

Hodkinson, S. & Hodkinson, H., 1981. 'Mantineia and the Mantinike: settlement and society in a Greek *polis*'. *Annual of the British School at Athens* 76: 239–96

Hodkinson, S. & Powell, A. (eds.), 1999. *Sparta: New Perspectives*. London: Duckworth

Holladay, A.J., 1982. 'Hoplites and heresies'. *Journal of Hellenic Studies* 102: 94–104

Hooker, J.T., 1980. *The Ancient Spartans*. London: J.M. Dent & Sons

Hope Simpson, R., 1972. 'Leonidas' decision'. *Phoenix* 26: 1–11

Hornblower, S., 1991. *A Commentary on Thucydides* (3 vols.). Oxford: Clarendon Press

Hornblower, S., 2002 (3rd edition). *The Greek World 479–323 BC*. London: Routledge

How, W.W., 1923. 'Arms, tactics and the strategy of the Persian War'. *Journal of Hellenic Studies* 43: 117–32

Isager, S. & Skydsgaard, J.E., 1995. *Ancient Greek Agriculture: An Introduction*. London: Routledge

Jones, A.H.M., 1957. *Athenian Democracy*. Oxford: Blackwell

Jones, A.H.M., 1967, 2008. *Sparta*. New York: Barnes & Noble

Jones, N., 1977. 'The topography and strategy of the battle of Amphipolis in 422 BC'. *California Studies in Classical Antiquity* 10: 71–104

Kagan, D., 1969. *The Outbreak of the Peloponnesian War*. Ithaca, NY: Cornell University Press

Kagan, D., 1974. *The Archidamian War*. Ithaca, NY: Cornell University Press

Kagan, D., 1981. *The Peace of Nicias and the Sicilian Expedition*. Ithaca, NY: Cornell University Press

Kagan, D., 1987. *Fall of the Athenian Empire*. Ithaca, NY: Cornell University Press

Kagan, D., 2003. *The Peloponnesian War: Athens and Sparta in Savage Conflict 431–404 BC*. London: Harper Collins

Keegan, J., 1987. *The Mask of Command*. London: Cape

Kellett, A., 1982. *Combat Motivation: The Behaviour of Soldiers in Battle*. Boston, MA: Kluwer Nijhoff Publishing

Kelly, D.H., 1981. 'Thucydides and Herodotus on the Pitanate *Lochos*'. *Greek, Roman & Byzantine Studies* 22: 31–8

Kelly, T., 1970. 'Did the Argives defeat the Spartans at Hysiai?' *American Journal of Philology* 91: 31–42

Kern, P.B., 1999. *Ancient Siege Warfare*. Bloomington, IN: Indiana University Press

Knigge, U., 1991. *The Athenian Kerameikos: History – Monuments – Excavations*. Athens: Deutsches Archäologisches Institut Athen

Krentz, P., 1985. 'The nature of hoplite battle'. *Cahiers Archéologica* 4: 50–61

Krentz, P., 1985. 'Casualties in hoplite battles'. *Greek, Roman & Byzantine Studies* 26: 13–20

Krentz, P., 2002. 'Fighting by the rules: the invention of the hoplite *agon*'. *Hesperia* 71: 23–39

Kroll, J.H., 1977. 'An archive of the Athenian cavalry'. *Hesperia* 46: 83–140

Lancaster, O., 1947. *Classical Landscape with Figures*. London: John Murray

Landels, J.G., 2000 (2nd edition). *Engineering in the Ancient World*. London: Constable

Lawrence, A.W., 1979. *Greek Aims in Fortification*. Oxford: Oxford University Press

Lawrence, A.W., 1996 (5th edition revised by R.A. Tomlinson). *Greek Architecture*. London: Yale University Press

Lazenby, J.F., 1985. *The Spartan Army*. Warminster: Aris & Phillips

Lazenby, J.F., 1993. *The Defence of Greece, 490–479 BC*. Warminster: Aris & Phillips

Lazenby, J.F., 1994. 'Logistics in classical Greek warfare'. *War in History* 1: 3–18

Lazenby, J.F., 1995. 'The *Archaia Moira*: a suggestion'. *Classical Quarterly* 45: 87–91

Lazenby, J.F., 1996. *The First Punic War: A Military History*. London: University of College London

Lazenby, J.F., 2004. *The Peloponnesian War: A Military Study*. London: Routledge

Lazenby, J.F. & Whitehead D., 1996. 'The myth of the hoplite's *hoplon*'. *Classical Quarterly* 46: 27–33

Leake, W.M., 1830. *Travels in Morea*, vols. I–III. London: John Murray

Leggett, W.F., 1944. *Ancient and Medieval Dyes*. New York: Chemical Publishing

Lengauer, W., 1979. *Greek Commanders in the 5th and 4th Centuries BC: Politics and Ideology: A Study of Militarism*. Warszawa: Wydawnictwa Uniwersytetu Warszawskiego (Studia Antiqua 2)

Lewis, D.M., 1977. *Sparta and Persia*. Leiden: E.J. Brill

Lefkowitz, M. & Fant, M.B., 1982 (2nd edition). *Women's Life in Greece and Rome*. Baltimore: Johns Hopkins University Press

Lloyd, A.B. (ed.), 1996. *Battle in Antiquity*. London: Duckworth

Lorimer, H.L., 1947. 'The hoplite phalanx'. *Annual of the British School at Athens* 42: 76–138

Luraghi, N. & Alcock, S. (eds.), 2004. *Helots and their Masters in Laconia and Messenia*. Cambridge, MA: Harvard University Press (Hellenic Studies 4)

McKechnie, P.R., 1989. *Outsiders in the Greek Cities in the Fourth Century BC*. London: Routledge

McKechnie, P.R., 1994. 'Greek mercenary troops and their equipment'. *Historia* 43: 297–305

MacDowell, D.M., 1986. *Spartan Law*. Edinburgh: Scottish Academic Press

Manfred, C., 1983. *Sparta. Einführung in seine Geschichte und Zivilisation*. Munich: C.H. Beck

Marsden, E.W., 1969, 1999. *Greek and Roman Artillery: Historical Development*. Oxford: Oxford University Press

Marshall, S.L.A., 1947. *Men Against Fire*. New York: William Morrow

Maurice, F., 1930. 'The size of the army of Xerxes in the invasion of Greece, 480 BC'. *Journal of Hellenic Studies* 50: 210–35

Mayor, A., 2003. *Greek Fire, Poison Arrows, and Scorpion Bombs: Biological and Chemical Warfare in the Ancient World*. Woodstock, NY: Overlook Press

Meiggs, R., 1972. *The Athenian Empire*. Oxford: Clarendon Press

Mitchell, B., 1991. 'Kleon's Amphipolitan campaign: aims and results'. *Historia* 40: 170–91

Mockler, A., 1986. *The New Mercenaries*. London: Sidgwick & Jackson

Montagu, J.D., 2006. *Greek and Roman Warfare: Battles, Tactics and Trickery*. London: Greenhill

Moore, J.M., 1983 (2nd edition). *Aristotle and Xenophon on Democracy and Oligarchy*. London: Chatto & Windus

Munn, M., 1993. *The Defense of Attica*. Berkeley & Los Angles: University of California Press

Munro, J.A.R., 1904. 'Some observations on the Persian Wars: 3. The campaign of Plataea'. *Journal of Hellenic Studies* 24: 144–65

Murray, O., 1993 (2nd edition). *Early Greece*. London: Fontana Press

Naussbaum, G., 1959. 'The captains in the army of the Ten Thousand'. *Classica et Mediaevalia* 20: 16–29

Nzongola-Ntalaja, G., 2002. *The Congo From Leopold to Kabila*. London & New York: Zed Books

Ober, J., 1985. *Fortress Attica: Defense of the Athenian Land Frontier, 404–322 BC*. Leiden: E.J. Brill

Ogden, D., 2004. *Aristomenes of Messene. Legend of Sparta's Nemesis*. Swansea: Classical Press of Wales

Osborne, R., 1987. *Classical Landscape with Figures: The Ancient Greek City and its Countryside*. London: George Philip

Packham, E.S., 1996. *Freedom and Anarchy*. Commack, NY: Nova Science Publishers

Parke, H.W., 1933. *Greek Mercenary Soldiers: From the Earliest Times to the Battle of Ipsus*. Oxford: Clarendon Press

Perlman, S., 1976–77. 'The Ten Thousand: a chapter in the military, social and economic history of the fourth century'. *Rivista Storica dell' Antichità* 6–7: 241–84

Petrakos, B., Ch., 1984. 'Ραμούντα'. *Τὸ Ἔργον τ–ς Ἀρχαιολογικκ–ς Ἑταίρεια κατὰ τὸ* 1984: 54.

Picard, O., 1980. *Les Grecs devant la menace Perse*. Paris: Société d' Éditions d' Enseignement Supérieur

Podlecki, A.J., 1963. 'Three Greek soldier-poets: Archilochus, Alcaeus, Solon'. *Classical Weekly* 63: 73–81

Pomeroy, S.B., 1976, 1995. *Goddesses, Whores, Wives and Slaves: Women in Classical Antiquity*. New York: Schocken Books

Pomeroy, S.B. (ed.), 1991. *Women's History and Ancient History*. Chapel Hill, NC: University of North Carolina Press

Pomeroy, S.B., 2002. *Spartan Women*. Oxford: Oxford University Press

Powell, A. (ed.), 1989. *Classical Sparta: Techniques behind Her Success*. London: Routledge

Powell, A., 2001 (2nd edition). *Athens and Sparta: Constructing Greek Political and Social History to 323 BC*. London: Routledge

Pritchett, W.K., 1957. 'New light on Plataea'. *American Journal of Archaeology* 61: 9–28

Pritchett, W.K., 1965–1985. *Studies in Ancient Greek Topography* (5 vols.). Berkeley & Los Angeles: University of California Press

Pritchett, W.K., 1971–1991. *The Greek State at War* (5 vols.). Berkeley & Los Angeles: University of California Press

Raaflaub, K.A. (ed.), 2007. *War and Peace in the Ancient World*. Oxford: Blackwell

Rahn, P.A., 1980. 'The military situation in western Asia on the eve of Cunaxa'. *American Journal of Philology* 101: 79–96

Rahn, P.A., 1981. 'The date of Xenophon's exile', in Shrimpton & McCargar (eds.) *Classical Contributions: Studies in Honour of M.F. McGregor*. New York: Locust Valley, 103–19

Rankin, H.D., 1977. *Archilochos of Paros*. New Jersey: Noyes Press

Ray, E., (ed.), 1980. *Dirty Work: The CIA in Africa*. London & New York: Zed Books

Rawlings, L., 2007. *The Ancient Greeks at War*. Manchester: Manchester University Press

Ridley, R.T., 1978. 'The hoplite as citizen: Athenian military institutions in social context'. *Archaeologica Classica* 48: 508–48

Roy, J., 1967. 'The mercenaries of Cyrus'. *Historia* 16: 287–323

Roy, J., 1968. 'Xenophon's evidence for the *Anabasis*'. *Athenaeum* 46: 37–46

Rusch, S.M., 2011. *Sparta at War: Strategy, Tactics, and Campaigns, 550–362 BC.* London: Frontline Books

Ruschenbusch, E. 1984. 'Die Bevölkerungszahl grieschelands im 5, und 4, Jh. v. Chr.' *Zeitschrift für Papyrologie und Epigraphik* 56: 55–7

Ruschenbusch, E., 1985. 'Die zahl der griechischen staaten und arealgrösse und bürgezahl der "normalpolis"'. *Zeitschrift für Papyrologie und Epigraphik* 59: 253–63

de Ste. Croix, G.E.M., 1972. *The Origins of the Peloponnesian War*. London: Duckworth

de Ste. Croix, G.E.M., 1981. *The Class Struggle in the Ancient Greek World: From the Archaic Age to the Arab Conquest*. Oxford: Clarendon Press

Salisbury, J.E., 2001. *Encyclopedia of Women in the Ancient World*. Santa Barbara, CA: ABC -CLIO

Sallares, J.R., 1991. *The Ecology of the Ancient Greek World*. London: Duckworth

Salmon, J.B., 1977. 'Political hoplites?' *Journal of Hellenic Studies* 97: 84–101

Schaps, D., 1979. *Economic Rights of Women in Ancient Greece*. Edinburgh: Edinburgh University Press

Schwertfeger, T., 1982. 'Der schild des Archilochos'. *Chiron* 12: 253–80

Scranton, R.L., 1941. *Greek Walls*. Cambridge, MA: Harvard University Press

Sealey, R., 1990. *Women and Law in Classical Greece*. Chapel Hill, NC: University of North Carolina Press

Sear, D.R., 1978. *Greek Coins*, vol. 1. London: Seaby

Sekunda, N.V., 1986. *The Ancient Greeks*. Oxford: Osprey (Elite 7)

Sekunda, N.V., 1992. *The Persian Army, 560–330 BC.* Oxford: Osprey (Elite 42)

Sekunda, N.V., 1998. *The Spartans*. Oxford: Osprey (Elite 66)

Sekunda, N.V., 2000. *Greek Hoplite, 480–323 BC.* Oxford: Osprey (Warrior 27)

Sekunda, N.V., 2002. *Marathon 490 BC: The First Persian Invasion of Greece*. Oxford: Osprey (Campaign 108)

Snodgrass, A.M., 1965. 'The hoplite reforms and history'. *Journal of Hellenic Studies* 85: 110–22

Snodgrass, A.M., 1967. *Arms and Armour of the Greeks*. London: Thames & Hudson

Snodgrass, A.M., 1971. *The Dark Age of Greece*. Edinburgh: Edinburgh University Press

de Souza, P., 2003. *The Greek and Persian Wars, 499–386 BC.* Oxford: Osprey (Essential Histories 36)

de Souza, P., 2003. *The Peloponnesian War, 431–404 BC.* London: Routledge

Spence, I.G., 1995. *The Cavalry of Classical Greece: A Social and Military History with Particular Reference to Athens*. Oxford: Clarendon Press

Starr, C.G., 1965. 'The credibility of early Spartan history'. *Historia* 14: 257–72

Strassler, R.B. (ed.), 1996. *The Landmark Thucydides: A Comprehensive Guide to the Peloponnesian War*. New York: Touchstone

Tickler, P., 1987. *The Modern Mercenary: Dog of War, or Soldier of Honour?* London: Patrick Stephens

Tiger, L., 1969. *Men in Groups*. London: Nelson

Tritle, L.A. (ed.), 1997. *The Greek World in the Fourth Century: From the Fall of Athens to the Successors of Alexander*. London: Routledge

Tritle, L.A., 2004. *The Peloponnesian War*. Westport, CT: Greenwood Press

Turney-High, H.H., 1971 (2nd edition). *Primitive War: Its Practice and Concepts*. Columbia, SC: University of South Carolina Press

Usher, S., 1988. *Herodotos, the Persian Wars: A Companion*. Bristol: Bristol Classical Press

Vanderpool, E., 1978. 'Roads and forts in northwestern Attica'. *California Studies in Classical Antiquity* 11: 227–45

Vernant, J-P. (ed.), 1968. *Problèmes de la guerre en Grèce ancienne*. Paris: Mouton Éditions

Wagoner, F.E., 1980. *Dragon Rouge*. Washington: National Defense University

Walker, W., 1860, 1985. *The War in Nicaragua*. Tucson, AR: University of Arizona Press

Wardman, A.E., 1959. 'Tactics and the tradition of the Persian Wars'. *Historia* 8: 49–60 van Wees, H., 2004. *Greek Warfare: Myths and Realities*. London: Duckworth

Weinberg, S., 1994. *The Last of the Pirates: The Search for Bob Denard*. London: Cape

Weissman, S.R., 1974. *American Foreign Policy in the Congo, 1960–1964*. Ithaca, NY: Cornell University Press

Westlake, H.D., 1968. *Individuals in Thucydides*. Cambridge: Cambridge University Press

Westlake, H.D., 1974. 'The naval battle at Pylos and its consequences'. *Classical Quarterly* 24: 211–26

Westlake, H.D., 1983. 'The progress of *epiteichismos*'. *Classical Quarterly* 33: 12–24

Wheeler, E.L., 1982. '*Hoplomachia* and Greek dances in arms'. *Greek, Roman & Byzantine Studies* 23: 223–33

Whitehead, D., 2001 (2nd edition). *Aineias the Tactician: How to Survive Under Siege*. Bristol: Bristol Classical Press

Wilson, J.B., 1979. *Pylos 425 BC*. Warminster: Aris & Phillips

Winter, F.E., 1971. *Greek Fortifications*. London: Routledge & Kegan Paul

Wood, N., 1964. 'Xenophon's theory of leadership'. *Classica et Mediaevalia* 25: 33–66

Woodhouse, W.J., 1898. 'The Greeks at Plataiai'. *Journal of Hellenic Studies* 18: 33–59

Worley, L.J., 1993. *Hippeis: The Cavalry of Ancient Greece*. Boulder, CO: Westview Press

Wycherley, R.E., 1976 (2nd edition). *How Greeks Built Cities*. London: Norton

Index